Matters of Culture

American sociology is in the midst o. _____ sociologists once spurned culture, today they embrace and explore it, seeking to understand the construction of social forms and the way culture matters. Problems of meaning, discourse, aesthetics, value, textuality, form, and narrativity, topics traditionally within the humanists' purview, have come to the fore as sociologists increasingly emphasize the role of meanings, symbols, cultural frames, and cognitive schema in their theorizations of social process and institution. *Matters of Culture* is an introduction to some of the best theorizing in cultural sociology, focusing in particular on questions of power, the sacred, and cultural production. With a major theoretical introduction that lays out the internal structure of the field and its relation to cultural studies and contributions from leading academics, *Matters of Culture* offers students and professors alike a representative range of the types of cultural sociological analysis available.

ROGER FRIEDLAND is Professor of Religious Studies and Sociology at the University of California, Santa Barbara and has published extensively in both disciplines. He is co-founder with John Mohr of the Cultural Turn conferences at the University of California, Santa Barbara.

JOHN W. MOHR is Associate Professor of Sociology at the University of California, Santa Barbara where he also serves as Associate Dean of the Graduate Division. He has published rticles across a wide range of topics in cultural sociology and is co-founder with Roger Friedland of the Cultural Turn onferences at the University of California, Santa Barbara.

Cambridge Cultural Social Studies

Series editors: JEFFREY C. ALEXANDER, *Department of Sociology, Yale University, and* STEVEN SEIDMAN, *Department of Sociology, University at Albany, State University of New York.*

Titles in the series

ILANA FRIEDRICH SILBER, *Virtuosity, Charisma, and Social Order* 0 521 41397 4 hardback

LINDA NICHOLSON AND STEVEN SEIDMAN (eds.), *Social Postmodernism* 0 521 47516 3 hardback   0 521 47571 6 paperback

WILLIAM BOGARD, *The Simulation of Surveillance* 0 521 55081 5 hardback   0 521 55561 2 paperback

SUZANNE R. KIRSHNER, *The Religious and Romantic Origins of Psychoanalysis* 0 521 44401 2 hardback   0 521 55560 4 paperback

PAUL LICHTERMAN, *The Search for Political Community* 0 521 48286 0 hardback   0 521 48343 3 paperback

ROGER FRIEDLAND AND RICHARD HECHT, *To Rule Jerusalem* 0 521 44046 7 hardback

KENNETH H. TUCKER, JR., *French Revolutionary Syndicalism and the Public Sphere* 0 521 56359 3 hardback

ERIK RINGMAR, *Identity, Interest and Action* 0 521 56314 3 hardback

ALBERTO MELUCCI, *The Playing Self* 0 521 56401 8 hardback 0 521 56482 4 paperback

ALBERTO MELUCCI, *Challenging Codes* 0 521 57051 4 hardback 0 521 57843 4 paperback

SARAH M. CORSE, *Nationalism and Literature* 0 521 57002 6 hardback   0 521 57912 0 paperback

DARNELL M. HUNT, *Screening the Los Angeles 'Riots'* 0 521 57087 5 hardback   0 521 57814 0 paperback

LYNETTE P. SPILLMAN, *Nation and Commemoration* 0 521 57404 8 hardback   0 521 57683 0 paperback

(list continues at end of book)

Matters of Culture: Cultural Sociology in Practice

EDITED BY

Roger Friedland and John Mohr

CAMBRIDGE
UNIVERSITY PRESS

PUBLISHED BY THE PRESS SYNDICATE OF THE UNIVERSITY OF CAMBRIDGE
The Pitt Building, Trumpington Street, Cambridge, United Kingdom

CAMBRIDGE UNIVERSITY PRESS
The Edinburgh Building, Cambridge CB2 2RU, UK
40 West 20th Street, New York, NY 10011–4211, USA
477 Williamstown Road, Port Melbourne, VIC 3207, Australia
Ruiz de Alarcón 13, 28014 Madrid, Spain
Dock House, The Waterfront, Cape Town 8001, South Africa

http://www.cambridge.org

First published 2004

Printed in the United Kingdom at the University Press, Cambridge

Typeface Times (monotype) 10/12.5 pt.   *System* LATEX 2_ε [TB]

A catalogue record for this book is available from the British Library

Library of Congress Cataloguing in Publication data
Matters of Culture : Cultural Sociology in Practice / edited by Roger Friedland and John Mohr.
    p.   cm. – (Cambridge Cultural Social Studies)
Includes bibliographical references and index.
ISBN 0 521 79162 6 (hardback) – ISBN 0 521 79545 1 (paperback)
1. Culture – Study and teaching – United States.   2. Culture.   I. Friedland, Roger.
II. Mohr, John.   III. Series.
HM623.M38   2004
306′.071 – dc22   2003055748 hardback

ISBN 0 521 79162 6 hardback
ISBN 0 521 79545 1 paperback

The publisher has used its best endeavours to ensure that URLs for external websites referred to
in this book are correct and active at the time of going to press. However, the publisher has no
responsibility for the websites and can make no guarantee that a site will remain live or that the
content is or will remain appropriate.

Contents

Part III   Culture and power

Part IV   Products and production of culture

Figures

Contributors

Jeffrey Alexander, Professor of Sociology at Yale University, works in the areas of theory, culture, and politics. An exponent of the "strong program" in cultural sociology, he has investigated the cultural codes and narratives that inform such diverse areas as computer technology, environmental politics, war-making, the Watergate crisis, and civil society. In the field of politics, Alexander is finishing a theory of the civil sphere and its contradictions. Alexander's work moves between the history of social thought, interpretive disputes, and the construction of systematic models. His most recent publication is *The Meanings of Social Life: A Cultural Sociology* (Oxford, 2003).

Denise D. Bielby is Professor of Sociology and Affiliated Faculty, Center for Film, Television, and New Media at the University of California, Santa Barbara. Her research focuses on sociology of culture, mass media, and gender. She is the author of numerous scholarly articles which have appeared in *American Sociological Review*, *American Journal of Sociology*, *Poetics*, *Journal of Popular Culture*, *Journal of Broadcasting and Electronic Media*, and *Television and New Media*.

William Bielby's research interests are in the areas of organizations and inequality, with a focus on workplace discrimination by gender, race, and age. Much of his work over the past decade, in collaboration with Denise Bielby, has applied those interests to the study of cultural production and labor market stratification in the entertainment industry. Currently, he is completing a study of the first wave of teenage rock and roll bands in the post-Elvis, pre-Beatles era.

Jon Cruz is Associate Professor of Sociology at the University of California, Santa Barbara. His is author of *Culture on the Margins: The Black Spiritual and the Rise of American Cultural Interpretation* (Princeton, 1999), and *Viewing, Reading, Listening: Audiences and Cultural Reception* (co-editor)

(Westview, 1994). Current primary research interests include the impact of digitization upon music culture, and the corporate uses of nostalgia.

Simonetta Falasca Zamponi teaches sociology at the University of California, Santa Barbara. Her publications include *Fascist Spectacle: The Aesthetics of Power in Mussolini's Italy* (Berkeley: University of California Press, 1997). She is currently working on a project that examines Bataille's Collège de sociologie and its vision of politics against the background of interwar Europe.

Nancy Fraser is the Henry and Louise A. Loeb Professor of Politics and Philosophy at the Graduate Faculty of the New School and co-editor of *Constellations: An International Journal of Critical and Democratic Theory*. Her books include *Redistribution or Recognition? A Political-Philosophical Exchange* (2003), with Axel Honneth; *Justice Interruptus: Critical Reflections on the "Postsocialist" Condition* (1997); *Feminist Contentions: A Philosophical Exchange* (1994) with Seyla Benhabib, Judith Butler, and Drucilla Cornell; and *Unruly Practices: Power, Discourse, and Gender in Contemporary Social Theory* (1989). She is a co-editor of *Pragmatism, Critique, Judgment: Essays for Richard J. Bernstein* (2003) and *Revaluing French Feminism: Critical Essays on Difference, Agency, and Culture* (1992). Her current research is on globalization.

Roger Friedland is Professor of Religious Studies and Sociology at the University of California, Santa Barbara. Together with John Mohr, he co-founded The Cultural Turn. Friedland, who is doing comparative research on religious nationalism, is author of "Money, Sex and God: The Erotic Logic of Religious Nationalism," *Sociological Theory*, 2002. He is currently finishing a study of Frank Lloyd Wright's Taliesin Fellowship with Harold Zellman, a Los Angeles-based architect.

John R. Hall is a Professor of Sociology and Director of the Center for History, Society, and Culture at the University of California – Davis. His most recent books are an edited volume – *Reworking Class* (Cornell University Press, 1997), *Cultures of Inquiry: From Epistemology to Discourse in the Methodological Practices of Sociohistorical Research* (Cambridge University Press, 1999), *Apocalypse Observed: Religious Movements and Violence in North America, Europe, and Japan*, coauthored by Philip D. Schuyler and Sylvaine Trinh (Routledge, 2000), and *Sociology on Culture*, co-authored by Mary Jo Neitz and Marshall Battani (Routledge, 2003). His current research concerns apocalyptic terrorism and modernity.

Richard D. Hecht is Professor of Religious Studies at the University of California, Santa Barbara. He is the author with Roger Friedland of *To Rule Jerusalem* (Cambridge University Press, 1996 and revised edition, University of California Press, 2000). Friedland and Hecht have written extensively on the politics and religion of sacred places. Hecht is the Associate Editor with Ninian Smart for the series *Religions of the World* (Laurence King in London and Prentice-Hall in New York) and is completing a book on religion and contemporary art.

Magali Sarfatti Larson is the author of, among other things, The *Rise of Professionalism* and *Beyond the Postmodern Façade: Architectural Change in Late Twentieth Century America*, which received awards from the American Institute of Architects and the Sociology of Culture section of the American Sociological Association. She has held the chair of Sociology of Labor at the University of Urbino in Italy from 1997 to 2001 and is Professor Emerita from Temple University. She lives in Philadelphia and her current interests are political culture and politics *tout court*.

John Mohr is Associate Professor of Sociology at the University of California, Santa Barbara where he also serves as Associate Dean of the Graduate Division. He has been a visiting professor at La Sapienza in Rome and at the Maison des Sciences de L'Homme, in Paris. He has published articles on the measurement of meaning structures, on the history of the American welfare state and (with Paul DiMaggio) on the measurement of cultural capital. He is currently studying organizational responses to the end of affirmative action in California higher education. He is the editor of a special issue of *Poetics* on the topic of "Relational Analysis and Institutional Meanings: Formal Models for the Study of Culture" (2000) and co-founder, with Roger Friedland, of the Cultural Turn conference series at the University of California, Santa Barbara.

Harvey Molotch's most recent book, *Where Stuff Comes From*, uses product design as a way to understand the link between culture and economy. Formerly on the faculty at the University of California, Santa Barbara (and Centennial Professor at the London School of Economics) he is now Professor of Sociology and Metropolitan Studies at New York University.

Orlando Patterson is John Cowles Professor of Sociology at Harvard University. He is the author of *The Sociology of Slavery* (1967), *Ethnic Chauvinism* (1977), *Slavery and Social Death* (1982), *Freedom in the Making of Western Culture* (1991), *The Ordeal of Integration* (1997), and *Rituals of Blood* (1999), as well as three novels. Patterson was awarded the Distinguished Contribution to Scholarship Award of the American Sociological Association in 1983 (The Sorokin Prize), and was co-winner of the Ralph Bunche Award of the American Political Science Association for the best scholarly work on the subject of pluralism. In 1991 he was awarded the National Book Award in non-fiction for

Volume 1 of *Freedom*. He is a Fellow of the American Academy of Arts and Sciences.

Steven Seidman is author most recently of *Beyond the Closet: The Transformation of Gay and Lesbian Life* (2002) and teaches sociology at the University at Albany.

Mark A. Schneider is Associate Professor of Sociology at Southern Illinois University-Carbondale. One of his central interests, pursued in *Culture and Enchantment* (University of Chicago Press, 1993), is the relationship between humanistic and scientific approaches to culture. He has published on a range of topics, including the structuralist character of Goethe's scientific writings, the social origins of the sacred, and olfactory mechanisms in incest avoidance. His next book is an exploration of sociological theorizing as a communicable skill.

Eviatar Zerubavel is Professor of Sociology at Rutgers University. He is the author of several books on the sociologies of time (*Time Maps, Hidden Rhythms, The Seven-Day Circle, Patterns of Time in Hospital Life*) and thinking (*The Fine Line, Social Mindscapes, Terra Cognita*) as well as on the art of writing books and dissertations (*The Clockwork Muse*). He is currently working on a book titled *The Elephant in the Room: The Social Organization of Silence and Denial*, for which he was awarded a 2003 Guggenheim Fellowship.

1

The cultural turn in American sociology

Roger Friedland and John Mohr

American sociology is in the midst of a cultural turn. Where sociologists once spurned culture, associated as it was with the normative premises of Parsonian theory or with other kinds of idealisms, today they embrace it. Problems of meaning, discourse, aesthetics, value, textuality, and narrativity, topics traditionally within the humanists' purview, are now coming to the fore as sociologists increasingly emphasize the role of meanings, symbols, cultural frames, and cognitive schema in their theorizations of social process and institution. This is happening across the intellectual landscape.

Political sociologists are analyzing the ritual construction of power (Alexander, 1988, 1993; Berezin, 1997; Falasca Zamponi, 1997; Falasca Zamponi, this volume.) Not only have they shown the cultural contingency of such things as nationalism, they have also turned the supposed objectivities of class and sexual position into cultural accomplishments, for example, insisting on the ways in which historically and societally variable meanings of work shape the nature of working-class demands or the ways in which conceptions of the market influence modalities of state intervention (Biernacki, 1995; Brubaker, 1998; Dobbin, 1994). Social movement theory once centered its attention on power balances and resource opportunities enabling challengers to aggregate, to find voice and reach for power (McCarthy and Zald, 1987; Tilly, 1978). It now increasingly analyzes the ways in which interpretations of grievances, understandings of situations, and repertoires of action shape the emergence, strategies, and course of social movements (Eyerman and Jamison, 1991; Friedland and Hecht, 2000; McAdam, 1982; Melucci, 1996; Snow and Benford, 1992).

Organizational theorists, long comfortable with conceptualizations of structure and strategy that depended on objective notions of resource relations, understood through competition and conflict, differentiation, and symbiosis, have increasingly recognized the conventional, and indeed fictional, quality of many organizational forms and strategies. Institutionalists who once looked to culture as a rushing in where rationality failed, where means–ends relations were uncertain or technologies untried, now increasingly recognize that culture plays a constitutive role in shaping organizational structures, strategies and technologies (Biggart and Guillen, 1999; DiMaggio, 1991; Dobbin, 1994; Fligstein, 1996, 1990; Friedland and Alford, 1991; Mohr and Guerra-Pearson, forthcoming; Scott, 2001; Scott et al., 2000).

Sociologists are increasingly taking bodies, space, and time – the elemental materials of social life – and analyzing the ways in which they figure in social signification. Feminists, and race and queer theorists are showing not only the ways in which the properties of the body are read, but how those readings are generative of the subjectivities inhabiting them (Seidman, 1991; Twine, 1998). Urbanists and sociologists of the built environment are analyzing the ways in which categories are materialized in physical form (Biernacki, 1995; Bourdieu, 1977, 1990; Gottdiener, 1995; Molotch, 1998; Zellman and Friedland, 2001; Zukin, 1995), and time, which has either been a staging ground or a fungible resource, is now increasingly understood as a culturally constructed and consequential foundation of social life, manifest in the social productivity of narrative forms, memorialization, and temporal classification (Irwin-Zarecka, 1994; Olick and Robbins, 1998; Somers, 1994; Zerubavel, 1985).

As sociologists maneuver across this new terrain, they confront the methods, theories, and insights of humanist scholars for whom questions of meaning and interpretation have long been at the core of their intellectual project. As sociologists enter this transdisciplinary zone, they are discovering that scholars in the humanities, particularly those in what is often called cultural studies, began making a sociological turn long ago (Grossberg, Nelson, and Treichler, 1992). Moving from canonical high culture to more popular forms, analyzing the ways in which cultural products are part of larger transformations in the ways of knowing in domains far from literature and art such as statecraft, cartography, and accounting, discerning the interests embedded in text, tune, image, and cultural forms of all sorts, the humanities drew heavily on post-structuralism, interpretive anthropology, and practice theory (Bermingham, 1986). Humanists increasingly came to assert that culture was not only a social product, but also integral to the production of the social. Scholars in the humanities moved away from a single-minded rereading of independent texts, increasingly analyzing the ways in which society itself could be read as a text. In making this move, they had at their disposal a wide array of analytical tools that had been developed for understanding and theorizing the production of meaning in texts, theories of genre, strategies of reading, types of rhetorical forms, the narrative process, and the nature of performance and sign systems. Inspired by linguistically grounded theorists who asserted that the subject is a position made speakable by language much more than a unitary consciousness speaking a language, humanists have pointed to the fictional quality of the social, to the logical and psychic contradictions immanent in the performativity of authority.

Where sociologists often hope to show that culture can be explained, and thus interpreted, through an analysis of its relation to social structure, sociologists have much less frequently addressed the cultural meanings themselves. In contrast, humanists bring an interpretative stance to whatever they encounter. While sociologists tend to socialize the text, analyzing the conditions of its production and reception, as well as the social interests it represents, humanists textualize society, assuming that the social order is an order of representation. Institutions, organizations, practices, and structures are all made into significations, texts to be read, grist for their exegetical mill. While they assume that the social is constituted in and through orders of language, code, symbol, and sign, humanists rarely, if ever, specify the contingent social conditions of its production or social productivity. For humanists, interpretation is explanation, whereas for sociologists it tends to be the reverse, in that sociologists make the assumption that their ability to isolate factors that co-vary with some cultural phenomenon constitutes its most useful interpretation.

The cultural turn in sociology and the sociological turn by humanists necessarily calls into question the division between them. This has provoked the calling of names and boundary defense from both sides of the aisle (Alexander, Smith, and Sherwood, 1993; Schudson, 1997; Bielby and Bielby, this volume; Clifford and Marcus, 1986; Schneider, this volume). "Sociology," Schudson writes, "can learn from cultural studies, but cultural studies is more in need of sociology than the other way around" (1997: 381). The territorial heat of partition indicates the existence of another space to be explored. The Cultural Turn conferences that we have organized at the University of California, Santa Barbara, from which this volume is composed, have been working forums where scholars from the social sciences and the humanities can explore together this shared and contested zone (http://www.soc.ucsb.edu/ct). It is our conviction that both communities have much to offer and much to learn, and it is this spirit that we seek to promote in this volume.

The place of culture in American sociology

Why the turn to culture in American sociology? Certainly it may reflect a new political–economic order in which image and identity increasingly matter. The collapse of the cold-war system and the steady erosion of the organizing power of left–right partisan politics, the politicization of sex, gender, and race, the return of religious cosmology to the public sphere, and the material productivity of software not only make the materiality of the sign abundantly clear, they point to ontology, to the very nature of the social, as a theoretical problem. They also point to the importance of identity and value-formation in social organization. Who we are and what we desire have become pressing theoretical and political problems. The theoretical status of the human is once again a question. All of this has brought culture to the fore. By this account it is the world that is becoming more cultural and we who must retool or reconceptualize if we are to stay abreast of the changes in that world.

This explanation is insufficient. If the cultural character of the social world is becoming increasingly apparent, that is not to say that culture was any less important for sociological explanation before these events. One need only rethink the classical theoretical texts. Durkheim's insight that the divine was a representation of the collectivity has been well-trodden sociological ground; its corollary, that the symbol was constitutive of the collectivity, has been relatively unexplored (Friedland, 2002). Weber, of course, pointed to forms of rationality that were structures not simply of organization, but of belief. And Marx's labor theory of value was not simply a materialist way of unlocking the laws of capitalist motion, it was a cultural account of valuation and category formation, values and categories integral to the operation of the economy. The entire project of sociological disenchantment presumed enchantment as the basis of the social order. Fictions have always been integral to the construction of social reality.

The cultural turn is neither an adaptation to changing social conditions nor is it a retreat from the core of social theory, from society as a theoretical object. It is rather a reconstitution of the sociological project, a transformation of its ontology and hence in the kinds of research problems that are likely to be most intellectually exciting and the theoretical specifications able to claim validity. It augurs, in short, a paradigm shift. What we are experiencing in American sociology can be better understood – in Thomas Kuhn's (1970) terms – as a recognition of the empirical, theoretical, methodological, and ontological limits of existing intellectual frameworks.

An increasing number of sociologists declare the inadequacy of their theoretical tools to address the problems confronting them. For example, Harrison White first developed a topological algebra for the study of kinship ties (1963) and then helped pioneer the field of social network analysis. These approaches insisted on the objectivity of the social, seeking to explain both social action and actors' accounts of that action in terms of the structure of social ties and one's position within them. White has rethought the utility of his objectivist approach. He now argues:

My theme proper is that mathematical and interpretative approaches should become indispensable to one another, partly because of this increasing scope and flexibility of mathematics . . . It is equally evident that, in avoiding and sidestepping the interpretative – and thus any direct access to the construction of social reality – *mathematical models have come to an era of decreasing returns to effort. Another way to say the same thing is that interpretative approaches are central to achieving a next level of adequacy in social data.*   (White, 1997: 57–58)

Respecifying one's model is no longer enough. White now seeks to study the co-implication of semantic and social spaces of institutional life, value sets, styles of use of those values, and social topologies. Changes in values, uses, and social networks typically occur together. Without understanding the semantic space and actions within it, one cannot understand the social space and its behaviors, and vice versa (White, 2003).[1]

The duality of the social and the cultural

Whatever new paradigm emerges, and it is too early to tell what that paradigm will look like, it will have to rethink the category of culture itself and the ways it is deployed in sociological practice. There is an enduring tendency in American sociology to hive meaning off, to treat it as something apart, inaccessible, and thus either beyond the sociologist's ken (Wuthnow, 1987), or an autonomous domain with its own symbolic logic or economy. This is evident in a wide range of dualities within the field. Perhaps the most fundamental of these is the split between the social and the cultural. The assumption that there is a gap between the old class-based social movements and the new identity-based movements, for example, is premised on a division between the social as an instrumental distributional system of things and the cultural as an expressive system of signs.

Albert Melucci, the social theorist of the "new" social movements, argues that their form and identity are a response to a new informatic mode of domination, a political economy where the commanding heights controls the production of symbols, not things.

In societies with high information density, production does not involve economic resources alone; it also concerns social relationships, symbols, identities, and individual needs. Control of social production does not coincide with its ownership by a recognizable social group. It instead shifts to the great apparatuses of technical and political decision-making. The development and management of complex systems is not secured by simply controlling the workforce and by transforming natural resources; more than that, it requires increasing intervention in the relational processes and symbolic systems on the social/cultural domain . . . The operation and efficiency of economic mechanisms and technological apparatuses depend on the management and control of relational systems where cultural dimensions predominate over "technical" variables. Nor does the market function simply to circulate material goods; it becomes increasingly a system in which symbols are exchanged.   (1996: 199–200)

"New" social movements, Melucci argues, oppose the "dominant codes upon which social relationships are founded," not control over the material means of production (1989).

It is widely presumed that there are material, objective "social" things that are separate, and fundamentally different, from more subjective, interpretive, cultural artifacts. This split, of course, derives from the long history of western philosophy, the Cartesian dualisms of mind and body, subject and object, ideal and material forces.

For example, in their anguished introductory essay to their collection, *Beyond the Cultural Turn*, Victoria Bonnell and Lynn Hunt express their concern that the cultural turn has eviscerated not only Marxism, but historical narration more generally. By its insistence on the discursive constitution of "social categories," they argue that the cultural turn threatens the social itself and, with it, the prospect for explanation and agency.[2] Having led and launched some of the best cultural historical analysis, it is a return of the social, displaced by the cultural, for which they now pine. They write of their contributors:

Although the authors in this collection have all been profoundly influenced by the cultural turn, they have refused to accept the obliteration of the social that is implied by the most radical forms of culturalism or post-structuralism. The status or meaning of the social may be in question, affecting both social history and historical sociology, but life without it has proved impossible.   (1999: 11)

And with what do Bonnell and Hunt identify the social? With the material (see also Schudson, 1997). They point approvingly to the growing study of "material culture" – of furniture, plastic madonnas, food – as an arena in which "culture and social life most obviously and significantly intersect, where culture takes concrete form." The implication is that the social is a domain of materiality, of hardness, thingness, objects with objectivity. It is not their aim, they say, to return to the days when it was legitimate to reduce the cultural to "the material world of economics and social relations" (Bonnell and Hunt, 1999: 26). But it is just this identification of the social with the material and the cultural with language, this maintenance of the duality of the social and the cultural, that blocks the way.

This duality is present in the most sophisticated of our theories. William Sewell's now-classic essay (Sewell, 1992) revises Giddens' concept of the duality of structure through the categories of "rules" and "resources." In Sewell's theory, rules refer to "cultural schemas": "society's fundamental tools of thought, but also the various recipes, scenarios, principles of action, and habitus of speech and gesture built up with these fundamental tools." Resources, in contrast, are objects and attributes of human beings that can be used to "enhance or maintain power." Schemas are virtual; resources are actual. Social structures conjoin the two.

While we like Sewell's definition of structure as the coupling of schema and resources, his resolution ends up privileging the social over the cultural. As Sewell's own discussion of the importance of schema in constituting the social power of resources suggests, it is not possible to delineate a concept of power with reference to the material world alone. Power, like structure, is known by the coupling of schema and resources. So not only does Sewell smuggle a particular end – power – into the definition of means, he de-culturalizes power, locating it in the control of resources which can be specified independently of the institutional sites in which they are produced/known/allocated. Resources, Sewell argues, are known as resources by their capacity to "enhance or maintain power" which is known by control of resources. The theory eats its tail.

One can see the problem when he distinguishes between two dimensions of structure: depth, a dimension of schema, and power, a dimension of resources. Deep structures are pervasive and unconscious. Powerful structures shift resources, typically creating inequities ("modest power concentrations," "shifting resources toward some speakers and away from others"). With this duality in place, Sewell can argue that linguistic structures are deep, but relatively powerless, a "neutral medium of exchange," which are therefore inappropriate to thinking about social structures where resources are really involved.

Not only is Sewell's analysis based on the official language as opposed to the way it is deployed, but, as Bourdieu and others have pointed out, linguistic competence is a powerful distributive force in modern societies (Bourdieu, 1991). The problems with this formulation, however, run deeper still. The use of resources, indeed the constitution of resources and the subjects who use them, are organized through institutions. Institutional reality is constructed through linguistic representation. As the philosopher John Searle has pointed out, all institutional facts – property, marriage, government – involve the conversion of collective intentionality into deontic powers – iterated, interlocked "status functions" – through linguistically mediated performative speech acts and constitutive rules. One cannot derive any institution, and hence its powers, even the organization of force, from "brute reality" itself (Searle, 1995). The state of nature, Searle points out, "is precisely one in which people do in fact accept systems of constitutive rules (1995: 91).

With regard to social life, language is not a neutral medium, but contains classifications/valuations which are productive of the things they denote. Languages author particular kinds of subjects in so far as they come into existence by speaking an authorized language. Linguistic practices, including the most ordinary, are part of the infrastructure of power. It is the unremarkable implication of the particular word in the particular social relation and vice versa that is power.

Conversely, Sewell can argue that most "state or political structures," while having enormous resource consequences, are generally not taken for granted. Sewell is here talking about state centralization and coercion. "One might argue that state structures are relatively mutable precisely because the massiveness (power) and obviousness (lack of depth) of their resource effects make them natural targets for open struggles." In the examples, his criteria are regime changes – new party systems in the United States for example, revolutions in the Third World. We would argue that it is precisely the taken-for-granted centrality of the state in allocating resources and in the schemas of social life, and of the democratic state in particular, that makes certain forms of political contest so durable. Thus Sewell, in the very next paragraph, can talk about "some political structures with immense power implications that are nevertheless relatively deep, that become 'second nature' and are accepted by all (or nearly all) political actors as essentially power-neutral, taken-for-granted means to political ends." These include the American constitution, the French public bureaucracy and the English community legal structure. Sewell concludes: "Durability, then, would appear to be determined more by a structure's depth than by its power." Sewell thus reintroduces the very duality he rejected, contradicting the whole point of the previous discussion of structure as the conjoining of schema and resources. It is precisely because these schema are materialized, that they are powerful. Depth is the result of past materiality, a forgotten history of materiality which has been naturalized. The distinction between depth and power alerts us to the attributes of institutionality and its decomposition, but it does not help us to explain them. They describe the problem, the joining and de-coupling of schema and resources; they do not point to a way toward explaining it.

More recently Sewell has taken on the duality of culture and practice, seeking to conceptualize their articulation (1999: 47). Sewell defines culture as the semiotic dimension of human social life, and practice as purposeful practical activity (1999: 44, 47–48). Sewell thus maintains his earlier dualism. He argues that "semiotic structure" is analytically independent of the economic, political, or geographical structure. Sewell politicizes a culture that he theorizes as having a "thin" coherence, a thinness due to the uncertainty and extension of reference, the resultant autonomy of culture, and the political contests that ensue. Linguistically constructed institutional facts – such as money or property – are anything but thin. Which objects, activities, and persons can be organized through different institutional categories is subject to political contest. The linguistically constructed institutional fact itself however is both enduring and epistemologically objective (Searle, 1995). While nowhere addressed, it is implicit in Sewell's approach that the purposes of practice are themselves not cultural, but what he takes to be objective considerations such as power and resources. In Sewell's approach it is, in fact, the struggle for power that organizes culture's coherence, its structured difference between the high and the low, the majority and the minority, the permitted and forbidden. "Authoritative cultural action, launched from the centers of power, has the effect of turning what otherwise might be a babble of cultural voices into a semiotically and politically ordered field of differences." If the purposes of practice were themselves cultural, the difference would not be hierarchical, but undecidable. Power, in that it is constituted by reference to values and legitimate uses of resources, which themselves are typically constituted by language, is anything but objective.

Although Sewell invokes institutional "nodes" wielding the most resources – like the state, business corporations and religions – as "sites of concentrated cultural practice" (1999: 56), it is in fact the logic of group contest that animates his theoretical machine. "The official cultural map may, of course, be criticized and resisted by those relegated to its margins. But subordinate groups must to some degree orient their local systems of meaning to those recognized as dominant; the act of contesting dominant meanings itself implies a recognition of their centrality" (1999: 56–57). Power struggles (like ours here) generate differences which are the basis of semiotic structure. The power of institutions and groups is located in part in their ability to structure semiotic difference. While these differences are supposed to refer to practices, practice is, in fact, absent – at both a theoretical and an empirical level – within his analysis. Without practices tied to institutional fields, Sewell can conflate the struggle between dominant groups over their position in a hierarchy of practices with the contradictions between incommensurable institutional logics. Even in his own terms, Sewell inadequately specifies the relation between culture and practice, for while he has pointed to the ways in which group conflict organizes meanings, he fails to specify the ways in which meanings organize group conflict.

Neither interests, powers, nor resources can be specified independently of the meanings which organize specific institutional fields. Materiality is a way of producing meaning; meaning is a way of producing materiality. Materiality and meaning are not exterior to each other, as the conceptual divide between social and cultural systems, or resource and structure, or the term "embedded," all variously imply.

Sociologists tend to make ideas and values into external variables which may add explanatory power once interests, which are attributes of individuals, organizations, and groups in social situations, have been taken into account. That culture might shape the formation of both the agents and their interests has not been a typical starting point. It is presumed that the social is knowable, observable, can be read from positionality in ostensibly objective relations between people and things. The social is presumed to be an instrument formed in consequence of the struggle for existence.

Jeffrey Alexander's post-Durkheimian school has grounded the autonomy of the cultural in the linguistic order of signs and symbols, in semiotic structure. Alexander and his students have looked on culture as a code or language with its own internal logic, insisting on its autonomy from the materiality of the social world (Alexander, 1998; Alexander and Smith, 1993; Kane, 1991). Alexander distinguishes between three "environments of action": social, cultural, and personality. The analytic autonomy of the cultural realm enables generalizable significations – both typifications and inventions – independent of the social conditions of their use. Autonomous, structured cultural codes provide the tools through and by which actors can recode themselves and the world and thereby create new worlds.

If Alexander grounds the autonomy of culture in semiotic order, he identifies the social system with an order of distribution. Reviewing Alain Touraine's theorization of post-industrial social movements, Alexander describes Parsons' distinction between values and norms, the latter involving "historically specific forms of organization that focus, not on general values, but on the distribution of rewards and sanctions" (1996). Alexander approves of how Touraine, unlike Parsons, does not conflate "existing forms of social organization with the cultural ideals that informed them." It is the gap between value and norm, between the cultural and the social, between cultural ideals and social norms, in which Alexander locates the possibility for reflexive agency and hence for social movements.

Pierre Bourdieu, whom Alexander has attacked for his materialist reductions, is not really that different (1985). Bourdieu refuses the idealist stance, arguing for the homology between categorical and social structures as they are mediated through incorporated non-discursive knowledges deposited in the habitus. Bourdieu does transform culture into an integral part of a general material economy, a form of capital like all others. However, like Alexander, for Bourdieu it is the gap between the symbolic and the social order, between habitus and the structure of domination, that makes both creative agency and critical social movement possible: things like the "fuzzy logic" of the habitus, its economic transposability, the mismatch between the conditions in which a habitus was acquired and the conditions in which it is expected to operate (Friedland, 2001).

In cultural sociology, relations to means – space, time, bodies, objects, and words – specify interests. Relations to ends tend to specify meanings. Social scientific theory has primarily sought a science of means, analyzing the ways in which the means are distributed or deployed, instrumentalizing means as sources of power. The ends are either exogenous and unanalyzed, as in economics, where preferences are exogenous, in organizational sociology where firm survival is taken as the organizing end, or assumed as in the pleasure principle of Freud's psychoanalytic theory, Marx's assumption of a progressive extension and appropriation of human faculties, or Bourdieu's assumption that the stake of stakes is the legitimate principle of domination. Culture is either transparent as ideology with regard to interests, instrumentalized as a schema or routines to be applied in those circumstances where the means–end connection has been ruptured, or opaque as dreams to be decoded in reference to interests derivable from one's relation to those means.

Sociologists have a strong tendency both to explain and interpret cultural forms through an objectively knowable social exterior, either making them into arbitrary markers to be produced, promoted, and defended by a community of cultural producers (Becker, 1982; Griswold, 1987; Peterson, 1976) or as status emblems for a class fraction (Biesel, 1993; Bourdieu, 1984). As a result, cultural meanings, both categorical and expressive, are usually subservient to a social logic and do not participate in its making. Or culture is treated as an exterior semiotic, symbolic, or classificatory order that shapes an already-existing social order.

The unmeaning of culture

A half a century ago, this split between the social and the cultural was less apparent. Many social scientists then took culture to be constitutive of social life. Both cultural anthropology and structural–functionalist sociology understood pre-modern and modern societies respectively as cosmologically ordered. Within the grand theories they had to offer, culture held up an important part of the tent. However, their conceptualizations of culture were attacked for consensuality, totalization, idealism, neglect of group power, the gap between attitude and action, abstraction from historical practice, and their inability to grapple with the material exigencies of production or reproduction. This kind of cultural sociology, it was said, simply reproduced dominant ideologies.

In consequence, in the mainstream there was a retreat from discourse altogether, from members' accounts, from meanings which, it was argued, were unobservable and hence unworthy of social scientific exploration. Sociology became a search for localized, objectively knowable materialities, whether of organization, social movement, family, state, or interpersonal interaction. The new paradigm was oriented toward a set of research practices, modalities of knowledge – from ethnography to quantitative analysis – that reflected an abiding skepticism of more abstract formulations. Only thus could one make the data speak, observe regularities, falsify hypotheses. Culture became a field unto itself, a specialized domain of semantic, cognitive, and attitudinal measurement dissociated from any larger sociological theory. Indeed, there was no encompassing theory, and hence no possibility of a cultural sociology, only a sociology of culture. Although culture was gradually rehabilitated, it was no longer an engine of social action nor a regulator of social order, but another lawful domain amenable to empirical study (Peterson, 1979).

True, culture continued to be understood as localized meanings by symbolic interactionists and ethnographers. However, those at the center of the sociological discipline tended to transform it into something that was decidedly unmeaningful (Mohr, 1998). Culture was largely instrumentalized, turned into a resource whose meaning could be reduced to its productivity in the struggle for social power. In the extensive empirical works of Pierre Bourdieu and those who have sought to apply his theory in the United States, culture is an instrument in the struggle for distinction, a resource in the distributional contest for prestige, power, and money, for the dominant a legitimating distancing from necessity (see also DiMaggio, 1982, DiMaggio and Mohr, 1985), or, in the work of Lamont (1992), a resource for the construction and maintenance of group boundaries. In institutional varieties of organizational theory, culture became a marker of legitimacy, a resource deployed by firms and agencies as they compete for clients, market share, and government authority and funding (DiMaggio and Powell, 1983; Meyer and Scott, 1983; Sutton, Dobbin, Meyer, and Scott, 1994; see also Ventresca and Mohr, 2002 and Mohr, forthcoming). Culture becomes a variable, an attribute, a property measured in the same manner as the distribution of birth order, educational certificates, or equities.

Ann Swidler, one of the leading figures in cultural sociology, articulated this new culture concept, taking the position that culture – as symbols, stories, and rituals – provides a set of modalities which people use to develop commonly understood and utilized strategies of action to solve their problems. Culture, she says, is like a "'tool kit' or repertoire . . . from which actors select differing pieces for constructing lines of action" (1986: 273; see also Swidler, 2001: 25). Swidler thus seeks to move away from Parsons' instrumental organization of means in pursuit of culturally defined, internalized ends, by stressing the external cultural delimitation of conceivable and actionable means.

The conditions under which it is possible to reject the classical Weberian approach that emphasizes the role of "world images" in shaping both the ends and means to and through which action is oriented must be specified (Weber, 1946). Culture is often not just a medium of individual or collective social action, it is very much what is at stake in both the means and the ends. Often there is an integral relation between instrumental and value rationality. While we endorse Swidler's freighting of strategy with cultural meaning, many important social movements cannot be analyzed if one analyzes culture, as she urges, as conditioning action, "not by shaping ends they ['its holders'] pursue, but by providing the characteristic repertoire from which they build lines of action" (1986: 284).

In Jerusalem, for instance, Friedland and Hecht found that the movements' strategies and organizational forms were conditioned not just by their powers, but by their particular world views (2000). Not only were the means chosen sometimes irrational as strategy, they were often suffused with meaning, emblems, or instances of the reality in which the movement was grounded. The strategies of Israeli and Palestinian social movements were dictated not just by resource constraints, but by their cosmology, by the ends they pursued, and by the means they considered appropriate to actualize those ends. Means and ends are associated. For instance, to understand the strategies of the religious Zionist movement that settled the West Bank after 1967 – its lack of concern for military defensibility or economic self-sufficiency in its settlement plan, its subordination of *halacha* – religious law – in its political program, its involvement in vigilanteism, its willingness to jeopardize major opportunities for peace with Israel's hostile neighbors, requires that one consider the co-implication of ends and means (see also Friedland, 2002; Rapoport, 1984).

Eyerman and Jamison have likewise shown the ways in which successful social movements – from environmentalism to socialism – create new public spaces in which new identities, new knowledges and new organizational forms conjointly emerge (1991: 66–93). "The environmental movement," they write, "embodied the concepts of ecology by contextualizing and politicizing them, but also by internalizing them . . . [It] transformed a scientific theory into a way of life, but even more into a set of beliefs" (1991: 72–73).

In the now-classic new institutionalist account of organizations, culture matters as a resource for demonstrating legitimacy and thereby access to resources. Particularly where means–ends relations are opaque, organizational forms and practices are templates that become invested with value independent of their contribution to efficiency or effectiveness (DiMaggio and Powell, 1983). This work approaches the problem with the assumption that the means–ends relation can be analyzed as an objectively knowable instrumental relation between means and ends (for instance, firm survival, the accumulation of profit or power, the control of uncertainty), such that the logical connections between means and ends derive instrumentally from the material constraints. The semiotic logic of culture is here a derivative of the material logic of practice.

Culture is part of the determination of both means and ends, of practices and values. Institutional facts are always relative to some purpose, some value by which the productivity of the powers they create is both gauged and legitimated.

This means that what counts as a resource always has a cultural specificity, and indeed an evaluative specificity. Institutional facts are necessarily regimes of valuation. In their work on the history of welfare organizations in New York City between 1888 and 1917, Mohr and Duquenne (1997) show the ways in which new modalities of action, the joining of repertoires of action (the provision of food, shelter, work) to particular categories of the poor, not only create categories of actor (indigent, deserving poor), but are integral to definition of the social problem and hence the ends which these organizations pursue.

Not only in social movements, but in organizations as well, the meaning and incidence of means and ends cannot be parsed so neatly. Between 1880 and 1980, Fligstein has shown how the very concept of the American firm, its organizational structure as well as the ends toward which its strategies are oriented, shifted over time from a unit of production, to one seeking to expand and control markets, to a bundle of financial assets (Fligstein, 1990). Likewise, in the San Francisco health field, Scott and his co-workers showed how dominant organizational forms, their practices of governance, and the values to which they were linked changed in tandem over the course of fifty years: from non-profit hospitals and independent physicians tied to the value of quality of care at the beginning, to profit-making hospitals, particularly HMOs, tied to the value of efficient delivery at the end (Scott et al., 2000). Action, actor, and the ends of action are implicated in each other in ways we need to understand better.

Swidler has specified an essential empirical agenda – understanding the conditions under which codes and symbols are internalized as common sense or electrically charged as self-conscious emblems of moral purpose or ideological templates. But social movements and organizations simultaneously develop particular motivations and purposes, as well as the categories of actor and the forms of action by which they can be realized. To inject meaning into means, while divorcing those means from the ends to which they are put may fit particular empirical instances of diffusion of models from one arena of social practice to another, but it also weakens our ability to analyze new strategies of action and the conditions for their institutionalization. It is precisely the conditions under which world views shape social practice across different institutional *loci* of social life that must be investigated, not their several empirical instances taken to normalize it as a transhistorical, trans-societal regularity. Culture's boundary conditions still elude us.

In Swidler's "Cultural Power and Social Movements," she stresses the critical role of "social context" in explaining the cultural determination of action (1995). What Swidler means by "context" is political polarization where "the conflict itself" generates clear ideological positions to which members must adhere in order to consolidate alliances or when social movements confront certain kinds of "institutions" which shape the kinds of demands they are likely to make. We can see the problem when Swidler argues that it is during "unsettled" times, "periods of social transformation," when ideologies are able to "establish new styles of strategies of action." She writes:

> In such periods . . . ideologies – explicit, articulated, highly organized meaning systems (both political and religious) – establish new styles or strategies of action. When people are learning new ways of organizing individual and collective action . . . then doctrine, symbol, and ritual directly shape action.   (1986: 278)

This takes as an explanatory variable precisely what needs to be explained.[3] Given that the genesis of "competing ways of organizing action" often define such "unsettled" times, this approach makes it difficult to explain under what conditions "new ways of organizing action" were possible in the first place. For "unsettled" times are precisely those periods when social movements or alternative institutional sites challenge existent world views, times when dominant world views that specify the good life and the way to realize it are breaking down or are in conflict. Swidler thus takes attributes of conditions under which social movements emerge or attributes of their emergence as predictors of the conditions under which social movement ideology will shape the behavior of those who participate in it. It is an astute analysis of how social movements operate, but not why they emerge or what they are about.

Swidler's own strategy to explain both the emergence and success of new ideologies is not then surprising. (Why, after all, should she escape the thrust of her own theory?) Swidler turns to Skocpol's "structural constraints," the culturally unmediated "real" social structure as the primary determinant. "Culture," she writes, "has independent causal influence in unsettled cultural periods because it makes possible new strategies of action . . . It is, however, the concrete situations in which these cultural models are enacted that determine which take root and thrive, which wither and die" (Swidler 1986: 280).

In her rich set of qualitative interviews of American adults, Swidler similarly interprets her subjects' talk of love. Swidler argues that when adults live "settled lives," a diffuse culture shapes action by providing taken-for-granted, often habitual, repertoires of action. These repertoires, "falling in love" for instance, are cultural media through which people pursue objective goals, "searching for a life partner" (2001: 105). These repertoires are loosely linked to articulated norms, a "toolkit" by which individuals can pursue shifting "values" – "happiness," "self-respect," "an exciting life" (2001: 106). In settled lives, values facilitate the enactment of one repertoire as opposed to another. In "unsettled" lives, in contrast, culture as ideology – organized, coherent with aspirations for comprehensiveness – allows the construction of new strategies of action. In "unsettled lives," Swidler writes:

Values do not usually determine how people act. Indeed people are likely to change their values while still holding on to the strategies with which they go about achieving their ends.   (2001: 106)

It is institutional insufficiency and incompleteness, Swidler argues, that generate problems of action to which cultural elaboration responds. Culture's coherence, its "logic" as a set of practices and semiotic codes, derives from these "dilemmas of action" (2001: 201). Swidler treats the institution of marriage as an objective structure to which the cultural construct of love, of which her informants talk incessantly, is a response. Mythic love is a cultural response to uncertain entry, of whether or to whom to marry. The emergence of a discourse of "prosaic" love, in which "love" is worked at through communication and compromise, is a response to the evident failure of actual marriages.

Love appears, however, to be an unchanging value. Swidler's informants, despite the widening incidence of divorce, their skepticism as to its singular, sudden, and exclusive qualities, and their invocation of another "prosaic" and "realistic" discourse of love, cannot let go of "mythic" love. Why? Swidler argues that it is because mythic love corresponds to the "structural reality" of marriage:

My argument is that the features of the love myth – an exclusive, unique passion, a decisive choice that expresses and resolves identity, a struggle to overcome obstacles, and a commitment that endures forever – correspond neither to personal experience nor to the observations people make of others they know. But its power is not an illusion. Rather, the love myth accurately describes the structural constraints of the institution of marriage.   (2001: 127–128)

Incomplete institutions here both provoke and constrain the formation of culture through "dilemmas of action" (2001: 201). Swidler rightly points out that we do not understand very well the contingent relation between semiotic codes and institutional orders (2001: 206). In this case, however, it is arguable that love is not a cultural outside to the institution of American marriage, but its inside. Love, like any value, is an unobservable substance, which can only be known by how it is produced and practiced (Friedland, 2001). Swidler's informants, by articulating new practices by which love is known and produced – more prosaic, voluntaristic, gradual learning to live with one another associated with less gender role-specificity within marriage – are seeking to align their practices with that value, which they refuse to abandon, which they believe is "there." It is the internality of value to institution, one typically performed and produced through an exclusive, eroticized, and emotional cohabitation, and the desire to sustain that value, that might account for the omnipresent effort evidenced by Swidler's informants to develop alternative culturally elaborated practices that will enable them to sustain marriage. In America, it may be the value of love as much as the material exigencies of reproduction and intimate sociality that accounts for the institutional structure of marriage. While Swidler shows the ways in which culturally elaborated strategies of action cannot be derived from institutions, she also shows that they cannot be separated from them either. Love, whether mythic or prosaic, appears to endure through changes in the institution of marriage. Values immanent in institutional life may be as important in shaping strategies of action during unsettled times as during settled ones. Just because the category is historically freighted with consensual normativity, we should not shun the domain of values, of ends, even as they appear to remain invariant, in accounting for the changing organization of social life. As Swidler's own work shows, changing repertoires of action are tied to regimes of valuation, instruments for the pursuit of purposes, techniques for producing, pursuing, and performing values, the social conditions of whose value we do not yet understand.

While Swidler is rightly concerned to move away from models that analyze culture as consensual, internalized subjectivities, her move toward publicly available externalized ways of organizing action, while it seeks to collapse the instrumental/expressive divide, simply reverses the old means–ends duality in which the instrumental world remains as an external, objective limit to cultural refashioning. The role of culture in constituting that world, in conjointly organizing its practices and its values, its means and its ends, drops from view.

When culture made its way back into American sociology, it did so as something that was either an independent domain, a discrete attribute or a localized activity, something that was measurable, or knowable in a grounded empirical sense, something that had demonstrable effects, and usually something which required little or no interpretation. While most would agree that these were important advances, a corrective to the older notion of a consensual cultural totality, meaning is often missing in this new cultural sociology, both in the sense of a rich hermeneutics and in the absence of a place for culture's constitutive role (Hall, this volume). If, in earlier understandings, there was little politics in culture, now there is little culture in politics.

If cultural sociologists have often reduced culture to meaningless media, cultural studies, its roots in the Birmingham Center for Cultural Studies, sought to interpret the meanings of cultural practice. Yet, they, too, operated out of the same binary that so vexes cultural sociological theory.

British cultural studies traditionally divided the world into a social realm, a world of experience, the *locus* of referents, and a cultural realm, a world of representation and meaning, of signs. Thus E. P. Thompson treated culture as the medium through which "class experience" was transformed into "class consciousness" (1966: 8–10). Likewise, Stuart Hall and Tony Jefferson define culture as:

that level at which social groups develop distinct patterns of life and give expressive form to their social and material . . . experience.   (1976)

But how to identify oppositional meanings in working-class culture? Much influenced by the Italian Marxist, Antonio Gramsci, the Birmingham School looked toward ideology not as political consciousness, but as social unconsciousness, as a fateful common sense. The cultural categories of the real were the foundations of legitimation. What is is and should be.

With a working class understood to be increasingly disillusioned with Labourite policies, in the same year that Margaret Thatcher's anti-statist regime would begin to roll back every form of social-democratic market regulation and redistribution gained in the post-World War II period, Dick Hebdige looked to young working-class men for signs of resistance (1979: 82–83). In his celebrated analysis of English working-class subcultures, Hebdige sought to show the ways in which working-class youth were able to recuperate in consumption expressions denied to them in production and politics. Hebdige argued that the objects of the mass commodity market could be resignified as style, which, when properly decoded, reveal resistance. "[C]ommodities," Hebdige writes, "can be symbolically 'repossessed' in everyday life, and endowed with implicitly oppositional meanings, by the very groups who originally produced them" (1979: 16). By the particular way in which they are consumed – through style – objects are made to speak "forbidden meanings" (1979: 103). Hebdige analyzed various styles of music and their associated dance and clothing to show the way in which the sign value of objects was contested by working-class youth. If one looked closely at the punks' safety pins in their earlobes, the Rastafarian dreadlocks, Teddy boy brothel creepers, ultra-neat mods on scooters, one could discern how the struggle over production and distribution of objects had been displaced by a struggle over their sign value, a challenge to the common sense of the commodity world (1979: 17–18). Through symbolic resistance, these "spectacular subcultures" forced things to speak otherwise, to denaturalize the code, creating a gap between sign and referent.

While Hebdige pointed to the contingent relation of subculture to class position, in his reconstruction it was "real relations under capitalism" that were the materialist rock and referent through which these subcultures were all interpreted (1979: 81). The experiences of inequality, powerlessness, and alienation were pre-categorical realities (1979: 121). Subculture is, he writes, the way in which "the experience of class found expression in culture" (1979: 74), and, "the challenge to hegemony which subcultures represent . . . is expressed obliquely, in style. The objections are lodged, the contradictions displayed . . . at the profoundly superficial level of appearances: that is, at the level of signs" (1979: 17). For example, noting the punk's "paralysed look," he writes:

its "dumbness" . . . found a silent voice in the smooth moulded surfaces of rubber and plastic, in the bondage and robotics which signify "punk" to the world. For at the heart of the punk subculture, forever arrested, lies this frozen dialectic between black and white cultures – a dialectic which beyond a certain point (i.e. ethnicity) is incapable of renewal, trapped, as it is, within its own history, imprisoned within its own irreducible antinomies.   (1979: 69–70)

Hebdige never studied whether, how, or even what this, or any subculture, actually signifies for those who consumed it, let alone those working-class youth who did not. This is a particularly glaring problem in that the oppositional meanings of these subcultures derive from their difference to white working- and middle-class cultures (1979: 73). If Bourdieu located cultural generation in the dominant class and its distancing from the dominated, cultural studies sought agency in the people. In Hebdige's account, the dominant culture remains largely unobserved, except as it shrieks needlessly, almost an implicit constant. Only the subcultures have any dynamism, any productivity. This does not mean that he actually reconstructs the dominant culture; in fact, Hebdige's account reads public rhetoric, the materials that make for the common intelligibility of the subcultures by followers and opponents. This method effaces difference. His study is not an ethnography, in that no mod or punk is ever observed in his/her particularity; no concrete scene is ever evoked; nor are any members of any of these cultures ever given any voice.

Hebdige narrates subcultural style as class resistance. He delicately con- structs the story of British music as a roadmap to the history of working-class subcultures. These subcultures are all ritually constituted, organized around par- ticular sounds and bodily practices – music, dress, and dance, a non-discursive world which is available to a quasi-illiterate population (not unlike the riots at football games). Embodied ritual, unlike written or spoken doctrine, is a priv- ileged site for popular resistance because it is a more ambiguous and hence concealable form of signification than are words. However, when bodies come to language, there is always a potential gap between bodily experience and the words in which it is conveyed. The meaning of bodily experience, much more than that of words, is unavailable to the outside observer. Saying what cannot be said, it need not be said, so what is said can easily account for what cannot be seen.

Deconstructionist and new historicist readings of culture through text and textual metaphor miss these bases for transgressive signification, the for- mer because they understand the body as always, already constituted through signs. Even so, the relation between non-discursive and discursive signification requires systematic analysis, for what is said has some bearing on what is done, on the translation of culture into politics, of style into struggle. Hebdige makes the young working-class body speak his language, but what discourse comes out of their mouths? We do not know.

Hebdige does not adequately problematize the specificity of the field – commodified consumption – in which the objects are put into practice, made to do particular forms of work, to signify and solidify, to resist and rally. The nature of the field in which these subcultures are constituted may have as much to do with the capacity for resignification as with its utter impotence. Thus Hebdige points out that style, including that of the punks, the most radical, is resistant only in its immaculate first instance, quickly becoming a magnet for mindless followers and a zone for new commodification. It is, as Hebdige says, diffused and defused (1979: 93). Whether you call it hegemony, repressive tolerance, or a capitalist circus, whether skinheads magically returning to an imagined class culture, mods magically moving up or punks magically jumping outside, these subcultures, as Hebdige remarks, are shooting blanks.[4] That it is organized around consumption of objects produced and distributed through capitalist commodity markets has as much to do with its capacity to carry resistant meanings as it does for its failure to produce any social effects. While Hebdige recognizes that capitalist commodification takes the sting out of subculture, it is perhaps also the case that commodification of consumption depends on sliding signification which makes play easy and resistance ineffective. Resistance depends on representations that are stable across time, on sticky signifiers. In Hebdige's analysis, the West Indians cohere, their words and their styles have effects on all the working-class subcultures despite dramatic changes in their population size and occupational chances in Britain, while the punks, the Teddies, the skinheads, and the Mods do not.

Speaking of the dialectic of cultural movement from black to white musical forms, Hebdige writes: "As the music and the various subcultures it supports or reproduces assume rigid and identifiable patterns, so new subcultures are created which demand or produce corresponding mutations in musical form. These mutations in their turn occur at those moments when forms and themes imported from contemporary black music break up the existing musical structure and force its elements into new configurations." In the 1960s, for instance, the Mods turned toward soul and ska from bop and romantic ballads; while the punks later moved from glam rock to reggae (1979: 68–69; see also 46–49).

Hebdige argues that the British blacks constituted a kind of symbolic constant, an inversion of white bourgeois convention, "a dark passage down into an imagined 'underworld'" (1979: 53–54). Indeed Hebdige contends that, although its meanings were periodically "laundered" or "suppressed" in white jazz or swing, black music signifies authentic resistance for white working-class youth who appropriated its forms because they wanted to reaffirm their difference from conventional, co-opted expressions.

Writing about the Mods, who, devaluing work, also parodied office dress by their compulsive neatness with one element out of place, Hebdige proclaims: "It was the Black Man who made all this possible: by a kind of sorcery, a sleight of hand, through 'soul,' he had stepped outside the white man's comprehension" (1979: 54). Even the chauvinist skinheads borrow West Indian clothing and speech, and dance to their music. It is a West Indian origin story for British working-class subculture, a classic diffusion tale with a Marxist plot.

Well, why do the West Indians function uniquely as the template, the font of white hipster and beat modalities, a reservoir for the white working class to imagine new working-class culture? Why, in short, is class expression inert; why does it depend on the appropriation of blackness, on racial reversals of otherness? Turning to Hall's notion that because counter-discourses are commonsensically repositioned through mass media, and hence to the analytic site of the public, explains nothing. Christian fundamentalism and radical Islam, feminism and racialized communities have all restructured the meaning of objects in ways that transform the very boundaries and constituent units of contemporary society, sometimes using the same mass media.

To explain why it has been possible to create socially potent subcultures around gender, religion, and race, it is necessary to give analytic autonomy and cultural specificity to institutional sites other than capitalism. As Hebdige notes, the persistence of a Jamaican subculture depended on the coincidence of biblical spaces of representation and racial difference, just as E. P. Thompson showed the ways in which the British working class formed itself through distinctive religious traditions. As McRobbie observes, while reassertions and redefinitions of masculinity were critical dimensions to these working-class subcultures, subcultures that were relentlessly male, Hebdige never examined the family as a source or site of this culture (1990). McRobbie also points out that these working subcultures were studied on the street, not in their sex, sleep, and sustenance, activities which were bound up with sexual divisions of labor. It was, she argues, relatively dangerous for women to participate in these street cultures with their drugs and drinking, and girls' subcultures were less extensive and more sparsely populated. To critique and organize collectively within a dominant institutional domain requires the importation of logics, of frames of interpretation and hence critique, from alternative institutional spaces (Friedland, 2002). This has been as true for women as for the working class as a whole.

The propulsive question behind cultural studies is what Stuart Hall calls the "transparency" of the relationship between class position and the creation of political subjects. While the issue can be observed at the level of subject formation, it cannot be adequately theorized there. Socialism has always involved the translation of the logic of capitalism into democracy, of exploitation/exchange into community/voice. Its critique is animated by the language of human need and its solidaristic fulfillment, the institutional logic of the family. Disappointed by democracy, by the failure of socialist movements, cultural studies have looked to other institutional sites, notably consumption and mass media, to explain the failure and to situate the promise. But their studies are dominated by the logic of group formation, not the logic of fields in which group formation takes place. Nicholas Dirks, Geoff Eley, and Sherry Ortner, for example, write: "there has been an explosion of studies, both contemporary and historical, on the cultural worlds of different classes, ethnic groups, racial groups, and so on and the way in which these cultural worlds interact" (1994: 3). While it is now recognized that the culture is not common, the agenda is still dominated by the question of who, of groups, not of where, from, in, and on behalf of what institution.

Cultural studies has failed to theorize the inter-institutional tracks. Why is class condition currently transmuted into consumption and not in politics, religion, or family life? To presume a priori that the subcultures formed express class as opposed to group formation rooted in other institutional spaces is warranted by political desire, not by empirical reality. One must return to the inter-institutional structure of the social formation and analyze the ways in which group conflicts in one arena carry or contradict the logic of other institutions – patriarchy, capitalism, the nation state, democracy, science, or religion. And, ironically, to explain or interpret the class meanings of culture requires that we engage in more persistent reexamination of the material and cultural organization of class, not in consumption, in living rooms and on dance floors, but in the ways in which work identities and practices do and do not suffuse our daily lives (Widick, 2003). Hebdige assumes a mechanism by which positions in production are transmuted into expressions in consumption; he does not study it. The working class, the class working, disappears. It is precisely those conditions under which expressions in commodity consumption reverberate in production and vice versa that require analysis. The cultural relationship between production and consumption, between the cultural meaning of class and the class meaning of culture, remains to be studied.

The cultural limits of critical theory

These are sad times for critical theory, with the global apotheosis of the market on the one side and the fissiparous explosion of particularisms on the other. Today's reigning "critical theories" – rational choice, institutional economics, population ecology, and socio-biology – mime the systemic rationality of the former while bemoaning the passionate irrationality of the latter. Cultural studies, in contrast, has attempted to harness the voices of excluded, dominated, or marginal groups as vehicles for critique and opposition. Class has become increasingly invisible just at that point when income inequities within both nations and the world are at record levels.

Traditional critical theory depended on alternative actionable standards stitched into social reality, contradictions internal and external to capitalism, on productive fissures through which one could launch practical utopian projects. Whether the unfolding of rationality, progress, freedom, or distributive justice, critical theory also depended on a unitary vision of what it meant, and could mean, to be human on this earth. Critical theories have traditionally grounded their critique on one or another abstract modern value immanent in the public sphere, whether justice, equality, tolerance, recognition, or authenticity. Crespi traces the lineage of this move to the Platonic and hence western metaphysical separation between absolutized, abstract thought and indeterminate, interested, practical action (Crespi, 1999). Crespi rejects this dualism as a basis for critical theory, for it either eventuates in a totalizing normative project of social control, which he discerns not only in Parsons and Durkheim but in Habermas as well, or it leads to a celebration of a Nietzschean will-to-power embodied in action to the neglect of action's dependence on normative order. However, even beyond this duality, with the disassembling of the subject into power's product and the partitioning of its perspectives into group points of view, the foundations for critique seem to have fallen away, reduced to a celebration of pluralities.

Critical theory once offered a cultural materialism, an understanding of capitalism as a cultural system that both produced and distributed a specific value, one whose codes of production were riven by internal and external contradictions. Marx refused a theory of the state, understanding capital as dependent on the power and form of the state and the power and form of that state as constituted by capital and its contradictions. Today, however, an institutionally de-localized power has become an ontological universal impassible to hermeneutic specificity. Whether in Sewell's identification of power with social structure, Bourdieu's interchangeable powers and capitals, or Foucault's power/knowledge couplet, power itself has become culturally void, an empty cell, pure potentiality, a relation. Instead of exploitation, we parse social reality through the grid of domination, of productive discourses, constituting exclusions and imposed binaries. Contradiction has been dissolved into the antinomies of power and powerlessness, for cultural studies, anxiety of an occupant of a subject position the reigning trope. These social theories have joined the logic of domination to signification through linguistic post-structuralisms, constricting the cultural to the categorical, reducing political purpose to power and representation, extruding value, beauty, desire, and sensuality from culture's contents.

Resistance to domination, the struggle for voice and for language, has become the underlying basis of critique, and the norms of the democratic public sphere its typical tracks.

But to do what? And how? Critical theory, Kozlarek writes, "looks for an orientation in that which has not yet become reality, but which is already inscribed in the existing social reality" (2001: 609). Critique depends on values, on style and passion; its oppositional languages must be joined to and derived from real social locations in which its practices are actionable across social groups. Cultural theorists have justly complained that the inherited critical theories have a delimited social address. Kozlarek points to the ways in which the universalism of the Frankfurt School's critical theory is inadequate to a critique of globalization because of its implication in the Eurocentric project of cosmopolitan unity. He argues that a renewed critical theory must derive it normative commitments out of the geographically multitudinous concrete and necessarily partial social processes, not out of the scenography of European reason. Our world is one of multiple modernities whose articulation must be part of the ethics of a new critical theory (Gole, 2001). Many look to dominated groups – women, people of color, the world's subaltern populations – as positions from and for which new forms of critical understanding and engagement can be deployed.

Locating critical positionality in dominated groups leads inexorably to coalition-building, to bases of alignments which must find their hermeneutic principle in that power, thereby eviscerating the cultural specificity of the groups themselves. When Marxism met post-structuralism, class evaporated into an atmosphere thick with difference. Ironically, the way was prepared by an Italian revolutionary, Antonio Gramsci, and a French academic Marxist, Louis Althusser. Gramsci, who pushed the notion of hegemony right to the Marxist frontier, sought to politicize the production of common sense, of consent, arguing that the naturalization of the power of the dominant class derives from a struggle, a balance of forces. Gramsci saw capitalism as the natural limit to the working class' ability to perform its hegemonic task of building a historic bloc that would be able to reconstitute state power and displace capitalism. Althusser, the structuralist Marxist, argued that ideology is not legitimation, but the discourse in which individuals are positioned, or interpellated, and through which they are known and know themselves. The subject is an ideological effect, not a prediscursive agent, an essential "man." But, although he granted them autonomy, Althusser transformed other institutions into reproductive supports – ideological state apparatuses – for the dominant logic of capital.

Although both Gramsci and Althusser asserted culture's autonomy, the reproduction of capitalism was the criterion by which the effects of ideology were to be known. Capitalism was culture's outside. But after Foucault and Derrida, culture's door opened on something absolutely unspeakable. There was no outside. Ernesto Laclau and Chantal Mouffe's *Hegemony and Socialist Strategy*, published in 1985, was emblematic of the transformation of capitalist society into a discursive formation, and has become a classic text in the effort to develop critical theory anew. Refracted through Marxism, post-structuralism pulverized the culturally specific contradictions of class, replacing them with the linguistic universals of difference and, as we shall show, the political universals of power.

While class formation has now disappeared as an analytic object in American cultural studies, Laclau and Mouffe originated their project in the contingent formation of a working-class political subject. Laclau and Mouffe reread socialist thinking about working-class politics to show that not just political action, but the identity of the collective political subjects who act, are contingent. These are not subjects with interests that require representation, but subject positions the meaning of whose action is governed by symbolic processes. Not only was politics interior, not exterior, to class, but politics did not necessarily produce class subjects. It depends on a contingent articulation of subject positions – worker, citizen, consumer – defined in different realms; it is a discursive contest, a struggle through which identities are constituted, visions of another order articulated. The proletariat is an imagined community.

Laclau and Mouffe argue that it is the inability to organize socialist politics around a morphological model of the totality and developmental historical laws that prompts the positing of hegemony. Democratic politics is not a representation of objective interests or identities constituted in production, but an articulation of multiple subject positions, including that of citizen itself. In socialist thought hegemony becomes the performative pathway to the popular – from the popular fronts against fascism to the popular revolutions of the Third World. The "people" return to Marxism as a set of subject positions not defined by class, positions all occupying an equivalent relation to the dominant position (1985: 62–63).

If the identity of actors in democratic politics is not fixed outside in class, but politically constructed in the articulation of citizen and worker, neither is the identity of worker and capitalist fixed inside of capitalism. Relations of production are not relations in production; exploitation requires domination not just external to, but also internal to, the organization of production. Neither capitalism nor capitalist society is an objectively "intelligible structure," and history therefore has no necessity, no immanent tendencies, no laws. Not only class formation, but also capitalism itself is contingent. There is no essential working-class identity, no objective interests, no basis for "privileging certain subject positions over others in the determination of the 'objective' interests of the agent as a whole" (1985: 84). The working class does not have an objective interest in socialism.

Joining Althusser to Derrida, and using the former's notion of overdetermination as the bridge, Laclau and Mouffe dissolve Marxism into difference. Although encased within capialism's necessity, Althusser appropriated psychoanalytic logic to argue that social relations were constituted symbolically. The identity of all social positions is constituted through unstable differences which have no outside producing the principle of their regularity. Social relations are not essential, not literal, but a symbolic order. Laclau and Mouffe make the constitution of every non-linguistic object conditional upon the discourse through which it is accountable (1985: 107). Discourse is a materialized language game. The world of things is sutured into the world of signs; the social is materialized metaphor. Shuck the economistic casing, introduce the sliding signifier and hence contingent meaning of every signified, and then objective interests, classes in themselves, society as a structure, even capitalism become so many discursive formations. "Society," they write, "is not a valid object of discourse. There is no single underlying principle fixing – and hence constituting – the whole field of differences" (1985: 111).

If identities float, with a multiplicity of possible signifieds, then politics becomes poetic, a struggle to create, or – as Laclau and Mouffe call it – articulate, privileged signifiers which fix the meaning of a signifying chain. If modern history is not the history of class struggle, in what does revolutionary politics consist? Laclau and Mouffe dare to posit a universal: antagonism. At first sight, it looks like a destabilizing move, one made possible by the surplus of meaning inherent in any and all identities. Antagonism, they claim, is not the mobilization around an objective relation of contradiction within capitalist society. Rather antagonism is the failure of difference, the erosion of objectivity (Laclau and Mouffe, 1985: 124–126; Laclau, 1988: 255). Antagonism makes possible hegemony, which is the "[a]ffirmation of a 'ground' which lives only by negating its fundamental character . . . of a 'meaning' which is constructed only as excess and paradox in the face of meaninglessness . . ." (1985: 193).

Antagonism is when reality is up for grabs, when the social reaches its limit and identity crumbles. "In an antagonistic relation," Laclau writes, "there is the peculiar possibility that the object, the entity that I am, is negated" (Laclau, 1988: 256). Antagonism does not reveal a hidden objective reality explaining it; it escapes language. Well, how do we know antagonisms? It is an empirical question. We know antagonism, they claim, through crises of identity. "If the subject is constructed through language, as a partial and metaphorical incorporation into a symbolic order, any putting into question of that order must necessarily constitute an identity crisis" (Laclau and Mouffe, 1985: 126). What Gramsci called an "organic crisis" is, in fact, a "generalized crisis of social identities" (Laclau and Mouffe, 1985: 136).

Although Laclau and Mouffe refuse the subject, antagonism is in fact revealed through subjectivity, through collective action (1985: 153). Theorized at the level of subject positions, antagonism is observed through oppositional political process. At the level of theory this is the old structuralist machine where discursive formations speak individuals, but at the level of observation it is American pluralism in continental dress. Subjects, they write, occupy "a plurality of weakly integrated and frequently contradictory subject positions." Democratic politics is organized according to a plurality of positionalities whose empirical *locus* is still the subjectivity of the citizens. Robert Dahl, the pluralist American political scientist, would grin. Laclau and Mouffe overwhelmingly explain and describe hegemony in terms of the formation of identities of subjects, groups, or social movements, whether or not they act on the politically political stage. Subject positions are known through political action, through the group conflicts, through the "struggle," the public affirmation and defense of identities, which constitute them (1985: 131–132). Indeed, what Laclau and Mouffe mean by a discursive formation is Gramsci's historical bloc, a group, and hegemony is about group conflict. (This, by the way, is not inconsistent with Gramsci's vision that a historical bloc centered on the working class could reconstitute in itself the institutional order of capitalist society.)

But, after the dust settles, a political ground is still there. For what are the conditions under which antagonism emerges: the conversion of difference into two opposing equivalences, a polarizing of its several social spaces. The people, for example, are constructed by homogenizing the signifiers of some Other into a series of equivalent elements which signify an anti-people. In this linguistic equivalent of the general strike, identity is poetically constructed by general negation. Antagonism always has the form of the construction of a social identity based on "the equivalence between a set of elements or values which expel or externalize those others to which they are opposed" (1985: 164–165). And what organizes these equivalences – subordination. "[O]ur task is to identify the conditions in which a relation of subordination becomes a relation of oppression, and thereby constitutes itself into the site of an antagonism" (1985: 153). Antagonism mediates between an objective subordination and an experienced oppression. And how is subordination defined: "a relation of subordination" is "that in which an agent is subject to the decisions of another." This is the pluralist binary of power. We know antagonism when there are collective conflicts organized around relations of subordination. Conflict is the empirical criterion for antagonism. This is decision-based power structure research. The capitalist West has become New Haven. Under conditions of modernity, the hegemonic task is to articulate a multiplicity of relations of subordination into relations of oppression, to destroy their differentiated positivity, to denaturalize them.

Politics is the construction of relations of domination out of relations of sub-ordination across a plurality of social spaces.

Class, they recognize, has clearly failed to extend the logic of equivalence across the entire social space. Laclau and Mouffe do not locate the source of antagonism in the relation of subordination itself; it requires a discursive exterior (1985: 153–154). So what creates the plurality of political spaces, called hegemonic formations, which are spaces of group conflict, spaces in which identities are negatively constituted? Given its long history of Marxist dismissal as so much bourgeois superstructure, the answer takes one's breath away: democracy. Democracy enables the articulation of struggles against subordination. The different forms of inequality now can appear as equivalents, as so many forms of oppression, as delegitimated subordination. Democracy is the liberatory language of equivalence, the "nodal point," the "discursive formation" which becomes the new "mode of institution of the social," which "would provide the discursive conditions which made it possible to propose the different forms of inequality as illegitimate and natural, and thus make them equivalent as forms of oppression" (1985: 154–155, 182). As Robert Dahl argued so very long ago, the democratic polity has no essential identity, which is why, we presume, he could be a socialist and a pluralist at the same time. Cultural studies has, at long last, caught up with him.

The over-meaning of culture

Humanists who have ventured outside the margins of their texts, who engage the social, make narratively organized interpretations, whether it is Michel Foucault's rise of disciplinarity or Donna Haraway's cyborg. These interpretations are readings of illustrative or exemplary texts and social practices. The humanists rarely examine whether these texts and practices signify to those who produce or appropriate them in the same way as they are interpreted by the analyst, nor the conditions under which that signification is successful (Schneider, 1987; Schudson, 1997). For example, not unlike the way the interpretive anthropologist Clifford Geertz read the Balinese cock-fight, the literary Marxist Frederic Jameson reads a postmodern structure of experience into cultural forms of art, architecture, film and music (Jameson, 1992; see Larson, this volume). The study of organizations, groups, social movements, and institutions through which and in which cultural products emerge, are disseminated, and take on particular meanings, has been mostly absent from their work.

Humanists tell a story. And, it is *a* story, a story whose telos is almost always the same – maintaining power, an impossible accomplishment, a unitary and ubiquitous structure whose reproduction is always unstable, unfounded, and often pathetic. For cultural theorists, power is the capacity to produce the dominant categories of social life, categories that organize its materiality. For many, linguistic ontology, not material organization, is the stake of stakes. While humanists have usefully stressed that culture is itself necessarily a structure of power, they have tended to make power into the primary content of culture. It is precisely because culture is presumed to be so constructive, that structures of power are understood to be so vulnerable. Humanists, however, tend to conflate the political mechanism by which meaning is produced for its content.

There has been a growing intersection between Anglo-American interpretive anthropology and social history. In a discussion that moves unselfconsciously between culture as power and power as culture, Dirks, Eley, and Ortner, in the introduction to their collection, write:

> there is a very specific convergence here, and "power," in the broad range of sense discussed earlier, is the point on which that convergence is taking place. Culture as emergent from relations of power and domination, culture as a form of power and domination, culture as a medium in which power is both constituted and resisted: it is around this set of issues that certain anthropologists and certain historians (as well as fellow travelers in sociology, philosophy, literary criticism, and other fields) are beginning to work out an exciting body of thought.   (1994: 6)

While the authors invoke the Foucauldian notion that power is culturally constituted, their treatment largely presumes a realist, objective notion. How else to read such statements as: "no examination of social relations or historical processes can be engaged without a relentless suspicion about power's displacements and effects"? "Suspicion" here refers to power, where the referent is "inequalities," lurking behind desire for love or tenderness. Or that social systems are "imposed by force from above – they embody relations of power." Inequality, force – these are transcultural categories.

For Marx, class relations were at once material relations of control and cultural relations of property. Whereas, in Marxism, the dominant figure was exploitation of natural man, in cultural studies the dominant trope is anxiety experienced by the occupant of a subject position. Where once explanation required interpretation, and the social was parsed through an interpretive grid of exploitation, a meaningful social relation also constituted through power, now cultural analysts interpret the social through a culturally empty relation of domination. They thus base their interpretations on what they presume is a noncultural foundation, making culture into an instrument of power, which is itself not culturally constituted. They thereby eviscerate both the cultural construction of the social and the social construction of the cultural. Their narratives bespeak an old emancipatory heroism, potential resistance located among the subjugated, in the margins, among those who can occupy the unspeakable, unimaginable spaces and use them to subvert or destabilize the structure.

We will take two examples, the psychoanalytically informed queer theory of Judith Butler and the feminist cultural history of science of Donna Haraway. Butler seeks to synthesize the Foucauldian perspective wherein sex functions as a regulatory ideal by which power produces subjects in the process of subjection, and a psychoanalytic framework wherein the "turning" of unsayable desire makes that subject possible.

Whereas most feminists refuse to ground gender in the body, making it the body's cultural reconstruction, Butler refuses the very choice between matter and sign, body and soul. She argues that the material body is neither social destiny, nor is it, as in the work of Bourdieu, a blank surface on which social writing takes place. Bodily desire is part of the production function of the social itself. Drawing on psychoanalytic theory, she argues that the erotic body is itself an instrument in the spatializing signification process by which the socialized subject is formed in the first place. Not only gender, but the ego itself, is a refraction of the social organization of a sexuality, the "turning" of an erotic relation with an other. The binary of masculine and feminine is tied to the normalization of heterosexual object choice. One cannot speak of gender without speaking of sex.

In *Bodies That Matter*, Butler wants to know how bodies come to matter. In western metaphysics, the body's materiality is premised on a sexist ontology, one where the feminine is its excluded, but necessary, condition, an ontology that denies difference. The female is formless matter, signifying nothing. "There may not be a materiality of sex," Butler writes, "that is not already burdened by the sex of materiality."

In psychoanalytic theory, the ego is first formed through an imagined, bounded material body, which is first apprehended as a sexed morphological imaginary. This culturally mediated narcissistic identification during the mirror stage is the precondition for the cognition of objects in the world, including other bodies. In Lacanian theory, sexually marked naming is the basis for the integrity of that bodily image, a naming that carries the authority of patriarchal kinship. Butler shows how psychoanalytic theory asserts a masculine, but dematerialized, form – the phallus – as the privileged signifier. Both Freud and Lacan, she suggests, fear the transferability of the phallus to other body parts.

As in almost all post-structuralist cultural studies, anxiety plays a critical role in her psychoanalytic approach. In *Bodies That Matter*, anxiety derives not from the lack of one's object of desire, but from the possibility of losing the lack and hence desire itself. Desire is constituted by the gap between desire and its object, a lack which, while unsymbolizable, is the Real. For reality to exist, the real must be unspoken, unsignifiable. Assimilating a temporal structure of loss to an atemporal structure of lack, Butler argues that the inhabitable, intelligible material body is constituted by an "illegible domain" of "unthinkable, abject, unlivable bodies" – here the feminized fag and the phallicized dyke. The terror of these positionalities, she argues, enforces same-sex identification and opposite-sex desire. (Indeed, Butler attributes the gendered form–matter duality to a panic at imagining "penetration" by the other, the phallic lesbian.)

In the normative resolution of the Oedipal complex, a boy's desire to have the mother as a sexual object is resolved through his ability to be the father, forbidden desire retained and resolved through gender identification. Butler points to the necessity of a previous prohibition, arguing that heterosexual desire is, in part, produced through a prior foreclosure of homosexual desire. In the *Psychic Life of Power*, Butler argues that a boy or a girl's homoerotic desire is both refused and retained in a melancholic gender identification, melancholy being an ungrievable loss (1997: 132–150). Gender identification, she argues, is a refraction of a socially foreclosed and unavowable same-sex desire, a refusal of its loss in which the same-sex erotic object is amorously incorporated in the ego as its ideal; while the rage at its loss, the beratement of its unlovability, and the anger at its necessarily imperfect habitability as an ego ideal are transformed into the violent demands of conscience toward the ego, a turned hatred toward the loved object whom one, in some sense, is (1997: 137). Strength of conscience is proportionate to the illegitimacy of the rage and the unavowability of the loss. Gender identification operates through the renunciation of homoerotic desire, a renunciation whose pleasure is sustained by the desire renounced. Gender identification is not given by the materiality of manhood.

Loss initiates the ego as a perceptual object, as a container for reflexively turned erotic desire and sadistic rage. The ego is a tropological formation, a metaphorical space resulting from the internalization of forbidden desire. Butler writes:

> Here it is not a question of love "escaping an extinction" mandated from elsewhere; rather, love itself withdraws or takes away the destruction of the object, takes it on as its own destructiveness. Instead of breaking with the object, or transforming the object through mourning, this *Aufhebung* – this active, negating, and transformative movement – is taken into the ego.   (1997: 176; see also 189–190)

The social divisions of desire produce the spatialized structures of the self, a reflexive inside generated in response to a forbidden outside, resulting in "a fabulation of psychic topography" (1997: 176). The first house we build is ourselves. The ego is not the body's pre-existent master, but an internalization of representations, "traces" of the body's object losses. It is an ambivalent homoerotic incorporation, the refused loss of an "other," where one's ego, one's sex, and one's gender are misrecognized forms of social regulation, regulation rendered invisible in the form of habitable gender ideals. Butler writes:

The straight man *becomes* (mimes, cites, appropriates, assumes the status of) the man he "never" loved and "never" grieved; the straight woman *becomes* the woman she "never" loved and "never" grieved. It is in this sense then, that what is most apparently performed as gender is the sign and symptom of pervasive disavowal.   (1997: 147)

The habitable space of gender is grounded in an uninhabitable space of sex.

If gender normally performs a repudiation of same-sex desire, which powers that identification, "gender performance" allegorizes the melancholic loss of prohibited desire. Drag, in which many straight men engage, then imitates the imitation of that ideal space. Butler asserts that by providing alternative morphological imaginaries, like the lesbian phallus, (confounding the having and being the phallus in Lacanian psychoanalysis) such performances might break the signifying chain. It is not woman, formless matter, but the lesbian butch, the woman who is and has the phallus, who is the force haunting heterosexist materiality and who is its condition of possibility. Resexing the subject might be possible, it is suggested, by bringing desire and identification back together again.

Sexed positions are citational practices, institutionalized significations, but reimagining our morphologies is contingent upon breaking the citational logic of patriarchal law, the coercive, performative process by which subjects are sexed as they are named. After cutting away the shriveled referent, she reproduces its tyranny by asserting the lesbian phallus as a revolutionary sword to upend heterosexist morphology. One would think that after deconstructing the sexed nature of materiality that one would want to dephallicize authority, but Butler just wants to change its sign. Rather than move out of the primal family scene, rather than resexualize, let alone desexualize, if that were possible, authority, Butler works the possessive sexual binary in which being is a refraction of having.

Butler courageously seeks to move beyond queer positionality and generalize the melancholic structure of ungrievable loss, the production of the ego as a substitute for lost objects, as the mechanism by which the social is made psychic more generally. As Freud points out, the loss of collective ideals can also function as lost objects, can substitute for loved persons, can set melancholia in motion. Butler writes:

In melancholia, not only is the loss of an other or an ideal lost to consciousness, but the social world in which such a loss became possible is also lost. The melancholic does not merely withdraw the lost object from consciousness, but withdraws into the psyche a configuration of the social world as well. The ego thus becomes a "polity" and conscience one of its "major institutions," precisely because psychic life withdraws a social world into itself in an effort to annul the losses that world demands.

(1997: 182)

Butler forwards melancholia as the psychic mechanism par excellence by which foreclosed, forbidden, or lost collective representations are retained and their loss concealed. She argues that "the violence of social regulation" works through the psychic process by which forbidden desires become transformed into the desiring individual's sense of worthlessness, into an impoverishment of the ego, a becoming of the loss itself (1997: 184, 187).

While the ambivalence of loss may apply equally to both persons and ideals, to model the psychic reaction to lost ideals on that to forbidden persons means that one has to make ideals unavowable, whereas, in fact, the most important ideals that animate the modern world – justice, equality, community, freedom, recognition, human rights – have a history of institutionalization, not only of avowal, but of accepted modalities of practice. Butler argues that conscience operates through the ungrievability of loss. But Butler has no theory about what might regulate the losses that can be grieved, nor the ways in which the cultural specificities of the relation between self and other might engender alternative subjectivities or psychic spaces. Justice denied is not the same as forbidden same-sex desire, nor even forbidden heterosexual desire. It is a legible, avowable domain. The conditions under which its denial, its prohibition, would produce self-beratement are outside her theory. Having shown that mourning is a subcategory of melancholia, she has no ways of distinguishing between the psychic mechanisms that might accompany avowable and unavowable losses. "Is the psychic violence of conscience," she asks, "not a refracted indictment of the social forms that have made certain kinds of losses ungrievable?" (1997: 185). Butler has no way to distinguish the conscience built on an economy of common pleasure and participation from one built on an economics of individual loss.

Butler flattens the social landscape. It is the gap between the ideal and the real generated out of forbidden desire that sets the social in motion, not the constitution of the real by the ideal or the plurality of alternative ideals. By placing the state and its law in place of the father, she thus can argue that melancholic incorporation provides a template by which to understand how the ideality of the state is made invisible in the psyche of the subject. "The process of forming the subject is a process of rendering the terrorizing power of the state invisible – and effective – as the ideality of conscience" (1997: 191).

For Butler, the ego is a political institution, a structure formed in reaction to the social "threat of judgment" about the love of an other (1997: 179). Butler's social ontology is grounded in eroticized dyads. One presumes the family as its institutional *locus*. Other social fields are reduced to generalizable homologues of these erotic dyads. In his *Use of Pleasure*, Foucault makes it clear that the meaning and operation of Hellenistic homoerotics is tied to the logic of the demos and the marketplace, not just to the family itself (1990). That other institutional codes and practices may inform the meaning and operation of that primary dyad Butler does not consider. Making the sovereign into the father implies that, for men at least, the authority of the state is psychically powered through a misrecognized homoerotic desire. The authority of the state is grounded not in our contractual consent, but in the forbidden love of the dominator. If Foucault neglects the psychic mechanisms by which subordination is made pleasurable, Butler neglects the possibility that other non-familial institutional sites may organize the content and structure of pleasure.

To make the ego a precipitate of a history of lost objects is an impoverished understanding of human development. Here, one's desire to destroy the objects one cannot have sets reflexivity in motion. By centering ego-formation in forbidden losses, in its refused pain, Butler neglects the permitted pleasures, of touching, feeding, kissing, laughter, and the gifts of being seen. Sensuous love, as in Pierre Bourdieu and Michel Foucault, has become social theory's most embarrassing topic. Butler eroticizes power but restricts the power of eros.

Unlike most humanists, Butler, a professor of rhetoric, has a sociological conception of power. But, unfortunately, citationality is simply institutionalized practice, convention, reiterated performative naming. Although power is a process ("a reiterated acting that is power in its persistence and instability," 1993: 225), and not a substance, in Butler's approach, not only is the power relation not sexed, it is essentialized and made exogenous to sexing. Because citational practices are reiterated, forever deferring the fact that authority is not a presence, Butler narcissistically imagines the counter-power of imagination or the deconstruction of the self. Given this approach to power, when combined with the fact that almost no actual citational practices and their variations are ever observed, it is no wonder that Butler does not provide us with an analysis of those conditions under which acting can be reiterated, or where renaming or resignification can be materialized. Butler, for example, never tells us when drag, or queer performativity, can destabilize, when it can reveal the arbitrary, can "dispute heterosexuality's claim on naturalness and originality" (Seidman, this volume). It a queer theoretical version of Nancy Reagan's "just say no campaign."

Because of its absorption of Foucault and Derrida's power/knowledge power/difference couplets, cultural studies does not problematize the production of power, tending to assume the process by which signs and representations, codes and discourses, are materialized. In this framework, means are meaningful, so universally meaningful that they are meaningless. We never know the conditions under which new cultural representation can be materialized, under what circumstances it actually has effects. One can find hegemony or resistance just about anywhere. One of the ironies of the refusal to specify the institutional content of power, and the tendency to make the logic of domination the homological basis of social order, is that the subject and his or her subjectivity then become the prime object of politics. Capillary power, the rejection of the state as a distinctive organ of social control, ends in a kind of methodological individualism, not as a constituent, but as the observational *locus*, of the social world.

Donna Haraway interprets scientific practice in the world of primatology. In one of the most widely read and beautifully written chapters from *Primate Visions*, "Teddy Bear Patriarchy: Taxidermy in the Garden of Eden, New York City, 1908–1936," Haraway analyzes the primate dioramas at the American Museum of Natural History as a "visual technology" which produces a particular narrative and ontology of nature, gender, and race (1989). Through his taxidermic scenography, Carl Akley, the man who stuffed Jumbo, stages a "morality play on the stage of nature." His dioramas are analyzed as ritual spaces which mime the white man's first siting of organically perfect primates, a siting achieved through the single squinted eye as it peered through the lens and the gunsight. Akley's taxidermy is grounded in a realist epistemology, striving to present the perfect forms of nature, not the average cases of realism, the "spermatic" mind telling nature's perfect organic truth.

Haraway's historical stage is foliated with agents: capitalist sportsmen shooting the species, capitalist benefactors financing their safaris and their memorialization, organicist scientists and taxidermists stuffing their quarry, the municipality of New York authorizing the site, misogynist men stealing the ideas and labors of their wives and secretaries, white people making the Africans an invisible intermediary to the pure state of nature. But everything is unified epistemologically around the eye as an organ of the spermatic mind of the white man, seeing nature from the outside.

Man is not in nature partly because he is not seen, is not the spectacle. A constitutive meaning of masculine gender for us is to be the unseen, the eye (I), the author, to be Linnaeus who fathers the primate order. That is part of the structure of experience in the Museum, one of the reasons one has, willy nilly, the moral status of a young boy undergoing initiation through visual experience. The Museum is a visual technology. It works through desire for communion, not separation, and one of its products is gender. Who needs infancy in the nuclear family when we have rebirth in the ritual spaces of Teddy Bear Patriarchy? (1989: 54)

For Haraway, the exhibit is a total social fact, revealing the logic of the totality. And a totality there is. For what motivates Akley's artifice? Haraway asserts:

Akley and his peers feared the disappearance of their world, of their social world in the new immigrations after 1890 amid the result dissolution of the old imagined hygienic, pre-industrial America. Civilization appeared to be a disease in the form of technological progress . . . The leaders of the American Museum were afraid for their health; that is, their manhood was endangered.   (1989: 42)

Akley's elephant is a figure for lost manhood. African Hall, she asserts, was meant "to cure the sick vision of civilized man." The museum intended a "regeneration of a miscellaneous, incoherent urban public threatened with genetic and social decadence, threatened with the prolific bodies of the new immigrants, threatened with the failure of manhood." Arresting the decay of a perfect nature was one among several conservationist technologies "for an endangered body politic," its racial stock threatened by immigration, its energies by the pace of industrial production, its social harmony by class war, its resources by unregulated exploitation. Exhibition, eugenics, and conservation, she asserts, "were prescriptions against decadence, the dream disease of imperialist, capitalist, white culture."

Wow. Capitalism, patriarchy, racism: Haraway makes the binaries of domination stand at attention, in tight parallel lines. Their institutional specificity and potential tensions are either eliminated or made mute. There are inherent tensions between capitalism and conservation, as Haraway well knows. Indeed although capitalism has its agents in Haraway's story, capitalism as culture is never present. How, for example, the museum dioramas speak to capitalism's perennial problem of naturalizing property is not addressed.

Culture – and the museum as an intellectual–organizational site – here lacks a politics. Haraway makes much of the fact that the museum hosted the Second International Eugenics Conference in 1921. However, as Schudson (1997) points out, it is precisely at this time that science, and particularly the anthropological science of Franz Boas, an American Museum of Natural History employee, was able to de-racialize human attributes, to assert culture's autonomy from biology. Indeed, by the time the African Hall opened, scientific racism was dead. In 1927, the museum hired one of Boas' students, Margaret Mead, as assistant curator. "By what screwball logic, then," Schudson writes, "does Haraway land on [Madison] Grant" – a museum trustee and popularizer of scientific racism – "as the animating spirit of the white male patriarchal capitalist vision that dominates American society?" (1997: 391). Not only did Grant's program fail as popular discourse but, as Schudson points out, Grant was concerned not with non-whites, but with non-Nordics, and Jews in particular. That Boas won was intimately connected to the huge waves of Jewish immigration and the Jewish entry into the public sphere, particularly the local literary and scientific milieu in which the museum was situated.

For somebody who is so concerned with multi-vocality, rescuing the silenced voices of the African porter, the ghost-writer secretary, it is strange that it is only Haraway's reading of this exhibit which is presented, which is never allowed to encounter readings of the exhibit at the time. Indeed, there is no study of the actual work of signification by the museum. Who went? What did they do? What did they say? What were their experiences? The museum is a text and Haraway its privileged reader, as all-consuming as any pot-shot seminal I.

In Haraway's later writings, the totality will become tighter still, nature's arti-factualism being organized around "hyper-productionism" and "humanism," a phallocentric Enlightenment project. Haraway writes:

This productionism is about man the tool-maker and -user, whose highest technical production is himself; i.e., the storyline of phallogocentrism. He gains access to this wondrous technology with a subject-constituting, self-deferring, and self-splitting entry into language, light, and law. Blinded by the sun, in thrall to the father, reproduced in the sacred image of the same, his reward is that he is self-born, an autotelic copy. That is the mythos of enlightenment transcendence.   (1992: 297)

In Haraway's analyses, human signification itself becomes a deadly toxin for the global collectivity, most of which does not sign its name the way we do. While Haraway brilliantly shows us how science is a cultural medium, how scientists become representatives for nature, where representation is premised on possession, a power relation that strips the generative power of actants, culture in her hands takes on an unnecessarily monstrous form. She conflates science, the logic of representation, rationality, individualism, capitalism, the bureaucratic state, the patriarchal family, the Eurocentric nation, sexism, and racism into a grand totality. This blond heliocentrism, some of whose agents would save nature, is deadly. "All people who care," she writes, speaking of the Peruvian Amazon, "cognitively, emotionally, and politically must articu-late their position in a field constrained by a new collective entity, made up of indigenous people and other human and unhuman actors." But, while repre-sentation depends on power and is itself a form of power, the logic of repre-sentation shifts across institutional orders. It is not homologous, not the same. Haraway, like Foucault, will posit an oppositional world which is chaotic and undecidable against the unitary and decidable phallocentric prison house of modernity.

Difference, wherein presence is erased either in exchange for a differen-tial and arbitrary string of signs, or as an unutterable outside, this iron cage whose bars hold by the way they abjectify outside, as opposed to objectify inside, suggests a new problematic, a different mood. To replace alienated man, divorced from the means of production, we now have an anxious incumbent in a subject position, unconsciously terrified that its social identity is illusory, an unspeakable gap. Because differences are inherently hierarchical, the project cycles back either to a quasi-Weberian problematic of relations of domination where the hope, *a là* Laclau and Mouffe, is to align the various binary relations into a giant structuralist firecracker, or to pluralism, wherein the differences become incommensurable group identities. The conditions under which either may be possible elude us because we cannot explain the conditions for new signification or its materialization. Alternating between the body and language, the human voice falls away. On the one hand, refusing an essential human subject who is not always, already a product of subjection, "man," and, on the other hand, collapsing the institutional specificity of Weber's "value spheres," each with its own ends and techniques, their basis for theorizing resistance remains startlingly weak. Unconcerned with the contingent and relative productivity of power's pathways, cultural studies largely tells functionalist stories, narratives of rationalization and subjection, not stories of exploitation and repression. One interprets, shows the alterity, the othering, speaking the unspeakable contained in alternative representations. What is to be done? The theory cannot begin to answer.

Humanists, too, have a distinctive habitus. It is, after all, the technology of "reading" that is the humanists' predominant methodological equivalent to the sociologist's formal measurement. Humanists assume, as a matter of course, that language is socially productive. They also assume that they can read the social world as if it were storied, not just a site in which stories are told, but that the social world is only interpretable as a story, and they its readers who can rewrite its underlying narrative. What a narrative does, by definition, is generate a story that subsumes the parts under the logic of the whole. The humanist reading of the social tends, likewise, to slice across the institutional terrain, rendering everything as if it were interpretable within the narrative. Stories, like music, work through tension and its resolution. Cultural studies also tells stories, but ones that are not very good because of their theories' totalizing tendencies. Haraway tells a historical story about techno-capitalist patriarchy; Butler tells a timeless story about the individual's inhabitation of heterosexist patriarchy. Lacking either a human subject or alternative institutional sites, the stories are cheerless and the call for resistance ungrounded.

Sociologists, on the other hand, no longer tell stories. We have not told a good story, since the classical stories of disenchantment and commodification, and their successors – secularization and modernization. Unlike imperialism, globalization, as a story, has zero content. Stories depend on ends, on contradictions, on contingent teleologies and collective intentions. Sociologists shy from collective purpose, avoid questions of "why?" in pursuit of the "how?" To study why would be to engage the accounts of the actors, to posit an intentional subject, to enter the meanings animating action. We need to recuperate the human and its meaningful actions, and to ground those meanings, those ends, and their possibility, in the irreducible plurality of institutional life.

The chapters

Cultural sociology

The next three chapters take up the task with which we began, considering how culture is and ought to be theoretically positioned in sociological work. It is culture's continuity, the stability of its forms over long periods of time, that both points to its potential explanatory power and invites slipshod arguments about its causal role. Orlando Patterson, whose historical sociological studies have explored the work of culture in the construction and perpetuation of slavery and freedom, examines how practices and beliefs persist over time. Patterson scores social theory for its neglect of the pathways of persistence, due in part to the sociologist's penchant for exploring change. Patterson lays out a taxonomy of four types of cultural continuity, each with its own kind of causal processes and type of sociocultural domain.

Qualitative cultural continuity involves cultural objects that are highly institutionalized and self-perpetuating, usually as a result of socialization processes, the persistence of samurai honorific individualism into the Meiji restoration and the modern Japanese corporation being an example. But cultural forms sometimes persist even though the cultural practices or values are not self-perpetuating. This occurs when there is a perduring configuration of structural factors that are causally associated with patterns of behavior that are not themselves institutionalized. Patterson refers to these as associative structural continuities pointing to the linkage of prostitution with the structural conditions of poverty in Cuba as an example. He also discusses the "culture of poverty" debates and suggests that the contentiousness of the issue in part derives from the confusion over whether patterns of behavior are qualitative cultural continuities or associative structural continuities.

A third type includes what Patterson terms event continuities. Here cultural behaviors that occur repeatedly across time are explained by their association with particular events. There are three sub-types. Some cultural patterns are explained by their association with regularly recurring events, lynching in the post-bellum South being an example. Other cultural continuities result from the occurrence of non-recurring events. One sub-type has to do with path dependency, the QWERTY keyboard being a classic example. Another sub-type concerns the effects of direct causal chains of non-recurring events. Here he points to the linkage – between the exile of the Ethiopian Emperor Haile Sellassie – in the 1930s and the emergence of a radical cult of the emperor that emerged in Jamaica around the same time and which ended up influencing the election of Michael Manley in 1972.

And finally there are invented continuities, and here Patterson criticizes Hobsbawm for the capacious quality of his category of "invented tradition," arguing that it should be delimited to secular, nonfaith-based practices associated with demonstrably false claims of historical continuity, as in the case of the "tradition" of Highland Scotland or Afrocentrism.

Patterson provides a useful methodological schema by which to understand the ways in which cultural practices, institutionalized forms of acting, might persist over time. However, his schema by which he would have us parse the patterns of persistence assumes a divide between "structural" contexts which are understood as objective, material, and social and cultural practices or "patterns" which are meaningful and contingently related to those contexts. There is an assumption here that social structural positions, like class or race, can be known outside of culture. While it is arguable that culture can be known independently of its material reference or the history of that reference, the reverse seems much more problematic. Patterson's schema for assessing continuity's forms itself faces an identity problem – what, in fact, is "structural"?

John Hall (this volume) is also concerned with time. Hall aims to reestablish the centrality of meaningful action in social theory, particularly through the medium of temporality, seeking to fuse the social phenomenological project of Alfred Schutz with the comparative historical hermeneutics of Max Weber. As a first step in this direction, Hall develops a typology of cultures of inquiry based upon two dimensions: first, whether phenomena are understood as meaningful or not and, second, whether the elements under consideration are understood systemically as opposed to structurally. If the first distinction rests on consideration of the subjective orientation toward action, the second rests on the interactional as opposed to architectural relations between elements.

The problem is that Hall seeks to hive off object from subject, thereby severing meaning from the social. This ultimately erodes the power of his useful attempt to develop a historically contingent, phenomenologically based hermeneutic approach. Let us look at the typological grid. Marx and Parsons are both treated as systemic theorists unconcerned with meaning, in the sense of subjective orientation to action. On the contrary, we would argue that Marx's understanding of property as a material force presumes its meaningfulness, the legitimacy of access to capital, the constructed quality of the processes by which accumulation takes place, not to mention commodity fetishism by which they are naturalized. On the other hand, Hall's category of meaningless structuralists includes such figures as Durkheim who developed the forms of division of labor and ritual, both of which are organized independently of content. However, again, Durkheim's form of the sacred or ritual cannot possibly be made to do any analytic work without presuming its meaningfulness. That same is true for the even more abstract linguistic structuralists like Saussure or Lévi-Strauss, likewise categorized by Hall as formal structural theorists, who operate with the meaning-producing forms of an empty category of difference. Given that we are dealing with practices of inquiry, it is important to remember that the utility of structuralist inquiry hinged on its ability to make new sense out of meaningful acts and categories. Hall confuses a level of analysis of meaning, its specificity, with a category of analysis – whether or not it is subjectively meaningful. Unfortunately, he replicates the old divide between objective and subjective meanings, making proper cultural history reside only in those forms of inquiry which rely upon subjectively available meanings. He thereby severs *langue* from *parole*, a distinction that will be critical to his study of culturally specific temporalities.

On the other "meaningful" side of the typology, which he divides into those interactional theorists, including rational choice and network theorists, who study meaningful interchanges and the structural theorists who study meanings intrinsic to actor's categories of action, for which, of course, Max Weber provides the classical template. One can see the problem of hiving off objective and subjective meanings, interactional and structural relations, by examining the work of John Mohr, whom Hall classifies as an interactional theorist who studies the meanings inherent in their practice. Mohr studies organizational discourse. Its meaning, in fact, is objective, inferred by the internal structure of its elements and its association with organizational survival and the distribution of resources. There is almost no subjective datum in Mohr's studies. Moreover, it is the fusion of the interactional and structural dimensions that makes Mohr's work distinctive. Mohr shows the ways in which competing organizational actors inhabit a resource space defined by a structure given by the distribution of both people and funds across categories of object and practice. In the process of organizational competition, the discursive structure of need and the legitimate forms by which it is managed are repeatedly reshaped.

Finally, Hall places Derrida along with Weber in the fourth structural hermeneutic approach. Hall is correct that Derrida does not study actual instances of interaction, analyzing instead ideal typical forms. But Derrida does study meaningful structures of interaction, meanings which inhere in the interaction, and meanings which are not subjectively available to the actors. Indeed, writing of religion, Derrida talks explicitly of structures of experience (Derrida, 1998: 18). Hall's examples all come from the study of apocalyptic religious temporalities. Deconstruction, like Marxism, plays off of the contingent relation between objective and subjective meanings that inhere in structures of interaction. Rather than externalize religion from the social world, a social to which religion is typically understood as a response, Derrida makes it immanent in the social bond itself, in the miraculous qualities of the relationship between every self and every other, in the logic of the response, the action elemental to all social relations. Derrida locates religion not in religious institutions, but in institution itself, in the unengendered, unnameable, unproducible conditions that precede and are immanent in social being. Religion both marks and draws from the conditions that must exist for the community to exist. Determinate religions, then, are refractions of a universal structure of experience, of the mystical bases of collectivity, its authorities, its values, its knowledges. In the very logic of address, of linguistic interaction with another person, there is both a promise to respond and a promise to tell the truth.

Presupposed at the origin of all address, coming from the other to whom it is also addressed, the wager (*gageure*) of a sworn promise, taking immediately God as its witness, cannot not but have already . . . engendered God quasi-mechanically. A priori ineluctable, a descent of God *ex machina* would stage a transcendental addressing machine. One would thus have begun by posing, retrospectively, the absolute right of anteriority, the absolute "birthright" (*le droit d'ainesse absolu*) of a One who is not born.
(Derrida, 1998: 27)

The faith demanded in bearing witness always exceeds both the order of proof and the limits of knowledge. For Derrida, the logic of the address contains both sources of religion, the faith that must undergird the promise to respond, the promise to tell the truth, that presumes an absolute witness guaranteeing iterability and truth, and the sacred, or the unscathed, in which the singularity of both self and other, which presumes an abstract space of inscription, which he calls a desert in the desert, in which the finite, embodied self and other, and the events of revelation, take place. If the first operates as an uncertain, temporal event forever repeated in the performative conventions of institutions, the second operates as a singular impassible space upon which all territorialities – both bodily and national – are premised. Derrida's project is not a hermeneutic project in Hall's sense, for it refuses the very divide between objective and subjective meanings, in that objective meanings are the very condition of possibility of the subjective ones.

Hall's call for a hermeneutic cultural history that theorizes meaningful temporalities as a way to avoid meta-narrative is an important way forward. Hall builds a typology of "alternative enactments of meaningful being-in-the-world" (p. 124 below). Drawing on his studies of Jonestown, the Branch Davidians at Waco, Texas, and the Solar Temple, Hall distinguishes between three modes of temporality: diachronic, synchronic, and apocalyptic. He crosses these with three modes of framing reality: natural, produced, and transcendental. Hall introduces, but constricts, the transcendental as "bracket[ing] social constructions of reality, so that non-cognitive experience can come to the fore" (p. 125).

The transcendental refers to those levels of reality which exceed the domain of things apprehended logically or empirically, by the mind or the senses. It is arguable that the transcendental is a necessary foundation for all social construction, whatever the subjective orientation of the actors. Given that these frames refer to subjectivity, the implications of the fact that all three may be simultaneously immanent in any social situation for the movement between these forms of framing cannot be addressed. For instance, do particular forms of culture generate particular incidences or forms of intentionality or naturalness, probabilities of denaturalization or renaturalization?

Hall's object is to understand how the apocalyptic form of temporality is transmitted and "developed through lifeworldly agencies of narrativity" (p. 128). The very way in which he narrates his cases shows the limits of the typology of discourses of inquiry. In all three cases, it is the interactional process between the group, its apostates, challengers, and the state that generates the evidence for and occasion for the members to interpret the occasion as an instance of apocalyptic time; and it is that interaction that generates new interpretive moves on the part of sect leaders which, as Hall shows, not only establish the onset of the apocalypse, but change the practices by which the group will mark it. Interactional and structural approaches are both necessary. In the case of the People's Temple, Hall argues that their adoption of ritualized revolutionary suicide was an adaptation to their failure "to achieve the post-apocalyptic sanctuary of an other-worldly sect in life." Branch Davidians emerged out of sectarian competition in response to the Seventh Day Adventist pursuit of the status of a legitimate denomination and were challenged by the state through the agency of apostate Davidians. The Branch Davidians, like the Peoples Temple, did not initially expect to die in the event of the apocalypse. In fact, Hall shows that the apocalyptic form held by Koresh had no determinate relation to the decision to remain in the fires that engulfed the Mount Carmel compound. Finally, the suicidal reinterpretation of "transit" by the followers of the Solar Temple, which had always held to a belief in the "transit" of souls to a transcendent domain, was likewise tied to state repression allied with apostates. Hall wants to argue that these sect adaptations are to "materially and socially constructed situations" (p. 135 below), but, in fact, the binary will not hold, because the construction of the sects by opponents and the state is as crucial in the generation of the situation as that by the sect of its opponents and the state. In this case at least, there is no situation outside these mutual, interactive interpretations. Culture must indeed be understood in practice, but dissociating interactional and structural, objective and subjective forms of analysis is likely to get in the way of an adequate account, rather than help us on our way.

Mark Schneider seeks a cultural sociology that will make interpretation scientific. In his book, *Culture and Enchantment*, Schneider (1993) shows how the classic works of cultural interpretation, from Geertz to Lévi-Strauss, depend upon rhetorical devices which persuade by the force of what he calls enchantment, a dazzling display of intriguing insights that satisfy as exotic and coherent narratives. But, as Schneider demonstrates with his own skilled textual exegesis, Geertz's analysis of the canonical cock-fight (1973) depends entirely on Geertz's reading of the action as opposed to the way it signified to those gathered around the killer roosters (1987). The believability that this was a story that the Balinese told themselves about themselves relies on no Balinese actually telling the story. Once, he claims, you get beyond the enchantment of an analyst's well-told story, there is little valid knowledge.

In his chapter for this volume Schneider examines the field of contemporary cultural studies, finding there a common set of impulses, a shared set of interpretative frames. He seeks to show that their frame of interpretation is itself a cultural structure, one not confined to academic scholarship. Schneider reads contemporary cultural studies in parallel with literary works from the late nineteenth-century "decadent" movement. Much like contemporary cultural studies scholars, authors in this literary genre shared a deep sense of revulsion at the decadence of empire and sought through their writing to criticize the pretension that they saw all around them. Their critique of bourgeois society was associated with three themes – the erosion of categorical differences, an affection for the artificial, and a fascination with paradox. The first of these finds expression in the ongoing erosion of boundaries around categories of gender and sexuality, as well as a fascination with the monstrous. "It is a rule of thumb," he writes, "that if a virgin is introduced, someone will soon be tortured or beheaded" (p. 142 below). This first move is associated with an effort to undermine the rationalist order characterizing western thought.

Fascination with the artificial found expression in stories of robots and other simulacra, as well as the rejection of the state of nature as a transcendental category on which to base the social order. "The dumb fecundity of nature," in general, and women as its emblems, were two favorite targets of ridicule in decadent literature. The decadents valorized homosexuality, precisely because it was non-reproductive and "unnatural." Here again, the celebration of artifice was part of an assault on the teleological sense of an orderly, rationalist, bourgeois world. The third literary theme is paradox, a practice through which the sense that rationality inevitably draws us toward its other is enacted, transporting us to the limits of a western "truth" warranting imperial power, an ignorance beyond truth challenging the West's right to rule.

Schneider then proceeds to show how these same literary impulses run throughout the writings of contemporary cultural studies. There is the same refusal of categorical thought and traditional identity categories, the same rejection of the certainties of reason as a guarantor of truth, its reconstruction as an expression of power. The parallelism is indeed convincing: the assertion and celebration of an inassimilable difference, the introduction of the cyborg and the actant, and the abyss of deconstruction.

Schneider thus shows that cultural studies is itself cultural, operating according to the logic of a particular literary genre. Schneider thus pushes beyond Max Weber's sense of "value relevance" as generating the problems one considers worthy of study, to the ways in which values shape both the ontology of the social and the procedures by which it is known. Here the conventions of this genre dictate the content of what passes for knowledge. Having used his skills in the name of science to debunk the interpretative work of cultural studies, Schneider uses his knowledge of literary theory to drive a deeper wedge between the humanities and the social sciences. The problem is that Schneider presumes that there is an alternative, that an unenchanted science of culture is possible. Statistical inference with its belief in a "general linear reality," and structural modeling with its assumption of a relational totality, are just as enchanted as forms by which magically to produce order out of chaos as the interpretive tactics of Haraway or Hebdige. In the end Schneider offers us no examples of what such an analysis would look like and no sense of how to achieve reliable and valid knowledge of the cultural word. What he offers instead are cautionary tales, readings of readings that we can either accept or reject. Ironically, Schneider has given us a cultural account of cultural studies. Schneider's problem is the assault on science; it is not yet his scientific object.

Sacred and profane: the Durkheimian tradition

Emile Durkheim's theory of the sacred has been critical for those who wish to argue for both culture's autonomy and its social productivity. In his *Elementary Forms of Religious Life*, Durkheim argued that social unity derives not from an observed social morphology, from how people exist materially on the land, but from a system of symbols that places them in relation to each other by the way it places them in relation to the species of nature. Without a locality, each composed of a multiplicity of kinship lines, lacking therefore in cohesion, for the clan, it is an image which makes the social possible (Durkheim, 1995: 235). "A clan is essentially a company of individuals who have the same name and rally around the same symbol. Take away the name and the symbol that gives it tangible form, and the clan can no longer even be imagined. [T]he clan was possible only on condition of being imaginable."

"I DID DRUGS WITH ELVIS" reads the graffiti on Graceland's wall. Richard Hecht, an historian of religions, returns to this late Durkheimian current as a vehicle to understand the profusion of popular forms of religiosity ranging from memorial sites for the freeway dead, "private devotions constructed in public spaces," to Elvis Presley and James Dean pilgrimages to Graceland mansion in Memphis and Cholame, California, where Dean's Spyder Porsche collided with another car. For Hecht, it is Durkheim's understanding of ritual, not as mythical narration, but as a vehicle for collective effervescence, that is key. New collectivities form through these places sacralized by the bodies which came into or left the earth there, bodies understood as media between human and divine world, *axes mundi* in the Eliadean sense. Like Mexican Catholics at the Virgin of Guadalupe, North African Jews in Meron, Palestinian Muslims at Nebi Musa or Iranian Shiites at Qom, the cult of the saints is very much with us, and, as he points out, the commodification of the pilgrimage of a pop hero is no different than the Christian cult of the saints, and the trade in relics by which pilgrims brought pieces of the center back to the periphery. Ritualized collective representation, and the energies it animates and that animate it, must be analytically recuperated in our day, in our lives. Elvis sightings, rather than bizarre curiosities about which to giggle, are important phenomena through which the sacred in cultural life can be repositioned. First, these sightings point to the import of religious ritual as a vehicle to create collective "mental states" beyond the limits of institutional religion in domains as diverse as the political sacralization of Evita Perón and the redemptive powers of popular cultural figures. And, second, they are part and parcel of an American form of religiosity, an Emersonian tradition that now joins adepts of the New Age and fundamentalists, which gives primacy to the private experience of a new birth, an unmediated experience of revelation, outside the boundaries of the established churches.

Eviatar Zerubavel was one of the first American sociologists of the post-Vietnam era to take cultural artifacts as objects of sociological analysis. Zerubavel's early work on the social meaning of time analyzed artifacts, such as the calendar and the week, as socially productive collective representations (Zerubavel, 1979, 1981, 1985). As he recounts in his contribution to this volume, it was only after he had begun the work of explaining the production and deployment of temporal meanings that he came to see his own work as part of a generalizable project of cultural analysis.

Analyzing the past as socially commemorated through the public ritual, Zerubavel argues for the consonance of structuralist linguistics and Durkheim's duality of sacred and profane as the elemental binary of culture. Zerubavel uses semiotics as the linkage allowing social scientists to advance Durkheim's cultural theory as an empirical project. He invokes two rules of structuralist theory: first, Saussure's suggestion that meanings are defined relationally through similarity and difference and, second, Trubetzkoy and Jakobson's notion that, in every contrastive pair, one item is actively defined or marked as different than the other which is left passively absent or unmarked. Zerubavel shows how these two structuralist principles can be identified in early sociological work from Simmel to Durkheim as well as their successors.

His own ideas about the social demarcation of time are implicitly a theory of cultural meaning that relies upon these two axial theorems of structuralist thought. Zerubavel points out that the "circular, calendrical time" seems a natural candidate for structuralist interpretation because it represents a closed and ordered system where the differentiation of elements appears to be a natural extension of the system. Moving to modernity's "linear, historical time" seems, at first sight, more intractable for structuralist understanding. Historical time seems to stretch out in a long unstructured and unsystemic ways. Zerubavel argues that the critical structuralist move, identified with Sorokin's work, was to analyze the social marking of time through social memorialization, clustering units of time into active periods and long "empty stretches" of uneventfulness, thus shifting the orderly mathematical patterning of time into something that is inherently "non-metric" in its shape. To study collective memory one must access the cultural frames of those groups who are doing the remembering, the ways these frames partition and mark time, and how these frames are ritually commemorated.

For Zerubavel, culture is a categorical order, a system of differences, a socially enformed cognitivism. This approach has a number of limitations. First, Zerubavel takes ritual commemorations as his primary social facts to be interpreted. There is no sense of the conditions under which one marking as opposed to another would be ritually institutionalized. Culture here has no politics. Second, structuralist marking is not the only way in which temporality is organized. The narrative device, and its study through narratology, is just as important and shapes not only what will be marked, but how (Abbott, 2002). And finally, cognitivism, even a social cognitivism, does not provide us with the interpretive tools to understand what energizes people's movements through times, their passions and ends, a domain of human experience that is much more amenable to analysis through narrative theory.

Jeffrey Alexander has given primacy to the analytic, as opposed to observational, autonomy of the cultural in contrast to the social. He grounds culture's autonomy in the structure of cultural codes. Whereas much of his recent work has centered on the codes of civil society, which he aligned with the axes of sacred and profane, in the essay published here, Alexander takes a new sociological look at the Holocaust, an instance of what Kant once termed "radical evil." In the previous work, the primary activity studied was the placement of people and actions in terms of these invariant codes of democratic modernity, reference being the primary stake, a politics of labeling. Here, not unlike the way that institutionalists moved from demonstrating isomorphism to the more vexing problem of how new forms are created, Alexander seeks to study the transformation of that democratic code and narrative structure in America through the introduction of a new category – a sacred evil.

For Alexander, as for Hall, narrative is productive. The Holocaust, Alexander points out, was not initially represented as such. During the course of the war and in its immediate aftermath, the mass-killing of Jews was understood as an "atrocity," yet another indicator of the apocalyptic struggle between the forces of universalistic liberal democracy and racist Nazi authoritarianism. Indeed, President Roosevelt did not even identify the victims of *Kristallnacht* as Jews, just as victims of fascism. Likewise, during the war anti-Semitism became un-patriotic in the United States, a violation of the democratic civil code, the Jew becoming the new embodiment of the universal citizen. The political invoca-tion of the Judeo-Christian tradition was born at this time. Anti-anti-Semitism became patriotic.

In the progressive narrative then dominant, the cultural structure was given by the opposition between the democratic and the anti-democratic, Germany being understood as an historical anomaly that would be and had to be defeated. "[T]his insistence on Naziism's anomalous historical status," he writes, "assured its ultimate defeat" (p. 205 below). In the progressive transcript, the radical evil was not the killings, but Naziism itself. The Jewish response was framed by the same narrative, seeking, on the one hand, to eliminate Jewish quotas in education and employment and, on the other hand, support for a new Jewish state in Palestine for Naziism's victims, as well as an analogue of American democracy, the Jews just another John Doe inside and a nation like any other on the outside.

But the progressive transcript would not stand. For the "atrocities" to become the "Holocaust," for them to become an icon of radical evil, they had to be separated from Naziism itself, "the mass killings . . . seen as not being typical of anything at all" (pp. 212–13 below). Indeed, Alexander argues, they became set apart in the way Durkheim described the sacred, and hence a "sacred evil." No longer mass murder, or even genocide, only in the 1960s did they become the Holocaust, a Hegelian "world historical event."

Through a variety of new representations, the narrative moved away from democratic progress toward a tragic drama of eternal return, a trauma that would forever mark modernity. The Holocaust was not something one could transcend, but "an event out of time" which demanded catharsis, a perpetual reliving and retelling, a universalized identification and a transferable symbol of transcendental suffering. This could easily happen again. Not only could any group become the Jew, but the Nazi was in us all. Through symbolic extension and emotional identification, this evil was "engorged" at the same time that modernity's progressive narrative was challenged. Alexander points out that the universalization of the Holocaust as a symbol of radical evil, evil's gold standard if you will, coincided with the decline of the United States as the paragon of democratic progress. Not only could anyone be Jews, who were now accepted as American citizens like anyone else, but any man and any country could act like Nazis, as indicated by America's behavior in Vietnam. Ironically, by transcending the non-human pair of Jew and Nazi, a new universal discourse of human rights was born. It was precisely the uniqueness of the event that allowed it to be universalized as a symbol of radical evil, to define "inhumanity."

This work shows that the codes of civil society are not static, that new symbolic structures can be fashioned, and that there may be alternative contradictory codes within modernity itself. Alexander has increasingly moved toward the narrative, as opposed to the categorical binary, as a primary cultural structure organizing experience and action. Here he narrates the narrations, both his data and his persuasiveness generated out of this narrative logic. While Alexander convincingly demonstrates the transformation in the framing of these events within the United States, he stays, like Geertz, within his interpretation of textual material itself. It is not just that the narratives are not located institutionally – within the field of commercialized popular culture, schools, international law, treaties between states, or museum world. There is no evidence about the ways in which these texts actually signify, the differential engagement in these significations by different groups, or any agents who wield interested power in the institutionalization or de-institutionalization of particular frames. The history of the public sphere is a narratable movement between narratives, and a relatively consensual one at that.

Alexander points to what he calls "the dilemma of uniqueness," the fact that this instance of evil could only serve as a universal symbol if it was empirically distinctive from other "evil acts." In fact there has been a constant struggle within both the United States and the world about the symbolic status of the Jews as world historical victims, not only by other groups who refuse to accord them uniqueness, but by the Jews themselves who resist any universalization of the Holocaust.

And, finally, Alexander wants to separate the ontological from the epistemological nature of the events, locating the impact of culture in their typification, but, as he himself shows, the revelations of 1945 led very quickly to a neologism – genocide, and a new charge, added in the last months before the Nuremberg trials began – crimes against humanity. This suggests that the nature of the event – this mass killing of marked bodies – may not have been unrelated to the erosion of the capacity of the progressive narrative to interpretively accommodate the events. This is not to suggest an essentialist historicism. However, social facts cannot be so easily dissociated, even at an analytic level, from the referential capacities of cultural codes. It is arguable that the failure of reference, not unlike Kuhn's account of the paradigm shift, generated a new code

(Kuhn, 1970). Alexander's obvious interpretive power, his ability to narrate the transformation in code, is not the same thing as specifying the conditions under which the interpretations he is interpreting have power.

Culture and state power

An important body of work has emphasized the centrality and the autonomy of the state as an institution understood to have a monopoly not only on legitimate physical violence but on the violence of legitimation. Pierre Bourdieu writes that it is the modern state:

> which possesses the means of imposition and inculcation of the durable principles of vision and division that conform to its own structure, is the site *par excellence* of the concentration of symbolic power.   (1998: 47)

Organizational institutionalism understands the state as the medium through which new organizational forms and procedures become diffused and legitimate (Meyer et al., 1977). However, most analyses treat the institutional specificity of the state and its powers as themselves culturally unproduced. Culture is part of the production function of state power, but the state is itself non-cultural.

The bounded territorial bodies that are nation states all have centers, the oculus through which the space is surveyed and classed, made "legible" in James Scott's phrasing. Scott, who makes the cultural work of the state central to his analysis, derives the social categorical order from the state's need for order, physically to choreograph its populace, to control its borders, and to capture as much economic activity within those borders as possible (Scott, 1999). Scott powers this drive materially to classify the population and the land through map and plan, through categorical and physical grids, in terms of the state's interests in tax revenues, soldiers for war, and the control of counter-state organization. State choreography, a manipulation to which legibility is integral, always fails to accommodate the spatio-temporal logic of practical knowledge, often with disastrous results. "The utopian, immanent, and continually frustrated goal of the modern state is to reduce the chaotic, disorderly, constantly changing social reality beneath it to something more closely resembling the administrative grid of its observations" (Scott, 1999: 80). State power generates powerful cultural categories.

If, in Scott's analysis of the state, materiality is culturally classified in the interests of state power, in some of the work of Nancy Fraser, the Marxist political philosopher, capitalist materiality is made into a non-cultural distributional fact. While Fraser's earlier work on the welfare state incisively analyzed the cultural construction of categories of state dependence, categories with enormous material and political consequence for those outside the workings of the market

(1989), Fraser's more recent work has sought to reinstate a binary between a politics of redistribution and a politics of recognition. Seeking to wend a way between the old politics and the new, class and identity, Fraser argues that we need to distinguish analytically between the politics of redistribution rooted in the social relations of class and a politics of recognition rooted in the cultural relations of status. These politics are distinguished by the nature of the collectivities that carry them – classes and status groups respectively. Fraser proposes a "bivalent" conception of justice drawing on both independent domains. For Fraser, "class is an artifact of an unjust political economy, which creates and exploits a proletariat. The core injustice is exploitation, an especially deep form of maldistribution, as the proletariat shoulders an undue share of the system's burdens, while being denied its fair share of the system's rewards" (p. 231 below).

By deriving class from material distribution, Fraser instrumentalizes the economy, making its politics into a conflictual problem of group share. She thereby evacuates the specificity of capitalism's institutional logic. Exploitation in Marxist theory, and hence in much socialist ideology, derives not from maldistribution, but from the cultural materiality of property relations and the commodification of labor it makes possible. Marx's theory of exploitation is a cultural theory, a theory of valuation, the labor theory of value asserting a specific regime of temporality through which value is produced, expanded, and reproduced. Institutional theorists, as well, have shown that property is not an objective material condition, but a legal performative, a transrational substance known by the manner in which it is performed. Distributional conflicts draw their transformative possibilities from their origin in capitalism's contradictory logic of production. The institutional specificity of capitalism does not afford a culturally empty power contest between the dominant and the dominated, but a struggle over commodification, over the production of capital. In Marxist theory, this is the source, the meaning, and the transformative end of distributional conflict. Like Bonnell and Hunt (1999), Fraser wants to save the analytic autonomy of the social. Contrary to Fraser, Marx's theory of capitalism is at once cultural and material.

Steven Seidman takes issue with the sociological and political adequacy of recognition as an analytic and moral category. Seidman here revisits the project of "coming out of the closet," which narrated both the personal lives and the social analysis of homosexuals seeking recognition as a respected minority. Seidman argues that, rather than the closet being simply a site of repression and sequestration of an authentic sexual self denied legitimate expression in the outside world, the closet was itself productive of America's post-Stonewall homosexual selves. ("Stonewall" here refers to an event that took place in 1969, the unprecedented physical resistance of men at a gay bar in lower Manhattan to a raid by policemen intending to arrest some of its patrons.) For example, Seidman writes, "[t]he interiority forced upon the individual by closeting practices compels making same-sex desire into an object of overdetermined investment and cathexis" (p. 257 below). The closet was also a space of fantasy and the staging ground for a particular project of citizenship.

Seidman argues that the romantic narrative of "coming out" was part and parcel of an emancipatory Enlightenment narrative of yet another repressed minority which was twinned in sociological analysis by the assumption of a pre-formed, stable, unitary, if non-normative, sexual self. In recent decades, Seidman argues, homosexuality has been normalized so that gay men internally accept their sexual desires, and routinized, so that the larger society accepts it. If the previous closet-based seeking of recognition functioned to reinforce the heterosexual/homosexual divide, the legitimation of homosexuality has led to both new practices of public sexualization and new forms of theoretical analysis.

Seidman argues that the closet has become decreasingly important as the center of homosexual life, sexuality becoming a deeply felt, but differentially revealable, aspect of self. On the one hand, given the pervasive awareness of homosexuality and the prospect of passing, its normalization had made it more important for heterosexuals to signal a heterosexual orientation in public. On the other hand, a queer theory has emerged which makes public recognition into a particular narrative rather than a political destiny, points to the problematic quality of a politics of visibility, shows the ways in which homosexuality is integral to the very formation of heterosexual identities, and takes issue with the sexualized quality of governmentality more generally (Seidman, 1997).

If Seidman calls into question the political and sociological logic of recognition, he also criticizes the sociological adequacy of the post-structuralism that has informed queer theory. While it can generate destabilizing readings of texts and television shows, it cannot analyze the sociological conditions under which those meanings are made. "This approach," he writes, "cannot alone account for processes of subject and identity formation, the creation of solidarities, and collective political mobilization." Seidman, a cultural sociologist closely identified with post-structuralism, with the Foucauldian turn, calls here for a new kind of analysis that will "rearticulate queer theory in a more sociological way" (p. 266 below). We could not agree more.

Michel Foucault re-read Karl Marx in an environment in which the ideological state apparatuses of Louis Althusser held sway. Unlike Fraser, Foucault refused to separate the social and the cultural. Foucault's pioneering work developed the cultural production and productivity of power. However, in the process, he effaced power's institutional, as opposed to its technical, specificity. Foucault, unlike Bourdieu, does not view power as resources that can be instrumentally controlled by particular individuals or groups, and hence accumulated and localized in a particular institution. For Foucault, power is diffuse – it circulates, is capillary, operating through corporeal techniques. Although Foucault locates the first forms of modern disciplinarity in segments of the state apparatus, he does not believe the space of modern society is built from a central nation state. Government is just another form of disciplinary discourse and technique aimed at the regulation of populations with the objective of increased collective productivity. Its science is political anatomy and its dominant technical means the enclosures in which bodies are contained, choreographed, partitioned, and hierarchically and sequentially ordered. The useful human body is the subjected human body (1979). Bodies of knowledge depend on the technical organization of bodies.

Foucault thus unhinges "governmentality" from any particular institutional configuration, and especially a central state. While Foucault recognizes that discipline allowed societies in the West to adjust the demographic explosion to the enormous burst in productive forces, indeed, that illegalities have a class organization, he refuses to give primacy to capitalism in shaping other institutional fields. "The 'invention' of this new political anatomy must not be seen as a sudden discovery," Foucault writes. "It is rather a multiplicity of often minor processes, of different origin and scattered location, which overlap, repeat, or imitate one another, support one another, distinguish themselves from one another according to their domain of application, converge and gradually produce the blueprint of a general method" (1979: 138).

Discipline is thus a technology, composed locally through mechanisms colonized and assembled in a plurality of sites as a "general method." It has no determinative social group origin or institutional *locus*. Wherever they arise, these disciplinary technologies break free of their institutional moorings and diffuse throughout the "whole social body." The techniques of power diffuse in an untheorized and unproblematic way, across a multiplicity of sites: prisons, almshouses, asylums, factories, and schools. As a result, all modern institutions tend to have a homologous structure. Foucault describes techniques; he does not study their institution. "I simply intend," he writes, "to map on a series of examples some of the essential techniques that most easily spread from one to another . . . disciplinary institution." His genealogical method seeks a "single process of 'epistemologico-juridicial formation'" (1979: 23).

Joining knowledge to power, Foucault cannot specify the conditions under which power or knowledge were possible and hence cannot specify the conditions of their production or productivity. Foucault helps to obviate the problem of specifying the historical conditions of modern disciplinarity because he fuses the modern bureaucratic state and capitalist production based on discipline as a "unitary technique." "The accumulation of men and the accumulation of capital," he writes, "cannot be separated; it would not have been possible to solve the problem of the accumulation of men without the growth of an apparatus of production capable of both sustaining them and using them; conversely, the techniques that made the cumulative multiplicity of men useful accelerated the accumulation of capital . . . Each makes the other possible and necessary; each provides a model for the other" (1979: 221). Institutional mimesis is driven by technical diffusion which is driven by the will to power, Weber's enchanted disenchantment, an effective claim to efficacy. Like Bourdieu, Foucault economizes power, making it into a technology of productive control. The power relation of the prison, he contends, is "an empty economic form." These two institutional spheres have homologous forms, the temporal quantification of the prison sentence, for example, paralleling the hourly wage.

In Foucault's theory, modern power is neither contractarian nor consensual, nor can it be localized in the sovereign state, but is situated in practices by which subjects are themselves produced. Power does not descend from the sovereign, but ascends from the aggregated homological order of micro-techniques diffused through the social body. Foucault thus moves toward a network conceptualization of the society rather than one based on the relations between bounded agentic actors. Foucault ignores the democratic movement, class struggles, nationalist uprisings and social revolutions that are ripping up Europe precisely at the time disciplinarity is being put in place. If Bourdieu neutralizes the popular, Foucault theoretically eliminates politics almost all together. Programs and their programmers, not politics and their parties and social movements, dominate his observational table. Politics becomes war, fought cell by cell.

Foucault relied on a hermeneutics of power, but lost, more precisely refused, the institutional specificity of the state, let alone the democratic state whose rights he also grounded in the self-same technical disciplinarity, the law dependent on the infra-law. Rethinking her important book on Italian fascism (1997), Simonetta Falasca Zamponi (this volume) argues that there are conditions under which one must return to the state as a particular site and source of power. In contrast to Foucault who argued that spectacular politics had been superceded in modernity, Falasca Zamponi argues that the representation of sovereign authority can still be a critical source of productive power. Indeed she argues, representation, the visible form in which the public understands itself as a collective subject, remains the core of modern politics. The public is constituted through its visibility. In the case of fascism, spectacle was both the medium and model for the formation of its collective subjectivity, the content of its identity. Fascist practices cannot be dissociated from the substance and subject they imply, in this case, the beautiful nation. Practice is necessarily meaningful. Fascist spectacle aimed through beautiful rite to display and thereby produce a beautiful collective subject. Italian fascism, she points out, also sought to control micro-interactions in parallel, through its prescription of anti-bourgeois forms of dress (black shirts versus white), forms of address (the salute versus the handshake), forms of body (the slim, hard versus the ample and soft), forms of speech (the use of informal *tu* versus the form *lei*, spare construction versus prolixity). As in Geertz's study of the theatre state in Bali, culture is constitutive of state power (Geertz, 1980).

These essays analyze the ways in which discursive elements are integral to the construction of the situation, as well as the nature of the agents and their agency deployed in this situation. Forms of understanding are integral to enabling both agents and action, and thus are formative of not only the structure of power, but its very nature.

Products and production of culture

Contemporary American cultural sociology developed in part through the doorway of the sociology of culture, that is the sociological study of aesthetic objects and practices, whether art, dance, theatre, or music. Traditionally these forms of culture were interpreted sociologically, that is as refraction, whether representation or ideology, of an exterior social structure. One read social structure through culture. In the mid-1970s, Pete Peterson, an organizational sociologist, revolutionized the field, analyzing rock music as an industrial field with its own organizational, production, and market dynamics and imperatives which shaped the levels and diversity of creative activity (Peterson and Berger, 1975). Today, with consequences that have not been fully examined, the differences between those who study the sociology of culture and those who make cultural sociological studies have been effaced at both rhetorical and practical levels. Indeed it is arguable that our Introduction recapitulates for post-structural interpretive studies some of the same critique that animated the original production of culture approach, with the difference that we wish to retain the meaningfulness of the products and the production themselves.

Denise and William Bielby criticize traditional "production of culture" approaches for ignoring the content of culture or at best treating the character of cultural forms as a dependent variable, as something which can be explained by industry structures and professional power. In contrast, the Bielbys argue that sociologists of culture need to embrace the aesthetics of artistic work itself, not just the "circumstances of its production and consumption," in order to develop a more effective sociological approach to cultural phenomena.

Without partaking of art historical interpretive approaches, the Bielbys seek to build on a new current of sociological work that makes attributes of the cultural products themselves integral to the institutionalization of new genres or the level of artistic creativity. If Dowd (1992) studied the ways in which song length and extent of instrumentation shaped product innovation in the rock industry, the Bielbys focus instead on how audiences experience and talk about television soap operas as works of art, the ways in which they understand their specific aesthetic attributes.

The Bielbys reject the assumption that popular art forms are lacking aesthetic content. Unlike high culture, which operates at a level which is frequently beyond the expectations of everyday experience, more popular forms, like television soap operas, differ, not in the relevance of complex aesthetic criteria, but in the level of familiarity with those criteria. "Because of their familiarity," they write, "narratives in popular genres are sufficiently 'open' for interpretation by different groups and relatively easily accessible. It is not uncommon for audience members to draw upon their own expert knowledge, participating alongside artists, producers, and critics in the evaluative process" (p. 301 below).

The Bielbys show that dedicated viewers of television soaps develop an expertise in the aesthetic qualities of the programs that they watch. The narrative elements are highly coded within genre conventions that are known and well understood. Soaps, with their open-ended narratives, depend more on character than plot, building characters who can operate in recognizable ways, no matter how the plots twist unexpectedly. Soap action works through recognizable emotional interactions in the viewer's actual lives. The soaps depend on loyal audiences who come to know those characters as well as their writers, director, and actors. As a result, viewers have very subtle and very well-developed aesthetic criteria that they apply to characterization and narrative flow. "Not only do viewers recognize the formulas, codes, and conventions that are uniform across the genre, they also understand that the styles of telling stories within the genre's parameters vary considerably by producer and headwriter" (pp. 305–6 below). This popular expertise is then turned back on the production process as dedicated viewers not only actively discuss and debate the aesthetic merits of particular programs, but also enter into the production process by making their critiques public. Because the art form is mediated by the market logic of mass production, these critical readings come to have an influence on how the art is produced. The masses play a role in the production of mass culture.

The difference between popular and high culture, the Bielbys argue, does not lie in the fact that popular culture is experienced in an emotionally direct manner, unmediated by aesthetic criteria. Aesthetic criteria can be just as relevant in the first as in the second. Mastering the aesthetic criteria for a soap opera or a science-fiction film, just like an opera or a piece of chamber music, involves investment in the acquisition of expertise. The Bielbys propose a research program that will study the "discourse of audience members' interaction." "Where and how are audience members acquiring, sharing, and refining expert knowledge about a genre's codes, formulas, conventions, and circumstances of production?" (p. 311 below).

At the very end of their essay the Bielbys open another door. Why, after all, would an audience member want to acquire such expert knowledge? Cultural sociologists, they argue, must look to the attributes of the cultural objects themselves in order to understand their capacity to elicit an "expressive experience" on the part of their audiences. This must necessarily move beyond the question of those attributes shaping accessibility, the Bielbys' chief interpretive criterion, to other aspects of culture. The Bielbys seek to retain their status as social scientists by studying the empirical regularities in what audience members say. But what is said is here reduced to pattern matching – violations of character, continuity, realism. Why these people watch, why they care so passionately about these forms in particular, is not part of their analysis. Nor are characterizations of what audiences say the same thing as understanding why they say them. Words do not exhaust meanings.

The sociology of culture is, logically, no different than economic sociology or the sociology of deviance. Just as we routinely use folk categories in the determination of corporate profitability and legal culpability in measuring organizational performance or crime, the Bielbys here make use of interpretive criteria institutionalized within the field of soap-opera production and reception as spoken by their informants. However, they do not wish to apply those criteria themselves to the soaps whose reception they study. They refuse that interpretive move as beyond the scientific realm. In fact, however, the Bielbys make an even stronger interpretive claim – adequacy of representation of an exterior social world. If one can interpret, as the Bielbys do, across the divide between the life of the viewers and the art of the genre to explain the accessibility of its aesthetic criteria, one should be able to use a more fulsome set of artistic interpretive techniques to explain other attributes of audience involvement and reaction – hatred of particular villains, pleasure in particular kinds of conflicts and resolutions, attractiveness of certain kinds of characters. Sociologists of culture should be able to deploy folk categories of cultural producers to develop reasonably reliable characterizations of different kinds of cultural products in order better to understand the conditions both of their production and its reception.

It is impossible to get at the "basis for audience members' pleasures," as the Bielbys suggest we must do, if we do not look more interpretively at the emotional, cognitive, narrative, and aesthetic forms deployed in both producers' and consumers' lives, and in the cultural products they produce and consume. The implication of the Bielbys' strong claim for representational adequacy, one consistent with dramaturgical approaches to the social, is that, in the case of the soap opera, non-experts, too, will have well-developed aesthetic criteria that they deploy because these criteria are integral to the ways in which they organize, narrate, dramatize, and experience their own lives. For example, by understanding how people deploy interpretive frames and aesthetic criteria derived from different forms of cultural products in their own lives when the television is turned off, or how they make sense of these dramas in terms of their own life narrations, is a direction by which we might aestheticize the social and socialize the aesthetic. Understanding the relation between art and social life remains a tempting and elusive sociological problem (Brown, 1987).

Magali Sarfatti Larson looks back at her classic study of the American architectural profession in the postwar period (Larson, 1993). Joining her theory of professionalization with the sociology of culture, Larson seeks to understand the social process by which postmodernism, whose original template was architectural, became, for a while, between 1966 and the mid-1980s, the most prestigious architectural form within the architectural profession. It was precisely its reading as an emblem of an era, indicating a larger cosmological shift or a new regime of capital accumulation, that made the advent of postmodern architecture so tempting a target for sociological analysis.

Larson argues that it is the very absence of architectural autonomy – the dependence of built forms on access to significant amounts of capital and government regulation, and the programmatic requirements of those who control them – that makes it difficult to interpret the architect's cultural production in terms of his or her artistic vision or social status. For Larson, the social meaning of architecture is to be found in its habitation, its use, what it does, not in the aesthetic sensibility or cosmological understanding of the architect. It is for this reason that Larson turned toward a production of culture perspective, one informed as much by Pete Peterson as by Pierre Bourdieu, analyzing the specific imperatives of architecture's production practices.

Suspicious of interpretive readings of buildings, Larson sought to locate postmodernism's condition of possibility in the social conditions of its architectural production. Larson does more than skewer Jameson's famous reading of the Bonaventura hotel in what passes for a downtown in Los Angeles for neglecting the conditions of its production, namely that its architect, uniquely, was able to function as his own developer. If architecture is so dependent on capital, to what can one attribute the rise of a new aesthetic doctrine? Larson argues that the architect's professional autonomy hinges certainly not on its command over buildability, but on the professional elite's claim to artistry, to their ability to imagine and produce beautiful forms. That claim is produced, disseminated, and enforced through elite-controlled discursive networks organized through juried shows, exhibitions, magazines, and prizes. It is the way in which language circulates around built forms that organizes their cultural meanings. "The field is held together by discourse" (p. 235 below).

Larson locates the agents of the postmodern architectural turn in professional space as mostly men from elite architectural schools early in their careers with small practices. In their struggle for symbolic capital, for authority in this cultural field, a struggle that could only be won based on their claim to be form-makers, these players were denied access to the large, modernist commissions, whether the office building or the planned development. They could not think in large scale – in terms of either an edifice or a landscape – because they could not build at that scale. Postmodernism, by implication, grows out of a community of aspirants to elite cultural authority who make a virtue out of necessity, out of preserving existent urban fabrics, of playing with the historicist potpourri of the American cityscape, out of the aesthetic powers of a simple house. The postmodern architects, Larson points out, were propelled first by a text, not a building – Robert Venturi's 1966 manifesto, *Complexity and Contradiction in Architecture*. As Larson regretfully admits, the thing itself, the semiotic or practical qualities of its form, is missing.

Harvey Molotch, in contrast, argues for the social productivity of art, the way in which, contrary to its useless, ornamental, feminine connotation, art "works." "[W]e can see art," he writes, "as a sociology of amazement; art involves encapsulating social forces in a form that yields a knowing ignorance." Contrary to Bourdieu, who focuses on the aesthetic as a basis of symbolic capital in a field whose logic depends on distance from capital in the economic field, Molotch centers his work on their intersection and co-constitution in profitable industrial production (Bourdieu, 1993).

Molotch, who has been conducting ethnographic work among product designers (Molotch, 2003), shows the ways in which the aesthetic, "a kind of lash-up of sensualities," has been integral to the imagination, design, production, and demand for economic goods and technologies of all sorts. Art as representation is a force of production of the collectivity that creates the object around which the collectivity will cohere. Modes of artistic representation, where technical and high-art genres and techniques of graphic representation develop in tandem, condition the capacity for imagining what is not yet, images critical to the enrollment of technological, organizational, and financial resources across time and space to produce a good and bring it to market. Whether the automobile or the brassiere, designers of practical objects appropriate from the arts.

To understand art's productive role, Molotch breaks with not only the division between cultural and social, but likewise that between the cognitive and the corporeal, rationality and the senses. Good technical solutions, whether for the scientist's equations or the product engineer's body moulding, are also beautiful, the pursuit of which is integral to their accomplishment and their reception. The pursuit of bodily pleasure, the site and source of the aesthetic domain, often animates the march of technical and economic progress, whether the way the use of copper metallurgy for the making of ornaments presages its use for the fabrication of weapons, blast lamps for making decorative beads led to the welding torch, the "rage for calico" stimulated the spinning jenny (Mukerji, 1983), and the demand for color that stimulated the pursuit of natural dyes and the first systematic botanical investigations.

The aesthetic cannot be assimilated to the structuralism of a cognitive grid. With its sensualities and feelings, the aesthetic is an essential and necessary productive mediator between the two. By pushing into material culture, Molotch also moves away from the dualism of subject and object. Not just words spoken by subjects, the center of Larson's analysis, but objects themselves, do signifying work, work necessary to their production and reception. The capacity of an object to objectify feeling and human pleasure, neither of which can be dissociated from social purpose, is its art. "When apprehending an object," he writes, "aesthetics and practicality combine as the very nature of the thing" (p. 359 below). "The feelings an object arouses guides the hand . . . in a certain direction, with a particular force, in a specific sequence" (p. 366 below). A product's very usability depends on in its ability to convey "the right kind of feeling."

We begin too late. Jon Cruz, like Mark Schneider above, argues that our historical understanding of cultural sociology begins too late. Cruz is concerned that scientism poses, not the greatest promise, but the greatest danger to cultural scholarship. For Cruz, the urge to subject cultural artifacts to scientific analysis tends to restrict our understanding of culture, limiting what we are willing to count as evidence, shrinking the scope of research and, ultimately, distancing us from the political implications of what we study.

When it is well done, Cruz contends, the analysis of cultural artifacts provides knowledge of the social world that stretches beyond the limitations of the particular case, out to a fuller understanding of the essential fissures and dilemmas confronting a given social order. For Cruz, the critical issue is the problem of the meaning of the social. An adequate interpretation, according to Cruz, "involves some conceptual double-duty. On the one hand there is the distinct inwardly *subjective* turn, the attempt to bring the meanings of group lives into view. On the other hand, there is a *social* turn, an attempt to examine groups as social sites that help highlight even larger horizons of social life" (p. 383 below).

Cruz first develops this argument through the concept of ethnosympathy, introduced in his book, *Culture on the Margins* (1999). Ethnosympathic understandings of subordinated groups, here racial minorities, but also the working class and women, emerged in tandem with both romanticism, with its "lament over the disappearance of environments, lives and livelihoods," and the social sciences which understood society as a malleable object subject to sociological, as opposed to teleological, explanation (p. 382 below). Cruz argues that this reformulation of collective subjectivity through the model of "ethnosympathy" is part and parcel of the emergence of new collective subjects themselves.

Cruz traces cultural sociology's lineage not to literary decadence, but to the cultural politics of racial emancipation. Culture is a racial project. Ethnic studies begins not in the wake of the Civil Rights movement, but in the new ethnosympathetic episteme used to interpret slave culture even before the American Civil War. This sensibility, seeking the humanity of people assumed to be less than human in their cultural products, was first applied to slave music – black spirituals – by abolitionists. The early writings of the ex-slave Frederick Douglass provided the impetus for studying this music, what he called the "songs of sorrow," as a "pathos-oriented" window into the broader dilemmas of black lives under slavery. "What was being discovered," Cruz writes, "in the abolitionist conjecture was the inner world of slaves as subjects, as makers of meaning, as possessors of authenticity, and as producers of cultural goods" (p. 386 below). This project, increasingly understood as a work of cultural retrieval, was carried forward after the war by early folklorists and the faculty of black colleges established during Reconstruction.

Ethnosympathetic hearings of black spirituals, Cruz argues, launched a "cultural turn," one that depended on "thick descriptions" of the black subjects, one that connected subjectivity to structure, one that delimited the meaningful coherence of a subculture. It is from here, Cruz argues, that the cultural sociologies of the next century would draw. It is to that legacy, Cruz suggests, one linking collective subjectivity to social structure, meaning to politics, that we should return, so that we might be able to understand both the social determinants of individual troubles and their critical, indeed dialectical, implications.

Cruz narrates the displacement of these original ethnosympathetic interpretations as the black spiritual became a relic subjected to scientific analysis. Classificatory taxonomies crowded out the broader interpretative readings and the spirituals began to be dissected in ways that severed them from the social conditions of their production. The ethnosympathetic approach was picked up again in the writings of the African American sociologist, W. E. B. Du Bois.

It is this same tension that Cruz sees at work today in the conflict between a more radical and politically meaningful cultural studies and what he sees as the more deadening and limiting scientific sociology of culture. What matters most, says Cruz, is that we constantly strive to see the ways in which subcultures and their cultural artifacts are used "as a lens that brings into focus and enables a broader range of people to grasp something larger, more systemic, transinstitutional, and deeply historical" (p. 396 below). Cultural sociologists need to see the social embedded in the "sub"-cultures they study, as well as the critical visions of that social those "sub"-cultures carry. Culture can be a struggle with social fate and, tied to that task, revision the social itself.

Cruz seeks to rehabilitate and democratize critical theory, whether Theodor Adorno's embrace of true culture as a medium of critical consciousness or Walter Benjamin's utopian reading of elements of material culture, as an empirical enterprise for our times, to re-fuse the tasks of explanation and interpretation. The hermeneutic circle haunts the project. Grounding himself in the historicity of suffering, Cruz has a humanistic warrant for the interpretation of the music, which, as he points out, was part and parcel of the emergence of the ethnosympathetic episteme in the first place. Ethnosympathy as a cultural sociological stance is in the very discourse of the interpreters whom he relies upon to interpret the music. Neither Larson, in the case of postmodern architecture, or the Bielbys, in the case of soap operas, draw out the critical understandings immanent in the cultural products whose production and reception they study. However, Cruz's understanding of Negro spirituals as critique has the same kind of warrant as Larson's understanding of postmodern architecture by architectural juries, and the Bielbys' readings of soap operas by dedicated soap fans.

Cruz is too quick to dismiss the critical and interpretive powers of explanatory social science. Under what conditions, in what forms, and with what effects critique emerges in culture cannot be specified within his approach, because he makes unitary interpretations of cultural forms in terms of an understanding of the social as a totality. It is not just that Cruz, unlike the Bielbys, provides us with no data on the signifying consequences of these spirituals either for slaves or freemen, it is an issue of how classifications of culture and social conditions might be mobilized as part of a critical interpretive project that would be better able to understand the fashioning of counter-power through culture.

The task is not easy. There is of course a broad gulf separating the hermeneutic tradition of the humanities from the explanatory project of the social sciences. While social scientists have potentially large contributions to make to the analysis of the order in the textual and the symbolic and its relation to social practices, these studies must ultimately be joined to the larger project of the social production and productivity of representation. Thorny issues of epistemology and ontology are at stake. Although each of the authors in this volume offers different starting points, all of their projects point in different ways to this gargantuan challenge and to the prospect of new disciplinary knowledges. While the sciences recombine and reconstitute, the humanities and the social sciences have remained oddly rigid.

Notes

1. Mohr (2000) traces the connection between traditional approaches to network analysis and the rise of a new structuralist institutional project that is being worked out by White and other network theorists.
2. Summarizing the import of Foucault and Derrida, they write: "Social categories were to be imagined not as preceding consciousness or culture or language, but as

depending on them. Social categories only came into being through their expressions or representations" (p. 9).

3. Swidler thus replicates the institutionalist claim that institutional routines make most difference when means–ends relations are opaque.

4. "Cuts and collages," Hebdige writes, "no matter how bizarre, do not change so much as rearrange things, and needless to say, the 'explosive junction' never occurs: no amount of stylistic incantation can alter the oppressive mode in which the commodities used in subculture have been produced" (1979: 130).

References

Abbott, H. Porter. 2002. *The Cambridge Introduction to Narrative*. Cambridge: Cambridge University Press.

Alexander, Jeffrey. 1988. "Culture and Political Crisis: 'Watergate' and Durkheimian Sociology," in Jeffrey Alexander, ed. *Durkheimian Sociology and Cultural Studies*. New York: Cambridge University Press. Pp. 187–224.

    1995. "The Reality of Reduction: The Failed Synthesis of Pierre Bourdieu," in Jeffrey Alexander, ed. *Fin de Siècle Social Theory: Relativism, Reduction and the Problem of Reason*. London: Verso. Pp. 128–217.

Alexander, Jeffrey and Phillip Smith. 1993. "The Discourse of American Civil Society: A New Proposal for Cultural Studies." *Theory and Society* 22:151–207.

Alexander, Jeffrey, Phil Smith, and Steven Sherwood. 1993. "The British Are Coming . . . Again! The Hidden Agenda of 'Cultural Studies.'" *Contemporary Sociology* 22/3:370–375.

Becker, Howard. 1982. *Art Worlds*. Berkeley: University of California Press.

Beisel, Nicola. 1993. "Morals Versus Art: Censorship, the Politics of Interpretation, and the Victorian Nude." *American Sociological Review* 58/2:145–162.

Berezin, Mabel. 1997. *Making the Fascist Self: The Political Culture of Inter-war Italy*. Ithaca: Cornell University Press.

Bermingham, Ann. 1986. *Landscape and Ideology: The English Rustic Tradition, 1740–1860*. Berkeley: University of California Press.

Biernacki, Richard. 1995, *The Fabrication of Labor: Germany and Britain, 1640–1914*. Berkeley: University of California Press.

Biggart, Nicole Woolsey and Mauro F. Guillen. 1999. "Developing Difference: Social Organization and the Rise of the Auto Industries of South Korea, Taiwan, Spain and Argentina." *American Sociological Review* 64:722–747.

Bonnell, Victoria A. and Lynn Hunt. 1999. "Introduction," in Victoria A. Bonnell and Lynn Hunt, eds. *Beyond the Cultural Turn*. Berkeley: University of California Press. Pp. 1–32.

Bourdieu, Pierre. 1977. *Outline of a Theory of Practice*, originally published in 1972, trans. Richard Nice. Cambridge: Cambridge University Press.

    1984. *Distinction: A Social Critique of the Judgement of Taste*. Cambridge: Harvard University Press.

    1990. *The Logic of Practice*, trans. Richard Nice. Stanford: Stanford University Press.

    1991. *Language and Symbolic Power*. Cambridge, MA: Harvard University Press.

    1995, *The Field of Cultural Production*. New York: Columbia University Press.

1998. *Practical Reason: On The Theory of Action.* Stanford: Stanford University Press.

Brown, Richard Harvey. 1987. *Society as Text: Essays on Rhetoric, Reason and Reality.* Chicago: University of Chicago Press.

Brubaker, Rogers. 1998. "Myths and Misconceptions in the Study of Nationalism," in John Hall, ed. *Ernest Gellner and the Theory of Nationalism.* Cambridge: Cambridge University Press.

Butler, Judith. 1993. *Bodies that Matter: On the Discursive Limits of "Sex."* New York: Routledge.

1997. *The Psychic Life of Power.* Stanford: Stanford University Press.

Clifford, James and George Marcus. 1986. *Writing Culture: The Poetics and Politics of Ethnography.* Berkeley: University of California Press.

Crespi, Franco. 1999. *Teoria dell'agire sociale.* Bologna: II Mulino.

Cruz, Jon. 1999. *Culture on the Margins.* Princeton: Princeton University Press.

Derrida, Jacques. 1998 [1996]. "Faith and Knowledge: The Sources of 'Religion' at the Limits of Reason Alone," in Jacques Demida and Gianni Vattimo, eds. *Religion.* Stanford: Stanford University Press. Pp. 1–78.

DiMaggio, Paul J. 1982. "Cultural Capital and School Success: The Impact of Status–Culture Participation on the Grades of U.S. High School Students." *American Sociological Review* 47:189–201.

1991. "Constructing an Organizational Field as a Professional Project: U.S. Art Museums, 1920–1940," in Walter W. Powell and Paul DiMaggio, eds. *The New Institutionalism in Organizational Analysis.* Chicago: University of Chicago Press. Pp. 267–292.

DiMaggio, Paul J. and John Mohr. 1985. "Cultural Capital, Educational Attainment and Marital Selection." *American Journal of Sociology* 90/6:1231–1261.

DiMaggio, Paul J. and Walter W. Powell. 1983. "The Iron Cage Revisited: Institutional Isomorphism and Collective Rationality in Organizational Fields." *American Sociological Review* 48:147–160.

Dirks, Nicholas B., Geoff Eley, and Sherry Ortner. 1994. "Introduction," in Dirks, Eley, and Ortner, eds. *Culture/Power/History: A Reader in Contemporary Social Theory.* Princeton: Princeton University Press. Pp. 3–45.

Dobbin, Frank R. 1994. *Forging Industrial Policy: The United States, Britain, and France in the Railway Age.* New York: Cambridge University Press.

Dowd, Timothy J. 1992. "The Musical Structure and Social Context of Number One Songs, 1955 to 1988: An Exploratory Analysis," in Robert Wothnow, ed. *Vocabularies of Public Life: Empirical Essays in Symbolic Structure.* London: Routledge. Pp. 130–134.

Durkheim, Emile. 1995 [1912]. *The Elementary Forms of Religious Life,* trans. Karen Fields. New York: Free Press.

Emirbayer, Mustafa. 1997. "Manifesto for a Relational Sociology." *American Journal of Sociology* 103:281–317.

Eyerman, Ron and Andrew Jamison. 1991. *Social Movements: A Cognitive Approach.* Cambridge: Polity Press in association with Basil Blackwell.

Falasca Zamponi, Simonetta. 1997. *Fascist Spectacle: The Aesthetics of Power in Mussolini's Italy*. Berkeley: University of California Press.

Fligstein, Neil. 1990. *The Transformation of Corporate Control*. Cambridge, MA: Harvard University Press.

1996. "Markets as Politics: A Political Culture Approach to Market Institutions." *American Sociological Review* 61:656–673.

Foucault, Michel. 1979 [1975]. *Discipline and Punish: The Birth of the Prison*. New York: Random House.

1990 [1984]. *The Use of Pleasure: Volume 2 of The History of Sexuality*, trans. Robert Hurley. New York: Random House.

Fraser, Nancy. 1989. *Unruly Practices: Power, Discourse and Gender in Contemporary Social Theory*. Minneapolis: University of Minnesota Press.

Friedland, Roger. 2001. "Religious Nationalism and the Problem of Collective Representation." *Annual Review of Sociology* 27:125–152.

2002. "Money, Sex and God: The Erotic Logic of Religious Nationalism." *Sociological Theory* 20/3:381–424.

Friedland, Roger and Robert Alford. 1991. "Bringing Society Back In: Symbols, Practices and Institutional Contradictions," in Walter Powell and Paul DiMaggio, eds. *The New Institutionalism in Organizational Analysis*. Chicago: University of Chicago Press. Pp. 232–263.

Friedland, Roger and Richard Hecht. 2000. *To Rule Jerusalem*. Berkeley: University of California Press.

Geertz, Clifford. 1973. "Deep Play: Notes on the Balinese Cockfight," in Geertz, *The Interpretation of Cultures*. New York: Basic Books. Pp. 412–454.

1980. *Negara: The Theatre State in Nineteenth Century Bali*. Princeton: Princeton University Press.

Giddens, Anthony. 1979. *Central Problems in Social Theory: Action, Structure and Contradiction in Social Theory*. Berkeley: University of California Press.

Gole, Nilufer. 2001. *The Forbidden Modern: Civilization and Veiling*. Ann Arbor: University of Michigan Press.

Gottdiener, Mark. 1995. *Postmodern Semiotics: Material Culture and the Forms of Postmodern Life*. Cambridge, MA: Blackwell.

Griswold, Wendy. 1987. "A Methodological Framework for the Sociology of Culture." *Sociological Methodology*, Washington, DC: American Sociological Association.

Grossberg, Lawrence, Cary Nelson, and Paula Treichler, eds. 1992. *Cultural Studies*. New York: Routledge.

Hall, John and Patrick Joyce. 1997. *Reworking Class*. Ithaca: Cornell University Press.

Hall, Stuart and Tony Jefferson. 1976. *Resistance Through Rituals: Youth Subculture in Post War Britain*. London: Hutchinson.

Haraway, Donna. 1989. *Primate Visions: Gender, Race, and Nature in the World of Modern Science*. New York: Routledge.

1992. "The Promises of Monsters: A Regenerative Politics of Inappropriate/d Others," in Lawrence Grossberg, Cary Nelson, and Paula Treichler, eds. *Cultural Studies*. New York: Routledge. Pp. 295–337.

Hebdige, Dick. 1979. *Subculture: The Meaning of Style.* New York and London: Methuen.

Irwin-Zarecka, Iwona. 1994. *Frames of Remembrance: The Dynamics of Collective Memory.* New Brunswick, NJ: Transaction Publishers.

Jameson, Fredric. 1992. *Postmodernism, Or, the Cultural Logic of Late Capitalism.* Durham: Duke University Press.

Kozlarek, Oliver. 2001. "Critical Theory and the Challenge of Globalization." *International Sociology* 16/4:607–622.

Kuhn, Thomas S. 1970. *The Structure of Scientific Revolutions.* Chicago: University of Chicago Press.

Lamont, Michèle. 1992. *Money, Morals, and Manners: The Culture of the French and the American Upper-Middle Class.* Chicago: University of Chicago Press.

Larson, Magali Sarfatti. 1993. *Behind the Postmodern Façade: Architectural Change in Late Twentieth Century America.* Berkeley: University of California Press.

Lazarsfeld, Paul F. 1961. "Notes on the History of Quantification in Sociology – Trends, Sources and Problems." *Isis* 52:277–333.

Madge, John. 1962. *The Origins of Scientific Sociology.* New York: Free Press.

McAdam, Doug. 1982. *Political Process and the Development of Black Insurgency 1930–1970.* Chicago: University of Chicago Press.

McCarthy, John and Mayer Zald. 1987. *Social Movements in an Organizational Society.* New Brunswick, NJ: Transaction Books.

McRobbie, Angela. 1990. *Feminism and Youth Culture: From "Jackie" to "Just Seventeen."* London: Macmillan.

Melucci, Alberto. 1989. "Social Movements and the Democratization of Everyday Life," in John Keane, ed. *Civil Society and the State.* London: Verso. Pp. 245–260.

   1996. *Challenging Codes: Collective Action in the Information Age.* Cambridge: Cambridge University Press.

Meyer, John and W. R. Scott, eds. 1983. *Organizational Environments: Ritual and Rationality.* Beverly Hills, CA: Sage.

Meyer, John W., John Boli, George M. Thomas, and Francisco O. Ramirez. 1997. "World Society and the Nation State." *American Journal of Sociology* 103:144–181.

Mohr, John W. 1998. "Measuring Meaning Structures." *Annual Review of Sociology* 24:345–370.

   2000. "Introduction: Structures, Institutions, and Cultural Analysis." *Poetics* 27/2: 357–368.

   Forthcoming. "Implicit Terrains: Meaning, Measurement, and Spatial Metaphors in Organizational Theory," in Joseph Porac and Marc Ventresca, eds. *Constructing Industries and Markets.* New York: Elsevier.

Mohr, John W. and Vincent Duquenne. 1997. "The Duality of Culture and Practice: Poverty Relief in New York City, 1888–1917." *Theory and Society* 26/2–3:305–356.

Mohr, John W. and Francesca Guerra-Pearson. Forthcoming. "The Differentiation of Institutional Space: Organizational Forms in the New York Social Welfare Sector, 1888–1917," in Walter Powell and Dan Jones, eds. *How Institutions Change.* Chicago: University of Chicago Press.

Molotch, Harvey. 1998. "L.A. as Product: How Art Counts in a Regional Economy," in Allen Scott and Edward Soja, eds. *Los Angeles: Geographic Essays*. Berkeley: University of California Press.

2003. *Where Stuff Comes From: How Toasters, Toilets, Cars, Computers and Many Others Things Come to Be as They Are*. New York and London: Routledge.

Mukerji, Chandra. 1983. *Graver Images: Patterns of Modern Materialism*. New York: Columbia University Press.

Oberschall, Anthony, ed. 1972. *The Establishment of Empirical Sociology*. New York: Harper and Row.

Olick, Jeffrey and Joyce Robbins. 1998. "Social Memory Studies: From Collective Memory to the Historical Sociology of Mnemonic Practices." *Annual Review of Sociology* 24:105–140.

Peterson, Richard A. 1976. "The Production of Culture." *American Behavioral Scientist* 19:669–683.

Peterson, Richard A. and D. Berger. 1975. "Cycles in Symbol Production: The Case of Popular Music," *American Sociological Review* 40:158–173.

Rapoport, David C. 1984. "Fear and Trembling: Terrorism in Three Religious Traditions." *American Political Science Review* 78/3:658–677.

Schneider, Mark. 1987. "Culture-as-Text in the Work of Clifford Geertz." *Theory and Society* 16:809–839.

1993. *Culture and Enchantment*. Chicago: University of Chicago Press.

Schudson, Michael. 1997. "Cultural Studies and the Social Construction of 'Social Construction': Notes on 'Teddy Bear Patriarchy,'" in Elizabeth Long, ed. *From Sociology to Cultural Studies*. Boston: Blackwell. Pp. 379–398.

Scott, James C. 1998. *Seeing Like A State: How Certain Schemes To Improve the Human Condition Have Failed*. New Haven: Yale University Press.

Scott, W. Richard. 2001. *Institutions and Organizations*. Thousands Oaks, CA: Sage.

Scott, W. Richard, Martin Ruef, Peter J. Mendel, and Carol A. Caronna. 2000. *Institutional Change and Healthcare Organizations: From Professional Dominance to Managed Care*. Chicago: University of Chicago Press.

Seidman, Steven. 1991. *Romantic Longings: Love in America 1830–1980*. New York: Routledge.

1997. *Difference Troubles: Queering Social Theory and Sexual Politics*. New York: Cambridge University Press.

Sewell, William H., Jr. 1992. "A Theory of Structure: Quality, Agency, and Transformation." *American Journal of Sociology* 98, 1:1–29.

1999. "The Concept(s) of Culture," in Victoria Bonnell and Lynn Hunt, eds., *Beyond the Cultural Turn: New Directions in the Study of Society and Culture*. Berkeley: University of California Press. Pp. 35–61.

Snow, David A. and Robert D. Benford. 1992. "Master Frames and Cycles of Protest," in Aldon D. Morris and Carol McClurg Mueller, eds. *Frontiers in Social Movement Theory*. New Haven: Yale University Press. Pp. 133–155.

Somers, Margaret R. 1994. "The Narrative Constitution of Identity: A Relational and Network Approach." *Theory and Society* 23:605–649.

Strang, David and John W. Meyer. 1993. "Institutional Conditions for Diffusion." *Theory and Society* 22:487–511.

Sutton, John R., Frank Dobbin, John W. Meyer, and Richard Scott. 1994. "The Legalization of the Workplace." *American Journal of Sociology* 99:944–971.

Swidler, Ann. 1986. "Culture in Action: Symbols and Strategies," *American Sociological Review* 51:273–286.

    1995. "Cultural Power and Social Movements," in Hank Johnston and Bert Klandermans, eds. *Social Movements and Culture*. Minneapolis: University of Minnesota Press. Pp. 25–40.

    2001. *Talk of Love: How Culture Matters*. Chicago: University of Chicago Press.

Thompson, E. P. 1966. *The Making of the English Working Class*. New York: Random House.

Tilly, Charles. 1978. *From Mobilization to Revolution*. New York: McGraw-Hill.

Twine, France Winddance. 1998. *Racism in a Racial Democracy: The Maintenance of White Supremacy in Brazil*. New Brunswick: Rutgers University Press.

Ventresca, Marc and John Mohr. 2002. "Archival Research Methods," in Joel A. C. Baum, ed. *The Blackwell Companion to Organizations*. Oxford, UK: Blackwell Publishers. Pp. 805–828.

Weber, Max. 1946. "The Social Psychology of the World Religions," in H. H. Gerth and C. Wright Mills, eds. *From Max Weber*. New York: Oxford University Press. Pp. 267–301.

White, Harrison C. 1997. "Can Mathematics be Social? Flexible Representations for Interaction Process and its Sociocultural Constructions." *Sociological Forum* 12/1:53–71.

    2003. "Innovation in Style." Paper given at Cultural Turn 4, University of California, Santa Barbara, March 7–8, 2003.

Widick, Richard. 2003. "Flesh and the Free Market: (On Taking Bordieu to the Options Exchange)." *Theory and Society*.

Wuthnow, Robert. 1987. *Meaning and Moral Order: Explorations in Cultural Analysis*. Berkeley: University of California Press.

Zellman, Harold and Roger Friedland. 2001. "Broadacre in Brentwood: The Politics of Architectural Aesthetics," in Michael Roth and Charles Salas, eds. *Looking for LA*. Los Angeles: Getty Research Institute. Pp. 167–210.

Zerubavel, Eviatar. 1979. *Patterns of Time in Hospital Life: A Sociological Perspective*. Chicago: University of Chicago Press.

    1981. *Hidden Rhythms: Schedules and Calendars in Social Life*. Chicago: University of Chicago Press.

    1985. *Hidden Rhythms: Schedules and Calendars in Social Life*. Berkeley: University of California Press.

Zukin, Sharon. 1995. *The Cultures of Cities*. Cambridge, MA: Blackwell.

PART I

The place of culture

2

Culture and continuity: causal structures in socio-cultural persistence

Orlando Patterson

The claim is frequently made that the past powerfully influences the present. Laymen and scholars alike constantly assume or assert that a given behavior or cultural pattern or belief is the persistence of a similar, previously existing pattern, or the consequence of conditions that existed in some earlier period. Thus, the historical sociologist, Charles Tilly, observes that "we bear the nineteenth century like an incubus," a continuity he finds agreeable in its "strong markings" on our urban landscape and the practices of everyday life, but deplorable in the way it encumbers our social thought (Tilly, 1984).

Continuities, however, are often as vehemently denied. One of the best-known cases is the controversy over the origins of African American gender and familial relations. A long tradition of African American scholarship from W. E. B. Du Bois, through Franklin Frazier, to Kenneth Clarke, had explained the distinctive gender and familial patterns of African Americans as, in part, a continuity from the slave past. However, after the Moynihan Report summarized these views in a policy report in the sixties, the ideological and scholarly tide turned sharply away from this claim of continuity toward a denial of any such connections (Rainwater and Yancy, 1967). More recently, there has been a swing back to the affirmation of continuity, not only in scholarly work, but also in legal arguments and popular culture. Thus, some legal activists in the slave reparations movement have rested their claims on the persistence of socioeconomic damages from the slave era; and a cover story in *Newsweek*, prompted by the Spielberg film, *Amistad*, led off with the assertion that slavery is "America's original sin . . . dogging our steps forward, projecting in black against the sunlight of democratic ideals" (Alter, 1997).

Regardless of where the truth lies, what is noteworthy is that none of the many scholars involved with this and similar controversies about the influence of the past has examined the grounds on which either the assertion or denial of continuity from the past can be made. An abundance of evidence from the past and the present is often cited, but just how the present is linked to the past remains unproblematized.

It is the objective of this chapter to explore this problem. After a brief reflection on the reasons why sociologists have neglected the problem, I explore some of the key theoretical issues relating to the problem of continuity, arguing that causal structures underlie all such claims. I then briefly examine how sociocultural processes are related to their contexts, paying special attention to the problem of contingencies which originate in, but are not identified with, their contexts, before exploring four basic kinds of sociocultural continuities. I conclude with a brief summary and a discussion of the main implications of our analysis.

Why sociology [and history!] neglects continuity

Sociologists and historians are, of course, aware of the fact that "most social practices," as Sewell notes, "tend to be consistently reproduced over relatively extended periods of time" (Sewell, 1996: 842). However, with some important exceptions to be noted later, most either take this overwhelming continuity for granted, finding little of theoretical interest in it, or, when they do approach it, especially via studies of institutionalization, they stop frustratingly short of the critical question of what exactly are the processes that constitute continuity.

Space constraints permit only the briefest discussion of the reasons for this neglect. One reason is the predominance of social constructionism in sociology. Its key notions are the relativism, contingency, and socially produced nature of social phenomena. In most versions, such an approach, by emphasizing the fluidity and meaning-dependent nature of social reality, is clearly antithetical to a concern with continuity. However, as Ian Hacking (1999: 19–34) recently emphasized, there are several versions of social constructionism involving different degrees of commitment to its philosophical and moral assumptions. Ironically, one of the earliest and best-known sociological works on social constructionism – that of Berger and Luckmann – was very concerned with the problem of continuity, with what they called the "awesome paradox" of how human activity is capable of creating a world of stable social objects (Berger and Luckman, 1967: 47–128); but equally mysterious is the problem of how these objects become things in themselves and maintain, for sometimes centuries – as is true of elements of Christianity, of the western culture of freedom, and of central features of American civil society – recognizable patterns of identity.

The second reason is an ingrained intellectual and ideological bias among many in the discipline against efforts toward an understanding of the nature of stable social entities and what explains their continuity. It is well known that sociologists who attempt to explain social problems such as ethnosomatic ("racial") inequality in terms of cultural continuities risk ostracism and occasional intellectual abuse. This bias originated partly in the reaction to what Tilly has called the "pernicious postulates" of nineteenth-century thought, especially its pseudo-evolutionary pretensions and problematic functionalism that culminated in the Parsonian system (Tilly, 1984; but see Alexander and Smith, 1993: 151–155). But it persists today, ironically, as a chronic disciplinary prejudice – a dogmatic anti-continuative intellectual continuity! Its counterpart is an entrenched transformational bias in the discipline. Most historical sociologists are relentlessly focused on the explanation of change: revolutions, peasant revolts, strikes, riots, movements of all kinds, are the standard fare of nearly all sociologists concerned with the past. So strong is this bias that even when a scholar has important things to say about stability he is careful to frame his argument in terms that signal his concern for change. William Sewell, for example, concludes his valuable analysis of social structure with the insightful statement that "structures can combine depth with great power and, consequently, can shape the experience of entire societies over many generations" (Sewell 1992: 26). Agreed! Nonetheless, and no doubt with a wary eye at his sociological audience, Sewell earlier in the same paper felt obliged to criticize "the language of structure" because it "lends itself readily to explanations of how social life is shaped into consistent patterns, but not to explanations of how these patterns change over time" (Sewell, 1992: 2–3).

Remarkably, this flight from continuity is as pronounced among professional historians – where we would least have expected it – as among their sociological counterparts. The historian Judith Bennett laments that among her professional colleagues, especially since the 1970s, "'transformation' is the accepted or even canonical story; 'continuity' is troublesome, worrisome, and even dismissible" (Bennett, 1997). As is true of sociology, the vogue for history as transformation sprang in part from a necessary reaction against the essentializing and universalizing tendencies of earlier histories, which either denied the agency of women and other oppressed groups and classes, or overemphasized continuities in problematic ways. A quote from D. C. Coleman nicely reflects current orthodoxy in history, as in sociology: "Change is the great temptress; continuity appears to be the bore to be avoided" (Coleman 1977: 91, cited in Bennett, 1997). Not only is continuity boring, however, but it is at odds with the dominant conception and method of historical writing which is "driven by the power of narrative, by the telling of stories that contain crisis, adjustment and resolution – without vast and clear differences between the past and the present, it seems that historical context – and with it the work of historians – might come to mean very little" (Bennett, 1997).

The closest that sociologists come to addressing the issue of continuity is in studies of institutionalization, especially the persistence of organizational forms. Arthur Stinchcombe's (1965) classic exploration of "internal tradition-alizing processes," and of what he termed the "liability of newness," is still one of the most illuminating approaches to the question of continuity, and its relation to change, in the literature. More recent scholarship by organizational sociologists, especially those working in the neo-institutionalist framework, has significantly contributed to our understanding of the problem posed by Stinchcombe four decades ago: the ways in which history "determines some aspects of the present structure of organizations" (Dobbin, 1994; Fligstein, 2001).

Nonetheless, even the newer generation of historically oriented institutional-ists tend to circle the problem of continuity rather than address it directly. Their emphasis has been on what Stinchcombe called "the motivation to organize," and on the groups that favor persistence, the vested interests that are served by it and the conditions favoring or reducing the "liability of newness." What is rarely addressed, and with a notable few exceptions (Abbott, 1999; Alexan-der and Smith 1993; Gerschenkron, 1968; Jepperson, 1991) remains largely unproblematized, is the nature of the "tradition" that is carried, the problem of what exactly is meant when we make the claim that a similarity or identity of form persists or is transmitted from one group to another, or from one period to the next. Thus DiMaggio and Powell (1983) in their influential paper on institutional isomorphism, which explicitly attempts "to explain homogeneity" rather than variation, in organizational forms, never actually explain what con-stitutes isomorphism between structures; it is simply taken for granted that we know what is meant when the claim is made that two structures are similar or isomorphous.[1]

The process of homogenization involves the spatio-temporal diffusion of a given social pattern that is assumed to remain stable. But this assumption is extremely problematic, both for the social entity that is the original model as well as for the imitators adopting it (Lillrank, 1995). What seems to be isomorphic may in fact be only isomeric or, worse, merely homologous, given the fluid and often ambiguous nature of social patterns and practices, not to mention the complexities of transmission processes. It is precisely these problems of spatio-temporal identity and the other main types of continuity in the social universe that this chapter addresses.

Some theoretical considerations

A continuity refers to any object, structural process, or type of event that per-sists between two or more periods of time. It entails something that persists and some mechanism that accounts for persistence and these are the central theo-retical issues to be dealt with in this part. I propose to argue that all claims of continuity – except those that are wholly invented – are really claims about the persistence of causal processes, and this is true even of persistence in the identity of objects.

Social scientists concerned with the continuity of social processes encounter at least four kinds of causal processes that I will call *identities* or *self-determining processes*, *direct processes*, *hierarchical processes*, and *post-inception* or *hysteretic processes*.

Identities or self-determining processes: an object persisting through time may be seen as a self-perpetuating or self-causing process. Following a tradition initiated by Russell (1948) but significantly modified by Quine (1950) and others, I take identity to be a "time-laden process," best understood with the metaphor of a stream. Each observation of an object is a temporal stage in its identity stream. The identity itself is the summation of all such moments, each being only a "time-slice" in a continuant process (Lewis, 1983). The object-stage at a given moment may be provisionally conceived as a "quasi-permanent" complex of related attributes. However, these attributes not only change values, but are shed and new ones included over time. None is essential although at given identity stages some may be more important than others (Hookway, 1988).

The "quasi-permanence" or continuity of identities, Russell argued, is due to a special kind of causal persistence that he sometimes calls intrinsic causation (Russell, 1948: 504). Identities are self-causing in that later phases of an object are held to "grow out of" or are caused by earlier phases. This is obviously true of biological objects (for example, embryo into adult), but we are inclined to agree with those who argue that it holds for most things – including social objects – with any identity through time (Armstrong, 1980: 67–78; Nozick, 1981: 35).

While identities have an objective reality, their boundaries are in good part socially determined or imputed. We observe existing patterns and epistemically demarcate, and socially construct them, both to explain them and to structure and control our environment (Hausman, 1998: 274; Putnam, 1991: 113–116). Such epistemic work is done in three ways: through the use of stereotypes which acknowledge the vagueness of boundaries that may go no further than family resemblances (Rosch and Mervis, 1975; Rosch, 1978; Wittgenstein, 1953); through the classical use of crisp sets of sharply defined categories (Pinker, 1997: 127, 2000: ch. 10); and by the symbolic processes of ritual enactments in secular and religious life, the human body being a major symbolic source (Douglas, 1966, 1986; Turner, 1995; White, 1992: 312–316; Zerubavel, 1993: chs. 2–3).

Direct processes shift the focus from the quasi-permanent identity of objects to the external link between such objects, as well as events, over time. Following

Lewis (1973, 2000), we view causation in counterfactual terms – "Event C causes event E if and only if there is a chain of dependencies running from C to E" (Lewis, 2000: 191) – and we do so in full awareness of the thorny theoretical issues involved, especially the persistent problems of trumping, preemption, and transitivity (Collins, 2000; Schaffer, 2000) as well as the need to take account of the fact that all causal claims are relative to the context of the problem at issue and to our notions of normalness (Hart and Honor, 1985: 32–41).

Hierarchical processes or multiple causal chains derive from the fact that an antecedent causal factor can generate several consequences, each of which may later become the causal ancestor of subordinate chains of consequences. With such chains we have a vertical network of causal influences, some of which may be more important than others; knowing where to draw the line is always problematic. If the causal chain is too short we end up with explanations that are likely to be not only trivial – as Lieberson (1997) warns – but inappropriate. With strong theory we can make more meaningful connections but, as Elster (1978: 184–185) observes, our conclusions are then more open to question.

Post-inception or hysteretic processes embrace several sub-classes of causal processes. All have in common the following kind of development. An event or object is generated in period T_1 by causal factors peculiar to period T_1. In the adjoining period, T_2, the event or object persists, but now it is due to an entirely different set of causal factors peculiar to T_2, and so on to period T_n. Thus between T_1 and T_n there has been an uninterrupted continuity of the object or (recurring) event in question, yet no apparent continuity in the set of factors causing it.

The two most important features of post-inception causal lines are their unpredictability and irreversibility. Nothing in the original or preceding cause on the nodes of the chain can predict subsequent causes since these seem to emerge either adventitiously or through some still to be understood process of causal attraction by the effected object.

The best-known sub-class is path-dependent processes, which will be discussed at greater length later. Another is the causal blowback in which the anticipation of a development, such as an economic downturn, brings it about (Kenney, 1979: ch. 1; Zellner, 1979). The final sub-category of this class of causal lines is self-interested regeneration. People benefiting from the existence of a given complex will devise means of perpetuating it even after it has outlived its uses or the original set of factors accounting for it. Organizational inertia is a classic instance of this.

I have, elsewhere, discussed one of these processes at some length in my case study of Jamaican lower-class familial patterns which have persisted from slavery to the present as a result of quite different sets of causal forces following each other from one period to the next over the past 160 years (Patterson, 1982).

Periodicity and the problem of weak and strong contingencies

Before we are ready to draw out the implications of the discussion above for the universe of sociocultural continuities, we must first address the conceptually prior problem of periodicity and its relation to continuity. This is necessary because very often when we try to establish a claim of continuity we are really more interested in showing that a given context or period has strongly influenced another period or some object in that period. We might, for example, be interested in exploring the extent to which the Puritan era left its mark on modern American values, or the period of antebellum slavery on modern "race" relations or certain practices of Afro-Americans.

Periods leave their marks on later ones through their influences on the qualitative objects, structures, and events that originated in them and persist into later periods. However, before we can make the claim that a period's influence has been mediated by these persisting entities and effects, we must first demonstrate that there was some intrinsic connection between the period in question and the originating entities or event which verify the claim of periodic continuity.

This is necessary because the mere existence of an originating entity or event within a period does not justify the claim that it mediates the influence of the period in question at a later time. It may have originated in a previous or different context, but continued to exist during period X, X being merely an uncontaminating historical conduit for the object. The Episcopalian Eucharist, Roman Catholic mass, and many of the central rituals and beliefs of Haitian Voudou or Jamaican Cumina, are cases in point.

More problematic and interesting, however, are those cases that stand in stark contradiction to Tilly's (1984: 79) claim "that the time and place in which a structure or process appears make a difference to its character." It sometimes happens that a historical process originated in, but was a wholly contingent element of, a given period, so that it cannot be claimed that its persistence transmits any influence from it. As Gordon Leff (1971: 42) observed, many "events happen which need not happen and which could frequently have happened differently." Such contingencies are, in a sense, sui generis, supervening in an established order. Contingencies introduce the play of human agency, of freedom, in history and culture. They may be the causal antecedents of later outcomes, sometimes even important ones, but they themselves are wholly adventitious in their appearance, bearing no particular mark of their context. For this reason, the later outcomes of the causal chains they set in motion cannot be claimed as continuities of the originating period.

To take an extreme case, the creation of the state of Israel occurred within the murderous context of Naziism. Nonetheless, we are reluctant to say that Israel is the legacy or effect of Nazi Germany or that this regime decisively influenced its character, and for good reason. While Naziism was a major aspect of the context out of which it emerged, it in no way necessitated or caused it. The state of Israel was envisioned long before Nazi Germany, and it is possible to imagine a range of possible worlds in which it might have been realized through determined human agency in conjunction with a favorable concatenation of other events.

The same goes for any number of other events and cultural objects. Jazz, for example, was largely the product of contingent forces and supreme human agency in the Jim Crow environment of lower-class and lower-caste New Orleans where it first made its appearance. Indeed, it is the very contingency of its origins, its transcendent supervention in the social nightmare of the old South, that made it so rapidly emerge as the first truly great all-American art form, as distinct from such other cultural creations as the slave songs and spirituals of the slave period, or the folk and urban blues of the rural, segregated South, or the blue-grass music of Appalachia, all of which are highly contextual and are meaningfully treated as legacies of their appropriate periods and contexts (Levine, 1978).

We naturally recoil from the idea that Israel was in any way a legacy or product of the Nazi terror, or that jazz was the product of racism, but we do so mainly on moral grounds. I am suggesting a more rational basis for our rejection of all such claims – the view that what emerges from the contingencies of a given context cannot be taken as a legacy or effect of that context.

The cases above are examples of what may be called strong contingencies, in contrast with a second set of weak contingencies, so called not because of their unimportance, but because they are usually minor events in their originating contexts, so minor that, as Paul David (1988: 11) observes, they "appeared not only insignificant, but entirely random in character." Nonetheless, they have major consequences in outcomes appearing later, as in path dependent processes. In a nutshell: strong contingencies, and their later outcomes, are unidentified with the contexts in which they emerged, in spite of seemingly strong counterfactual evidence to the contrary. Weak contingencies, and their contexts, have powerful identifying connections to later outcomes, in spite of seemingly weak counterfactual evidence to the contrary.

Four types of continuities

I distinguish between four types of continuities based partly on the kind of causal processes involved and the domain of the sociocultural universe to which they pertain: qualitative, structural, event, and commemorative.

Qualitative continuities

These are persisting cultural objects or quasi-permanent identity streams in the sociocultural domain. What we observe at any given moment will be a bounded complex of inter-related qualities, but it is only a socio-temporal stage, a sampled occurrence of many closely similar, adjoining occurrences of this complex along the historical line that constitutes, in its entirety, the identity of the cultural object in question (Burger, 1976: 75).

I am firmly in the school of social thought that views culture as an information system and specific cultural objects as packages of information, or native models of behavior, values, and ideals (Boyd and Richerson, 1985; D'Andrade, 1995; Goodenough, 1989; Keesing, 1987). They must be distinguished from actual behavior, for which they provide blueprints. The interaction between models and performance is reciprocal. The point is best made with the familiar metaphor of an open software package and its relation to long-term usage. Models guide behavior; but behavior, over the long run, leads to adjustments in models: for example, the various editions of a software package in response to the demands and tinkering of end-users. And, in the same way that in the physical human-made world everything ultimately has a software dimension – is the embodiment of some information package – so it is that ultimately all areas of social life are cultural in that they are embodiments or enactments of iterated cultural models responding to social uses. Material and other artifacts are simply the embodiment of cultural software. Social structures – from informal routines to highly structured organizations – are more fluid, and interactive, enactments of cultural models. Note that the software (culture), hardware (structural enactments) metaphor includes a critical feature of all cultural processes missed, or downplayed by analogous images such as "schemas" or "toolkits" (Swidler, 1986), namely, the fact that they are all rule-based, though varying in degrees of tightness (Emmett, 1966). Further, this approach allows for an even greater play of human agency. I can write anything with my Word Perfect software, from Jamaican short stories to American sociological abstractions. It is a highly rule-bound instrument; but it is a powerfully enabling set of rules. It is stable, predictable, and has a clearly defined identity, but it is not static; and it is collectively constructed and reconstructed. As Alexander and Smith (1993: 158) note, "cultural codes are elastic because individuals can ad-hoc from event to code and from code to event," but not so elastic that they lack causal influence.

The software metaphor also gets around the thorny problem of cultural coherence (Swidler, 2001: 181–186). The fact that people are often contradictory, confused, and downright incoherent in their views and rationalizations is not inconsistent with a conception of cultural models as rule-based and coherent.

My word-processing software is very coherent – except when it occasionally crashes. It is what I do with it that is too often contradictory. A sociology of culture should be careful not to operate at so particularistic a level that it gets entangled with the minutiae of ordinary social intercourse – this is the province of ethnographers and novelists. The difference is similar to that between what linguists do and what language journalists pontificate about in the Sunday papers.

Qualitative cultural objects are causally self-perpetuating. They are "chronically reproduced" identities that "owe their survival to relatively self-activating social processes" (Jepperson, 1991: 145). What this means in practical sociological terms is that they are normative, taken-for-granted, social processes that are believed in, valorized, and acted on simply because they have always been there, or are believed to have always been there, and are among the social things that make life meaningful and "real." As Lynne G. Zucker (1977: 726) pointed out some time ago, "it is sufficient for one person simply to tell another that this is how things are done. Each individual is motivated to comply because otherwise his actions and those of others in the system cannot be understood ... the fundamental process is one in which the moral becomes factual." Processes vary in the degree to which they are encultured, that is, rule bound and self-perpetuating. They are most encultured when they become institutions. This immediately raises the question of how such self-reproducing complexes are transmitted.

Although sociologists have neglected this problem, it is one focus of the landmark work of Boyd and Richerson (1988: ch. 3) on cultural processes. The main mechanism, they show, is through social learning, defined as "the transmission of stable behavioral dispositions by teaching or imitation." Integrating the findings of social learning theory and socialization studies within their own theory of culture as a dual transmission process, Boyd and Richerson present a powerful case for cultural persistence or, to use their own language, for cultural inertia, in the face of environmental variation, for why "history should explain a significant fraction of present behavior and a common past should cause significant similarities between societies." Their argument is summarized as follows:

Because they have many effects that are spread over a long period of time, it is difficult for individuals to determine the best choice by trial and error; because the consequences of alternate choices depend on a complex, variable, hard to understand environment, it is difficult for individuals to deduce the optimal behavior. The result is that a reliance on individual learning [i.e. trial and error] will lead to frequent errors. If this intuition is correct, and if the social learning theorists are also correct that information can be acquired easily and accurately by social learning, then ... a strong dependence on cultural transmission usually provides a better way to acquire beliefs about the environment than a strong dependence on individual learning.   (Boyd and Richerson, 1988: 117)

Because of the structuralist and transformative bias of most historical sociology, there are only a few studies that systematically unravels the historical paths by which cultural continuities originate, become institutionalized or self-causing, are transmitted from one period to another and causally interact with social organization, and it is striking how many of these few are by non-sociologists (see, for examples: Bennett, 1996; Degler, 1977; Greif, 1998; Hall and Soskice, 2001; Reed, 1972; Wood, 2001). Let us briefly examine one of the finest examples of this small group of studies exploring the interaction between cultural processes and what Hall and Soskice (2001) call "behavioral logics," over a long period of time: Eiko Ikegami's (1997) brilliant study of the samurai tradition of honorific individualism in Tokugawa and later Japan. Honorific individualism was an integral part of the samurai honor culture that emerged during the medieval period "as a sense of warrior pride" by men fiercely devoted to the defense, management, and expansion of the sovereignty and familial honor of their *ie* (house) or landed estate and its position in the competitive ranking system of the broader society.

The Tokugawa regime removed the unstable militaristic foundation that originally generated samurai honorific individualism, but the new leadership shrewdly preserved the ethic and redirected it toward its own ends of state formation and sociocultural consolidation. The samurai were "tamed" into loyal bureaucrats and servants of the state. It was during this period that status, power, and occupation were given objective and external expression in the enactments of elaborate public ceremonies as well as sumptuary rules and other symbolic instruments legitimized by the state. This domestication of the warrior class and its ethic naturally generated tension, sometimes verging on disorder, and hence the need for control, out of which emerged an overarching, self-reproducing identity. The samurai expressed their sense of mutual resistance in the cultural identity known as the ethic of *ichibum*, which Ikegami (1997) translates as "'one part' of the core of a person's pride that cannot be compromised." She observes further:

The spirit of *ichibum* was observed in various political milieus during the Tokugawa period. *It was this sense of honor that provided an ethical impetus for all kinds of early modern ideologies regardless of their behavioral manifestations.* If anything, the culture of honor increasingly became a prized moral resource through its provision of idioms for the expression of spiritual and social individuality in the cultural setting of the Tokugawa samurai – a setting in which unconditional loyalty and obedience received an ever stronger emphasis. (italics added)

With the Meiji restoration we find yet another radical change in the social context of samurai honorific individualism, this time the abolition of the samurai as a class along with most of their privileges. Nonetheless, as Ikegami (1997) shows, the "legacy of the samurai honor culture remained," and precisely because it was decoupled from its social creators it could be more creatively and expansively used as a powerful cultural resource by the modern Japanese state. And use it they did, in the promotion of the secondary traditions of Japanese nationalism, militarism, imperial expansion, and later in the development of the special form of Japanese business organization and culture with its distinctive emphasis on loyalty and collective solidarity. So successful was the use of this resource in the modernization period that it became conventional wisdom among Japanese and western scholars that most of the modernizers were from the samurai class, a view that has been challenged by more recent revisionist scholars (Yamamura, 1977: ch. 7).

Here we have a prime example of an identity stream as a self-perpetuating causal process. We see clearly what quasi-permanence means in cultural terms: the interrelation of qualities that constituted the Japanese culture of honor, its spirit of *ichibum*, went through important changes from one period to another, responding to the changing environment even as the environment itself changed reciprocally to enable its persistence. Today, the Japanese culture of honor remains pervasive in its capitalist system, accounting for much that is distinctive and successful (as well as problematic) in this most modern of economic macro-cultures.

Identity persists through many sources of change. One source, as indicated earlier, is inherent in the very nature of culture and its reciprocal relation to behavior. People tinker with their cultural models in the course of using them and adapting them to their own purposes, although in so doing they have to adjust to other people's tinkering. Changes are also introduced in the process of transmission. Those who teach often misinterpret or offer idiosyncratic versions of the model. Naive learners often misunderstand what they have been taught. And variations are also introduced in the process of learning through observations of the behavior of role models. There are also the deliberate attempts at change by cultural innovators and deviants. And, finally, there are those new variants of a complex that emerge as a result of unplanned trial and error (Boyd and Richerson, 1988: ch. 4). Through all these changes, however, it is possible for identities to continue by means of the joint interplay of epistemic imputation, symbolic manipulation, and some constancy in the resemblance of objectively real bundles of attributes "out there" in the shifting stuff of social reality.

Structural continuities

Layers of structural analysis   A structure is a system of relations. It is a quite straightforward concept and there is no need to get entangled in frightful sociological metaphysics when we talk about it. In the broadest terms, it is any persisting, relatively stable system of interacting elements. Following Russell

(1948: 271), we say that two observed systems of interaction have identical structures if there is a direct correspondence in all the fields of relations that constitute them. Underlying all structural continuities are hierarchical causal chains.

All but the most elementary structures tend to be nested in broader systems and can be viewed on different levels of analysis. Hannan (1992) has observed, correctly, that social structures are usually only partly nested in each other, in that different levels – elementary interactions, informal groups, formal organizations – may sometimes interact, but may also singly generate outcomes at the highest systemic or macro-levels. We are inclined to agree with him, too, that the endless agonizing about the integration of micro- and macro-relations may be a waste of time. The discipline lacks the capacity to deal with more than two levels and, in any event, levels are so loosely coupled that analytic failure at lower, micro-levels may not preclude quite robust theorizing at the macro-level. He notes that this was true of Darwin, whose macro-theory of evolution survived his erroneous micro-theory of (blending) genetics. It is not unreasonable to assume that the same may hold for sociology.

In both sociology and neo-institutional economics significant progress has been made in reconciling human agency and structure and in avoiding the twin dangers of oversocialized holism, on the one hand, and undersocialized reductionist individualism, on the other (Alexander and Smith, 1993; Granovetter, 1985; Groenewegen and Vromen, 1999; Sewell, 1992). Agents and structural processes mutually reinforce and constitute each other in ongoing, relatively stable reproductive patterns. A striking convergence of views has also emerged in both fields, often independently, that in complex modern societies it is institutions, and especially organizations, that mediate between different levels, and function, as Samuels (1994) has most forcefully argued, as transmission mechanisms between them (see also Jepperson, 1991). Ann Swidler's (2001) fine recent study of love in America, well illustrates the ways in which the institution of marriage mediates between different levels and "logics" of the wider culture.

There are many ways to interpret and analyze such structures. I draw attention to three basic layers. First, we refer to the surface structure of objects, and what is meant here is simply the stable interrelations that are observed to exist between objects or events. The patterns in the sounds people make; the way they are combined to form symbols; and the stable arrangement of these symbols into sentences, constitute the surface structure of language. To speak a language we must have an implicit knowledge of its surface structure or grammar, and the same holds for our performance of all other areas of culture and social interaction (Pinker, 2000). However, we can move either downward to deeper layers of structure, or outward to higher, emergent or macro-layers. It is usually the case that the deeper or the higher we move, the more stable (or quasi-permanent) the structures, but also the less aware of them are native performers of the surface object or event being explained (Lieberson, 1985: 107–115).

The exploration of the continuities that are deeper structures has long been the preoccupation of linguists and one school of symbolic anthropologists, as well as psychologists. Underlying syntactical structures reaching down to a Chomskian universal grammar; the search for the deep structures of myths famously associated with the work of Lévi-Strauss; and the use of component analysis and other reduction techniques to probe latent psychological states or structures are among the better known examples of the search for latent quasi-permanent continuities (Mohr, 1998).

Eschewing psychological reductions, network methods and analyses would seem to offer the best prospects for the sociological exploration of deep structures and, indeed, that was the explicit goal of the approach in its early days. The aim, as one network scholar recently put it, was to find some kind of synchronization in which "certain patterns on the structural level" are found to coexist on a regular basis "with a specific texture of events on the contact level at the same time" (Krempel, 1990). Unfortunately, network studies have yet to live up to this promise.

It is the exploration of outer, emergent structures that have drawn the lion's share of sociological interest. How structures operate, especially at lower, more accessible levels, has been the subject of considerable theoretical attention, some of which I have already mentioned. Jonathan Turner's (1989: ch. 11) synthesis strikes me as the most illuminating. He has persuasively argued that they emerge through the overlapping mechanisms of categorization, regionalization, normalization, ritualization, routinization, and the stabilization of resource transfers.

I will briefly discuss here mainly intra-societal emergent structures, although there are far grander levels (Tilly, 1984: ch. 4). Labor markets and class inequality more generally, as well as racial and gender stratification and discrimination, are classic instances of structural continuities that have different behavioral and cultural outcomes in different periods.

Brinton and Kariya's (1998) richly textured study of the labor market for elite graduates in Japan nicely illustrates how continuities at different macrolevels overlay surface variations. In response to threatened sanctions from government following public criticisms of the closed-door recruitment process, whereby certain firms exclusively hired from certain universities in a mutually beneficial arrangement that was judged unfair to many Japanese graduates (the *reserved school* system), outward changes were made in the recruitment process. Nonetheless, in spite of these changes there remain "considerable continuity in the recruiting relationship between particular prestigious universities and employers." This continuity is explained by a shift toward a new outward pattern – reliance on alumni–student relations – which completely subverted the other new pattern of meritocractic recruitment that the firms rather cynically instituted in response to public pressure. However, behind the institutional continuity of the reserved school system is an even more enduring continuity in Japanese culture: the propensity to operate through exclusive collective groupings based on a system of mutual trust and loyalty that can be traced all the way back to the medieval era. This pattern of mutual trust is reinforced, on the individual level, by the persisting, if modernized, culture of honor shared by the top officers of the interacting universities and businesses.

A vast body of literature has demonstrated the persistence of class as a principle of social organization in western societies and its changing sociocultural consequences (Dahrenndorf, 1965; Hall, 1997; Grusky and Sorensen, 1998; Portes, 2000). The problem with most sociological studies of class is that they aim at too high a level of aggregation. As Grusky and Sorensen (1998) have sensibly observed, if sociologists aimed at more modest levels they would discover "deeply institutionalized groupings" such as those that emerge from the socioeconomic domain. Such institutionalized groupings are precisely the social expressions of persisting, hierarchical causal processes, and it is here that we see most clearly the ways in which institutions act as transmission mechanisms between levels of social phenomena.

Hierarchically linked, structural continuities accompanied by surface changes are also strikingly demonstrated by the history and current socio-economic status of women. As Judith Bennett (1997: 73–94) shows, it is essential to distinguish between the experiences of women – what may be called the surface level of women's social life – and "transformations in women's status." For example, in the fourteenth century, when women dominated brewing, it was "low-skilled, low-profit, low-status work – that is, work then seen as appropriate for a woman." By the seventeenth century, brewing had become a highly skilled, profitable, and very prestigious craft, now suitable mainly for men. Women were still working in the trade, but in the unskilled, low-status, and low-paying areas. In other words, Bennett concludes, beneath the radical changes in the brewing industry and in the surface experiences of women, was one unrelenting continuity: the persistence of women's work as low status, low skill, and low profit. Today, over four centuries later, a leading sociologist of gender can still lament in a recent article that the wage-gap and all its ramifications remains one of "the most enduring manifestations of sex inequality in industrial and postindustrial society" (Reskin, 1991). A common explanation of this gap among sociologists is the high level of job segregation in modern industries (Bielby and Baron, 1984). However, Reskin (1991) observes that job segregation is of limited explanatory value precisely because it is too close to the surface of what is being explained. This more basic cause is one of the most ancient continuities in human history: "men's desire to preserve their advantaged position and their ability to do so by establishing rules to distribute valued resources in their favor" (Reskin, 1991: 143).

Much the same holds for our explanation of the surface realities of ethnosomatic ("racial") inequalities. According to Lieberson (1985), the traditional explanation that the persistent income gap between Afro-Americans and Euro-Americans has been due to the educational differences between them is superficial because changes in the former are not commensurate with declines in the latter. When educational access was denied Afro-Americans this may indeed have been a significant proximate cause, but with access to education, he argues, Euro-Americans have found other ways of maintaining their superordinate position. While this explanation certainly holds for the post-bellum South up to the eve of the Civil Rights movement, it carries far less weight in explaining ethnosomatic inequalities over the past half century. Since the late 1950s, education has proven to be a major factor in reducing the income gap between African Americans and Euro-Americans. And a recent study suggests that the skills gap between the groups explains nearly all the income discrepancy between them (Jencks and Philips, 1998). Racism and racial discrimination persist, but educational attainment now trumps it as an explanation.

What this suggests is the time-sensitive nature of causal structures: conditions that were causally important in one period may lose their causal potency in a later one, or vice versa.

Associative and non-associative structural continuities   There is a complex relationship between enduring structural processes and the surface manifestations, especially sociocultural objects, associated with them that raises contentious social and political issues. It is often the case that a persisting configuration of structural factors is causally associated with persisting patterns of behavior that, however, are not institutionalized. In other words, they never become self-generating qualitative or cultural continuities. Once the structural factors that generate them are discontinued they cease to exist. I call these associative structural effects or continuities. Most forms of deviant behavior are of this nature. The association of prostitution with the structural forces of poverty is a case in point, well illustrated by their joint history in Cuba. Thus, prostitution was rampant before the revolution, became nearly extinct during the more economically secure decades of Soviet subsidies after the revolution, and then, almost on cue, has rapidly returned with the economic troubles that began after the collapse of the Soviet Union and the termination of its economic aid.

Some scholars who explore the relationship between culture and poverty are basically arguing for what I am here calling associative structural continuities (Rainwater, 1970; Wilson, 1997). At their best, the works of Oscar Lewis (1959, 1966) did make a strong case of such continuities. Problems began only when he and others attempted to make the case that these structurally generated patterns could, and did, become institutionalized, that is, non-associated. There is no dead horse that sociologists and policy analysts love to flog more than this one (Burton, 1992; Katz, 1989; Leacock, 1971; Valentine, 1970). While I do not wish to reprise the debate here, it now seems that the extreme attacks on all attempts to explore the relationship between culture and poverty amounted to sociological overkill and political bias. The truth of the matter is that there are well-documented associations between the structural condition of poverty and distinctive behavioral patterns, a fact acknowledged even by the most severe of critics (Valentine, 1970).

It is not unreasonable to suggest that an associative structural continuity can, under certain circumstances, become non-associative, self-perpetuating cultural continuities. Indeed, it is very likely that this is an important way in which many (non-controversial) cultural patterns originated. What bedevils this debate is the all or nothing approach of both advocates and critics of "the culture of poverty." The term "culture of poverty" should perhaps be avoided, along with its implication that the totality of a class's subculture is entirely the product of class position. But so, too, should the equally totalistic view that no area of the behavior of the poor is a cultural adaptation to their present or former condition that has become self-perpetuating. Some attitudes, and patterns of thought and behavior among some groups – some of which may be problematic, some desirable – may be cultural continuities, or they may simply be associated structural continuities pure and simple, or they may be associated structural continuities in the process of becoming dissociated and institutionalized into cultural continuities. Deciding what they are is a matter for empirical verification, as Herbert Gans (1962: 244; 1965) wisely observed years ago, not something to be decided by theoretical or ideological fiat.

An understanding of the factors accounting for the effects of persisting structures and the ways they are associated with social objects on the surface is best found in fine-grained sociohistorical and field-based studies of localities. Thus, the British social historian, Peter Laslett (1980), and his collaborators, have demonstrated the existence of generations of bastardy in certain parts of England from the Middle Ages through to modern times; a clear case of non-associative, cultured practices growing out of formerly structurally associative ones. In America, the regional sociologists Susan Hanson and Geraldine Pratt (1995) have provided several instances of sustained associative structural effects in their detailed historical geography of the Massachusetts city of Worcester. For example, they have found a long tradition of deep antipathy toward collective bargaining in Worcester, which stands in stark contrast with vigorous support for trade unions in Boston and other cities of the state. "The Worcester of the past," they argue, "shines through the Worcester of the present," in the presence of a distinctive configuration of structural continuities in Worcester's social economy. These are its ethnic diversity; the plurality of skills and industries that made union organizations difficult; the fact that ethnic and geographic communities have always coincided with occupational differences, creating further problems of union organization; extreme gender segregation at the workplace; and a socially close-knit, politically united business and civic leadership. Closely associated with these structural continuities is a tradition of extreme hostility to unionism on the part of both the local bosses and workers, undermining any kind of working-class solidarity and radical leadership (Hanson and Pratt, 1995).

What is true of Worcester may hold for the ghettoes of America. As William Julius Wilson (1997) frequently comments on his years of study of unemployment and joblessness in the African American ghettoes of Chicago, there is a world of difference between being unemployed in a neighborhood where the unemployment rate is the national norm of 5 percent, and one in which the vast majority of persons of working age are unemployed. When work disappears, when unemployment persists from generation to generation, a small but significant proportion of those not employed fall from the categories of being unemployed (i.e. with no job but actively seeking one) or discouraged worker (no longer in the labor force but still would like to work) and become unemployable or what Marta Tienda and Haya Stier (1991) call the "shiftless." At that point, and for this small group only, what we are calling a pattern of associative structural effects phases into what begins to look like a weakly institutionalized kind of non-associative continuity, at least in the Chicago communities studied by Tienda and Stier (1991) as well as Wilson (1997). Whether or not such early signs of institutionalization are to be found in other African American ghettoes such as those of Boston and New York is a matter for empirical research.

Event continuities

Events figure prominently in all theories of causation and, hence, any explicit or implied notion of continuity. Indeed, for philosophers such as Quine (following Russell) all objects are ultimately held to be constituted entirely by events (Hookway, 1998: 100–104). All this may come as a surprise to most sociologists whose structuralist bias, as Harrison White (1992: 76–77, 135–136) has wryly observed, often leads them to disdain events. However, because of the discipline's transformationist bias, even those scholars who call for greater attention

to events commit the serious error of defining them as sociohistorically important only when they are momentous and are so considered or constructed by
agents (Abbott, 1992; Griffen, 1992; Abrams, 1982; Sewell, 1966a, b). This
restriction is a serious conceptual flaw, for the simple reason that consequential
events are often themselves quite minor and may even be wholly neglected
when they occurred. A proper sociological theory of events must allow for the
possibility that all events are potentially important.

An important distinction should be made from the start. When we claim
that an event is the cause of an outcome we may be referring to the event
as a concrete object in its entirety, or as Hart and Honore (1985: ch. 5) have
emphasized, to "the *fact* that an event was of a certain type or possessed a certain
feature causally relevant to the outcome." The distinction, often referred to as
one between token (or singular) and type (or property) causation, has grown in
importance among students of causality, controversy focusing on the question of
which is more fundamental (Galvotti, 2001). I am inclined to agree with Judea
Pearl (2000: 310) that the really important question is "what tangible claims do
type and token statements make about our world and how is causal knowledge
organized so as to substantiate such claims?" My own view is that this is the
fundamental difference between qualitative and positivistic sociologists rather
than a preference for the use of statistical methods which are now equally
amenable to qualitative and quantitative approaches. Positivists tend to refer to
causally relevant attributes of events, in contrast with more cultural and case-
oriented sociologists who tend to refer to the entirety of the concrete event as
the causal antecedent.

Recent studies of lynching in the post-bellum South well illustrate the distinction. The historical sociologists Stewart Tolnay and E. M. Beck (1992) have
recently added to a long line of scholars who have treated lynching as a recurring series of events. However, there are many detailed treatments of particular
lynchings which explore them as complex, unique social objects (McGovern,
1982). And I, along with others, have recently examined them comparatively
as cultural objects, attempting to uncover their quasi-permanent qualities and
internal structure (Patterson, 1998).

It is interesting that the one major attempt at theorizing continuity in the social
sciences emphasizes events rather than social objects. Unfortunately, Alexander
Gerschenkron's (1968) classic paper betrays not only his economist disciplinary
bias in that he has nothing to say about the kinds of cultural and structural
continuities we have discussed so far, but a disquieting subjectivism. "At all
times and in all cases," he asserts, "continuity must be regarded as a tool forged
by the historian rather than something inherently and invariably contained in
the historical matter" (Gerschenkron, 1968: 38). Concentrating on the problems
of continuity and discontinuity in economic change, he distinguishes between

five ways in which we use the term continuity. It may mean simply growth or constancy of direction, such as the development of institutions and ideas; or the periodic recurrence over time such as cycles and stages in which the causal mechanism from one stage to another remains constant; or endogeneity, which largely derives from the scholar's approach to his material; or length of causal regress, meaning continuity as a long causal chain.

It is the fifth meaning that most interests him, namely, continuity as stability of the rate of change in things such as price and national income, and he focuses on constancy of a low rate of change. Discontinuity then, means an increase in the rate of change from previously low levels. Although Gerschenkron has many useful insights to offer, on some of which we will draw later, this view of continuity is far too narrow, even for the domain of economic events. Continuities in events are found not only in constant rates, but in the variance profiles of regular recurrences. There is, for example, a variation of seasons each year; but the unfailing regularity of their variation comes as close to our notion of a continuity as anything else, and it is odd that Gerschenkron would want to exclude these from our conception of continuity.

Continuities underlying recurring events   Let us begin with the standard distinction between recurring and unique events. Both may entail continuities, though in different ways.

Continuities are found in the patterns that underlie the surface rates and direction of recurring events. This is true even of the trends and cycles uncovered in the time-domain approach which employs models that attempt to predict the present as a regression on the past, although what emerges from such studies is an admittedly weak version of continuity. We are on surer footing with frequency domain approaches which attempt to explain the behavior of the series in terms of underlying periodic and structural variations in some other phenomena driving it (Shumway and Stoffer, 2000). When, for example, we explore whether there is an underlying warming trend in global temperature measurements, we are searching for continuities beneath the surface variations of the climate. Similarly, continuous cycles in the price of cotton in the American South during the first half of the century persistently drove the rate at which African American men were lynched.

However, there are major potential pitfalls in the use of time-series events, involving a distortion of history as a temporal process and of any meaningful notion of continuity. Larry Isaac and Larry Griffin (1989) have drawn our attention to these problems, although they themselves go on to commit a serious error in their remarks concerning the nature of continuity. After reviewing a large number of such studies in sociology and economics they concluded that nearly all these studies work with a wholly ahistorical conception of time.

Among the many historical and methodological problems noted by Isaac and Griffin in what are often considered landmark studies in historical sociology are: neglecting the time-ordered nature of the series' units in their treatment of missing data; unwarranted linearity in their estimation equations; obviating the search for time-sensitive parameter estimates by the usually untenable assumption that time-series coefficients are stable over the entire period – sometimes spanning a century and a half – for which their equations are estimated; arbitrarily "slicing into" history and ending the series at the convenience of the researcher in wanton disregard for the substantive significance of the starting and ending dates in question; and using coefficients from one part of the series to "predict" values in the dependent variable in another stretch of the series in total disregard for sometimes major structural changes that have taken place between the two stretches of time in question.

I fully endorse these criticisms by Isaac and Griffin (1989) as well as their plea for the historicization of quantitative methodology, for taking periodization and structural context seriously, and for sensitivity to the play of the contingent in history. I also agree with them that this is not a problem of quantitative analysis, per se, but of ahistorical theorizing and often improper statistical procedures.

However, Griffin and Isaac undermine an otherwise excellent paper by completely confusing continuity with ahistoricism, failing to see how change and continuity are inextricably linked. Ahistoricism, they assert incorrectly, is manifested "in the emphasis on the continuity of history or the history of continuity. Here history is conceived to be the continual unfolding of the same underlying historical communality. Such a preoccupation with the continuity between past and present tends to homogenize or average away the difference between 'then and there' and 'here and now'" (Griffin and Isaac, 1989: 876). With such a naive and distorted view of continuity – as simply the absence of change – it is no wonder that Isaac and Griffin are convinced that the goal of historical sociology is to "explain social change" (1989: 882). Second, their position fails to acknowledge the role of underlying structural continuities beneath surface changes. Third, they are unaware of how causal processes can establish continuous links between wholly different objects, assuming that continuity must mean continuity of the same thing or of recurring events.

Continuities from non-recurring events: path-dependency   Continuities emerge from non-recurring events in two ways: through the persisting effects of initial events or, more properly, initial sequences of events, on the later course of events, better known as path-dependency; and through the operation of causal chains. This sub-section discusses path-dependency; the next takes up the role of continuity in causal chains.

"A path-dependent process," writes a leading authority on the subject (David, 1993), is one in which systems "cannot shake off the effects of past events," and the task of the researcher is to understand "the reasons why particular sequences of events in the past are capable of exerting persisting effects upon current conditions; [of] how adventitious, seemingly transient actions may become so magnified as to exercise a controlling (and sometimes pernicious) influence over matters of far greater economic and social significance." The classic example from economic history is the QWERTY keyboard layout, which is a relatively inefficient system that was deliberately designed to slow down typing speed by the early producers of the typewriter. Nonetheless, we are locked into the old technology and still continue to use this system (David, 1995). Other examples are the choice and persistence of water-cooled instead of gas-cooled nuclear reactors, the concentration of particular industries in certain cities, such as the auto industry in Detroit, and the adoption of the VHS over the more efficient Sony BETA format in VCRs.

Economic historians became interested in path-dependent systems because it appears to contradict a few well-established economic principles, although such claims have recently been strongly contested or qualified. Competitive market forces fail to reward and select out the most efficient technology due to the switching costs of learning and installing the better system. And the law of diminishing returns is upended by what appears to be an inertial network effect: people adopt the technology because many people already know how to use it; and because many people are comfortable with it, producers stick with it. Economists refer to these feedback effects as network externalities, the triumph of the crash-prone Microsoft operating system being the favorite modern example (Garrouste and Ioannides, 2001; Liebowitz and Margolis, 1995; Magnusson and Ottosson, 1997; North, 1997).

It is important to understand that path-dependency means more than is implied by the phrase, "history matters," or even that given patterns of behavior are outcomes of their past. This is all true, but trite. It is, rather, a stochastic process in which the outcome is strongly determined or "locked in" by initiating conditions, and in which each point or branch in the sequence of events leading to the outcome is a function of previous transition states of the system. This is what is meant by calling it a non-ergodic process – each transient state is unique and the outcome is unpredictable, the classic instance being the evolutionary process in biology (David, 2001). Two other features of such processes are to be noted. One is extreme sensitivity to small changes in the originating variables, a process best known to sociologists in tipping point patterns of ethnosomatic ("racial") segregation, where one move by a Euro-American or African American can result in white flight and the "catastrophic" transition of a neighborhood. The other is irreversibility: once the selection process is completed it is locked in and can usually only be changed by concerted public action – which is why Microsoft had to be sued by the government.

While path-dependency processes are more clearly recognizable with economic data, they are found in all areas of social life and have attracted considerable interest among political scientists and historical sociologists. However, there is a real danger among non-economists of claiming to identify path-dependent processes where none exists; that is, of confusing it with what amounts to ordinary cultural processes. Thus, I wholly disagree with Lars Magnusson and Jan Ottosson (1997: 1–9) that path-dependency can be identified as "genuine rule following" whether in the form of the selection of information in situations of uncertainty or just plain, inertial rule-following independent of situational constraints. Rule-following is the essential feature of what we have earlier called qualitative continuities. It is what happens when behavior becomes normative and what makes cultural complexes self-reproducing. Thus the persistence of the British system of measurement in the USA and UK instead of the more efficient metric system is not, as is often claimed, a path-dependent outcome, but a straightforward cultural persistence (Grabher, 1995).

So far, I have emphasized the need to distinguish path-dependent from purely cultural processes. However, path-dependent processes can become cultural and often do. What is the difference? When the practice in question is learned behavior that is passed down from one generation to the next. This is what happened with the QWERTY typewriter layout. It may now be happening with the Microsoft operating system. These can sometimes be of long duration as Avner Greif (1998) shows in his study of the cultural orientations of Maghribi and Genoese merchants during in the late Middle Ages. In the contemporary world, the plantation economy is a classic path-dependent outcome of Caribbean economic history which, as many noted Caribbean economists have shown, is now a powerful cultural model that continues to shape and explain many of the problems and failures of industrialization in the region. So powerful is it, that it has survived nearly a half century of a communist "revolution" in Cuba that began with the explicit aim of removing all traces of the plantation and its humiliating vestiges of slavery (Beckford, 1972, 1975).

Non-recurring events: direct causal chains   Let us now consider the final way in which events are implicated in continuities. If an event, Y, in a later period can be shown to be the outcome of a series of non-recurring events initiated by an event, X, in an earlier period, we are entitled to claim that a continuity exits between them. The continuity, which may be direct or hierarchical, is constituted by the causal chain that links them.

Let me give an example. The radical cultural transformation of Jamaica during the 1970s may seem to have absolutely nothing to do with the Italian fascist conquest of Ethiopia in the 1930s (Barrett, 1997; Brodber and Greene, 1981; Chevannes, 1995; Nettleford, 1972). Nonetheless, this brutal imperial conquest, and the exile of the young and attractive Emperor Haile Sellassie of Ethiopia suddenly thrust the formerly obscure African kingdom and its monarch into prominence. Lower-class Afro-Jamaicans of the 1930s, who had suffered centuries of British slavery, colonialism, and denigration of all things African, and were then going through mass unemployment during the worst years of the Great Depression (which devastated the Caribbean sugar industry), suddenly learned that there was a great and ancient kingdom in Africa with an emperor who claimed a lineage that not only far surpassed that of the British colonial emperor in ancestry, but also traced its roots back to the biblical Queen of Sheba. It was not long before a cult of the emperor emerged among the Afro-Jamaican poor, and then a syncretic, millenarian religion blending elements of Hebrew Old Testament history with its emphasis on exile with a new vision of Ethiopia as an earthly heaven and the emperor as a living God.

Like many millenarian cults, it survived a major crisis during the late 1950s when prophecy failed and the Emperor did not turn up to take them back on the day appointed by their local leader (Patterson, 1964, 1965). The cult attracted many of the newly emerging popular singers of the late 1950s and early 1960s, most notably Bob Marley and his group, the Wailers. Its close identification with reggae music and the success of that music internationally finally won the admiration of radical middle-class political leaders, especially Michael Manley, son of one of the founding fathers of the Jamaican nation. Reggae singers and the Rastafarian cult were a decisive factor in the political victory of Michael Manley's party in the 1972 elections (Waters, 1989). In repaying his political debt to the cult, Manley not only gave it the legitimacy it sought (it was, for example, allowed equal free time on the National radio station with the established churches) but encouraged a massive rehabilitation of Jamaican cultural symbols, shifting from its traditional bias in favor of cultural complexes of British ancestry as well as light complexion, to a celebration of Africa, the African heritage, and dark complexion, in Jamaica (Anglès, 1994; Panton, 1993). We have, in this way, established a causal chain between the radical, left-wing cultural revolution of Jamaica in the 1970s and the conquest of Ethiopia during the 1930s.

This kind of continuity is similar to what Gerschenkron (1968: 29) called the causal regress, and his qualifications about when it is appropriate are worth repeating. First, to be meaningful, it should entail "more than simply the fact that the existence of any given complex of events at any given time can be conceived as having been occasioned by events preceding it in time," since such connections are "inherent in the very concept of history" (Gerschenkron, 1968: 29–30). To go beyond such truisms, the historian must make the "concrete" research decision to "single out a certain occurrence as the 'beginning' of the causal chain . . . In all cases it will be his task to make the selection plausible in terms of the specific strength of the cause chain that is attached, link by link, to the 'original' cause. He will have to show how it compares and intertwines with other chains that run in the same direction" (Gerschenkron, 1968: 29–30). In other words, all good counterfactual explanations must be guided by an explicitly developed theory or argument. In doing so, Hart and Honore's criterion of relativity to the contexts of both the case in question and the perspective of the enquiry is decisive. For example, I did not go back to the founding of fascism in Italy because it was irrelevant to my inquiry. But that was the easy part. More problematic is the fact that I could have traced the causal tree much farther back in Jamaican history. For example, I could have decided that the denigration of things African in colonial Jamaica and the yearning of lower-class Afro-Jamaicans for pride in something African had to be explained, in which case the chain would have had to go all the way back to the introduction of slavery in Jamaica during the seventeenth century.

Quite apart from the question of where to begin the historical chain, however, is the more serious problem of competing theories. There was, for example, a long tradition of cultural nationalism in Jamaica, which increased in momentum with independence in 1962, having its roots in intellectual and artistic circles that were independent of the Rastafarian movement. This other movement had close links to the People's National Party of Michael Manley, his own mother, the British-born sculptor Edna Manley, being a powerful early force in its development. A counterfactual argument could be made for a causal chain running along strongly bourgeois nationalist lines to some point in the forties as the source of the cultural revolution of the 1970s in Jamaica. Michael Manley's family background and his education at the radical London School of Economics where he came under the influence of the liberal radical thinker, Harold Laski, and the British trade union movement, were sufficient to account for his radical leanings. His promotion of lower-class Afro-Jamaican culture, in this scenario, was more determined by astute political calculations.

In spite of the enormous popularity of backward causal chains, their complexity and potential precariousness are not often appreciated. Every node on such chains involves a counterfactual open to challenge. Might the Jamaican working classes have discovered Ethiopia and developed the cult of Sellassie without the fascist invasion of Ethiopia? Would Manley have won the culturally decisive election of 1972 without the strong support of the reggae singers and culture-conscious urban lumpenproletariat? A reasonable case could be made for any of these counterfactuals.

These problems are even more acute when we are dealing with complex chains. An extreme case in point is Fernand Braudel's (1985–87) huge and unwieldy three-volume study of Mediterranean civilization and the rise of capitalism between the fifteenth and eighteenth centuries. This elaborate study might serve as a classic example of how not to explore the continuities of history through elaborate causal chains, every node and branch of which stands open to question (Tilly, 1984: 65–74).

Commemorative or "invented" continuities

We come finally to the problem of invented continuities, which is peculiar to the social universe. People are not only conscious of their past and very concerned about how it is interpreted, but are highly invested in the notion that there is continuity between them and their ancestors, as well as between their lives now and life as lived in the past. This raises important epistemic as well as ontic issues pertaining to history and collective memory (David, 1988: 13–14).

There is a lively tradition of scholarship on collective memory, going back to Halbwachs (1980), which we do not have the space to discuss here at any length. Barry Schwartz (1996) recently distinguished between two broad bodies of research. There is, first, a strongly instrumentalist tradition which sees collective memory as an ever changing construction that serves the interests of the present generation. Commemorative icons, official histories, historic parks and monuments, holidays and other ritualized occasions, as well as what Connerton (1989) calls bodily practices are adapted to the needs of each generation. At its most extreme, this view sees the past as a malleable resource completely at the mercy of present needs and values. The second body of scholarship is no less constructionist, differing mainly in its view that there are competing constructions of collective memory rather than the generalized memory of the Halbwachs School. There are two strands of this second school: one approaches the subject from a neo-Marxian, conflict perspective, best represented by Eric Hobsbawm (1992) and his associates in their studies of the invention of tradition in British society. The second is a pluralist branch which sees collective memories emerging from a diversity of cross-cutting interests. Perhaps the best example of this branch is Joseph Rhea's (1997) excellent study (published after Schwartz's review) of the struggle for collective cultural representation by America's ethno-racial minorities.

I wish to draw attention to the two main ways in which the problem of collective memory intersects with those raised by the study of continuities. The first is the potential tension between native and scholarly claims of continuity; the second has to do with the treatment of collective memory itself as a kind of continuity.

First, invented continuities constitute one (problematic) means of collective commemoration and it is important that we distinguish it from other such means as well as cultural processes in general. Most of the ways in which societies collectively remember, and what they select for commemoration, present no special problem for the historian or historical sociologist, as Alon Confino (1977) recently emphasized. In other words, selectively idealizing and mythologizing the past is a normal cultural process, true of all societies. We either suspend disbelief in such matters, or see them as belonging to the domain of faith and belief and not subject to the dictates of reason. For these and other reasons, I have serious problems with Hobsbawm's (1992: 2–3) view of invented tradition, as "a set of practices, normally governed by overtly or tacitly accepted rules and of a ritual or symbolic nature, which seek to inculcate certain values and norms of behavior by repetition, which automatically implies continuity with the past." The problem with this definition and Hobsbawm's subsequent attempt to defend it, is that it applies to pretty nearly all areas of culture and fails to discriminate a meaningful analytic set. All enduring social customs seek "the sanction of precedent, social continuity and natural law as expressed in history" (Hobsbawm, 1992: 2). Least persuasive of all is the argument that invented traditions differ in "the use of ancient materials to construct invented traditions of a novel type for quite novel purposes" (Hobsbawm 1992: 6). The adaptation of old traditions to new uses is an important and long-recognized aspect of all cultural life, in all periods. All secular and religious pageantry is collective play and ritual, and an element of make-believe is always involved. It really does not matter whether the cultural objects used on such occasions are historically accurate or have been culturally decontextualized. There is a willing suspension of disbelief on such occasions and the question of invention is simply inappropriate in our consideration of them.

To be sure, the historian has an obligation to distinguish between fact and dogma, both in his or her interpretation of secular history as well as in accounts of the history of the religion in question (Scholem, 1971). The distinction becomes especially important where believers over-reach and attempt to impose their dogmas as historical truth on non-believers, for example, the attempt of some Southern fundamentalists to teach the biblical version of creation instead of, or as an alternate theory of, evolution.

What then is left of invented traditions? What category of cultural life can be meaningfully included under such a category? My view is that the term is non-redundant and analytically useful only in reference to those cases where a set of *secular* practices and beliefs are defined by their practitioners as traditional *and* demonstrably false claims are made about their past, especially about the continuity of the tradition from a previous period of practice. In such cases we are no longer willing to suspend disbelief about claims of authenticity. If we are actors or participants of the practice, we believe them to be true, or have been duped into believing them to be authentic, and are offended if someone questions their authenticity. If we are not practitioners, we are offended by the deception and cry fraud. When, further, such beliefs are presented as the authentic record of history rather than fanciful idealizations or mythmaking and are taught in schools as true history, we have a fully developed invented tradition.

One of the case studies in Hobsbawm's and Ranger's (1992) collection satisfies this narrowed definition, and indeed may be viewed as paradigmatic. This is the Highland tradition of Scotland, which Trevor-Roper shows to be shot through with fraudulent claims and deceptions, *especially about history and continuity*. The whole thing was a "retrospective invention," in which the history of the relation between Ireland and Scotland was completely inverted, "culminating in the claim that Scotland – Celtic Scotland – was the 'mother nation' and Ireland the cultural dependency" which is the complete opposite of the historical facts (Trevor-Roper, 1992: 14). Not only was history fraudulently "stolen from the Irish," but even the most distinctive and symbolically cherished artifact of Highland culture – the kilt – turns out not to be of ancient Scottish origin, but something dreamt up by an enterprising English Quaker from Lancashire sometime during the 1720s! A modern, American example is the Afrocentric interpretation of African American history which advocates have succeeded in imposing on several of the nation's secondary school systems.

There is a second way in which the study of continuities intersect with that of collective memory. We can treat the processes of collective memory like any other cultural process and then ask whether there are continuities and discontinuities in them. In so doing, however, we step right into one of the most heated controversies in collective memory studies. As we previously noted, scholars working in the Halbwachs tradition are inclined to see the processes of collective memory to be themselves in flux, beliefs about the past changing from one generation to the next. Another group of scholars, however, tracing their ancestry back to Durkheim, have insisted that societies can maintain their identity and stability only by preserving some continuity in their conceptions of the past and this is achieved "by periodic commemoration rites whose function is not to transform the past by bending it to serve the present, but to reproduce the past, to make it live as it once did" (Schwartz, 1991). People need an "available past" that is stable and self-sustaining as well as an enduring "constitutive narrative" if they are to constitute a viable "community of memory" (Schudson, 1989: 222).

Schwartz nicely adjudicates between these two extremes in coming to a position similar to what we have advocated earlier in this chapter. He shows how the commemoration of George Washington over the centuries has changed in some respects from one period to another to meet changing collective needs, and yet there were striking continuities across generations having "a logic and force of [their] own," that undermine the radical constructionist position. There is no anomaly in the simultaneity of continuity and change for, as we have seen, it is normal for cultural processes to change even while maintaining their identities: in the commemoration of Washington "there remains an assemblage of old beliefs coexisting with the new, including old beliefs about the past itself" (Schwartz, 1991: 234). The extreme constructionists and advocates of generational change have badly underestimated "the present's carrying power," Schwartz correctly observes, and have failed "to see that the same present can sustain different memories and that different presents can sustain the same memory" (Schwartz, 1991: 234).

This eloquent statement holds true not only for the objects and processes of collective memory, but for all cultural objects and processes, and I can think of no better way to segue into my own final remarks.

Conclusions

In this chapter I have drawn attention to the dimension of continuity in social analysis. I have argued that the neglect of and ingrained bias against this subject are the result of ignorance about the nature and mechanisms of continuity and the necessary relationship between continuity and change.

One of the main reasons for the misunderstanding of continuity is the limited view that it is primarily about the persistence of identity or of similar objects between periods. While this is certainly an important kind of continuity, I have shown that it is only one of several ways in which continuities exist over time. Further, I emphasized that identity through time does not mean the persistence of an essence, or a fixed set of attributes, but rather a "time-laden" stream of potentially changeable attributes with a quasi-permanent internal causal (relational) structure.

It may be objected, at this point, that if continuities are basically causal processes (other than cultural objects), then they appear to be nothing more than traditional explanations in sociology. This is an easily made error because of the common misconception, especially among quantitative sociologists, that most explanations in the discipline are causal. In fact, they are not. Sociologists have come to rely heavily on statistical models that predict dependent or outcome variables based on patterns of association in non-experimental data. A prediction, especially one based on atemporal data, is not a causal statement. As Clogg and Haritou – among others – (Clogg and Haritou, 1997; Kim and Ferree Jr., 1981) have recently reemphasized: "Finding models that predict well or fit the data well has little or nothing to do with estimating the presence, absence, or size of causal effects" (Clogg and Haritou, 1997: 110). To their credit, mainstream neo-classical economists have long recognized the importance of the distinction between models that are functional relations between variables in which effects are mathematically derived from ahistorical independent variables, on the one hand, and models that explain an effect as the outcome of a causal process, on the other; and at least since Milton Friedman have explicitly embraced the former over the latter (Cowan and Rizzo, 1996).

I would like to conclude by emphasizing a few practical implications of what I have just summarized. First, now that we understand how attributes may change, even as identities persist, we should be careful how quickly we dismiss the operation of continuities simply on the basis of appearances. The more quasi-permanent internal causal structure may remain stable, even when one or more attributes of an identity has either been shed or ceases to be important. I have shown elsewhere, for example, that, between the period of slavery and late into the share-cropping era, many of the cultural complexes of slavery persisted in the attitudes and practices of Euro-Americans and African Americans and in their interactions; and, indeed, that several of these cultural complexes persist to this day. We often fail to recognize these because in many cases a persisting cultural complex may be expressed in behavioral attributes that seem very different from those that appeared important in the earlier period (Patterson, 1998). The fact that African Americans had high marriage rates during the share-cropping period, in contrast with their currently low marriage rates, does not prove that there was a decisive break with the gender and familial relations of the slave past, as is so often simple-mindedly claimed by sociologists and historians of the African American family. Marriage is merely one attribute of the complex of cultural relations that constitute gender and familial patterns. Furthermore, behind these changes may have been powerful persisting environmental forces (for example, racism, economic and cultural exclusion, and the relentless effort to emasculate, and demonize, the African American male, all originating in, and bearing the mark of slavery) and equally powerful persisting cultural models learned while surviving the brutal challenges of the slave period. Examples include: the importance of paternity in defining manhood and the refusal to consider resources in making the decision to have a child, among men; and the absolute importance of motherhood in giving meaning and purpose to life, and to ensure racial survival, among women. What is true of African Americans, is also true of Euro-American Southerners, among whom slavery was an equally powerful "molder of peculiarly southern attitudes and social development," and of deeply ingrained continuities, as Carl Degler (1977) and others have shown. We also saw how the seeming changes in the economic situation of women over several centuries masked powerful underlying continuities in occupational status, skill level, and relative income.

Second, it should now be clear that when we ask a question such as how the institution of slavery influenced some area of modern life, the answer is not necessarily found in the identification of cultural patterns that are similar to those found during the period of slavery. Continuities may, and usually do, exist where there are no similarities in cultural objects. This is because of the operation of continuities through causal chains. By these means, one cultural complex or event in one period can have a relation of continuity with an entirely different object or type of event in a later period. In the case of path-dependent processes we have seen how practices in a later period can remain trapped in an irreversible zone of reinforcing externalities that are the outcome of a wholly adventitious sequence of initiating events in an earlier period. The economies and industrial relations of modern Jamaica and Cuba are profoundly different from the plantation economies and labor relations of the slave past; yet, it is possible to demonstrate striking causal chains of continuity between past and present. A recent study of labor relations in Jamaica, for example, finds attitudes toward managers and authority in the workplace which can be traced directly back in a dismal causal chain through the post-emancipation plantation system to the patterns prevailing during slavery (Carter, 1977).

Third, in the discussion of structural continuities I drew attention to the special problem of the extent to which sociocultural objects are associated with them (are therefore structurally induced) or have become non-associated and self-perpetuating. It is hoped that my discussion of the nature of cultural objects will be of some use here. A good deal of the heat surrounding discussions of the so-called "culture of poverty" springs from simple-minded notions of cultural processes, as well as equally simplistic ideas about cultural and structural continuities. By now it should be clear that there is nothing static about cultural processes, that indeed they often change faster than structural ones.

Ironically, many sociologists and social historians imagine that an analysis which finds that behavior is structurally associated is more "progressive" than one which suggests non-association and self-sustaining identity. But the opposite, we now see, may well be the case. It is much harder to change structural processes and continuities than cultural ones. Thus, in a single generation the vast, oppressive system of cultural complexes we know as Southern Jim Crow – from institutions of legal repression to gratuitous petty insults – was undermined and largely removed. But the class system of the South continues, indeed has grown more entrenched judging by recent figures on inequality of income – with class divisions among African Americans greater than among Euro-Americans.

I close by emphasizing what should already have been apparent. My objective has not been to downplay the role or importance of change in human affairs and history. I do not seek to replace one bias with another, but to restore some balance to our attempts at understanding how the past matters. Change and continuity are two sides of the same temporal coin, whether we approach the matter psychologically or philosophically or historically. Psychologists have long known that our sense of time comes from both the things that happen in time and the intervals between them (Fraise, 1964: ch. 5). Change entails the end of a continuity and hence the persistence of some object that sheds or acquires one or more (or sometimes all) properties. The two are so intimately bound up, so constitutive of each other, that there is a danger of circularity when we try too hard to decipher them apart from each other. "Time is not just an abstract beast," complains the philosopher Newton-Smith, "but also is a most promiscuous beast who regularly couples with equally elusive partners," such as change, entropy, continuity, and causality (1980).

These are very big issues, which we will gladly leave to the philosophers. For practical intellectual purposes, historians and sociologists will do well to remember what the historical sociologist, Berkhofer (1969: 238–239), wisely observed many years ago, that "the analysis of change in the fullest sense must . . . involve a study of continuity," and that "this would seem to mean that change as sequence must be measured against continuity as setting and duration" (Berkhover 1969: 238–239).

Notes

I would like to thank Professors John Mohr, Steven Pinker, and Ann Swidler for their extremely valuable comments and criticisms of earlier drafts of this chapter. All remaining deficiencies, however, are entirely my own.

1. In a personal communication, Paul DiMaggio has, with his usual graciousness, acknowledged that their paper "focused on the diffusion of particular structures while bracketing the issue of identity, touching upon it only lightly through the notion of 'legitimacy.'"

References

Abbott, Andrew. 1992. "From Causes to Events." *Sociological Methods and Research* 20:428–453.

1999. *Department and Discipline*. Chicago: University of Chicago Press.

Abrams, Philip. 1982. *Historical Sociology*. Ithaca: Cornell University Press.

Alexander, Jeffrey C. and Philip Smith. 1993. "The Discourse of American Civil Society: A New Proposal for Cultural Studies." *Theory and Society* 22:151–207.

Alter, Jonathan. 1997. "The Long Shadow of Slavery." *Newsweek* December 8.

Anglès, Eric, Chris Hensley, and Denis-Constant Martin. 1994. *Les tambours de Jah et les sirènes de Babylone: rastafarisme et reggae dans la société jamaïcaine*. Paris: Fondation Nationale des Sciences Politiques; Centre d'Études et de Recherches Internationales.

Armstrong, D. M. 1980. "Identity Through Time," in Peter Van Inwagen, ed. *Time and Cause*. Boston, MA: D. Reidel Publishing. Pp. 67–78.

Barrett, Leonard. 1997. *The Rastafarians*. Boston, MA: Beacon Press.

Bazzoli, Laure and Veronique Dutraive. 1999. "The Legacy of J. R. Commons' Conception of Economics as a Science of Behavior," in John Groenewegen and Jack Vromen, eds. *Institutions and the Evolutionary Capitalism*. Pp. 52–77

Beckford, George. 1972. *Persistent Poverty: Underdevelopment in Plantation Economies of the Third World*. New York: Oxford University Press.

1975. *The Caribbean Economy: Dependence and Backwardness*. Mona, Jamaica: Institute of Social and Economic Research.

Bennett, Judith M. 1996. *Ale, Beer and Brewsters in England: Women's Work in a Changing World, 1300–1600*. New York: Oxford University Press.

1997. "Confronting Continuity." *The Journal of Women's History* 9/3:73–94.

Berger, Peter and Thomas Luckmann. 1967. *The Social Construction of Reality: A Treatise on the Sociology of Knowledge*. New York: Anchor Books.

Berkhofer, Jr., Robert F. 1969. *A Behavioral Approach to Historical Analysis*. New York: Free Press.

Bielby, W. T. and J. N. Baron. 1984. "A Woman's Place is With Other Women," in B. F. Reskins, ed. *Sex Segregation in the Workplace: Trends, Explanations and Remedies*. Washington: National Academy Press. Pp. 27–55.

Boyd, Robert and Peter J. Richerson. 1988. *Culture and the Evolutionary Process*. Chicago: University of Chicago Press.

Braudel, Fernand. 1985–1987. *Civilization and Capitalism, 15th–18th Century*. 3 vols. New York: Harper and Row.

Brinton, Mary C. and Takehiko Kariya. 1998. "Institutional Embeddedness in Japanese Labor Markets," in Mary C. Brinton and Victor Nee, eds. *The New Institutionalism in Sociology*. New York: Russell Sage. Pp. 181–207.

Brodber, Erna and J. Edward Greene. 1981. *Reggae and Cultural Identity in Jamaica*. St. Augustine, Trinidad and Tobago: Department of Sociology.

Burger, Thomas. 1976. *Max Weber's Theory of Concept Formation*. Durham, NC: Duke University Press.

Burton, C. Emory. 1992. *The Poverty Debate*. Westport, CT: Greenwood Press.

Carter, Kenneth. 1997. *Why Workers Won't Work*. London: Macmillan.

Chevannes, Barry. 1995. *Rastafari: Roots and Ideology*. Syracuse, NY: Syracuse University Press.

Clogg, Clifford and Adamaniktos Haritou. 1997. "The Regression Method of Causal Inference and a Dilemma Confronting This Method," in Vaughn R. McKim and Stephen P. Turner, eds. *Causality in Crisis*. P. 110.

Coleman, D. C. 1977. *The Economy of England, 1450–1750*. London, England: Oxford University Press.

Collins, John. 2000. "Preemptive Prevention." *The Journal of Philosophy* 97:223–234.

Confino, Alon. 1977. "Collective Memory and Cultural History: Problems of Method." *American Historical Review* 102:1386–1403.

Connerton, Paul. 1989. *How Societies Remember*. New York: Cambridge University Press.

Cowan, Robin and Mario Rizzo. 1996. "The Genetic-Causal Tradition and Modern Economic Theory." New York University, C.V. Starr Center – Working Paper 9529.

D'Andrade, Roy. 1995. *The Development of Cognitive Anthropology.* New York: Cambridge University Press.

Dahrenndorf, Ralf. 1965. *Class and Class Conflict in Industrial Society.* Stanford, CA: Stanford University Press.

David, Paul A. 2001. "Path Dependence, Its Critics, and the Quest for 'Historical Economics,'" in Garrouste and Ioannides, eds. *Evolution and Path Dependence in Economic Ideas.* Cheltenham, England: Edward Elgar. Pp. 15–40.

David, Paul. 1985. "Clio and the Economics of QWERTY." *The American Economic Review* 75/2:332–337.

1988. "Path Dependence: Putting the Past Into The Future of Economics." Institute for Mathematical Studies in the Social Sciences, Stanford University, Technical Report No. 533.

1993. "Historical Economics in the Longrun: Some Implications of Path-Dependence," in G. D. Snooks, ed. *Historical Analysis in Economics.* London: Routledge. Pp. 29–40.

Degler, Carl N. 1977. *Place over Time: The Continuity of Southern Distinctiveness.* Baton Rouge, LA: Louisiana State University Press.

DiMaggio, Paul and Walter W. Powell. 1983. "The Iron Cage Revisited: Institutional Isomorphism and Collective Rationality in Organizational Fields." *American Sociological Review* 48:148.

Dobbin, Frank. 1994. *Forging Industrial Policy.* New York: Cambridge University Press.

Douglas, Mary. 1966. *Purity and Danger.* London: Routledge.

1986. *How Institutions Think.* Syracuse, NY: Syracuse University Press.

Elster, Jon. 1978. *Logic and Society: Contradiction and Possible Worlds.* New York: John Wiley & Sons.

Emmet, Dorothy. 1966. *Rules, Roles and Relations.* New York: St. Martin's Press.

Fligstein, Neil. 2001. *The Architecture of Markets.* Princeton: Princeton University Press.

Fraise, Paul. 1964. *The Psychology of Time.* London: Eyre and Spottiswoode.

Galvotti, Maria. 2001. "Causality, Mechanisms and Manipulation," in Maria Galvotti, Patrick Suppes, and Domenico Constantini, eds. *Stochastic Causality,* Stanford, CA: CSLI Publication. Pp. 1–13.

Gans, Herbert. 1962. *The Urban Villagers.* New York: Macmillan.

1965. "Subcultures and Class," in Louis Ferman, et al. *Poverty In America.* Ann Arbor, MI: University of Michigan Press.

Garrouste, Pierre and Stavros Ioannides, eds. 2001. *Evolution and Path Dependence in Economic Ideas.* Cheltenham, England: Edward Elgar.

Gerschenkron, Alexander. 1968. "On the Concept of Continuity in History," in Gerschenkron, ed., *Continuity in History and Other Essays.* Cambridge, MA: Harvard University Press. Pp. 11–39.

Goodenough, Ward. 1989. "Culture: Concept and Phenomenon," in Morris Freilich, ed. *The Relevance of Culture.* New York: Bergin and Garvey. Pp. 93–97.

Grabher, G. 1995. "The Elegance of Incoherence: Economic Transformation in East Germany and Hungary," in E. Dittrich, Gert Schmidt, and Richard Whitley, eds. *Industrial Transformation in Europe*. London: Sage.

Granovetter, Mark. 1985. "Economic Action and Social Structure: The Problem of Embeddedness." *American Journal of Sociology* 91:481–510.

1998. "Cultural Beliefs and the Organization of Society: A Historical and Theoretical Reflection on Collectivist and Individualist Societies," in Mary C. Brinton and Victor Nee, eds. *The New Institutionalism in Sociology*. Stanford, CA: Stanford University Press. Pp. 77–104.

Griffen, Larry. 1992. "Temporality, Events, and Explanation in Historical Sociology." *Sociological Methods and Research*. 20:403–427.

Groenewegen, John and Jack Vromen. 1999. "Implications of Evolutionary Economics: Theory, Method and Policits," in Groenewegen and Vromen, eds. *Institutions and the Evolution of Capitalism: Implications of Evolutionary Economics*. Northampton, MA: Edward Elgar. Pp. 1–16.

Grusky, D. B. and J. B. Sorensen. 1998. "Can Class Analysis Be Salvaged?" *American Journal of Sociology*. 103:1187–1234.

Hacking, Ian. 1999. *The Social Construction of What?* Cambridge, MA: Harvard University Press.

Halbwachs, Maurice. 1980. *The Collective Memory*. New York: Harper and Row.

Hall, J. R., ed. 1997. *Reworking Class*. Ithaca, NY: Cornell University Press.

Hall, Peter and David Soskice. 2001. "Introduction to Varieties of Capitalism," in Peter Hall and David Soskice, eds. *Varieties of Capitalism: The Institutional Foundations of Comparative Advantage*. New York: Oxford University Press.

Hannan, Michael T. 1992. "Rationality and Robustness in Multilevel Systems," in James S. Coleman and Thomas Fararo, eds. *Rational Choice Theory: Advocacy and Critique*. New York: Sage Publications. Pp. 120–136.

Hanson, Susan and Geraldine Pratt. 1995. *Gender, Work and Space*. New York: Routledge.

Hart, H. L. A. and Tony Honore. 1985. *Causation in the Law*. Oxford: Clarendon Press.

Hausman, Daniel. 1998. *Causal Asymmetries*. New York: Cambridge University Press.

Hobsbawm, Eric. 1992. "Introduction," in Eric Hobsbawm and Terence Ranger, eds. *The Invention of Tradition*. Cambridge, MA: Cambridge University Press.

Hobsbawm, Eric and Terence Ranger. 1992. *The Invention of Tradition*. New York, Cambridge University Press.

Hookway, Christopher. 1988. *Quine: Language, Experience and Reality*. Polity Press.

Ikegami, Eiko. 1997. *The Taming of the Samurai*. Cambridge, MA: Harvard University Press.

Isaac, Larry W. and Larry J. Griffin. 1989. "Ahistoricism in Time-Series Analyses of Historical Process: Critique, Redirection, and Illustrations from U.S. Labor History." *American Sociological Review* 54:873–890.

Jencks, Christopher and Meredith Phillips, eds. 1998. *The Black White Test Score Gap*. Washington, DC: Brookings Institution.

Jepperson, Ronald L. 1991. "Institutions, Institutional Effects, and Institutionalism," in Walter W. Powell and Paul J. DiMaggio, eds. *The New Institutionalism in Organizational Analysis.* Chicago, IL: University of Chicago Press. Pp. 143–161.

Katz, Michael. 1989. *The Undeserving Poor.* New York: Pantheon.

Keesing, Roger. 1987. "Models, 'Folk' and 'Cultural': Paradigm Regained," in Dorothy Holland and Naomi Quinn, eds. *Cultural Models in Language and Thought.* New York: Cambridge University Press.

Kenny, David. 1979. *Correlation and Causality.* New York: John Wiley and Sons.

Kim, Jae-On and G. Donald Ferree, Jr. 1981. "Standardization in Causal Analysis," in Peter Marsden, ed. *Linear Models in Social Research.* Beverly Hills, CA: Sage. Pp. 22–43.

Krempel, Lothar. 1990. "Interpersonal Structure and Contact," in Jeroen Weesie and Henk Flap, eds. *Social Networks Through Time.* Utrecht: ISOR. Pp. 65–90.

Laslett, Peter, ed. 1980. *Bastardy and its Comparative History.* London: Edward Arnold.

Leacock, Eleanor Burke, ed. 1971. *The Culture of Poverty: A Critique.* New York: Simon and Schuster.

Leff, Gordon. 1971. *History and Social Theory.* New York: Anchor Books.

Levine, Lawrence. 1978. *Black Culture and Clack Consciousness; Afro-American Folk Thought from Slavery to Freedom.* New York: Oxford University Press.

Lewis, David. 1973. *Counterfactuals.* Oxford: Blackwell.

  1983. "Survival and Identity." *Philosophical Papers, Vol. 1.* New York: Oxford University Press.

  2000. "Causation as Influence." *Journal of Philosophy* 97:182–197.

Lewis, Oscar. 1959. *Five Families: Mexican Case Studies in the Culture of Poverty.* New York: Basic Books.

  1966. "The Culture of Poverty." *Scientific American* 215:19–25.

Lieberson, Stanley. 1980. *Piece of the Pie.* Berkeley, CA: University of California Press.

  1985. *Making it Count.* Berkeley, CA: University of California Press.

  1997. "The Big Broad Issues in Society and Social History," in V. R. McKim and Stephen P. Turner, eds. *Causality in Crisis?* Notre Dame, IN: University of Notre Dame Press. Pp. 378–379.

Liebowitz, S. J. and S. E. Margolis. 1995. "Path Dependence, Lock-In and History." *The Journal of Law, Economics and Organization* 11:205–226.

Lillrank, Paul. 1995. "The Transfer of Management Innovations from Japan." *Organization Studies* 16:971–989.

Magnusson, Lars and Jan Ottosson. 1997. *Evolutionary Economics and Path Dependence.* Cheltenham, England: Edward Elgar.

McGovern, James R. 1982. *Anatomy of a Lynching: The Killing of Claude Neal.* Baton Rouge, LA: Louisiana State University Press.

Mohr, John. 1998. "Measuring Meaning Structures." *Annual Review of Sociology* 24:345–370.

Nettleford, Rex. 1972. *Identity, Race and Protest in Jamaica.* New York: William Morrow.

North, Douglas. 1997. "Some Fundamental Puzzles in Economic History/ Development," in W. Brian Arthur, S. N. Durlauf, and D. A. Lane, eds. *The Economy as an Evolving Complex System II*. Reading, MA: Addison-Wesley.

Nozick, Robert. 1981. *Philosophical Explanations*. Oxford: Clarendon Press.

Panton, David. 1993. *Jamaica's Michael Manley: The Great Transformation (1972–92)*. Kingston, Jamaica: Kingston Publishers Limited.

Patterson, Orlando. 1964. *The Children of Sisyphus*. London: Hutchinsons.

1965. "Ras Tafari: Cult of Outcasts." *New Society* 1:15–17.

1982. "Persistence, Continuity and Change in the Jamaican Working Class Family." *The Journal of Family History* 7:135–161.

1991. *Freedom in the Making of Western Culture*. New York: Basic Books.

1998. *Rituals of Blood: Consequences of Slavery in Two American Centuries*. New York: Basic Books.

Pearl, Judea. 2000. *Causality*. Cambridge, MA: Cambridge University Press.

Pinker, Steven. 1997. *How the Mind Works*. New York: Norton, 1997.

2000. *Words and Rules: The Ingredients of Language*. New York: HarperCollins.

Portes, Alejandro. 2000. "The Resilient Importance of Class: A Nominalist Interpretation." *Political Power and Social Theory* 14: 249–284.

Putnam, Hilary. 1991. *Representation and Reality*. Cambridge, MA: MIT Press.

Quine, W. V. 1950. "Identity, Ostension, and Hypostasis." *The Journal of Philosophy* 47/22:623–624.

Rainwater, Lee. 1970. *Behind Ghetto Walls: Black Families in a Federal Slum*. Chicago, IL: Aldine.

Rainwater, Lee and William Yancey. 1967. *The Moynihan Report and The Politics of Controversy*. Cambridge, MA: MIT Press.

Reed, John Shelton. 1972. *The Enduring South: Subcultural Persistence in Mass Society*. Lexington, MA: D. C. Heath.

Reskin, Barbara F. 1991. "Bringing the Men Back In: Sex Differentiation and the Devaluation of Women's Work," in Judith Lorber and Susan A. Farrell, eds. *The Social Construction of Gender*. Newbury Park, CA: Sage. Pp. 141–161.

Rhea, Joseph T. 1997. *Race Pride and the American Identity*. Cambridge, MA: Harvard University Press.

Rosch, Eleanor. 1978. "Principles of Categorization," in Eleanor Rosch and Barbara Lloyd, eds. *Cognition and Categorization*. New York: John Wiley and Sons. Pp. 27–47.

Rosch, Eleanor and Carolyn B. Mervis. 1975. "Family Resemblances: Studies in the Internal Structure of Categories." *Cognitive Psychology* 7:573–605.

Russell, Bertrand. 1948. *Human Knowledge: Its Scope and Limits*. London: George Allen and Unwin.

Samuels, W. J. 1994. "Part–Whole Relationships," in F. M. Hodgson, M. Tool, and W. J. Samuels, eds. *The Elgar Companion to Institutional and Evolutionary Economics*. Cheltenham, England: Edward Elgar Publishing.

Schaffer, Jonathan. 2000. "Trumping Preemption." *The Journal of Philosophy* 97/4:165–181.

Scholem, Gershom. 1971. *The Messianic Idea in Judaism: And Other Essays in Jewish Spirituality*. New York: Schocken Books.

Schudson, Michael. 1989. "The Present in the Past Versus the Past in the Present." *Communication* 11:105–113.

Schwartz, Barry. 1982. "The Social Context of Commemoration: A Study of Collective Memory." *Social Forces* 61:374–402.

1991. "Social Change and Collective Memory: The Democratization of George Washington." *American Sociological Review* 56:221–236.

1996. "Memory as a Cultural System: Abraham Lincoln in World War II." *American Sociological Review* 61:908–927.

Sewell, William H. 1966. "Three Temporalities: Toward an Eventful Sociology," in Terrence McDonald, ed. *The Historic Turn in the Human Sciences*. Ann Arbor, MI: University of Michigan Press.

1992. "A Theory of Structure: Duality, Agency and Transformation." *American Journal of Sociology* 98:1–29.

1996. "Historical Events as Transformation of Structures: Inventing Revolution at the Bastille." *Theory and Society* 25:841–881.

Shumway, Robert H. and David S. Stoffer. 2000. *Time Series Analysis and Its Applications*. New York: Springer.

Stevenson, Renda. 1995. "Black Family Structure in Colonial and Antebellum Virginia: Amending the Revisionist Perspective," in M. B. Tucker and C. Mitchell-Kernan, eds. *The Decline in Marriage Among African Americans*. New York: Russell Sage. Pp. 27–56.

Stinchcombe, Arthur L. 1965. "Social Structure and Organizations," in James G. March, ed. *Handbook of Organizations*. Chicago, IL: Rand McNally. Pp. 153–193.

Swidler, Ann. 1986. "Culture and Action: Symbol and Strategies." *American Sociological Review* 51:273–286.

2001. *Talk of Love: How Culture Matters*. Chicago, IL: University of Chicago Press.

Tienda, Marta and Haya Stier. 1991. "Joblessness and Shiftlessness: Labor Force Activity in Chicago's Inner City," in C. Jencks and P. Peterson, eds. *The Urban Underclass*. Washington, DC: Brookings. Pp. 135–154.

Tilly, Charles. 1984. *Big Structures, Large Processes, Huge Comparisons*. New York: Russell Sage.

Tolnay and Beck. 1992. *A Festival of Violence: An Analysis of Southern Lynchings, 1882–1930*. Urbana, IL: University of Illinois Press.

Trevor-Roper, Hugh. 1992. "The Invention of Tradition: The Highland Tradition of Scotland," in Terence Ranger, ed. *The Invention of Tradition*. New York: Cambridge University Press. P. 14.

Turner, Jonathan H. 1989. *A Theory of Social Interaction*. Stanford, CA: Stanford University Press.

Turner, Victor. 1995. *The Ritual Process*. New York: Aldine.

Valentine, Charles. 1970. *Culture and Poverty: Critique and Counter-Proposals*. Chicago, IL: University of Chicago Press.

Waters, Anita M. 1989. *Race, Class and Political Symbols: Rastafari and Reggae in Jamaican Politics*. New Brunswick: Transaction Publishers.

White, Harrison C. 1992. *Identity and Control: A Structural Theory of Action*. Princeton, NJ: Princeton University Press.

Wilson, W. J. 1997. *When Work Disappears: The World of the New Urban Poor*. New York: Vintage.

Wittgenstein, L. 1953. *Philosophical Investigations*. New York: Macmillan.

Wood, Stewart. 2001. "Business, Government, and Patterns of Labor Market Policy in Britain and the Federal Republic of Germany," in Peter Hall and David Soskice, ed. *Varieties of Capitalism*. New York: Oxford University Press. Pp. 247–274.

Yamamura, Kozo, ed. 1977. *The Economic Emergence of Modern Japan*. New York: Cambridge University Press, 1977.

Zellner, A. 1979. "Causality and Econometrics," in K. Brunner and A. Melzer, eds. *Three Aspects of Policy and Policymaking: Knowledge, Data and Institutions*. Amsterdam: North-Holland.

Zerubavel, Eviatar. 1993. *The Fine Line*. Chicago, IL: University of Chicago Press.

Zucker, Lynne G. 1977. "The Role of Institutionalization in Cultural Persistence." *American Sociological Review* 42:726.

3

Theorizing hermeneutic cultural history

John R. Hall

The tensions between cultural studies and cultural history likely derive from their differential similarities: cultural studies are carried out in relatively new intellectual domains precariously established outside any formal academic discipline, whereas history is a rather old intellectual domain precariously established outside any formal academic discipline. Describing the older domain, Carl Schorske has remarked, "The historian is singularly unfertile in devising concepts. It is not too much to say that historians are conceptual parasites . . . They reconstitute the past by relativizing the particulars to the concepts and the concepts to the particulars, doing full justice to neither, yet binding and bonding them into an integrated life as an account under the ordinance of time" (1995: 383–384). Practitioners of cultural studies are sometimes troubled by history precisely because of what can seem entailed by that "ordinance of time" which Schorske invoked – namely, the specters of meta-narrative, objectivity, representation – all the historians' dirt that had been hidden under the scholarly carpets until the deconstructive cleaners came along. As for historians, even ones sympathetic to cultural studies worry about a full linguistic turn. If they give up the ordinance of time – real events as the contexts of other real events, even textual ones – they fear finding themselves, as Peter Jelavich (1995: 77) put it, "in a sphere of free-floating interpretation that is certainly justifiable as a realm of human inquiry, but which is no longer 'history.'"

In the face of these anxieties, the challenge for cultural history is to study cultural meanings in their shifting temporal connectedness to social life, yet without succumbing to the idealism, historicism, or teleology that sometimes afflict histories of culture. Yet to rise to that challenge, Schorske's "ordinance of time" needs to be unpacked, for historicity is not reducible to the modernist notion of objective linear time (Hall, 1980).

How, then, to proceed? I appreciate what Robert Dawidoff (1995: 371) has suggested about history – that the many ailments afflicting it are not always best treated with strong prescription pharmaceuticals. Sometimes, an off-the-shelf, over-the-counter drug will do, and sometimes nothing works quite as well as homeopathic medicine, voodoo, or a good home remedy. But the ordinance of time is a difficult problem in the philosophy of history, and no great purchase on it will be gained by revisiting recent discussions and exemplars of cultural history (for example, Eley, 1995; Hall, 1990, 1994, 2003; Halttunen and Perry, 1998; Hunt, 1989; Rioux and Sirinelli, 1997). The reason is that absent the most self-conscious methodological consideration, historical inquiry remains highly resistant to reconstruction. Cultural history can easily serve as a seemingly new banner around which to organize inquiry, but actually replicate the problems of the old practices that it is supposed to displace. In part this situation obtains because narrative discourse is capable of absorbing shifts in aesthetics of style without necessarily altering the enduring practices which employ it. Thus, in order to obtain a fresh assay of the prospects for cultural history, we need to understand the practice of history as a form of culture. To do so here, I step back and consider its "theoretical" position, beginning at the point of epistemology – specifically, a cultural epistemology.

Epistemology and cultures of inquiry

The problems of epistemology that now afflict the entire range of cultural, historical, and social studies are no doubt substantial, but they derive from an overdrawn binary opposition between the disciplinarity, objectivism, and scientism of modernism, and postmodern transdisciplinarity and skepticism. We need to declare an end to the modernist search for purity (Latour, 1993) that sometimes infects even its dialectical reversals. A different resolution emerges if we acknowledge the *cultural* (rather than purely *logical*) construction of inquiry's diverse methodological practices, and embark on critique of practices as "cultural logics" (Hall, 1999). In brief, the modernist goal of completely rationalizing various "pure" logics of inquiry is beyond our reach because any concrete practice of inquiry is an amalgam that draws together different *forms of discourse*. *Theory* is one such form, *narrative* is another. Other discourses particularly important to inquiry are those concerning *values*, and the discursive terrain concerned with *adjudication of accounts* about sociohistorical phenomena.

As Lyotard (1988: esp. 84, 129, 158, 160) argued, any genre or form of discourse has something "at stake," which he described as based on "a single universal principle, shall we say that of 'winning' or 'gaining.'" But the stakes of different discursive forms are distinctive and heterogeneous, and there is thus no single *logical* way to harmonize relations among them. For this reason, inquiry cannot be reduced to a coherent enterprise informed solely by principles of what Kant called pure reason. There can be no final rationalization of method-ology that creates pure, unalloyed knowledge. Instead, we are left with "impure reason," in which alternative *practices of inquiry* coexist as different *cultural* possibilities. Yet these alternative possibilities are not isolated from one another; to the contrary, it can be shown that the diverse practices – science and universal history, critical theory and the new historicism – are connected by their conven-tional but divergent ways of drawing upon shared forms of discourse – i.e., value discourse, theory, narrative, and adjudication. There are two implications. First, divisions between both disciplines and interdisciplinary programs in history, the social sciences, and the humanities turn out to be arbitrary. Second, no disci-pline or program can make any special claim to define the scope or methodology appropriate to cultural studies, either on logical or on moral grounds.

Adopting discourse, rather than putatively pure logic, as an organizing metaphor for *social* epistemology (Fuller, 1988) yields an entirely different way of understanding inquiry – as one or another cultural practice. Once we acknowl-edge that practices of inquiry are shaped by alternative cultural amalgams of discourses through which they proceed, it becomes possible to subject the prac-tices of inquiry themselves to deconstruction and, thereby, to cultural critique. As both Michel Foucault (1972) and Jean-François Lyotard (1988) anticipated, acknowledging the cultural character of inquiry opens to exploration the inter-plays and infusions of multiple forms of discourse in relation to one another, for example, establishing more self-conscious relations between theory and narrative. Becoming clearer about the cultural constructions of inquiry makes it possible to reformulate cultural practices on a critical basis, rather than pursuing a drunken random walk, fleeing one epistemological position, only unwittingly to take on the baggage of another.

In order to assay the prospects for cultural history, I propose to consider it as a cultural practice of inquiry. To do so, I will (1) address the question of narrative; and (2) consider alternative approaches to theoretical concept formation. I will then (3) sketch a phenomenology of temporality in relation to the hermeneutic problem of meaning and cultural history. Finally, I will (4) illustrate the hermeneutic approach by sketching vignettes from my colleagues' and my own research on a cultural history of the apocalyptic.

Extrinsic and intrinsic narrative in cultural history

Narrativity is a subject of continuing debate among scholars as diverse as hermeneutic philosopher Paul Ricoeur, theorists of rhetoric, speech–act theo-rists, sociologists, and even rational-choice theorists (Hall, 1999: ch. 3). Partly because narrative has diverse possibilities that are deeply embedded in our own historicities, it is not an epistemologically tidy enterprise. Any narrative is partly a narration of narrations, the interpretation of preinterpretations, a journey into the hall of mirrors. Yet paradoxically, pieced-together fragments of reflected images can provide readers a rich sense of experiencing events. In part this trick works because stories stand in reflexive relationship to readers' everyday and imaginative experiences. Evocations of a "seedy jungle town" or a "refusal of the judge to rush to a decision concerning a person of political stature" can allow the reader to apprehend a situation and "come to rest" at a subsequent point in the story. Given this characteristic, even when a historical narrative is carefully constructed on the basis of evidence, it produces something like a tour of a Potemkin village: the thickly described world gains its verisimilitude by the installation of images along the route of the text. In an odyssey constructed through voice, emplotment, flashbacks, and other strategies, meaning is opened up through illusion (Kellner, 1989).

Given the diverse possibilities, there can be no hope of identifying a definitive method for narrative discourse. My interest is much less ambitious: I simply want to differentiate two broad points of view that are often mixed with each other in narratives. Georg Simmel (1977: 149–155) alluded to the two possibilities when he distinguished between event-sequences of history, and the formulation of some external scheme, teleology, or theory that would assign historical importance to manifold events. Simmel thus posited a strong distinction between sociohistorical science and metaphysics. Here, I push Simmel's insight in a different – constructivist and hermeneutic – direction, by distinguishing between inquiry that is driven by extrinsic schemes of interpretation versus inquiry oriented to the intrinsic meanings in play in events themselves. What does this distinction entail?

The first possibility I will call *extrinsic narrative*. In this approach, the axial principle holding narrative together is a consequence of inquiry's frame of reference, rather than a plot posited to emerge out of events themselves. The extrinsic version of cultural history is an exercise in theoretical argument, functional identification of a series, or the use of some other historian's plot device to arrange a discussion of cultural materials, practices, motifs, and meanings that have no obvious connections with one another in sequences of historical events themselves (for example, privacy in different historical epochs, sexuality over centuries, dieting in heterogeneous cultural circumstances; Hall, 1990).

In limiting cases, extrinsic narrative is completely subordinated to some other enterprise such as analytic history or historical sociology. But far short of these possibilities, the goal of "objectivity" in much historical writing (Novick, 1988) has made it important simultaneously to *have* an external ordering principle and to *obscure* that principle so as to give the historical account a "natural" quality. As Sande Cohen's (1986) deconstructive analysis of historical writing shows, the sense of "aboutness" in such narratives depends on expository devices that transcend whatever empirically demonstrable connections may exist among events: at least some narrative connections are *extrinsic* products of inquiry's frame of reference.

The problem with the narrative claim of "objectivity" is that it closes off any reflexive account of the axial principle that orders its practice. However, if extrinsic narrative is self-conscious and explicit about its ordering principles, as it ought to be, Cohen's deconstructive critique loses its force. The use of transcendent staging devices to constitute the object of inquiry need not mask a failure to "represent" reality; rather, the transcendent devices of linkage may derive from some other rationale of inquiry than the representation of events claimed to have their own coherence. In these analytic circumstances, "meta-narrative" is simply a pejorative label for narrative in which the plot is – or ought to be – a narrator's self-conscious model, theory, argument, or set of juxtapositions. Culture often has what Benjamin called a "suchness" that is external to subjectivity, and it is thus amenable to extrinsic narrative. Yet to avoid the deconstructive critique, such a practice must be explicit about the theoretical principles that organize it.

By contrast with extrinsic cultural history, if narrative instead focuses on the lifeworld as the domain where history is acted out, the task of uncovering what Simmel called immanent meaning leads in the hermeneutic direction of discovering how events are patterned *intrinsically* – by social actors themselves. Although no observer can reproduce the viewpoint of any other subject, the observer can seek to discern social actors' emplotments, thus directing inquiry to construction of an *intrinsic narrative* meant to describe a constellation of historically emergent lifeworldly actions and meanings connected to one another by the mutual orientations of actors. Intrinsic narratives thus seek to identify how unfolding events and actions are made meaningful by social actors who themselves narrate stories – to themselves and others.

In unfolding life, people invoke narratives ("stories," we can call them, so long as we do not take this term to signify any judgments about truth status) in a variety of ways. They can use narratives to "construct" reality for people by representing events beyond the listeners' own personal knowledge. People also individually and jointly compose other kinds of narratives – "scripts" and "scenarios" – to make sense of projects they plan to undertake in the future. In a different way, narratives can be used to "reconstruct" past events as "memories," and they can "deconstruct" competing narratives in advance, as events unfold, and after the fact (Carr, 1986: 65; Polkinghorne, 1988). In short, lifeworldly narratives are central to the meaningful construction of social life.

Construed as the excavation of enacted narratives, intrinsic narrative in inquiry connects historicity directly to Max Weber's methodological goal of *Verstehen* – interpretive understanding of subjectively meaningful action. This connection can be indexed briefly via the efforts of phenomenology to escape the frameworks of deterministic social science in order to apprehend the character of meanings in existential social life itself. As Jean-François Lyotard argued in his 1950s assessment of phenomenology,

Between the simplistic subjectivism which amounts to the ruin of all social or psychological science, and the brutal objectivism whose laws ultimately lack objects, there remains a place for a *recovery* of explanatory data which seeks to express the unity of their latent meaning.   (1991: 99)

This unity phenomenologists have located in the relationship between consciousness and temporality. As Edmund Husserl (1964) and Alfred Schutz (1967) both showed, subjective meaning is a *temporally* constituted phenomenon in the individual's unfolding stream of life experience. That is, in brief, the stream of individual consciousness is a temporal stream, in which meaning is made at a series of existential moments – in relation to present experience, recalled memories that reconstruct meanings from past experiences, and anticipations of future events and projected goals. Any subjective meaning is both located in time and constituted through acts of consciousness that construct meaningful temporal accentuations of the moment (for example, "we're late!" or "you need to plan for the future!"). Therefore, any project of *verstehende* narrative involves a textual representation of temporality (Wood, 1989).

The connection between time and narrative has been described by, among others, Mikhail Bakhtin, who showed how various genres of fiction are infused with alternative forms of temporality – adventure time, everyday time, and so forth – forms, he argued, that establish continuities between the novel and temporalities of actual life (Bakhtin, 1981: 38–40, 99). In a related way, Paul Ricoeur (1984, 1985, 1988) has argued that the lived engagement of sociohistorical actors in meaningful social relationships gives shape *to* time. There will be lived time of one sort in a bureaucratically ordered realm, another in the interplay of pure sociability, an altogether different one in the performance of ritual, yet another in the conduct of war and revolution (Hall, 1978, 1980). In turn, the lived temporal enactments of unfolding dramas in any one episode frequently become connected in path-dependent chains of action linked in serial but temporally discontinuous and transepisodic "plots" – social interactions with stakes – that are themselves the foci of social conflict, cooperation, ploys, and stratagems. People engaged in a political campaign, for example, are not just acting in a seemingly self-contained here and now; at a given present moment, they make coordinated plans for future activities, the success of which in turn is affected by events subsequent to the formulation of plans, which the campaigners may or may not learn about in time to take into account. In this instance, and in general, narrative emplotment is not just an observer's account of events after the fact. As Wilhelm Dilthey made it his life's work to show, narrative is a basic rubric constitutive of social life itself (Owensby, 1994). In other words, intrinsic narrative in inquiry is an effort to describe an emergent plot enacted through what Margaret Somers (1997, 1995; Somers and Gibson, 1994) calls "ontological narratives" that bear the projective, unfolding, and retrospective interpretive activities of diverse individuals and groups oriented toward a shared problematic.

In these terms, a specifically *cultural* history approximates the intrinsic criterion when it describes the temporally enacted narratives of mutually oriented social actors through time, who, as the living bearers of culture, either *serially* replicate or *sequentially* modify meanings and practices. Intrinsic cultural history thus concentrates on the socially mediated historical lineages of replication, innovation, distribution, and diffusion of culture, and their consequences in unfolding time. Culture does not float autonomously; it is tied to its bearers, their predecessors, and the historical contexts and consequences of their actions.

Whether cultural history employs intrinsic narrative, extrinsic narrative, or some combination, it bears a double relation to social theory. On the one hand, any one who has tried to take up theoretical issues in the midst of a narrative knows that this involves a discursive shift not easily smoothed over. On the other hand, as Schorske's comment quoted earlier suggests, in its own terms narrative is a sponge that can absorb all manner of implicitly theoretical discourse. Yet doing so presumes that theoretical constructs exist in their own right, in ways that are not preeminently narratological. It is thus important to come to terms directly with the question of how theoretical concepts "work" in various cultural constructions of cultural history.

Social theory

How to theorize "culture" remains controversial, since culture is not so easily subjected to the rationalizations, in the Weberian sense of the term, of social science methodology. Like tourists on a safari taking photographs of the natives, when objectivist social science develops its film, the prints display only the perspectives of visitors to a simulacratic village of culture – a circumstance eloquently addressed by Trinh (1989). It is all too easy to take culture into account by bringing it under control, framing it within some analytic lens that drains it of its meaningful significance (Alexander and Smith, 1993).

Establishing relations between theory and culture is thus tricky. One approach is to treat the world as a text. However, no matter what gains there might be from the basic insight, taken alone, it paradoxically reestablishes the essentialist contradiction of totalizing a practice of representation – just the sort of thing that deconstructive critique was supposed to undermine. In a different unsatisfactory way, cultural studies can loosely invoke critical theories rhetorically committed to a radical (but also romantic) meta-narrative of resistance. Or, cultural studies can latch onto some single fashionable theorist – Gramsci or Foucault, Bourdieu or Habermas – as avatar. These gestures simultaneously invoke theory yet avoid entering the terrain of theoretical logic, where, as Jeffrey Alexander (1982) has argued, theoretical ideas are subject to reasoning in their own terms.

Given the inadequacy of theory as gesture, the New Historicism might seem to offer an attractive alternative – avoiding any engagement of theory whatsoever. But the New Historicism does not escape problems of theory any more than the old historicism did. Superficially, both seem theoryless, but both depend upon some implicit theory that gives "history" qualities of coherence and significance (Hall, 1999: ch. 8). In short, as Martin Jay (1996) has shown, efforts to purge theory from inquiry more easily repress than eliminate it.

In turn, the abstract character of theory tends to obscure its consequences for inquiry. Therefore, we must lay bare the implications that one choice of theory bears over another. To do so, I bring coals to Newcastle, using an analytic strategy popularized in the 1950s and 1960s by sociologists such as Talcott Parsons, Paul Lazersfeld, and Robert Merton – crosstabulating two binary analytic distinctions to create a typology with four possible combinations. However, my crosstabulation does not theorize empirical phenomena; instead it theorizes the discursive domain of theoretical logic, via a typology that identifies four alternative but interrelated generic approaches to theoretical discourse.

The first binary distinction differentiates theoretical constructs in terms of whether they conceptualize phenomena in *meaningful* versus *non-meaningful* terms. Here, and in the discussion that follows, "meaning" is defined in Weber's (1978: 4–7) narrow sense as *subjective* orientation toward action by a social actor; concepts not concerned with subjective meaning do not necessarily exclude the consideration of meaning from sociological analysis, but they tend to focus on objective meanings and their circumstances of production and consequences, rather than subjective meanings per se.

The second dimension differentiates between conceptualizations of phenomena that emphasize their *structural* versus *systemic* aspects. A "structural" conceptualization I define as representing a phenomenon in terms of a single, relatively bounded pattern of mutually determined or articulated elements, such as a person, episode, or concrete organization. "Systemic" concepts, on the other hand, designate interactive relationships among multiple, differentially located, relatively autonomous elements (for example, social actors, organizations, texts, social classes, subsystems) that are theorized as operating in relation to one another within broader bounded contexts, such as communities, organizational fields, markets, discursive universes, or social totalities.

Table 3.1 *Four approaches to theoretical discourse with associated types of case-pattern concepts, according to subjective meaning adequacy and basis of concept formation, with type of analytic-element relation used to specify case-pattern concept listed in brackets (Hall 1999: 127)*

		BASIS OF CONCEPT FORMATION	
		Systemic	**Structural**
		Dialectical/functional approach	*Formal/structural approach*
BASIS IN	**Absent**	**FUNCTIONAL/ DIALECTICAL**	**FORM**
MEANING		[functional/dialectical]	[causal/conditional]
ADEQUACY		*Interchange approach*	*Hermeneutic approach*
	Present	**"MARKET"**	**IDEAL TYPE**
		[exchange/interchange]	[meaning elements]

A crosstabulation of the two dimensions – meaningful versus non-meaningful, and structural versus systemic – maps ideal typically four alternative approaches to theoretical discourse. Like dialects in ordinary language, these regimens are not inherently isolated from one another; in the case of theory, this means that actual theories are not necessarily purely of one type or another. But insofar as these four types of theoretical discourse are meaningfully coherent, like dialects, they are subject to examination in their own terms (see Table 3.1).

1. The *dialectical and functional approach* does not deny the importance of meaningful action, but its core analysis centers on posited "objective" (i.e., action transcendent) consequences of actions along with social and material processes, all of which interact with one another, thereby creating a systemic or dialectical dynamic theorized as tending toward equilibrium and evolution, or dysfunction, crisis, and transformation. Karl Marx and Talcott Parsons (both in their later works) and functionalist theorists of world systems have employed this conceptual approach.

Functional and dialectical systems theories can yield models of societal integration and contradictions, and by their incorporation of evolutionary or revolutionary dynamics, they can theorize secular (i.e., long-term) change, such as proletarianization or the emergence of value contradictions in societal cultures. But, as critics have emphasized, they face difficulties in addressing what has come to be called the micro–macro problem (Alexander et al., 1987). In their core logics, functionalist and dialectical theories obtain coherence by way of the system as a construct, without any necessary conceptualization of the concrete processes that connect action with either functions or contradictions at work in sociohistorical processes. Thus, actual social relations tend to drop out of the analysis. The result is remarkably similar for otherwise diverse approaches that theorize a systemic "totality." On the one hand, Parsons' social systems theory has the widely noted tendency of emphasizing order, consensus, equilibrium, evolution, and teleology. By contrast, in Marxist dialectical analysis, the totality is a dynamic system of revolutionary ruptures and transformations. What both approaches have difficulty theorizing are the system's relationships to the relativity of means and ends of diverse social actors, and the contingent historicity of their interplay.

Although systems and dialectical theories have been widely criticized as having reductionist, totalizing, and teleological tendencies, this has not stopped some cultural historians from unwittingly falling into implicitly functionalist teleological discourse – I think here of the new historicist Steven Mullaney's otherwise very interesting book, *The Place of the Stage* (1988). More generally, systemic discourse is attractive precisely because it offers a way of considering developmental tendencies of culture within complex societies. Using this theoretical approach, in their own ways, Daniel Bell (1976) and Anthony Giddens (1990) both analyze disjunctures between an increasingly consumption/leisure/self-fulfillment/therapy culture and the presumed work imperatives of still rationally oriented postmodern organizations. Cultural history is written as the relation between cultural elements, their affinities in coherent subsystems, and the dialectical systemic emergence of contradictions, harmonizations, and ruptures between these and other elements of a social whole.

2. A *formal/structural approach* theorizes about parallel patterns that obtain in otherwise diverse social arenas despite differences in the specific subjective meanings in play; the patterns are conditioned by causal externalities and structural features of social interaction, organization, culture, and the like (exemplars range from Georg Simmel's delineation of "forms" like "secrecy" and "the party," to various structuralisms, to many versions of quantitative empiricism). Although Simmel is not typically seen as a compatriot of Emile Durkheim in social theory, their affinities come to the surface once the structural character of Simmel's basic theoretical construct – the form – is acknowledged. For his part, Durkheim identified forms like the division of labor, solidarity, and religious ritual which have structures that shape how meanings operate within them.

Beyond Simmel and Durkheim, formal/structural theoretical discourse has been widely applied during the twentieth century. On the one hand, symbolic structuralism can be traced in linguistics, literature, and anthropology, in the works of Ferdinand de Saussure, the Russian formalist Roman Jakobson, Roland Barthes, Claude Lévi-Strauss, and Mary Douglas. On the other hand, societal structuralism and the identification of social forms find their micro-sociological development in certain approaches to symbolic interaction, and in the works of Erving Goffman. And, in the late twentieth-century Los Angeles school of cultural sociology, a neo-Durkheimian social–semiotic model of ritual has been used to explain the application and transformation of cultural and ideo-logical codes (see, for example, contributions to Alexander, 1988; Alexander and Smith, 1992; Kane, 1997). There is great variety in the specifics of these theoretical approaches, but they all share a generic interest in identifying struc-tured social patterns and processes that may operate in relation to meaning, with mechanisms that can be identified independently of meaning. Under this regimen, as Simmel explicitly insisted, and as Durkheim showed in practice, the structures of cultural processes are matters that can be analyzed in rela-tive autonomy from the specific *contents* of culture on which they operate. For Simmel (1950), the form of sociability obtains across multiple meaningful con-texts, just as for Durkheim (1965) the process by which the sacred becomes socially fixed for a community is open with respect to its cultural contents. Cultural history based strongly in this theoretical discourse is thus a history of forms, structures, or codes, and the results of their (formal/structural) processes of transformation.

3. Of the two approaches to theorizing that embed subjective meaning (in Weber's specific sense) *within* concepts, the *interchange approach* manifests the "system" possibility. However, instead of theorizing dialectics and func-tions as abstractions, interchange concepts theorize systems as concrete mean-ingful social relationships of exchange and interchange, and their media of transmission. From diverse intellectual sources, the interchange approach now converges on two broad and interrelated alternatives – *networks* and *markets* as systems of meaningful social interaction. On the one hand, the network emphasis on the social *relationships* that produce exchange moves in the direc-tions of game theories, including the sort proposed by rational-choice theorists, and network theories such as those developed by Simmel, Harrison White, Ronald Burt, Roger Gould, and Mustafa Emirbayer and Jeff Goodwin. On the other hand, market theories that emphasize economic, human, cultural, or social "capital" draw on the same basic theoretical approach, but empha-size the *medium* of exchange. This emphasis yields not only the well-known theories of economic markets, but also models of cultural, social, and political interchange.

Examples of cultural inquiries that employ the interchange approach include: gift-giving theorized by Marcel Mauss and Claude Lévi-Strauss; credential systems in the work of Randall Collins; class-status distinction systems in Pierre Bourdieu's work on cultural capital; John Mohr's work on competition for "market" niches among New York City welfare agencies a century ago; and even a "political economy of signs" in the work of Jean Baudrillard. In this approach, cultural history concerns meaningful social actions directed toward market positionings, competition, exchange, status distinctions, niche positions, and boundary structures. Mapping these dynamics quantitatively over objective time remains a methodological challenge. Nevertheless, by taking atemporal snapshots at various historical junctures, the interchange approach can bring into view historically emergent cultural systems of meaning as they are produced through the institutionalized routinization of social actions of exchange and interchange.

4. Finally, *hermeneutic theoretical approaches* draw on "meaning elements" – binary oppositions, continua, and tropes of meaning – using configurations of these elements to specify "ideal types," that is, interpretive models intended to describe distinctive complexes of subjectively meaningful social action and interaction (including organized action), and the developmental tendencies of their enactment.

Max Weber's consolidation of *verstehende Soziologie* is the classic exemplar of this theoretical discourse. Overall, the strategy for cultural analysis that Weber put forward (in his sociology of religion) is to investigate the relations among four poles – (1) ideas, (2) practitioners, (3) social organization, and (4) audiences or participants – all in the context of wider social formations. Thus, Weber's famous cultural history, *The Protestant Ethic and the Spirit of Capitalism* (1958), theorized ideal types as configurations of meaning elements, in order to explore the shift from socially organized Catholic asceticism to the innovative "inner-worldly" asceticism in different Protestant movements – from Lutheranism's proto-asceticism through Calvinism, Methodism, the Baptist sects, and the Quakers – and their economic affinities. In this analysis, the subjective meanings of actions and their historical specificities are not divorced from concepts, but embedded within them.

Broadly hermeneutic theories have been developed on diverse fronts. Scholars like Alfred Schutz, Hans-Georg Gadamer, and Charles Taylor have explored epistemological considerations. Norbert Elias has elaborated a historical sociology of "the civilizing process," and Clifford Geertz has championed an interpretive anthropology. Peter Berger and Thomas Luckmann have developed the approach within empirical sociology, and Dorothy Smith (influenced in part by Schutz) has taken the actor's personal knowledge to develop a feminist standpoint sociology. In literary criticism, speech-act and phenomenological theories of reception and discourse analysis, when historicized, follow a parallel hermeneutic track; and, though it may seem odd at first glance to locate Michel Foucault and Jacques Derrida in relation to this theoretical discourse because of their intellectual origins in the French structuralist tradition, both are centrally concerned with meaning in hermeneutic ways. Derrida, after all, wants to deconstruct texts precisely to get at meanings that are occluded in structuralist reductions of them; and Foucault excavated the epistemic shifts in historically specific webs of meaning that occupy social–semiotic categories such as "madness."

I have only sketched these four theoretical approaches, and I have emphasized their distinctiveness rather than the many ways that they have been and might be articulated in relation to one another (meaningful action, for example, often is oriented toward fulfillment of systemic functions, and as economic sociologists persuasively argue, markets have their structural conditions of operation). These issues of theoretical development are topics in their own right.

The phenomenology of meaning and hermeneutic cultural history

Here, keeping to the problem of cultural history, I want to consider the hermeneutic theoretical approach further. The reason for this focus is simple: the hermeneutic approach seems particularly important to cultural history, yet, because its practitioners tend toward repression of theory, the theory behind the approach remains obscure. As I will argue, because phenomenology links meaning and different kinds of temporality, it offers a way of bringing to light the embedded meaningful temporalities in the flux of history, thus offering a basis for theorizing intrinsic cultural history. To demonstrate the implications of this argument for concrete analysis, I will propose a typology of temporally grounded hermeneutic concepts, and I will sketch the application of these in relation to three apocalyptic social movements.

Today, all the elements for a new hermeneutic cultural history are available. They can be found in the works of scholars that include Max Scheler, Karl Mannheim, Weber, Schutz, Habermas, and Foucault. But they have not yet been brought together effectively. In part this story is about the uneven development and reception of phenomenology.

Max Scheler (1961) clearly demonstrated the possibility of a phenomeno-logical–hermeneutic analysis that probes deeply into the meaningful structure of complex sentiments such as *ressentiment* – the simultaneous attitude of envy and disdain that people are especially prone to adopting toward others in order to displace their anger when they are unable to achieve their own desires; in Scheler's analysis, *ressentiment* surfaces especially in social situations of powerlessness and decline, for example, among women insofar as they are dependent on men, the aged in relation to the young, and in class hatreds among the petty bourgeoisie, artisans, and minor officials.

Karl Mannheim (1953) showed that sociological analysis of meanings can be historical, for example, in his rich and complex study tracing the origins of "conservative thought" and its transmission through actual social carrier groups. Describing conservative thought as conceiving the past brought into the present in a sort of spatial simultaneity, Mannheim argued that its self-conscious development occurred historically only when adherents to the old order were confronted with forces of modernistic rationalization. Modern conservatism was a reaction against the Enlightenment, forged in an alliance of the nobility with intellectuals who became ideologues of the movement, injecting sentiments of romanticism and mystic contemplation into conceptions of organic groups such as "community" and "nation." Yet, as Mannheim argued, the origins of a mode of thought do not circumscribe its diffusion, and the feudalistic origins and anti-Enlightenment character of conservative thought have not prevented it from finding its way into even radical social movements, for example, through the Hegelian dialectic, to Marxism as "romantic opposition."

Criticizing Scheler for not transcending the opposition between timeless essence and historicism (1952: 139–140), Mannheim steered away from phenomenology. Thus, an odd disjuncture became embedded in Mannheim's work. His study of ideological and utopian mentalities (1937) was centrally concerned with temporalities, specifically, of conservatism, liberal-humanitarianism, socialist-communism, and orgiastic chiasm as utopian mentalities. But, despite Mannheim's own interest in history and temporality, given his resistance to Scheler's phenomenology, he failed to explore the relevance of Edmund Husserl's phenomenology of time, and he did not follow the move by Alfred Schutz from Husserl's analysis of *internal* time consciousness to a social phenomenology of the temporality of meaningful action in the *lifeworld*. Lacking these intellectual resources, Mannheim failed to connect the temporalities of utopian *mentalities* to the historical dynamics of utopian movements as social *groups*.

On the other hand, Alfred Schutz (1967) drew on Husserl's phenomenology of time consciousness to mount an effective critique of Max Weber's conceptualization of subjectively meaningful action. Showing that Weber only constructed an *external observer's* model of subjective action, Schutz demonstrated that a phenomenological approach oriented to analyzing the actor's temporal stream of consciousness could be used to develop sociological concepts that describe meaning as it is constructed in the actor's internal temporal flow of consciousness – through conscious acts of remembrance of the past, anticipation of the future, and paying attention in the here-and-now. But, though Schutz possessed an analysis of temporal structures of meaning construction, he lacked the comparative and historical interests of a Max Weber that would allow him to demonstrate the substantive importance of this analysis.

Given these theoretical disjunctures, the hermeneutic project mostly has been represented by the brilliant interpretive studies of exemplars like Clifford

Geertz, himself a recovering modernist and a bit of an antitheorist. Even the most direct appropriation of Schutz's phenomenology, by Jürgen Habermas (1987), ends up casting an opposition between lifeworld and "system" that ignores the lifeworldly structurations of systems. Equally problematic, Habermas in effect essentializes the lifeworld by failing to explore its multiple constructions. Or consider Michel Foucault: he resolutely salvaged deep cultural meanings in a way appropriately considered hermeneutic, and he began to connect cultural meanings to the organizational forms that construct their disciplines (in both senses of the term). But, deeply suspicious of agency as a narrative that denies the effects of both power and culture, and disdainful of "history" as a discipline, Foucault shied away from any close examination of the complex relations between culture, disciplines, and meaningful social action.

The lacunae in these projects do not overshadow their great illuminations, but they do leave open the possibility that a richer theorization of hermeneutic cultural history can be achieved. As my sketch suggests, in the hermeneutic project, the basic disjunctures – from Scheler to Foucault – have to do with the gaps between theories of meaning, temporality, and historicity. Most notably, Mannheim lacked the phenomenological method that would have linked his temporalized utopian mentalities to the dynamics of concrete social action and organization, while Schutz lacked the interest in historical analysis that would have given his work more than "merely philosophical" import. Such disjunctures have impeded the formulation of a hermeneutic approach to inquiry adequately grounded in theoretical concept formation – an approach that would bring hermeneutics into common cause with the project of cultural history, where the challenge today is to connect concrete events to narratives that bring us to new meaningful understandings of history, without falling into metanarrative (Lethen, 1995). The key to a hermeneutic cultural history, I submit, is to move beyond Schutz's general phenomenology of the temporality of meaningful action, to theorize the connections of manifold meaningful temporalities to history. For this purpose, Schutz's social phenomenology can be used to develop a typology of alternative enactments of meaningful being-in-the-world. Of course, any typology is a product of a historically located culture of inquiry, but, precisely on this basis, typifications of temporalized social enactments can help orient the study of meaningful cultural phenomena and their courses of historical development.

A typology of meaningful social enactments can be defined by two axes: first, a differentiation of alternative subjective and socially organized *temporalities* of gearing into the lifeworld, and, second, a distinction among alternative modes of *framing* how *social reality* is construed. On the basis of these distinctions, Figure 3.1 specifies alternative types of social enactment. On the first axis, three alternative modes of temporality are distinguished – *synchronic* being in

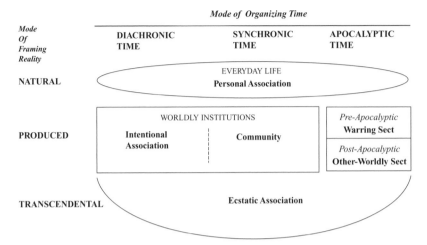

Figure 3.1   Ideal types of meaningful social enactment.
Source: Adapted from Hall (1978).

the here-and-now; *diachronic* gearing into temporal flux on the basis of a constructed linear progression of externally rationalized and measured time; and the *apocalyptic* positing of a coming-to-a-head of events, followed by a radical rupture that initiates a different (typically "timeless") tableau. On the second dimension, possibilities of framing reality include (1) the taken-for-granted *natural* frame – related to what Schutz called the "natural attitude" – where experiences are "taken for granted" as real, existing in relation to events "out there," and no socially unifying philosophy, system of belief, or set of ethics provides collectively legitimated rules for the interpretation of experience; (2) the *produced* frame of a social domain that is orchestrated according to some institutional pattern legitimated through ideology, and enforced through norms, ethics, and social control; and (3) the *transcendental* production of a social domain in which the operant ethos is to bracket social constructions of reality, so that non-cognitive experience can come to the fore.

I originally developed this typology in order to draw a relation between Mannheim's utopian *mentalities* and concrete utopian *social movements* of the US counterculture (Hall, 1978). More recently, analysts of social movements such as Anne Kane (1997) have become interested in understanding ideologies constituted in movements not just as utilitarian appropriations of symbols or frames, but in their constructions of meaning – an interest that can be addressed on the basis of cultural histories that construct intrinsic narratives. And, as Alain Touraine (1981) has argued, the tensions between social movements and an established social order display the fault lines and stakes of social change.

The phenomenological typology of meaningful social enactments offers a way to link these interests in social movement ideologies, their construction in historical time, their cultural tensions in concrete social-movement organizations, and the fault lines between movements and society-at-large that interest Touraine.

However, the tensed relationship between ideology and enactment is not unique to social movements; it has long been recognized as a generic feature of social life. Thus, if we accept Schutz's phenomenological claim that temporality is a general feature of subjective meaning, the typology of social enactment should be equally capable of identifying ideological meanings and modes of social enactment within societies more generally. This is so because the phenomenological types clarify basic social logics of enactment that are "polysemic" in their potential lines of social elaboration, and open to multiple meaningful constructions through alternative mediations of culture (Sewell, 1992).

This ensemble of claims about the typology of social enactment depicted in Figure 3.1 can be sketched more concretely. For synchronic and diachronic times, the ideal typical possibilities include: (1) the world of *personal association* in the natural attitude that moves among different temporal enactments without resort to their institutional structuring; (2) the diachronic world of *intentional association*, where enactment patterned by external regulations, laws, and governmental procedures, including republican democracy; (3) the world of a normatively integrated *community* of status-group members that operates in the here-and-now on the basis of direct personal relationships warranted by either tradition (to be sure, often reworked or "invented") or charisma, including the charisma of direct democracy; and (4) the world of *ecstatic association* experienced through meditation or sensual action (lovemaking, dance, the cold shower) in absolute presentness of the here-and-now. Under the regime of apocalyptic time, two broad possibilities obtain. (5) The positing of an *impending* radical denouement or rupture mobilizes a *warring sect* against opponents, in a struggle to win the stakes of the struggle through strategic action – ranging from relatively institutionalized competition and conflict in economic and political domains, through conflict between law enforcement authorities and organized crime (or between two nationalist groups vying for supremacy), to the anti-establishment struggles of revolutionary social movements. Finally, (6) counterculturalists who reject the established social order may seek to establish an *other-worldly sect* – a "heaven-on-earth" construed as somehow *temporally* "past" or *spatially* "beyond" the (political, environmental, religious) apocalypse deemed to have unfolded in the world at large.

These ideal types – identified temporally, and by the framing of social reality construction – are very broad constructs that could be elaborated in different directions in order to study, say, terrorism or war, the construction of systemic social organization through bureaucracy, or the tensions within a given social movement between cultural motifs of rationality and ones of community, right-wing survivalists or left-wing revolutionary cells. But, to be quite clear, the alternative types of enactment are not specific in their cultural *contents* of meaning. Rather, they are something like Aristotle's *topoi*: they identify historically relevant general types of meaningful enactment that can be used to analyze specific cultural structurations of meanings. A hermeneutic cultural history is not a history of these ideal types; rather, these ideal types (and others like them) serve as benchmarks of generic meanings by which to chart cultural narrativities as they play out in lifeworldly enactments of the social.

This returns us to the issue of the relation between theory and narrative: because the ideal types are constructed phenomenologically in relation to temporalities and modes of framing reality, they conceptualize alternative meaning-agency complexes that embody different kinds of narrativity in a way that parallels Bakhtin's ideas about the differences among adventure time, everyday time, and so forth. In turn, if we follow Bakhtin, Max Weber, Kenneth Burke, Paul Ricoeur, and Margaret Somers, we will acknowledge that lifeworldly meanings obtain *through action*, and that narrativity is the medium of enacted culture. In other words, if the typology I have proposed has analytic value, it will offer conceptual aid in the interpretation of alternative enacted cultural narrativities.

Apocalypse as exemplar

The implications of hermeneutic concept formation can be illustrated by focusing on apocalyptic time. Here, we encounter all the problems of how to do cultural history. It would be disarmingly easy to write a meta-narrative of the millennium that wove "History" out of a series of disconnected episodes, each of which could be functionally classified as having some millennial or apocalyptic dimension. We live with the moral tragedies and carnage of the twentieth-century's major historical debacles – from the ultimately failed Soviet revolution, World War I, the Holocaust, World War II, Hiroshima and Nagasaki, and the wars in Indo-China, to the episodes of "ethnic cleansing" in Africa and the Balkans, and the slow but undeniable ecological apocalypse. These all could be folded into a universal history from a moral standpoint, of the sort that Kant (1963) proposed, albeit in a decidedly more tragic vein (for a feminist and theological reflection, see Keller, 1996).

It would also be possible to provide a theoretically organized *extrinsic* narrative of how different versions of apocalyptic ideas about history emerged historically over the *longue durée*. As Norman Cohn (1993, 1970) has shown, the wellsprings of apocalyptic thought lie deep in ancient religions of the Middle

East, and apocalyptic motifs have a rich and complex history. They animated Christian religious movements of the Middle Ages and early modern era in Europe. They found their way into Islam. And sometimes, through independent invention, or colonization and diffusion, they have surfaced in non-western religions and social movements, such as Hindu sects, the Taiping rebellion, and the Mau Mau rebellion. On a different front, apocalyptic elements can be found in the theories, ideologies, and social movements of Marxism. The diversity of these examples suggests a widely distributed apocalyptic *topos* that has become diversely nuanced in specific historical and cultural contexts.

However, a very different cultural history, an *intrinsic* one, moves beyond functional juxtaposition, moral meta-narrative, or extrinsic narratives of culture as either *zeitgeist* or material object, to ask about specific cultural motifs of apocalypse, their origins and conduits of transmission, and the ways they have developed through lifeworldly agencies of narrativity. As Mannheim (1953) argued for conservative thought, the apocalyptic has no standing outside of its historically embedded invocation in concrete carrier groups and the cultural materials that they appropriate, produce, maintain, mediate, and rework. Apocalyptic motifs, like any other cultural material, have no existence outside either consciousness or material instantiations (including electronic ones). There is no preestablished trope, ahistorical configuration of signs, significations, and text, or discursive regimen with a stable meaning which fixes the interactions that occur under the sign of the apocalyptic. Nor is the apocalypse sitting in a general cultural storeroom, available to be "used" in some instrumentalist fashion as the occasion warrants (as the most naive invocations of culture as a "toolbox" imply). Apocalypse is neither code nor ephemeral *zeitgeist*. Instead, the situation is far more dialectical: the apocalyptic *topos* describes a generic meaningful situation relevant to the empirical analysis of how various parties within both social movements and the dominant society invoke, transform, and play out specific meaningful motifs in the course of intrinsic unfolding narrative plots. Social actors simultaneously interpret and enact the apocalypse in emergent and interactional constructions of meanings. As Biernacki (1997) has shown for labor, intrinsic cultural history concerns culture embodied in practice.

To explore how this formulation can inform the study of cultural history, let us consider three contemporary episodes in which apocalyptic meanings have been enacted in religious social movements – the apocalypse at Jonestown, "Waco," and the "Transit" of the Solar Temple. Sociologically, there is what Arthur Stinchcombe (1978) calls a "deep analogy" among the episodes involving the three groups: all three groups established strong boundaries between themselves and an established social order, and they all galvanized conflicts between movements, cultural countermovement opponents, and the state over the legitimacy of apocalyptic narratives and counternarratives. In the Tourainian sense the episodes thus connect lived enactment to broader cultural conflicts between countercultures and an established social order (for an extended discussion, see Hall, Schuyler, and Trinh, 2000).

Peoples Temple   Arguably, the murders and mass suicide at Jonestown, Guyana, in 1978 represent the iconic case of apocalyptic religious conflict. As I showed in *Gone From the Promised Land* (2004b), a number of cultural elements became transmuted within Peoples Temple into a doctrine of "revolutionary suicide" and, in turn, revolutionary suicide became translated into mass suicide through a conflict that unfolded between Peoples Temple, its cultural countermovement opponents (who called themselves the Concerned Relatives), and the state (personified in the San Mateo, California US congressman assassinated by Peoples Temple operatives, Leo Ryan). In this cultural history, there is a convergence of multiple apocalyptic themes. Jim Jones, the white, self-styled pentecostal preacher who founded Peoples Temple as an interracial congregation in Indiana in the 1950s, both claimed a political inspiration in communism and invoked Messianic Christian theology. Jones's movement was centrally oriented toward black liberation and racial integration, and Jones elaborated these goals by way of Judeo-Christian and socialist visions of a post-apocalyptic communitarian promised land – most centrally connected historically to various back-to-Africa and black liberation motifs that Jones copied from Father M. J. Divine, who had founded a series of "Promised Lands" in upstate New York during the 1930s. From quite a different direction, Jones became enamored with the doctrine of "revolutionary suicide" that Black Panther Huey Newton advanced in the early 1970s. In Newton's formulation, the slow suicide of life in the ghetto was to be displaced by revolutionary suicide that would end only in victory or death (Hall, 2004b: 136). Thus, revolutionary suicide signified a characteristic element of apocalyptic enactment – *metanoia*, or a radical shift of consciousness, in which individuals give up their old identities and become reborn to the revolutionary movement against racist capitalism (Weber, 1978: 1117; Hall, 1978).

Yet in Peoples Temple, the other-worldly post-apocalyptic image of a promised land carried sufficient potency that the group did not embark on the sort of armed revolutionary struggle undertaken by the Symbionese Liberation Army and similar warring sects, nor did it provoke direct social confrontations like another movement of which Jones was aware – the Philadelphia group called MOVE (Hall, 2004b: 148, 237; Wagner-Pacifici, 1994). Instead, anticipating difficulties with the US Internal Revenue Service, and facing both concerted opposition by the Concerned Relatives and exposés in the San Francisco Bay area media, during the summer of 1977 Jones led his followers in a collective migration to the colony that they had established at Jonestown, Guyana. But fleeing Babylon did not achieve the other-worldly sanctuary beyond the apocalypse of "this" world that a promised land ought to offer. Instead, the Jonestown community became embroiled in an even deeper struggle with opponents over custody of children, including the boy Jim Jones claimed as his biological son. Opponents seeking custody charged that Jonestown was a "concentration camp." The struggle reached a climax when the opponents brought state authority to their side in the "fact-finding" mission of Congressman Ryan to Jonestown. Jones and his committed followers viewed Ryan as biased against them, and they regarded the Congressman's departure with Jonestown apostates under the glare of television cameras as the biggest step yet in their opponents' unrelenting efforts to destabilize the community. In these circumstances, on November 18, 1978, the true believers of Jonestown translated Huey Newton's doctrine of revolutionary suicide into a final decisive act against their opponents, killing Leo Ryan, three journalists, and a defector, then orchestrating the deaths of 913 members of the community in ritualized murders and mass suicide, departing their own promised land through death. At the end, invoking Huey Newton's words, Jones preached to the dying: "This is a revolutionary suicide. This is not a self-destructive suicide." Unable to achieve the post-apocalyptic sanctuary of an other-worldly sect in life, the faithful at Jonestown had mounted a last pre-apocalyptic act of strategic war against their opponents, and then shut themselves off from further conflict by abandoning their failed sanctuary in this world for a different other-worldly sanctuary – of death.

The Branch Davidians   "Waco," as the disastrous conflict between the Branch Davidians and the Bureau of Alcohol, Tobacco, and Firearms (ATF) and FBI has come to be known, is often compared to Jonestown, but for the wrong reasons. Like Peoples Temple, the Branch Davidians under David Koresh adopted the siege mentality of a militant yet other-worldly apocalyptic sect, but the specific meaning of apocalypse and the process by which it emerged were different.

The Branch Davidians came out of the apolitical Christian tradition of Seventh-Day Adventism that surfaced in the nineteenth century, keyed to that most apocalyptic of texts, the New Testament's Book of Revelation. In the twentieth century, Seventh-Day Adventists sought to attain a legitimate status as a denomination, and these very efforts inspired sectarian adventist splinter groups to claim the "true faith" on the basis of new interpretations of scripture that fanned intense expectations about the end of the world. The Davidians were one such group, started in 1929 by a man named Victor Houteff, who designed a clock with its hands to be set near 11 : 00 to symbolize life at the end of time. At the Mount Carmel colony established in 1935 near Waco, Texas, the Davidians lived a strict, hard-scrapple quasi-communal life. After Houteff's death in 1955, a series of contestations for the mantel of prophetic succession ensued. The last occurred in the 1980s, when a man in his twenties who came to be known as David Koresh won a protracted struggle that included one skirmish where gunfire was exchanged between the Koresh group and the son of a former Davidian leader.

If anything, Koresh reasserted the doctrine of end times more strongly than some of his less prophetically gifted predecessors. He took on the Messianic mission of opening the seven seals described in the Book of Revelation that would unveil the actual events of the end times, which he characterized as the fall of Babylon. And Koresh legitimated his right to take multiple wives (his so-called "New Light" doctrine) by claiming that he was founding the new House of David that would rule the world after the anticipated collapse of Babylon (Bromley and Silver, 1995). Koresh thus seems to have envisioned his group surviving a wrenching apocalyptic cataclysm that would leave him and his followers to people the earth as God's chosen lineage. Not strictly a warring sect, neither were the Branch Davidians other-worldly in any sense of claiming that they had escaped the final conflagration. Instead, they were survivalists who would live through the end days and beyond.

The shootout with the ATF SWAT team on February 28, 1993, the ensuing fifty-day siege by the FBI, and the final conflagration on April 19 precipitated by the FBI teargas tank assault on the Mount Carmel compound could only be regarded by the Branch Davidians as a particular enactment of the very apocalypse that Koresh had prophesied in general terms. But, deep as the apocalyptic culture of the Branch Davidians was, the explanation of the events is different than a survivalist scenario would imply. As has been shown elsewhere (Hall, Schuyler, and Trinh, 2000: ch. 2), the genesis of the siege had much to do with efforts of apostate Davidians to raise the alarm against them. These cultural opponents, nicknamed the "Cult Busters" by their leader, spoke like Adventists before them in a highly symbol-laden and metaphoric language, but, instead of using this language to narrate events in the wider world, like the Arab oil embargo, as signs of the apocalypse, they employed it to inscribe stories about Koresh's Branch Davidians. Specifically, the Cult Busters took up the trope of "mass suicide" given such potency at Jonestown, and used it as a convenient apocalyptic symbol of the horrible danger that they believed the Davidians posed. Eventually, the symbol of mass suicide as the ultimate cult threat became transferred into narratives composed within a different interpretive register, that of law enforcement. Specifically, Bureau of Alcohol, Tobacco, and Firearms operatives appropriated the atrocity tales of the apostates as an evidentiary basis that would justify obtaining a search warrant (which the ATF had previously failed to obtain on the basis of more conventional evidence), and they inserted the symbolic trope of mass suicide into strategic narratives of law enforcement, specifically, in ATF scenarios about how to serve the warrant.

The failed raid and the deaths of ATF agents in February 1993 set the stage for the protracted FBI siege, and the FBI's frustration at their inability to end the siege led to their fateful decision to assault the compound, and the terrible tragedy that ensued. This outcome cannot be traced to any essential characteristic of the Branch Davidians or the apocalyptic vision that David Koresh had unveiled. To the contrary, in various ways up until the end, Koresh showed himself to being looking for the signs that would reveal to him what direction the apocalypse would take. Those signs finally came in the way of tanks rolling up to the compound's woodframe building complex in the early morning hours of April 19 to launch tear-gas canisters, and, toward noon, the use of the tanks to destroy walls of the Mount Carmel compound itself. Under this assault, however the fires started, the Davidians chose to remain in the apocalypse that engulfed them, rather than submit to the forces of Babylon. Some seventy-four Branch Davidians died in the inferno.

The Solar Temple   The third case is less well known in the United States, but it is an important one for theorizing cultural history because it shows how apocalyptic meanings can become amalgamated with other meanings, specifically, ecstatic mysticism. On the morning of October 5, 1994, police in Switzerland discovered bodies of forty-eight members of the Solar Temple who had died in ritualized ceremonies in two Swiss villages. These events were quickly connected to the murders of three people and the suicides of two other Solar Templars in a resort town near Montreal, Canada. Letters left behind in Switzerland insisted that the deaths in the fires were a "Transit" to the distant star of Sirius, "which is in no way a suicide in the human sense of the term." Over a year later, on the winter solstice of 1995, sixteen more people associated with the sect died in a similar ceremony in a wooded mountain area in southern France, near the Swiss border and, in March 1997, five more Templars took their lives in Quebec.

Whereas Peoples Temple and the Branch Davidians included mostly ordinary folk and the dispossessed, largely from American Protestant backgrounds, Solar Temple participants were overwhelmingly Catholic; many were wealthy and socially established; and most others participated in the New Age culture of the relatively educated new middle class. Their leaders, a mystagogue named Jo DiMambro and a younger charismatic homeopathic doctor named Luc Jouret, trafficked in an admixture of apocalyptic and mystical ideas. As "front man," Jouret traveled an elite lecture circuit where he portrayed the apocalypse as a traumatic but tremendously positive transition from a sick and exhausted era to the Age of Aquarius. The group initially keyed this imagery to the task of convincing followers to give all their wealth to the organization's leaders and gather together on a survival farm, to pave the way for the New Age. Beyond its public façade the group operated as a secret society dominated by DiMambro. Highly elaborate rituals invoked medieval and Enlightenment European traditions of the Knights Templar and Rosicrucianism – both historically reputed to possess gnostic secrets of human divinity – and offered a quasi-traditional faux Catholicism to substitute for the traditional Catholicism that had declined with the reforms of Vatican II. These mystical ceremonies ritualized participants' connection with divine eternity via contact with "Ascended Masters" reputed to live outside of conventional time and space.

Events that led to the Solar Temple's so-called Transit in October 1994 bear a marked resemblance to both Peoples Temple and the Branch Davidians. In all three cases, scenarios of conflict were played out between (1) the group, (2) apostates allied with countermovement organizations, (3) mass media that came to portray the group as a "cult," and (4) representatives of state power that intervened in ways interpreted within the group as acts of persecution. In the case of the Solar Temple, one apostate worked through an anticult organization to make public accusations of extortion and, around the same time, Quebec police arrested Luc Jouret and two followers in a sting operation for trying to purchase handguns with silencers in Canada – an episode that quickly became labeled in law-enforcement circles and the press as "arms trafficking." A Transit letter claimed that the Solar Temple had been the target of a "pseudoplot."

However, persecution was not the whole story: the Solar Temple had long held to a secret doctrine of soul travel between earthly existence and eternal transcendence, tied to the ideas of a French metaphysician, Jacques Breyer, who calculated the beginning of the third millennium such that "The Grand Monarchy ought to Leave this world around 1995–96," that is, around the time of the *second* Transit, at the winter solstice of 1995. Thus, a key question is whether the Temple might still have attempted a Transit in the absence of the negative apostate publicity and the gun incident. The Transit letters describe the October 1994 Transit as "premature," a description which implies a plan for a Transit, independent of external opposition, but for many years the Solar Temple was oriented toward other-worldly survival on earth. Moreover, even a fixed prophecy is open to recalculation, as numerous cases of millennial numerology demonstrate. Even if Breyer's calculations had been the Solar Temple's sole theological resource, they left considerable flexibility to put off the big apocalypse for decades or even centuries.

On the other hand, given Breyer's theory, it is certainly not implausible that the Transit would have taken place even in the absence of the apocalyptic conflict that *did* occur. How, then, would such a hypothetical *non*-confrontational Transit be understood? This question brings us to core issues about the valences of mass suicide with cultural narratives of apocalypticism and mysticism in the Solar Temple. On the one hand, a Transit seems contradictory to any known cultural narrative of mysticism, since ecstatic association does not acknowledge either time in its social construction or a strong dualism between this world and some eternal world (Hall, 1978). On the other hand, in the cases of Jonestown and Waco, mass suicide is the outcome of a direct apocalyptic confrontation between a religious sect and external opponents. In other words, mysticism has other routes to eternity than physical death, and without a manifest social opposition, mass suicide lacks any compelling apocalyptic *raison d'être*.

These considerations suggest that the Solar Temple was a cultural hybrid – neither purely apocalyptic nor purely mystical in orientation. And indeed, if we look to the specific mechanism by which religious experience was provided in the Solar Temple, it depended on a spiritual hierarchy in which a mystagogue acted as priestly intermediary between divinity (the Ascended Masters) and the audience of religious seekers, who were, in effect, clients receiving a mystical experience produced through participation in ritual. But here another puzzle arises, for "client mysticism" is a staple of New Age spirituality in groups where mass suicide seems an extremely unlikely development.

The difficulty in squaring the Transit with either pure mysticism or client mysticism on their own suggests that a cultural narrative oriented only to one of these lifeworldly enactments would not be adequate to explain the Transit. A much more likely cultural source is the apocalyptically tinged western culture of mystical dualism that equates life with temporality, death with eternity and (potentially) transcendence. After all, the Temple drew from the deep well of the western tradition that mixes the client mysticism of dispensed salvation with quasi-apocalyptic struggles for the true faith – in the death of Jesus, the martyrdom of early Christians, and particularly the cultural memorialization of fourteenth-century burnings at the stake of the Knights Templar who refused to recant allegiance to their order.

In sum, a meaningfully coherent model that posits a purely *apocalyptic*, purely *mystical*, or *client mystical* enactment of mass suicide is difficult to con- solidate. When this meaningful complexity is traced in relation to historical forms of religiosity, its source is to be found in the ways Solar Temple mysti- cism was colored both by dualism and by connections with Christian apocalyptic martyrdom. Yet it would be mistaken to consider this cultural fixing as teleo- logically inevitable, for Jo DiMambro was flexible and syncretic in appropri- ating theological sources and principles as occasion required (Mayer, 1996: 70–78). From what empirical information is available, it seems that there was a shift from earthly apocalyptic survivalism to passage beyond the earthly apoc- alypse in the early 1990s, but the Solar Temple's leaders only elaborated this theology as "departure" when they began to perceive increasing earthly opposition, from February 1993 onward. As with Jonestown and Waco, it was the social conflict with opponents that gave way to an apocalyptic denouement of mass suicide in the initial Transit of October 1994. Whether a collective suicide of the Solar Temple would have occurred in the absence of this perceived opposition is a mental experiment that cannot be completed (Hall, Schuyler, and Trinh, 2000: ch. 4).

As these vignettes show, the production of apocalyptic meanings in the intrinsic narratives of religious movements were fed by the appropriation, reworking, and combination of particular meanings available through specific lines of transmission in uneven relations to a wider world. It was possible to sketch the relations between these emergent and nuanced cultural meanings and a variety of analytic facets: temporal phenomenological possibilities of enactment (i.e., warring and other-worldly apocalypse, and the ecstatic association oriented to timeless mysticism); materially and socially constructed situations; cultural structures of social organization; shifts from one interpretive register to another; the trajectories of conflicts between religious movements, countermovements, and forces of the established social order; and the ways in which these conflicted social interactions shade apocalypse into nuanced new meanings with potentially tragic implications. To explore these intrinsic cultural histories is to recognize that wider events and more encompassing narratives are not detached from the apocalyptic meanings that play out in the struggles between religious movements and countermovements (Hall, 2004a). As Walter Benjamin reminded us, historians need to understand how a given present time is "shot through with chips of Messianic time" (1969: 263).

Conclusion

In a short compass, I have traced a wide arc. Beginning with cultural studies, I turned its gaze reflexively toward the cultures *of* studies by arguing that diverse methodological practices of inquiry are impure hybrids, deeply connected to one another. Such reflexivity suggested the need to think about the discourse of narrative in theoretical terms, and to consider how social theoretical discourses shape narrative discourses. Among theoretical approaches to concept formation, I singled out hermeneutic theories that conceptualize meaningful action in relation to lived temporality for their importance to intrinsic narratives of cultural history. I proposed a phenomenological typology in order to theorize temporality in alternative narratologically structured modes of socially organized being-in-the-world, and I illustrated the potential of this approach with interpretive historical vignettes of apocalyptic meanings in the intrinsic narrative trajectories of three religious social movements.

The vignettes hardly scratch the surfaces of the cultural histories that they describe. But, even at this first pass, the hermeneutic approach begins to reveal cultural history in terms quite different than would be suggested by positing some relatively autonomous *zeitgeist* or externalized cultural code with the status of a social fact. The trajectories revealed in the hermeneutic analysis suggest that culture cannot adequately be understood solely by attending to either its functional implications or the structural properties and processes of its transmissions and transformations, and that cultural meanings are more than just signs, texts, codes, discourses, or tools with putative existence outside their social production and reproduction, more as well than either "frames" or "vocabularies of motives" invoked *by* actors to make sense of their own actions and those of others. In addition, and centrally, culture is constitutive *of* social enactments in their narratively lived (and thereby reworked) meanings. This conclusion poses an epistemological challenge. Much cultural history is neither deeply historical nor does it connect culture to unfolding life. It is thus ill-equipped to fulfill programs such as the one suggested by Walter Benjamin's concern with the "chips of Messianic time." In this light, to paraphrase Clifford Geertz, we need to understand the relation of culture to history "all the way down."

Note

I wish to thank the fellows of New College, Oxford University, and the Centre d'Analyse et d'Intervention Sociologiques, Ecole des Hautes Etudes en Science Sociales, Paris, for providing auspices under which I could pursue the issues addressed in this chapter, and audiences at the February 1997 conference on "Cultural Sociology and Cultural Studies," University of California – Santa Barbara, and at a September 1997 seminar at the Department of Sociology, University of Arizona, for their helpful comments.

References

Alexander, Jeffrey C. 1982. *Theoretical Logic in Sociology, Vol. I: Positivism, Presuppositions, and Current Controversies*. Berkeley, CA: University of California Press.
　ed. 1988. *Durkheimian Sociology: Cultural Studies*. New York: Cambridge University Press.
Alexander, Jeffrey C., Bernhard Giesen, Richard Münch, and Neil J. Smelser, eds. 1987. *The Micro–Macro Link*. Berkeley, CA: University of California Press.
Alexander, Jeffrey C. and Philip Smith. 1993. "The Discourse of American Civil Society: A New Proposal for Cultural Studies." *Theory & Society* 22:151–207.
Bakhtin, Mikhail M. 1981. *The Dialogic Imagination*. Austin, TX: University of Texas Press.
Bell, Daniel. 1976. *The Cultural Contradictions of Capitalism*. New York: Basic.

Benjamin, Walter. 1969. *Illuminations*. New York: Schocken.

Biernacki, Richard. 1997. "Work and Culture in the Reception of Class Ideologies." Ch. 5 in John R. Hall, ed. *Reworking Class*. Ithaca, NY: Cornell University Press.

Bromley, David G. and Edward D. Silver. 1995. "The Davidian Tradition: From Patronal Clan to Prophetic Movement," in Stuart A. Wright, ed. *Armageddon in Waco*. Chicago, IL: University of Chicago Press. Pp. 43–72.

Carr, David. 1986. *Time, Narrative, and History*. Bloomington, IL: Indiana University Press.

Cohen, Sande. 1986. *Historical Culture*. Berkeley, CA: University of California Press.

Cohn, Norman. [1957] 1970. *Pursuit of the Millennium*. Oxford: Oxford University Press.

1993. *Cosmos, Chaos and the World to Come: The Ancient Roots of Apocalyptic Faith*. New Haven, CT: Yale University Press.

Dawidoff, Robert. 1995. "History . . . But," in Cohen and Roth, eds. *History and– : Histories within the Human Sciences*. Pp. 370–381.

Durkheim, Emile. [1915] 1965. *The Elementary Forms of Religious Life*. New York: Free Press.

Eley, Geoffrey. 1995. "What is Cultural History?" *New German Critique* 65:19–35.

Foucault, Michel. [1969] 1972. *The Archaeology of Knowledge*. London: Tavistock.

Fuller, Steve. 1988. *Social Epistemology*. Bloomington, IN: Indiana University Press.

Giddens, Anthony. 1990. *The Consequences of Modernity*. Stanford, CA: Stanford University Press.

Habermas, Jürgen. [1981] 1987. *The Theory of Communicative Action, Vol. 2: Lifeworld and System*. Boston, MA: Beacon Press.

Hall, John R. 1978. *The Ways Out: Utopian Communal Groups in an Age of Babylon*. Boston, MA: Routledge & Kegan Paul.

1980. "The Time of History and the History of Times." *History and Theory* 19:113–131.

1990. "Social Interaction, Culture, and Historical Studies," in Howard S. Becker and Michal McCall, eds. *Symbolic Interactionism and Cultural Studies*. Chicago, IL: University of Chicago Press. Pp. 16–45.

1994. "Cultural history," in Peter N. Sterns, ed. *Encyclopedia of Social History*. New York: Garland. Pp. 185–187.

1999. *Cultures of Inquiry: From Epistemology to Discourse in Sociohistorical Research*. Cambridge: Cambridge University Press.

2003. "Cultural history is dead (long live the Hydra)," in Gerard Delanty and Engin Isin, eds. *Handbook for Historical Sociology*. Beverly Hills, CA: Sage, Pp. 151–67.

2004a. "Apocalypse 9/11," in Phillip Lucas and Thomas Robbins, eds. *New Religious Movements in the Twenty-First Century: Legal, Political, and Social Challenges in Global Perspective*. London: Routledge. Pp. 265–82.

2004b. *Gone from the Promised Land: Jonestown in American Cultural History*, second edition, with a new introduction. New Brunswick, NJ: Transaction.

Hall, John R., with Philip D. Schuyler and Sylvaine Trinh. 2000. *Apocalypse Observed: Religious Movements and Violence in North America, Europe, and Japan*. London: Routledge.

Halttunen, Karen and Lewis Perry, eds. 1998. *Moral Problems in American Life: New Perspectives on Cultural History*. Ithaca, NY: Cornell University Press.

Hunt, Lynn, ed. 1989. *The New Cultural History*. Berkeley, CA: University of California Press.

Husserl, Edmund. [1905] 1964. *The Phenomenology of Internal Time Consciousness*, trans. J. S. Churchill. Bloomington, IN: Indiana University Press.

Jay, Martin. 1996. "For Theory." *Theory and Society* 25:167–183.

Jelavich, Peter. 1995. "Method? What Method? Confessions of a Failed Structuralist." *New German Critique* 65:75–86.

Kane, Anne. 1997. "Theorizing Meaning Construction in Social Movements: Symbolic Structures and Interpretation during the Irish Land War, 1879–1882." *Sociological Theory* 15: 249–276.

Kant, Immanuel. [1784] 1963. "Idea for a Universal History from a Cosmopolitan Point of View," in Lews W. Beck, ed. *On History*. Indianapolis, IN: Bobbs-Merrill. Pp. 11–26.

Keller, Catherine. 1996. *Apocalypse Now and Then: A Feminist Guide to the End of the World*. Boston, MA: Beacon Press.

Kellner, Hans D. 1989. *Language and Historical Representation*. Madison, WI: University of Wisconsin Press.

Latour, Bruno. 1993. *We Have Never Been Modern*. Cambridge, MA: Harvard University Press.

Lethen, Helmut. 1995. "Kracauer's Pendulum: Thoughts on German Cultural History." *New German Critique* 65:37–45.

Lyotard, Jean-François. 1988. *The Differend: Phrases in Dispute*. Minneapolis, MN: University of Minnesota Press.

   [1954] 1991. *Phenomenology*. Albany, NY: State University of New York Press.

Mannheim, Karl. 1937. *Ideology and Utopia*. New York: Harcourt, Brace & Company.

   1952. "The Problem of a Sociology of Knowledge," in Mannheim, *Essays on the Sociology of Knowledge*. London: Routledge & Kegan Paul. Pp. 139–90.

   1953. "Conservative Thought," in Mannheim, *Essays on Sociology and Social Psychology*. London: Routledge & Kegan Paul. Pp. 74–164.

Mayer, Jean-François. 1996. *Les Mythes du Temple Solaire*. Geneva: Georg Editeur.

Mullaney, Steven. 1988. *The Place of the Stage: License, Play, and Power in Renaissance England*. Chicago, IL: University of Chicago Press.

Novick, Peter. 1988. *That Noble Dream: The "Objectivity Question" and the American Historical Profession*. New York: Cambridge University Press.

Owensby, Jacob. 1994. *Dilthey and the Narrative of History*. Ithaca, NY: Cornell University Press.

Polkinghorne, Donald. 1988. *Narrative Knowing and the Human Sciences*. Albany, NY: State University of New York Press.

Ricoeur, Paul. 1984, 1985, 1988. *Time and Narrative*. 3 vols. Chicago, IL: University of Chicago Press.

Rioux, Jean-Pierre, and Jean-François Sirinelli, eds. 1997. *Pour une histoire culturelle.* Paris, France: Seuil.

Scheler, Max. [1915] 1961. *Ressentiment.* New York: Free Press.

Schorske, Carl E. 1995. "History and the Study of Culture," in Cohen and Roth, eds. *History and– : Histories within the Human Sciences.* Pp. 382–395.

Schutz, Alfred. [1932] 1967. *The Phenomenology of the Social World.* Evanston, IL: Northwestern University Press.

Sewell, William H., Jr. 1992. "A Theory of Structure: Duality, Agency, and Transformation." *American Journal of Sociology* 98: 1–29.

Simmel, Georg. [1908/1917] 1950. *The Sociology of Georg Simmel.* New York, NY: Free Press.

[1905] 1977. *The Problems of the Philosophy of History.* New York, NY: Free Press.

Somers, Margaret R. 1995. "Narrating and Naturalizing Civil Society and Citizenship Theory: The Place of Political Culture and the Public Sphere." *Sociological Theory* 13:229–74.

1997 [1992]. "Deconstructing and Reconstructing Class Formation Theory: Narrativity, Relational Analysis, and Social Theory," in John R. Hall, ed. *Reworking Class.* Ithaca, NY: Cornell University Press. Pp. 73–105.

Somers, Margaret R. and Gloria Gibson. 1994. "Reclaiming the 'Epistemological Other': Narrative and the Social Constitution of Identity," in Craig Calhoun, ed. *Social Theory and the Politics of Identity.* Boston: Blackwell. Pp. 37–99.

Stinchcombe, Arthur L. 1978. *Theoretical Methods in Social History.* New York, NY: Academic Press.

Touraine, Alain. 1981. *The Voice and the Eye: An Analysis of Social Movements.* Cambridge: Cambridge University Press.

Trinh, T. Minh-ha. 1989. *Woman, Native, Other.* Bloomington, IN: Indiana University Press.

Wagner-Pacifici, Robin. 1994. *Discourse and Destruction: The City of Philadelphia versus MOVE.* Chicago, IL: The University of Chicago Press.

Weber, Max. 1958. The *Protestant Ethic and the Spirit of Capitalism.* New York: Schribners.

1978. *Economy and Society,* ed. Guenther Roth and Claus Wittich. Berkeley, CA: University of California Press.

Wood, David. 1989. *The Deconstruction of Time.* Atlantic Highlands, NJ: Humanities Press.

4

Cultural studies as *fin-de-siècle* culture

Mark A. Schneider

The field of cultural studies is no more coherent today than when it first appeared a quarter century ago, and this makes characterizing it – especially in broad strokes – difficult. As an interdisciplinary enterprise, it shelters work ranging from relatively standard sociological or anthropological inquiry to more textualist engagements dependent upon literary theory or psychoanalysis – which makes for very odd bedfellows, drawn to one another largely by shared political sentiments. Yet, though we need to recognize this diversity, and pay respect to the Birmingham tradition out of which cultural studies grew, what is novel in the field today, and what accounts for its quite striking rise in visibility over the last decade, is found in its postmodern exemplifications. These often advertise themselves in terms of the break they have made with the tenets of modernism-writ-large, and the very frequency with which this break is styled "radical" underscores the claim to novelty.[1] Yet at the same time there is a vague feeling, within and without the field, of déjà vu: despite the banner of newness, post-modern forms of cultural studies are reminiscent of the *fin de siècle*.[2] I want to give this vague feeling greater concreteness, since it allows us to view the project of cultural studies from a different critical angle.[3]

Of course it would be odd, chronologically at least, if the *fin-de-siècle* quality of postmodern cultural studies were other than a coincidence. The existence of a pattern to centuries in which their closings evoke a common sense of time running out or down – of decadence – is highly problematic.[4] Perceptions of such patterns normally result from dubious sampling procedures and in the wake of rather heavy interpretation, so that we are left to wonder whether *fin de siècle* names a real phenomenon or is merely an interpretive fiction that finds regularity where none in fact exists. Yet, if we drop our concern with the sociological warrant for the concept and use it simply as an interpretive tool, it proves illuminating. It allows us to see analogies between some postmodernist themes and a set of attitudes that have been seen before, particularly in the literary movement we style "Decadence."

It is true that "decadent" is normally a term of abuse, especially as used by the larger modernism, that of the Enlightenment, to which postmodernists join the Decadents in objecting. I hope to give it more standing here, for if we can get past its lurid reputation and ignore the generally mediocre quality of its literary representations, decadence presents an interesting moral and philosophical profile. Postmodernists may be initially distrustful of an association with decadence, but they should recall the imprimatur given it by Nietzsche, who wrote in *Ecce Homo* (1969: 223) that his philosophy sprang from the fertile balance between a "rich life" and "the secret work of the instinct of decadence."

The instinct of decadence

What is this instinct? In characterizing it, I will concentrate on three themes consistently represented in decadent literature: the erosion of categorical differences and boundaries; an affection for the artificial; and a fascination with paradox. These themes were used by writers in the *fin de siècle* for a particular purpose: to sever their connection to civilizational developments such as the Enlightenment, its belief in progress, and the bourgeois society they saw as growing out of it. By severing this connection, they hoped to become innocent of the West, that is, be relieved of its historical burden, which they found absurd and suffocating. Having explored their project, taking up these three themes in some detail, I will return to postmodern cultural studies to build the comparison.

The literature of decadence – I have in mind centrally Huysmans, Lorrain, Rachilde, Villiers de l'Isle-Adam, and Oscar Wilde, as well as associated Symbolists from Baudelaire to Maeterlinck – is everywhere furnished with entities or activities that violate conventional categorical distinctions as well as our sense of boundaries. A main locus of activity here is gender categories. The title of one of Rachilde's works, *Monsieur Venus*, illustrates this nicely by intermingling the categories of male and female. The *"Monsieur"* of the title might refer equally to the feminized male protagonist or the masculinized heroine, Raoule de Venerande, who dresses in men's clothes and adopts the male role in seducing Jacques Silvert, an artist whose physical beauty is deeply androgynous. Raoule refers to Jacques consistently as her mistress and uses the feminine gender in addressing him, while her fondest hope is to make him her wife. Later, when their affair sours, she has him killed and his hair removed to be placed on a wax simulacrum, introducing the theme of artificiality I will turn to later.

Similarly, when Des Esseintes, the hero of Huysmans' classic *A rebours*, takes a mistress, he quite naturally settles upon a trapeze artist; that is, upon a woman whose finely muscled body makes her the *fin-de-siècle* equivalent of today's bodybuilders. Throughout the literature, the violation of gendered expectations is inscribed in the bodies of the characters: they *look* unclassifiable as to gender, and, if they do not, they cross-dress. Rachilde herself, whose real name was Marguerite Valette, had a visiting card inscribed "Rachilde – Man of Letters."

An analogous tendency is to link sex with asexuality, and both with destruction. Raoule is a virgin, but like her counterparts Salome and Turandot, is hyper-sexualized in result. Virginity of her sort is consistently linked to sadism. In fact it seems a rule of thumb in decadent literature that, if a virgin is introduced, someone will soon be tortured or beheaded. This is obviously done for shock effect, but it has a deeper purpose as well: to show that the category of purity, as traditionally applied to virgins, is intermixed with a perversity of unusual proportions. Indeed, it is suggested, and said directly of Salomé by Herod in Wilde's play, that virgins are *monstrous*, in the sense of psychological grotesques.[5] Extremes of purity and monstrousness are thus characterized as inhabiting one another.

The monstrous itself is used in decadence to annihilate our sense of limits. A truly astounding novel associated with decadence, Flaubert's *Salambo*, overwhelms us with excess, using it, in Victor Brombert's (1966: 212) words, to "explode the boundaries of the human." The dust jacket of my English edition (Flaubert, 1932) gives a nice sense of the flavor of this historical novel set in the time of the Punic wars: "Against a background of bloody, religious warfare, rape, lust, and sadistic torture, [Flaubert] tells of the violent love of Salambo and the barbaric mercenary, Matho, which culminates in the tragic death of both, by excruciating torture at the hands of a roaring mob, maddened with the lust of religious frenzy." This is not hyperbole; the novel attempts to stupefy us with the presumably commonplace excesses of a barbarous time.

In contrast to this extreme, other decadent works emphasize languor, acedia, torpor, abulia, apathy, lassitude, and neurasthenia – as if they were thesauruses of exhaustion. At one level, this of course expresses a conviction that civilization is slowly failing of energy. But something more is going on: the frequent juxtaposition of spectacular violence on the one hand and languor on the other, as if to link excess and defect, seems aimed at underscoring the banality of the mean or the measured. To the extent that western civilization had seemed to value the mean, the measured, and the reasonable, decadent recourse to excess and defect challenged it. Similarly, to the extent that the intellectual work of the West, from Aristotle through the Enlightenment, was premised on the utility of sharp categorical distinctions, the erosion of differences championed by decadence sought to blunt its tools, to destroy the implements of its intellectual economy. As that peculiar exponent and analyst of Decadence, the

Romanian-French essayist E. M. Cioran, has claimed (1968: 133), "It is by undermining the idea of reason, of order, of harmony that we gain consciousness of ourselves."

More broadly, the Decadents created a counter-world that reversed the principles Aristotle had laid down for household economy in his *Politics*. Whereas, for Aristotle, households aimed at increasing their wealth through the rational use of tools designed for specific applications, the Decadents pictured the inexorable squandering of wealth, having deconstructed the instruments through which they believed it had been accumulated. They present, as role models, rentier aesthetes (like Huysmans' Des Esseintes) who spend beyond their means and are generally incapable of maintaining, let alone increasing, them. In figures like Wilde and Mallarmé, the very language of business and commerce, of "getting," is seen as spiritually polluted: art aims to distance itself from this as much as possible.

Thus, though we are apt to dismiss all the androgynes and hermaphrodites, the fire-and-ice, sadistic virgins, and the continual vacillation between excess and defect in Decadence as no more than the sensationalism of second-rate literature, they represent something more serious: an erosion of categories and limits that is aimed against the principles by which western thought had theretofore "worked" so as to accumulate wealth and knowledge.

A similar attitude underlies decadent celebration of the artificial. For literary historian A. E. Carter (1958: 25):

Artificiality . . . is the chief characteristic of decadence as the nineteenth century understood the word. By a voluntary contradiction of the nature-cult, writers were able to see all traditional Romantic themes in a new light and a new perspective. The whole approach . . . was entirely deliberate: from Gautier to Mirbeau, everybody who took up a pen realized that he was going "against the grain."

This preference is perhaps nowhere better symbolized than in *The Future Eve* by Villiers de l'Isle-Adam, whose protagonist has Edison create a robot – a simulacrum – which is physically identical to his fiancée but intellectually superior to her, with which he then elopes. Similarly, when Des Esseintes decides to add a living tortoise to his collection of objets d'art, he must transform it by gilding its carapace. Not entirely satisfied with the result, he proceeds to encrust it with gems. To watch this creature, now transformed by art, plod slowly through his study throwing off reflected light, proves immensely satisfying to him. Here, as with Wilde, nature exists only to be improved upon by art.

While the Decadents faulted the natural order variously, a foremost sin was its incessant generativity: it could not stop reproducing itself. To be involved in this was, for them, slavery to the dictates of nature – a slavery to which no self-respecting person would submit. In one of the first essays exploring a decadent sensibility, Gautier (1930[1868], cited by Carter, 1958: 3) says of Baudelaire that, "For him, everything that distanced man, and above all woman, from the state of nature appeared a happy invention." The dumb fecundity of nature stood as a symbol for that of humankind, and it made all the more objectionable Rousseau's resort to the state of nature as a foil with which to pillory "civilization." Taken as an artificial phenomenon, civilization could only improve upon human nature, as Wilde stressed in "The Decay of Lying." More generally, decadent figures transformed "natural" behavior through the application to it of intelligence and sensibility, at once claiming it for civilization and setting themselves above the bourgeoisie, who were neither very reflective nor "reflexive" in this way.

Hostility to nature and to generation also reinforced the Decadents' misogyny: since women both gave birth and were assumed somehow to be "nearer nature" than men, they were tainted by association with nature's dumb fecundity. Disgust with fecundity also influenced the decadent's aesthetic appreciation for homosexuality, which had the double advantage of being by the day's lights perverse – against the grain – and incapable of eventuating in issue.[6]

The celebration of artifice had a central impact upon literary style. Gautier (1930[1868], cited by Carter 1958: 129–130) saw the origin of decadent style in Baudelaire, and he characterized it as "an ingenious style, complicated, knowledgeable, full of nuance and research," Anatole Baju (1886), editor of the journal *Le Décadent*, called for a style "*rare et tourmenté*" – which is to say excessively cultivated. Here the enemy does not seem so much to be nature or the natural as it is the commonplace and the commercial. Baju went on to say that cultivation was necessary to escape the "banality of the *fin de siècle*," and the masthead of his journal was blazoned with the exhortation "Everything! Except Banality." Banality for the decadents meant the stolid world of the bourgeois, and they aimed for a style that would express their disdain for this. This effort was carried furthest by Mallarmé, the poet whose difficult syntax Paul Valery termed "sadistic." One of Mallarmé's justifications for his difficulty was that it distanced his work as far as possible from linguistic forms associated with commerce and practical action. Similarly, in the Preface to *Dorian Gray* Oscar Wilde (1982: 236) encouraged us to "forgive a man for making a useful thing as long as he does not admire it." Art, he suggested (1968: 176), functioned to keep the world of utility, indeed all "reality," at bay, using "the impenetrable barrier of beautiful style, of decorative or ideal treatment."

The sense that reality was profoundly inferior to art underlay the Decadents' emphasis upon style. As Cioran (1968: 135) has written: "Every idolatry of style starts from the belief that reality is even more hollow than its verbal figuration." From this perspective, style has prophylactic capacities: it separates one securely from hollow mundanity. It also can transmute it: Mallarmé is famous for having insisted that the world existed to wind up in a book, transformed by artifice into something more acceptable. A faintly absurd twist was given this by Villiers de l'Isle-Adam at the conclusion of his play *Axël*, when the brilliant and immensely wealthy lovers conclude that the imaginative pictures they can paint of their future together are so far superior to what they could actually experience that they have no option but to kill themselves.

Edmund Wilson (1948) saw in *Axël* the charter for the literary modernism of Yeats, Eliot, and Pound. Certainly modernists shared with decadents a visceral disgust with bourgeois society and a deep pessimism about the culture it produced (a pessimism shared by the Frankfurt School of critical sociologists). The difficulty and artificiality of style that both adopted would, they hoped, provide the "impenetrable barrier" of which Wilde spoke, on the other side of which a spiritually superior life might be led.

Our third theme is a fascination with paradox. A love of verbal conundra of course infused Wilde's epigrams, as when he says in *The Decay of Lying* (1968: 172) that "the only real people are the people who never existed" meaning figures in books. He once even claimed that his homosexuality expressed in the moral domain his intellectual intrigue with paradox.[7] With Wilde much paradox is only a display of wit – though he would object to my disparaging "only" – but with Mallarmé, I think, one finds an artistically more fertile commitment to paradox. Though it is risky to see specific meanings in his mature poetry, *Un coup de dés* certainly seems to be reflecting on a mirroring relation between chance and necessity, as if to see chance as paradoxically necessary and necessity itself as constructed out of chance – ideas that John Cage was later to explore.

The function of paradox in the decadents' aesthetic toolkit seems clear. As Cioran writes (1975: 116), "A civilization evolves from agriculture to paradox." Paradox is the "natural" culmination of Reason, which begins productively but, in becoming excessively cultivated, turns reflexive and ties itself in knots. Paul Valery (1947: 36) has his Monsieur Teste say: "That by which I know makes me ignorant. I am ignorant inasmuch, and insofar, as I know." A conviction that Reason would eventually stymie itself, and that this was in fact its *telos*, allowed the decadents to feel above bourgeois satisfaction with science and progress.

But their appreciation of paradox was also driven by the conviction that Truth – of the sort Reason had championed – occasioned the sins of which the West was guilty. The decadents wanted out of this – as did Nietzsche in his own way. Indeed, though it may seem odd to claim that their indulgence in paradox, alongside the imaginative perversions and excesses, was an effort to purify themselves, I suggest it *was*. Contrast their sense of the telos of Reason with that of Edmund Husserl. At roughly the same time as the decadents were writing, Husserl had become convinced that Truth – the apodictic, the demonstrably certain – was the telos of Occidental thought and the emblem of our civilization. In that telos, he wrote (1965: 157), "lies something unique, which all other human groups, too, feel with regard to us, something that, apart from considerations of expediency, becomes a motivation for them – despite their determination to retain their spiritual autonomy – constantly to Europeanize themselves, whereas we, if we understood ourselves properly, will never, for example, Indianize ourselves." Thus, in Husserl's eyes, Truth was the warrant for cultural imperialism, the proof of the superiority of our civilization over any other. In contrast to this, as Cioran (1975: 115) says, the attraction of decadence is that of "ages when truths have no further life, when they pile up like skeletons in . . . the boneyard of dreams." Paradox was thus the tool by which Truth could be shown not to be the telos of the West but a symptom of its adolescence, a necessary but juvenile stage on the road from agriculture to paradox.

Each of the themes I have discussed – the erosion of categories, the pursuit of the artificial, and the fascination with paradox – is underlain by a dissatisfaction with the West as it manifested itself in bourgeois society, with its belief in science, progress, and cultural imperialism. The most effective way of summarizing the overall attitude of Decadence is to join Cioran (1975: 123) in his view of it as a "discipline of sterility." The meaning of "discipline" here is monastic: to submit to decadence would be to devote oneself, as if religiously, to being sterile, to being without issue or effect in the world. The opposite, fecundity, is something the decadents found repulsive. They objected to fecundity as physical reproduction, but they also saw it, metaphorically, as being caught up in the generative, "progressive" projects associated with western civilization – from commerce to empire – which they ridiculed. In an effort to opt out of this, they championed a deep inconsequentiality. For them sterility was a route to cultural innocence; inconsequentiality would protect them from the disease of Reason. As their contemporary, the French literary critic Paul Bourget, noted (1924: 22), they thus made little contribution to the grandeur of France. Indeed, having become disgusted with the "advance" of bourgeois civilization, they strove, through their work, to set themselves apart from it.

Decadence, then, employed its distaste for the natural and the real to sufflate the realm of culture, the domain of words. Decadent culture was a gymnasium for spiritual athletes who sought through it a freedom from consequence, an escape from Husserl's apodictic sickness and its presumed sociopolitical sequelae. By eroding categories, emphasizing artifice, and promoting paradox they sought to be innocent of the *telos* and history of the West.

The *fin de siècle* in cultural studies

The hurried sketch I have drawn of Decadence as a literary movement should make it clear why postmodern efforts in cultural studies appear at least vaguely *fin de siècle*: they express certain convictions and attitudes in common with Decadence. Foremost among these is the rejection of Reason – of science or philosophy – as capable of generating Truth, which is to say knowledge that would hold good for all times and places. Postmodernism sees the pursuit of Truth as the key flaw of the larger modernism that begins with the Enlightenment. Truth is the epistemological disguise of Power, the outgrowth of an urge to tame and discipline an unruly universe. Consequently, an ambition of postmodernism is to stigmatize Truth and replace it with multiple knowledges that are regulated by local rather than universal conventions.

To this end, it uses tools very similar to those used by the Decadents. Traditional categorical thinking has been aggressively prosecuted by postmodern cultural studies, just as it was by the decadents – for being a tool of Reason. Categorical thinking is seen either as by its nature privileging – as deconstruction attempted to hammer home – or as insensitive to the bottomless particularity of people, a concern evident in the recent stylistic proliferation of plurals in book titles: sexualities, masculinities, and so on. In fact, developments within (or allied with) postmodern cultural studies, such as queer theory, make the effort to categorize into their principal demon.[8]

Where my comparison will be more controversial, but also more interesting, is with the themes of artificiality and paradox. I want to approach the theme of artificiality from two angles, one stylistic and the other theoretical. As to style, it seems evident that postmodernist analysts of culture often use a reflexive style, sometimes itself *rare et tourmenté*, to underscore the constructedness of their own position. They do this to avoid relapsing into the naturalistic rhetoric through which, they suggest, the Enlightenment managed to obscure its social constructedness. On this view, by continually remarking our own rhetorical practices, we can alert our readers to the very provisionality and localism of our understanding. For instance, Scott Baker (1990: 241) has recommended that we proceed by "*questioning* and then textually *revealing*" our own writing practices, in result of which "the sometimes false mystique surrounding the academic paper would be deconstructed further, but in such a way as to enhance both the honesty and the humility of the author." The worry here is interestingly parallel to that of figures like Wilde and Mallarmé, who sought through stylistic artifice to keep a barrier between their work and common, unreflective, practical speech.

This stylistic attraction to artifice is mirrored at a deeper level, however, in the assumption of social constructedness. In viewing all our knowledge as founded more by rhetorical practices than by engagement with the world, constructivism encourages us to see all culture as artificial. And artificialness is seen as "good" in that it suggests how easy it would be in principle to replace "poor" art – the repressive, truth-seeking art of the Enlightenment – with "better" – that subscribing to the postmodernist aesthetic. Particularly in some postmodernist attitudes toward science, we are presented with a position Oscar Wilde took long ago when he wrote (1968: 174) in *The Decay of Lying* that, "If . . . we regard Nature as the collection of phenomena external to man, people only discover in her what they bring to her. She has no suggestions of her own." Being mute, Nature is unable to contribute the essentialist props that have shorn up now-outdated ways of thinking.

However, this is too crude a characterization of the postmodernist position. The artificiality of the world is not seen as exclusively good because so much of it is produced under the taint of "getting." In this regard, "late capitalism," as instanced in corporations like Disney, has taken over the role the decadents ascribed to bourgeois commerce at the end of the last century. The thoroughly artifactual quality of the cultural environment, especially as it serves corporate profit, is seen as deeply problematic. Yet the "natural" response to this, which would be to seek support for opposition to late capitalism in a return to Nature, is blocked by Nature's complicity as the underwriter of essentialist props referred to above. Thus a new oppositional space for the artificial must be developed. As Donna Haraway (1992: 313) writes in an essay that undertakes this project:

> Some . . . scholars have been terrified to criticize their constructivist formulations because the only alternative seems to be some retrograde kind of "going back" to nature and to philosophical realism. But . . . these scholars should know that "nature" and "realism" are precisely the consequences of representational practices. Where we need to move is not "back" to nature, but *elsewhere*, through and within an artifactual social nature.

Echoing Derrida, Haraway characterizes this "elsewhere" as a monstrous birth from within the belly of an already monstrous present. It opens a space for science no longer in the service of oppression or in thrall to progress: "The shape of my amodern history will have a different geometry, not of progress, but of permanent and multi-patterned interaction through which lives and worlds get built, human and unhuman. This Pilgrim's Progress is taking a monstrous turn" (1992: 304). The enterprise develops "outside the premises of enlightenment," and in part by eroding its categorical structures: "When the pieties of belief in the modern are dismissed, [categorical differences] collapse into each other as into a black hole" (1992: 330). Haraway concludes her essay with a meditation on a painting by Lynn Randolph titled "Cyborg." She notes (1992: 329) that:

> This cyborg does not have an Aristotelian structure . . . S/he is not utopian nor imaginary; s/he is virtual. Generated . . . by the collapse into each other of the technical, organic, mythic, textual, and political, s/he is constituted by articulations of critical differences within and without each figure.

Thus Haraway's analysis instances the themes I have identified as central to literary decadence. Here, as for Cioran, "reality" is found to be considerably more hollow than its verbal figuration. Of course, a world exterior to the mind exists, but we can only address it as a text – just as Mallarmé contended.

Let us turn finally, and most controversially, to the theme of paradox. I suggested the decadents saw paradox as the unwitting telos of Reason, the natural outcome of extended reflection – which arrived not at the doorstep of Truth, but was waylaid, in effect by *itself*, along the route. From this perspective, extended cogitation leaves us more stupid than when we began – a consequence Flaubert satirized in *Bouvard and Pécuchet*. The decadents pointed to paradoxes in the works of others, so as to show them derailing themselves, and embraced it themselves, as a way of achieving inconsequentiality.

Now this theme of paradox is overwhelmingly evident in certain strands of postmodern inquiry such as deconstruction. For instance, Paul de Man's (1971) suggestion that we achieve our greatest insights in being blind to the principles we claim to govern our inquiry is certainly paradoxical, as is much of Derrida's work; but, although deconstruction influenced cultural studies, the latter has taken a somewhat less involuted stance. Indeed, much of the allure of cultural studies has lain in its ambitions to political effectivity – and this seems very different from the inconsequentiality the decadents expected out of paradox.

Yet it is clear to many external observers and to some adherents that the field of cultural studies has waylaid itself, and in a way that suggests an "objective" pursuit of inconsequentiality. The easiest way to put this is to suggest that cultural studies guarantees, by the very sophistication and reflexivity of its analytical strategies, that it will have no practical political consequence in the wider world whatsoever, unless it be the negative one of serving as a shibboleth for conservative forces, or as the butt of parodies such that foisted on the cultural studies journal *Social Text*.[9]

This conundrum of postmodern cultural studies, that its analytical means subvert its political ambitions, is so evident to friendly observers like Stanley Fish that in *Professional Correctness* (1995) he is barely able to rein in his dismay. How can the extraordinarily subtle analysis we find in Haraway, for instance, pointing as it does toward a difficult-to-define "elsewhere," possibly enter into the realm of practical politics? It is not that anything in principle forbids this, Fish points out, but the initiative simply isn't in the court of cultural studies: "[T]he initiative has to come from the other direction, from those who are so situated as to have the power (although they do not yet have the reasons) to introduce into their councils news from the world of cultural studies" (1995: 97). But there is no prospect of this, and Fish comments sarcastically (1995: 123) that: "Only academics, invested as they are in some version of idealism, think that because they have come up with an elegant account of what non-academics are doing those same non-academics will be moved, in admiration, to join forces with the academy." Only inside universities does the ambition of cultural studies to effectivity seem reasonable: elsewhere this sort of work "is not subversive, but irrelevant: *it cannot be heard* except as the alien murmurings of a galaxy far away" (1995: 91).

Occasionally, proponents seem to recognize the conundrum themselves: in an interesting article on postmodern social theory in the journal *Sociological Theory*, Scott Baker (1990: 232) notes that "postmodernism can add a *paradoxical quality* to our own self-images as textual–rhetorical social scientists." This is because "a tension arises between the permanently immanent self-critique that a rhetorical notion of scientific inquiry imposes and a suspicion that such scholarship is socially and politically meaningless" (1990: 238). He responds to this paradox by arguing for a rhetorical approach that self-reflexively points out its own socially constructed quality, in hopes that its very humility will prove appealing to a wide audience. Yet this seems unlikely in the extreme. Fish notes numerous similar instances where proponents of cultural studies recognize their inconsequentiality in one paragraph, only to announce a new, but similarly vexed, strategy to escape it in the next.

I believe this straining against a conclusion whose inevitability is almost admitted – that postmodernism and cultural studies are politically sterile practices – indicates that proponents have not seen with quite the clarity of their antecedents in Decadence.[10] Looking back to them, we would see that, in hobbling its own impulse to effectivity, however unwittingly, cultural studies assures its innocence. From outside postmodern cultural studies, this search for purity, for relief from the historical burden of the West, seems its distinguishing mark. The decadents saw that innocence and effectivity did not easily mix, and Derrida occasionally seems to recognize that you cannot "get out of" the business of the West – call it logocentrism or whatever – simply by getting into another one. You have to get out of business altogether, and enter the monastery – there to embark upon the discipline of sterility. In practice, postmodernist cultural studies has submitted to this discipline; it lacks only the self-understanding to embrace it.

A postmodernist lesson by way of conclusion.

This brief exercise in historical comparison has a moral – and a postmodern one at that. The construction by postmodernists of "modernism" as a foil against which to claim radical newness has been insensitive to the complexity and difference that modernism has always included. It included the Decadents – foes of Truth – just as much as it did Husserl – its champion. In fact the attitudes of the Decadents were far more important to the ideology of literary modernism than were Husserl's.[11] Of course postmodernism *is* new in many respects, but in an important sense we have already been there and done that. Further, we have already done that in a context that reveals the complex inter-weavings of postmodernist themes within the variegated tapestry of the modern. Indeed, though it may be a rhetorical necessity for postmodernism to ignore this, since foils are useful in self-promotion, it represents a violation of some of the insights upon which postmodernism stakes its claim to novelty. The modern has no clear categorical structure; it never has been as monolithic as its critics imagine.

In the end, the example of the postmodern constitution of the modern does not, it appears, support de Man's thesis in *Blindness and Insight*. Though we may occasionally achieve insights by being blind to our announced critical principles, we just as often go astray. Vagrancy of this sort can be vivifying, but its results are not necessarily new: in thinking of postmodern cultural studies as *fin de siècle*, we are apt to be reminded of Wilde's (1982: 346) aside in "The Artist as Critic" that, "It has all the vitality of error, and all the tediousness of an old friend."

Notes

1. For instance, Scott Baker (1990) uses the honorific "radical" with embarrassing frequency in characterizing postmodernism.
2. Within postmodern cultural studies, Lemert (1992) appears to recognize its *fin de siècle* character. From without, Alexander (1991: 149) notes that "Postmodernism . . . is surely the expression of a *fin de siècle* antimodernist mood." Flanagan (1996) gives extensive consideration to the relation between postmodernism and the moral and aesthetic climate of the *fin de siècle*, though primarily from a moralistic angle.
3. An interesting compilation of mostly intramural criticisms of cultural studies will be found in Ferguson and Golding (1997).
4. The case for a consistent pattern to ends of centuries is made by Schwartz (1990). DeJean (1997) argues that the seventeenth and the twentieth centuries evidence a common complex of cultural themes distinctly different from the classic *fin de siècle*.
5. After Salomé has received the head of Iokanaan, Herod (Wilde, 1925: 181) says to Herodias, "She is monstrous, thy daughter; I tell thee she is monstrous."
6. As Carter (1958: 23) writes, "Varieties of homosexuality were especially popular. It is certain that this craving for the sexually abnormal arose from the belief that it was somehow artificial. Verlaine defined pederasty as '*un affranchissement de la lourde nature.*'"
7. Hyde (1975: 321) quotes Wilde as writing that "I became spendthrift of my genius, and to waste an eternal youth gave me a curious joy. Tired of being on the heights, I deliberately went to the depths in search of a new sensation. What paradox was to me in the sphere of thought, perversity became to me in the sphere of passion." A source is not given, but is presumably *De Profundis*.

8. See Seidman (1996). It is tempting to see an analogy to Henri Bergson's vitalism in this point of view.
9. For a relatively brief overview of the so-called Sokal incident and a bibliography of the primary documents, see Jardine and Frasca-Spada (1997). I note that decadent literature was also subjected to pastiche and parody: see, for instance, Gabriel Vicaire's *Les Déliquescences: poèmes décadents d'Adoré Floupette* of 1885.
10. Indeed, not all the Decadents themselves saw clearly. Anatole Baju, the peculiar figure who edited *Le Décadent*, often seems to have thought Decadence was a progressive movement about to effect change.
11. See again Wilson (1948). I note also that the portrait of artistic modernism by analysts subscribing to traditional critical standards often bears little resemblance to the postmodernist portrait. Take, for instance, Irving Howe in "The Idea of the Modern" (1967: 19, 26):

> Disdainful of certainties, disengaged from the eternal or any of its surrogates, fixated upon minute particulars of subjective experience, the modernist writer regards settled assumptions as a mask of death and literature as an agent of metaphysical revolt . . . Weariness sets in, and not merely with this or the other belief, but with the whole idea of belief.

References

Alexander, Jeffrey. 1991. "Sociological Theory and the Claim to Reason: Why the End is not in Sight." *Sociological Theory* 9:147–153.

Baju, Anatole. 1886. Article in *Le Décadent*, October 16.

Baker, Scott. 1990. "Reflection, Doubt, and the Place of Rhetoric in Postmodern Social Theory." *Sociological Theory* 8:232–245.

Bourget, Paul. 1924. *Essais de psychologie contemporaine*. Vol. 1. Paris: Plon.

Brombert, Victor. 1966. *The Novels of Flaubert: A Study of Themes and Techniques*. Princeton, NJ: Princeton University Press.

Carter, A. E. 1958. *The Idea of Decadence in French Literature*. Toronto: University of Toronto Press.

Cioran, E. M. 1968. *The Temptation to Exist*, trans. Richard Howard. Chicago, IL: Quadrangle Books.

1975. *A Short History of Decay*, trans. Richard Howard. New York: Viking Press.

DeJean, Joan. 1997. *Ancients Against Moderns: Culture Wars and the Making of a Fin de Siècle*. Chicago, IL: University of Chicago Press.

De Man, Paul. 1971. *Blindness and Insight: Essays in the Rhetoric of Contemporary Criticism*. New York: Oxford University Press.

Ferguson, Marjorie and Peter Golding, eds. 1997. *Cultural Studies in Question*. London: Sage Publications.

Fish, Stanley. 1995. *Professional Correctness: Literary Studies and Political Change*. Oxford: Clarendon Press.

Flanagan, Kieran. 1996. *The Enchantment of Sociology: A Study of Theology and Culture*. New York: St. Martin's Press.

Flaubert, Gustave. 1932. *Salambo*, trans. E. Powys Mathers. New York: Rarity Press.

Gautier, Theophile. 1930[1868]. "Notice" to Charles Baudelaire, *Fleurs du mal*. Paris: Calmann-Lévy.

Haraway, Donna. 1992. "The Promises of Monsters: A Regenerative Politics for Inappropriate/d Others," in Grossberg, Nelson, and Treichler, eds. *Cultural Studies*. New York: Routledge. Pp. 295–337.

Howe, Irving. 1967. "Introduction: The Idea of the Modern," in Irving Howe, ed. *The Idea of the Modern in Literature and the Arts*. New York: Horizon Press.

Husserl, Edmund. 1965. "The Crisis of European Man," in Husserl, *Phenomenology and the Crisis of Philosophy*, trans. Quentin Lauer. New York: Harper & Row Publishers.

Hyde, H. Montgomery. 1975. *Oscar Wilde*. New York: Farrar, Straus and Giroux.

Jardine, Nick and Marina Frasca-Spada. 1997. "Splendours and Miseries of the Science Wars." *Studies in History and Philosophy of Science* 28:219–235.

Lemert, Charles, 1992. "Series Editor's Preface," in Norman Denzin, ed. *Symbolic Interactionism and Cultural Studies: The Politics of Interpretation*. Oxford: Blackwell Publishers.

Nietzsche, Friedrich. 1969. *Ecce Homo*, trans. Walter Kaufmann, in *On the Genealogy of Morals/Ecce Homo*. New York: Vintage Books.

Schwartz, Hillel. 1990. *Century's End: A Cultural History of the Fin de Siècle from the 990s through the 1990s*. New York: Doubleday.

Seidman, Steven. 1996. "Introduction," in *Queer Theory/Sociology*, edited by Seidman. Cambridge, MA: Blackwell.

Valéry, Paul. 1947. *Monsieur Teste*, trans. Jackson Mathews. New York: A. A. Knopf.

Wilde, Oscar. 1925. *Salome*, trans. Alfred Douglas, in *The Writings of Oscar Wilde*, vol. IX. New York: Gabriel Wells.

 1968. *Literary Criticism of Oscar Wilde*, ed. Stanley Weintraub. Lincoln, NE: University of Nebraska Press.

 1982. *The Artist as Critic: Critical Writings of Oscar Wilde*, ed. Richard Ellmann. Chicago, IL: University of Chicago Press.

Wilson, Edmund. 1948. *Axel's Castle: A Study in the Imaginative Literature of 1870–1930*. New York: Charles Scribner's Sons.

PART II

Sacred and profane

5

Private devotions and the sacred heart of Elvis: the Durkheimians and the [re]turn of the sacred

Richard D. Hecht

It's not the corpse of that woman but the destiny of Argentina. Or both things, which to so many people seem to be one. Heaven only knows how the useless dead body of Eva Duarte came to be confused with the country. Not for people like you or me. To the poverty-stricken, to the immigrant, to those who are outside of history. They would let themselves be killed for the corpse. If it had rotted away, that would have been the end of that. But by embalming it, you made history change place. You left history inside. Whoever has the woman has the country in the palm of their hand, do you realize? The government cannot allow a corpse like that to drift about.

Tomás Eloy Martínes, Santa Evita

Social theorists of the first half of our century reached consensus or at least widely agreed that economic progress and the modernization of society would lead to the withering away and perhaps even the disappearance altogether of religion by the century's end. Religion was moribund, a procrustean remnant that had persisted into modernity largely as result of superstition, myth, and irrationalism, bound to be replaced, they argued, by an emergent society which would be tolerant, rational, pragmatic, progressive, humanistic, and secular. Of course, the second half of the century has not gone according to plan. Economic and social modernization became global, leaving no society or social order untouched, but this was unexpectedly accompanied by a similarly omnipresent global "awakening" of religion.

Some extreme forms of this global revival of religion, what one scholar has called *la revanche de Dieu*, are well documented and well studied. Here, I am speaking of that curious form of religiosity given name as "fundamentalism" by journalists in the late 1970s. But these forms of religious resurgence which have swept significant portions of the global community, represent only the tip of the iceberg, a relatively small portion of this phenomenon. Samuel Huntington notes that, despite the dramatic and explosive quality of these religious movements, they are "only the surface waves of a much broader and more fundamental religious tide that is giving a different cast to human life at the end of the twentieth century. The renewal of religion throughout the world far transcends the activities of fundamentalist extremists" (Huntington, 1996: 96). Religion pervades daily life in society after society, and it does so unexplosively, unspectacularly, undramatically; it is part of the normal business of human social life.

There is much good news in this particular failure of prophecy. Not only should the study of religion thrive in this environment, I would hope that this resurgence will reposition religion as a central domain in the human sciences for reflection on social life. The manifestations of the sacred, its constructions and deconstructions can no longer be relegated to the periphery, to alienation, projection, false-consciousness, meta-justifications for the structuration of the material world. Religion is as central to our projects of understanding and analysis as gender, class, and race; indeed, it may eclipse them.

Irrespective of the failed prophecy of the disappearance of religion, the social theorists' model had an important flaw. It presumed that religion was continually disappearing, being eroded by progressive social policy, economic development, and the unrelenting march of rationalism. This may have been more a wish than an accurate analysis of the place of religion in twentieth-century life. Indeed, the argument could be made that religion continued to be a substantial element in social life and only appeared to erupt in the forms of "divine vengeance" which have characterized the revival of religion in the last decades of our century. Here I would like to argue that, like the social theorists, students of religion have overlooked the analytic power and implications of what many refer to as the "later Durkheim." Durkheim is not just one of the powerful ancestors whose name and thought must be mastered as part of the history of our disciplines and fields. There is still much to be learned from him and, in some respects, his analysis of the relationships between religion and society have profound implications for how we understand religion at the end of the century. But, I would also like to suggest that Durkheim's later thought in which he attempted to trace out these comprehensive relationships is missing an important element, an analysis of language which undergirds the symbolic order. Durkheim saw what he called "effervescence" as the dynamic which created collective representations. He saw this dynamic only in explosive situations. Effervescence may be short-lived or more durative but it appears when the order of society or its central institutions are threatened. Here, I will argue that effervescence is a much more common phenomenon than he was able to establish in his later work. Indeed, the processes of the sacral construction of society and culture are ever-present. They are not extraordinary, but thoroughly normal and ordinary.

Trouble with corpses

Andrew Lloyd Weber and Madonna have given us nothing short of a popular musical hagiography of a contemporary saint, so popular that "Evita" (alongside "Cats") has remained one of the most omnipresent contemporary "light operas" of the past fifty years. Eva Perón's ballad from the balcony of La Casa Rossatta as the regime seems to be on the verge of collapse and her own death draws near has been transformed into a love song, a love song which conceals the multiple evils of Perónist politics, a political order modeled on the fascisms of Italy, Spain, and Germany. Audiences are enthralled by the young woman, so beautiful, who "works" her way up from tawdry "hostess" and bar singer to the very centers of Argentine wealth and power, and by the end has taken it all. Her life and death were infused with the hopes and desires of landless peasants and impoverished laborers.

Andrew Lloyd Weber and Madonna got it right. Eva Duarte had become a saint and in many respects the social and religious processes surrounding her exemplify the dynamics of sacralizing the body so well described by Peter Brown in the world of late antiquity and in the rise of Latin Christianity. Brown rejects what he calls the "two-tiered" model of the growth of Christianity in which the assumed mass conversions of Roman citizens in the wake of Constantine's conversion forced the hands of the church's leaders into accepting a wide variety of pagan practices, most importantly the cult of the saints, which represents a repackaging of the older and classical ideas surrounding mythological heroes. By rejecting this model, Brown has demonstrated that what is often called "popular religion" of late antiquity and the early Middle Ages becomes a dynamic process of religious change and transformation which reflects the changing patterns of human relations in late-Roman society. He writes that the rise of the cult of saints is not a dialogue between the elite and the common people or the few and the many, but rather "part of a greater whole – the lurching forward of an increasing proportion of late-antique society toward radically new forms of reverence, shown to new objects in new places, orchestrated by new leaders, and deriving momentum from the need to play out the common preoccupation of all, the few and the 'vulgar' alike with new forms of the exercise of power, new bonds of human dependence, new, intimate, hopes for protection and justice in a changing world" (Brown, 1981: 21–22).

Brown provides many examples of this dynamic process, but one is instructive for our purposes here. In 385 the residents of Milan were greatly excited by the discovery of the relics of Saints Gervasius and Protasius. Already the hillsides around Milan were dotted with the *memoriae* or graves of martyrs, but this was the first time that relics had been discovered in Milan. Brown notes that what was most unusual about this discovery was the speed and determination with which

Milan's Bishop Ambrose laid claim to and appropriated the relics. The relics were quickly moved from the shrine of Saints Felix and Nabor where they had been uncovered to the new basilica which Bishop Ambrose had built for himself, placing them under the new altar. Through this act, Gervasius and Protasius were linked to the liturgy of the community in the central church built by the bishop. They would no longer be available to only the few select people who visited the shrine of Saints Felix and Nabor but to the whole community. Encased in the altar, the relics were now directly related to the episcopal eucharistic liturgy. Brown concludes that "Ambrose had not 'introduced' the cult of the martyrs into Milan, still less had he merely acquiesced passively to previous practices. His initiatives had been firm and in many ways unusual: he had been prepared both to move the bodies and to link them decisively to the altar of a new church. Rather, he was like an electrician who rewires an antiquated wiring system: more power could pass through stronger, better-insulated wires toward the bishop as leader of the community" (Brown, 1981: 37).

Using Brown's metaphor, Ambrose created a new wiring system through which power flowed to the bishop and his community. Brown then sees the integration of the relics of Gervasius and Protasius as a reflection of the centralizing power of the church, indeed that centralizing power is dependent upon the integration of some specialized *memoriae* downtown and not in suburbia. In short, there is no acquiescence to what the church might have understood as *superstitio* but a conscious politic involving corpses. Of course, the potency of the corpse is overlooked by Andrew Lloyd Weber and Madonna. Better get out the handkerchiefs and shed a few tears for the withering beauty, her body slowly dissipating through the ravages of cancer. But the troubling and powerful dimension of the body or the corpse is not overlooked by Tomás Eloy Martínes who makes the control of the corpse central to his recasting of the narrative of Santa Evita. He clearly understands that the body symbolizes something else. In life and death it has become a representation of the collectivity. His detective tells the embalmer who had sought to make Evita more beautiful in death than in life at the order of Juan Perón that "by embalming it, you made history change place. You left history inside. Whoever has the woman has the country in the palm of their hand, do you realize? The government cannot allow a corpse like that to drift about."

But let us not leave the dead too quickly. We continue with two more exemplary phenomena, both having to do with corpses as suggested by my epigraph, closer to us in time and space than either Evita or Saints Gervasius and Protasiusas. The urban landscape is increasingly marked by instant memorial shrines which appear at street corners, store-fronts, freeway overpasses, sidewalks, telephone poles, and parks. These memorials mark the places where a child was run down by a drunk-driver, where teenagers where killed in a shoot-out with a rival gang, where a store-owner was murdered in a holdup gone awry, or where an individual jumped to his death from a freeway bridge. These memorial shrines, perhaps very comparable to the *memoriae* around the urban center of fourth-century Milan, are often quite simple, made of jumbled collections of flowers, candles, testimonials, cards, photographs, offerings of food, and poems. We, of course, are now much more aware of these instant *memoria* in their massive forms after the bombing of the Alfred P. Murrah Federal Building in Oklahoma City, the deaths of Princess Diana and John F. Kennedy Jr., and the destruction of the World Trade Center. Rituals emerge at these sites. The last journeys of those to whom the shrines are dedicated are traced as ritual peregrinations; where they went from the restaurant to the movie theater and then the walk to where they died. In the simple, local *memoriae*, a mother visits the shrine marking the place where her son committed suicide and weekly reads a poem she wrote and first read at the church memorial service: "The woman sits in her garden under her geraniums and listens to the cars . . . on Lincoln Boulevard and thinks about that awful day. She cries, great heaves from her chest, her face old like her grandmother's." They are private devotions constructed in public spaces. Some disintegrate and vanish as quickly as they appear, while others seem to take on a more lasting quality, attracting relatively large numbers of people who regularly visit them and replace their flowers and candles, and who did not know the individuals for whom these private devotions were originally intended. For example, in Los Angeles a shrine appeared at the Denker Avenue Recreation Center near Exposition Park in April 1993 for a former member of the Crips gang slain by rival Bloods as he sat on a park bench. This gang member's shrine was made up of flowers in 800 malt liquor bottle "vases" and a paper plate of fried chicken. Another memorial is for an aspiring actor, well known in his neighborhood, who was shot and killed in an apparent robbery while walking home, hand-in-hand with his lover. One visitor left the following note: "I don't know you but I miss you. You will not be forgotten." In Santa Monica, another shrine marks the place where four young people were killed by a drunk driver in 1992. This shrine is tended by one of the victims' fathers, who faithfully visits the site on his way to work. He sweeps up around the shrine, replaces the wilted flowers, and, from time to time, adds a new composite photograph of the four victims and ties a new Mothers Against Drunk Driving ribbon to a pole near the shrine. At an intersection in the middle of the agricultural plain north of Camarillo, California is a small shrine made of three simple white crosses, marking the place where the car carrying three teenagers sped off the road and crashed into an irrigation ditch, killing all three. Their deaths were alcohol-related and, once a month, one of the mothers of those teenagers visits the site, strengthens the crosses blown over by the wind, and replaces the flowers she has brought every week for five years since the accident occurred.

One is tempted to interpret these shrines to the dead through psychologisms. One Los Angeles professor of religion commented that Americans as a nation in particular "have difficulty making public statements about tragic deaths. This [the shrines] fulfills a social need, an emotional need, perhaps even a religious need. In some countries," he continued, "the wailing is very, very vocal, very public, but we don't like the idea of public spectacles where people tear their hair and cry out in agony. This is a public statement that is acceptable" (Beyette, 1996). In other words, in the face of meaningless and random death, our emotional need is to mourn, but that is done with almost Quaker sobriety. However, I think that these shrines are really more important than an acceptable public demonstration of private pain and loss. Something else may be lurking here which draws them closer to the *memoriae* around Milan in the fourth century than to a modern psychological release.[1]

Edward T. Linenthal has written the best study of American memorial culture as it is seen in the memorialization of the bombing and its victims at the Federal Building in Oklahoma City. He speaks of a "memorial energy" which burst forth and infused a fence and tree near the site of the bombing. He writes that these memorializations were "in part a protest against the anonymity of mass death. These victims of violence would not be forgotten. Their deaths would be redeemed by becoming public. The specter of meaningless death would be contained through the physical presence of individual memorial chairs and through the civic rhetoric of 'lessons' of the bombing" (Linenthal, 2001: 233). This memorial energy is often unplanned for and unexpected, as we have seen in the Vietnam Veterans Memorial. Kristin Ann Hass (1996) has shown at the Vietnam Memorial that this energy has also been very difficult to control and shape. She understands that the rubbings of names and the now hundreds of thousands of objects and notes left at the Wall represent a democratization of the desire to memorialize. But, it is also the case that these memorial energies, as Linenthal describes them, have the power to transform landscapes, as Kenneth E. Foote (1997) has shown through the dynamics of sanctification, designation, rectification, and obliteration.

The second exemplary phenomenon is the decennial anniversary of the death of Elvis Presley held in Memphis over a nine-day period in August 1987 and heralded as "The Elvis International Tribute Week." The national press estimated that the events of the decennial drew approximately 50,000 participants, while the Memphis Chamber of Commerce put the number much higher.[2] The "pilgrims" and "devotees" as they were called in almost all of the accounts were treated to a myriad of memorials, including an Elvis trivia contest (which was won by knowing which Elvis movie was based on the novel *Kiss My Firm But Pliant Lips*; the correct answer was *Live a Little, Love a Little*), an Elvis Legacy Laser-light Show, the World Elvis Impersonator Competition (including the midget Elvis impersonators), and the Elvis Presley Karate Tournament. Much of the city's business community participated in the anniversary, with many stores installing tributes to the singer in their shop windows or announcing the schedule of autograph sessions with those who knew Elvis. The Memphis Hyatt Regency hotel advertised a "rare intimate dining experience" for the pilgrims which featured the family-style "food he loved, prepared the way he loved it by his trusted friend and cook, Nancy Rooks." The courtyard of the Days Inn near the Graceland mansion was transformed into an American town square dedicated to Presley. The motel's windows framed vivid tableaux with hand-sequined jump suits, memorabilia, American flags, hand-painted signs, and buttons with slogans such as "Don't Blame Me I Voted for Elvis."

Every night during the anniversary, the pilgrims congregated for memorials, candle-lightings, and vigils outside the walled Graceland compound and plazas throughout the city. Like pilgrims to any religious site they brought flowered gifts which were placed at the foot of the statue of Elvis in downtown Memphis or at the gate of the mansion. They left their pilgrim's mark, ex-votos, on the stones of Graceland's walls; "ELVIS IS LOVE," "I DID DRUGS WITH ELVIS," and "ELVIS DIDN'T DESERVE TO BE WHITE." Like any other major religious center, the pilgrims maintained a fixed itinerary, first standing in long lines to visit the Graceland mansion, posing for photographs entering the mansion or with Elvis' horse, then following the guided tours through the compound, beginning with the house where they visited Elvis' mirrored TV room, displays of the clothes he and Priscilla wore on their wedding day and the replica of their wedding cake, his motorcycle, his jumpsuits and army uniform, a hallway of his gold records, ending with a graveside visit in the meditation garden, and then finally to the emergency entrance of the city's Baptist Hospital where Elvis was pronounced dead at 3:30 P.M. on August 16, 1977. Prayer services were held in the hospital's parking lot and each day, men and women would collapse in uncontrollable weeping, overcome by the emotion of the site, and the heat and humidity.[3] Memphis became a complex sacred space for the pilgrims with Graceland the very center, the *axis mundi* which connects the human world to the divine. For Karal Ann Marling the small hill upon which the mansion is perched made it closer to heaven, much like the complex symbolisms of elevation in sacred centers. She writes "[P]hysically aloof from the road below, the house had even more private and secret zones inside, determined solely by elevation. Friends hung out in the basement and played pool. Visitors were entertained on the main floor. But the staircase to the second floor was always a kind of Jacob's Ladder, often contemplated, seldom climbed. The King's Room was at the top, at the apex of the mystery, behind a pair of golden doors." The upstairs is closed to the pilgrims, but Marling notes that, as they pass through the foyer, all eyes turn to the staircase that leads to some ethereal realm. In death, she continues, he lay at the foot of the staircase "to say goodbye to his fans before he disappeared forever into the final mystery that lingers over Graceland still, like a stormcloud above the earthly Jerusalem, confounding understanding" (Marling, 1996: 153). Of course "The King" is not only "King" of rock and roll, but still another symbol of the center. Universally, kings are the centers of the world, the navel of the world which connects the mundane to the transcendent. In its ancient Near Eastern formulation, the king is the pivot between the world of humans and the world of gods. He represents the people to the divine and the divine to the people.

In many respects, the pilgrimage to Graceland is similar to pilgrimages involving other mythical figures of modernity. For example, James Dean has maintained an intense following here and abroad. Two important pilgrimages have developed around Dean. The first is to Fairmont, Indiana, the small farming-town where Dean was born. This pilgrimage is held on the last full weekend of September to commemorate Dean's death on September 30, 1955. Each year the pilgrimage of the curious and Dean devotees has grown since "Museum Days" and "James Dean Weekend" were established in 1968. Approximately 20,000 visitors come to the town where the James Dean Gallery is usually the first stop on the pilgrims' itinerary. Here they gaze upon one of the largest collections of James Dean sacred memorabilia in the world, including the jeans he wore in the movie "Giant," faded scripts bearing notations in his own handwriting, and a host of mementos from his high-school days. The "Deaners," as Fairmont's residents refer to them, participate in rituals of identity which bond them to the presence of this saint-figure, including a James Dean look-alike contest, a memorial service at the local church, a James Dean street fair, and, finally, a visit to his grave. Throughout the year, visitors leave their ex-votos at the graveside, including cigarettes, flowers, candles, love notes, pictures, medallions, and even cans of beer. In some cases, the pilgrims stand in silent devotion while others sing songs, recite poetry, or play music.[4]

On the West Coast, on the same weekend, a second pilgrimage is organized by We Remember Dean International, the star's fan club. Each year approximately 100 members of the fan club participate in what they refer to as the James Dean Memorial Run from Santa Monica City College, where Dean attended classes before going on to UCLA, to Cholame, 40 miles east of Paso Robles, approximately 230 miles north of Los Angeles, where Dean's Porsche Spyder collided with another car. The largest group of participants has been the South Bay Cruisers, a car club whose members all drive hotrods from the 1930s, 40s, 50s, and 60s. There are chop-jobs, mag wheels, chrome headers, tuck-and-roll, superchargers, and fuel-injection on all these muscle cars. The pilgrims leave Santa Monica at 6:00 A.M. and reach Cholame at noon, after breakfasting in different locations in Santa Barbara, San Luis Obispo, and Paso Robles. They first stop at a restaurant, approximately a quarter-mile from the scene of the accident. The restaurant has long since stopped serving any food and now specializes in selling the memorabilia of pilgrimage, t-shirts, jackets, sweat-shirts, key chains, replica movie posters, books, coffee mugs, high-ball glasses, cigarette lighters, and pictures, all with the James Dean theme.

In 1987, I accompanied the pilgrims from Santa Barbara to Cholame. The souvenirs and memorabilia are part of the economy of pilgrimage, in which pilgrims want to take something back from the center of the world to their homes on the periphery, far from where the presence of the semi-divine being is located. After the pilgrims have purchased these sacred artifacts, they reassemble in a circle around a tree which they call the Tree of Heaven next to the restaurant. At the base of the tree is a memorial sculpture done by the Japanese artist Seita Ohnishi. The leader of the run recites the narrative which is inscribed on the sculpture. The narrative notes that very near here Dean was killed in the crash, summarizes the list of films he appeared in, and then concludes the brief life of the saint with these words: "Everyday, somewhere in the world, at the cinema or on television, James Dean lives on. Cinema is no longer just celluloid. Every day we find reminders that the drama of James Dean is the theme that we live." He is, in short, a universal saint. He is accessible everywhere through his films. And then the narration provides his power to save and redeem, to heal and mediate. What is the drama we all live which is presented in the paradigm of his life?

He was a youth yearning for one precious touch of warmth between parents and their off-spring. He was an individual struggling in this huge land of infinite promise and many races. He was a rebel searching for that cause we must all possess. This young man, seemingly ordinary yet possessing a talent and individuality that were unique in their combination, has come to personify a generation awakened.

Many are those who feel strongly that James Dean should not be forgotten. There are some things, like the hatred that accompanies war, that are best forgotten. There are others, like the nobler qualities of man, to which this young actor directed our attention, that should be preserved for all time.

James Dean is all the more with us today because his life was so fleeting. In Japan, we say that his death came as suddenly as it does to cherry blossoms. The petals of early spring fall at the height of their ephemeral brilliance.

Death in youth is life that glows eternal.[5]

In this hagiolatric aretology, Dean becomes the patron saint of families and those individuals who are in their hearts rebels with a cause. He awakens a generation to their full potential as individuals.

However, the decennial anniversary for Elvis Presley was in scale and scope a much larger phenomenon and was the first real inkling that most Americans who did not read the tabloids had of the depth and extent of the adoration of Elvis Presley, a strange new piety which seemed to have its origins in the American south and attracted increasing numbers of the lower middle class. The often presumed bizarre quality of his devotion now began to register in the mainsteam of American society and religion. One of the most popular icons of this devotion drawn by Christopher Rywalt, reprinted time and time again, was a portrait of Elvis in the traditional role of the Virgin Mary. Around his head is a halo; his upper torso draped in the robes of the Virgin; his right hand raised in the gesture of the crucifixion; in the center of his chest, the sacred heart of Jesus. In popular iconography, this thoroughly American saint had become completely androgynous.

By the decennial, there was already an extensive body of documents attesting to post-mortem sightings of Elvis or counter-narratives which provided the faithful with an alternative to the official account of his death. Consider the following as only one very abbreviated account:

A self-centered Yuppie, just coming out of a bitter and ruinous divorce, goes hiking on the Appalachian Trail in search of peace and some answers to the meaning of his meaningless lifestyle. He meets a fellow hiker, a tall quiet man named . . . John Burrows. They camp together, share a fire and a meal. That night, under the stars, Burrows relates his philosophy, a mixture of Christianity and Buddhism, tough love and New Age mysticism. He gently guides the Yuppie to a reevaluation of his wasted life, his shallow values, and his lapsed religious convictions, leading him toward an understanding of the magnitude of God's works and the bottomless resources of God's mercy and love. They talk all night, and by the time the first hint of dawn touches a nearby mountain, the Yuppie has faith to move that mountain, and he literally sees the light.

When he awakens later that day, the wise stranger has vanished. He has left a note, admitting that his name is not John Burrows, but he cannot reveal his true identity. He wishes the young man "the best, in your long struggle into the light."

Days later, back home, he sees a TV show about Elvis Presley and learns that John Burrows was an alias he often used.   (Strausbaugh, 1995: 134)

Those familiar with the New Testament will immediately recognize the genre of this "Elvis sighting" narrative. It belongs to the genre of post-resurrection appearances of the risen Christ. But, it also belongs to a more widespread genre involving the reappearance of sacred personages, equally present in narratives of traditional shamans, the *theos aner* of the Hellenistic world, or traditions of the Buddha's reappearance after death or his successive incarnations in other Buddhas. For example, Philostratus' third-century biography of the holy man Apollonius of Tyana whose life spanned the first century concludes with Apollonius' disappearance, or assumption into heaven, from a temple in

Crete. According to the narrative, Apollonius came to the temple of Dictynna late at night. The temple was guarded by savage dogs who became silent as the holy man approached. The custodians of the temple, who accused him of using some magical or charmed morsel to silence the canine guardians, seized Apollonius and bound him, accusing him of being a wizard or a temple robber. However, at the midnight hour he released himself and ran to the doors of the temple which opened for him. He entered and disappeared in its darkened interior, the doors closing after him as mysteriously as they had opened. From within the temple came the sound of maidens singing, "Go from the earth; go into Heaven; go." This aretology concludes with Apollonius appearing to mortals after his assumption in order to preach that the soul is immortal (Conybeare, 1969: 401–405). Philostratus wrote this account under the patronage of the empress Julia Domna, who perhaps saw this holy man's aretology as a counter-narrative to the aretologies of Jesus. Apparently, Philostratus did his work so well that Alexander Severus placed a statue of Apollonius in his private chapel alongside Orpheus, Alexander the Great, Abraham, and Jesus.

Of course some would argue that the contemporary *memoriae* and the sacralization of Elvis Presley or James Dean are fundamentally different from the late-antique religious transformations described by Peter Brown or in classical aretologies. For example, Mark Gottdiener argues that the "Dead Elvis" is a complex sign system in which the "vast commodified domain of material objects that signify Elvis functions principally through images that iconically represent his body" (Gottdiener, 1997: 197). The sign system is manifested in the thousands of objects which are identified with the Dead Elvis, from ashtrays, drinking glasses, liquor decanters, buttons, etc., and the growing number of Elvis impersonators. For Gottdiener, this endless replication of Elvis is a result of the commodification of late capitalism and is thus distinctive from earlier forms of religious expression; and he reasons that, as commodification continues in an ever-expanding circle of production, the adoration of the Dead Elvis will become stronger. Commodification produces its own logic of consumption, of supply and demand. But is this commodification any different than the proliferation of relics of earlier saint figures or the symbolic economic system which dominates all pilgrimage centers and which allows the pilgrim to connect the center and the periphery? Certainly the *translationes* narratives from the mid-tenth century through mid-twelfth century which depict a large-scale industry of production and movement of saint relics from place to place attest to a similar commodification (Geary, 1978). Here the only difference can be one of scale.

Just as contemporary memorials are counter-narratives to the dominant forms of memorialization, there are counter-narratives to the Dead Elvis. This has been brilliant argued by José David Saldivar who has interpreted the southern

California performance artist El Vez (Robert Lopez) whose political songs not only reflect *la frontera*, the Borderland, but also construct it. In his 1994 song "Immigration Time," which blends Elvis' "Suspicious Minds" with the Rolling Stones "Sympathy for the Devil," El Vez reveals and subverts the moral hypocrisy of California's and the US government's immigration policy as it relates to undocumented Mexican workers. Saldivar transcribes the following verses:

> I'm caught in a trap, I can't walk out
> Because my foot's caught in the border fence
> Why can't you see, Statue of Liberty
> I'm your homeless, tired, and weary.
> We can go on together, it's Immigration Time.
> And we can build our dreams, it's Immigration Time.
> Yes I'm trying to go, get out of Mexico
> The promised land waits on the other side.
> Here they come again, they're trying to fence me in
> Wanting to live with the brave and the home of the free . . .

Saldivar argues that El Vez's "Immigration Time" is a ritual practice enacting Americanization. He does not reject other ethno-racial groups whose icons and narratives have become the national archetypes, but rather captures them, aligning, Saldivar writes, "the plight of undocumented Mexican workers with those archetypes and symbologies" that are part and parcel of the national imaginary (Saldivar, 1997: 193–194). El Vez's "Immigration Time" neutralizes the American nativist tradition of which Elvis as "Good Ol' Boy" (in which he is a miracle of native southern soil, the righteous vindication of an oppressed region and its people, a folk hero, and an angel loved by God) is central and replaces it with a link to the most central paradigms of American consciousness – the immigrant.

The Durkheimian tradition lost and found

The private devotions and body of Elvis are embedded in complex social systems and come to represent more than what they appear to be, isolated social phenomena. They are in short examples of what Emile Durkheim described as collective representations. Collective representation was one of the central dynamics of Durkheim's analysis of the relationship between religion and society and in many ways the very heart of his *Les Formes élémentaires de la vie religieuse*, published in 1912. Most histories of the study of religion mark 1912 and the publication of Durkheim's *The Elementary Forms of the Religious Life* as a watershed year; for some it marks the beginning of the modern study of religion, bringing to closure many of the intellectual trends of the nineteenth century while initiating new methods with more enduring results.[6] Durkheim rejects most, if not all, the evolutionary theories of religion that appeared in the second half of the nineteenth century, including E. B. Tylor's "animism," R. R. Marett's "pre-animism," and also Sir James Frazer's implicit distinction between "magic" and "religion." Certainly, he was interested in the totem, the fetish, and magic but not because they reflected the earliest forms of religion. His use of *élémentaires* does not mean the simplest in an evolutionary scheme. Durkheim understood "elementary" to mean the simplest, that which would allow us to see precisely the religious nature of humans, and to reveal to us an essential and permanent aspect of all human life. Karen E. Field suggests that *élémentaire* has the sense of "elemental" or the "elementary particles" of particle physics, the fundamental building blocks of reality. Paraphrasing a physicist, she writes these forms have an underlying identity that persists despite unceasing change and limitless diversity (Durkheim, 1995: lix–lx).

The second dynamic in his analysis of the elementary particles of religion is the fundamental dichotomy between sacred and profane. This dichotomy is built into his very definition of religion. He writes "[A] religion is a unified system of beliefs and practices relative to sacred things, that is to say, things set apart and forbidden – beliefs and practices which unite into a single moral community called a Church, all those who adhere to them" (Durkheim, 1995: 44). He quickly adds that the idea of religion cannot be separated from the idea of a church and thus religion is always a matter of the collective. In other words, religion cannot be separate from the social order. The sacred and profane are bound to the social order and this is precisely how he understood collective representations. They are not "representations" but always *collective* representations. Durkheim underscores this time and again. He writes, for example, "[T]he general conclusion of the chapters to follow is that religion is an eminently social thing. Religious representations are collective representations that express collective realities; rites are ways of acting that are born only in the midst of assembled groups and whose purpose is to evoke, maintain, or recreate certain mental states of those groups" (Durkheim, 1995: 9). Further, these collective representations are the result, according to Durkheim, of immense cooperation which extends through time and space. The production of these representations is thus the result of multitudes of different minds who have combined their ideas over generations of experience and elaboration (Durkheim, 1995: 15). The collective representation then is a much richer and more complex "intellectuality" than that of any individual. This leads Durkheim to a very specific anthropology. The human being is a dual being. On the one hand, the human is limited to his or her immediate sphere of influence. But each is also a social being. Durkheim concludes that "[I]n the realm of practice, the consequence of this duality in our nature is the irreducibility of the moral idea to the utilitarian motive; in the realm of thought, it is the irreducibility of reason to individual experience. As part of society, the individual naturally transcends himself both when he thinks and when he acts" (Durkheim, 1995: 16).

Certainly, the dichotomy of the sacred and profane has proven to be one of the most long-lasting contributions of the *Elementary Forms*, and he had advanced components of dichotomy long before its publication in 1912. Indeed, his students, Henri Hubert and Marcel Mauss, first made this dichotomy central to their interpretation of the generic and structural unity of sacrifice more than a decade before Durkheim enunciated his complete theory. For Hubert and Mauss, sacrifice is a ritual procedure which establishes a connection between the sacred and the profane through the mediation of the sacrificial victim or offering (Hubert and Mauss, 1899). Durkheim's thinking on this dichotomy continued to evolve in his work. In the *Elementary Forms*, the sacred and profane are described as oppositional categories, but in later work they appear to be more dialectically related.

Durkheim did not ontologize the sacred which remains here a relational category. The radical ontologizing of the sacred was left to Rudolf Otto whose *Das Heilige*, published in 1917, made the sacred into a *sui generis* category of experience, irreducible to the sum total of the empirical world. Otto, very much the Protestant theologian, does not construe his argument as a positive science as Durkheim had. There are no elemental particles in Otto, just the Holy which breaks into the world of human experience throughout history. Otto was of course a comparativist of sorts and he uses the Holy as a convention for moving between and among religious traditions. For Otto, the argument is essentially textual. In all languages where there is a term which can be translated as the holy or the sacred their essential meaning is that which is separate. The manifestation of the holy is characterized by the sacred's *mysterium tremendum* and its *fascinans*. The *mysterium* suggests the total otherness of the holy, its radical alterity from the empirical world. The *tremendum* frightens us, fills us with awe, and repels us. But the manifestation of the holy is also accompanied by *fascinans*. It fascinates and draws us to it. Otto's formulation is squarely located within the Kantian tradition of establishing the *sine qua non* of religion and is essentially a category of individual experience, interpretation, and valuation peculiar to religion, not the social order. While Durkheim rejects evolutionary ideas about religion in favor of his elemental particles of analysis, Otto returns to the evolutionary account of religion. The experience of sacred, with its twin human responses, leads Otto to consider how the awesome power of the sacred is lost or dissipated. He describes this as "schematization" in which gradually the *mysterium tremendum* and the *fascinans* are balanced and thus filled with ethical content. So, for Otto, still the Christian theologian, the New Testament reveals a higher level of schematization than the Old Testament or Hebrew Bible, the Church Fathers still higher, the medieval scholastics still higher, and the very pinnacle is reached in Martin Luther. In Luther there is a perfect balance between God's wrath and God's love. Protestantism in its earliest formulation is the highest expression of religion. Yet, Otto's formulation of the irreducibility of the sacred stands as the foundation of much of the phenomenology of religion in later decades of the century.

The *Elementary Forms of the Religious Life* is the watershed text for the study of religion. But students of religion know little of Durkheim's earlier work. And the opposite situation applies to the social theorists who identify Durkheim most with his works from the early to mid-1890s, *The Division of Labor in Society* (1893), *The Rules of the Sociological Method* (1895), and *Suicide* (1897), where collective representation and the dichotomy of sacred and profane are virtually absent and where his emphasis is on the social operations of external constraints and coercive social facts. In these works Durkheim's methods are positivistic and quantitative. The later Durkheim has been lost for the social theorists.

Jeffrey Alexander has underscored how different Durkheim's work from the mid-1890s to his death is from the earlier, purely sociological works. For Alexander, the later works reveal a profound change and attest to the emergence of what he describes as a cultural program in which Durkheim came to understand that secular social processes have to be modeled upon the sacred world. Alexander writes that, in his monographs and lectures from this period, "Durkheim developed a theory of secular society that emphasized the independent causal importance of symbolic classification, the pivotal role of the symbolic division between sacred and profane, the social significance of ritual behavior, and the close interrelationship between symbolic classifications, ritual processes and the formation of social solidarities" (Alexander, 1988: 2). Alexander further notes Durkheim chose to announce and systematically begin the development of this new theory which he called his "religious sociology" in a work that largely appears to be about archaic or aboriginal religion and thus today about concerns other than sociological.

Durkheim, however, was keenly aware that this might be a possible reading of *Elementary Forms* and in the introduction tells the reader that his work is not solely of interest to what he calls "science of religion." He continues that there "is an aspect of every religion that transcends the realm of specifically religious ideas. Through it, the study of religious phenomena provides a means of revisiting problems that until now have been debated only among philosophers" (Durkheim, 1995: 8). Durkheim's project is thus not limited to specific religious traditions but generalizable to something more universal, epistemological and metaphysical problems which have long occupied the attention of philosophers. But he hints at his larger agenda and project as he continues. The first systems of representations that humans made of their worlds and themselves were religious in origin. He writes that there "is no religion that is not both a cosmology and a speculation about the divine. If philosophy and the sciences were born in religion, it is because religion itself began by serving as science and philosophy. Further, and less often noted, religion has not merely enriched a human intellect already formed but in fact has helped to form it. Men owe to religion not only the content of their knowledge, in significant part, but also the form in which that knowledge is elaborated" (Durkheim, 1995: 8). Here, Durkheim does not make the argument as so many of his generation did that religion was a kind of primitive science and philosophy generated by human fear and a desperate desire to control the forces of a hostile world around them. Religion is not only the content of thought, but informs and structures it. By making this argument he sets the foundation for a much bolder analysis in which all of society could be understood as structured by the fundamentals of religion, the sacred and the profane. And that is exactly how Alexander reads Durkheim. In *Elementary Forms* he selects aboriginal religion not simply because of the pleasures which ensue from describing its peculiarities, but because it yields the essential religious nature of humans and shows us a permanent aspect of human society. Alexander reasons that, if Durkheim had lived longer, he would have demonstrated that education, politics, professional organization, morality, and the law must be studied in terms of symbolic classifications. They are structured by tensions between the sacred and profane; their central social processes are ritualistic; their most significant structural dynamics concern the construction and destruction of social solidarities (Alexander, 1988: 3). The sacred and the profane becomes the master dialectic which produces all of society.

Alexander sketches out the history of the Durkheimian project pointing to its influence in both the semiotics of Ferdinand Saussure and the structuralism of Claude Lévi-Strauss. From both Saussure and Lévi-Strauss, according to Alexander, come some of the most important contemporary cultural movements, including Roland Barthes' examination of the systems of symbolic classification that regulate a wide array of secular institutions and social processes, from fashions and food production to civil conflict. And, for Alexander, postmodernists like Foucault have carried the Durkheimian emphasis on central social power of the sacred and profane even further into the social domain through the structuring power of symbolic patterns or discourses (Alexander, 1988: 5). But the larger and more comprehensive Durkheimian cultural program was mostly lost in the study of religion and in sociological studies. In part, this was the result of the search for more elaborate quantifiable methods of research among social scientists. Likewise, among students of religion, little was done with Durkheim's work accept to enter it into to the genealogy of the modern study of religion, especially with regard to how it provided a theoretical justification for the sacralization of society. Among students of religion the Durkheimian program was seen to conceal a subtle reduction of the sacred to the social. The latter, of course, was the result of a very narrow reading of Durkheim, especially when the study of religion had not fully emancipated itself from theology and when Otto's argument for the irreducibility of the sacred held a great promise to protect the sacred from precisely this kind of reduction. And it must be remembered that among the "lost generation" of World War I were some of Durkheim's most brilliant students. The Durkheimian School, especially as it drew from the later works, waned in the decades following the Great War. The Annales school of history, which initially held the promise for the continuation of the Durkheim cultural program, turned more and more to demographic and socio-political structures and away from the symbolic and cultural. Those students of Durkheim who survived the war, like Marcel Mauss, were influential in turning the tradition toward ethnography and case studies which proved much less theoretically rich than what was latent in the later Durkheim.

Normalizing the sacred

Despite the importance of Durkheim's conceptualization of collective representations and the dichotomy of sacred and profane, little or no attention has been given to the central dynamic which produced the collective representations or brought together the seemingly polar opposites of sacred and profane. Durkheim called that dynamic "effervescence." In his *Elementary Forms* he saw effervescence, the hyper-excitement of physical and mental life, as the very origin of religion (Durkheim, 1995: 218–220). In one very well-known passage Durkheim describes effervescence in the following way:

It is not difficult to imagine a man in such a state of exaltation should no longer know himself. Feeling possessed and led on by some sort of external power that makes him think and act differently than he normally does, he naturally feels he is no longer himself. It seems to him that he has become a new being . . . And because his companions feel transformed in the same way at the same moment, and express this feeling by their shouts, movements, and bearing, it is as if he was in reality transported into a special world inhabited by exceptionally intense forces that invade and transform him. Especially when repeated for weeks, day after day, how would experiences like these not leave him with the conviction that two heterogeneous and incommensurable worlds exist in fact? In one world he languidly carries on his daily life; the other is one that he cannot enter without abruptly entering into relations with extraordinary powers that excite him to the point of frenzy. The first is the profane world and the second, the world of sacred things.   (Durkheim, 1995: 220)

He noted that this hyper-excitement of the mind and body could not be sustained over long periods, but was normalized or prolonged in ritual. This, of course, comes very close to Weber's understanding of routinization of charisma, but nowhere to my knowledge does Durkheim offer this specific terminological reading of effervescence. He further noted that great religious leaders show signs of extreme or pathological excitability and that individual or group effervescence changes or alters human beings and their surroundings. It is thus related to the primary dichotomy of sacred and profane which underlies his analysis of the social workings of religion. Ritual for Durkheim is only a form of effervescence and may not have any meaning beyond that form. He rejects ideas of ritual which link it to forms of play or entertainment, and is against the myth-ritualists, who at the time of the publication of the *Elementary Forms* were arguing that ritual's main power or function was explanatory (Durkheim, 1995: 385–386). For Durkheim, ritual's power is in the structuring, the normalizing, and the social reproduction of effervescence.

It is instructive to examine a number of handbooks on the study of religion published during the past three decades to see how they understood Durkheim. Each of these handbooks has proven to be very influential in shaping how we have understood the history of theory in the study of religion. Consider first Jan de Vries' *The Study of Religion: A Historical Approach*. De Vries links Durkheim almost exclusively to the study of totemism. He argues that Durkheim was wrong in placing totemism at the earliest stages of religious development. Such an argument, de Vries suggests, cannot comprehend the presence of a creator–god or high god among small-scale traditional peoples. He does not summarize Durkheim's collective representations, but hints at them in his summary of the totem. He writes: "totemism has a religious and a social aspect. The mystical relation between the clan and the totem is religious, the clan organization and exogamy are social by nature. The question may be raised as to which of these aspects is the primary one. For a sociologist like E. Durkheim the answer is not hard. Totemism, which he calls nothing but the symbol of the clan's community, represents for him the foundation of religious forms. In a totem, he sees the sign by which a clan makes itself distinct. Since a totem is also the manifest form of a totem god, Durkheim draws the following forced conclusion: if a totem means at the same time a deity and a community, are not that god and the community the same thing?" (de Vries, 1967: 129).

When de Vries turns to the *Elementary Forms* he underscores that Durkheim proposes an objective study. Social facts are to be analyzed without subjective prejudice. This is indeed what Durkheim meant by science. But, he finds problems in Durkheim's definition of religion. First, when Durkheim writes that religion deals with "things set apart and forbidden" he must mean the phenomenon of taboo, but not all taboos are religious. There are many things, de Vries reasons, in our society that have a strong social sanction but are not considered religious. "Sacred things," de Vries writes, "can become forbidden and be set apart from the profane world, but what is intriguing is to find out just what characteristic element necessitates this setting apart" (de Vries, 1967: 158). He notes that the "word 'church' is altogether misleading; it suggests a special religious fellowship. In spite of the best scholarly intentions, the word is quite inappropriate for primitive communities that exist on a sacred foundation. All that is left of the definition now is that certain things are declared tabu and such rules are valid for a community. This is a thin picture of religion" (de Vries, 1967: 158).

But de Vries reserves his harshest criticism for Durkheim's analysis of totemism. Totemism reduces God to community. In de Vries' words, Durkheim has brought "religion to the level of a cult of the idea of community" (de Vries, 1967: 159). Durkheim is a reductionist and an evolutionist to boot! De Vries is obsessed in his desire to reveal the twin evils of Durkheim. He writes, "[C]learly, what is lacking in this theory [i.e., the theory of totemism] is precisely the idea of religion. The totem is the hypostasized community, and everything else is illusory. Indeed, if one considers the social facts *'comme des choses'* ('as things') and classifies them only *'par certains charactères extérieurs'* ('by certain typical external features'), it may happen that what is essentially religious vanishes in the process" (de Vries, 1967: 160). Durkheim would have us believe that totemism is a very "primitive" and general form of religion. But, de Vries notes that it is neither. De Vries concludes that "Durkheim erred by his fixation on totemism, whose social character is quite pronounced; but to explain all other forms of religion as sociological forms on that basis is staggeringly lopsided and shows little understanding of any serious religious awareness." And so this Dutchman dispatches Durkheim.

Eric J. Sharpe is much less interested in demonstrating Durkheim's evolutionary thinking than de Vries, who I believe misread what Durkheim meant by the *élémentaires* of his title. Other things trouble him. He begins by observing that Durkheim's work was conceived in sharp reaction against the psychologically oriented individualism of the late nineteenth-century social thought. Hence, Durkheim's emphasis is not on individuals, but on groups and thus religion becomes the most characteristic product of the collective mind (Sharpe, 1986: 83). The science of religion as it existed in the second half of the nineteenth century and in the first decades of the twentieth century had explored religion as though it belonged to no social system at all and hence, Sharpe grudgingly admits that Durkheim's efforts to ground it in the social group were important and positive. Rather than focusing on totemism as de Vries had done, Sharpe underscores the obligatory nature of religious beliefs and ritual actions. It is obligation which characterizes them as religious; there is something obligatory to the sacred. In Sharpe's summary, "obligation presupposes an authority: and to Durkheim, the only conceivable authority is that of the group of which the individual is part. It follows that 'society' prescribes to the faithful the dogmas which he must believe and the rites which he must observe; religion then, originates in collective states of mind (*états de l'âme collective*)" (Sharpe, 1986: 84–85). The distinction between the sacred and the profane is then the achievement of collective mind and accounts for Durkheim's definitional phrase "religion is a unified system of beliefs and practices relative to sacred things, that is to say, things set apart and forbidden." "Relative" here implies the systematic workings of obligation. Sharpe concludes that religion "involves the formation of communities bound together by a common attitude to certain 'sacred' objects, places and persons. The individual can only accept this common attitude; nothing more is expected of him, and nothing more is acceptable" (Sharpe, 1986: 85).

Totemism best illustrates how this obligation and collective representation work together, and not because totemism is the earliest form of religion. The deity is the tribe or clan; god and totem are simply alternative expressions of society, the collective. In this simple equation is the greatest problem in Durkheim for Sharpe. There is no autonomous realm of religion. The sacred is the profane and the dichotomy ultimately collapses in what Sharpe understands as a reductionist move. He writes: "Durkheim was so dominated by the desire to explain away the phenomenon of religion that his theories about the origin of religion are of little consequence. His failure to accept mankind's belief in the actual existence of an unseen supernatural order – a failure in which he was to have many followers – led him into serious errors of interpretation" (Sharpe, 1986: 86). Of course, such a reading of Durkheim would seem to negate much of what Durkheim has to say about the autonomy of the sacred and profane, and, more importantly, Alexander's argument that, in Durkheim's positioning of both collective representation and the dichotomy of the sacred and profane in the very center of his societal analysis, Durkheim begins a much larger and comprehensive analysis which he described as "a religious sociology."

Lastly, we bring one of the most recent commentators in the study of religion on Durkheim. Like Sharpe, Walter Capps rejects understanding Durkheim as an evolutionary thinker. Durkheim is most important for his contribution to the morphology of religion, which Capps believes he employed to "demonstrate that there are exact (and not simply continuous) evolutionary correlations between elementary and contemporary forms of religious life" (Capps, 1995: 160). Capps, like de Vries and Sharpe, summarizes Durkheim's idea of collective representation which he sees as the way social groups articulate a "we-feeling." Collective representation, as all commentators note, is directly connected to social processes of solidarity. Capps writes that collective representation gives evidence "of the way in which the group forms its conception of reality. In other words, reality is constituted by social order and the 'collective conscience' is the source and sustainer of moral values, cultural ideals, religious aspirations, and all other determinants of prevailing collectivity" (Capps, 1995: 160). All of this is in line with all interpreters of Durkheim.

However, Capps introduces something distinctive in how he understands Durkheim's importance in the history of the study of religion. For Capps, Durkheim is also interested in how religion functioned and continues to function in the formation of the intellect. This leads him to consider religion in a much broader context, and come to the same interpretation reached by Alexander. Here, Capps notes that Durkheim is interested in the ideal. This interest is critical throughout his *Elementary Forms* and Capps pushes him away from the reductionist interpretation that Sharpe tries to make in his reading of Durkheim. "In society," Capps writes, "via the instrumentation of religion, the ideal is formulated. Thus society is always forming itself in light of the ideal it envisions and the ideal is always in process of formulation" (Capps, 1995: 162). Not only does Capps read Durkheim as every bit an idealist as he was a materialist, but he also sees the dynamic function of religion in Durkheim as the force which drives human history; and, perhaps most importantly, Capps understands that the origins of religion for Durkheim, "lie in something more universal than a particular capacity or idiosyncrasy of the earliest humans. Religion bespeaks a fundamental human tendency. It is a perennial and permanent feature of human nature" (Capps, 1995: 160). Religion then is not a moment in the beginning of human history, but a normal element of all human life. Here, I think that Capps has recaptured the insight drawn long ago by Talcott Parsons that the real significance of Durkheim is not that he was the first to understand that religion is a social phenomenon, but that he was the first to understand society as a religious phenomenon (Parsons, 1937: 427). In Parsons and Capps the central implication of Durkheim's work is the normalization of the sacred.

What is absent however in de Vries', Sharpe's, and Capps' summaries is Durkheim's theory of effervescence. This is an extraordinary oversight given the importance that effervescence has in the formation of collective representations. Why is this? For many commentators the central role played by effervescence has suggested that in his theory real efficacy, potency, or power as an analytic structure is in the explosive or convulsive moments of social history like the assassination of a president or some other great tragedy. Others have limited their use of Durkheim to the traditional forms of religion because of Durkheim's use of the term "Church." Only in the world-historical traditions like Judaism, Christianity, Islam, or Hinduism is there real history which can demonstrate the role and power of these collective representations. Their histories are punctuated by these explosive and convulsive moments. There is, of course, one notable exception to this pattern: those scholars who have used Durkheim to understand "civil religion" in a number of contexts. But, there is suggestive evidence in the corpus of Durkheim's work from its early phases that suggests that he imagines something more routine or normal in religion. In 1887, Durkheim published a lengthy review of Jean-Marie Guyau's *L'irréligion de l'avenir, étude de sociologie* published that same year. Guyau (1854–1888) was a follower of Auguste Comte and, much like the social theorist of the twentieth century, had confidently predicted the demise of all religion, and the creation of a more or less anarchic and utopian state. Durkheim argued in this early study that Guyau was essentially incorrect. Religion would not disappear, but in the future of Europe would become a socially diffused metaphysic, an expression of the social order which went beyond institutions.

Let us consider one additional example of collective representation. In March 1988 a truckload of regional police arrived in a small village in Jaipur, India in time to stop the widow of a Rajput from immolating herself on his funeral pyre. They found his widow Jasvant Kanvar lying next to her husband on the pyre, covered from her shoulders to her feet with coconuts and garlands, her face concealed by a gossamer veil. Her hand was extended from underneath the coconuts and garlands, bent almost at a ninety-degree angle to her forearm in the *samkalpa* gesture, the oath of a widow who is determined freely to accompany her husband in death and become a *suttee*. The police ordered the priests to stand away from the pyre while the widow was uncovered and lifted from it. She was carried to the police truck and driven away, while the police remained to watch the completion of the ritual burning of the dead.

Thirty women burned themselves to death in Rajasthan alone between 1943 and 1987. There may have been many more who became *sati* and whose cases were unreported or unregistered. For many interpreters of contemporary India and social activists, widow-burning is a particularly vicious form of what Ashis Nandy has called "internal colonialism" carried out by vicious and powerful men (Nandy, 1980: 1–31 and Nandy, 1994: 27–53). However, in a recent and very important study Catherine Weinberger-Thomas makes the issue of the *suttee* much more complex. She demonstrates that the individual *suttee* is completely mythologized, related to the foundational events of the cosmos and thus becomes a paradigmatic figure, who internalizes the entire society of the village around her. Indeed, Jasvant Kanvar whom the regional constabulary liberated from a horrible death quickly became a living *suttee*, the object of extensive veneration, with her own temple, her own religious organization, and who was at one and the same time the living image of the goddess, the officiant at her own cult, and also its primary benefactor (Weinberger-Thomas, 1996). Weinberger-Thomas' analysis of the *suttee* clearly makes it the elemental Durkheimian phenomenon. The widow becomes the goddess and feminine power which is completely woven into the social fabric of the village, a true collective representation, embodying the divine and human, the sacred and profane. Even the collective effervescence is present. The men and women standing around the pyre were not there to see an individual woman burning. Instead they assembled to see a goddess manifest herself. The crowd itself is transformed; it is a religious act to watch the manifestation of the goddess. But, more important, the effervescence did not happen as the result of a cataclysmic event, a rupturing of the social fabric. The ritual of *suttee* was completely normal. There was no frenzy associated with the ritual, and the normalcy of the event was further underscored when the police interrupted the ritual so that Jasvant Kanvar would not immolate herself. Indeed, the breaking of the ritual only contributed to the normalization of the goddess.

The analytic power of Durkheim's collective representations is not confined its ability to make understandable only the extreme moments of effervescence. The sacred is a normal, everyday component of human life. Durkheim's collective representations thus open the way for us to understand many contemporary forms of religion. For example, Catherine L. Albanese suggests that two major forms of contemporary American religion, fundamentalism and the New Age religiosity, are characterized by what she calls the democratization of the sacred. She traces both of these contemporary movements, which she calls "curious partners," to Ralph Waldo Emerson's transcendentalism, following literary critic Harold Bloom's description that Emerson invented American religion, a religion that replaced God-reliance with self-reliance. She writes that both fundamentalists and New Agers:

hear voices more than see visions: their mysticism comes clad in a rhetoric of newness that is expressed as ongoing revelation. For fundamentalists, the word of the gospel continues in and through private experience of the new birth. Conversations with Jesus are real and potent. Fundamentalists have them out loud, and preachers regularly report their content to congregations in rural churches or in television studios. New Agers hear the word in channeled messages or in voice of intuition. They travel in body to places where heightened earth energy increases their ability to hear and answer. They travel in mind through hypnotic regressions that help them to recall past lives or through shamanic journeys that increase their sense of mastery.   (Albanese, 1988: 349)

Both fundamentalism and the New Age represent new forms of the voluntarism which has characterized American religions and this new voluntarism is expressed in the popular, non-elite, do-it-yourself quality that characterizes both. She reasons that both arouse the ire of the traditional American denominations because they are:

sociological upstarts, untrained to ministry, untutored in the seminary tradition of most of the mainline. Clearly, both groups – fundamentalists and New Agers – are celebrators of a spiritual democracy. Their mysticism is a mysticism discovered in action and deed, created by language and shaped by the rhetorical 'falling forward' that Harold Bloom identified with Emerson. And for both the falling forward is a fall into the millennium: for fundamentalists, in the end, in the premillennial voice of the returned Jesus; for New Agers, in their inheritance of a postmillennial call.   (Albanese, 1988: 350)

In one respect we have come full-circle back to Durkheim. The fundamentalists and the New Agers are confirmation of Durkheim's early view that religion would not disappear, but would become a new metaphysic outside of the boundaries of traditional religions.

As sociology and the study of religion turn to the analysis and interpretation of culture they both will have to return to old problems which have not vanished and withered away. Sociologists will have to return to the problem of the sacred which continues to be one of the central elements in the production and reproduction of culture. The study of religion which over the past three decades has been intensely interested in deep contextualization of religion in history and society must still confront the old problem of the sacred. We began this chapter with private memorials and the growing devotion to a popular cultural icon. Both are collective representations for societal processes which reached deep into late-twentieth-century America. The later Durkheimian tradition provides immense possibility to understand the continued power of the sacred, but its challenge and, indeed, its utility are not confined only to the sociologists of culture. Much of the twentieth century's work in the study of religion has separated religion from the processes of culture and society. For us, too, the Durkheimian tradition holds substantial promise for new understandings of how religion is a significant *locus* for cultural production.

Notes

1. It should not be overlooked that the tradition of *memoriae* which Brown sees as central to the rewiring of late-antique religious expressions is itself exceedingly variegated. Perhaps one of the best examples of this cultural variation is in the Mexican and Mexican American *retablo* tradition in which an individual presents an iconographic narrative done on tin-sheet, a stylized *ex-voto*, as an offering of public thanks to a divine image for a miracle or favor received. See Dunnington (1997); Durand and Massey (1995); Egan (1991); Steele (1974); and Worth (1991). The altar, the *santos*, and the *retablo* also are prominent in Chicano/a contemporary art.

See for example, "Amalia Mesa-Bains" in Weintraub, Danto, and McEvilley (1996), pp. 92–96.

2. See, e.g., Jim Miller, "Forever Elvis – In a summer of books, recordings and TV specials, Elvis Presley lives on as a complex American legend: a saint who loved his mom and gave away Cadillacs – and a hungry good ole boy whose appetites killed him," *Newsweek*, August 3, 1987, pp. 48–55.

3. Paul Feldman, "To Honor Elvis' Memory, Star's Mentor Puts on a Show Himself," *The Los Angeles Times*, August 13, 1987; Patricia Leigh Brown, "10 Years After Elvis: the Faithful at the Shrine," *The New York Times*, August 14, 1987; Pat H. Broeske, "After Death, It was War: Even Elvis' Coffin Made It to the Front Page," *Calendar, The Los Angeles Times*, August 16, 1987; and Patricia Leigh Brown, "Candles in the Dark: 2 Sides of Elvis," *The New York Times*, August 17, 1987.

4. Laura A. Galloway, "Deaners bring annual revel without a pause," *The Los Angeles Times*, February 8, 1993.

5. Sylvia M. Bongiovanni, ed., "James Dean – We Remember Dean International Newsletter" (Fullerton, California, September, 1987), p. 1.

6. For example, Eliade (1969), pp. 12–36 notes that, in addition to Durkheim's *Elementary Forms of the Religious Life*, 1912 saw the publication of: the first volume of Wilhelm Schmidt's *Ursprung der Gottesidee* which would be completed posthumously with the appearance of volumes XI and XII in 1954 and 1955; Raffaele Pettazzoni's first important monograph, *La religione primitiva in Sardegna*; and C. G. Jung's *Wandlungen und Symbole der Libido*; and Sigmund Freud correcting the proofs of *Totem und Tabu* which was published the following year. For Eliade, these works reflected four different approaches to the study of religion – the sociological, the ethnographical, the psychological, and the historical. None of these was completely new. The only new approach, that of the phenomenological study of religion, was not to be attempted for another ten years. Nevertheless, Durkheim, Jung, Schmidt, Pettazzoni, and Freud applied new methods and claimed to have obtained more enduring results than their predecessors.

References

Albanese, Catherine L. 1988. "Religion and the American Experience: A Century After." *Church History* 57:337–351.

Alexander, Jeffrey C., ed. 1988. *Durkheimian Sociology: Cultural Studies*. New York: Cambridge University Press.

Beyette, Beverly. 1996. "Public Devotions: When Someone Dies on the Mean Streets of L. A., Loved Ones and Strangers Grieve Together at Imprompta Curbside Shrines," *The Los Angeles Times* December 14.

Brown, Peter. 1981. *The Cult of the Saints: Its Rise and Function in Latin Christianity*. Chicago, IL: University of Chicago Press.

Capps, Walter H. 1995. *Religious Studies: The Making of a Discipline*. Minneapolis, MN: Augsburg Fortress Press.

Conybeare, F. C. 1969. *Philostratus: The Life of Apollonius of Tyana*. Cambridge: Harvard University Press and William Heinemann Ltd.

de Vries, Jan. 1967. *The Study of Religion: A Historical Approach*, trans. Kees W. Bolle. New York: Harcourt, Brace & World.

Dunnington, Jacqueline Orsini. 1997. *Viva Guadalupe! The Virgin in New Mexican Popular Art*. Santa Fe, NM: Museum of New Mexico Press.

Durand, Jorge and Douglas S. Massey. 1995. *Miracles on the Border: Retablos of Mexican Migrants to the United States*. Tucson, AZ: University of Arizona Press.

Durkheim, Emile. [1912] 1995. *The Elementary Forms of Religious Life*, trans. Karen E. Fields. New York: The Free Press.

Egan, Martha. 1991. *Milagros: Votive Offerings from the Americas*. Santa Fe, NM: Museum of New Mexico Press.

Eliade, Mircea. [1963] 1969. "The History of Religions in Retrospect: 1912 and After," in *The Quest: History and Meaning in Religion*. Chicago, IL: University of Chicago Press. Pp. 12–36.

Foote, Kenneth E. 1997. *Shadowed Ground: America's Landscapes of Violence and Tragedy*. Austin, TX: University of Texas Press.

Geary, Patrick J. 1978. *Furta Sacra: Thefts of Relics in the Central Middle Ages*. Princeton, NJ: Princeton University Press.

Gottdiener Mark. 1997. "Dead Elvis as Other Jesus," in Vernon Chadwick, ed. *In Search of Elvis: Music, Race, Art, Religion*. Boulder, CO: Westview Press.

Hass, Kristin Ann. 1996. *Carried to the Wall: American Memory and the Vietnam Veterans Memorial*. Berkeley, CA: University of California Press.

Huntington, Samuel P. 1996. *The Clash of Civilizations and the Remaking of the World Order*. New York: Simon and Schuster.

Linenthal, Edward T. 2001. *The Unfinished Bombing: Oklahoma City in American Memory*. New York: Oxford University Press.

Marling, Karal Ann. 1996. *Graceland: Going Home with Elvis* Cambridge, MA: Harvard University Press.

Nandy, Ashish. 1980. *At the Edge of Psychology. Essays on Politics and Culture*. New Delhi: Oxford University Press.

1994. "Sati as Profit versus Sati as a Spectacle: The Public Debate on Roop Kanvar's Death," in J. S. Hawley, ed. *Sati, the Blessing and the Curse. The Burning of Wives in India*. Albany, NY: State University of New York Press.

Parsons, Talcott. 1937. *The Structure of Social Action*. New York: McGraw-Hill.

Saldivar, José David. 1997. *Border Matters: Remapping American Cultural Studies*. Berkeley, CA: University of California Press.

Sharpe, Eric J. [1975] 1986. *Comparative Religion: A History*. La Salle, IL: Open Court Publishing Company.

Steele, Thomas J. 1974. *Santos and Saints: The Religious Folk Art of Hispanic New Mexico*. Santa Fe, NM: Ancient City Press.

Strausbaugh, John. 1995. *Reflections on the Birth of the Elvis Faith*. New York: Blast Books.

Weinberger-Thomas, Catherine. 1996. *Cendres d'immortalité: La crémation des veuves en Inde*. Paris: Seuil.

Weintraub, Linda, Arthur Danto, and Thomas McEvilley, eds. 1996. "Amalia Mesa-Bains," in *Art on the Edge and Over: Searching for Art's Meaning in Contemporary Society – 1970s–1990s*. Litchfield, CT: Art Insights. Pp. 92–96.

Worth, William. 1991. *Images of Penance, Images of Mercy: Southwestern Santos in the Late Nineteenth Century*. London: University of Oklahoma Press.

6

The social marking of the past: toward a socio-semiotics of memory

Eviatar Zerubavel

The present chapter is part of a larger project dedicated to the development of what I envision as a *socio-mental topography*.[1] As such, it has a threefold agenda distinctively characterized by my concern with both the social and cognitive aspects of the past as well as with its structure.

The "mental" component of this "socio-mental topography" refers to the *cognitive* thrust of my concern. Unlike most historians, for example, I am interested here not in what actually happened in history but in the way it is *remembered*. After all, while things happen all the time, only some of them are preserved in our minds as memories.

The "socio-" component of this "socio-mental topography" pertains to my general effort to develop a *sociology* of the past.[2] Ever since Maurice Halbwachs (1992: 37–189) introduced the notion of "collective memory" in 1925, there has been growing interest among historians and social scientists in the social dimension of human memory. In marked contrast to the psychology of memory, a "*socio*-mental topography" relates to what we remember not as individuals but as social beings, members of particular "mnemonic communities" with distinctive "mnemonic traditions" (Zerubavel, 1997: 17–18, 87–91, 95–96).

The "topography" component of this "socio-mental topography" has to do with my particular concern with the *structure* of collective memory.[3] Whereas most of the study of this phenomenon has thus far been essentially confined to the content of what we collectively remember, I am mainly interested in exploring here the "patterning" of those memories.

Given my concern with the structure of collective memory, I will draw extensively on the general theoretical approach commonly known as *structuralism*. Specifically, I will draw on two main ideas developed by some of its originators within the context of semiotics. The essence of the first one lies in the simple yet quite radical claim made by Ferdinand de Saussure that, "in any semiological system, whatever *distinguishes* one sign from the others constitutes it.

Difference makes character."[4] (Using language as a prototypical example of such a system, he adds: "In language there are only differences . . . A linguistic system is a series of differences of sound combined with a series of differences of ideas."[5]) The second, jointly developed by fellow linguists Nikolaj Trubetzkoy and Roman Jakobson, is based on the epistemologically intriguing observation that, in every contrastive pair of phonemes ("b" and "p," "d" and "t"), one item is always defined actively in terms of the presence of the particular feature that marks the contrast, whereas the other remains passively defined by its absence.[6] The first idea underscores the centrality of the mental act of *differentiation* to the way we assign meaning. The second revolves around the basic notion of semiotic *markedness*. As we shall see, both of them can be of great use to anyone trying to understand the structure of collective memory.

The social marking of time

Saussure's general "semiological" agenda was never meant to be confined to linguistics alone (Saussure, 1959: 15–17), which may indeed help account for the considerable impact structuralism has had on other disciplines both in the humanities and in the social sciences. One major exception, however, is sociology, which has been rather slow to recognize what it has to offer its practitioners.

It is particularly ironic, therefore, to discover that some of the most notable precursors of structuralism can actually be found within sociology! A perfect example of such "pre-structuralist" scholarship is Georg Simmel's 1904 essay on the social organization of fashion, which, more than sixty years before Roland Barthes, underscores our "need of differentiation," "tendency towards dissimilarity," or "desire for contrast" as a major theme underlying many of the choices we make in matters of dress (Simmel, 1971: 296). An even better-known example of such scholarship, of course, is Emile Durkheim's 1912 magnum opus, *The Elementary Forms of Religious Life*, also published several years before Saussure's *Course in General Linguistics*.

Structuralism is essential, for example, for understanding Durkheim's distinctive vision of sanctity as articulated in *The Elementary Forms*. After all, despite the fact that most of the book revolves around the notion of "the sacred," nowhere does Durkheim even try to define the latter in a direct, affirmative manner. (In fact, just as he did earlier with regard to crime, he even claims that, at least in theory, *anything* might be considered sacred [Durkheim, 1982: 97–104, 1995: 230].) Rather, he defines it in terms of the way it is structurally situated mentally in opposition to "the profane," thereby implicitly suggesting that it is anything that is not profane (Durkheim, 1995: 34–38).

Indeed, as if anticipating Trubetzkoy's and Jakobson's discussions of markedness twenty years later, he also posits a fundamental semiotic asymmetry between the two, whereby everything is considered by default profane unless explicitly marked as sacred. In other words, he defines the sacred as that which is specifically marked as *non*-profane.

Durkheim's "pre-structuralist" thrust is also quite evident in the way he approaches time, claiming in the introduction to *The Elementary Forms* that "we can conceive of time only if we differentiate between moments" (Durkheim, 1995: 9). It is the mental act of differentiating, in other words, that enables us to experience temporality.

Durkheim himself, unfortunately, never takes that idea any further. However, when making that statement, he is actually restating an idea that had already been fully developed in a paper (which he cites later in that paragraph) published seven years earlier by his own student Henri Hubert, "A Brief Study of the Representation of Time in Religion and Magic."[7] In that paper, arguably the earliest contribution to the sociology of time, Hubert essentially presents, ten years before Saussure, an unmistakably "Saussurian" analysis of time as a semiotic system; and, like another student of Durkheim, Robert Hertz, in a somewhat parallel "pre-structuralist" semiotic analysis of social space (Hertz, 1973: 3–31), Hubert bases it on the nature of the relations between the sacred and the profane (or more generally, as I would like to argue here, the marked and the unmarked).

Drawing on Henri Bergson's revolutionary ideas regarding the qualitative heterogeneity of experienced duration,[8] Hubert attributes the rhythmic, "spasmodic" nature of time in religion to the fundamental epistemological distinction between socially marked "critical dates" such as holidays and the essentially unmarked intervals between them.[9] Durkheim himself reiterates that idea, practically "out-Saussuring" Saussure:

> There is no religion, and hence no society, that has not known and practiced this division of time into two distinct parts that alternate with one another . . . In fact, probably the necessity of that alternation led men to insert distinctions and differentiations into the homogeneity and continuity of duration that it does not naturally have.
>
> (Durkheim, 1995: 313)

I first came across this intriguing idea twenty-five years ago, as I was working on my book *Hidden Rhythms* and slowly beginning to appreciate the unmistakably "structural" essence of the Jewish Sabbath as a sacred block of time that is basically defined in terms of the way in which it contrasts with "profane days" (as they are commonly known in Hebrew) such as Monday or Thursday.[10] Yet Durkheim's notion of "religion" is practically synonymous with "society," and he was actually making that claim not only about time in religion but about social time in general. That the distinction between what I had initially identified as "sacred" and "profane" time was, in fact, only a particular manifestation of a more fundamental *epistemological distinction between marked and unmarked time* finally dawned on me four years later, as I was working on my book *The Seven-Day Circle* and trying to understand the essence of the unmistakably social rhythm we call "the week." As I compared my earlier vision of the essentially religious Sabbath with my evolving vision of the pronouncedly secular weekend, I began to realize that there really *is* no fundamental difference between the two, and that the latter is actually the modern structural equivalent of the former! I soon came to understand that there is also no fundamental difference between either of those structurally defined "peak days" and the market day in a four-day West African market cycle or the day of communal reunion in the nineteen-day Baha'i week, for that matter (see Zerubavel, 1989: 45–50. See also 28–43).

Although I ended up calling my book *The Seven-Day Circle*, my own preferred title was actually *The Seven-Day Beat*, a far more appropriate reflection of my deepening appreciation of the "pre-structuralist" thrust of Hubert's and Durkheim's general approach to social time, the essence of which is beautifully captured in Edmund Leach's "pendular" vision of time as a "sequence of oscillations between opposites," an "alternation between contraries," a "discontinuity of repeated contrasts" (Leach, 1961: 126, 129, 133–134). (As a true structuralist, Leach does not fail to remind us explicitly that "the essence of the matter is not the pendulum but the alternation" [Leach, 1961: 134].) I thus came to regard the four-day West African market week, the nineteen-day Baha'i week, as well as other structural cousins of the seven-day Jewish week and its modern secular offspring such as the ancient eight-day Roman market cycle or the ten-day French Republican *décade* as but different variants of the same phenomenon,[11] which I basically ended up characterizing as a "pulsating" cycle of periodically alternating marked and unmarked days (Zerubavel, 1989: 117, 113–120). In other words, I came to view our week (in marked contradistinction to various *non*pulsating distant relatives such as the Mexican and Indonesian divinatory cycles or even its "etically" similar yet "emically" different seven-day astrological counterpart, which are basically made up of days that are *all* marked)[12] as a *system of periodically alternating marked and unmarked blocks of time* signifying a socio-semiotic contrast between marked and unmarked chunks of cultural, political, and economic reality.[13]

The social shape of history

Is it possible, at all, to "translate" any of this from the language of circular, calendrical time to that of essentially linear, historical time? If there can actually be "pulsating" weeks and a seven-day "beat," can one possibly also hear the "pulse" or "beat" of history?[14] If we indeed experientially single out "peak days" such as Saturdays and Sundays, do we then also have particularly intense memories of "peak" historical periods such as the Industrial Revolution or the so-called Renaissance?

It was Pitirim Sorokin who first saw the possibility of applying Hubert's and Durkheim's essentially "structural" view of time to the study of history when he noted the curious distinction we often make between "pregnant periods packed with eventfulness" and "empty stretches" during which nothing of major significance seems to have happened (Sorokin, 1943: 212), thereby implicitly identifying a hitherto-unnoticed important variable one might call the *socio-mental "amplitude" of history*. While such a distinction may even seem to have actual ontological resonance for someone like a devout Catholic friend who once asked my wife, "So how do you account for the fact that nothing major actually happened from the time of Moses until the birth of Christ?" one need not adopt such an extreme reificatory stance to appreciate the *epistemological* distinction we often make between historical periods we consider "eventful" and those we regard as "uneventful" or "empty."

Such an intriguing distinction has also been noted by Claude Lévi-Strauss, the most influential proponent of structuralism to date. Viewing chronology as a semiotic code, Lévi-Strauss identifies what he calls the "pressure" of history as a subtle signifier of cultural significance:

> We use a large number of dates to code some periods of history; and fewer for others. This variable quantity of dates applied to periods of equal duration are a gauge of what might be called the pressure of history: there are "hot" chronologies which are those of periods where . . . numerous events appear as differential elements; others, on the contrary, where . . . very little or *nothing took place*.
>
> (Lévi-Strauss, 1966: 259, emphasis added)

> Historical knowledge thus proceeds in the same way as a wireless with frequency modulation: like a nerve, it codes a continuous quantity . . . by frequencies of impulses proportional to its variations.   (Lévi-Strauss, 1966: 259)

Following Lévi-Strauss' ideas as well as his highly evocative almost-graphic imagery, I would like to extend here my "structural" analysis of calendrical time to history and argue that the general "shape" of our collective memory basically resembles a cardiogram in that it follows a fundamental "tidal" pattern of mental rotation between extraordinary, "epochal," marked historical periods during which a lot seems to have happened and ordinary, unmarked "lulls" that seem relatively uneventful. To get a somewhat better "feel" of the latter, consider, for example, the seemingly empty so-called Dark Ages, which may very well prove to be a generic, universal category,[15] not to mention long historical stretches that remain virtually nameless, like the "negative" spaces that are typically left between buildings or pieces of furniture.[16] Following the normal pattern of the social organization of human attention (Zerubavel, 1997: 35–52), our collective memory thus tends to inflate telescopically what appears to be historically "momentous" while essentially compressing, or even entirely ignoring, what seems to be uneventful. As a result, "history" usually consists of small pockets of "eventful" marked periods interspersed between long stretches of seemingly "empty" unmarked ones.

Patterning historical time in such a manner presupposes a pronouncedly *non-metric* mode of experiencing duration that is altogether different from the essentially mathematical manner in which we often process temporality in that it basically entails a "Bergsonian" sensitivity to the "qualitative" heterogeneity of mathematically equal durations.[17] It presupposes, for example, our ability to inflate the mental "weight"[18] of the single year 1492 in the way we collectively remember the history of the Western Hemisphere while at the same time essentially compressing that of the three preceding centuries to near-oblivion.

The ritual marking of the past

Yet mnemonic "cardiograms" are more than just a philosophical curiosity. Indeed, they are an extremely important methodological tool that allows students of memory to move from the strictly theoretical to a more empirical level of exploring the social marking of the past.

One can quite easily generate such "cardiograms" by asking individuals to draw "timelines" of particular stretches of history or by reconstructing such timelines from life-history narratives. It is based on such narratives, for example, that historian Ulrich Herbert characterizes the years 1935–1942 as a relatively unmarked period in elderly Germans' memory (Herbert, 1986: 44).

Yet *collective* memory is more than just the sum of the memories of particular individuals.[19] In order to produce a *sociology* of memory, one therefore needs to try to construct *socio*-mnemonic "cardiograms" for entire "mnemonic *communities*" (Zerubavel, 1997: 6, 17–18, 90, 95–96).

Drawing on Durkheim's vision of the sacred as manifested in ritual displays of collective sentiments (Durkheim, 1995: 303–417), I suggest that we look at the way historical events are ritually commemorated. After all, the act of commemorating entails the mental lifting of socially marked periods and events from a backdrop of unmarked historical sequences, thereby allowing us access to what mnemonic communities *collectively* regard as eventful or historically "sacred." To quote Barry Schwartz:

commemoration lifts from an ordinary historical sequence those extraordinary events which embody our deepest and most fundamental values. *Commemoration . . . is in this sense a register of sacred history.*　　　　　　　　(Schwartz, 1982: 377, emphasis added)

Hence the theoretical as well as methodological value of *commemorative rituals* (Zerubavel, 1995) as significant "sites" of collective memory.[20]

Consider, for example, ritual processions. Indeed, the first one to study the social marking of the past empirically, Lloyd Warner, actually looked at the chronological distribution of the events chosen by the people of Newburyport, Massachusetts to be represented in a parade marking the first three-hundred years of their town's history. What he discovered was that the events that enter our collective memory (that is, what memonic communities come to regard as "history") are unevenly distributed chronologically, rarely following patterns one would expect based on the laws of statistical probability:

The forty-three floats of the Procession . . . were spread throughout the three hundred years being officially celebrated . . . Further inspection demonstrates that *chronologically they are not spread equally* throughout the three centuries. There are *sharp divergencies between the social time of the Procession and the chronology of objective time . . .* Since three hundred years were being celebrated, if only the statistical probability of pure chance were at work each century would receive a third of the scenes displayed and each half- and quarter-century be given its proportion of symbolic events. The criteria of objective time and "probablility" would both be served. But in fact, one brief period of little more than a decade received as much attention as the previous hundred years. One full quarter-century was not represented at all.

(Warner, 1959: 129–130, emphasis added)

As evident from a chart he titled "Social Time and Chronology" thereby explicitly contrasting the two, Warner was referring to uneven chronological distribution patterns such as having the twenty-five-year interval from 1780 to 1805 represented by nine floats yet the mathematically identical interval from 1705 to 1730 by practically none![21] As Hubert first noted when applying Bergson's non-metric vision of temporality to social reality, mathematically equal time intervals are often made *socially* unequal.[22]

Consider also, along these lines, ritual displays of art in museums and other public galleries (such as the collection of Diego Rivera murals displayed at the National Palace in Mexico City) that are designed to offer mnemonic communities a visual encapsulation of their collective past. Indeed, the very same basic American socio-mnemonic pattern identified by Warner at the Newburyport tricentennial procession was also identified by Schwartz in a somewhat parallel examination of the chronological distribution of the historical events commemorated in the paintings, statues, murals, frescoes, and busts that are stored in the United States Capitol's art collection in Washington, DC (Schwartz, 1982).

One only needs to compare the public commemoration of the virtually barren 1760s and the highly eventful 1770s, for example, to appreciate the fundamental difference between sacred and profane stretches of history (Schwartz, 1982: 381–383).

Finally, consider calendars, which often include an annual cycle of holidays and other *memorial days* specifically designed to commemorate "sacred" historical events. As such, they play a major role in socializing members of a mnemonic community to its history[23] as well as distinctive mnemonic traditions (as manifested in its distinctive socio-mnemonic "commemograms"). By examining which events are publicly commemorated as memorial days, we can thus identify "sacred" periods in a community's collective past.[24]

The Israeli calendar of the 1950s and 1960s offers a perfect illustration of the general socio-mnemonic pattern identified by both Warner and Schwartz in the United States.[25] Indeed, since it actually "covered" more than thirty centuries of Jewish history as seen through a modern Zionist mnemonic lens, it underscores the *uneven chronological distribution of socially "memorable" and "negligible" historical events* even more forcefully. Particularly remarkable, in this regard, is the striking contrast between brief yet commemoratively "dense" historical intervals such as the period surrounding the biblical Exodus or the one from 1920 to 1948, each of which is calendrically associated with no fewer than three days of remembrance (the former with Passover, Sukkoth, and Shavuoth, and the latter with the Eleventh of Adar, the Holocaust Memorial Day, and the Day of Independence), and the practically barren 1,785-year "lull" between 135 and 1920, which is associated with virtually none! Such a striking calendrical contrast represents most spectacularly the sharp cultural contrast between sacred and profane themes (national birth and revival vs. exile) in Zionist historiography.[26]

Meaning and social memorability

Meaning presupposes being able to differentiate marked chunks of reality from essentially unmarked ones. It is virtually impossible meaningfully to "grasp" anything without mentally detaching it first from its surroundings, which we must basically ignore as mere "background" (Zerubavel, 1993: 1, 6, 118–119). It is likewise impossible to appreciate the musical quality of sounds we hear without also recognizing the major role of silence in this process.

The inherent tension between sound and silence in the phenomenological construction of what we call "music" is quite analogous to the fundamental tension between marked and unmarked blocks of time in the social construction of what we regard as a meaningful "history."[27] After all, it is the mental act of differentiating marked from unmarked chunks of the past that allows us to assign the former any social significance. As Lévi-Strauss puts it, "in so far as history aspires to meaning, it is doomed to select [certain historical periods] . . . and to make them stand out, as discontinuous figures, against a continuity . . . used as a backdrop" (Lévi-Strauss, 1966: 257).

The process of semiotic marking offers a rare window into what we socially value (Waugh, 1982; Brekhus, 1998). Hence the importance of studying the social marking of time in general (such as the act of delineating a certain phase of the female reproductive cycle as "premenstrual" [Foster, 1996] or of the life course as "adolescence") and the *social construction of memorability* in particular. Just as creating a cycle with a single "sacred" day helped the ancient Israelites articulate to themselves, as well as to pagan users of the nonpulsating seven-day astrological week around them, the rather elusive idea of monotheism (Zerubavel, 1989: 113), creating a history with certain "sacred" periods helps a mnemonic community explicitly articulate what it considers memorable (and therefore socially significant).

By examining how a particular mnemonic community differentiates "sacred" from "profane" chunks of its collective past, we thus tacitly gain access to what it values in the present. By observing how commemoratively "densely" Zionism marks the period from 1920 to 1948 in sharp contrast to the calendrical wilderness of the preceding eighteen centuries of Jewish history, we also gain a somewhat deeper understanding of the fundamental Zionist distinction between "Israeli" and "Jew" (Zerubavel, 1995). By observing how intensely Americans commemorate the 1770s and 1780s, we likewise gain access to what they collectively regard as their origins as a nation.[28]

Hence the need to study what social communities consider historically memorable. By essentially examining how they construct their history, we also learn who they are both culturally and politically. Studying how we collectively construct our past is therefore also a tacit way of studying our present social condition.

Notes

1. An earlier version of this chapter was presented at the Cultural Turn conference at Santa Barbara, February 1997. I wish to thank Wayne Brekhus, Yael Zerubavel, and Johanna Foster for their valuable comments on an earlier version of this chapter.
2. See, e.g., Zerubavel (1996a).
3. For a somewhat similar attempt to approach the structure of human memory from an "archaeological" perspective, see Freud (1961), pp. 16–18.
4. Saussure (1959), p. 121. Emphasis added. See also Zerubavel (1997), pp. 72–75.
5. Saussure (1959), p. 120. See also pp. 116–122.
6. Waugh (1982), pp. 300–301. On the particular usefulness of the notion of semiotic markedness for sociology, see Brekhus, 1996, and 1998.

7. Hubert (1909). Although the paper cited by Durkheim appeared only in 1909, it was actually a reprinted version of a paper originally published in 1905. See Isambert (1979), p. 203.
8. Hubert (1909), p. 210. See, e.g., Bergson (1960), pp. 90–128, 222–240.
9. Hubert (1909), pp. 197–205. See also Sorokin (1943), pp. 182–184.
10. Zerubavel (1985), pp. 110–126. On the distinction between sacred and profane time, see also Durkheim (1995), pp. 311–313; Eliade (1959), pp. 68–72.
11. On "etically" different yet "emically" similar units of meaning, see Pike (1967), pp. 44–46; Zerubavel (1993), pp. 16–17, 63, 78; Zerubavel (1996b), pp. 422–423.
12. Zerubavel (1989), pp. 12–20, 50–59. On "etically" similar yet "emically" different units of meaning, see Pike (1967), pp. 42–44.
13. For a somewhat similar socio-semiotic "mapping" of the menstrual cycle, see Foster (1996), pp. 525–528.
14. Personal communication from Wayne Brekhus.
15. Personal communication from Karen Cerulo. See also Velikovsky (1977), p. 5.
16. See Zerubavel (1998). See also Zerubavel (1993), p. 97; Brekhus (1998).
17. See Bergson (1960). On the pronouncedly non-mathematical nature of "socio-cultural" time, see also Sorokin (1943), pp. 158–225.
18. I borrow this metaphor from Jamie Mullaney (1999).
19. Zerubavel (1997), pp. 95–96. See also Frisch (1989).
20. On "sites" of collective memory, see Nora (1989); Zerubavel (1997), pp. 92–95. On their centrality to commemoration, see Zerubavel (1995), pp. 138–144.
21. Warner (1959), p. 133.
22. Hubert (1909), pp. 207–208. See also Sorokin (1943), p. 184; Zerubavel (1979), pp. 113–117.
23. Connerton (1989), pp. 41–71; Zerubavel (1995), pp. 216–221. On "mnemonic socialization," see also Zerubavel (1997), pp. 87–89, 96–98.
24. Zerubavel (2003b), pp. 25–34.
25. For a 191-nation comparative study of national calendars, see Zerubavel (2003a).
26. Zerubavel and Zerubavel (1999). On the socio-mental organization of Jewish history in Zionist historiography, see Zerubavel (1995), pp. 13–36.
27. Personal communication from Ira Cohen.
28. Schwartz, 1982. On the commemoration of "origins," see also Connerton (1989), pp. 41–71.

References

Bergson, Henri. [1889] 1960. *Time and Free Will: An Essay on the Immediate Data of Consciousness*. New York: Harper and Row.

Brekhus, Wayne. 1996. "Social Marking and the Mental Coloring of Identity: Sexual Identity Construction and Maintenance in the United States." *Sociological Forum* 11:497–522.

1998. "A Sociology of the Unmarked: Redirecting Our Focus." *Sociological Theory* 16:34–49.

Connerton, Paul. 1989. *How Societies Remember*. Cambridge: Cambridge University Press.

Durkheim, Emile. [1895] 1982. *The Rules of Sociological Method*. New York: Free Press.

[1912] 1995. *The Elementary Forms of Religious Life*. New York: Free Press.

Eliade, Mircea. [1957] 1959. *The Sacred and the Profane: The Nature of Religion*. New York: Harcourt, Brace & World.

Foster, Johanna. 1996. "Menstrual Time: The Sociocognitive Mapping of 'The Menstrual Cycle.'" *Sociological Forum* 11:523–547.

Freud, Sigmund. [1930] 1961. *Civilization and Its Discontents*. New York: W. W. Norton.

Frisch, Michael. 1989. "American History and the Structures of Collective Memory: A Modest Exercise in Empirical Iconography." *Journal of American History* 75:1130–1155.

Halbwachs, Maurice. [1925] 1992. *The Social Frameworks of Memory*. In Lewis A. Coser, ed. *Maurice Halbwachs on Collective Memory*. Chicago, IL: University of Chicago Press. Pp. 37–189.

Herbert, Ulrich. 1986. "Good Times, Bad Times." *History Today* 36:42–48.

Hertz, Robert. [1909] 1973. "The Pre-eminence of the Right Hand: A Study in Religious Polarity," in Rodney Needham, ed. *Right and Left: Essays on Dual Symbolic Classification*. Chicago, IL: University of Chicago Press. Pp. 3–31.

Hubert, Henri. [1905] 1909. "Etude Sommaire de la Représentation du Temps dans la Religion et la Magie," in Henri Hubert and Marcel Mauss, eds. *Mélanges d'Histoire des Religions*. Paris: Félix Alcan and Guillaumin. Pp. 189–229.

Isambert, François A. 1979. "Henri Hubert et la Sociologie du Temps." *Revue Française de Sociologie* 20:183–204.

Leach, Edmund. 1961. "Two Essays Concerning the Symbolic Representation of Time," in *Rethinking Anthropology*. London: Athlone. Pp. 124–136.

Lévi-Strauss, Claude. [1962] 1966. *The Savage Mind*. Chicago, IL: University of Chicago Press.

Mullaney, Jamie. 1999. "Making It Count: Mental Weighing and Identity Attribution." *Symbolic Interaction* 22:269–283.

Nora, Pierre. 1989. "Between Memory and History: Les Lieux de Memoire." *Representations* 26:7–25.

Pike, Kenneth L. [1954] 1967. *Language in Relation to a Unified Theory of the Structure of Human Behavior*. Rev. edn. The Hague: Mouton.

Saussure, Ferdinand de. [1915] 1959. *Course in General Linguistics*. New York: Philosophical Library.

Schwartz, Barry. 1982. "The Social Context of Commemoration: A Study in Collective Memory." *Social Forces* 61:374–396.

Simmel, Georg. [1904] 1971. "Fashion," in Donald N. Levine, ed. *Georg Simmel On Individuality and Social Forms*. Chicago, IL: University of Chicago Press. Pp. 294–323.

Sorokin, Pitirim A. 1943. *Sociocultural Causality, Space, Time: A Study of Referential Principles of Sociology and Social Science*. Durham, NC: Duke University Press.

Velikovsky, Immanuel. 1977. *Peoples of the Sea*. Garden City, NY: Doubleday.

Warner, W. Lloyd. 1959. *The Living and the Dead*. New Haven: Yale University Press.

Waugh, Linda R. 1982. "Marked and Unmarked: A Choice between Unequals in Semiotic Structure." *Semiotica* 38:299–318.

Zerubavel, Eviatar. 1979. *Patterns of Time in Hospital Life: A Sociological Perspective*. Chicago, IL: University of Chicago Press.

  [1981] 1985. *Hidden Rhythms: Schedules and Calendars in Social Life*. Berkeley, CA: University of California Press.

  [1985] 1989. *The Seven-Day Circle: The History and Meaning of the Week*. Chicago, IL: University of Chicago Press.

  [1991] 1993. *The Fine Line: Making Distinctions in Everyday Life*. Chicago, IL: University of Chicago Press.

  1996a. "Social Memories: Steps to a Sociology of the Past." *Qualitative Sociology* 19:283–299.

  1996b. "Lumping and Splitting: Notes on Social Classification." *Sociological Forum* 11:421–433.

  1997. *Social Mindscapes: An Invitation to Cognitive Sociology*. Cambridge, MA: Harvard University Press.

  1998. "Language and Memory: 'Pre-Columbian' America and the Social Logic of Periodization." *Social Research* 65:315–330.

  2003a. "Calendars and History: A Comparative Study of the Social Organization of National Memory," in Jeffrey K. Olick, ed. *States of Memory: Continuities, Conflicts, and Transformations in National Retrospection*. Durham, NC: Duke University Press. Pp. 315–337.

  2003b. *Time Maps: Collective Memory and the Social Shape of the Past*. Chicago, IL: University of Chicago Press.

Zerubavel, Eviatar and Yael Zerubavel. 1999. "Re(cycling) the Past: Calendars and Collective Memory." Paper presented at the annual meeting of the American Sociological Association, Chicago, IL.

Zerubavel, Yael. 1995. *Recovered Roots: Collective Memory and the Making of Israeli National Tradition*. Chicago, IL: University of Chicago Press.

7

On the social construction of moral universals: the "Holocaust" from war crime to trauma drama

Jeffrey C. Alexander

> If we bear this suffering, and if there are still Jews left, when it is over, then Jews, instead of being doomed, will be held up as an example. Who knows, it might even be our religion from which the world and all peoples learn good, and for that reason and for that alone do we have to suffer now.
>
> Anne Frank, 1944

How did a specific and situated historical event, an event marked by ethnic and racial hatred, violence, and war, become transformed into a generalized symbol of human suffering and moral evil, a universalized symbol whose very existence has created historically unprecedented opportunities for ethnic, racial, and religious justice, for mutual recognition, and for global conflicts to become regulated in a more civil way? This cultural transformation has been achieved because the originating historical event, traumatic in the extreme for a delimited particular group, has come over the past fifty years to be redefined as a traumatic event for all of humankind. Now free floating rather than situated – universal rather than particular – this traumatic event vividly "lives" in the memories of contemporaries whose parents and grandparents never felt themselves even remotely related to it. In what follows, I explore the social creation of a cultural fact, and the effects of this cultural fact upon social and moral life.

Mass murder under the progressive narrative

In the beginning, in April 1945, the Holocaust was not the "Holocaust." In the torrent of newspaper, radio, and magazine stories reporting the discovery by American infantrymen of the Nazi concentration camps, the empirical remains of what had transpired were typified as "atrocities." Their obvious awfulness, and indeed their strangeness, placed them for contemporary observers at the borderline of that unfortunately abused category of behavior known as "man's inhumanity to man." Nonetheless, qua atrocity, the discoveries were placed side by side – metonymically and semantically – with a whole series of other brutalities that were considered to be the natural results of the ill wind of this second, very unnatural, and most inhuman world war.

The first American reports on "atrocities" during that second world war had not, in fact, even referred to actions by German Nazis, let alone to their Jewish victims, but to the Japanese army's brutal treatment of American and other allied prisoners of war after the loss of Corregidor in 1943. On January 27, 1944, the US released sworn statements by military officers who had escaped the so-called Bataan Death March. In the words of contemporary journals and magazines, these officers had related "atrocity stories" revealing "the inhuman treatment and murder of American and Filipino soldiers who were taken prisoner when Bataan and Corregidor fell." In response to these accounts, the US State Department had lodged protests to the Japanese government about its failure to live up to the provisions of the Geneva Prisoners of War Convention (*Current History*, March 1944, 6: 249). Atrocities, in other words, were a signifier specifically connected to war. They referred to war-generated events that transgressed the rules circumscribing how national killing could normally be carried out. Responding to the same incident, *Newsweek*, in a section entitled "The Enemy" and under the headline "Nation Replies in Grim Fury to Jap Brutality to Prisoners," reported that "with the first impact of the news, people had shuddered at the story of savage *atrocity* upon Allied prisoners of war by the Japanese" (vol. 23 [6], February 7, 1944: 19, italics added). It is hardly surprising, then, that it was this nationally specific and particular war-related term that was employed to represent the grisly Jewish mass murders discovered by American GIs when they liberated the Nazi camps. Through April, 1945, as one camp after another was discovered, this collective representation was applied time after time. When, toward the end of that month, a well-known Protestant minister explored the moral implications of the discoveries, he declared that, no matter how horrifying and repulsive, "it is important that the full truth be made known so that a clear indication may be had of the nature of the enemy we have been dealing with, as well as of a realization *of the sheer brutalities that have become the accompaniment to war.*" The *New York Times* reported this sermon under the headline, "Bonnell Denounces German Atrocities" (April 23, 1945: 23, italics added). When alarmed American Congressmen visited Buchenwald, the *Times* headlined that they had witnessed first hand the *"War Camp Horror"* (April 26, 1945: 12, italics added). When a few days later the US Army released a report on the extent of the killings in Buchenwald, the *Times* headlined it an "Atrocity Report" (April 29, 1945: 20). A few days after that, under the headline "Enemy Atrocities in France Bared," the *Times* wrote that a just released report had shown that "in France, German brutality was not limited to the French underground or even to the thousands of hostages whom the Germans killed for disorders they had nothing to do with, but was practiced almost systematically against entirely innocent French people" (May 4, 1945: 6).

The Nazis' anti-Jewish mass murders had once been only putative atrocities. From the late thirties on, reports about them had been greeted with widespread public doubt about their authenticity. Analogizing to the allegations about German atrocities during World War I that later had been thoroughly discredited, they were dismissed as a kind of Jewish moral panic. Only three months before the GIs' "discovery" of the camps, in introducing a first-hand report on Nazi mass murder from a Soviet-liberated camp in Poland, *Collier's* magazine acknowledged: "A lot of Americans simply do not believe the stories of Nazi mass executions of Jews and anti-Nazi Gentiles in eastern Europe by means of gas chambers, freight cars partly loaded with lime and other horrifying devices. These stories are so foreign to most Americans' experience of life in this country that they seem incredible. Then too some of the atrocity stories of World War I were later proved false" (January 6, 1945: 62). From April 3, 1945, however, the date when the GIs first liberated the concentration camps, all such earlier reports were retrospectively accepted as facts, as the realistic signifiers of Peirce rather than the "arbitrary" symbols of Saussure. That systematic efforts at Jewish mass murder had occurred, and that the numerous victims and the few survivors had been severely traumatized, the American and world-wide audience now had little doubt. Their particular and unique fate, however, even while it was widely recognized as representing the grossest of injustices, did not itself become a traumatic experience for the audience to which the mass media's collective representations were transmitted, that is, for those looking on, either from near or from far. Why this was not so defines my initial explanatory effort here.

Symbolic extension and psychological identification

For an audience to be traumatized by an experience which they themselves do not directly share, symbolic extension and psychological identification are required. This did not occur. For the American infantrymen who first made contact, for the general officers who supervised the rehabilitation, for the reporters who broadcast the descriptions, for the commissions of Congressmen and influentials who quickly traveled to Germany to conduct on-site investigations, the starving, depleted, often weird-looking and sometimes weird-acting Jewish camp survivors seemed like a foreign race. They could just as well have been from Mars, or from Hell. The identities and characters of these Jewish survivors rarely were personalized through interviews or individualized through biographical sketches; rather, they were presented as a mass, and often as a mess, a petrified, degrading, and smelly one, not only by newspaper reporters but by some of the most powerful general officers in the Allied high command. This depersonalization made it more difficult for the survivors' trauma to generate compelling identification.

Possibilities for universalizing the trauma were blocked not only by the depersonalization of its victims but by their historical and sociological specification. As I have indicated, the mass murders semantically were immediately linked to other "horrors" in the bloody history of the century's second great war and to the historically specific national and ethnic conflicts that underlay it. Above all, it was never forgotten that these victims were Jews. In retrospect, it is bitterly ironic, but it is also sociologically understandable, that the American audience's sympathy and feelings of identity flowed much more easily to the non-Jewish survivors, whether German or Polish, who had been kept in better conditions and looked more normal, more composed, more human. Jewish survivors were kept in the worst areas and under the worst conditions of what had become, temporarily, displaced-persons camps. American and British administrators felt impatient with many Jewish survivors, even personal repugnance for them, sometimes resorting to threats and even to punishing them. The depth of this initial failure of identification can be seen in the fact that, when American citizens and their leaders expressed opinions and made decisions about national quotas for emergency postwar immigration, displaced German citizens ranked first, Jewish survivors last.

How could this have happened? Was it not obvious to any human observer that this mass murder was fundamentally different than the other traumatic and bloody events in a modern history already dripping in blood, that it represented not simply evil but "radical evil," in Kant's remarkable phrase (Kant, 1960), that it was unique? To understand why none of this was obvious, to understand how and why each of these initial understandings and behaviors was radically changed, and how this transformation had vast repercussions for establishing, not only new moral standards for social and political behavior, but unprecedented, if still embryonic, regulatory controls, it is important to see the inadequacy of common-sense naturalistic understandings of traumatic events.

The cultural construction of trauma: coding, weighting, narrating

Elie Wiesel asserted in the 1970s that the Holocaust represents an "ontological evil." From a sociological perspective, however, evil is epistemological, not ontological. For a traumatic event to have the status of evil is a matter of its *becoming* evil. It is a matter of how the trauma is known, how it is coded. "At first glance it may appear a paradox," Diner has noted – and certainly it does – but, considered only in and of itself, "Auschwitz *has* no appropriate narrative, only a set of statistics" (Diner, 2000: 178). Becoming evil is a matter, first and foremost, of representation. Depending on the nature of representation, a traumatic event may be regarded as ontologically evil, or its badness, its "evility," may be conceived as contingent and relative, as something that can be ameliorated and overcome. This distinction is theoretical, but it is also practical. In fact, decisions about the ontological versus contingent status of the Holocaust were of overriding importance in its changing representation.

If we can deconstruct this ontological assertion even further, I would like to suggest that the very existence of the category "evil" must be seen not as something that naturally exists but as an arbitrary construction, the product of cultural and sociological work. This contrived binary, which simplifies empirical complexity to two antagonistic forms, has been an essential feature of all human societies. This rigid opposition between the sacred and profane, which in western philosophy has typically been constructed as a conflict between normativity and instrumentality, not only defines what people care about but establishes vital safeguards around the shared normative "good." At the same time, it places powerful, even aggressive, barriers against anything construed as threatening the good, forces defined not merely as things to be avoided but as sources of horror and pollution that must be contained at all costs.

The material "base": controlling the means of symbolic production

Yet, if this grid is a kind of functional necessity, how it is applied very much depends on who is telling the story, and how. This is first of all a matter of cultural power in the most mundane, materialist sense: who controls the means of symbolic production? It was certainly not incidental to the public understanding of the Nazis' policies of mass murder, for example, that for an extended period of time it was the Nazis themselves who were in control of the physical and cultural terrain of their enactment. This fact of brute power made it much more difficult to frame the mass killings in a distinctive way. Nor is it incidental that, once the extermination of the Jews was physically interrupted by Allied armies in 1945, it was America's "imperial republic" – the perspective of the triumphant, forward-looking, militantly and militarily democratic new world warrior – that directed the organizational and cultural responses to the mass murders and their survivors. The contingency of this knowledge is so powerful that it might well be said that, if the Allies had not won the war and "liberated" most of the camps, the "Holocaust" would never have been discovered. It was, in other words, precisely and only because the means of symbolic production were not controlled by a victorious postwar Nazi regime, or even by a triumphant communist one, that the mass killings could be called the Holocaust and coded as evil.

Creating the culture structure

After a phenomenon is coded as evil, the question that immediately follows is, how evil is it? In theorizing evil, this refers to the problem, not of coding, but of weighting. For there are degrees of evil, and these degrees have great implications in terms of responsibility, punishment, remedial action, and future behavior. Normal evil and radical evil cannot be the same.

Finally, alongside these problems of coding and weighting, the meaning of a trauma cannot be defined unless we determine exactly what the "it" is. This is a question of narrative: what were the evil and traumatizing actions in question? Who was responsible? Who were the victims? What were the immediate and long-term results of the traumatizing actions? What can be done by way of remediation or prevention?

What these theoretical considerations suggest is that even after the physical force of the Allied triumph and the physical discovery of the Nazi concentration camps, the nature of what was seen and discovered had to be coded, weighted, and narrated. This complex cultural construction, moreover, had to be achieved immediately. History does not wait; it demands that representations be made. Whether or not some newly reported event is startling, strange, terrible, or inexpressibly weird, it must be "typified," in the sense of Husserl and Schutz, that is, it must be explained as a typical and even anticipated example of some thing or category that was known about before. Even the vastly unfamiliar must somehow be made familiar. To the cultural process of coding, weighting, and narrating, in other words, what comes before is all-important. Historical background is critical, both for the first "view" of the traumatic event and, as "history" changes, for later views as well. Once again, these shifting cultural constructions are fatefully affected by the power and identity of the agents in charge, by the competition for symbolic control, and the structures of power and distribution of resources that condition it.

Naziism as the representation of absolute evil

What was the historical structure of "good and evil" within which, on April 3, 1945, the "news" of the Nazi concentration camps was first confirmed to the American audience? In the deeply disturbing wake of World War I, there was a pervasive sense of disillusionment and cynicism among mass and elite members of the western "audience," a distancing from protagonists and antagonists that, as Paul Fussell has shown, made irony the master trope of that first postwar era. This trope transformed "demonology" – the very act of coding and weighting evil – into what many considered to be an act of bad faith. Good and evil became less distinct from one another, and relativism became the dominant motif of the time. In such conditions, coherent narration of contemporary events becomes difficult if not impossible. Thus it was that, not only for many intellectuals and artists of this period but for many ordinary people as well, the startling upheavals of these interwar years could not easily be sorted out in a conclusive and satisfying way.

In this context of the breakdown of representation, racism and revolution, whether fascist or communist, emerged as compelling frames, not only in Europe but also in the United States. Against a revolutionary narrative of dogmatic and authoritarian modernism on the Left, there arose the narrative of reactionary modernism, equally revolutionary but fervently opposed to rationality and cosmopolitanism. Many democrats in western Europe and the United States withdrew from the field of representation itself, becoming confused and equivocating advocates of disarmament, non-violence, and peace "at any price." This formed the cultural frame for isolationist political policy in both Britain and the United States.

Eventually, the aggressive military ambition of Naziism made such equivocation impossible to sustain. While racialism, relativism, and narrative confusion continued in the United States and Britain until the very beginning of World War II, and even well into it, these constructions were countered by increasingly confident representations of good and evil that coded liberal democracy and universalism as unalloyed goods, and Naziism, racism, and prejudice as representations of the polluting and profane.

From the late 1930s on, there emerged an eventually dominant anti-fascist narrative in western societies. Naziism was coded, weighted, and narrated in apocalyptic, Old Testament terms as "the dominant evil of our time." Because this radical evil aligned itself with violence and massive death, it not merely justified, but compelled, the risking of life in opposing it, a compulsion that motivated and justified massive human sacrifice in what came later to be known as the last "good war." That Naziism was an absolute, unmitigated evil, a radical evil that threatened the very future of human civilization, formed the presupposition of America's four-year prosecution of the world war.

The representation of Naziism as an absolute evil emphasized not only its association with sustained coercion and violence, but also, and perhaps even especially, the manner in which Naziism linked violence with ethnic, racial, and religious hatred. In this way, the most conspicuous example of the practice of Nazi evil – its policy of systematic discrimination, coercion, and, eventually, mass violence against the Jews – was initially interpreted as "simply" another horrifying example of the subhumanism of Nazi action.

Interpreting "Kristallnacht": Nazi evil as anti-Semitism

The American public's reaction to *Kristallnacht* demonstrates how important the Nazis' anti-Jewish activities were in crystallizing the polluted status of

Naziism in American eyes. It also provides a prototypical example of how such representations of the evils of anti-Semitism were folded into the broader and more encompassing symbolism of Naziism. *Kristallnacht* refers, of course, to the rhetorically virulent and physically violent expansion of the Nazi repression of Jews that unfolded throughout German towns and cities on November 9 and 10, 1938. These activities were widely reported. Exactly why these events assumed such critical importance in the American public's continuing effort to understand "what Hitlerism stood for" (Diamond, 1969: 201) goes beyond the simple fact that violent and repressive activities were, perhaps for the first time, openly, even brazenly displayed in direct view of the world public sphere. Equally important was the altered cultural framework within which these activities were observed. For *Kristallnacht* occurred just six weeks after the now infamous Munich agreements, acts of appeasement to Hitler's expansion which at that time were understood, not only by isolationists but by many opponents of Naziism, indeed by the vast majority of the American people, as possibly reasonable accessions to a possibly reasonable man (Diamond, 1969: 197). What occurred, in other words, was a process of understanding fuelled by symbolic contrast, not simply observation.

What was interpretively constructed was the cultural difference between Germany's previously apparent reasonableness – representations of the good in the discourse of American civil society – and its subsequent demonstration of violence and irrationality, which were taken to be representations of anti-civic evil. Central to the ability to draw this contrast was the ethnic and religious hatred Germans demonstrated in their violence against Jews. If one examines the American public's reactions, it is this anti-Jewish violence that is taken to represent Naziism's evil. The *New York Times* employed the rhetoric of pollution further to code and weight Nazi evil: "No foreign propagandist bent upon blackening the name of Germany before the world could outdo the tale of beating, of blackguardly assaults upon defenseless and innocent people, which degraded that country yesterday" (quoted in Diamond, 1969: 198). The *Washington Post* identified the Nazi activities as "one of the worst setbacks for mankind since the Massacre of St. Bartholomew" (quoted in Diamond, 1969: 198–199).

This broadening identification of Naziism with evil, both triggered and reinforced by *Kristallnacht*'s anti-Jewish violence, stimulated influential political figures to make more definitive judgments about the antipathy between American democracy and German Naziism than they had up until that point. Speaking on NBC radio, Al Smith, the former New York governor and democratic presidential candidate, observed that the events confirmed that the German people were "incapable of living under a democratic government" (quoted in Diamond, 1969: 200). Having initially underplayed America's official reaction to the events, four days later President Franklin Roosevelt now emphasized the purity of the American nation and its distance from this emerging representation of violence and ethnic hatred: "The news of the past few days from Germany deeply shocked public opinion in the United States . . . I myself could scarcely believe that such things could occur in a twentieth century civilization" (quoted in Diamond, 1969: 205). Judging from these reactions, it seems only logical that, as one historian has put it, "most American newspapers or journals" could "no longer . . . view Hitler as a pliable and reasonable man, but as an aggressive and contemptible dictator [who] would have to be restrained" (quoted in Diamond, 1969: 207).

What is equally striking, however, is that in almost none of the American public's statements is there explicit reference to the identity of *Kristallnacht*'s victims as Jews. Instead, they are referred to as a "defenseless and innocent people," as "others," and as a "defenseless people" (quoted in Diamond, 1969: 198, 199, 201). In fact, President Roosevelt goes well out of his way to present his polluting judgment of the events as reflecting a typically American standard, strenuously removing his moral outrage from any link to a specific concern for the fate of the Jews. "Such news from *any part* of the world," the President insists, "would inevitably produce similar profound reaction among Americans *in any part* of the nation" (Diamond, 1969: 205, italics added). In other words, despite the centrality of the Nazis' anti-Jewish violence to the emerging American symbolization of Naziism as evil, there existed – at that point in historical and cultural time – a reluctance for non-Jewish Americans to identify with Jewish people as such. The fate of the Jews would be understood only in relation to the German horror that threatened democratic civilization in America and Europe. This failure of identification would be reflected seven years later in the distantiation of the American soldiers and domestic audience from the traumatized Jewish camp survivors and their even less fortunate Jewish compatriots whom the Nazis had killed.

Anti-anti-Semitism: fighting Nazi evil by fighting for the Jews

During the 1930s, in the context of the Nazi persecution of German Jews, there also emerged in the United States an historically unprecedented attack on anti-Semitism. It was not that Christians suddenly felt genuine affection for, or identification with, those whom they had vilified for countless centuries as the killers of Christ. It was that the logic of symbolic association had dramatically changed. Naziism was increasingly viewed as the vile enemy of universalism and the most hated enemies of Naziism were the Jews. If Naziism singled out the Jews as their enemies, then that negation must be countered by democrats and anti-Nazis. Anti-Semitism, tolerated and condoned for centuries in every western nation, and for the preceding fifty years embraced fervently by proponents of American "nativism," suddenly became distinctly unpopular in progressive circles throughout the United States (Gleason, 1981; Higham, 1984).

What I will call "anti-anti-Semitism" became particularly intense after the USA declared war on Nazi Germany. For the first time, positive representations of Jewish people proliferated in popular and high culture alike. It was during this period that the phrase "Judeo-Christian tradition" was born. Fighting anti-Semitism and defending American democracy were now of a piece.

Constructing the progressive narrative in the war against Naziism

Naziism marked a traumatic epoch in modern history. Yet, while coded as evil, it was narrated inside a framework that offered the promise of salvation and triggered actions that generated confidence and hope. What I will call the "progressive narrative" proclaimed that the trauma created by social evil would be overcome, that Naziism would be defeated and eliminated from the world, eventually be relegated to a traumatic past whose darkness would be obliterated by a new and powerful social light. The progressivity of this narrative depended on keeping Naziism situated and historical, which prevented this representation of absolute evil from being universalized and its cultural power from being equated, in any way, with the power possessed by the good. In narrative terms, this asymmetry, this insistence on Naziism's anomalous historical status, assured its ultimate defeat. In the popular consciousness and in the dramas created by cultural specialists, the origins of Naziism were linked to specific events in the interwar period and to particular organizations and actors within it, to a political party, to a crazy and inhuman leader, to an anomalous nation that had demonstrated militaristic and violent tendencies over the previous one hundred years.

The trauma was dark and threatening, but it was, at the same time, anomalous and, in principle at least, temporary. As such, the trauma could and would be removed, via a just war and a wise and forgiving peace. The vast human sacrifices demanded were measured and judged in terms of this progressive narrative and the salvation it promised. The blood spilled in the war sanctified the future peace and obliterated the past. The sacrifice of millions could be redeemed, not by dwelling in a lachrymose manner on their deaths, but by eliminating Naziism, the force that had caused their deaths, and by planning the future which would establish a world in which there could never be Naziism again.

While initially received with surprise, and always conceived with loathing, the gradual, halting but eventually definitive revelations of Nazi plans for murdering the entirety of European Jewry actually confirmed the categorizing of evil already in place: Naziism as an inhuman, absolutely evil force. What had been experienced as an extraordinary trauma by the Jewish victims, was experienced by the audience of others as a kind of categorical vindication. In this way, and for this reason, the democratic audience for the reports on the mass murders experienced distance from, rather than identification with, the trauma's victims. The revelations had the effect, in some perverse sense, of normalizing the abnormal.

The empirical existence of Nazi plans for the "Final Solution," as well as extensive documentation of their ongoing extermination activities, had been publicly documented by June 1942 (Dawidowicz, 1982; Laqueur, 1980; Norich, 1998–99). In July of that year more than 20,000 persons rallied in Madison Square Garden to protest the Nazis' war against the Jews. Though he did not attend in person, President Franklin Roosevelt sent a special message that what he called "these crimes" would be redeemed by the "final accounting" following the Allied victory over Naziism. In March, 1943, the American Jewish Congress announced that two million Jews had already been massacred and that millions more were slated for death. Its detailed descriptions of the "extermination" were widely reported in the American press. By March, 1944, when the Germans occupied Hungary and their intention to liquidate its entire Jewish population became known, Dawidowicz shows that, for Americans, Auschwitz was no longer an unfamiliar name (Dawidowicz, 1982).

Yet, it was this very familiarity that seemed to undermine the sense of astonishment that might have stimulated immediate action. For Auschwitz was typified in terms of the progressive narrative of war, a narrative that made it impossible to de-normalize the mass killings. What eventually came to be called the Holocaust was reported to contemporaries as a war story, nothing less but nothing more. In private conferences with the American president, Jewish leaders demanded that Allied forces make special efforts to target and destroy the death camps. In describing these failed efforts to trigger intervention, a leading historian explains that the leaders "couldn't convince a preoccupied American President and the American public of the significance of Auschwitz for their time in history" (Feingold, 1974: 250). In other words, while Auschwitz was coded as evil, it simply was not weighted in a sufficiently dire way.

In these symbolically mediated confrontations, attention was not focused on the mass killings in and of themselves, the discovery of an evil unique in human history. The evil of that time had already been discovered, and it was Naziism, not the massive killing of European Jews. The trauma which this evil had created was a second world war. The trauma that the Jews experienced in the midst of their liquidation was represented as one among a series of effects of Nazi evil. As one historian has put it, "the processed mass murders became merely another atrocity in a particularly cruel war" (quoted in Benn, 1995: 102). The mass murders were explained, and they would be redeemed, within the framework of the progressive struggle against Naziism.

To understand the initial, frame-establishing encounter between Americans and the Jewish mass murder, it is vital to remember that narratives, no matter how progressive and future-oriented, are composed of both antagonists and protagonists. The antagonists and their crimes were well established: the German Nazis had murdered the Jews in a gigantic, heinous atrocity of war. The protagonists were the American GIs, and their entrance into the concentration camps was portrayed, not only as a discovery of such horrendous atrocities, but as another, culminating stage in a long and equally well-known sequence of "liberation," with all the ameliorating expectations that utopian term implies (Zelizer, 1998: 63). When readers of the *New York Times* and *Los Angeles Times* were confronted, on April 16, with the photo from Buchenwald of bunk-beds stuffed to overflowing with haunted, pathetically undernourished male prisoners, they were informed that they were looking at "freed slave laborers" (Zelizer, 1998: 183).

It was within this highly particularized progressive narrative that the first steps toward universalization actually took place. Because the Jewish mass killings came at the conclusion of the war, and because they without doubt represented the most gruesome illustration of Nazi atrocities, they came very quickly to be viewed not merely as symptoms but as emblems and iconic representations of the evil that the progressive narrative promised to leave behind. As the novelist and war correspondent Meyer Levin wrote of his visit to Ohrdruf, the first camp American soldiers liberated, "it was as though we had penetrated at last to the center of the black heart, to the very crawling inside of the vicious heart" (quoted in Abzug, 1985: 19). On the one hand, the trauma was localized and particularized – it occurred in this war, in this place, with these persons. On the other hand, the mass murder was universalized. Within months of the initial revelations, indeed, the murders frequently were framed by a new term, "genocide," a crime defined as the effort to destroy an entire people which, while introduced earlier, during the war period itself, became publicly available and widely employed only after the discovery of the Nazi atrocities.

In response to this new representation, the scope of the Nuremberg War Crimes Tribunal was enlarged. Conceived as a vehicle for linking the postwar Allied cause to progressive redemption, the Trials were now to go beyond prosecuting the Nazi leaders for crimes of war to considering their role in the mass murder against the Jewish people. Justice Robert Jackson, the chief American prosecutor, promised that the trial would not only prosecute those responsible for the war but would present "undeniable proofs of incredible events" – the Nazi crimes (quoted in Benn, 1995: 102). The first three counts of the 20,000-word indictment against the twenty-three high-ranking Nazi officials concerned the prosecution of the war itself. They charged conspiracy, conducting a war of aggression, and violating the rules of war. The fourth count, added only in the months immediately preceding the October trial in Nuremberg, accused the Nazi leaders of something new, namely of "crimes against humanity." This was the first step toward universalizing the public representation of the Jewish mass murder. From the perspective of the present day, however, it appears as a relatively limited one, for it functioned to confirm the innocent virtue and national ambitions of one particular side. In its first report on the indictments, for example, the *New York Times* linked the Jewish mass murder directly to the war itself, and placed its punishment within the effort to prevent any future "war of aggression." The Nuremberg Trial was not, in other words, perceived as preventing genocide or crimes against humanity as such. At that time, the commission of such crimes could not be conceived apart from the Nazis and the recently concluded aggressive war.

The force of the progressive narrative meant that, while the 1945 revelations confirmed the Jewish mass murder, in themselves they did not create a trauma for the postwar audience. Victory and the Nuremberg war trials would put an end to Naziism and alleviate its evil effects. Postwar redemption depended on putting mass murder "behind us," moving on, and getting on with the construction of the new world (Lipstadt, 1996: 195–214; Rosenfield, 1995: 37–38). This was as true for Jewish as for non-Jewish Americans, whose leaders unanimously rejected a proposal for a Holocaust memorial in New York City (Novick, 1994: 160).

It was neither emotional repression nor good moral sense that created the early responses to the mass murder of the Jews. It was, rather, a system of collective representations that focused its narrative light on the triumphant expulsion of evil. Most Americans did not identify with the victims of the Jewish trauma. Far from being implicated in it, Americans had defeated those responsible for the mass murders and righteously engaged in restructuring the social and political arrangements that had facilitated them. This did not mean that the mass murder of Jews was viewed with relativism or equanimity. According to the progressive narrative, it was America's solemn task to redeem the sacrifice of this largest of all categories of Nazi victims. In postwar America, the public redeemed the sacrifices of war by demanding the thorough de-Nazification, not only of German but also of American society. As Sumner Welles eloquently framed the issue a month after the GIs had entered the Nazi death camps, "the crimes committed by the Nazis and by their accomplices against the Jewish people are indelible stains upon the whole of our modern civilization" (Welles, 1945: 511).

Making progress: purifying America and redeeming the murder of the Jews

Propelled by the logic of this progressive understanding of redemption, the long-standing anti-anti-Semitism culminated in the immediate postwar period in a massive shift of American public opinion on the Jewish question (Stember, 1966). Only days after the hostilities ceased, in response to an appeal from the National Council of Christians and Jews, the three candidates for Mayor of New York city pledged to "refrain from appeals to racial and religious divisiveness during the campaign." One of them made explicit the connection of this public anti-anti-Semitism to the effort to remain connected to, and enlarge upon, the meaning of America's triumph in the anti-Nazi war.

This election will be the first held in the City of New York since our victory over nazism and Japanese fascism. It will therefore be an occasion for a practical demonstration of democracy in action – a democracy in which all are equal citizens, in which there is not and never must be a second class citizenship and in which . . . the religion of a candidate must play no part in the campaign.   (*The New York Times*, October 1, 1945: 32)

Political activism of Jewish groups rose dramatically in the immediate post-war period from 1945 to 1948 (Dinnerstein, 1981). Newly surfaced, and often newly formed, groups held conferences, wrote editorials, and issued specific proposals for legal and institutional changes. By 1950, these activities had successfully exposed and often defeated anti-Jewish quotas and, more generally, created an extraordinary shift in the practical and cultural position of American Jews. During the same month that New York's mayoral candidates announced their anti-anti-Semitism, *The American Mercury* published an article, "Discrimination in Medical Colleges," replete with graphs and copious documentation, detailing the existence of anti-Jewish quotas in some of America's most prestigious professional institutions. While the specific focus was anti-Jewish discrimination, these facts were narrated in terms of the overarching promise of America and democracy:

[He] made an excellent scholastic record [but] upon graduation . . . his first application for admission to a medical school . . . was mysteriously turned down. He filed another and another – at eighty-seven schools – always with the same heartbreaking result . . . Not one of the schools had the courage to inform Leo frankly that he was being excluded because he was a Jew . . . The excuse for imposing a quota system usually advanced is that there ought to be some correlation between the number of physicians of any racial or religious strain and the proportion of that race or religion in the general population [but] the surface logic of this arithmetic collapses as soon as one subjects it to *democratic or sheerly human*, let alone scientific, tests. [It is] spurious and *un-American* arithmetic.
(vol. LXI, no. 262, October, 1945: 391–399, italics added)

In the years that followed, the fight against quotas continued to be informed by similar themes (Dodson, 1946: 268). In 1949, *Collier's* published an article describing the "scores of college men to whom fraternities" for "'full-blooded Aryans' are a little nauseating *in this day.*" Quoting the finding of an Amherst College alumni committee that exclusive fraternities gave young men "a false and undemocratic sense of superiority," the article claimed that "the anti-discrimination movement is hopping from campus to campus" (Whitman, 1949: 34–35).

Newly formed Jewish voluntary organizations entered the American public sphere as aggressive political advocates only after 1945, the first time Jews had forcefully entered the civil sphere as advocates for their own rather than others' causes. In the prewar period, such an explicit and aggressively Jewish public intervention would certainly have made anti-Semitism worse. In the postwar period, however, despite their failure to identify with the Jewish victims of Naziism, the American non-Jewish audience was determined to redeem them. If, as Dinnerstein writes, Jewish groups intended to "mobilize public opinion against intolerance, and [thus to] utilize the courts and legislative bodies" in their anti-Semitic fight, they were able to carry on these political activities only because postwar public opinion had already been defined as committed to "tolerance." Progress toward establishing civil relations between religious and ethnic groups was woven into the patriotic postwar narratives of the nation's mass circulation magazines.

The anti-anti-Semitism theme also entered popular culture through the movies. In the 1945 box office hit, *Pride of the Marines*, the Jewish protagonist Larry Diamond chided a friend for pessimism about the possibility of eliminating prejudice in the postwar years. He did so by connecting their present situation to the progressive ideals that had sustained their anti-Nazi war: "Ah, come on, climb out of your foxholes, what's a matter you guys, don't you think anybody learned anything since 1930? Think everybody's had their eyes shut and brains in cold storage?" As the movie's closing music turns into "America the Beautiful," Diamond wraps it up this way: "One happy afternoon when God was feeling good, he sat down and thought of a rich beautiful country and he named it the USA. All of it, Al, the hills, the rivers, the lands, the whole works. Don't tell me we can't make it work in peace like we do in war. Don't tell me we can't pull together. Don't you see it guys, can't you see it?" Two years later, a movie promoting anti-anti-Semitism, *Gentleman's Agreement*, won the Academy Award for best motion picture. In the final dialogue of *Gentlemen's Agreement*, the film's future-oriented, utopian theme could not be more clear. "Wouldn't it be wonderful," Mrs. Green asks Phil, "if it turned out to be everybody's century, when people all over the world, free people, found a way to live together? I'd like to be around to see some of that, even a beginning" (quoted in Short, 1981: 180).

As they had immediately before and during the war, "Jews" held symbolic pride of place in these popular narratives because their persecution had been preeminently associated with the Nazi evil. In fact, it was not tolerance as such that the progressive narrative demanded, but tolerance of the Jews. Thus, despite their feelings of solidarity with their foreign coreligionists, Jewish leaders carefully refrained from publicly endorsing the wholesale lifting of anti-immigration quotas after 1945. They realized that the idea of immigration remained so polluted by association with stigmatized others that it might have the power to counteract the ongoing purification of Jewishness. In the preceding half century, anti-immigration and anti-Semitism had been closely linked, and Jews did not want to pollute "Jewishness" with this identity again. While demonstrating their support in private, Jewish leaders resolutely refused to make any public pronouncements against lifting the immigration quotas (Dinnerstein, 1981–82: 140).

What Dinnerstein has called the "turnabout in anti-Semitic feelings" represented the triumph over Naziism, not recognition of the Holocaust trauma. News about the mass murder, and any ruminations about it, disappeared from newspapers and magazines rather quickly after the initial reports about the camps' liberation, and the Nazis' Jewish victims became represented as displaced persons, potential immigrants, and potential settlers in Palestine, where a majority of Americans wanted to see a new, and redemptive, Jewish state. This interpretation suggests that it was by no means simply real politik that led President Truman to champion, against his former French and British allies, the postwar creation of Israel, the new Jewish state. The progressive narrative demanded a future-oriented renewal. Zionists argued that the Jewish trauma could be redeemed, that Jews could both sanctify the victims and put the trauma behind them, only if they returned to Jerusalem. According to the Zionist world view, if Israel were allowed to exist, it would create a new race of confident and powerful Jewish farmer–warriors, who would redeem the anti-Jewish atrocities by developing such an imposing military power that the massive murdering of the Jews would never, anywhere in the world, be allowed to happen again. In important respects, it was this convergence of progressive narratives in relation to the war and the Jewish mass killings that led the postwar paths of the United States and the state of Israel to become so fundamentally intertwined. Israel would have to prosper and survive for the redemptive telos of America's progressive narrative to be maintained.

These cultural–sociological considerations do not suggest that the postwar American fight against anti-Semitism was in any way morally inauthentic.

It was triggered by grassroots feelings as deep as those that had motivated the earlier anti-Nazi fight. When one looks at these powerful new arguments against anti-Semitism, it is only retrospectively surprising to realize that the "atrocities" revealed in 1945 – the events and experiences that defined the trauma for European Jews – figure hardly at all. This absence is explained by the powerful symbolic logic of the progressive narrative, which already had been established in the prewar period. With the victory in 1945, the United States got down to the work of establishing the new world order. In creating a Nazi-free future, Jewishness came for the first time to be analogically connected with core American symbols of "democracy" and "nation."

In the course of this postwar transformation, American Jews also became identified with democracy in a more primordial and less universalistic way, namely as newly minted, patriotic representations of the nation. "After 1945," a leading historian of that period remarks, "other Americans no longer viewed the Jews as merely another of the many exotic groups within America's ethnic and religious mosaic. Instead, they were now seen as comprising one of the country's three major religions" (Shapiro, 1992: 28). This patriotic-national definition was expressed by the Jewish theologian Will Herberg's insistence on the "Judeo-Christian" rather than "Christian" identity of the religious heritage of the USA (Shapiro, 1992: 53). What motivated this intense identification of anti-anti-Semitism with the American nation was neither simple emotional revulsion for the horrors of the Jewish mass killings nor common sense morality. It was, rather, the progressive narrative frame. To end anti-Semitism, in President Truman's words, was to place America alongside "the moral forces of the world" (quoted in Shapiro, 1992: 143). It was to redeem those who had sacrificed themselves for the American nation, and, according to the teleology of the progressive narrative, this emphatically included the masses of murdered European Jews.

Deepening evil: Jewish mass murder under the tragic narrative

In the second part of this chapter, I will show how a different kind of narrative developed in relation to the Nazis' mass murder of the Jews, one which gave the evil represented significantly greater symbolic weight. In the formation of a new culture structure, the coding of the Jewish mass killings as evil remained, but its weighting substantially changed. It became burdened with extraordinary gravitas. The symbolization of the Jewish mass killings became generalized and reified, and, in the process, the evil done to the Jews became separated from the profanation of Naziism per se. Rather than seeming to "typify" Naziism, or even the nefarious machinations of any particular social movement, political formation, or historical time, the mass killings came to be seen as not being typical of anything at all. They came to be understood as a unique, historically unprecedented event, as evil on a scale that had never occurred before. The mass killings entered into universal history, becoming a "world historical" event in Hegel's original sense, an event whose emergence onto the world stage threatened, or promised, to change the fundamental course of the world. In the introduction to an English collection of his essays on Nazi history and the Holocaust, the German–Israeli historian Dan Diner observes that "well into the 1970s, wide-ranging portraits of the epoch would grant the Holocaust a modest (if any) mention." By contrast, "it now tends to fill the entire picture" (Diner, 2000: 1).

The Jewish mass killings became what we might identify, in Durkheimian terms, as a sacred-evil, an evil that recalled a trauma of such enormity and horror that it had to be radically set apart from the world, an evil which became inexplicable in ordinary, rational terms. As part of the Nazi scheme of world domination, the Jewish mass killing was heinous but understandable. As a sacred evil, set apart from ordinary evil things, it had become mysterious and inexplicable. One of the first to characterize this post-progressive inexplicability was the Marxist historian, Isaac Deutscher. This great biographer of Trotsky, who had already faced the consequences of Stalinism for the myth of communist progress, was no doubt already conditioned to see the tragic dimensions of the Holocaust. In 1968, in "The Jewish Tragedy and the Historian," Deutscher suggested that comprehending the Holocaust "will not be just a matter of time."

I doubt whether even in a thousand years people will understand Hitler, Auschwitz, Majdanek, and Treblinka better than we do now. Will they have a better historical perspective? On the contrary, posterity may even understand it all even less than we do.

Who can analyze the motives and the interests behind the enormities of Auschwitz . . . We are confronted here by a huge and ominous mystery of the generation of the human character that will forever baffle and terrify mankind.   (Deutcher, 1968: 163)

For Deutscher, such a huge and mysterious evil, so resistant to the normal progress of human rationality, suggested tragedy and art, not scientific fact-gathering, something exceeding the limits of "historical interpretation and explanation." Historians and commentators increasingly discerned some excess, some surplus in the event itself that resists interpretation (Hartman, 1996: 3–4; van Gelder, 1999: 1).

This separateness of sacred-evil demanded that the trauma be renamed, for the concept of "mass murder," and even the notion of "genocide," now appeared unacceptably to normalize the trauma, to place it too close to the banal and mundane. In contrast, despite the fact that the word "Holocaust" did have a formally established English meaning – according to the *OED*, "something wholly burnt up" (Garber and Zuckerman, 1989: 199) – it no longer performed this sign function in everyday speech. Rather, the term entered into ordinary English usage, in the early 1960s, as a proper rather than a common noun. Only several years after the Nazis' mass murder did Israelis begin to employ the Hebrew word *shoah*, the term by which the Torah evoked the kind of extraordinary sufferings God had periodically consigned to the Jews. In the official English translation of the phrase "Nazi *shoah*" in the preamble to the 1948 Israeli Declaration of Independence, one can already find the reference to "Nazi holocaust" (Novick, 1999: 132). With the decline of the progressive narrative, in other words, as "Holocaust" became the dominant representation for the trauma, it implied the sacral mystery, the "awe-fullness," of the transcendental tradition. "Holocaust" became part of contemporary language as an English symbol that stood for that thing that could not be named. As David Roskies once wrote, "it was precisely the nonreferential quality of 'Holocaust' that made it so appealing" (quoted in Garber and Zuckerman, 1989: 201).

This new linguistic identity allowed the mass killings of the Jews to become what might be called a bridge metaphor: it provided the symbolic extension so necessary if the trauma of the Jewish people was to become a trauma for all humankind. The other necessary ingredient, psychological identification, was not far behind. It depended on configuring this newly weighted symbolization of evil in a different narrative frame.

Suffering, catharsis, and identification

The darkness of this new postwar symbolization of evil cast a shadow over the progressive story that had thus far narrated its course. The story of redeeming Naziism's victims by creating a democratic world order could be called an ascending narrative; it suggested confidence that things would be better over time. Insofar as the mass killings were defined as a Holocaust, and insofar as it was the very emergence of this sacred-evil, not its eventual defeat, that threatened to become emblematic of "our time," the progressive narrative was blocked, and in some manner overwhelmed, by a sense of historical descent, by a falling away from the good.

In dramaturgical terms, the issue concerns the position occupied by evil in the historical narrative. When Aristotle first defined tragedy in the *Poetics*, he linked what I have here called the weight of the representation of suffering to temporal location of an event in the plot, a representation with a beginning, a middle, and a conclusion. Well-constructed plots do not begin from a random point (Aristotle, 1987: 3.2.1).

In the progressive narrative, the Jewish mass killings were not an end but a beginning. In the postwar period they and related incidents of Nazi horror were regarded as a birth trauma, a crossroads in a chronology that would eventually be set right. By contrast, the newly emerging world-historical status of the mass murders suggested that they represented an end point, not a new beginning, a cause for despair, not the beginning of hope. In place of the progressive story, then, there began to emerge the narrative of tragedy. The endpoint of a narrative defines its telos. In this tragic understanding of the Jewish mass murder, suffering, not progress, became the telos toward which the narrative was aimed.

In this tragic narrative, the Jewish mass killings become not an event in history but an archetype, an event out-of-time. As archetype, the sacred evil evoked an experience of trauma greater than anything that could be defined by religion, race, class, region – indeed, by any conceivable sociological configuration or historical conjuncture. This transcendental status, this separation from any particular time or space, provided the basis for psychological identification on an unprecedented scale. The contemporary audience cares little about the second and third installments of Sophocles' archetypal story of Oedipus, the tragic hero. What we are obsessed with is Oedipus' awful, unrecognized, and irredeemable mistake, how he finally comes to recognize his responsibility for it, and how he blinds himself from guilt when he understands its full meaning. Tragic narratives focus attention not on some future effort at reversal or amelioration – "progress," in the terms I have employed here – but on the nature of the crime, its immediate aftermath, and on the motives and relationships that led up to it.

A tragic narrative offers no redemption in the traditionally religious, Judeo-Christian sense, no sense that something else could have been done, and no belief that the future could, or can, necessarily be changed. Indeed, protagonists are tragic precisely because they are in the grip of forces larger than themselves, impersonal, even inhuman forces that often are not only beyond control but, during the tragic action itself, beyond comprehension. This sense of being overwhelmed by unjust force or fate explains the abjection and helplessness that permeates the genre of tragedy, and the experience of pity it arouses.

Instead of redemption through progress, the tragic narrative offers what Nietzsche called the drama of the eternal return. Now there was no "getting beyond" the story of the Holocaust. There was only the possibility of returning to it: not transcendence but catharsis (Hartman, 1996: 2, 5). As Aristotle explained, catharsis clarifies feeling and emotion. It does so not by allowing the audience to separate itself from the story's characters, a separation, according to Frye, that defines the very essence of comedy (Frye, 1971). Rather, catharsis clarifies feeling and emotion by forcing the audience to identify with the story's characters, compelling them to experience their suffering and to learn, as often they did not, the true causes of their death. That we survive and they do not, that we can get up and leave the theater while they remain forever prostrate – this allows the possibility of catharsis, that strange combination of cleansing and relief, that humbling feeling of having been exposed to the dark and sinister forces that lay just beneath the surface of human life, and of having survived. We seek catharsis because our identification with the tragic narrative compels us to experience dark and sinister forces that are also inside of ourselves, not only inside others. We "redeem" tragedy by experiencing it, but, despite this redemption, we do not get over it. Rather, to achieve redemption we are compelled to dramatize and re-dramatize, experience and re-experience the archetypal trauma. We pity the victims of the trauma, identifying and sympathizing with their horrible fate.

Aristotle argued the tragic genre could be utilized only for the "sorts of occurrence [that] arouse dread, or compassion in us" (Aristotle, 1987: 4.1.2). The blackness of tragedy can be achieved only if, "first and foremost, the [suffering] characters should be good," for "the plot should be constructed in such a way that, even without seeing it, someone who hears about the incidents will shudder and feel pity at the outcome, as someone may feel upon hearing the plot of the Oedipus" (Aristotle, 1987: 4.2.1, 4.1.1.3). It is not only the fact of identification, however, but its complexity that makes the experience of trauma as tragedy so central to the assumption of moral responsibility, for we identify not only with the victims but with the perpetrators as well. The creation of this cultural form allows the psychological activity of internalization rather than projection, acceptance rather than displacement.

The trauma drama: eternal return and the problem of progress

In the tragic narration of the Holocaust, the primal event became a "trauma drama" to which the "audience" returned time and again. This became, paradoxically, the only way to ensure that such an event would happen "never again." This quality of compulsively returning to the trauma drama transformed it into the archetypical sacred-evil of our time. Insofar as it achieved this status as a dominant myth, the tragedy of the Holocaust challenged the ethical self-identification, the self-esteem, of modernity – indeed, the very self-confidence that such a thing as "modern progress" could continue to exist. For to return to the Holocaust, to identify over and over again with the suffering and helplessness of its victims, was in some sense to give that confidence-shattering event a continuing existence in contemporary life. It was, in effect, to acknowledge that it *could* happen again.

In this way, the tragic framing of the Holocaust fundamentally contributed to postmodern relativism and disquiet. Because the tragic replaced the progressive narrative of the Nazi mass murder, the ethical standards protecting good from evil seemed not nearly as powerful as modernity's confident pronouncements had promised they would be. When the progressive narrative had organized understanding, the Nazi crimes had been temporalized as "medieval," in order to contrast them with the supposedly civilizing standards of modernity. With the emergence of the more tragic perspective, the barbarism was lodged within the essential nature of modernity itself (Bauman, 1989).

It would be wrong, however, to imagine that because a trauma drama lies at the center of the Holocaust's tragic narration, with all the ambition of exciting pity and emotional catharsis that this implies, that this lachrymose narrative and symbol actually became disconnected from the ethical and the good. While the mass killings of Jews came to assume a dramaturgical form, their significance hardly became aestheticized, i.e., turned into a free-floating, amoral symbol whose function was to entertain rather than to instruct. The events of the Holocaust were not dramatized for the sake of drama itself, but rather to provide what Martha Nussbaum once described as "the social benefits of pity" (Nussbaum, 1992).

The project of renaming, dramatizing, reifying, and ritualizing the Holocaust contributed to a moral remaking of the (post)modern (western) world. The Holocaust story has been told and retold in response to not only an emotional need but a moral ambition. Its characters, its plot, and its pitiable denouement have been transformed into an increasingly less nationally bound, less temporally specific, and more universal drama. This dramatic universalization has deepened contemporary sensitivity to social evil. The trauma drama's message, as every tragedy's, is that evil is inside all of us, and in every society. If we are all the victims, and all the perpetrators, then there is no audience that can legitimately distance itself from collective suffering, from either its victims or its perpetrators.

This psychological identification with the Jewish mass killings and the symbolic extension of its moral implications beyond the immediate parties involved has stimulated an unprecedented universalization of political and moral responsibility. To have created this symbol of sacred-evil in contemporary time, then, is to have so enlarged the human imagination that it is capable, for the first time in human history, of identifying, understanding, and judging the kinds of genocidal mass killings in which national, ethnic, and ideological groupings continue to engage today. This enlargement has made it possible to comprehend that heinous prejudice with the intent to commit mass murder is not something from an earlier, more "primitive" time or a different, "foreign" place, committed by people with values we do not share. The implication of the tragic narrative is not that progress has become impossible. It has had the salutary effect, rather, of demonstrating that progress is much more difficult to achieve than moderns once believed. If progress is to be made, morality must be universalized beyond any particular time and place. These bathetic events, once experienced as traumatic only by their Jewish victims, became generalized and universalized. The representation of Jewish mass death no longer referred to events that took place at a particular time and place but to a trauma that had became emblematic, and iconic, of human suffering as such. The horrific trauma of the Jews became the trauma of all humankind.

The symbolic reconstruction was a slow concatenated process. Through personalized dramas, such as the *Diary of Anne Frank*, and dramatized trials, such as the 1961 Adolf Eichmann trial, both the victims and the perpetrators became everyman and everywoman. Steven Spielberg's *Schindler's List* suggested that anybody could be good. Holocaust museums, designed to facilitate identification with the Jewish victims, proliferated. The United States steadily lost control over the the means of symbolic production of this drama. During the Vietnam War, the United States was increasingly positioned as a Nazi analogue. As America became "Amerika," napalm bombs were analogized with gas pellets, and the flaming jungles of Vietnam with the gas chambers. The powerful American army that claimed to be prosecuting a "good war" against Vietnamese communists – in analogy with the lessons that western democracies had learned in their earlier struggle against Naziism – came to be identified, by influential intellectuals and a wide swath of the educated western public, as perpetrating genocide against the helpless and pathetic inhabitants of Vietnam. Bertrand Russell and Jean-Paul Sartre established a kind of counter-"War Crimes Tribunal" to apply the logic of Nuremberg to the United States. Indefensible incidents of civilian killing, like the My Lai Massacre of 1968, were represented, not as anomalous incidents, but as typifications of this new American-made tragedy.

This process of material deconstruction and symbolic inversion further contributed to the universalization of the Holocaust: it allowed the moral criteria generated by its earlier interpretation to be applied in a less nationally specific and thus less particularistic way. This inversion undermined still further the progressive narrative under which the mass killings of the Jews had early been framed. For the ability to leave the trauma drama behind, and to press ahead toward the future, depended on the material and symbolic existence of an unsullied protagonist who could provide salvation for survivors by leading them into the promised land. "Vietnam" and "the sixties" undercut the main agent of this progressive narrative. The result was a dramatic decline in the confidence that a new world order could be constructed in opposition to violence and coercion; if the United States itself committed war crimes, what chance could there be for modern and democratic societies ever to leave mass murder safely behind?

Perhaps the most visible and paradoxical effect of this loss of the American government's control over the means of symbolic production control was that the morality of American leadership in World War II came to be questioned in a manner that established polluting analogies with Naziism. One issue that now became "troubling," for example, was the justification for the Allied fire bombings of Dresden and Tokyo. The growing climate of relativism and reconfiguration threatened to undermine the coding, weighting, and narrating that once had provided a compelling rationale for those earlier events that were, in themselves, so massively destructive of civilian life. In a similar manner, but with much more significant repercussions, the symbolic implications of the atomic bombings of Hiroshima and Nagasaki began to be fundamentally reconfigured. From being conceived as stages in the unfolding of the progressive narrative, influential groups of westerners came to understand the atomic bombings as vast human tragedies. Younger generations of Americans, in fact, were increasingly responsive to the view of these events that had once been promoted exclusively by Japan, the fascist Axis power against which their elders had waged war. The interpretation of the suffering caused by the atomic bombings became separated from the historical specifics of time and place. With this generalization, the very events that had once appeared as high points of the progressive narrative came to be constructed as unjustifiable, as human tragedies, as slaughters of hundreds of thousands of innocent and pathetic human beings – in short, as typifications of the "Holocaust."

Perhaps the most pointed example of what could happen after America lost control over the Holocaust story was the manner in which its redemptive role in the narrative was challenged. Rather than being portrayed as the chief prosecutor of Nazi perpetrators – as chief prosecutor, the narrative's protagonist along with the victims themselves – the American and the British war-time governments were accused of having at least indirect responsibility for allowing the Nazis to carry out their brutal work. A steady stream of revisionist historical scholarship emerged, beginning in the 1970s, suggesting that the anti-Semitism of Roosevelt and Churchill, and of their American and British citizens, had prevented them from acting to block the mass killings. For they had received authenticated information about German plans and activities as early as June, 1942.

This analogical linkage between the Allies and the Perpetrators quickly became widely accepted as historical fact. On September 27, 1979, when the President's Commission on the Victims of the Holocaust issued a report recommending the American establishment of a Holocaust Museum, it listed as one of its primary justifications that such a public construction would give the American nation an opportunity to compensate for its early, "disastrous" indifference to the plight of the Jews (quoted in Linenthal, 1995: 37). When the museum itself was eventually constructed, it enshrined this inversion of the progressive narrative in the exhibitions themselves. The third floor of the museum is filled with powerfully negative images of the death camps, and is attached by an internal bridge to a tower whose rooms display actual artifacts from the camps.

As visitors approach this bridge, in the midst of the iconic representations of evil, they confront a photomural of a US Air Force intelligence photograph of Auschwitz–Birkenau, taken on May 31, 1944. The text attached to the mural informs visitors: "Two freight trains with Hungarian Jews arrived in Birkenau that day; the large-scale gassing of these Jews was beginning. The four Birkenau crematoria are visible at the top of the photograph" (quoted in Linenthal, 1995: 217). Placed next to the photomural is what the principal ethnographer of the museum project, Edward Linenthal, has called "an artifactual indictment of American indifference." It is a letter, dated August 14, 1944, from Assistant Secretary of War John J. McCloy. According to the text, McCoy "rejected a request by the World Jewish Congress to bomb the Auschwitz concentration camp." This rejection is framed in the context not of physical impossibility, nor in terms of the vicissitudes of a world war, but as the result of moral diminution. Visitors are informed that the US Air Force "could have bombed Auschwitz as early as May 1944," since US bombers had "struck Buna, a synthetic-rubber works relying on slave labor, located less than five miles east of Auschwitz-Birkenau." But, despite this physical possibility, the text goes on to note, the death camp "remained untouched."

The alignment of Allied armies with Nazi perpetrators is more than implicit: "Although bombing Auschwitz would have killed many prisoners, it would also have halted the operation of the gas chambers and, ultimately, saved the lives of many more" (quoted in Linenthal, 1995: 217–218). This authoritative reconstruction, it is important to emphasize, is not a brute empirical fact, any more than the framework which had earlier previous sway. In fact, within the discipline of American history, the issue of Allied indifference remains subject to intensive debate (Linenthal, 1995: 219–224). At every point in the construction of a public discourse, however, factual chronicles must be encased in symbolically coded and narrated frames.

Eventually, this revision of the progressive narrative about exclusively Nazi perpetrators extended, with perhaps even more profound consequences, to other Allied powers and to the neutrals in that earlier conflict as well. As the charismatic symbol of French resistance to German occupation, Charles de Gaulle had woven a narrative, during and after the war, that purified his nation by describing his nation as first the victim, and later the courageous opponent, of Nazi domination and the "foreign" collaborators in Vichy. By the late 1970s and 1980s, however, a younger generation of French and non-French historians challenged this definition, seriously polluting the earlier Republican government, and even some of its postwar socialist successors, by documenting massive French collaboration with the anti-democratic, anti-Semitic regime.

In the wake of these reversals, it seemed only a matter of time until the nations who had been "neutral" during the earlier conflict would also be forced to relinquish symbolic control over how the telling of their own stories, at least in the theatre of western opinion if not on their own national stage. Austria, for example, had long depicted itself as a helpless victim of Nazi Germany. When Kurt Waldheim ascended to Secretary-General of the United Nations, however, his hidden association with the Hitler regime was revealed, and the symbolic status of the Austrian nation, which rallied behind their ex-president, began to be publicly polluted as a result. Less than a decade later, Switzerland became subject to similar inversion of its symbolic fortunes. The tiny republic had prided itself on its long history of decentralized canton democracy and the kind of benevolent, universalizing neutrality of its Red Cross. In the mid-nineties, journalists and historians documented that the wartime Swiss government had laundered, that is, "purified," Nazi gold. In return for gold that had been plundered from the bodies of condemned and already dead Jews, Swiss bankers gave to Nazi authorities acceptable, unmarked currency that could much more readily be used to finance the war.

This discussion of how the non-Jewish agents of the Progressive Narrative were undercut by "real world" developments would be incomplete without some mention of how the Israeli government, which represented the other principal agent of the early, progressive Holocaust story, also came to be threatened with symbolic reconfiguration. The rise of Palestinian liberation movements inverted the Jewish nation's progressive myth of origin, for it suggested, at least to more liberally inclined groups, an equation between Nazi and Israeli treatment of subordinate ethnic and religious groups. The battle for cultural position was not, of course, given up without a fight. When West German Chancellor Helmut Schmidt spoke of Palestinian rights, Israeli Prime Minister Menachem Begin retorted that Schmidt, a Wehrmacht officer in World War II, had "remained faithful to Hitler until the last moment," insisting that the Palestine Liberation Organization was a "neo-Nazi organization" (quoted in Novick, 1994: 161). This symbolic inversion vis-à-vis the newly generalized and reconfigured Holocaust symbol was deepened by the not unrelated complicity of Israel in the massacres that followed the Lebanon invasion, and by the documented reports of Palestinian torture and occasional death in Israeli prisons.

The engorgement of evil and its ethical manifestation

Each of the cultural transformations and social processes I have described has had the effect of universalizing the moral questions provoked by the mass killings of the Jews, of detaching the issues surrounding the systematic exercise of violence against ethnic groups from any particular ethnicity, religion, nationality, time, or place. These processes of detachment and deepening emotional identification are thoroughly intertwined. If the Holocaust were not conceived as a tragedy, it would not attract such continuous, even obsessive attention; this attention would not be rewarded, in turn, if the Holocaust were not understood in a detached and universalizing way. Symbolic extension and emotional identification both are necessary if the audience for a trauma, and its social relevance, are to be dramatically enlarged. The effect of this enlargement is an "engorgement of evil."

Norms provide standards for moral judgment. What is defined as evil in any historical period provides the most transcendental content for such judgments. What Kant called radical evil, and what I would call, drawing on Durkheim, sacred-evil, refers to something considered absolutely essential to defining the good "in our time." Insofar as the "Holocaust" came to define inhumanity in our time, then, it served a fundamental moral function. "Post-Holocaust morality" could perform this role, however, only in a sociological way: it became a bridging metaphor that social groups of uneven power and legitimacy applied to parse ongoing events as good and evil in real historical time. What the "Holocaust" named as the most fundamental evil was the intentional, systematic, and organized employment of violence against members of a stigmatized collective group, whether defined in a primordial or an ideological way. Not only did this representation identify as radical evil the perpetrators and their actions but it polluted as evil non-actors as well. According to the standards of post-Holocaust morality, one became normatively required to make an effort to intervene against any Holocaust, regardless of personal consequences and cost. For as a crime against humanity, a "Holocaust" is taken to be a threat to the continuing existence of humanity itself. It is impossible, in this sense, to imagine a sacrifice that would be too great when humanity itself is at stake.

Despite the moral content of the Holocaust symbol, then, the primary, first order effects of this sacred-evil do not work in a ratiocinative way. Radical evil is a philosophical term, and it suggests that evil's moral content can be defined and discussed rationally. Sacred-evil, by contrast, is a sociological term, and it suggests that defining radical evil, and applying it, involves motives and relationships, and institutions, that work more like those associated with religious institutions than with ethical doctrine. In order for a prohibited social action to be powerfully moralized, the symbol of this evil must become engorged. An engorged evil overflows with badness. Evil becomes labile and liquid; it drips and seeps, ruining everything it touches. Under the sign of the tragic narrative, the Holocaust became engorged, and its seepage polluted everything with which it came into contact.

Note

A longer version of this chapter appeared in the *European Journal of Social Theory* 5/1 (2002), and in Professor Alexander's *The Meanings of Social Life: A Cultural Sociology* (New York: Oxford University Press, 2003).

References

Abzug, Robert H. 1985. *Inside the Vicious Heart: Americans and the Liberation of Nazi Concentration Camps.* New York: Oxford University Press.

Aristotle. 1987. *Poetics I*, trans. Richard Janko. Indianapolis: Hacket.

Bauman, Zygmut. 1989. *Modernity and the Holocaust*, Cambridge: Polity Press.

Benn, David Wedgood. 1995. "Perceptions of the Holocaust: Then and Now," *World Today* 51:102.

Dawidowicz, Lucy. 1982. *On Equal Terms: Jews in America, 1881–1981.* New York: Holt, Rinehart, and Winston.

Deutscher, Isaac. 1968. "The Jewish Tragedy and the Historian," in Tamara Deutscher, ed. *The Non-Jewish Jew and Other Essays.* London: Oxford University Press.

Diamond, Sander A. 1969. "The *Kristallnacht* and the Reaction in America," *Yivo Annual of Jewish Social Science*, 14:196–208.

Diner, Dan. 2000. *Beyond the Conceivable: Studies on Germany, Naziism, and the Holocaust.* Berkeley and Los Angeles: University of California Press.

Dinnerstein, Leonard. 1981–1982. "Anti-Semitism Exposed and Attacked, 1945–1950." *American Jewish History* 71:134–149.

Dodson, Dan W. 1946. "College Quotas and American Democracy." *The American Scholar* 15/3:267–276.

Feingold, Henry L. 1974. *Zion in America: the Jewish Experience from Colonial Times to the Present.* Boston: Twayne.

Frye, Northrup. 1971. *The Anatomy of Criticism.* Princeton, NJ: Princeton University Press.

Garber, Zev and Bruce Zuckerman. 1989. "Why Do We Call the Holocaust 'The Holocaust'? An Inquiry into the Psychology of Labels." *Modern Judaism* 9/2:197–211.

Hartman, Geoffrey H. 1996. *The Longest Shadow: In the Aftermath of the Holocaust.* Bloomington: Indiana University Press.

Kant, Immanuel. 1960. *Religion within the Limits of Reason Alone*, trans. Theodore M. Greene and Hoyt H. Hudson. New York: Harper.

Laqueur, Walter. 1980. *The Terrible Secret: Suppression of the Truth about Hitler's "Final Solution."* Boston: Little, Brown.

Linenthal, Edward T. 1995. *Preserving Memory: The Struggle to Create the Holocaust Museum.* New York: Viking.

Lipstadt, Deborah E. 1996. "America and the Memory of the Holocaust, 1950–1965." *Modern Judaism* 16:195–214.

Norich, Anita. 1998–1999. "Harbe Sugyes/Puzzling Questions: Yiddish and English Culture in America during the Holocaust." *Jewish Social Studies* 1–2:91–110.

Novick, Peter. 1994. "Holocaust and Memory in America," in James E. Young, ed. *The Art of Memory: Holocaust Memorials in History*. Munich: Prestel-Verlag. Pp. 159–176.

1999. *The Holocaust in American Life*. New York: Houghton Mifflin.

Nussbaum, Martha. 1992. "Tragedy and Self-sufficiency: Plato and Aristotle on Fear and Pity," in Amelie Oksenberg Rorty, ed. *Essays on Aristotle's Poetics*. Princeton, NJ: Princeton University Press. Pp. 261–290.

Rosenfeld, Alvin H. 1995. "The Americanization of the Holocaust." *Commentary* 90/6:35–40.

Shapiro, Edward S. 1992. *A Time for Healing: American Jewry since World War II*. Baltimore: Johns Hopkins University Press.

Short, K. R. M. 1981. "Hollywood Fights Anti-Semitism, 1945–47," in K. R. M. Short, ed. *Feature Films as History*. Knoxville: University of Tennessee Press.

Stember, Charles Herbert. 1966. *Jews in the Mind of America*. New York: Basic Books.

van Gelder, Lawrence. 1999. "After the Holocaust, if There Can Indeed Be an After." *The New York Times*, May 5, Section D: 1.

Welles, Sumner. 1945. "New Hope for the Jewish People." *The Nation*, no. 160, May 5: 511–513.

Whitman, Howard. 1949. "The College Fraternity Crisis." *Collier's* no. 123, January 8: 34–35.

Zelizer, Barbie. 1998. *Remembering to Forget: Holocaust Memory through the Camera's Eye*. University of Chicago Press.

PART III

Culture and power

8

Social justice in the age of identity politics: redistribution, recognition, and participation

Nancy Fraser

In today's world, claims for social justice seem increasingly to divide into two types. First, and most familiar, are redistributive claims, which seek a more just distribution of resources and goods. Examples include claims for redistribution from the North to the South, from the rich to the poor, and (not so long ago) from the owners to the workers. To be sure, the recent resurgence of free-market thinking has put proponents of redistribution on the defensive. Nevertheless, egalitarian redistributive claims have supplied the paradigm case for most theorizing about social justice for the past 150 years.[1]

Today, however, we increasingly encounter a second type of social-justice claim in the "politics of recognition." Here the goal, in its most plausible form, is a difference-friendly world, where assimilation to majority or dominant cultural norms is no longer the price of equal respect. Examples include claims for the recognition of the distinctive perspectives of ethnic, "racial," and sexual minorities, as well as of gender difference. This type of claim has recently attracted the interest of political philosophers, moreover, some of whom are seeking to develop a new paradigm of justice that puts recognition at its center.

In general, then, we are confronted with a new constellation. The discourse of social justice, once centered on distribution, is now increasingly divided between claims for redistribution, on the one hand, and claims for recognition, on the other. Increasingly, too, recognition claims tend to predominate. The demise of communism, the surge of free-market ideology, the rise of "identity politics" in both its fundamentalist and progressive forms – all these developments have conspired to decenter, if not to extinguish, claims for egalitarian redistribution.

In this new constellation, the two kinds of justice claims are often dissociated from one another – both practically and intellectually. Within social movements such as feminism, for example, activist tendencies that look to redistribution as the remedy for male domination are increasingly dissociated from tendencies that look instead to recognition of gender difference; and the same is true of their counterparts in the US academy, where feminist social theorizing and feminist cultural theorizing maintain an uneasy arm's-length coexistence. The feminist case exemplifies a more general tendency in the United States (and elsewhere) to decouple the cultural politics of difference from the social politics of equality.

In some cases, moreover, the dissociation has become a polarization. Some proponents of redistribution reject the politics of recognition outright, casting claims for the recognition of difference as "false consciousness," a hindrance to the pursuit of social justice. Conversely, some proponents of recognition approve the relative eclipse of the politics of redistribution, construing the latter as an outmoded materialism, simultaneously blind to and complicit with many injustices. In such cases, we are effectively presented with what is constructed as an either/or choice: redistribution or recognition? class politics or identity politics? multiculturalism or social democracy?

These, I maintain, are false antitheses. It is my general thesis that justice today requires *both* redistribution *and* recognition. Neither alone is sufficient. As soon as one embraces this thesis, however, the question of how to combine them becomes paramount. I contend that the emancipatory aspects of the two paradigms need to be integrated in a single, comprehensive framework. Theoretically, the task is to devise a "two-dimensional" conception of justice that can accommodate both defensible claims for social equality and defensible claims for the recognition of difference. Practically, the task is to devise a programmatic political orientation that integrates the best of the politics of redistribution with the best of the politics of recognition.

My argument proceeds in four steps. I outline the key points of contrast between the two political paradigms, as they are presently understood. Then I problematize their current dissociation from one another by introducing a case of injustice that cannot be redressed by either one of them alone, but that requires their integration. Finally, I consider some normative philosophical questions and some social-theoretical questions that arise when we contemplate integrating redistribution and recognition in a single comprehensive framework.

Redistribution or recognition? Anatomy of a false antithesis

I begin with some denotative definitions. The paradigm of redistribution, as I shall understand it, encompasses not only class-centered orientations, such as New Deal liberalism, social-democracy, and socialism, but also those forms of feminism and anti-racism that look to socioeconomic transformation or reform as the remedy for gender and racial–ethnic injustice. Thus, it is broader than class politics in the conventional sense. The paradigm of recognition, in contrast, encompasses not only movements aiming to revalue unjustly devalued identities, for example, cultural feminism, black cultural nationalism, and gay identity politics, but also deconstructive tendencies, such as queer politics, critical "race" politics, and deconstructive feminism, which reject the "essentialism" of traditional identity politics. Thus, it is broader than identity politics in the conventional sense.

With these definitions, I mean to contest one widespread misunderstanding of these matters. It is often assumed that the politics of redistribution means class politics, while the politics of recognition means "identity politics," which in turn means the politics of sexuality, gender, and "race." This view is erroneous and misleading. For one thing, it treats recognition-oriented currents within the feminist, anti-heterosexist, and anti-racist movements as the whole story, rendering invisible alternative currents dedicated to righting gender-specific, "race"-specific, and sex-specific forms of economic injustice that traditional class movements ignored. For another, it forecloses the recognition dimensions of class struggles. Finally, it reduces what is actually a plurality of different kinds of recognition claims (including universalist claims and deconstructive claims) to a single type, namely, claims for the affirmation of difference.

For all these reasons, the definitions I have proposed here are far preferable. They take account of the complexity of contemporary politics by treating redistribution and recognition as *dimensions of justice that can cut across all social movements.*

Understood in this way, the paradigm of redistribution and the paradigm of recognition can be contrasted in four key respects: first, the two paradigms assume different conceptions of injustice. The redistribution paradigm focuses on injustices it defines as socioeconomic and presumes to be rooted in the political economy. Examples include exploitation, economic marginalization, and deprivation. The recognition paradigm, in contrast, targets injustices it understands as cultural, which it presumes to be rooted in social patterns of representation, interpretation, and communication. Examples include cultural domination, nonrecognition, and disrespect.

Second, the two paradigms propose different sorts of remedies for injustice. In the redistribution paradigm, the remedy for injustice is political-economic restructuring. This might involve redistributing income, reorganizing the division of labor, or transforming other basic economic structures. (Although these various remedies differ importantly from one another, I mean to refer to the whole group of them by the generic term "redistribution.") In the paradigm of recognition, in contrast, the remedy for injustice is cultural or symbolic change. This could involve upwardly revaluing disrespected identities, positively valorizing cultural diversity, or the wholesale transformation of societal patterns of representation, interpretation, and communication in ways that would change everyone's social identity. (Although these remedies, too, differ importantly from one another, I refer once again to the whole group of them by the generic term "recognition.")

Third, the two paradigms assume different conceptions of the collectivities who suffer injustice. In the redistribution paradigm, the collective subjects of injustice are classes or class-like collectivities, which are defined economically by a distinctive relation to the market or the means of production. The classic case in the Marxian paradigm is the exploited working class, whose members must sell their labor power in order to receive the means of subsistence. But the conception can cover other cases as well. Also included are racialized groups of immigrants or ethnic minorities that can be economically defined, whether as a pool of low-paid menial laborers or as an "underclass" largely excluded from regular waged work, deemed "superfluous" and unworthy of exploitation. When the notion of the economy is broadened to encompass unwaged labor, moreover, women become visible as a collective subject of economic injustice, as the gender burdened with the lion's share of unwaged carework and consequently disadvantaged in employment and disempowered in relations with men. Also included, finally, are the complexly defined groupings that result when we theorize the political economy in terms of the intersection of class, "race," and gender.

In the recognition paradigm, in contrast, the victims of injustice are more like Weberian status groups than Marxian classes. Defined not by the relations of production, but rather by the relations of recognition, they are distinguished by the lesser esteem, honor, and prestige they enjoy relative to other groups in society. The classic case in the Weberian paradigm is the low-status ethnic group, whom dominant patterns of cultural value mark as different and less worthy, but the conception can cover other cases as well. In the current constellation, it has been extended to gays and lesbians, who suffer pervasive effects of institutionalized stigma; to racialized groups, who are marked as different and lesser; and to women, who are trivialized, sexually objectified, and disrespected in myriad ways. It is also being extended, finally, to encompass the complexly defined groupings that result when we theorize the relations of recognition in terms of race, gender, and sexuality simultaneously as intersecting cultural codes.

It follows, and this is the fourth point, that the two approaches assume different understandings of group differences. The redistribution paradigm treats such differences as unjust differentials that should be abolished. The recognition paradigm, in contrast, treats differences either as cultural variations that should be celebrated or as discursively constructed hierarchical oppositions that should be deconstructed.

Increasingly, as I noted at the outset, redistribution and recognition are posed as mutually exclusive alternatives. Some proponents of the former, such as Richard Rorty (1998) and Todd Gitlin (1995), insist that identity politics is a counterproductive diversion from the real economic issues, one that balkanizes groups and rejects universalist moral norms. They claim, in effect, that "it's the economy, stupid." Conversely, some proponents of the politics of recognition, such as Charles Taylor (1994), insist that a difference-blind politics of redistribution can reinforce injustice by falsely universalizing dominant group norms, requiring subordinate groups to assimilate to them, and misrecognizing the latter's distinctiveness. They claim, in effect, that "it's the culture, stupid."

This, however, is a false antithesis.

Exploited classes, despised sexualities, and two-dimensional categories: a critique of justice truncated

To see why, imagine a conceptual spectrum of different kinds of social differentiations. At one extreme are differentiations that fit the paradigm of redistribution. At the other extreme are differentiations that fit the paradigm of recognition. In between are cases that prove difficult because they fit both paradigms of justice simultaneously.[2]

Consider, first, the redistribution end of the spectrum. At this end let us posit an ideal–typical social differentiation rooted in the economic structure, as opposed to the status order, of society. By definition, any structural injustices attaching to this differentiation will be traceable ultimately to the political economy. The root of the injustice, as well as its core, will be socioeconomic maldistribution, while any attendant cultural injustices will derive ultimately from that economic root. At bottom, therefore, the remedy required to redress the injustice will be redistribution, as opposed to recognition.

An example that appears to approximate this ideal type is class differentiation, as understood in orthodox, economistic Marxism. In this conception, class is an artifact of an unjust political economy, which creates, and exploits, a proletariat. The core injustice is exploitation, an especially deep form of maldistribution in which the proletariat's own energies are turned against it, usurped to sustain a social system that disproportionately burdens it and benefits others. To be sure, its members also suffer serious cultural injustices, the "hidden (and not so hidden) injuries of class" (Sennett and Cobb, 1973). But, far from being rooted directly in an autonomously unjust status order, these derive from the political economy, as ideologies of class inferiority proliferate to justify exploitation. The remedy for the injustice, consequently, is redistribution, not recognition. The last thing the proletariat needs is recognition of its difference. On the contrary, the only way to remedy the injustice is to restructure the political economy in such a way as to put the proletariat out of business as a distinctive group.

Now consider the other end of the conceptual spectrum. At this end let us posit an ideal–typical social differentiation that fits the paradigm of recognition.

A differentiation of this type is rooted in the status order, as opposed to the economic structure, of society. Thus, any structural injustices implicated here will be traceable ultimately to the reigning patterns of cultural value. The root of the injustice, as well as its core, will be cultural misrecognition, while any attendant economic injustices will derive ultimately from that root. The remedy required to redress the injustice will be recognition, as opposed to redistribution.

An example that appears to approximate this ideal type is sexual differentiation, understood through the prism of the Weberian conception of status. In this conception, the social differentiation between heterosexuals and homosexuals is not grounded in the political economy, as homosexuals are distributed throughout the entire class structure of capitalist society, occupy no distinctive position in the division of labor, and do not constitute an exploited class. The differentiation is rooted, rather, in the status order of society, as institutionalized patterns of meaning and value constitute heterosexuality as natural and normative, while simultaneously constituting homosexuality as perverse and despised. When such heteronormative meanings are pervasively institutionalized, for example, in law, state policy, social practices, and interaction, gays and lesbians become a *despised sexuality*. As a result, they suffer sexually specific forms of *status subordination*, including shaming and assault, exclusion from the rights and privileges of marriage and parenthood, curbs on their rights of expression and association, and denial of full legal rights and equal protections. These harms are injustices of misrecognition. To be sure, gays and lesbians also suffer serious economic injustices: they can be summarily dismissed from civilian employment and military service, are denied a broad range of family-based social-welfare benefits, and face major tax and inheritance liabilities. But, far from being rooted directly in the economic structure of society, these injustices derive instead from the status order, as the institutionalization of heterosexist norms produces a category of despised persons who incur economic disadvantages as a byproduct. The remedy for the injustice, accordingly, is recognition, not redistribution. Overcoming homophobia and heterosexism requires changing the sexual status order, deinstitutionalizing the heteronormative patterns that deny equal respect to gays and lesbians. Change the relations of recognition, and the maldistribution will disappear.

Matters are thus fairly straightforward at the two extremes of our conceptual spectrum. When we deal with groups that approach the ideal type of the exploited working class, we face distributive injustices requiring redistributive remedies. What is needed is a politics of redistribution. When we deal with groups that approach the ideal type of the despised sexuality, in contrast, we face injustices of misrecognition. What is needed *here* is a politics of recognition.

Matters become murkier, however, once we move away from these extremes. When we posit a type of social differentiation located in the middle of the conceptual spectrum, we encounter a hybrid form that combines features of the exploited class with features of the despised sexuality. I call such differentiations "two-dimensional." Rooted at once in the economic structure and the status order of society, they may entrench injustices that are traceable to both political economy and culture simultaneously. Two-dimensionally oppressed groups, accordingly, may suffer both maldistribution and misrecognition *in forms where neither of these injustices is an indirect effect of the other, but where both are primary and co-original.* In their case, neither the politics of redistribution alone nor the politics of recognition alone will suffice. Two-dimensionally oppressed groups need both.

Gender, I contend, is a two-dimensional social differentiation. Neither simply a class, nor simply a status group, it is a hybrid category with roots in both culture and political economy. From the economic perspective, gender structures the fundamental division between paid "productive" labor and unpaid "reproductive" and domestic labor, as well as the divisions within paid labor between higher-paid, male-dominated, manufacturing and professional occupations and lower-paid, female-dominated "pink collar" and domestic service occupations. The result is an economic structure that generates gender-specific modes of exploitation, economic marginalization, and deprivation. Here, gender appears as a class-like differentiation; and gender injustice appears as a species of maldistribution that cries out for redistributive redress.

From the perspective of the status order, however, gender encompasses elements that are more like sexuality than class and that bring it squarely within the problematic of recognition. Gender codes pervasive patterns of cultural interpretation and evaluation, which are central to the status order as a whole. As a result, not just women, but all low-status groups, risk being feminized and thereby demeaned. Thus, a major feature of gender injustice is androcentrism: an institutionalized pattern of culture value that privileges traits associated with masculinity, while pervasively devaluing things coded as "feminine," paradigmatically – but not only – women. Institutionalized in law, state policies, social practices, and interaction, this value pattern saddles women with gender-specific forms of *status subordination*, including sexual assault and domestic violence; trivializing, objectifying, and demeaning stereotypical depictions in the media; harassment and disparagement in everyday life; and denial of full legal rights and equal protections. These harms are injustices of recognition. They cannot be remedied by redistribution alone but require additional independent remedies of recognition.

Gender, in sum, is a "two-dimensional" social differentiation. It encompasses a class-like aspect that brings it within the ambit of redistribution, while also including a status aspect that brings it simultaneously within the ambit of recognition. Redressing gender injustice, therefore, requires changing both the economic structure and the status order of society.

The two-dimensional character of gender wreaks havoc on the idea of an either/or choice between the paradigm of redistribution and the paradigm of recognition. That construction assumes that the collective subjects of injustice are either classes or status groups, but not both; that the root injustice they suffer is either maldistribution or misrecognition, but not both; that the group differences at issue are either unjust differentials or unjustly devalued cultural variations, but not both; that the remedy for injustice is either redistribution or recognition, but not both.

Gender, we can now see, explodes this whole series of false antitheses. Here we have a category that is a compound of both status and class, that implicates injustices of both maldistribution and misrecognition, whose distinctiveness is compounded of both economic differentials and culturally constructed distinctions. Gender injustice can only be remedied, therefore, by an approach that encompasses both a politics of redistribution and a politics of recognition.

Gender, moreover, is not unusual in this regard. "Race," too, is a two-dimensional social differentiation, a compound of status and class. Rooted simultaneously in the economic structure and the status order of capitalist society, racism's injustices include both maldistribution and misrecognition. Yet neither dimension of racism is wholly an indirect effect of the other. Thus, overcoming the injustices of racism, too, requires both redistribution and recognition. Neither alone will suffice.

Class, too, is probably best understood as two-dimensional for practical purposes. To be sure, the ultimate cause of class injustice is the economic structure of capitalist society.[3] But the resulting harms include misrecognition as well as maldistribution (Thompson, 1963). And cultural harms that originated as byproducts of economic structure may have since developed a life of their own. Left unattended, moreover, class misrecognition may impede the capacity to mobilize against maldistribution. Thus, a politics of class recognition may be needed to get a politics of redistribution off the ground.[4]

Sexuality, too, is for practical purposes two-dimensional. To be sure, the ultimate cause of heterosexist injustice is the heteronormative value pattern that is institutionalized in the status order of contemporary society.[5] But the resulting harms include maldistribution as well as misrecognition; and economic harms that originate as byproducts of the status order have an undeniable weight of their own. Left unattended, moreover, they may impede the capacity to mobilize against misrecognition. Thus, a politics of sexual redistribution may be needed to get a politics of recognition off the ground.

For practical purposes, then, virtually all real-world axes of subordination are two-dimensional. Virtually all implicate both maldistribution and misrecognition in forms where each of those injustices has some independent weight, whatever its ultimate roots. To be sure, not all axes of subordination are two-dimensional in the same way, nor to the same degree. Some, such as class, tilt more heavily toward the distribution end of the spectrum; others, such as sexuality, incline more to the recognition end; while still others, such as gender and "race," cluster closer to the center. Nevertheless, in virtually every case, the harms at issue comprise both maldistribution and misrecognition in forms where neither of those injustices can be redressed entirely indirectly but where each requires some practical attention. As a practical matter, therefore, overcoming injustice in virtually every case requires both redistribution and recognition.

The need for this sort of two-pronged approach becomes more pressing, moreover, as soon as we cease considering such axes of injustice singly and begin instead to consider them together as mutually intersecting. After all, gender, "race," sexuality, and class are not neatly cordoned off from one another. Rather, all these axes of injustice intersect one another in ways that affect everyone's interests and identities. Thus, anyone who is both gay and working class will need both redistribution and recognition. Seen this way, moreover, virtually every individual who suffers injustice needs to integrate both those two kinds of claims and so, furthermore, will anyone who cares about social justice, regardless of their own personal social location.

In general, then, one should roundly reject the construction of redistribution and recognition as mutually exclusive alternatives. The goal should be, rather, to develop an integrated approach that can encompass, and harmonize, both dimensions of social justice.

Normative–philosophical issues: for a two-dimensional theory of justice

Integrating redistribution and recognition in a single comprehensive paradigm is no simple matter, however. To contemplate such a project is to be plunged immediately into deep and difficult problems spanning several major fields of inquiry. In moral philosophy, for example, the task is to devise an overarching conception of justice that can accommodate both defensible claims for social equality and defensible claims for the recognition of difference. In social theory, by contrast, the task is to devise an account of our contemporary social formation that can accommodate not only the differentiation of class from status, economy from culture, but also their mutual imbrication. In political theory, meanwhile, the task is to envision a set of institutional arrangements and associated policy reforms that can remedy both maldistribution and misrecognition, while mini- mizing the mutual interferences likely to arise when the two sorts of redress are sought simultaneously. In practical politics, finally, the task is to foster democratic engagement across current divides in order to build a broad-based programmatic orientation that integrates the best of the politics of redistribution with the best of the politics of recognition.

This, of course, is far too much to take on here. In the present section, I limit myself to some of the moral–theoretical dimensions of this project. (In the next, I turn to some issues in social theory.) I shall consider three normative philosophical questions that arise when we contemplate integrating redistribution and recognition in a single comprehensive account of social justice: first, is recognition really a matter of justice, or is it a matter of self-realization? Second, do distributive justice and recognition constitute two distinct, *sui generis*, normative paradigms, or can either of them be subsumed within the other? And third, does justice require the recognition of what is distinctive about individuals or groups, or is recognition of our common humanity sufficient? (I omit here a fourth crucial question, discussed in my contribution to Fraser and Honneth [2003]: how can we distinguish justified from unjustified claims for recognition?)

On the first question, two major theorists, Charles Taylor and Axel Honneth, understand recognition as a matter of self-realization. Unlike them, however, I propose to treat it as an issue of justice. Thus, one should not answer the question "what's wrong with misrecognition?" by reference to a thick theory of the good, as Taylor (1994) does. Nor should one follow Honneth (1995) and appeal to a "formal conception of ethical life" premised on an account of the "intersubjective conditions" for an "undistorted practical relation-to-self." One should say, rather, that it is unjust that some individuals and groups are denied the status of full partners in social interaction simply as a consequence of institutionalized patterns of cultural value in whose construction they have not equally participated and which disparage their distinctive characteristics or the distinctive characteristics assigned to them.

Let me explain. To view recognition as a matter of justice is to treat it as an issue of *social status*. This means examining institutionalized patterns of cultural value for their effects on the *relative standing* of social actors. If and when such patterns constitute actors as *peers*, capable of participating on a par with one another in social life, then we can speak of *reciprocal recognition* and *status equality*. When, in contrast, institutionalized patterns of cultural value constitute some actors as inferior, excluded, wholly other, or simply invisible, hence as less than full partners in social interaction, then we should speak of *misrecognition* and *status subordination*.

I shall call this the *status model of recognition*.[6] On the status model, misrecognition is an institutionalized relation of *subordination* and a violation of justice. To be misrecognized, accordingly, is to be constituted by *institutionalized patterns of cultural value* in ways that prevent one from participating as a peer in social life. On the status model, then, misrecognition is relayed not through deprecatory attitudes or free-standing discourses but, rather, through social institutions. It arises, more precisely, when institutions structure interaction according to cultural norms that impede parity of participation. Examples include marriage laws that exclude same-sex partnerships as illegitimate and perverse, social-welfare policies that stigmatize single mothers as sexually irresponsible scroungers, and policing practices such as "racial profiling" that associate racialized persons with criminality. In each of these cases, interaction is regulated by an institutionalized pattern of cultural value that constitutes some categories of social actors as normative and others as deficient or inferior: straight is normal, gay is perverse; "male-headed households" are proper, "female-headed households" are not; "whites" are law-abiding, "blacks" are dangerous. In each case, the effect is to create a class of devalued persons who are impeded from participating on a par with others in social life.

In each case, accordingly, a claim for recognition is in order. But note precisely what this means: aimed at overcoming subordination, claims for recognition in the status model seek to establish the subordinated party as a full partner in social life, able to interact with others as a peer. They aim, that is, *to deinstitutionalize patterns of cultural value that impede parity of participation and to replace them with patterns that foster it*. The status model offers several advantages. First, by appealing to the norm of participatory parity, it permits us to sidestep unresolvable disagreements about self-realization and the good; as a result, it allows us to justify claims for recognition as morally binding under modern conditions of value pluralism. Second, by conceiving misrecognition as status subordination, this approach locates the wrong in social relations, not in individual or interpersonal psychology. As a result, it avoids identifying misrecognition with internal distortions in the structure of self-consciousness of the oppressed, an approach that leads easily to victim blaming. Finally, the status model avoids the patently untenable view that everyone has an equal right to social esteem. What it *does* entail is that everyone has an equal right to pursue social esteem under fair conditions of equal opportunity. And such conditions do not obtain when, for example, institutionalized patterns of cultural value pervasively downgrade femininity, "non-whiteness," homosexuality, and everything culturally associated with them. For all these reasons, recognition is better viewed as a matter of justice than as a matter of self-realization.[7] But what follows for the theory of justice?

Does it follow, turning now to the second question, that distribution and recognition constitute two distinct, *sui generis* conceptions of justice? Or can either of them be reduced to the other? The question of reduction must be considered from two different sides. From one side, the issue is whether standard theories of distributive justice can adequately subsume problems of recognition.

In my view, the answer is no. To be sure, many distributive theorists appreciate the importance of status over and above the allocation of resources and seek to accommodate it in their accounts,[8] but the results are not wholly satisfactory. Most such theorists assume a reductive economistic-cum-legalistic view of status, supposing that a just distribution of resources and rights is sufficient to preclude misrecognition. In fact, however, as we saw, not all misrecognition is a byproduct of maldistribution, nor of maldistribution plus legal discrimination. Witness the case of the African American Wall Street banker who cannot get a taxi to pick him up. To handle such cases, a theory of justice must reach beyond the distribution of rights and goods to examine patterns of cultural value. It must consider whether institutionalized patterns of cultural value impede parity of participation in social life.[9]

What, then, of the other side of the question? Can existing theories of recognition adequately subsume problems of distribution? Here, too, I contend the answer is no. To be sure, some theorists of recognition appreciate the importance of economic equality and seek to accommodate it in their accounts, but once again the results are not wholly satisfactory. Such theorists tend to assume a reductive culturalist view of distribution. Supposing that economic inequalities are rooted in a cultural order that privileges some kinds of labor over others, they assume that changing that cultural order is sufficient to preclude maldistribution (Honneth, 1995). In fact, however, as we saw, and as I shall argue more extensively later, not all maldistribution is a byproduct of misrecognition. Witness the case of the skilled white male industrial worker who becomes unemployed due to a factory closing resulting from a speculative corporate merger. In that case, the injustice of maldistribution has little to do with misrecognition. It is rather a consequence of imperatives intrinsic to an order of specialized economic relations whose *raison d'être* is the accumulation of profits. To handle such cases, a theory of justice must reach beyond cultural value patterns to examine the structure of capitalism. It must consider whether economic mechanisms that are relatively decoupled from cultural value patterns and that operate in a relatively impersonal way can impede parity of participation in social life.

In general then, neither distribution theorists nor recognition theorists have so far succeeded in adequately subsuming the concerns of the other. Thus, instead of endorsing either one of their paradigms to the exclusion of the other, I propose to develop what I shall call a "two-dimensional" conception of justice. A two-dimensional conception treats distribution and recognition as distinct perspectives on, and dimensions of, justice. Without reducing either one of them to the other, it encompasses both dimensions within a broader, overarching framework.

The normative core of my conception, which I have mentioned several times, is the notion of *parity of participation*.[10] According to this norm, justice requires social arrangements that permit all (adult) members of society to interact with one another as peers. For participatory parity to be possible, I claim, at least two conditions must be satisfied.[11] First, the distribution of material resources must be such as to ensure participants' independence and "voice." This I call the "objective" precondition of participatory parity. It precludes forms and levels of material inequality and economic dependence that impede parity of participation. Precluded, therefore, are social arrangements that institutionalize deprivation, exploitation, and gross disparities in wealth, income, and leisure time, thereby denying some people the means and opportunities to interact with others as peers.[12]

In contrast, the second additional condition for participatory parity I call "intersubjective." It requires that institutionalized patterns of cultural value express equal respect for all participants and ensure equal opportunity for achieving social esteem. This condition precludes institutionalized patterns that systematically depreciate some categories of people and the qualities associated with them. Precluded, therefore, are institutionalized value schemata that deny some people the status of full partners in interaction – whether by burdening them with excessive ascribed "difference" from others or by failing to acknowledge their distinctiveness.

Both the objective precondition and the intersubjective precondition are necessary for participatory parity; neither alone is sufficient. The objective condition brings into focus concerns traditionally associated with the theory of distributive justice, especially concerns pertaining to the economic structure of society and to economically defined class differentials. The intersubjective precondition brings into focus concerns recently highlighted in the philosophy of recognition, especially concerns pertaining to the status order of society and to culturally defined hierarchies of status. Thus, a two-dimensional conception of justice oriented to the norm of participatory parity encompasses both redistribution and recognition, without reducing either one to the other.

This brings us to the third question: does justice require the recognition of what is distinctive about individuals or groups, over and above the recognition of our common humanity? Here it is important to note that participatory parity is a universalist norm in two senses. First, it encompasses all (adult) partners to interaction; and, second, it presupposes the equal moral worth of human beings. But moral universalism in these senses still leaves open the question whether recognition of individual or group distinctiveness could be required by justice as one element among others of the intersubjective condition for participatory parity.

This question cannot be answered, I contend, by an a priori account of the kinds of recognition that everyone always needs. It needs rather to be approached in the spirit of pragmatism as informed by the insights of a critical social theory. From this perspective, recognition is a remedy for injustice, not a generic human need. Thus, the form(s) of recognition justice requires in any given case depend(s) on the form(s) of *mis*recognition to be redressed. In cases where misrecognition involves denying the common humanity of some participants, the remedy is universalist recognition. Where, in contrast, misrecognition involves denying some participants' distinctiveness, the remedy could be recognition of difference.[13] In every case, the remedy should be tailored to the harm.

This approach overcomes the liabilities of two other views that are mirror opposites and equally decontextualized. First, it avoids the view, espoused by some distributive theorists, that justice requires limiting public recognition to those capacities all humans share. That approach dogmatically forecloses recognition of what distinguishes people from one another, without considering whether the latter might be needed in some cases to overcome obstacles to participatory parity. Second, the pragmatist approach avoids the opposite view, also decontextualized, that everyone always needs their distinctiveness recognized. Favored by some prominent theorists of recognition, (Honneth, 1995; Taylor, 1994) this view cannot explain why it is that only some social differences generate claims for recognition, nor why only some of those that do are morally justified. More specifically, it cannot explain why dominant groups, such as men and heterosexuals, usually shun recognition of their (gender and sexual) distinctiveness, claiming not specificity but universality. By contrast, the approach proposed here sees claims for the recognition of difference pragmatically and contextually – as remedial responses to specific harms. Putting questions of justice at the center, it appreciates that the recognition needs of subordinate groups differ from those of dominant groups; and that only those claims that promote participatory parity are morally justified.

For the pragmatist, accordingly, everything depends on precisely what currently misrecognized people need in order to be able to participate as peers in social life, and there is no reason to assume that all of them need the same thing in every context. In some cases, they may need to be unburdened of excessive ascribed or constructed distinctiveness. In other cases, they may need to have hitherto underacknowledged distinctiveness taken into account. In still other cases, they may need to shift the focus onto dominant or advantaged groups, outing the latter's distinctiveness, which has been falsely parading as universality. Alternatively, they may need to deconstruct the very terms in which attributed differences are currently elaborated. Finally, they may need all of the above, or several of the above, in combination with one another and in combination with redistribution. Which people need which kind(s) of recognition in which contexts depends on the nature of the obstacles they face with regard to participatory parity. That, however, cannot be determined by abstract philosophical argument. It can only be determined with the aid of a critical social theory, a theory that is normatively oriented, empirically informed, and guided by the practical intent of overcoming injustice.

Social–theoretical issues: an argument for "perspectival dualism"

This brings us to the social-theoretical issues that arise when we try to encompass redistribution and recognition in a single framework. Here, the principal task is to theorize the relations between class and status, and between maldistribution and misrecognition, in contemporary society. An adequate approach must allow for the full complexity of these relations. It must account *both for the differentiation of class from status and for the causal interactions between them.* It must accommodate, as well, *both the mutual irreducibility of maldistribution and misrecognition and their practical entwinement with one another.* Such an account must, moreover, be historical. Sensitive to shifts in social structure and political culture, it must identify the distinctive dynamics and conflict tendencies of the present conjuncture. Attentive both to national specificities and to transnational forces and frames, it must explain why today's grammar of social conflict takes the form that it does: why, that is, struggles for recognition have recently become so salient; why egalitarian redistribution struggles, hitherto central to social life, have lately receded to the margins; and why, finally, the two kinds of claims for social justice have become decoupled and antagonistically counterposed.[14]

First, however, some conceptual clarifications. The terms class and status, as I use them here, denote socially entrenched orders of subordination. To say that a society has a class structure is to say that it institutionalizes economic mechanisms of distribution that systematically deny some of its members the means and opportunities they need in order to participate on a par with others in social life. To say, likewise, that a society has a status hierarchy is to say that it institutionalizes patterns of cultural value that pervasively deny some of its members the recognition they need in order to be full, participating partners in interaction. The existence of either a class structure or a status hierarchy constitutes an obstacle to parity of participation and thus an injustice.

These understandings differ from some more familiar definitions of status and class. Unlike stratification theory in postwar US sociology, for example, I do not conceive status as a prestige quotient that is ascribable to an individual and compounded of quantitatively measurable factors, including economic indices such as income. In my conception, in contrast, status represents an order of intersubjective subordination derived from institutionalized patterns of cultural value that constitute some members of society as less than full partners in interaction. Unlike Marxist theory, likewise, I do not conceive class as a relation to the means of production. In my conception, rather, class is an order of objective subordination derived from economic arrangements that deny some actors the means and resources they need for participatory parity.[15]

According to my conceptions, moreover, status and class do not map neatly onto current folk distinctions among social movements. Struggles against sexism and racism, for example, do not aim solely at transforming the status order, as gender and "race" implicate class structure as well. Nor, likewise, should labor struggles be reduced exclusively to matters of economic class, as they properly concern status hierarchies, too. More generally, as I noted earlier, virtually all axes of subordination partake simultaneously of the status order and the class structure, albeit in different proportions. Thus, far from corresponding to folk distinctions, status and class represent analytically distinct orders of subordination, which typically cut across social movements.

What status and class *do* correspond to, however, are misrecognition and maldistribution respectively. Each of them is associated with an analytically distinct type of impediment to participatory parity – hence with an analytically distinct dimension of justice. Status corresponds to the recognition dimension, which concerns the effects of institutionalized meanings and norms on the relative standing of social actors. Class, in contrast, corresponds to the distributive dimension, which concerns the allocation of economic resources and wealth. In general, then, the paradigmatic status injustice is misrecognition, which *may*, however, be accompanied by maldistribution, whereas the quintessential class injustice is maldistribution, which *may* in turn be accompanied by misrecognition.

Given these clarifications, we can now supply the counterpart in social theory to the moral theory of the previous section. The key point is that each of the two dimensions of justice is associated with an analytically distinct aspect of social order. The recognition dimension corresponds to the *status order* of society, hence to the constitution, by socially entrenched patterns of cultural value, of culturally defined categories of social actors – statuses – each distinguished by the relative respect, prestige, and esteem it enjoys vis-à-vis the others. The distributive dimension, in contrast, corresponds to the *economic structure* of society, hence to the constitution, by property regimes and labor markets, of economically defined categories of actors, or classes, distinguished by their differential endowments of resources. Each dimension, too, corresponds to an analytically distinct form of subordination: the recognition dimension corresponds to *status subordination*, rooted in institutionalized patterns of cultural value; the distributive dimension, in contrast, corresponds to *economic class subordination*, rooted in structural features of the economic system.

These correspondences enable us to situate the problem of integrating redistribution and recognition within a broad social-theoretical frame. From this perspective, societies appear as complex fields that encompass at least two ana-lytically distinct modes of social ordering: an economic mode, in which inter-action is regulated by the functional interlacing of strategic imperatives, and a cultural mode, in which interaction is regulated by institutionalized patterns of cultural value. Economic ordering is typically institutionalized in markets; cultural ordering may work through a variety of different institutions, including kinship, religion, and law. In all societies economic ordering and cultural order-ing are mutually imbricated. The question arises, however, as to how precisely they relate to each other in a given social formation. Is the economic struc-ture institutionally differentiated from the cultural order, or are they effectively fused? Do the class structure and the status hierarchy diverge from one another, or do they coincide? Do maldistribution and misrecognition convert into each other, or are such conversions effectively blocked?

The answers to these questions depend on the nature of the society under consideration. Consider, for example, an ideal–typical pre-state society of the sort described in the classical anthropological literature, while bracketing the question of ethnographic accuracy.[16] In such a society, the master idiom of social relations is kinship. Kinship organizes not only marriage and sexual relations, but also the labor process and the distribution of goods; relations of authority, reciprocity, and obligation; and symbolic hierarchies of status and prestige. Of course, it could well be the case that such a society has never existed in pure form. Still, we can imagine a world in which neither distinctively economic institutions nor distinctively cultural institutions exist. A single order of social relations secures (what *we* would call) both the economic integration and the cultural integration of the society. Class structure and status order are accordingly fused. Because kinship constitutes the overarching principle of distribution, kinship status dictates class position. In the absence of any quasi-autonomous economic institutions, status injuries translate immediately into (what *we* would consider to be) distributive injustices. Misrecognition directly entails maldistribution.

Now consider the opposite extreme of a fully marketized society, in which economic structure dictates cultural value. In such a society, the master deter-mining instance is the market. Markets organize not only the labor process and the distribution of goods, but also marriage and sexual relations; political rela-tions of authority, reciprocity, and obligation; and symbolic hierarchies of status and prestige. Granted, such a society has never existed, and it is doubtful that one ever could.[17] For heuristic purposes, however, we can imagine a world in which a single order of social relations secures not only the economic integration but also the cultural integration of society. Here, too, as in the fully kin-governed society, class structure and status order are effectively fused, but the determina-tions run in the opposite direction. Because the market constitutes the sole and all-pervasive mechanism of valuation, market position dictates social status. In the absence of any quasi-autonomous cultural value patterns, distributive injustices translate immediately into status injuries. Maldistribution directly entails misrecognition.

As mirror-opposites of each other, these two imagined societies share a common feature: the absence of any meaningful differentiation of the economy from the larger culture. In both of them, accordingly, (what *we* would call) class and status map perfectly onto each other. So, as well, do (what *we* would call) maldistribution and misrecognition, which convert fully and without remainder into one another. As a result, one can understand both these societies reasonably well by attending exclusively to a single dimension of social life. For the fully kin-governed society, one can read off the economic dimension of subordination directly from the cultural; one can infer class directly from status and maldistribution directly from misrecognition. For the fully marketized society, conversely, one can read off the cultural dimension of subordination directly from the economic; one can infer status directly from class and misrecognition directly from maldistribution. For understanding the forms of subordination proper to the fully kin-governed society, therefore, culturalism is a perfectly appropriate social theory.[18] If, in contrast, one is seeking to understand the fully marketized society, one could hardly improve on economism.[19]

When we turn to other types of societies, however, such simple and elegant approaches no longer suffice. They are patently inappropriate for our own society, which contains both marketized arenas, in which strategic action predominates, and non-marketized arenas, in which value-oriented interaction predominates. Here, accordingly, zones of economic ordering are differentiated from zones of cultural ordering, the economic structure from the cultural order. The result is a partial uncoupling of economic mechanisms of distribution from structures of prestige – thus – a gap between status and class. The class structure ceases perfectly to mirror the status order, even as each of them influences the other. Because the market does not constitute the sole and all-pervasive mechanism of valuation, market position does not dictate social status. Partially market-resistant cultural value patterns prevent distributive injustices from converting fully and without remainder into status injuries. Maldistribution does not directly entail misrecognition, although it certainly contributes to the latter. Conversely, because no single status principle such as kinship constitutes the sole and all-pervasive principle of distribution, status does not dictate class position. Relatively autonomous economic institutions prevent status injuries from converting fully and without remainder into distributive injustices. Misrecognition does not directly entail maldistribution, although it, too, surely contributes to the latter.

As a result, one cannot understand this society by attending exclusively to a single dimension of social life. One cannot read off the economic dimension of subordination directly from the cultural, nor the cultural directly from the economic. Likewise, one cannot infer class directly from status, nor status directly from class. Finally, one cannot deduce maldistribution directly from misrecognition, nor misrecognition directly from maldistribution. It follows that neither culturalism nor economism suffices for understanding capitalist society. Instead, one needs an approach that can accommodate differentiation, divergence, and interaction at every level.

What sort of social theory can handle this task? What approach can theorize both the differentiation of status from class and the causal interactions between them? What kind of theory can accommodate the complex relations between maldistribution and misrecognition in contemporary society, grasping at once their conceptual irreducibility, empirical divergence, and practical entwinement? And what approach can do all this *without reinforcing the current dissociation of the politics of recognition from the politics of redistribution*? If neither economism nor culturalism is up to the task, what alternative approaches are possible?

Two possibilities present themselves, both of them species of dualism.[20] The first approach I call "substantive dualism." It treats redistribution and recognition as two different "spheres of justice," pertaining to two different societal domains. The former pertains to the economic domain of society, the relations of production. The latter pertains to the cultural domain, the relations of recognition. When we consider economic matters, such as the structure of labor markets, we should assume the standpoint of distributive justice, attending to the impact of economic structures and institutions on the relative economic position of social actors. When, in contrast, we consider cultural matters, such as the representation of female sexuality on MTV, we should assume the standpoint of recognition, attending to the impact of institutionalized patterns of interpretation and value on the status and relative standing of social actors.

Substantive dualism may be preferable to economism and culturalism, but it is nevertheless inadequate – both conceptually and politically. Conceptually, it erects a dichotomy that opposes economy to culture and treats them as two separate spheres. It thereby mistakes the differentiations of capitalist society for institutional divisions that are impermeable and sharply bounded. In fact, these differentiations mark orders of social relations that can overlap one another institutionally and are more or less permeable in different regimes. Thus, the economy is not a culture-free zone, but a culture-instrumentalizing and -resignifying one. What presents itself as "the economy" is always already permeated with cultural interpretations and norms – witness the distinctions between "working" and "caregiving," "men's jobs" and "women's jobs," which are so fundamental to historical capitalism. In these cases, gender meanings and norms have been appropriated from the larger culture and bent to capitalist purposes, with major consequences for both distribution and recognition. Likewise, what presents itself as "the cultural sphere" is deeply permeated by "the bottom line" – witness global mass entertainment, the art market, and transnational advertising, all fundamental to contemporary culture. Once again, the consequences are significant for both distribution and recognition. *Contra* substantive dualism, then, nominally economic matters usually affect not only the economic position but also the status and identities of social actors. Likewise, nominally cultural matters affect not only status but also economic position. In neither case, therefore, are we dealing with separate spheres.[21]

Practically, moreover, substantive dualism fails to challenge the current dissociation of cultural politics from social politics. On the contrary, it reinforces that dissociation. Casting the economy and the culture as impermeable, sharply bounded separate spheres, it assigns the politics of redistribution to the former and the politics of recognition to the latter. The result is effectively to constitute two separate political tasks requiring two separate political struggles. Decoupling cultural injustices from economic injustices, cultural struggles from social struggles, it reproduces the very dissociation we are seeking to overcome. Substantive dualism is not a solution to, but a symptom of, our problem. It reflects, but does not critically interrogate, the institutional differentiations of modern capitalism.

A genuinely critical perspective, in contrast, cannot take the appearance of separate spheres at face value. Rather, it must probe beneath appearances to reveal the hidden connections between distribution and recognition. It must make visible, and *criticizable*, both the cultural subtexts of nominally economic processes and the economic subtexts of nominally cultural practices. Treating *every* practice as simultaneously economic and cultural, albeit not necessarily in equal proportions, it must assess each of them from two different perspectives. It must assume both the standpoint of distribution and the standpoint of recognition, without reducing either one of these perspectives to the other.

Such an approach I call "perspectival dualism." Here redistribution and recognition do not correspond to two substantive societal domains, economy and culture; rather, they constitute two analytical perspectives that can be assumed with respect to any domain. These perspectives can be deployed critically, moreover, against the ideological grain. One can use the recognition perspective to identify the cultural dimensions of what are usually viewed as redistributive economic policies. By focusing on the production and circulation of interpretations and norms in welfare programs, for example, one can assess the effects of institutionalized maldistribution on the identities and social status of single mothers.[22] Conversely, one can use the redistribution perspective to bring into focus the economic dimensions of what are usually viewed as issues of recognition. By focusing on the high "transaction costs" of living in the closet, for example, one can assess the effects of heterosexist misrecognition on the economic position of gays and lesbians.[23] With perspectival dualism, then, one can assess the justice of any social practice, regardless of where it is institutionally located, from either or both of two analytically distinct normative vantage points, asking: does the practice in question work to ensure both the objective and intersubjective conditions of participatory parity? Or does it, rather, undermine them?

The advantages of this approach should be clear. Unlike economism and culturalism, perspectival dualism permits us to consider both distribution and recognition, without reducing either one of them to the other. Unlike substantive dualism, moreover, it does not reinforce their dissociation. Because it avoids dichotomizing economy and culture, it allows us to grasp their imbrication and the crossover effects of each. And, finally, because it avoids reducing classes to statuses or vice versa, it permits us to examine the causal interactions between those two orders of domination. Understood perspectivally, then, the distinction between redistribution and recognition does not simply reproduce the ideological dissociations of our time. Rather, it provides an indispensable conceptual tool for interrogating, working through, and eventually overcoming those dissociations.

Perspectival dualism offers another advantage as well. Of all the approaches considered here, it alone allows us to conceptualize some practical difficulties that can arise in the course of political struggles for redistribution and recognition. Conceiving the economic and the cultural as differentiated but interpenetrating social orders, perspectival dualism appreciates that neither claims for redistribution nor claims for recognition can be contained within a separate sphere. On the contrary, they impinge on one another in ways that may give rise to unintended effects.

Consider, first, that redistribution impinges on recognition. Virtually any claim for redistribution will have some recognition effects, whether intended or unintended. Proposals to redistribute income through social welfare, for example, have an irreducible expressive dimension;[24] they convey interpretations of the meaning and value of different activities, for example, "childrearing" versus "wage-earning," while also constituting and ranking different subject positions, for example "welfare mothers" versus "taxpayers" (Fraser, 1993). Thus, redistributive claims invariably affect the status and social identities of social actors. These effects must be thematized and scrutinized, lest one end up fueling misrecognition in the course of remedying maldistribution.

The classic example, once again, is "welfare." Means-tested benefits aimed specifically at the poor are the most directly redistributive form of social welfare. Yet such benefits tend to stigmatize recipients, casting them as deviants and scroungers and invidiously distinguishing them from "wage-earners" and "taxpayers" who "pay their own way." Welfare programs of this type "target" the poor – not only for material aid but also for public hostility. The end result is often to add the insult of misrecognition to the injury of deprivation.

Redistributive policies have misrecognition effects when background patterns of cultural value skew the meaning of economic reforms, when, for example, a pervasive cultural devaluation of female caregiving inflected Aid to Families with Dependent Children as "getting something for nothing."[25] In such contexts, welfare reform cannot succeed unless it is joined with struggles for cultural change aimed at revaluing caregiving and the feminine associations that code it.[26] In short, *no redistribution without recognition.*

Consider, next, the converse dynamic, whereby recognition impinges on distribution. Virtually any claim for recognition will have some distributive effects, whether intended or unintended. Proposals to redress androcentric evaluative patterns, for example, have economic implications, which work sometimes to the detriment of the intended beneficiaries. For example, campaigns to suppress prostitution and pornography for the sake of enhancing women's status may have negative effects on the economic position of sex workers, while no-fault divorce reforms, which appeared to dovetail with feminist efforts to enhance women's status, may have had at least short-term negative effects on the economic position of some divorced women, although their extent has apparently been exaggerated and is currently in dispute (Weitzman, 1985). Thus, recognition claims can affect economic position, above and beyond their effects on status. These effects, too, must be scrutinized, lest one end up fueling maldistribution in the course of trying to remedy misrecognition. Recognition claims, moreover, are liable to the charge of being "merely symbolic."[27] When pursued in contexts marked by gross disparities in economic position, reforms aimed at recognizing distinctiveness tend to devolve into empty gestures; like the sort of recognition that would put women on a pedestal, they mock, rather than redress, serious harms. In such contexts, recognition reforms cannot succeed unless they are joined with struggles for redistribution. In short, *no recognition without redistribution.*

The need, in all cases, is to think integratively, as in the example of comparable worth. Here a claim to redistribute income between men and women is expressly integrated with a claim to change gender-coded patterns of cultural value. The underlying premise is that gender injustices of distribution and recognition are so complexly intertwined that neither can be redressed entirely independently of the other. Thus, efforts to reduce the gender wage gap cannot fully succeed if, remaining wholly "economic," they fail to challenge the gender meanings that code low-paying service occupations as "women's work," largely devoid of intelligence and skill. Likewise, efforts to revalue female-coded traits such as interpersonal sensitivity and nurturance cannot succeed if, remaining wholly "cultural," they fail to challenge the structural economic conditions that connect those traits with dependency and powerlessness. Only an approach that redresses the cultural devaluation of the "feminine" precisely *within* the economy (and elsewhere) can deliver serious redistribution and genuine recognition.

Conclusion

Let me conclude by recapitulating my overall argument. I have argued that to pose an either/or choice between the politics of redistribution and the politics of recognition is to posit a false antithesis. On the contrary, justice today requires both. Thus, I have argued for a comprehensive framework that encompasses both redistribution and recognition so as to challenge injustice on both fronts.

I then examined two sets of issues that arise once we contemplate devising such a framework. On the plane of moral theory, I argued for a single, overarching, but two-dimensional conception of justice that encompasses both redistribution and recognition, without reducing either one of them to the other. And I proposed two key components of such a conception: a *status model of recognition* and the principle of *parity of participation*. On the plane of social theory, I argued for a *perspectival dualism* of redistribution and recognition. This approach alone, I contended, can accommodate both the differentiation of class from status in capitalist society and also their causal interaction, and it alone can alert us to potential practical tensions between claims for redistribution and claims for recognition.

Perspectival dualism in social theory complements participatory parity in moral theory. Taken together, these two notions constitute a portion of the conceptual resources one needs to begin answering what I take to be the key political question of our day: how can we develop a coherent programmatic perspective that integrates redistribution and recognition? How can we develop a framework that integrates what remains cogent and unsurpassable in the socialist vision with what is defensible and compelling in the apparently "postsocialist" vision of multiculturalism?

If we fail to ask this question, if we cling instead to false antitheses and misleading either/or dichotomies, we will miss the chance to envision social arrangements that can redress both economic and cultural injustices. Only by looking to integrative approaches that unite redistribution and recognition can we meet the requirements of justice for all.

Notes

1. Portions of this chapter are adapted and excerpted from my first chapter in Fraser and Honneth (2003) and from my Tanner Lecture on Human Values (Fraser 1998) both titled, "Social Justice in the Age of Identity Politics: Redistribution, Recognition and Participation." I am grateful to the Tanner Foundation for Human Values for permission to adapt and reprint this material. I thank Elizabeth Anderson and Axel Honneth

for their thoughtful responses to the Tanner Lecture, and Rainer Forst, Theodore Koditschek, Eli Zaretsky, and especially Erik Olin Wright for helpful comments on earlier drafts.

2. The following discussion revises a subsection of Fraser (1995).

3. It is true that pre-existing status distinctions, for example, between lords and commoners, shaped the emergence of the capitalist system. Nevertheless, it was only the creation of a differentiated economic order with a relatively autonomous life of its own that gave rise to the distinction between capitalists and workers.

4. I am grateful to Erik Olin Wright (personal communication, 1997) for several of the formulations in this paragraph.

5. In capitalist society, the regulation of sexuality is relatively decoupled from the economic structure, which comprises an order of economic relations that is differentiated from kinship and oriented to the expansion of surplus value. In the current "post-Fordist" phase of capitalism, moreover, sexuality increasingly finds its *locus* in the relatively new, late-modern sphere of "personal life," where intimate relations that can no longer be identified with the family are lived as disconnected from the imperatives of production and reproduction. Today, accordingly, the heteronormative regulation of sexuality is increasingly removed from, and not necessarily functional for, the capitalist economic order. As a result, the economic harms of heterosexism do not derive in any straightforward way from the economic structure. They are rooted, rather, in the heterosexist status order, which is increasingly out of phase with the economy. For a fuller argument, see Fraser (1997b). For the counterargument, see Butler (1997).

6. For a fuller discussion of the status model, see Fraser (2000).

7. The advantages of the status model are more fully discussed in Fraser (2000, 2001a) and in my contribution to Fraser and Honneth (2003).

8. John Rawls, for example, at times conceives "primary goods" such as income and jobs as "social bases of self-respect," while also speaking of self-respect itself as an especially important primary good whose distribution is a matter of justice (see Rawls, 1971: sections 67 and 82; and 1993: 82, 181, and 318 ff.). Dworkin (1981), likewise, defends the idea of "equality of resources" as the distributive expression of the "equal moral worth of persons." Sen (1985), finally, considers both a "sense of self" and the capacity "to appear in public without shame" as relevant to the "capability to function," hence as falling within the scope of an account of justice that enjoins the equal distribution of basic capabilities.

9. The outstanding exception of a theorist who has sought to encompass issues of culture within a distributive framework is Will Kymlicka. Kymlicka proposes to treat access to an "intact cultural structure" as a primary good to be fairly distributed. This approach was tailored for multinational polities, such as Canada, as opposed to polyethnic polities, such as the United States. It becomes problematic, however, in cases where mobilized claimants for recognition do not divide neatly into territorially concentrated groups with distinct and bounded cultures. It also has difficulty dealing with cases in which claims for recognition do not take the form of demands for political autonomy or sovereignty but aim rather at parity of participation within a polity that is cross-cut by multiple, intersecting lines of difference and

inequality. For the argument that an intact cultural structure is a primary good, see Kymlicka (1989). For the distinction between multinational and polyethnic politics, see Kymlicka (1996).

10. Since I coined this phrase in 1995, the term "parité" has come to play a central role in feminist politics in France. There, it signifies the demand that women occupy a full 50 percent of seats in parliament and other representative bodies. "Parité" in France, accordingly, means strict numerical gender equality in political representation. For me, in contrast, "parity" means the condition of being a *peer*, of being on a *par* with others, of standing on an equal footing. I leave the question open as to exactly what degree or level of equality is necessary to ensure such parity. In my formulation, moreover, the moral requirement is that members of society be ensured the *possibility* of parity, if and when they choose to participate in a given activity or interaction. There is no requirement that everyone actually participate in any such activity. For a fuller account of the differences between my usage and the French, see Fraser (2001b).

11. I say "*at least* two additional conditions must be satisfied" in order to allow for the possibility of more than two. I have in mind specifically a possible third class of obstacles to participatory parity that could be called "political," as opposed to economic or cultural. Such obstacles would include decision-making procedures that systematically marginalize some people even in the absence of maldistribution and misrecognition, for example, single-district winner-take-all electoral rules that deny voice to quasi-permanent minorities. For an insightful account of this example, see Guinier (1994). The possibility of a third class of "political" obstacles to participatory parity adds a further Weberian twist to my use of the class/status distinction. Weber's own distinction was tripartite not bipartite: "class, status, and party." This third, "political" kind of obstacle to participatory parity might be called "misrepresentation." For further discussion, see my contribution to Fraser and Honneth (2003).

12. It is an open question as to how much economic inequality is consistent with parity of participation. Some such inequality is inevitable and unobjectionable, but there is a threshold at which resource disparities become so gross as to impede participatory parity. Where exactly that threshold lies is a matter for further investigation.

13. I say the remedy *could* be recognition of difference, not that it must be. Elsewhere I discuss alternative remedies for the sort of misrecognition that involves denying distinctiveness. See Fraser (2001a) and my contribution to Fraser and Honneth (2003).

14. In this brief chapter I lack the space to consider these questions of contemporary historical sociology. See, however, my contributions in Fraser and Honneth (2003).

15. To be sure, these economic arrangements can be theorized in Marxian terms; but my emphasis here is less on the mechanisms of exploitation than on their normative consequences, which I conceive in terms of the impact of distributive outcomes on social participation.

16. For example, Mauss (1954) and Lévi-Strauss (1969).

17. For an argument against the possibility of a fully marketized society, see Polanyi (1957).

18. By culturalism, I mean a monistic social theory that holds that political economy is reducible to culture and that class is reducible to status. As I read him, Honneth (1995) subscribes to such a theory.

19. By economism, I mean a monistic social theory that holds that culture is reducible to political economy and that status is reducible to class. Karl Marx is often (mis)read as subscribing to such a theory.

20. In what follows, I leave aside a third possibility, which I call "deconstructive anti-dualism." Rejecting the economy/culture distinction as "dichotomizing," this approach seeks to deconstruct it altogether. The claim is that culture and economy are so deeply interconnected that it doesn't make sense to distinguish them. A related claim is that contemporary capitalist society is so monolithically systematic that a struggle against one aspect of it necessarily threatens the whole; hence, it is illegitimate, unnecessary, and counterproductive to distinguish maldistribution from misrecognition. In my view, deconstructive anti-dualism is deeply misguided. For one thing, simply to stipulate that all injustices, and all claims to remedy them, are simultaneously economic and cultural, evacuates the actually existing divergence of status from class. For another, treating capitalism as a monolithic system of perfectly interlocking oppressions evacuates its actual complexity and differentiation. For two rather different versions of deconstructive anti-dualism, see Young (1997) and Butler (1997). For detailed rebuttals, see Fraser (1997b, 1997c) and my contribution to Fraser and Honneth (2003).

21. For more detailed criticism of an influential example of substantive dualism, see Fraser (1985).

22. See Fraser (1994, 1990) and Fraser and Gordon (1994).

23. Jeffrey Escoffier has discussed these issues insightfully in "The Political Economy of the Closet: Toward an Economic History of Gay and Lesbian Life before Stonewall," in Escoffier (1998: 65–78).

24. This formulation was suggested to me by Elizabeth Anderson in her comments on my Tanner Lecture, presented at Stanford University, April 30–May 2, 1996.

25. Aid to Families with Dependent Children (AFDC) was the major means-tested welfare program in the United States. Claimed overwhelmingly by solo-mother families living below the poverty line, AFDC became a lightning rod for racist and sexist anti-welfare sentiments in the 1990s. In 1997, it was "reformed" in such a way as to eliminate the federal entitlement that had guaranteed (some, inadequate) income support to the poor.

26. This formulation, too, was suggested to me by Elizabeth Anderson's comments on my Tanner Lecture, presented at Stanford University, April 30–May 2, 1996.

27. I am grateful to Steven Lukes for insisting on this point in conversation.

References

Butler, Judith. 1998. "Merely Cultural." *Social Text* 53/54.

Dworkin, Ronald. 1981. "What is Equality? Part 2: Equality of Resources." *Philosophy and Public Affairs* 10:283–345.

Escoffier, Jeffrey. 1998. "The Political Economy of the Closet: Toward an Economic History of Gay and Lesbian Life before Stonewall," in Escoffier, ed. *American Homo: Community and Perversity*. Berkeley, CA: University of California Press. Pp. 65–78.

Fraser, Nancy. 1985. "What's Critical About Critical Theory? The Case of Habermas and Gender." *New German Critique* no. 35: 97–131. Reprinted in Fraser 1989.

　1987. "Women, Welfare, and the Politics of Need Interpretation." *Hypatia: A Journal of Feminist Philosophy* 2/1: 103–121. Reprinted in Fraser 1989.

　1990. "Struggle over Needs: Outline of a Socialist-Feminist Critical Theory of Late-Capitalist Political Culture," in Linda Gordon, ed. *Women, the State, and Welfare: Historical and Theoretical Perspective*. Madison WI: University of Wisconsin Press. Pp. 205–231. Reprinted in Fraser 1989.

　1993. "Clintonism, Welfare, and the Antisocial Wage: The Emergence of a Neoliberal Political Imaginary." *Rethinking Marxism* 6/1:9–23.

　1995. "From Redistribution to Recognition? Dilemmas of Justice in a 'Postsocialist' Age." *New Left Review* no. 212: 68–93. Reprinted in Fraser 1997.

　1997a. *Justice Interruptus: Critical Reflections on the "Postsocialist" Condition*. New York: Routledge.

　1997b. "Heterosexism, Misrecognition, and Capitalism: A Response to Judith Butler." *Social Text* 52/53: 279–289.

　1997c. "A Rejoinder to Iris Young." *New Left Review*, no. 223:126–129.

　1998. "Social Justice in the Age of Identity Politics: Redistribution, Recognition and Participation," in Grethe B. Peterson, ed. *The Tanner Lectures on Human Values*, vol. XIX. The University of Utah Press. Pp. 1–67.

　2000. "Rethinking Recognition: Overcoming Displacement and Reification in Cultural Politics." *New Left Review* 3:107–120.

　2001a. "Recognition without Ethics?" *Theory, Culture & Society* 18/2–3: 21–42.

　2001b. "Pour une politique féministe à l'âge de la reconnaissance: approche bi-dimensionnelle et justice entre les sexes." *Actuel Marx*, no. 30: 153–172.

Fraser, Nancy and Linda Gordon. 1994. "A Genealogy of 'Dependency': Tracing a Keyword of the U.S. Welfare State." *Signs* 9/2:309–336. Reprinted in Fraser 1997.

Fraser, Nancy and Axel Honneth. 2003. *Redistribution or Recognition? A Political–Philosophical Exchange*, trans. Joel Golb, James Ingram, and Christiane Wilke. London: Verso.

Gitlin, Todd. 1995. *The Twilight of Common Dreams: Why America is Wracked by Culture Wars*. New York: Metropolitan Books.

Guinier, Lani. 1994. *The Tyranny of the Majority*. New York: The Free Press.

Honneth, Axel. 1995. *The Struggle for Recognition: The Moral Grammar of Social Conflicts*, trans. Joel Anderson. Cambridge, MA: Polity Press.

Kymlicka, Will. 1989. *Liberalism, Community and Culture*. Oxford: Oxford University Press.

　1996. "Three Forms of Group-Differentiated Citizenship in Canada," in Seyla Benhabib, ed. *Democracy and Difference*. Princeton, NJ: Princeton University Press.

Lévi-Strauss, Claude. 1969. *The Elementary Structures of Kinship*, trans. James H. Bell. Boston, MA: Beacon Press.

Mauss, Marcel. 1954. *The Gift*, trans. Ian Cunnison. Glencoe, IL: Free Press.

Polanyi, Karl. 1957. *The Great Transformation*. Boston, MA: Beacon Press.

Rawls, John. 1971. *A Theory of Justice*. Cambridge, MA: Harvard University Press.
    1993. *Political Liberalism*. New York: Columbia University Press.

Rorty, Richard. 1998. *Achieving Our Country: Leftist Thought in Twentieth-Century America*. Cambridge, MA: Harvard University Press.

Sen, Amartya. 1985. *Commodities and Capabilities*. New York: North-Holland: Dordecht.

Sennett, Richard and Jonathan Cobb. 1973. *The Hidden Injuries of Class*. New York: Knopf.

Taylor, Charles. 1994. "The Politics of Recognition," in Amy Gutmann, ed. *Multiculturalism: Examining the Politics of Recognition*. Princeton, NJ: Princeton University Press.

Thompson, E. P. 1963. *The Making of the English Working Class*. New York: Random House.

Weitzman, Lenore. 1985. *The Divorce Revolution: The Unexpected Social Consequences for Women and Children in America*. New York: The Free Press.

Young, Iris Marion. 1997. "Unruly Categories: A Critique of Nancy Fraser's Dual Systems Theory." *New Left Review* 222:147–160.

9

Are we all in the closet? Notes toward a sociological and cultural turn in Queer Theory

Steven Seidman

The concept of the homosexual closet is a core category of knowledge and politics in postwar American public culture. More specifically, it has been integral to the discourses of homosexual life that are associated with what I will call post-Stonewall culture, that is, the lesbian and gay culture that took shape roughly in the early seventies and eighties in the United States (Duberman, 1993; D'Emilio, 1983). The category of the closet has been central to the way individuals who identify as lesbian and gay – and individuals who analyze those who identify as lesbian and gay – narrate homosexual experience (e.g., Gross, 1993; Russo, 1981; Sedgwick, 1990; Woods, 1993). Post-Stonewall culture fashioned a romantic narrative of the homosexual heroically struggling to be free of the oppression of the closet. "Out of the closets and into the streets" was the rallying cry of liberationist politics in the 1970s (Humphreys, 1972; Jay and Young, 1992 [1972]) and, as the politics of "outing" in the 1990s suggests (Gross, 1993; Signorile, 1993, 1995), a politics of visibility or coming out of the closet remains at the center of the lesbian and gay movement.

This chapter has two purposes. First, I intend to raise some questions about the implicit sociology and politics of the closet that has dominated post-Stonewall culture. I will do this in a sketchy, largely programmatic way. I outline a perspective that underscores the "productive" aspects of the closet, that emphasizes its limited sociohistorical applicability, and that underscores the limits of the politics of visibility or recognition (see Seidman, 2000). Second, the theme of the closet as an organizing principle of American life is used to explore some reservations regarding recent queer theory. In this regard, I make the case for a stronger sociological and cultural turn in queer studies.

The productivity of the closet

The dominant discourses of post-Stonewall culture have framed the closet in a way that assumes an already formed homosexual self. Repressed in the closet the homosexual is liberated through the act of coming out. However, a queer critique or a perspective which makes the making of the subject into a problem has opened up a line of inquiry that has been unthinkable in post-Stonewall culture – namely, the role of the closet in the formation of a homosexual self. To what extent is the closet or the condition of concealment and "global" self management productive of homosexual selves?

Post-Stonewall narratives have understood the closet as referring to the concealment of homosexual desire and identity. The closet is said to describe a state of self alienation and inauthenticity. However, the experience of concealment implies not only repression but the making of a desire and self around homosexuality. The interiority forced upon the individual by closeting practices compels making same-sex desire into an object of overdetermined investment and cathexsis. Does not the closet indicate a condition where homosexual desires are imagined and cultivated, and where a self is formed around this desire? Does not the concept of the closet presume an experience where the individual invests homosexual desire not only with shame but with pleasure and the longing for an imaginary integrated, whole self?

Consider, for example, Paul Monette's *Becoming a Man* (1992). This exquisitely moving memoir is organized around the theme of Paul's youthful awareness of his homosexuality and the simultaneous concealment of this desire. He describes a closeted life involving secrecy, deception, a pervasive fear of exposure, and a heightened management of daily life. Indeed, the closet makes its appearance, signaling its key role in the thematic framing of this autobiographical essay, on the very first page:

Everybody else had a childhood, for one thing – where they were coaxed and coached and taught all the shorthand. Or that's how it always seemed to me, eavesdropping my way through twenty-five years, filling in the stories of straight men's lives. First they had their shining boyhood, which made them strong and psyched them up for the leap across the chasm to adolescence, where the real rites of manhood began.

And every year they leaped further ahead, leaving me in the dust with all my doors closed, and each with a new and better deadbolt. Until I was twenty-five, I was the only man I knew who had no story at all . . . That's how the closet feels, once you've made your nest in it and learned to call it home.

I speak for no one else here . . . Yet, I've come to learn that all our stories add up to the same imprisonment . . . The gutting of all our passions till we are a bunch of eunuchs . . . Most of all, the ventriloquism, the learning how to pass for straight. Such obedient slaves we make, with such very tidy rooms.

Monette details the deep psychic and social costs to the self of a society that imposes the conditions of the closet on some of its citizens. And yet, Monette's own descriptions of the "closeted life" point less to a pre-existing homosexual self than to a homosexual self in formation. It was, after all, in the closet that Paul began to fantasize or construct a sense of self around a homosexual desire and life. "I couldn't tell my claque of girls how riveted I'd been on the Prom King's grinding hips – his football hands stroking Connie's bare back up and down" (1992: 45). Similarly, Paul speaks of the terrors of the High School locker room. His struggles to suppress his impulse to stare at the other boys undressing or showering is described as repressive, indeed as castrating. Yet, Paul relates that such experiences were productive of homosexual desires and fantasies. "Jerking off every night in the dark thinking about them, summoning them in their nakedness . . . I was able to picture in stupefying detail a hundred different naked bodies from Andover – my pantheon, unchanged by time" (1992: 70–71). It was these homosexual fantasies and longings that ultimately drove Paul to begin a journey out of the closet: "I had no choice but to keep on looking for the thing I'd never seen: two men in love and laughing. For that was the image in my head, though I'd never read it in any book or seen it in any movie. I'd fashioned it out of bits of dreams . . . The vision of the laughing men dogged me and wouldn't be shaken . . . The searching became as compulsive as any insatiable need, till I sometimes thought I'd lost my mind – but I also think it kept me alive" (1992: 178).

Thus, while Monette self-consciously relates a story of how social domination produces a dominated self, he also – unconsciously it seems – narrates a tale of the making of a resisting homosexual self. The chief drama of his own story is that of a dominated, shadowy, inauthentic self who ultimately rebels against the closet, comes out, recovers his self and demands personal and collective freedom. If we take the closet as indicating only a state of repression and the loss of self, we cannot explain how this dominated self manages, in the end, to resist and rebel in order to recover a whole, authentic self.

Proposing a notion of the productivity of the closet parallels the way the concept of a women's sphere, the colonized other, and the racial ghetto are now often understood. Each of these concepts have been pivotal for analyzing dynamics of social oppression. Feminists and critical race theorists, for example, have analyzed how the power to enforce social invisibility works internally to produce dominated selves, but also, feminists, postcolonial, and antiracist theorists have inquired into how this very same condensation of the self around a particular identity is productive of new subaltern subjects who resist domination.

Beyond the closet?

I have come to believe that the social texture of American lesbian and gay life today is considerably different from the way it is represented in the dominant discourses of post-Stonewall culture (see Seidman, 2000; 2002). By investigating the social conditions that make the closet narrative central to post-Stonewall culture, it is perhaps possible to begin to delineate its historical boundaries. Specifically, to what extent is it plausible to speak of the emergence of at least the contours of a gay culture in which the closet, coming out, and declaring a public sexual identity are no longer the key narrative figures in terms of which homosexuality is understood?[1]

My argument in this regard turns on the claim that there is occurring a trend toward the "normalization" (internal acceptance) and social routinization (social acceptance) of homosexuality (see Seidman, 2002).

I found strong support for this claim in interviews I conducted in 1996–97. My initial aim was to research what it means to be "in" the closet. How did social domination shape a homosexual subject? How did concealment and sequestration make possible a resisting homosexual subject? However, from the very first interview I found that my respondents reported lives that were in a significant sense "beyond the closet." I interviewed individuals who lived in small towns or mid-sized cities, who are not strongly integrated into a gay subculture, and therefore would be expected to be "closeted." However, many individuals described a degree of internal normalization and social routinization that was inconsistent with the idea of the closet.

Typical in many ways is Lenny, a 40-year-old gay man. Until recently, Lenny lived in a small upstate New York town, the place where he grew up and where his working-class, religious family still lives. Coming of age at the very beginning of the making of a public gay culture (mid-1970s), Lenny's only ideas about homosexuality were very negative. He recalls hearing words like "fag" and "queer" from peers and family as derogatory and shaming – a message reinforced by his church. He grew up being aware of, yet suppressing, his homosexuality. Lenny lived an almost classically defined "closeted" life until he was about 30. The suppression of his homosexuality, in other words, shaped key life decisions such as getting married and joining the Marines. Concealment, moreover, meant disassociating his inner and outer life, and maintaining a vigilant, intense self management, driven by extreme fear, to avoid exposure. No one knew of his homosexuality, except those few men with whom he had anonymous, guilt-ridden sex.

This changed when he turned 30 years of age. Lenny "came out" – initially to a lesbian friend, then to gay men at bars and community events, and finally to family, friends, and co-workers. For example, Lenny reports that today his supervisor and co-workers know about his homosexuality. More importantly as an indicator of normalization and social routinization, they know about his homosexuality not merely as an abstract identity but as something that is interwoven into his life. That is, his co-workers know about his homosexuality as it relates to his friends, dates or lovers, gay community events and politics, and so on. Pressing further into the extent to which his homosexuality has become normalized and routinized, Lenny reports that he talks about his life to his co-workers in an open, easy way that is no different than if he were heterosexual. Like heterosexually identified individuals, Lenny does not tell everyone everything about the homosexual aspects of his life. Disclosure decisions are determined by a series of factors including feeling safe, the closeness or intimacy of the relationship, determining whether the other can handle it, and judging whether disclosure will result in being treated as a mere label or as a complex, multidimensional person: "I just feel everybody out, one at a time. I think first of all would they be supportive and more importantly was it any of their business. I would ask myself that. And in a lot of cases, I feel like its more important that they get to know me, who I am, you know without that aspect, so that they really won't be so prejudiced when they do find out. I try to prepare people and I try to feel them out, because some people just can't handle it and don't want to know it."

Make no mistake – heterosexuality remains very definitely normative and homosexuality and the homosexual is still freighted with connotations of moral pollution. As the above statement by Lenny indicates, and as many interviews make clear, concealment and disclosure decisions, and sexual identity management are still part of the lives of lesbian and gay men in America. Homosexuals still suffer and, for many, the closet and coming out remains not merely a phase of their lives but its center. Yet, whether the evidence is individual reports of the normalization and routinization of their homosexuality, or shifts in popular culture (for example, television, novels, news coverage) and politics, a trend toward normalization and social routinization seems to be one prominent current in contemporary America.

Trends toward normalization and social routinization would suggest shifts in the relation of homosexuality and identity. In this regard, respondents often speak as if they are searching for ways to express a change in the meaning and place of homosexuality in their lives. Homosexuality is often likened to something personal such as an intimate relationship or a deep religious conviction that one only tells some people not out of fear or shame but depending on the degree of familiarity or intimacy established or desired. In many of my interviews, homosexuality is described less as a core identity than a thread, one among many, woven into respondents' lives. For example, Jeff describes the identity aspect of his homosexuality in terms of the metaphor of a theme – one among many (religion, gender, occupation, ableness) that shapes his life: "Being gay is not a separate part of me; it's just an overall theme that affects different parts of my personality. Being gay has a little bit of influence in how I behave at work, a little bit of influence in the way I go shopping, and why and whom I'm seeing." To the extent that homosexuality becomes a thread, and to the extent that it is routinely managed, respondents report that the dramatic center of their lives is not the closet. Thus, when I asked Jeff what is the chief problem that homosexuality presents today for him, the closet or coming out is not mentioned: "[Being gay] makes it a little bit tougher to walk hand in hand with my boyfriend in public. That's really where the impact is now." Jeff's comments are, in fact, typical of many respondents who highlighted the second-class status of their intimate relationships: "I feel like as much as we as a society want to be culturally diverse, we are not . . . If I [as a woman] develop a relationship with a woman, and we're together for an extended period of time, and I choose to spend my life with this person, and this person is an intricate part of my life, then that person should be able to share in all of the things that we have together, e.g., my pension or health benefits. That's a really big focus for me right now."

I am not arguing that concealment is no longer part of lesbian and gay life but that this practice is less compellingly framed in terms of the closet and that the dynamic of concealment and disclosure is less the focus of the lives of many lesbian-and-gay-identified Americans. Moreover, I believe that queer theory and politics has, in part, taken shape in response to gay normalization and routinization. The public tolerance of homosexuality, which coexists with the continued pathologizing and polluting of non-normative sexual, gender, and intimate practices, has made criticizing normalization per se – apart from the critique of heteronormativity – into a new political focus. I will return to this point toward the end of the chapter.

Simultaneously, normalization and routinization suggests that practices associated with the homosexual closet are becoming a social force for heterosexual America. As gays become a visible, even routine part of public life, one effect is that the issue of who is or is not a homosexual matters less. However, to the extent that homosexuality is not normative, the more significant effect of trends toward social routinization is that homosexual suspicion is generalized to all Americans as there will be a pervasive awareness of the closet and the practice of passing. No matter how masterful a performance of heterosexuality, individuals will not be free of such suspicion. A certain gesture or posture, an unguarded slip or a certain intonation, a prolonged single status, perhaps a close association with publicly known homosexuals or homosexually identified occupations, might elicit suspicion. If normalization and routinization generalizes and heightens homosexual suspicion, there will likely be a more concerted effort by many Americans to project a heterosexual identity. This may involve intentionally avoiding practices that circulate as signs of homosexuality (e.g., deviant gender behavior, participation in pride or protest marches); or, it might involve a more assertive effort by individuals publicly to flag signs of heterosexuality such as wearing a wedding ring, letting others know one is heterosexually involved, engaging in homophobic displays, or simply being more deliberate about exhibiting conventional gender practices. The point is that for many Americans there is a new deliberateness about managing and publicizing sexual identity in daily life, a deliberateness that has been considered unique to the homosexual (Seidman, 2000).

Rethinking Queer Studies

For some time I have been thinking about the epistemology of homosexuality. Like many sociologists who study sexuality, I was challenged by the rise of queer theory (see De Lauretis, 1991; Seidman, 1996; Warner, 1994). From Stonewall through the 1980s, it was historians and social scientists who fashioned the key knowledges about homosexuality. These scholars analyzed the social making of the homosexual and his or her struggle to transform a polluted into a legitimate social identity. The focus of these perspectives was on the social processes that made same-sex desire into a homosexual identity and into a new social minority (Duberman et al., 1989).

Queer theory challenged these sociological knowledges, in a way paralleling so-called "postmodern" critiques of gynocentric approaches to gender (see Butler and Scott, 1992; Nicholson, 1990). Unlike the sociological turn of lesbian and gay perspectives in the 1980s, queer theory had its institutional roots in English departments, and drew considerably from post-structuralism – a tradition largely foreign to historians and social scientists. Queer theorists raised doubts about the conceptual underpinnings of lesbian and gay and sexuality studies, in much the same way that Derrida and Foucault wreaked havoc on the social sciences by questioning assumptions about the duality of knowledge and power, Whiggish notions of history, and unitary ideas of subjectivity and identity. Many sociologists and historians have defended lesbian and gay studies against the interventions of queer theory – much the same as sociologists, including many cultural sociologists, have resisted and sometimes scandalized post-structuralism as a sign of unreason. Although I made the post-structural turn, I have been troubled by the thin sociology and politics of queer theory. I have imagined the idea of a sociologically informed queer theory but wanted to fathom this not as a purely metatheoretical possibility, but in the context of a research project.

A sociology of homosexuality had typically accepted the categories of homosexual and heterosexual as if they were natural, universal features of "human sexuality" (Stein and Plummer, 1996). A pre-existing sexual subject was assumed and homosexuals were taken to be a distinct subset of the human population. Researchers analyzed the social forces that facilitated the formation of a public homosexual identity and community (for example, Hoffman, 1968; Humphreys, 1979; Warren, 1974). From this perspective, the closet came to signify social repression while coming out indicated the opening act to the recovery and liberation of the homosexual. Sociologists crafted an heroic narrative that charted a movement from invisiblity to visibility, assuming that the latter marked authenticity and the inaugural act of freedom. In effect, lesbian and gay sociological studies rehearsed the liberation narrative of the Enlightenment – that is, a story of the power of reason to transform the world by revealing the truth of a transparent, essential humanity. Sociologists imagined themselves disclosing the truth of the homosexual's agonizing progress toward authenticity, and indeed this sociological truth expedited liberation by freeing the homosexual from myth and tradition which enforced the closet. These sociological knowledges rearticulated a Whiggish history in the service of a political project – the demand for the recognition of a homosexual minority.

Queer theory substituted for this realist narrative of the making of the homosexual an ironic, deconstructive perspective (for example, Butler, 1990; Sedgwick, 1990). For example, instead of understanding the closet, coming out, and asserting a sexual identification in realist terms, these categories were said to acquire meaning as part of a discursive or narrative order. This semiotic perspective does not deny the integrity of people's reported experiences. Rather, it contests the notion that the closet is a term necessary to describe the experience of concealment. The closet is part of a narrative framing of self and society, and as such, it shapes the experience of concealment or is productive of homosexual life. Similarly, once concealment is understood in terms of the category of the closet, with its resonances of self denial and alienation, then disclosure or the act of coming out signifies a liberatory act. Queer theorists criticized a view of coming out as an objectified process rather than as a narrative that shapes the dynamic of disclosure and indeed makes public recognition into the supreme political act. They question the interpretation of coming out as a process of self discovery and criticize this narrative's millenarian investment in coming out as an act of emancipation. Coming out is renarrativized as an act of self construction (e.g. Butler, 1991; Cohen, 1991). Moreover, public self-identification, no matter how personally courageous and psychically empowering, is said to be ambivalently linked to resisting heteronormativity. Clearly, visibility is a condition of community building and political mobilization. Yet, such an identity politic not only has marginalizing and exclusionary effects but reinforces a regime of sexuality (see Seidman, 1997). Affirming a lesbian and gay sexual identity still sexualizes the self, reproduces the hetero/homosexual binary as a majority/minority relation, and subjects selves to sexual normalization. Queer theorists do not advocate abandoning an identity based politics – a naive move since the only way to resist a mode of oppression that deploys identity categories is to own and contest their meaning. Who can doubt the importance of affirming identities whose pollution have been integral to social oppression? Queers aim though to trouble the epistemological basis of a politic that assumes a unitary sexual identity; they contest the necessity or desirability of a politic narrowly wedded to visibility. Queer theoretical perspectives approach identity in terms of non-substantialist notions of affinity, hybridity, and multiplicity while pressing beyond a politic of identity to a critique of the social forces that compel the organization of selves and social relations in sexual identity terms and to be regulated by norms of normality and health (e.g. Namaste, 1996; Warner, 1993).

Queer theorists intend to shift the center of sexual theory away from the minority discourse of lesbian and gay studies. This means abandoning the concept of the homosexual as a foundational category and the homosexual as an oppressed and resisting social minority. The new focus is on the social force of the hetero/homosexual cultural figure. To the extent that this cultural code or definition is structured into official knowledges, laws, social policies, folk mores, institutional cultures, and media representations, it defines and regulates selves and social relations. To say it differently, queer theorists delineate, as characteristic of societies such as the United States and England, an analytically distinct process of "sexualization" or the sexual formation of the self and social life – a central aspect of which is the normative status of heterosexuality (see Sedgwick, 1990; Seidman, 1997).

Given the social imposition of normative heterosexuality, and the intent to extinguish all traces of homosexuality from public and private life or to permit its visibility but only as the inferior, scandalized other to heterosexuality, one aim of queer theorists is to show how homosexuality is an active social presence, even if disguised or coded. Contesting the assumed exclusive heterosexualization of public and private life, queer theorists document the way homosexuality is present in practices and texts that are explicitly heteronormative.

For example, in *Making It Perfectly Queer*, Alexander Doty (1993) analyzes the ways homosexuality functions as a dramatic presence in television shows which assume normative heterosexuality: "What is so interesting about series such as *I Love Lucy*, *Laverne and Shirley*, *Designing Women*, *The Golden Girls*, *Babes*, *The Mary Tyler Moore Show*, *Kate and Alice*, and *Alice* is their crucial investment in constructing narratives that connect an audience's pleasure to the activities and relationships of women – which results in situating most male characters as potential threats to the spectator's narrative pleasure." Not only are relations between women the dramatic center of these shows, but viewers (women and men), says Doty, derive pleasure from these same-sex intimacies, get invested in these "lesbian" bonds, or identify with women who bond primarily with women. While men's presence in such TV shows (as husbands or boyfriends) is meant to signal that these women are heterosexual, their marginality makes the emotional and erotic bonds between women the sustaining drama and source of viewer pleasure. Accordingly, the (ostensibly) straight-identified viewer assumes a lesbian or queer subject position.

In a similarly provocative way, Eve Sedgwick (1990) has sought to trace the ways homosexuality gets coded in non-sexual terms. For example, she argues that the organization of twentieth-century thought and culture around binaries such as private/public, knowledge/ignorance, and secrecy/disclosure is connected to the dynamics of the closet which foregrounds the organization of experience around secrecy and disclosure, privacy and publicity: "The *Epistemology of the Closet . . .* will argue that an understanding of virtually any aspect of modern western culture must be, not merely incomplete, but damaged in its central substance to the degree that it does not incorporate a critical analysis of modern homo/heterosexual definition."

My own research moves in a decidedly queer terrain. I intend to explore how homosexuality might be analyzed less as a minority identity than as a general social and symbolic condition. In this regard, I trace the way some key features of homosexual life become general social conditions of American society. For example, coming out creates the conditions of homosexuality – that is, the closet, coming out, and publicizing a sexual identity – for straight Americans. The daughter who comes out to her parents creates for them the condition of the closet and the dilemma of whether to come out to their relatives, friends, and co-workers. The parents' coming out creates once again the same social condition of the closet for those to whom they come out. One father describes himself as somewhat in the closet about his son's homosexuality: "I'm not entirely out of the closet. There are some people who I may not ever admit to them that my son is gay. I don't think it's fear on my part. I just don't want to get into a big argument with these people, primarily family, about my son. I don't feel like it's their business." In fact, this man revealed that he has never told any friend, co-worker, or relative, about his son. The reproduction of the closet as a social practice with every act of coming out proceeds continuously, thereby becoming a general social force in American society. Similarly, if normalization and routinization make passing and homosexual suspicion a general feature of American society, homosexuality refers less to the identity of some Americans than to practices involving reading sexual signs and managing sexual identity that are no longer unique to the homosexual.

While the post-structural grounding of queer theory has made it possible for lesbian and gay studies to become a general analysis of sexuality and society, it is also the cause of some unease. Queer theory is not of course a uniform discourse. Yet its chief currents exhibit a cultural reductionism. Queer theorists have skillfully traced the social productivity of the hetero/homosexual cultural definition, but have not analyzed the social creation and context of these meanings. Unfortunately, this culturalism sometimes leads to a call for a Marxist materialist analysis (for example, Morton, 1996). I say unfortunate because it is in my view regrettable to think that social structure and institutional dynamics can be comprehended by another retreading of Marxism – as if the critique of Marxism's materialist and class reductionism by sociologists, semioticians, critical theorists, post-structuralists, feminists, and others had never happened. Moreover, post-structuralism makes for a thin cultural social analysis. Social meanings are analyzed in terms of relations of contrast and similarity among signs. This approach cannot alone account for processes of subject and identity formation, the creation of solidarities, and collective political mobilization. In this regard, a queer cultural analysis could profit from the work of cultural anthropologists such as Mary Douglas (1966) or Marshall Sahlins (1976) and cultural sociologists such as Durkheim (1965), Bellah (1975), and Alexander (1993). Also problematic is that queer theorists often assume that the meanings in texts such as television programs, literature, or popular songs are directly socially effective. Unlike the recent turn in cultural studies toward reception studies (Press, 1994), there has been little effort among queer theorists to analyze the way textual meanings are processed by agents. Queer theorists minimize the contextual, agentic aspects of meaning making.

Post-structuralism cannot stand alone as the basis of a cultural social analysis. Neither a deconstructive nor a Lacanian perspective can provide the kind of analytical frameworks for understanding histories, complex structural and cultural processes, and power dynamics that operate at subjective, interpersonal, and macrosocial levels. One of my aims in studying the closet is to rearticulate queer theory in a more sociological way – balancing discursive with institutional analysis, attending to both textual meanings and the meaning making of agents, bringing richer cultural and historical perspectives to bear, and analyzing power beyond the power of discourse to legitimate or interpellate. As I mentioned at the very beginning of this chapter, one reason the closet appeals to me as a focus of study is that it raises the problem of power in interesting ways. On the one hand, there is the question of the power to create closets, to enforce social invisibility, which involves an analysis of both juridical–repressive and disciplinary power, that is, dynamics of surveillance, sequestration, and normalization. On the other hand, not only does power operate to create a dominated self, but the power of the closet is productive of a homosexual self.

From the vantage point of the closet, resistance involves not only a politic of citizenship but also an anti-normalizing politic.

From recognition to anti-normalizing politics

Let me conclude by making explicit some of the political implications of the sort of sociology of the closet I am beginning to sketch. To the extent that the closet has functioned as the chief signifier of homosexual oppression, the act of smashing the closet or of coming out has been at the center of the politics of homosexual liberation (Humphreys, 1972; Signorile, 1993, 1995). However important coming out and public visibility is for personal empowerment and as a condition of community building and political mobilization, it is not in itself a transformative political act. Public disclosure, whether as a personal act or a collective act such as during National Coming Out Day or Pride Marches, does not change the institutional, cultural, and gender bases of normative hetero-sexuality. Nor am I convinced that mere exposure to homosexuality changes people's attitudes or behaviors.[2]

The closet and coming out has figured so prominently in lesbian and gay politics because its primary aim has been the legitimation of same-sex prefer-ence and a homosexual identity. The lesbian and gay movement has sought to extend full citizenship rights to a new category of Americans – the homosexual. Some intellectuals and activists criticize this as assimilationist. I think they are partly mistaken. Citizenship rights make it possible for individuals to protect themselves against social threat, to participate in public decision-making, to make claims about national policy and culture, and so on. At stake is how the lesbian and gay movement approaches questions of citizenship. Contestation should be over the basis of citizenship and the meaning of sexual and intimate citizenship. In short, we need a queer articulation of democratic theory. In part, its absence reflects queer intellectuals' preoccupation with questions of identity and visibility – not with discovering, celebrating, and creating a national iden-tity, but with deconstructing identities. And, if queer theorists have raised doubts about the politics of coming out, they have at times surrendered to an equally narrow politics of transgressive play – as if the mere exposure of the multiple and unstable character of identity is sufficient to inaugurate social change.

There is though a positive side to queer politics. Queers hold that the legit-imation of same sex preferences and a lesbian and gay or bisexual identity leaves in place and non-politicized social norms and practices that patholo-gize and control non-normative social practices. That is, the mainstream of the lesbian and gay movement has sought to legitimate homosexuality without contesting the norms and conventions that regulate the broader sexual, gender, and social context of everyday life. Returning to the more radical roots of gay liberationism and lesbian-feminism, a queer politics makes these norms of personal and public life an object of political struggle. For example, queer politics would politicize sexual norms that stipulate legitimate, healthy, and normal sex as exclusively tender, romantic, genital-centered, monogamous, and romantic or it would politicize norms regarding the deportment, aesthetics, and everyday management of the body.

Queer politics proposes an antinormalizing type of sexual politics. Thus, queer nation and transgendered activists have challenged social institutions and discourses that aim to impose upon selves norms of normality and health that assume that sex – an assigned status of female or male – dictates correct gender identity – i.e. socially appropriate feminine and masculine behaviors – which, in turn, dictates a correct, normal, or healthy sexuality, i.e. heterosexuality. A queer anti-normalizing politics aims ultimately to remove wide stretches of personal and intimate life from social and especially state regulation. This renegotiating of moral boundaries entails a considerable shift in the culture of sexuality. For example, hard-and-fast judgments of sex acts as normal/abnormal, healthy/sick, and natural/unnatural would give way to looser judgments about the communicative context of sex acts. Shifting the site of ethical judgment from the sex act to the social exchange, a pragmatic language of intent, responsibility, consent, and consequence, would provide rough guidelines for practice. In other words, while a minimalist ethic would continue to provide moral regulation, sexuality would be placed more squarely in the realm of aesthetic taste, as a personal inclination which does not carry much of any moral and social weight (see Seidman, 1992, 1997; Weeks, 1995).

Notes

1. Even where the narrative of the closet continues to be used, the texture of the experience it describes is often quite different for a post-Stonewall generation. For example, a younger American generation (say born between 1970 and 1980) coming of age today will often take for granted the institutionalization of a Stonewall culture. Many in this generation will not anguish like the Stonewall generation (say born between 1940 and 1950) over the normality of homosexuality, will not necessarily feel the same isolation, and will not delay the "coming out" process until adulthood, sometimes late adulthood. Many youth in this generation will be subculturally identified. Their struggles will often revolve around the tension between their subjective experience of the normalization of their homosexuality and their dependence on families and a school system that are still homophobic and heterosexist.

2. My sense is that many nonhomosexually identified Americans either live with the dissonance of being homophobic while maintaining good feelings to lesbian and gay friends or acquaintances or they de-homosexualize the person, thereby preserving their antigay feelings. To be sure, there are many (heterosexual) Americans for whom

homosexuality has been "normalized." Yet, the number of Americans who accept homosexuals and also accept homosexuality as the psychological, social, and moral equal of heterosexuality is, in my estimation, still probably a fairly small minority.

References

Alexander, Jeffrey. 1993. "The Discourse of Civil Society: A New Proposal for Cultural Studies." *Theory and Society* 22:151–207.

Bellah, Robert. 1975. *The Broken Covenant*. New York. Seabury Press.

Butler, Judith. 1990. *Gender Trouble*. New York: Routledge.

1991. "Imitation and Gender Insubordination," in Diana Fuss, ed. *Inside/Out*. New York: Routledge.

Butler, Judith and Joan Scott, eds. 1992. *Feminists Theorize the Political*. New York: Routledge.

Cohen, Ed. 1991. "Why are 'We'? Gay 'Identity' as Political (E)motion (A Theoretical Rumination)," in Diana Fuss, ed. *Inside/Out*. New York: Routledge.

D'Emilio, John. 1983. *Sexual Politics, Sexual Communities*. Chicago, IL: University of Chicago Press.

De Lauretis, Teresa. 1991. "Queer Theory: Lesbian and Gay Sexualities." *Differences* 3:iii–xviii.

Doty, Alexander. 1993. *Making Things Perfectly Queer*. Minneapolis, MN: University of Minnesota.

Douglas, Mary. 1966. *Purity and Danger*. London: Penguin.

Duberman, Martin Bauml. 1993. *Stonewall*. New York: Plume.

Duberman, Martin Bauml, Martha Vicinus, and George Chauncay, In eds. 1989. *Hidden From History*. New York: Meridan.

Durkheim, Emile. 1965. *The Elementary Forms of the Religious Life*. New York: Free Press.

Gross, Larry. 1993. *Contested Closets*. Minneapolis, MN: University of Minnesota Press.

Hoffman, Martin. 1968. *The Gay World*. New York: Basic Books.

Humphreys, Laud. 1972. *Out of the Closets*. Englewood Cliffs, NJ: Prentice-Hall.

1979. "Exodus and Identity: The Emerging Gay Culture," in Martin Levine, ed. *Gay Men*. New York: Harper and Row.

Jay, Karla and Allen Young, eds. [1972] 1992. *Out of the Closets*. New York: New York University Press.

Monette, Paul. 1992. *Becoming a Man*. New York: HarperCollins.

Morton, Donald, ed. 1996. *The Material Queer*. Boulder, CO: Westview.

Namaste, Ki. 1996. "The Politics of Inside/Out: Queer Theory, Post-structuralism, and a Sociological Approach to Sexuality," in Steven Seidman, ed. *Queer Theory/ Sociology*. Oxford: Blackwell.

Press, Andrea. 1994. "The Sociology of Cultural Reception: Notes toward an Emerging Paradigm," in Diana Crane, ed. *The Sociology of Culture*. Oxford: Blackwell.

Russo, Vito. 1981. *The Celluloid Closet*. New York: Harper & Row.

Sahlins, Marshall. 1976. *Culture and Practical Reason*. Chicago, IL: University of Chicago Press.

Sedgwick, Eve. 1990. *Epistemology of the Closet*. Berkeley, CA: University of California Press.

Seidman, Steven. 1992. *Embattled Eros*. New York: Routledge.

1996, ed. *Queer Theory/Sociology*. Oxford: Blackwell.

1997. *Difference Troubles*. Cambridge: Cambridge University Press.

2000. "The Rise and Fall of the Closet: From the Hetero/Homo to the Good/Bad Sexual Citizen." Unpublished Ms.

2002. *Beyond the Closets: The Transformation of Gay and Lesbian Life*. New York: Routledge.

Signorile, Michelangelo. 1993. *Queer in America*. New York: Random House.

1995. *Outing Yourself*. New York: Simon & Schuster.

Stein, Arlene and Ken Plummer. 1996. "I Can't Even Think Straight: Queer Theory and the Missing Sexual Revolution in Sociology," in Steven Seidman, ed. *Queer Theory/Sociology*. Oxford: Blackwell.

Warner, Michael, ed. 1994. *Fear of a Queer Planet*. Minneapolis, MN: University of Minnesota Press.

Warren, Carol. 1974. *Identity and Community in the Gay World*. New York: Wiley.

Weeks, Jeffrey. 1995. *Invented Moralities*. New York: Columbia University Press.

Woods, James with Jay Lucas. 1993. *The Corporate Closet*. New York: Free Press.

10

Why (not) Foucault? Reflections on power, fascism, and aesthetics

Simonetta Falasca Zamponi

In a 1977 interview with Michel Foucault, Alessandro Fontana and Pasquale Pasquino invited the French philosopher to clarify his analysis of the mechanics of power and his critique of the concept of repression. Foucault replied to his interlocutors' solicitation with an illuminating passage that both exposed the limits of the traditional understanding of power as repressive and encouraged an innovative approach to the study of modern power's modalities, the multiplicity of its operations:

[T]he notion of repression is quite inadequate for capturing what is precisely the productive aspect of power. In defining the effects of power as repression, one adopts a purely juridical conception of such power, one identifies power with a law which says no, power is taken above all as carrying the force of a prohibition. Now I believe that this is a wholly negative, narrow, skeletal conception of power, one which has been curiously widespread. If power were never anything but repressive, if it never did anything but to say no, do you really think one would be brought to obey it? What makes power hold good, what makes it accepted, is simply the fact that it doesn't only weigh on us as a force that says no, but that it traverses and produces things, it induces pleasure, forms knowledge, produces discourse. It needs to be considered as a productive network which runs through the whole social body.[1]

By emphasizing the articulation between power and knowledge, Foucault condemned the term repression as analytically and empirically inadequate to the study of modern power. He argued that the identification of power with a forbidding law – with prohibitions – hides power's fundamentally creative potential. The modern age in particular, according to Foucault, witnessed the emergence in the seventeenth and eighteenth centuries of a new economy of power that supposedly amplified power's productivity, its effects.[2] Foucault's historical analyses of disciplinary institutions, such as prisons, focused on this process. His studies showed that modern power operates broadly in everyday social practices through micro-techniques that are less costly and more efficient as compared to the spectacular, ostentatious, and discontinuous procedures of the *ancien régime*. Foucault directed attention to the continuous, local, and capillary character of modern power, its inscription in people's lives. Against political theory's "obsession" with sovereignty, he claimed that power is not vertical, is not merely located in a decision- or policy-making apparatus, nor is it confined at the level of the state. In contrast, modern power needs to be examined as a cluster of relations, an intricate and complex system of desubjectivized strategies working within the social body,[3] an ensemble of rebounding effects that both constitute subjects and redefine power.

When I first began to research the relationship between politics and aesthetics in Italian fascism, which culminated in *Fascist Spectacle: The Aesthetics of Power in Mussolini's Italy*, the greatest challenge I encountered was the established and obviously sensible identification of fascism with authoritarianism and repression. Classical interpretations of fascism commonly defined it as a negative and coercive exercise of power denying any autonomous rights to individuals.[4] The questions raised by this perspective tended to concern fascism's means and effectiveness in organizing and controlling civil society. On the one hand, totalitarian theory emphasized totalitarian power's recourse to the scientific application of propaganda, the use of mass terror, the monopoly of technological instruments of control.[5] Although exponents of this theory focused on totalitarian states' need to mobilize depoliticized masses toward goals established by the system (the element of mobilization being what differentiated totalitarian regimes from classical tyrannies), they still defined the political as a mainly negative project of terrorizing and atomizing citizens. For the Marxists, on the other hand, fascism exemplified the dictatorship of monopoly capitalism, capitalism's most coercive and open form of rule. Fascist leaders were portrayed as agents of big industrialists and agrarian proprietors, and the general analysis focused on the question of class struggle, as the political factor was submerged by the economic one.[6] The Marxists downplayed the political, or rather insisted upon its coercive elements. Their model, as well as the totalitarian one, laid stress on the negating, repressive force of fascist power and offered a mechanical theory of the way (no doubt, still pernicious) in which fascism operated as a regime.

In contrast, I was interested in the process through which fascism came to form its identity as "fascism" and made its power, the process through which it constructed its destructive goals and defined its ends. To be sure, any social formation could be analyzed in its making. I was, however, convinced that the loosely structured nature of fascism, its anti-party ideology, its self-proclaimed rejection of programs, and its "movementist" character more rightly required an approach that would focus on fascism's historical development and shaping, rather than consider fascism a ready-made construct. One needs to remember that, spanning over two decades, Mussolini's regime was a new political formation established only three years after the foundation in 1919 of the fascist movement (*Fasci Italiani di Combattimento*), and one year after the newly organized party (*Partito Nazionale Fascista*) vowed to maintain the features of ideological and political flexibility characterizing the movement. Within this perspective, and drawing on a theory of narrative that establishes a close link between the production of power and its representation,[7] I examined fascism's symbolic discourse (that is, cults, rituals, speeches, etc.) as a text that told the story of fascism at the same time that it made its history. If representation is the very essence of power, as some argue, if we assume that power cannot exist without being represented, then, I believe, narratives also produce power while representing it. Fascism's cults, rituals, and speeches can be seen as constitutive, essential elements in the process of the regime's self-definition and in the construction and unfolding of its developmental trajectory. The centrality of aesthetic politics in fascism, so brilliantly theorized by Walter Benjamin,[8] also convinced me that the analysis of fascist rituals, cults, and myths was necessary better to penetrate fascism's logic and further our knowledge of a social and political phenomenon whose pernicious nature still remains enigmatic.

The historian George Mosse had already explored fascist politics' symbolic dimensions in the case of Nazi Germany. His work on the cultural sources of National Socialism focused on the role that secular religion, the German tradition of volkish mass movements, and aesthetic ideas born in the eighteenth and nineteenth centuries assumed in informing the nascent Nazi politics.[9] Other scholars paralleled or followed Mosse's lead in their analyses of the Italian and German dictatorships. In the Italian case, the opening of the archives of fascism in the 1960s allowed researchers to complement their theoretical discussion of fascism's origins with the study of how the fascist regime functioned. Historians and social scientists were turning their attention to the analysis of the relationship between culture and politics.

Yet, I found that culture in fascism most often tended to be identified with ideology, as questions were raised about how fascism succeeded in holding onto power and how it organized consent.[10] Even though force and coercion had been replaced as terms of analysis, manipulation still seemed to dominate the terms of interpretation of fascism. Within this context, rituals, festivals, and symbols were interpreted in connection with the issue of legitimation.[11] I believed, however, that fascism's relationship with the symbolic dimensions of politics was not merely strategic. And here is where Foucault's conceptualization of power became important in my study.

So, why Foucault? In what follows I will answer the question I originally posed in my title by retracing the theoretical path that led me, an interpretive sociologist educated in the Weberian tradition, to embrace the French philosopher. By taking Foucault as the catalyst of my discussion I will present some of the main points characterizing *Fascist Spectacle*, and will make an argument about the central and controversial role of aesthetics in modern political processes. Later, I will also explain why in the end, and paradoxically, *Fascist Spectacle* did not turn out to be a study *à la* Foucault.

The spectacle of power

In several of his writings and interviews Foucault argued that power's practices, not its intentions, reveal the nature of relations of domination. His dismissal of ideology, concurrently with his critique of repression, emphasized the overlap between means and expressions of power, while also insisting on modern power's productive character and creative potential. Foucault focused on the way power generates new habits, touches individual bodies, pervades people's actions. Thus, he both overcame the tendency to analyze power's operations in terms of their functional role in the legitimation process, and undermined the question of consent which typically sprouts from the conception of power as operating with manipulative devices and propaganda.

Although Foucault relied on the concepts of "tactics," "strategy," and "effectiveness" in his account of power, thus revealing a tendency toward teleology, he offered a stimulating alternative to the classical Weberian definition of power as the ability to impose one's will on others in order to attain specific goals. To be sure, Weber's formulation raises crucial sociological questions about the legitimacy of power's operation, the role of force and violence involved in the exercise of power, and the problem of consent, but it leaves little space for an analysis of power's internal logic and development, its construction of goals and definition of ends, its establishment of new social relationships. Steven Lukes sought to modify the Weberian conception of power by introducing the concept of "objective interest."[12] Lukes rightly argues that we cannot identify the exercise of power only when there is an openly conflictual relationship between subject A and subject B, as the pluralists' view of power seems to imply. If force is what characterizes the exercise of power, if "power turns out to be the affirmation of one's will against opposition," then all we look for when identifying a relation of power is conflict, Lukes says. When A acts with force over B, this means that B is forced to do what s/he would not otherwise do. Yet, sometimes A exerts power over B by simply "preventing B's demands from being made." In this sense, Lukes claims, power refers to all situations where

"A affects B in a manner contrary to B's interests,"[13] even though a conflict is not immediately present.

Lukes highlights the manipulative role of power in situations where conflicts of interest are latent. Since he understands power in a vertical manner and interprets it in a teleological sense, within his frame, however, power still negates and prevents. Both Weber and Lukes single out crucial questions one needs to take into account when studying power, including issues of manipulation, violence, and coercion; but, for the purposes of my study, Foucault's culturally founded notion of power as productive, with its lesser emphasis on power's negative dimensions, seemed to offer a working concept more suitable to the goal of tracing fascist power's creative process.

This said, Foucault's notion was not devoid of problems. Two critical points, in particular, immediately surfaced that distanced my study from Foucault's theoretical model. First, Foucault's critique of classical interpretations of power was founded on the dismissal of a state-centered understanding of power, an understanding which he identified with theorizing power as the source of decision-making instances, the *locus* of policy elaboration. According to Foucault, excessive insistence on the state as playing an exclusive role in the system of domination "leads to the risk of overlooking all the mechanisms and effects of power which don't pass directly via the State apparatus, yet often sustain the State more effectively than its own institutions, enlarging and maximising its effectiveness."[14] Since he believed in the importance of examining power in its multiple relational forms and diverse, local sites, Foucault also needed to dismantle the category of sovereignty with the related identification, inherited from the theory of social contract, between the legitimate rights of sovereignty and the legal obligation to obey it. Foucault therefore rejected the idea of analyzing power as the domination of one individual over others; rather power was circulating and not localized in anybody's hands. Ultimately, for Foucault, "*le*" *pouvoir* did not exist, and any field of inquiry that might have reinstated the idea of the centrality of power, sovereignty and the state was to be avoided. Following this theoretical standpoint, Foucault overlooked political power strictly speaking – all power was political for him. According to his schema, any domain of the social is involved and participates in the general strategy of power. Foucault's own analysis of disciplinary institutions, and of techniques to govern the population, pointedly proved the novel embodiments taken by modern power and showed the multiple, capillary ways in which modern power anonymously operates.

In my study, on the contrary, I was more interested in that dimension of the political that Foucault downplays, or rather submerges, within his theory of the micro-relations of power. By looking at fascism, I focused on a form of government that was characterized by a strong, central political presence, the dictator, and his authoritarian, bureaucratic state. I wanted to analyze the most visibly manifest form of political power, the one directly connected to the ruler. Thus, while Foucault's analytic of power focused on the peripheral, dispersed sites of power, I analyzed the top; and I contended that modern power's productivity can also stem from the legal and symbolic center constituted by the state. Even in its centralized form, power can creatively construct new social relations and new definitions of the world without resorting to purely coercive means.

To be sure, Foucault did not deny instances in which relations of power are engendered from the top. But, according to him, even those cases need to be analyzed in connection with the parallel, synchronic process of a capillary movement from below. Foucault's ultimate goal was, after all, to explain and show why power works. In contrast, I was not concerned with the effectiveness of power. Rather, my study aimed at determining how the regime formed its identity while constructing its means of power. Furthermore, I believed that the analysis of power's intentions was not opposed to the examination of power's practices. Mussolini's aesthetic conception of politics guided his notion of the politician's role and informed his actions at several, and not only plainly governmental, levels.

The other issue that distanced my study from Foucault's theoretical model concerned the role of the "visibility" of power and the question of representation. As is well known, Foucault attributed crucial importance to the "gaze" as one of the disciplinary techniques at work since the end of the eighteenth century within the new economy of power.[15] He argued that, while monarchical power before the eighteenth century operated discontinuously, via exemplary actions that involved great expenditure and proportionally less efficacy, inventors of disciplinary institutions made power more efficient. Bentham's utopian idea of the panopticon, very popular during the 1700s, permitted the surveillance of pupils, inmates, soldiers from a central site with little expense and high effectiveness. This new technology of power seemed to serve well the nascent modern preoccupation with the management of a growing population. The idea of the panopticon also revealed as outdated the technique of spectacular punishment that characterized monarchical power in the years of the *ancien régime*. Spectacular executions, Foucault argued, did not match the relentless control of modern power, and represented an uneconomic expenditure. Foucault thus declared the era of spectacle over. This conclusion derived from his conceptualization of modern power as capillary, anonymous, continuous, dispersed, and omnipresent, and also followed from his opposition to the theory of sovereignty, with its tendency to subjectivize power.

In contrast, I believe that although the irrational expenditure of regal ceremonies and the pageant spectacle *à la* Louis XIV might well be finished, forms of representation founded on the display of authority, whether the king's or the people's, are still present today.[16] Their role and scope, as well as the modalities of their use, might be different from the era of spectacular executions; but they still constitute an important element in "political" rule as a vehicle for establishing a relationship between government and governed. They also contribute to power's self-transformation. Foucault indirectly acknowledged that free-floating strategies in power struggles can produce new effects.[17] But his reliance on terms such as strategy and tactics, although appropriate to Foucault's conception of history as war,[18] appears nevertheless limited when asked to account for power's creativity. In general, I believe that Foucault failed to recognize the new role of representations in the genealogy of modern power, the importance of means of visibility that are also spectacular and not merely surreptitiously inspective.

There are two perspectives from which we can draw on the historical issue of visibility. One considers the crucial role that the medium of vision played in the creation of a new politics that tried to respond to the entrance of the "masses" onto the political scene. In his work on political symbolism, George Mosse has shown that a new political style, mainly founded on rituals, imagery, and festivals, originated in the eighteenth century from the idea of popular sovereignty then transformed by Rousseau into the concept of general will. This latter concept fueled the creation of myths and their symbols. "The general will became a secular religion, the people worshipping themselves," Mosse writes.[19] The worship of the people then combined with emergent nationalist sentiments. The nation, seen as founded on the people, developed into a cult, and the new politics sought to express the unity between nation and its subjects through a new political style. This style, according to Mosse, actually became a secularized religion in which the people were directly and publicly involved. It was adopted by many European nations in the course of the nineteenth century, and later in the twentieth, when it became the dominion of fascism and Naziism.

The presence of the spectacle as portrayed in Mosse's study does not imply a return to seventeenth-century politics. The newly visible, public style of power was related rather to the formation of an enlarged public for politics. During the French revolution the principle of visibility was connected to the building of a good citizen through one's self-consciousness of everybody else's opinion.[20] Visibility made things public, but it also made a public. Thus, paraphrasing Foucault, one could state that the rising problem of population growth, and its management, due to the formation of workers' associations, opinion movements, and so on, required the development of new disciplinary techniques, but also gave rise to new political models that responded to the populace's demands for participation in political decisions.

The other perspective on the issue of visibility focuses on the development of new media of communication, and refers to contemporary societies as "accumulations of spectacles," the reign of representations.[21] According to Guy Debord, who popularized this concept, the spectacle cannot be reduced to being the effect of new techniques of the creation of images. Rather, it constitutes the way through which people understand themselves. Spectacle is an administered image or narrative which absorbs a passive and privatized audience whose members are detached from their own creative, productive powers; people do not realize that the world around them is a product of their own labor. In this guise, the spectacle plays a totalizing role and becomes "the present model of socially dominant life," with its propaganda, advertisement, and entertainment consumption. For Debord, this society has a very negative connotation: it represents the ubiquity of power and its mystifying functions.

Debord does not exactly state when the new society of the spectacle established itself, but other scholars have emphasized the emergence of a quest for high visibility in public space characterizing western culture at the end of the nineteenth century.[22] Theories might differ over what defines "spectacle." But whether it was the emergence of a new phase of commodity production, the expansion of commercialization and mass consumption, or the perfecting of new means of technological reproduction, the role of the spectacle has certainly grown during the last century, implicating the political realm. Politics has become the site of a more or less open struggle for the monopolization of public spaces. And the development of mass media has complicated the issue of politics' relation to spectacle and convergently to the public. In summary, whether we understand spectacle as a totalizing social relation or simply as one form of representation, the two perspectives above suggest that spectacular power still characterizes modern political processes.

In the case of fascism, I argue, spectacle was indeed at the heart of the regime's rule – a self-proclaimed sign of distinction from the supposedly dry, legalistic style of past liberal governments. Ever since its foundation in 1919, the fascist movement heavily relied on a plethora of public symbols, myths, and rituals that over the years became staples of the established regime. Festivals and ceremonies were continuously staged punctuating the fascist calendar at anniversaries and special events. The movement's embryonic history was institutionalized and made official via commemorations that at first affirmed fascism's existence, and later sanctioned fascism's legitimate role in Italian political life. In terms of symbols, Mussolini constituted from the beginning the mythical fulcrum of fascism, its sacred center. In an uninterrupted hagiographic operation, he continued to be deified during the regime and elevated to the status of superhuman. Mussolini's image, words, and deeds circulated widely, saturating the public sphere. He represented and interpreted fascism's strength. In addition, the regime's interventions in public works, agricultural campaigns, artistic initiatives, and war enterprises were spectacular, as were the rituals that fascism imposed on daily life.

In a famous essay published in 1936, Walter Benjamin defined fascism's reliance on cultic values and ritualistic processes as the aestheticization of politics, the ultimately destructive path of totalitarian power.[23] Benjamin argued that the prevalence of aesthetic form over ethical norms characterized fascism's version of aesthetic politics and linked it closely to the *l'art pour l'art* movement. Like *l'art pour l'art* movement, fascism was an expression of the contradictory nature of modernity, an attempt to bring back aura to the disenchanted modern world.

In line with Benjamin, in my book I make the argument that fascism's version of aesthetic politics was based on a notion of absolute self-referentiality that led the regime to privilege aesthetic and totalitarian aspirations over any other value. I also characterize fascism's aesthetic politics as an intrinsic, if extreme, product of turn-of-the-century political events and culture, the result of, or the response to, modernity's contradictory achievements. In this sense, contrary to Foucault, I believe that the recourse to aesthetic, "spectacular" means also constitutes an important feature of modern power's modalities. Foucault's desire to counteract intentionalist analyses mistakenly led him to disregard the role of representations in modern power and to emphasize power's effectiveness and usefulness, its intrinsic "rationality." In contrast, I believe that power is not always useful or effective, although I do not mean to imply that aesthetics is merely a source of irrational drives. (Nor can the application of aesthetics to the political realm be identified only with the suspension of normative considerations or the prevalence of illusory and violent goals in the exercise of power, as is the case with fascism. There is, indeed, a long-standing democratic tradition, going back to the Greek polis, that has relied on aesthetics as an element to establish the ideal political state.[24])

In the next section, and for the purposes of a comparison with Foucault, I will focus on the issue of modern power's effectiveness and "rationality" and will present some examples of the way in which the fascist regime applied aesthetics to politics. More specifically, I will examine briefly a few cases of fascism's intervention in everyday life.[25] This choice will allow me better to characterize my difference from Foucault by challenging him on his own terrain. Thus, following Foucault, I will show how fascism strove to enforce, through regulatory processes, a calculated, rational control over daily routines, gestures, and practices affecting the body of individual subjects. Yet, *pace* Foucault, I will also make the argument that discipline in fascism took an aesthetic turn. And it directly spilled into the organization of everyday activities through a ritualizing process that, while directed at people's style, both represented and transformed fascist power. The regime's rules of compliance, I claim, were aesthetically inspired and propelled; capillary, yet also "spectacular." They did not ultimately prove useful or effective in mobilizing and molding a controlled population. The rules rather affected and defined fascist power's self-understanding and goals, at the same time that they displayed the identity and aims of fascist power.

Fascism and the aesthetics of style

Beginning in the early 1930s an endless number of rulings issued by the Fascist Party Secretariat targeted the formal aspect of the Italians' way of living. People's daily conduct in its most minute aspects was scrutinized, attacked, and regulated. In particular, everything connected to appearance fell under the range of intervention of a campaign later defined as the "reform of customs." Ways of dressing, speaking, walking, saluting became the target of the regime's daily injunctions following a speech of Mussolini delivered on March 4, 1931, in which he stated: "I am deeply convinced that our way of eating, dressing, working and sleeping, the entire complex of our daily habits must be reformed."[26]

One of the first targets of fascism's scrutiny concerned the use of clothing, and especially of the black shirt. A symbol of fascism's origins, the black shirt constituted the basic piece of party-members' uniforms and a constant of fascist attire, spanning more than twenty years of variations in fashion. All participants in the numerous fascist organizations, from women's and children's groups to school associations and sport clubs, also wore the black shirt. In November 1934, even infants and children up to eight years old were organized under the umbrella name of "Sons and Daughters of the She-Wolf," and outfitted in miniature black shirts.

Mussolini assigned a highly sacred value to the shirt. As he proclaimed in 1925: "The black shirt is not the everyday shirt, and is not a uniform either. It is a combat outfit and can only be worn by those who harbor a pure soul in their heart."[27] In the 1920s, however, use of the black shirt was not strictly regulated. Only in 1932 the statute of the Fascist Party for the first time included an article stating: "The black shirt constitutes the fascist uniform and must be worn only when it is prescribed."[28] Following this precept, party secretary Achille Starace began to give instructions on the occasions when it was appropriate to dress in a black shirt. He also specified the proper combination of accessories. When required, the black shirt needed to be complemented with care in all details. Injunction 93 of March 22, 1933, discussed the young fascists' summer outfit; youth were allowed to wear the black shirt without the tie and with the open collar, but they were absolutely forbidden to roll up the sleeves.[29] On

August 7, 1933, Starace reiterated that a fluttering tie was not allowed. On May 23, 1934, he "absolutely forbade" wearing the black shirt with a starched collar. A September 13, 1937, *disposizione* ordered party members not to wear decorations on their uniforms at the Exhibit of the Revolution.[30]

Accessories, ornaments, and medals demonstrated a person's position in the regime's organization. Uniforms came to epitomize change and differentiated fascist spirit from "bourgeois" values. Within this context, failure to wear the fascist outfit supposedly revealed one's bourgeois attitude. In his *disposizione* of April 25, 1936, Starace lamented what he called "a common reluctance" to wear the fascist uniform at prescribed events. He defined those attitudes as "emanating from a bourgeois spirit that is absolutely in contrast with the fascist mentality."[31]

The "bourgeoisie," intended as a moral category, was the main concept in opposition to which fascism built itself as a movement. Bourgeois clothes thus constituted only one of Starace's targets. He issued several other *disposizioni* indicating how fascists needed to demonstrate their spiritual and material contrast with the bourgeois individual. The new Italian was supposed to change his style, to follow new values, to transform his way of living. The persistence of bourgeois practices denoted an unfulfilled *fascistizzazione*. Thus, in 1932 the regime took another initiative toward the reform of Italians: the Roman salute as the substitute for the bourgeois handshake. A few years earlier, the salute had already officially become part of the regime. Mussolini had ordered all state civil administrations at the center and the periphery, including schools, to adopt it as of December 1, 1925. The salute, which consisted in raising the right arm in a straight and perpendicular manner, was supposed to reflect a sense of discipline, as it addressed a superior as a sign of respect from an inferior in the ranks. But there were also rules concerning the salute between *gerarchi* (high-ranking fascists) of equal importance. In 1932, the salute began to be specifically opposed to handshake; in his *disposizioni*, Starace wished that "the year XI signs the twilight of shaking hands."[32] The salute was considered "more hygienic, more aesthetic and shorter,"[33] in the words of Mussolini, and the regime defined itself as anti-bourgeois through the Roman salute. On August 28, 1932, Starace hinted that "[t]o salute the Roman way by remaining sitting is . . . little Roman" – that is, little fascist.[34] And on September 9, 1933, he reprimanded *gerarchi* who in a dispute had used the bourgeois formula: "[T]hey reconciled with a handshake." They should have adopted instead the sentence: "[T]hey reconciled with a Roman salute."[35]

Unlike ugly, slow bourgeois culture, fascism was efficient, harmonic, and dynamic. The aesthetics of order and discipline combined with the regime's emphasis on character; and the Roman salute came to represent the physical sign of a truly new man, whose gestures reflected his intimate fascist nature. Theories began to circulate about the Roman salute being an expression of the fascists' decisive spirit, firmness, and seriousness, an unfailing proof of fascist character. The regime was so persuaded by these theories that the improper execution of the salute raised fears about a person's character.[36] Within this context, shaking hands was naturally considered a disgrace, a true betrayal of fascist principles. Starace ordered that a note be put in the personal file of people who continued to shake hands. The note would say, "Devoted to hand shaking," as a sign of a lesser fascist spirit.[37] In 1938, a party *disposizione* stated that hand shaking was abolished in films and theatrical representations.[38] On November 21, 1938, the Ministry of Popular Culture issued orders not to "publish photographs showing hand shaking, even if those gestures were performed by very high dignitaries."[39] The bourgeois gesture was supposed to disappear from the view of Italians. In contrast, the regime was eager to emphasize the adoption of the Roman salute for important occasions. On March 23, 1939, the daily orders to the press invited journalists to write that during her visit to the Chamber, the queen had saluted with a straight arm and not by reclining her head.[40]

The regime's identification of symbols with character also led to fascism's intervention into language. On December 11, 1934, Starace asked the federal secretaries to be concise in their reports.[41] On June 21, 1937, Starace condemned prolixity: "The prolix man in writing and speaking is to be compared to the plump man who is uncertain and slow in action and thought, since fat exercises an influence over the muscular and cerebral systems. Prolixity is a characteristic of sedentary, rhetorical, exhibitionist people and inexorably leads to waste, and makes others waste, time. Anything but 'new men'!" The following year Starace made clearer the identification of speaking style with physical characteristics: "Those who show bureaucratic tendencies end up becoming also physically heavy" – he stated in his injunction of October 10. [42] According to Starace's interpretation, slimness denoted fascist spirit and was more aesthetic.

Starace generally emphasized dynamism in his *disposizioni*. Thus, in the injunctions on office correspondence of April 13, 1938, he ordered: no "dear such and such" – an address sufficed; nor should there be "cordial greetings" or worse "fascist greetings" and other bad bourgeois and servile formulas. And he concluded: "Shortness! We still write too much, despite the numerous encouragements to write little. A *gerarca* stuck to his table, constantly dealing with paper, takes away very useful time from the activity he should be engaging in outside the office, and runs the risk of losing that dynamism which must characterize him."[43]

Starace's preoccupation with language focused in particular on the use of *lei*, the third-person singular, as a formal mode of addressing people. Bruno Cicognani, a Tuscan writer, ignited this polemic with a January 15, 1938 article published in the daily *Corriere della Sera*. Cicognani condemned the *lei* as a "grammatical aberration" imported from Spain, a sign of serfdom and abjection unfit to the new fascist Italy. Thus he wrote:

The fascist revolution intends to bring back the spirit of our race to its authentic origins, freeing it from any pollution. Then, let us go back to the use of Rome, to the Christian and Roman *tu* which expresses the universal value of Rome and Christianity. Let the *voi* be a sign of respect and of hierarchical recognition. But in any other case let the *tu* be the form of communicating, writing or speaking: the grammatically, logically and spiritually true, immediate, genuine and Italian form.

Cicognani's reference to Rome and spirituality, and the critique of the *lei* as a foreign expression, corresponded well with the regime's aspirations to establish a new national and fascist style. Thus, the regime endorsed Cicognani's plea for the substitution of the *lei* with the *tu* and the *voi* in the spirit of the Roman tradition. The formal *lei* came to be considered one of the worst signs of bourgeois behavior, unfit for the new reality fascism had created. Starace suggested ignoring any correspondence not written in fascist style, that is with the adoption of the *tu*.[44] Then, in 1939 he planned an Anti-*lei* exhibit and deplored those who still insisted on using the *lei*. According to him, they revealed "the absence of that fascist temperament which must be able to carry out in every circumstance the style of Mussolini's time"; and he continued: "The federal secretaries must call upon the *gerarchi* and talk clearly to them without omitting to indicate that when the injunctions I have ordered regarding this matter are not followed, it may mean either little sense of discipline or even little fascist faith. This is one of those cases in which form, by definitively affecting customs, expresses its deep content with exactitude."[45]

Following Mussolini, Starace identified form and style with character and spirit. People's observance of rituals and symbols, their adoption of new habits, testified to their acquired fascist identity, their relinquishing of bourgeois habits. Hence, in a final apotheosis, Starace called for the organization of an Anti-Bourgeois Exhibit aimed at denouncing what the regime defined as "the typical aspects of bourgeois mentality."[46] Announced in an injunction of November 29, 1938, the exhibit invited artists to submit caricatures ridiculing bourgeois lifestyle. The listed topics covered: hand shaking, afternoon tea, top hats. Starace wanted to purge the Italians from any attachment to old ways of living. Daily practices and gestures attracted the regime's attention.

The regime assigned an enormous importance to the execution of fascist rituals as signs of a transformation in the Italian spirit. The insistence on petty rules, and the sustained equation between form and substance, appearance and content, style and spirit, often led the regime to privilege the aesthetic dimension of changes over changes themselves. In an acute observation written in his diary on January 30, 1939, Galeazzo Ciano, Mussolini's son-in-law and Minister of Foreign Affairs, exposed this danger:

The Duce is all involved . . . with the preparation of the Milizia for the parade of February 1. He takes care in person of the minutest details. He spends hours at the window of his office hidden behind the blue curtains, spying the movements of the troops . . . He has ordered the bandmaster to use a baton, and he teaches in person the right movements and corrects the proportions and the style of the club. He more and more believes that form, in the army, also determines the substance . . . He often accuses the King of having diminished the physical prestige of the army in order to harmonize it to his "unhappy figure."[47]

Ciano perspicaciously singled out what I believe are the two important dimensions characterizing fascism's totalitarian approach to power.[48] On the one hand, fascism exercised a disciplining eye that aimed at touching people's lives in their most capillary details and at extending control over old habits and traditional behavior. As theorized by Foucault, power circulated in the private sphere, traversed people's lives and invaded their personal space. On the other hand, the regime's quest of total control was guided by an impulse to create, an emphasis on the effectiveness of formal display, and an aesthetic understanding of politics. Fascism's infatuation with aesthetics guided fascism's vision of creating an homogeneous body of citizen–soldiers, while destroying individuals. Fascism's disciplining project, I conclude, was indissolubly linked to the lethal pursuit of beauty.

Conclusion

In this chapter I have argued that analyses of modern power have been greatly enhanced by Foucault's new focus on power's creative potentiality, its capillary nature and embeddedness in people's everyday life and practices. Foucault's critique of power as negative and forbidding, in particular, has benefited my research on fascism, a regime that all too naturally seemed to fit the category of "repressive." Building on Foucault's culturally founded approach to power, in my work on Mussolini's Italy I have stressed the creative relationship that connects the making of fascism's totalitarian power to the regime's self-representations. In so doing, however, I have also at the same time distanced myself from Foucault, whose interest in the effectiveness of modern power hampered him from conceiving the role that representations play in the formation of political regimes. Foucault's impatience with the concept of sovereignty, and his dismissal of a state-centered understanding of power, led him to steer his attention away from political power strictly speaking. Within his theoretical frame, there was no space for the analysis of a dictator, let alone his spectacular symbolic politics.[49]

Foucault continued to uphold his notion of power's strategic rationality until the end of his life. In the 1979 Tanner Lectures delivered at Stanford, for example, he addressed the relationship between rationalization and the excesses of political power. Through an historical analysis of what he called "pastoral power" and the formation of the modern state, Foucault assessed the crucial role of rationality in the modern art of government and singled out the elaboration of technologies directed toward the individual as a typical form of modern power's modalities. In line with his other writings on the capillary, relentless, and efficient nature of power, Foucault affirmed the enormous growth of political rationality in western societies. He concluded his lectures stating: "Liberation can only come from attacking . . . political rationality's very roots."[50] Not instrumental violence, Foucault claimed, but rationalization was responsible for the excesses of modern power. Resistance could only be directed against the logic of power's strategic practices.

Habermas points out that Foucault "borrows his concept of power from the empiricist tradition."[51] In this dry, objectified form, his notion of power lacks "the experiential potential of an at once terrifying and attracting fascination, from which the aesthetic avant-garde from Baudelaire to the Surrealists was nourished."[52] For Foucault, modern power was not a spectacle, and its distinguishing trait was the dominating role of reason. Within this context, Habermas claims, Foucault went against his masters Nietzsche and Bataille, whose concepts of "will to power" and "sovereignty" were founded on aesthetic dimensions.[53]

Foucault's emphasis on the domination of reason has been widely recognized, and it has led critics to question Foucault's failure to distinguish between types of rationality, his lack of normative standards in the portrayal of power, and his preclusion of any alternative proposition to the existing excesses of power.[54] To these criticisms, I want to add that his model also fails to recognize that the modern process of rationalization has been accompanied by nostalgic longings and efforts to rejoin the increasingly separated value-spheres. The retreat of religion from worldly matters, as Weber so insightfully explained in his thesis on the disenchantment of the world, spurred the secularization of economy, politics, and art; but this process, I argue, has also been punctuated by a pursuit of the sacred and passion through other means. Fascism, as well as Naziism, constituted only the most extreme examples of the meshing of sacred and profane – a reliance on modern rationality's achievements while assaulting instrumental reason. Mussolini believed that feelings and emotions needed to be reinstated in political life in order to neutralize the dry effects of democracy's formal procedures and parliamentary institutions. According to him, politics' mystical side was important, indeed necessary, to refurbish the spirit of the nation and rejuvenate a country dominated by bourgeois, philistine interests. He relied on aesthetics to develop his peculiar version of totalitarian power.

Foucault chose to ignore aesthetics in his analysis of modern power.[55] In this way, he both missed the opportunity to expose modern power's inner conflicts, and also failed to disentangle aesthetics' meanings and contradictions. This latter point is particularly critical since, as I am going to argue in the remainder of these conclusions, Foucault developed his own attraction to aesthetics at the end of the 1970s and early 1980s. This attraction, because it went unquestioned, affected Foucault's severe stance on power and further undermined the theoretical strength of Foucault's approach to power.

Foucault's attraction for aesthetics emerges *mutatis mutandis* in his later writings on the "arts of existence" or the "aesthetics of existence." Foucault defined the "arts of existence" as "those intentional and voluntary actions by which men not only set themselves rules of conduct, but also seek to transform themselves, to change themselves in their singular being, and to make their life into an *oeuvre* that carries certain aesthetic values and meets certain stylistic criteria."[56] Foucault explained his theoretical journey into aesthetics as the necessary step to assess the historical experience of sexuality. The latter, Foucault argued, could be understood as the interrelations of three axes that included: the formation of sciences studying sexuality; the systems of power that regulate sexuality's practices; and the forms within which individuals are able to, are obliged to, recognize themselves as subjects of sexuality.[57] While Foucault had earlier explored questions related to fields of knowledge and types of normativity, he believed that the self-formation of the desiring subject remained to be accounted for. Thus, he engaged in an analysis of Greek and Roman antiquity and found that "the will to be a moral subject and the search for an ethics of existence were . . . mainly an attempt to affirm one's liberty and to give to one's own life a certain form in which one could recognize oneself, be recognized by others."[58] Morality was founded on self-mastery; one "had to be able to look at a beautiful girl or a beautiful boy without having any desire for her or him."[59] In this process of reaching sexual austerity, more beauty was added to life. The constitution of the desiring subject, of his or her moral existence, took place via aesthetics, as one's life became a "personal work of art."[60] While assessing the decline of aesthetics with Christianity's reliance on a code of rules, Foucault revealed his admiration for the Graeco-Roman world. There, ethical norms derived from aesthetic choices, and the search for one's self was supposed to give life a certain form.

The importance of aesthetics as the source of life's meaning became paramount for Foucault, a precept for our own society. As he declared in one of his interviews: "[I]f I was interested in Antiquity it was because, for a whole series of reasons, the idea of a morality as obedience to a code of rules is now disappearing, has already disappeared. And to this absence of morality corresponds, must correspond, the search for an aesthetics of existence."[61] Foucault did not advocate a nostalgic return to Greek antiquity, but he yearned for a form of ethics that, as in Greece, resulted from an aesthetics of existence, a personal choice.[62] In an interview with Rabinow and Dreyfus he admitted: "The idea of the bios as a material for an aesthetic piece of art is something which fascinates me . . . What strikes me is the fact that in our society, art has become something which is related only to objects and not to individuals, or to life. That art is something which is specialized or which is done by experts who are artists. But couldn't everyone's life become a work of art? Why should the lamp or the house be an art object, but not our life?"[63] Foucault's advocacy of aesthetics was absolute; his identification of ethics with aesthetics irrefutable.

Foucault's aesthetic inclination and insistence on personal choice has led some critics to define his notion of ethics as "aesthetic decisionism"[64] – a position that would ally him with Nietzsche and bring him close to an undemocratic position, as it inevitably leads to disregard other people's lives. To be sure, Foucault's stress on self-domination as the prerequisite to dominate others is problematic when applied to political power. It turns power into the expression of one's aesthetic fulfillment or determination, as is evident in the case of the King of Cyprus whom Foucault cites in *The Use of Pleasure*. For Foucault, Nicocles' austere self-control, his superiority over the majority, does not reside in the moral value of Nicocles' behavior; it "does not owe its political value simply to the fact that it is an honorable behavior in everyone's eyes." Rather, it is the "relationship with the self that modulates and regulates the use the prince makes of the power he exercises over others. It is therefore important in itself, for the visible excellence it displays."[65] In line with his posture of normative neutrality Foucault's interest in power focused on style. His fascination with aesthetics inevitably left him vulnerable to political indifference.[66]

Aesthetics is not, however, a value-free category, a neutral or exclusively positive sphere. As the case of fascism demonstrates, the privileging of an aesthetic approach to life and politics can bear deleterious consequences when based on the suspension of ethical and moral values, and it might entail the establishment of a system of rule that, in the name of beauty and style, obliterates common rights. Foucault's unconditional embrace of aesthetics blinds him to the potential danger of an exclusively aesthetic world view. Within this context, I maintain, Foucault's aesthetic turn further mars his seemingly neutral approach to power.

To summarize: Foucault's analysis of power as anonymous and capillary, decentered and continuous, ascending and productive, provides critical tools for deciphering the multiple ways in which modern power operates. His emphasis on modern power's dual process of individuation and totalization is also a brilliant accomplishment. Yet, historical shifts notwithstanding, on the one hand, I believe that modern power is less rational than Foucault would like to portray it. On the other hand, though Foucault refused to take a normative stand in his discussion of power, or opposed the idea of characterizing reason as the contrary entity of non-reason, he failed to reconcile theoretical austerity with the longing for an aesthetics of existence. This is why, in the end, I had to give up Foucault.

Notes

1. Michel Foucault, "Truth and Power," in Foucault (1980: 119).
2. One might argue that Foucault's model conceives all power as productive. However, for Foucault, this is a typical operation of modern power.
3. On the question of strategy without subjects in Foucault see Michel Foucault, "Powers and Strategies" and "The Confession of the Flesh" in Foucault (1980). Also see Colin Gordon's afterword; Foucault (1980: 250–252).
4. De Felice (1977); Gregor (1974); Nolte (1965).
5. Arendt (1951); Friedrich and Brzezinski (1956).
6. There are however different degrees in the way in which these theses have been applied by Marxists. For example, Paul Baran and Paul Sweezy argue that fascism is not the inevitable outcome of capitalism. On the contrary, they claim that financial oligarchies in capitalist countries generally prefer democratic governments to authoritarian ones because a democratic system is supposedly better able to serve their interests. See Baran and Sweezy (1966).
7. See Marin (1987, and 1989). Marin goes to the extreme of affirming that because power has no reality beyond its representation, representation is the very essence of power.
8. "The Work of Art in the Age of Mechanical Reproduction" in Benjamin (1973). We can define aesthetic politics as the prevalence in politics of form over ethical norms.
9. Mosse (1970).
10. The literature in this tradition is vast, especially in Italian. A very valuable contribution in English is De Grazia (1981). Studies on consent do not necessarily claim that fascism's cultural practices succeeded in generating popularity for Mussolini's government. They do, however, approach culture from the point of view of its instrumental use.
11. For a different approach see Gentile (1995).
12. Lukes (1974).
13. Lukes (1974: 34).
14. Foucault, "Questions on Geography" in Foucault (1980: 73).
15. Foucault stated: "[T]he gaze has had great importance among the techniques of power developed in the modern era, but . . . it is far from being the only or even the principal system employed." See Foucault (1980: 155).
16. See, e.g., Rogin (1985).

17. "The Confessions of the Flesh" in Foucault (1980: 200). However, for Foucault, all relations are strategic, even when they produce new social fields.
18. "Truth and Power," in Foucault (1980: 123). See Honneth (1991) for a critique of Foucault on this issue and on the question of the stabilization of power.
19. Mosse (1970: 2).
20. Rousseau's ideal was that of a transparent society. Each individual was able to see the whole of society and could thus fully participate in a community founded on virtue. See Starobinski (1988).
21. Debord (1983).
22. Fisher (1986).
23. Benjamin, "The Work of Art," in Benjamin (1973).
24. On the double-edged notion of aesthetics see my discussion in Falasca Zamponi (1997).
25. See ch. 3, "The Politics of Symbols: From Content to Form," in Falasca Zamponi (1997).
26. Mussolini (1934–1939: VIII, 21).
27. Mussolini (1934–1939: v, 110–111).
28. See article 3 of the Statute in Missori (1986: 379).
29. Archivio Centrale dello Stato, Partito Nazionale Fascista, Direttorio (Uff. Stralcio), 369.
30. Gravelli (1940).
31. Archivio Centrale dello Stato, Partito Nazionale Fascista, Direttorio (Uff. Stralcio), 370. no. 577.
32. Archivio Centrale dello Stato, Partito Nazionale Fascista, Direttorio (Uff. Stralcio), 369, no. 50.
33. Ludwig (1932: 110).
34. Gravelli (1940: 33).
35. Gravelli (1940: 80).
36. Archivio Centrale dello Stato, Presidenza del Consiglio dei Ministri, 1934–1936, 1.7.6024.
37. Archivio Centrale dello Stato, Partito Nazionale Fascista, Direttorio (Uff. Stralcio), 370, no. 706.
38. Biondi (1967: 311).
39. Flora (1945: 20).
40. Flora (1945: 19).
41. Gravelli (1940: 183).
42. Gravelli (1940: 236).
43. Archivio Centrale dello Stato, Partito Nazionale Fascista, Direttorio (Uff. Stralcio), 371, no. 828.
44. Archivio Centrale dello Stato, Partito Nazionale Fascista, Direttorio (Uff. Stralcio), 371, no. 1046.
45. Gravelli (1940: 286–287).
46. Archivio Centrale dello Stato, Partito Nazionale Fascista, Foglio di Disposizioni, no. 1200.

47. Ciano (1980: 245).
48. The term "totalitarianism" generally refers to political entities; it is a political qual-ification that describes a political phenomenon. In contrast, I use the term as a cultural qualification that describes fascism's project of transforming the Italians totally and creating a new social world. In this sense, the issue of fascism's actual "effectiveness" in organizing and controlling civil society is not relevant to my argument.
49. Foucault opposed the hermeneutic tradition.
50. "Politics and Reason" in Foucault (1988: 85).
51. "Some Questions Concerning the Theory of Power: Foucault Again" in Habermas (1987: 285). Habermas, however, recognizes a literal relation of aesthetics to power in Foucault via the perceptive body as the target of power.
52. Habermas (1987: 285).
53. Ibid.
54. Fraser (1981: 272–286).
55. With reference to fascism, however, Foucault recognized the inadequacy of main-stream analyses. He talked about "a general complicity in the refusal to decipher what fascism really was . . . The non-analysis of fascism is one of the important political facts of the past thirty years." See "Power and Strategies" in Foucault (1980: 139).
56. Foucault (1985).
57. Foucault (1985: 4).
58. "An Aesthetics of Existence" in Foucault (1988: 49).
59. Dreyfus and Rabinow (1983: 236).
60. "An Aesthetics of Existence," in Foucault (1988: 49).
61. Ibid.
62. "Greek ethics is centered on a problem of personal choice, of aesthetics of existence," Dreyfus and Rabinow (1983: 235).
63. Dreyfus and Rabinow (1983: 235–236).
64. Wolin (1986: 71–86). Wolin's rich and suggestive essay specifically examines the aesthetic dimensions of Foucault's theory.
65. Foucault (1985: 173).
66. According to Maria Daraki, Foucault's interpretation of ancient Greece and Rome is inaccurate. In particular in relationship to politics, Foucault totally ignores the centrality of freedom in Greek society, and is indifferent to its democratic idea. See her essay "Michel Foucault's Journey to Greece," in Daraki (1986: 87–110).

References

Arendt, Hannah. 1951. *The Origins of Totalitarianism*. New York: Harcourt Brace Jovanovich.
Baran, Paul and Paul Sweezy. 1966. *Monopoly Capital: An Essay on the American Economic and Social Order*. New York: Monthly Review Press.
Benjamin, Walter. 1973. *Illuminations*. New York: Schocken Books.

Biondi, Dino. 1967. *La fabbrica del Duce*. Florence: Vallecchi.

Ciano, Galeazzo. 1980. *Diario (1937–43)*. Milan: Rizzoli.

Daraki, Maria. 1986. "Michel Foucault's Journey to Greece." *Telos* 67:87–110.

Debord, Guy. 1983. *Society of the Spectacle*. Detroit, MI: Black and Red.

De Felice, Renzo. 1977. *Interpretations of Fascism*. Cambridge, MA: Harvard University Press.

De Grazia,Victoria. 1981. *The Culture of Consent: Mass Organization of Leisure in Fascist Italy*. Cambridge: Cambridge University Press.

Dreyfus, Herbert and Paul Rabinow. 1983. *Michel Foucault: Beyond Structuralism and Hermeneutics*. Chicago, IL: University of Chicago Press.

Falasca Zamponi, Simonetta. 1997. *Fascist Spectacle: The Aesthetics of Power in Mussolini's Italy*. Berkeley, CA: University of California Press.

Fisher, Philip. 1986. "Appearing and Disappearing in Public: Social Space in Late-Nineteenth-Century Literature and Culture," in Sacvan Bercovitch, ed. *Reconstructing American Literary History*. Cambridge, MA: Harvard University Press.

Flora, Francesco, ed. 1945. *Stampa dell'era fascista: Le note di servizio*. Rome: Mondadori.

Foucault, Michel. 1980. *Power/Knowledge: Selected Interviews and Other Writings 1972–1977*, ed. Colin Gordon. New York: Pantheon.

1985. *The Use of Pleasure*. New York: Vintage.

1988. *Politics, Philosophy, Culture: Interviews and Other Writings 1977–1984*, edited with intro. by Lawrence Kritzman. New York: Routledge.

Fraser, Nancy. 1981. "Foucault on Modern Power: Empirical Insights and Normative Confusions." *Praxis International* 6:272–286.

Friedrich, Carl J. and Zbigniew K. Brzezinski. 1956. *Totalitarian Dictatorship and Autocracy*. Cambridge, MA: Harvard University Press.

Gentile, Emilio. 1995. *Il culto del Littorio: La sacralizzazione della politica nell'Italia fascista*. Rome-Bari: Laterza.

Gravelli, Asvero, ed. 1940. *Vademecum dello stile fascista*. Rome: Nuova Europa.

Gregor, James. 1974. *Interpretations of Fascism*. Morristown, NJ: General Learning Press.

Habermas, Jürgen. 1987. *The Philosophical Discourse of Modernity*. Cambridge, MA: MIT Press.

Honneth, Axel. 1991. *The Critique of Power: Reflective Stages in a Critical Social Theory*. Cambridge, MA: MIT Press.

Ludwig, Emil. 1932. *Colloqui con Mussolini*. Milan: Mondadori.

Lukes, Steven. 1974. *Power: A Radical View*. London: Macmillan.

Marin, Louis. 1987. *Portrait of the King*. Minneapolis, MN: University of Minnesota Press.

1989. "The Narrative Trap: The Conquest of Power," in Mike Gane, ed. *Ideological Representation and Power in Social Relations*. London: Routledge.

Missori, Mario. 1986. *Gerarchie e statuti del P.N.F.: Gran Consiglio, Direttorio Nazionale, Federazioni Provinciali: Quadri e biografie*. Rome: Bonacci.

Mosse, George. 1970. *The Nationalization of the Masses*. New York: Howard Fertig.

Mussolini, Benito. 1934–1939. *Scritti e discorsi*. 12 vols. Milan: Hoepli.

Nolte, Ernst. 1965. *Three Faces of Fascism: Action Française, Italian Fascism, National Socialism*. New York: Holt, Rinehart and Winston.

Rogin, Michael. 1985. *Ronald Reagan the Movie: And Other Essays in Political Demonology*. Berkeley, CA: University of California Press.

Starobinski, Jean. 1988. *Jean-Jacques Rousseau: Transparency and Obstruction*. Chicago, IL: University of Chicago Press.

Wolin, Richard. 1986. "Foucault's Aesthetic Decisionism." *Telos* 67:71–86.

PART IV

Products and production
of culture

11

Audience aesthetics and popular culture

Denise D. Bielby and William T. Bielby

Introduction

Aesthetics are systems through which attributions of value are made regarding cultural objects. If asked, cultural sociologists would acknowledge that aesthetic systems are socially constructed, but there is little agreement among cultural sociologists about whether the concept of aesthetics is a topic worthy of empirical analysis. Some take the position that engagement with the qualities or properties of the cultural object should be avoided altogether. This stance assumes neutrality toward the analysis of artistic works and practices as objects of inquiry in their own right. Guided by the production of culture perspective which attends to the "objective facts of production and consumption . . . found in the social relations governing the production of art: 'the socialization and careers, the social positions and roles' of artists, 'the distribution and reward systems' [and] 'tastemakers and publics'" (Bird, 1979: 30, cited by Bowler, 1994: 251), sociologists who circumvent engagement with the cultural object do so to avoid questions of meaning and value. To these sociologists, meaning is a subjective state that is inaccessible to sociological analysis (Wuthnow, 1987). In this view, such matters are best left to art historians and literary critics.

Emerging more recently is a stance among cultural sociologists that poses questions designed to yield insight into cultural meanings and creative practices underlying the production and reception of cultural objects. In an early contribution to this stance, Barbara Rosenblum's (1978a, b) work on contemporary professional photographers sought to explain variation in photographic styles. While her work on the effects of different distribution channels underscored the importance of production contexts, it also sought to explain recognized differences in style and the aesthetic expectations those styles, in turn, embedded in production contexts. This stance acknowledges how cultural forms and practices play a constitutive role in society. That is, art or cultural objects are not simply reflections of structural features or material conditions; cultural forms themselves can shape society. Ann Bowler (1994: 253) refers to this as a methodological position arguing for the autonomy of art:

Specifically, it allows for the conceptualization of artistic production as a sphere always connected with but not reducible to other social processes. Similarly, it allows for the analysis of aesthetic works and practices without recourse to the myth of the transcendent object or artist-as-genius. Finally, this approach positions the relationship of artistic works and practices with social processes at the center of analysis. For the autonomy of art in both of these definitions does not imply that art and society are somehow "separate" in some absolute sense but that the autonomy of art as either a differentiated sphere or an object not reducible to some other social factor *itself* becomes an important focus of the analysis.

Although aesthetics is integral to the operation of art worlds, its contribution to sociological analysis has largely been limited to exploring how aesthetic conventions shape the social organization of cultural production (for example, Becker, 1982) or how distinctions between types of art articulate with class differences or other social groupings (Bourdieu, 1984; Gans, 1974; Halle, 1993). Analysis of aesthetic systems themselves has remained in the domain of art historians and literary critics, because sociologists believed that to study them would reinforce the notion of the solitary, creative artist-as-genius and generate unreflexive, canonical classifications of "great works." Ironically, as Bowler (1994: 254) observes, sociologists' avoidance of aesthetic analysis contributes to that value-laden divide because, "the very act of choosing what *kind* of art to study entails an evaluative component which assigns significance to the objects selected for analysis."

The problematic status of aesthetics as an analytical focus is evident in sociological analyses of all forms of artistic creation, particularly so in studies of the complex art worlds of popular culture such as television and film, where creative interests must co-exist with commercial ones. The issue that frames our analysis is the importance of considering the aesthetic properties of the cultural product itself, not just the circumstances of its production and consumption. While some might argue that issues of aesthetic value are absent, by definition, in the popular realm, in fact popular culture is an important venue for studying aesthetic systems precisely because audiences, as well as creators and critics, can legitimately make judgments about the value of cultural objects. In this chapter, we address the place of aesthetics in the analysis of popular culture through discussion of scholarship and evidence pertaining to two interrelated topics: the critical capacity of audiences in popular culture, and the properties of aesthetics in popular genres. We conclude with a discussion of why sociological understanding of popular culture requires analysis of the interdependence among aesthetics, the production process, and audience reception.

Aesthetics in sociological analysis of culture

Aesthetic principles and aesthetic systems are part of the package of inter-dependent practices that make up art worlds (Becker, 1982). Aesthetic systems – criteria for classifying works of art as "beautiful," "good," "not art," "bad," and other expressive categories used to "handle" art – are formulated by those expert with the art form and applied by critics and connoisseurs to arrive at judgments of value or worth of the object in question. In complex and highly developed art worlds, aesthetic consensus provides working participants in the production of specific art works a set of stable values which help regularize practice.

Aesthetician D. W. Prall wrote that aesthetics is "knowledge of qualities in their immediacy and their immediately grasped relations, directly apprehended in sensuous structures" (1967: 30–31). Aesthetic analysis is the demonstra-tion of the relations among elements comprising a scheme or "structure," and, according to Prall, those constituent elements or properties must attain a known or understood coherence before the object can be understood (Prall, 1967: 25). That understanding is achieved because we are "already familiar with them as wholes or types, or with their kind of elements and the kinds of relations native or possible to these elements in complexes" (1967: 41); but, is this kind of understanding of aesthetic elements necessary for a *sociological* analysis of cultural objects and the contexts in which they are produced and received?

Sociologists' disagreement on this question centers on whether the discipline ought to embrace or avoid aesthetics as an independent variable in the analy-sis of art. Even among those who subscribe to a production of culture view of art worlds, a perspective which generally ignores aesthetics, opinion varies. Some attend only to the socioeconomic strata, market systems, or organiza-tional arrangements through which cultural objects are produced. Examples include: work by DiMaggio (1982), whose study of aesthetic entrepreneurs of the visual and musical arts in nineteenth-century Boston revealed that those cultural forms succeeded because they coincided with class-based interests; Faulkner and Anderson (1987), whose analysis of the film industry showed that directors' careers develop because of economic success on past projects, not artistic innovation; Peterson and Berger (1975), who studied aesthetic innova-tion in the popular music industry but defined innovation as organizational, not product, diversity; and Bielby and Bielby (1994), who analyzed the organiza-tional context of prime-time television programming as one in which network executives claim to choose innovative programming but instead select from those with prior successes. To the extent that aesthetics is addressed among these cultural scholars, it is as a dependent variable determined by market structure or industrial organization.

Becker, who also studies the organizational or collective processes through which cultural objects are created, addresses aesthetics in art worlds but asserts: "developing an aesthetic in the world of sociology would be an idle exercise, since only aesthetics developed in connection with the operation of art worlds are likely to have much influence in them" (Becker, 1982: 145). While eschewing the content of aesthetic systems, Becker endorses the concept of "institutional aesthetics," systems which account for the emergence of new aesthetics from existing ones and legitimate artists and their work as art. An example of Becker's approach is Peterson's (1972) study of jazz as a musical style, in which he elaborates sociopolitical conditions and the circumstances of the music industry which led to the aesthetic mobility of jazz from folk to popular to fine art (see also Gilmore's [1987] analysis of the New York concert world, and Gitlin's [1983] of the factors that shape the quality of prime-time television series).

Compared to scholars working in the production of culture perspective, sociologists of art take stronger positions on all sides of this debate, although they disagree among themselves. Among those pressing to forego analysis of aesthetic content altogether is Crane (1987: 148), who argues that "systematic analysis of visual materials by social scientists has rarely been done and few guidelines exist for a sociological examination of aesthetic and expressive content in art objects." In opposition to Crane's position is Wolff (see also Balfe and Wyszomirski, 1985), who centrally locates aesthetic content in analysis of art and art worlds, for "art always encodes values and ideology, and . . . art criticism itself, though operating within a relatively autonomous discourse, is never innocent of the political and ideological processes in which that discourse has been constituted" (1981: 143). While acknowledging that the sociology of art demonstrates the "very arbitrariness [of aesthetics] in laying bare its historical construction" (1981: 141), to Wolff, "it is an historical fact that there is, in contemporary industrial societies, a distinct sphere of life (or level of experience, or discourse) which we designate the aesthetic." While she is agnostic on what is involved in assigning value to cultural products, Wolff stakes out a clear position on the causal status of aesthetics: "although I would argue that any aesthetic judgment is the product of other, non-aesthetic, values, it does not seem to me to have been demonstrated that it is entirely reducible to these" (1981: 142).

The problem lies, according to Wolff, in sociology's inability "to acknowledge the constitutive role of culture and representation *in* social relations"

(1992: 710). For Bowler (1994), it lies specifically in the discipline's avoiding the problem of meaning, interpreted by some to be nothing more than the subjective, psychological experience of individuals (e.g., Wuthnow, 1987). But to Bowler, meaning occurs in social interaction and, as Griswold asserts, it can be studied "as a property of specifiable social categories and groups, which are empirically accessible and comparable" (Griswold, 1987: 3–4).

Two examples illustrate this point. Lachmann's (1988) work on New York subway graffiti artists studied how social relations, aesthetics, and ideological meaning fostered graffiti artists' careers. Taggers' "corners," where subway lines intersect, allowed art from different neighborhoods to pass on display and individual muralists' work to become known throughout the community of graffiti artists. Notions of fame, reputation, and territory organized writers' communities and the audiences they addressed. Fundamental to their social organization was "a qualitative conception of style [which] allowed them to develop a total art world, formulating aesthetic standards for evaluating one another's murals and determining which innovations of content and technique would be judged advances in graffiti style" (1988: 242). In their words, the audience of these muralists' art world is appreciative "'cause we's bringing style around" (1988: 244). In another example, Dowd (1993), coming from an avowed "production of culture" perspective, attempts to incorporate elements of "musical attributes" to further understanding of cyclical diversity in the music industry. Specifically, he incorporated the measures of song length and of portion of the song devoted to instrumental passages as aesthetic characteristics affecting the potential for variation in musical innovation, independent of market structure or other product characteristics. In findings that upheld his hypotheses, Dowd demonstrated that musical diversity is something that inheres within the form of the cultural product itself, and is not fully explained by market structure or organizational diversity.

In sum, sociologists who favor analysis of the social structural and institutional determinants of cultural production typically forego altogether any consideration of the qualities of cultural products that make them interesting or appealing to those who engage, utilize, or otherwise appreciate them and create demand for them in the first place. Aesthetic qualities matter, as other scholars demonstrate; they must resonate coherently before a product can be understood, appropriated, or otherwise used in ways that carry its impact outward. Moreover, aesthetic considerations are important if for no other reason than that they serve as the basis for artistic innovation (Becker, 1982). Thus, the constitutive role of aesthetics, culture, and representation in the social relations that comprise everyday interaction and social institutions cannot be overlooked.

Aesthetics, audiences, and popular culture

The contribution of aesthetics to the analysis of cultural products becomes particularly salient when considering popular vs. high art or popular vs. high culture because of the still pervasive assumption that aesthetic quality is lacking in popular art forms (see, for example, Adorno, 1976 [1962]; Shrum, 1991). Gans (1974) challenged such claims, arguing instead that aesthetic criteria apply equally to popular art forms and warrant the sociological analyst's attention. In discussing aesthetic considerations in popular culture, he says:

I use the term aesthetic broadly, referring not only to standards of beauty and taste but also to a variety of other emotional and intellectual values which people express or satisfy when they choose content from a culture, and I assume, of course, that people apply aesthetic standards in all taste cultures, and not just in high culture.   (1974: 14)

Gans raises two important considerations by including popular art in the world of so-called legitimate art. The first is that there are recognizable and observable aesthetic elements or properties (his reference to standards of beauty and taste) in popular cultural forms, and the second is that those properties are aligned with the expression of emotional and intellectual values. That is, even though the cultural object is popular, individuals are applying aesthetic judgments in their selection and engagement of those objects. Gans identifies the collective expression of those judgments as "taste publics"; whether individual or collective, those taste publics are the manifestation of human interest in an art form.

While Gans proposes a multidimensional view of aesthetics in both popular and "high" art worlds, theoretical and empirical research on relevant underlying dimensions is still at an early stage. However, empirical research on audience reception has been pivotal in opening up direct examination of popular aesthetics. That research originated from literary scholarship of texts and their meanings (see, for example, Eco, 1990; Holland, 1975; Holub, 1984; and Iser, 1978), and it became especially relevant when scholars focused on how reception of intended meaning, particularly of popular written and televisual texts, was "negotiated," "resisted," or otherwise transformed though alternative uses (see Press' 1994 review of these developments). Scholarship on readers of romance novels (Radway, 1984), and studies of viewers' reception of "Dallas" in the Netherlands and Israel (Ang, 1985; Liebes and Katz, 1990), along with studies of alternative "Star Trek" fan communities (Bacon-Smith, 1992; Jenkins, 1992; and Penley, 1991) unequivocally revealed the potential for interpretations among popular audiences, autonomous from producers' intended meaning. Scholarship on dedicated viewers of daytime serials (Harrington and Bielby, 1995) introduced another element to understanding audience autonomy by demonstrating that resistance and marginalized status are not essential for audience authority. This was also the case in Long's (1986; 1987) research on book choices of reading groups, which focused specifically upon the bases for cultural authority in members' selections and textual interpretations. She found that group selections and interpretations are informed by both literary critics and readers' own experientially based preferences. In particular, her work reveals how cultural autonomy is present even among those attuned to the literary criteria of cultural authorities. Although Long's findings do not speak to the bases and content of audience aesthetics as they engage strictly popular art forms, her findings are consistent with work showing how audiences readily partake in their own aesthetic judgments as they engage products of art worlds.

What should be key elements of a sociological approach to the study of a popular culture aesthetic? To achieve broad appeal, the aesthetics of popular cultural objects necessarily emphasize a sense of the familiar and of cultural knowledge widely shared, while simultaneously incorporating sufficient novelty to perpetuate interest. Popular art is understood to be "essentially a conventionalized art which restates in an intense form, values and attitudes already known; which reassures and reaffirms, but brings to this something of the surprise of art as well as the shock of recognition" (Hall and Whannel, 1967: 66). Thus, textual elements such as cultural themes, medium, myth, and formula all warrant attention (Cawelti, 1973). Formula assures entertainment and recreation, which are essential ingredients of popular culture. Formula in particular, engages shared social and cultural rituals and synthesizes cultural values, and thus guarantees the patterned experience of excitement, suspense, and release within the realm of fantasy.

Because of their familiarity, narratives in popular genres are sufficiently "open" for interpretation by different groups and are relatively easily accessible. It is not uncommon for audience members to draw upon their own expert knowledge, participating alongside artists, producers, and critics in the evaluative process (Dunlop, 1975). As a result, popular art forms elicit audience-based critical insight about the worth or value of cultural products which competes with expert authority in popular art worlds. "Word-of-mouth" and other personal endorsements are potentially as influential as the evaluations of professional critics on a cultural product's reception (Shrum, 1991). Thus, consideration of audience-based criticism is a key element of a sociological analysis of popular culture aesthetics.

Not only do popular audiences contribute to critical authority, they also make claims to ownership which take the form of debate over who a text "belongs to," regardless of who actually creates it. Indeed, in many popular artistic realms, the issue of who "owns" the text, who can legitimately speak for it, and who has rights to it is often ambiguous and contested. For example, Star Trek fans contest or "poach" the narrative in order to write homoerotic fan fiction that transcends the heterosexual specifications of the text (Jenkins, 1992; Penley, 1991), fans of comic-book superheroes vigorously debate the authenticity of screen portrayals of heroes and villains alike (Bacon Smith and Yarbrough, 1991), and fans of country music evaluate whether artists are remaining true to rural traditions (Peterson, 1997). In the remainder of this chapter we explore critical authority, audience criticism, and claims to ownership in popular genres by examining how viewers of daytime serials frame their discussions about aesthetic quality. Doing so allows us to suggest general principals for sociological analysis of popular aesthetics.

Critical authority and claims to ownership: an example from the world of "soaps"

The issues of aesthetic criteria and judgments and of critical distance from popular cultural texts arise in interesting ways within the audience of the daytime serial genre – the "soaps." Ever since soap operas began as a genre of storytelling on radio in the 1930s, cultural and moral gatekeepers have claimed its audience is unable to distinguish fantasy from reality (see, for example, Berg, quoted in Thurber, 1948). Domestic in content and initially targeted to housewives, soaps were devalued by both scholars and media critics. Consequently, the actual critical practices of soap viewers have been overlooked, even though they provide a unique opportunity in which to explore the interconnections between audience aesthetics, evaluation, and popular culture.

   Like audiences of other popular media, soap opera viewers frame issues of quality in terms of contested ownership of expert knowledge (Harrington and Bielby, 1995). Critics play an important role in other artistic mediums, and audience members often debate the value of critics' interpretations. For example, film critics mediate between industry and audience, basing their assessments upon specialized, scholarly knowledge that is not readily available to popular audiences (see Bordwell, 1989). Although the content of critics' insights may be questioned, their presence is generally understood and accepted as a legitimate part of the art world of cinema. In contrast, in the world of daytime serials, the role of professional critics has not been fully institutionalized, and soap opera critics rarely represent themselves as having unique, expert knowledge about the aesthetic qualities of the soap opera form. Consequently, audiences directly engage industry producers about issues of quality. Debates typically arise when continuity in storyline or characterization is perceived to have gone astray, and they become arguments about who possesses the most expertise about the history of the narrative or character in question. Thus, in the absence of professional critics, soap audiences assume that role and feel entitled to make claims to ownership of the narrative. That is, they feel that they know the narrative and its qualities better than the producers do (Bielby, Harrington, and Bielby, 1999; Harrington and Bielby, 1995).

This unique interconnection between the industry and its audience has its origin in the unique properties of the genre. Soap operas are open-ended narratives with storylines that never achieve closure (Cassata, 1985; Intintoli, 1984; LaGuardia, 1974; Whetmore and Kielwasser, 1983). To sustain continuity, soap producers must make the narrative appear authorially seamless, despite the fact that soaps are collaboratively authored by many different participants – producers, writers, directors, actors, and others – who come and go in the world of soap production (Allen, 1985). Ironically, it is soaps' very success at creating and sustaining a seamless fictional world that opens up a space for viewers to assert their claims when they perceive continuity is broken (Harrington and Bielby, 1995).

The distinctive features of the genre's narrative content and structure establish a long-term loyalty in its audience that can last for decades (Hobson, 1982; Seiter et al., 1989; Williams, 1992). As a result, viewers acquire a stock of knowledge and expertise that generates a unique relationship between soap producers and writers, on the one hand, and the daytime audience on the other. Soap audiences believe that their expert knowledge is comparable if not superior to that of the serials' producers and writers, and for this reason they feel entitled to pass judgment on their shows. A typical example of the soap audience's critical capacity is illustrated in the following excerpt from a letter to a daytime magazine. In it, a viewer directly criticizes a show, and by implication its headwriter and executive producer, for debasing the continuity of a narrative that is an audience favorite:

Patrick's proposal to Margaret on OLTL should have been so beautiful. Instead, it was anticlimactic and hollow, because their love has been forever contaminated by the fact that Patrick slept with Blair and got her pregnant . . . The wonderful unbridled spontaneity of their connection is now forever strained by the wretched new "history" in which they have now been mired. It seems like a trite, cheap melodramatic ploy with no consideration for the fans, the rich history of the show or the integrity of the characters as we remember them, and can only serve to leave us feeling unfulfilled and betrayed by this storyline no matter how it proceeds.   (viewer letter, *Soap Opera Weekly*, March 25, 1997: 44)

Soap operas specialize in narratives about emotional life, often told in real time, foregrounding character over plot. Characters are written to exist in many different situations; thus, they have lives and in effect are potentially as knowable as friends and family are in real life (Modleski, 1982). For viewers, "watching over a long period of time leads to an understanding of what makes a certain character tick – why he or she will seem conniving at times and at other times unselfish. Plays and movies may give an insight into what people are like when they are caught in a certain specific situation – but only soaps can show what people are like in a thousand different situations" (LaGuardia, 1974: 3). Also, soaps' fictional world parallels the vicissitudes of real life. As an art form, soap operas represent lives that are separate from but continuous with those of its viewers. "Fate is the only real villain of daytime serials – and that point is brought home again and again by the death of 'good' characters and the sudden sadnesses inflicted on happy families. In real life people are trapped by fate, and *that* is upsetting . . . All viewers implicitly understand these parallels and react to the serials the way they react to life" (LaGuardia, 1974: 4). Consequently, unexpected plot turns are accepted only if they are perceived as authentic to the patterns of everyday life. Otherwise, viewers reject them as contrived and as violations of the tacit understanding between producer and audience, as the following viewer makes clear:

In all the 30 years of watching soap operas, I have never felt more outraged, sick to my stomach and betrayed as I did today watching *Sunset Beach*. I've invested a year of my time in Ben and Meg's romance, and I am absolutely appalled that Ben is the killer. Executive producer Aaron Spelling [producer of *Melrose Place*] can get away with this kind of sensational stuff in prime time, but on daytime, where viewers like me watch our soaps every day and feel like they know these characters inside and out, to have your leading romantic male character turn out to be a psychotic killer is just the worst kind of betrayal imaginable. I feel like I've been stabbed in the back – or should I say the heart. I really loved Ben and Meg.   (letter in *Soap Opera Weekly*, February 10, 1998)

Character development is central to soap narratives, and viewers consider soap characters engaging when they resonate "true to their conceptualization." Especially important in this regard is the consistency with which characters are written and the authenticity of the emotions they express. Dedicated viewers know when a soap is failing to deliver the emotional authenticity they seek, and because they closely monitor the telling of a given story, they feel entitled to complain publicly about how the quality of the show has been compromised, and by whom (Harrington and Bielby, 1995; Hobson, 1982). The criticism is often intense and direct, as can be seen in the following Internet newsgroup posting:

For me OLTL is soulless now, filled with new characters I don't care about, old ones that are unrecognizable, idiotic stories . . . I *want* to return to Llanview, hopefully I will be able to soon, when a writer who cares about Llanview and its characters gets hired.
(rec.arts.abc, August 15, 1997)

Soap opera producers often seek to interject social issues with topical relevance into storylines (Gledhill, 1992). "Soap writers and producers, unlike most
of their counterparts on the evening shows, are socially concerned enough to
run storylines with the specific purpose of conveying socially important information to the viewers" (LaGuardia, 1974: 6–7). One might expect such stories
to complement successfully the narratives about everyday experience that are
the staple of soap operas. However, as is sometimes the case, the social realism
interjected through topical storylines competes with or even undermines the
emotional verisimilitude of the fictional narrative. Consequently, soap viewers
do not always appreciate these stories when their purpose supplants the overarching goal of soaps, which is to offer "a day-to-day world that palatably combines realism and fantasy" (LaGuardia, 1977: 1). Said one fan about a critically
acclaimed and popular storyline about AIDS that appeared on *General Hospital*
a few years ago:

I did like the Stone [the hero] story, because I loved Michael Sutton [the actor portraying
Stone], and Claire Labine [the headwriter] did a wonderful job with it. And it was
incredibly educational, a story and subject that needs to be told about in a medium
that reaches people emotionally. But, here again, that's a social awareness story, which
soaps in general do a good job with. I'm more impressed when soaps use more creative
approaches in storytelling, rather than relying on social relevance all the time.

Because soap opera narratives and characters are observed closely by audiences over extended periods of time, the critical capacity of soap opera viewers
develops into an understanding of the genre's conventions and codes, its narrative structure and appeal, and even its cultural marginalization. In the following
communication to a fan e-mail group, a viewer articulates how the commercial
purpose of soap operas can undermine its aesthetic accomplishments:

You have to justify relationship with characters as much as you can, otherwise people go
HUH? where did that come from? That, in my opinion, is where soap operas go wrong
again and again. They put in these little plot twists that do not necessarily have anything
to do with the continuity of their characters. But maddening as it is, unfortunately,
too often, it works. People keep watching hoping that their favorite characters will get
straightened out. Then they wait too long to straighten things out, hoping to string you
along a little longer and by the time they finally resolve things it is in a rush, some people
are already turned off, and they give the characters a few days to be themselves until they
are off on along long plot device . . . I think it is more the nature of the beast. They like to
manipulate your emotions. As long as you watch the show, they don't necessarily care
what you think of their plots. But the bottom line is this industry's chief purpose is to
entertain and bring in the ratings. They are always going to do this to us guys.

Not only do viewers recognize the formulas, codes, and conventions that are
uniform across the genre, they also understand that styles of telling stories within

the genre's parameters vary considerably by producer and headwriter. That variation is analyzed in discussions among viewers, generating dialog about their own preferences for the stylistic differences of one headwriter over another. For example, one long-term viewer's analysis of a former headwriter compares him to his predecessor and to his successor after his firing. Communicating with another viewer, she wrote:

As for Michael Malone, I'll admit he wrote 3 or 4 good stories, but that's all I'll admit to. And most of the stories he wrote fell apart at the end or were destroyed down the line . . . Michael Malone and Linda Gottleib (the executive producer) wanted to reinvent the wheel but the wheel had been working just fine. His movie-of-the-week plots – or short arc stories – as he called them didn't work in the soap format. His inability to write more than one or two stories at a time is not something I want to go back to either . . . Just like these [the then-current headwriters], his story pacing was awful. Storylines stopped and started on a regular basis. But his worst crime was destroying all the characters I gave a darn about.

Even when viewers accept variation across soap writers' narrative styles, they still debate the ways in which particular writers tell stories. For example, the central importance of romance to soap operas virtually assures that there will be debate among viewers about the ways in which it is portrayed. In the following illustration, viewers differ in their preferences for idealized versus cynical visions of romance, and they articulate their own scenarios for a troubled married couple and a possible interloper. One viewer prefers the "endless seesaw action" of a constantly shifting triangle, while the other feels it is important to have a couple that viewers care for and for whom some payoff and resolution is assured.

My dream storyline for these three [characters] is not one couple over another, but a true threesome. In this scenario . . . Todd will not allow himself to have a physical relationship with the wife for whom he is beginning to have romantic feelings. He will not subject a woman he admires and desires to the "beast" within him. But Todd would realize that because he cares for her, he wants his unfulfilled wife to achieve fulfillment. He will try to put his dangerous jealousy in the deep-freeze and give Tea tacit approval for her to exercise her pre-nup granted to other relationships . . . In the other corner at the base of this triangle is Andrew . . . At the apex of the triangle sits Tea, who is genuinely attracted to both of her possible partners, but is laboring under a heavy burden . . . Now this is the stuff of good soap opera, or at least the soap opera I grew up on. Couples who are thwarted from truly uniting stay viable, become legendary. Couples who get together must break up or suffer horrible conflict within months of that "happy ending."

(rec.arts.abc, January 7, 1998)

In response to this posting, another viewer voices her own preferences for how romantic stories should be told:

I couldn't disagree with you more strongly. I believe the audience needs couples, solid couples, to invest in and root for, and I think that the lack of good romantic couples is absolutely OLTL's [*One Life to Live*'s] weakest point. Soaps, especially OLTL under the Labines, have become overloaded with artificially-induced, by-the-numbers triangles, which instead of providing obstacles for the average couple, seem to have taken the place of the relationship entirely . . . Since the writers seem determined to keep their options opinion and perfectly balanced, making sure that whoever is in the middle can go either way at any time, little emotional depth is found in any of these triangles IMO [in my opinion]. I want to see great couples developing. I want to see why these TWO people are together, what makes them right for each other, how they build their relationship and make it unique. To do that, we need to see couples who are united and together – not always and forever, but enough so that they acutely face their problems together.

(rec.arts.abc, January 8, 1998)

In sum, our analysis of the soap world shows that audiences who engage popular genres have the capacity to do so analytically, and that their critical capacity is not undermined by the high value they place on the emotional authenticity of popular narratives. Indeed, as this example suggests, that capacity may be strengthened by the emotional value of a narrative.[1] Engaged audiences are well informed about the genre's conventions, formulas, narrative structures, production process, and industry context. Equally important, they fully understand the aesthetic qualities of the cultural form and share among themselves their assessments of how successful a cultural product is in delivering those qualities. When it fails to deliver, engaged audience members feel entitled to critique the decisions made by those who produce the product, and they draw upon the full range of their knowledge to diagnose what went wrong and what it would take to restore "their" cultural form to the level of quality the audience deserves.

Distinctive features of the soap genre, such as the open-ended storylines, narrative emphasis on everyday life, and illusion of authorial seamlessness, invite audiences to assert their claims to pass judgment on the quality of the cultural product; but, to varying degrees, all popular genres invite such claims, and the proliferation of print and electronic media for news about entertainment provides audience members with the requisite knowledge for both understanding the production process and making judgments about quality. Moreover, the expansion of electronic sites for airing critical assessments, such as Internet newsgroups and electronic bulletin boards, provides autonomous space for audiences to assert their claims to critical authority (Bielby et al., 1999).

Emotion, critics, and the popular aesthetic

To what extent does a popular aesthetic mediate an audience's understanding of popular art forms? Does an audience's vigorous and often vocal quest for elements such as emotional authenticity, narrative continuity, and consistency of characterization, as observed among soap viewers, indicate that audiences of popular genres are not sufficiently distanced to form reasoned judgments about quality? According to work in the sociology of culture (see Bourdieu, 1984; Gans, 1974), audiences approach highbrow culture with a "cultivated detachment" which allows meaning to be constructed in a way that is abstracted from the world of direct everyday experience. Emotions theorist Thomas Scheff (1979) describes this as an "overdistanced" reading position: the consumer is all observer, with no emotional participation in the unfolding drama. In contrast, the consumption of mass or popular culture is assumed to be largely unmediated and is based on the consumer's direct experience of the cultural product: "For genres such as revues and cabarets, as well as for soap operas, the world of everyday experience is sufficient grounds for understanding and appreciation" (Shrum, 1991: 370). Following this logic, the popular culture consumer is thought to hold an "underdistanced" reading position, one consisting entirely of emotional participation with no critical reflection or observation.

To Shrum, high art and popular art are differentiated by the extent to which understanding of the cultural object is mediated by professional critics. In high art, an audience member does not make an autonomous personal judgment about the quality of an art form but instead defers to the expert judgment of cultural critics. As Shrum argues, critics are "tastemakers . . . gatekeepers, structuring the experiences of audiences and cultural consumers" (1991: 352). That is, the audience's aesthetic values and preferences are interpreted, mediated, and shaped by the assessments of cultural authorities (Cameron, 1995). Thus, unlike Bourdieu (1968, 1984), Shrum does not equate highbrow culture with the class position and associated cultural capital of its consumers. A high status individual might embrace both high- and popular-art forms; the relevant distinction is the degree to which that individual defers to the authority of knowledgeable experts in the consumption of each (DiMaggio and Useem, 1978). At the same time, according to Shrum, consumers of highbrow art enter into a form of symbolic exchange or "status bargaining" whereby they relinquish in part their right to form an autonomous judgment in exchange for the prestige that accrues to participation in highbrow culture.

To both Shrum and Bourdieu, the experience of popular art forms is direct and unmediated, and the audience for such art is "undiscriminating," suggesting that there is little room for an articulated popular aesthetic. Thus, they avoid addressing questions about whether and how audiences make judgments about the quality of popular cultural art forms. We agree with Shrum that the "status bargain" associated with the consumption of highbrow culture involves a deferral of critical authority to the judgment of elite experts who interpret a cultural form's aesthetic value; and we agree that, in popular genres such as soap operas, professional critics play only a limited role, serving mainly as advocates for the genre, not as tastemakers (Harrington and Bielby, 1995; also see Lang, 1958, about television criticism more generally). However, we take issue with the conclusion he draws, that the experience of popular art forms is direct and unmediated by aesthetic valuation. Shrum (1996: 198) seems to acknowledge that critical discourse is possible among audiences of popular art forms; what makes it popular is not the absence of critical discourse but an absence of deferral to critical authority, but, ultimately, he retreats to the position that popular art forms are directly experienced and avoids analysis of a popular aesthetic.

Our point is that appreciation and evaluation of popular art forms is highly mediated, but by an aesthetic that is fully accessible to engaged audiences. Our analysis of the soap genre suggests that consideration of the popular aesthetic must focus not only on the audience's understanding of the production context, but also on the aesthetic's grounding in shared cultural knowledge about emotion. In short, the prevailing view of popular culture consumption as a direct, underdistanced mode of experiencing reality fails to capture the complexity of audiences' relationship to cultural products. In the soap genre, for example, soap viewers distinguish between "realism" and authenticity; it is the latter that dedicated soap viewers seek, respond to, and critique. They do so from an understanding of a complex popular aesthetic, comprised of knowledge about the genre's codes and conventions about representations of emotion in everyday life.

In the soap opera genre, emotion, and the pleasure of experiencing it, are generated by the use of elements of melodrama as a stylistic form (cf. Williams, 1992). As Gledhill (1992: 107) describes, melodrama seeks "to prove (by making visible) the presence of ethical forces at work in everyday life, and thereby to endow the behavior of ordinary persons with dramatic and ethical consequence." In other words, melodrama efficiently conjoins the consequences of reality with the liberation of the imagination. As Peter Brooks (1976) articulates, melodramatic aesthetics push facts from the real world toward the symbolic activity of metaphor. Soap viewers are familiar with this stylistic form, recognizing that encoded in the personal talk that comprise soaps are the psychic and social contradictions that constitute soaps' fictional world of family and personal relationships.

To many, melodrama is not considered an aesthetic precisely because it plays to emotions. However, it is not simply the portrayal of emotions that defines the quality of the cultural form, it is doing so in a way that resonates with and has symbolic meaning to the audience. Melodrama is a stylistic form that provides that meaning. As Gledhill (1992: 108) explains,

In melodrama what people feel and do, how they relate to each other, is of utmost consequence – the source of meaning, the justification for human action. Personalization in this respect is not simply a realist technique for individualizing the social world. Nor does it simply, as is often said, "displace" social and political issues into personal or familial terms in order to achieve a bourgeois fantasy resolution. Personalization is melodrama's primary strength. The webs of economic, political, and social power in which melodrama's characters get caught up are represented not as abstract forces but in terms of desires which express conflicting ethical and political identities and which erupt in the actions and transactions of daily life.

Not all fictional narratives that attempt to execute this stylistic form are successful. The audience for this form is not simply responding to the portrayal of emotions. Instead, they fully understand the melodramatic aesthetic, which mediates their appreciation of the narrative (Ang, 1985).[2] As we have observed in our example from the soap opera genre, audiences can and do make evaluations based on the success of a cultural production's realization of this aesthetic. They distinguish between good melodrama and "bad art," and they do so by relying on shared cultural knowledge and without deferring to the authority of professional critics (Harrington and Bielby, 1995).[3]

In the realm of popular drama portrayed in novels, plays, film, and television, melodrama is, of course, just one type of stylistic form among many that can serve as an accessible aesthetic understood by both producers and consumers of an art form. Our point is that what makes a popular culture art form both "culture" and "popular" is that appreciation and evaluation are mediated by a widely shared and understood aesthetic, and both the art form and the aesthetic are accessible to an engaged audience that invests in acquiring the requisite knowledge without deferring to cultural authorities. For example, the everyday experience required to make both professional wrestling and science fiction films accessible is likely to be shared by a large segment of the population, but that does not mean that nearly everyone can distinguish good art from bad art in each of those genres. To become a fan of either genre requires a personal investment to become expert in the subtleties of the genre's aesthetic and knowledgeable about the production context. A fan of science-fiction films who can differentiate a mediocre production from one that realizes the full potential of the genre is unlikely to have the capacity to appreciate and critique a professional wrestling exhibition, and vice versa; but fans of either genre can and do discuss among themselves what constitutes a successful or unsuccessful production, they bring a sophisticated level of cultural expertise to their critiques, and they know how and where to obtain further knowledge of both stylistic forms and production contexts that allow them to enhance their understanding and refine their critical capacity. Most important to the cultural sociologist, much of the social interaction around and discourse about popular aesthetics is public and observable, providing the opportunity for empirical examination of aesthetics, interpretation, and meaning in popular culture.

Conclusion: toward an empirical sociology of popular aesthetics

Popular audiences do not defer to the judgment of elite critical authority, but that implies neither a direct, unmediated, and underdistanced experience of the cultural form nor an inability to respond critically and analytically. Research on the world of daytime serials shows that appreciation and evaluation of the cultural form is mediated by a popular aesthetic that is well understood by both an engaged audience and those who write and produce the serials. Critical authority in popular genres such as soap operas resides among those audience members who choose to invest in acquiring expertise about the genre's conventions, codes, and stylistic forms, and knowledge about the organization of production and its business context.

While our argument is based largely on empirical research on the world of daytime serials, we believe it applies to popular culture genres more generally. More importantly, to cultural sociologists, the ways in which it does so can be evaluated through systematic empirical research. In our view, three elements are essential to an empirical research program on popular culture and popular aesthetics. First, the distinctive feature of a popular aesthetic is the critical capacity of an engaged audience, which is revealed through social interaction. Thus, the starting point for an empirical research program is study of the discourse of audience members' interaction. Doing so will reveal where claims about quality and value are being made, who is making them, the criteria that are being applied, and the basis for the legitimacy of those claims. The cultural sociologist should ask: Where and how are audience members acquiring, sharing, and refining expert knowledge about a genre's codes, formulas, conventions, and circumstances of production? Central to studies of audience discourse should be an analysis of how the social organization of the audience allows critical communities to emerge and to survive. For example, what is it about the social networks and social relationships in which audience members are embedded that allows them to find opportunities for repeated interaction around critical discourse? One might explore the extent to which the proliferation of electronic forums such as Internet newsgroup discussion groups (covering popular genres as diverse as alt.comedy.standup, alt.music.christian.rock, alt.culture.bullfight, rec.sports.pro-wrestling, alt.gothic.fashion, and alt.graffiti, among thousands of others) and other commercial and audience-supported venues expand audience members' capacity to define, participate in, and refine a popular aesthetic.

Second, while critical discourse among audience members is a key ingredient of an empirical research program on popular aesthetics, cultural sociologists simply cannot avoid empirical analysis of the features of popular culture art forms that allow accessibility to a popular audience and motivate its members to invest in acquiring the expert knowledge that builds critical capacity. Here, cultural sociologists must confront the reality that appreciation of a popular art form (or a high art form, for that matter) is an *expressive* experience; what makes it art is the emotional experience it elicits in the audience, and what makes it popular is the extensiveness of the shared experience. Thus, the cultural sociologist must study the cultural form's styles, formulas, genres, narrative themes and structures, media, and conventions to gain an understanding of points of accessibility and the basis for audience members' pleasures.

Third, while studying shared discourse and meaning among the audiences of popular art forms, the cultural sociologist must also attend to difference. A shared community of critical discourse does not imply uniformity in the value attributed to cultural forms or the criteria audience members use to assign value. Dedicated audience members are themselves cultural authorities, and in the relative absence of professional critics, their vigorous and vocal quest for authenticity and quality will often lead to vehement disagreements with one another about both the value of specific cultural products and the appropriate criteria to be applied in assigning value. Popular audiences are heterogeneous, and differences over aesthetic value and criteria most likely derive in part from the differentiated gender, class, and ethnic origins of audience communities and subcultures. A systematic approach to empirical analysis should consider how disagreements over a cultural form vary by an audience's needs and uses. However, the extent to which various audience segments evaluate cultural forms from a stance of "resistance" is an empirical question, as is the degree to which individuals of different race, class, or gender background participate in the same networks of discourse, share an appreciation for a specific form, or agree on how it is to be evaluated.

In sum, debates over the existence of a popular aesthetic and the degree to which audience members' understanding and evaluation of popular genres is culturally mediated fall squarely within the domain of sociological theory and research. Issues of aesthetics and meaning in popular culture can and should be topics of empirical inquiry of cultural sociologists, but those issues are not accessible in any scientifically interesting way when analysis is limited to interpretive readings of cultural texts. Instead, as sociologists we are uniquely qualified to contribute to debates about aesthetics and meaning by empirically examining the social interaction and discursive exchanges through which audience members reveal and debate their understandings and assessments of a cultural form's qualities. Moreover, since audience members engage popular culture from a stance informed by knowledge of a genre's conventions, codes, stylistic forms, and production context, an informed sociology of popular aesthetics must proceed from a framework that attends as carefully to issues of the production of culture as it does to analysis of discourse and texts.

To many of those who have embraced the "cultural turn" in the humanities and social sciences, work in the production of culture tradition is often dismissed or devalued as nothing more than an application of industrial sociology to a distinctive kind of market. From this perspective, analyzing cultural production as any other kind of productive system may yield insights into the social organization of art worlds, but it is disconnected from sociological analysis of issues of aesthetics and meaning. To the contrary, from the perspective we have presented in this chapter, it should be clear that sociological analysis of the popular aesthetic requires asking questions about the properties of the cultural form and the circumstances of its production and consumption that allow for contestation between producers and audiences about meaning and aesthetic value. To understand how popular culture audiences ascribe value to cultural objects necessarily requires understanding of features of the production context that allows audiences, with some legitimacy, to make claims that they are as capable as creators to judge the value or meaning of the cultural object.

Notes

A version of this chapter was presented at the annual meetings of the American Sociological Association, Washington, DC, August, 2000. We wish to thank Krista Paulsen and Michele Wakin, and our colleagues in the Comparative Institutions Seminar at the University of California, Santa Barbara, for their helpful feedback on an earlier version of this chapter. We especially thank Carol Traynor Williams at Roosevelt University for her insights.

1. We thank Carol Williams for this insight.
2. Melodrama is one of a variety of storytelling forms that are used in soap operas. Among others are fairy tales and folk tales (Williams, 1992).
3. On the other hand, critics are not completely absent from the world of soap viewers. Indeed, the role of the soap columnist–critic evolved in response to the increased visibility of a diverse and sophisticated viewing audience. As opportunities for public, fan-generated criticism proliferated (see Bielby et al., 1999), the daytime press found and acknowledged an audience for critical perspectives on issues within the medium. A sophisticated segment of the soap audience became an important resource to the daytime press. Increasingly, columnists–critics–editors began to monitor the boundaries of the soap genre and its audience, taking issue with commentary that failed to rise above outsiders' stereotypes of the subculture of soap-opera viewers. For example, soap columnists now regularly take the mainstream media to task for stereotyping or being condescending toward the soap industry and its viewers. In short, while soap critics generally do not perform the cultural mediation of their counterparts in highbrow genres, they are not simply extensions of the industry's

publicity apparatus. Instead, they perform an important institutional function, legitimating viewers' interests and concerns to the industry and representing the genre to outsiders who marginalize the status of the medium and its viewers.

References

Adorno, Theodor. [1962] 1976. *Introduction to the Sociology of Music*. New York: Seabury Press.
Allen, Robert C. 1985. *Speaking of Soap Operas*. Chapel Hill, NC: University of North Carolina Press.
Ang, Ian. 1985. *Watching Dallas: Soap Opera and the Melodramatic Imagination*. New York: Methuen.
Bacon-Smith, Camille. 1992. *Enterprising Women: Television Fandom and the Creation of Popular Myth*. Philadelphia, PA: University of Pennsylvania Press.
Bacon-Smith, Camille and Tyrone Yarbrough. 1991. "Batman: The Ethnography," in William Urrichio and Roberta Pearson, eds. *The Many Faces of Batman: Critical Approaches to a Superhero and His Media*. New York: Routledge, Chapman, and Hall. Pp. 90–116.
Balfe, Judith and Margaret Wyszomirski. 1985. *Art, Ideology, and Politics*. New York: Praeger.
Becker, Howard. 1982. *Art Worlds*. Berkeley, CA: University of California Press.
Bielby, Denise, Lee Harrington, and William Bielby. 1999. "Whose Stories Are These? Fan Engagement with Soap Opera Narratives in Three Sites of Fan Activity." *Journal of Broadcasting and Electronic Media* 43:35–51.
Bielby, William and Denise Bielby. 1994. "'All Hits Are Flukes': Institutionalized Decision-Making and the Rhetoric of Network Prime-Time Television Program Development." *American Journal of Sociology* 99:1287–1313.
Bird, Elizabeth. 1979. "Aesthetic Neutrality and the Sociology of Art," in Michele Barrett, Philip Corrigan, Annette Kuhn, and Janet Wolff, eds. *Ideology and Cultural Production*. New York: St. Martin's. Pp. 26–48.
Bordwell, David. 1989. *Making Meaning: Inference and Rhetoric in the Interpretation of Cinema*. Cambridge, MA: Harvard University Press.
Bourdieu, Pierre. 1968. "Outline of a Sociological Theory of Art Perception." *International Social Science Journal* 20:589–612.
   1984. *Distinction. A Social Critique of the Judgement of Taste*. London: Routledge and Kegan Paul.
Bowler, Anne. 1994. "Methodological Dilemmas in the Sociology of Art," in Diana Crane, ed. *The Sociology of Culture*. Oxford: Blackwell. Pp. 247–266.
Brooks, Peter. 1976. *The Melodramatic Imagination: Balzac, Henry James, Melodrama and the Mode of Excess*. New Haven, CT: Yale University Press.
Cameron, S. 1995. "On the Role of Critics in the Culture Industry." *Journal of Cultural Economics* 19:321–331.
Cassata, Mary. 1985. "The Soap Opera," in Brian Rose, ed. *TV Genres: A Handbook and Reference Guide*. Westport, CT: Greenwood. Pp. 131–149.

Cawelti, John G. 1973. "The Concept of Formula in the Study of Popular Literature," in Ray B. Browne, ed. *Popular Culture and the Expanding Consciousness*. New York: John Wiley. Pp. 109–119.

Crane, Diana. 1987. *The Transformation of the Avant-Garde: The New York Art World 1940–1985*. Chicago, IL: University of Chicago Press.

DiMaggio, Paul. 1982. "Cultural Entrepreneurship in Nineteenth-Century Boston: The Creation of an Organizational Base for High Culture in America." *Media, Culture and Society* 4:33–50.

DiMaggio, Paul and Michael Useem. 1978. "Social Class and Arts Consumption: The Origins and Consequences of Class Differences in Exposure to the Arts in America." *Theory and Society* 5:41–61.

Dowd, Timothy. 1993. *The Song Remains the Same? The Musical Diversity and Industry Context of Number One Songs, 1955–1988*. Princeton University, Department of Sociology Working Paper Series, I-93.

Dunlop, Donald. 1975. "Popular Culture and Methodology." *Journal of Popular Culture* 9:375–383.

Eco, Umberto. 1990. "Innovation and Repetition: Between Modern and Postmodern Aesthetics." *Daedalus* 114:161–184.

Faulkner, Robert and Andy B. Anderson. 1987. "Short-Term Projects and Emergent Careers: Evidence from Hollywood." *American Journal of Sociology* 92:879–909.

Gans, Herbert. 1974. *Popular Culture and High Culture: An Analysis and Evaluation of Taste*. New York: Basic Books.

Gilmore, Samuel. 1987. "Coordination and Convention: The Organization of the Concert World." *Symbolic Interaction* 10:209–227.

Gitlin, Todd. 1983. *Inside Prime Time*. New York: Pantheon.

Gledhill, Christine. 1992. "Speculations on the Relationship between Soap Opera and Melodrama." *Quarterly Review of Film and Video* 14:103–124.

Griswold, Wendy. 1987. "A Methodological Framework for the Sociological of Culture," in Clifford Clogg, ed. *Sociological Methodology*. Washington, DC: American Sociological Association. Pp. 1–35.

Hall, Stuart and Paddy Whannel. 1967. *The Popular Arts: A Critical Guide to the Mass Media*. Boston, MA: Beacon Press.

Halle, David. 1993. *Inside Culture: Art and Class in the American Home*. Chicago, IL: University of Chicago Press.

Harrington, C. Lee and Denise Bielby. 1995. *Soap Fans: Pursuing Pleasure and Making Meaning in Everyday Life*. Philadelphia, PA: Temple University Press.

Hobson, Dorothy. 1982. *Crosswords: The Drama of a Soap Opera*. London: Methuen.

Holland, Norman N. 1975. *5 Readers Reading*. New Haven, CT: Yale University Press.

Holub, Robert C. 1984. *Reception Theory. A Critical Introduction*. London: Methuen.

Iser, Wolfgang. 1978. *The Act of Reading: A Theory of Aesthetic Response*. London: Routledge and Kegan Paul.

Jenkins, Henry. 1992. *Textual Poachers: Television Fans and Participatory Culture*. New York: Routledge.

Lachmann, Richard. 1988. "Graffiti as Career and Ideology." *American Journal of Sociology* 94:229–250.

LaGuardia, Robert. 1974. *The Wonderful World of TV Soaps.* New York: Ballantine.

1977. *From Ma Perkins to Mary Hartman: The Illustrated History of Soap Operas.* New York: Ballantine.

Lang, Kurt. 1958. "Mass, Class, and the Reviewer." *Social Problems* 6:11–21.

Liebes, Tamar and Elihu Katz. 1990. *The Export of Meaning: Cross-Cultural Readings of Dallas.* New York: Oxford University Press.

Long, Elizabeth. 1986. "Women, Reading, and Cultural Authority: Some Implications of the Audience Perspective in Cultural Studies." *American Quarterly* 38:591–612.

1987. "Reading Groups and the Postmodern Crisis of Cultural Authority." *Cultural Studies* 1:306–327.

Modleski, Tania. 1982. *Loving with a Vengeance: Mass Produced Fantasies for Women.* New York: Methuen.

Penley, Constance. 1991. "Brownian Motion: Women, Tactics, and Technology," in C. Penley and A. Ross, eds. *Technoculture.* Minneapolis, MN: University of Minnesota Press. Pp. 135–161.

Peterson, Richard A. 1972. "A Process Model of the Folk, Pop, and Fine Art Phases of Jazz," in C. Nanry, ed. *American Music: From Storyville to Woodstock.* New Brunswick, NJ: Transaction Books. Pp. 135–151.

1997. *Creating Country Music: Fabricating Authenticity.* Chicago, IL: University of Chicago Press.

Peterson, Richard A. and D. Berger. 1975. "Cycles in Symbol Production: The Case of Popular Music." *American Sociological Review* 40:158–173.

Prall, D. W. 1967 [1936]. *Aesthetic Analysis.* New York: Thomas Y. Crowell Company.

Press, Andrea. 1994. "The Sociology of Cultural Reception: Notes Toward an Emerging Paradigm," in Diana Crane, ed. *The Sociology of Culture.* Oxford: Blackwell. Pp. 221–245.

Radway, Janice. 1984. *Reading the Romance: Women, Patriarchy, and Popular Literature.* Chapel Hill, NC: University of North Carolina Press.

Rosenblum, Barbara. 1978a. *Photographers At Work: An Empirical Study in the Sociology of Aesthetics.* New York: Holmes and Meyer.

1978b. "Style as Social Process." *American Sociological Review* 43:422–438.

Scheff, Thomas J. 1979. *Catharsis in Healing, Ritual, and Drama.* Berkeley, CA: University of California Press.

1996. *Fringe and Fortune: The Role of Critics in High and Popular Art.* Princeton, NJ: Princeton University Press.

Seiter, Ellen, Hans Borchers, Gabriele Kreutzner, and Eva-Maria Warth. 1989. "Don't Treat Us Like We're So Stupid and Naive: Toward an Ethnography of Soap Opera Viewers," in E. Seiter, H. Borchers, G. Kreutzner, and E. Warth, eds. *Remote Control.* New York: Routledge. Pp. 223–247.

Thurber, James. 1948. "Soapland," in James Thurber, ed. *The Beast in Me and Other Animals.* New York: Harcourt. Pp. 189–260.

Whetmore, Edward Jay and Alfred P. Kielwasser. 1983. "The Soap Opera Audience Speaks: a Preliminary Report." *Journal of American Culture* 6:110–116.

Williams, Carol. 1992. *It's Time for My Story: Soap Opera Sources, Structure, and Response*. Westport, CT: Praeger.

Wolff, Janet. 1981. *The Social Production of Art*. New York: New York University Press.

1992. "Excess and Inhibition: Interdisciplinarity and the Study of Art," in L. Grossberg, C. Nelson, and P. Teichler, eds. *Cultural Studies*. New York: Routledge. Pp. 706–718.

Wuthnow, Robert. 1987. *Meaning and Moral Order: Explorations in Cultural Analysis*. Berkeley, CA: University of California Press.

12

Grounding the postmodern: a story of empirical research on fuzzy concepts

Magali Sarfatti Larson

Consider the experiences I had visiting two monumental buildings last summer: in the Duke's Palace at Urbino, one of the gems of the fifteenth century, Duke Federico di Montefeltro placed *his* initials *FD: Federico Dux* on pediments and windows all over the building. Yet even the briefest guidebooks speak of the Dalmatian architect, Luciano Laurana, who summoned Bramante and Francesco di Giorgio Martini to help with the project. Some five hundred and thirty years later and an ocean away, in the Civic Center of Mississagua, Ontario, heralded as one of the most important "postmodern" monuments of the continent, I could not find a trace of the architects' name – Jones and Kirkland of Toronto – nor were they mentioned until the end of our guided tour. Yet the name and the semblance of Hazel McCallion, Mississagua's colorful and effective mayor for over eighteen years, were visible from the beginning, in the small auditorium where the visit started with a video about the city.

While doing research for my book on postmodernism in American architecture, *Behind the Postmodern Façade* (Larson, 1993), I tried hard not to become a "fan" of the architects (as for "going native," incompetence is a good safeguard!). But I admit that my heart went out to the ignored architects in Mississagua: so much work – to win a competition, to plan such a monumental building, to "come in" on budget (a remarkably small budget for such an enormous project), and to merit but two words at the end of a guide's spiel! The pathos of the architect's disputed authorial position seemed to resonate across the centuries, competing with the patron for history's attention. Yet this double experience confirmed to me the characteristics of architecture as an art.

It is, first of all, an *impersonal* art. Roger Scruton explains the difference between artistic expression that must be "seen as personal" and "that which must be seen as abstract and detached":

In the latter case we do not attribute, even in imagination, an *emotion* to a *subject*, for there is no subject to imagine and rarely any emotion to attribute. Expression is more like a display of atmosphere, an abstract presentation of character.

(Scruton, 1979: 189)

A building does not so much express an emotion, as wear a certain expression . . . We regard a building as "imbued with character," and this "character" is not only immediate . . . but also observable in principle by anyone.   (Scruton, 1979: 196)

Surely we can see this as a continuum, in which twentieth-century painting, for one, moved resolutely toward abstraction, basing its discourse, as the historian Bruno Zevi notes, "on lines planes surfaces volumes, interpenetrations of figures and geometric solids, in sum on categories of pure visibility which until then had been considered pertinent especially for architecture" (Zevi, 1961: 26, my trans.). It is thus from the aesthetic region *already* inhabited by architecture that cubism and its derivations communicated their rationalizing aesthetics to modern architects.

A building, indeed, cannot convey individual feeling, or the *private* subjectivity of those who claim a position of authorship with regard to it. A building does not represent anything, and expresses only itself, its own public existence. This is not to say that a building does not convey individual intentions, but they are inseparable from what the building *publicly* does: a building intervenes in public space, and appropriates it. The act of appropriation asserts control, and it is fraught with the implications of power. We could say, oversimplifying, that from the Renaissance on, kings and merchant princes vied with the Church in the public erection of palaces and monumental symbolic displays of their power. Today, the symbolism remains, even though the celebration of power itself is cloaked and muted by the utilitarian and commercial reasons invoked to justify construction. Not infrequently, projects that have an impact on the environment or on public finance are resisted, and resistance, even if it is unsuccessful, even if it only obtains trivial results, even if it rises after the fact and too late, confirms the political nature of architecture. A building is presumed to serve the sponsors' program, to embody their intentions in space: in challenging the building and its architects, users and public contest the program defined by the clients, and the clients' power.[1] It is therefore particularly difficult in this art for the author to express herself in the object as her "statement," independently from any other intention than the enunciative.

Architecture is, secondly, always a *collective* enterprise. The architect may conceive the building, translating the client's intentions (as well as the users' and his or her own) into form, he or she may choose and command materials, but, in fact, it is not the architect who *builds*. Others realize the plans, bringing materials together to give them a durable organic existence as realized architectural forms. Therefore, it is not even the case that trivial details in the realization can reveal, as in painting or a craft, the hand of the master better than the more striking traits of the composition. It is impossible in architecture to imagine the artist's individuality revealing itself in "elements outside conscious control" (Ginzburg, 1989: 101).

Yet the disputed and elusive notion of authorship is important in western architecture, imbued since the Quattrocento with the dialectic of genius and renown (Larson, 1983a). However, the author's claim must be marked by something else than the building or its reproducible and imitable details: by a signature, initials, a plaque, a name, which arguably belong to another order of discourse than the building itself. Architects have the upper hand over patrons in this spread-out discourse, of which their *confrérie* controls the core, and the core in turn determines what a peripheral but widely read testimony like a guidebook will say. My story about Urbino and Mississagua was intended to suggest that architectural objects by themselves are silent, not only about their obscure and always ignored executors (as Brecht asked: "Who built the seven gates of Thebes?") but also about the architect and even the client, the two overt contenders to embodied immortality. The discourse as a whole, with its contested boundaries, its chronological evolution and its various parts, with the critics educating the public's attention to tone and detail, with historians recording names and commissions, is needed to connect style and manner to an author, or even a building to its time. The complexity makes the "production perspective" indispensable.

This perspective emerged in the 1970s, "largely in response to the failure of the earlier dominant idea that culture and social structure mirror each other." Both structure and culture emerge in social practice, and their relationship is always problematic (Peterson, 1994: 164–165). We can no longer assume that structure (the "social background" of the artists, and the relevant features of the social context in which they work, expressible in "hard data") determines "soft" culture; but the sociology of culture must also reject the ideological view that separates art from the economy, and insulates the creation of culture from all except aesthetics and the dilemmas of pure creation. Thus, on the one hand, the specialized practices that constitute recorded or embodied culture exist in as "hard" a matrix as any other productive practice in contemporary society, a matrix in which social networks give access to differential resources and rewards, determining to a large extent the development of careers and the complex dynamics of cultural fields. On the other hand, in each field, the producers are free to advance in specific ways their own claims to recognition, although this freedom does not give them control over the reception of their products; sociologists cannot ignore that the products themselves respond to physical, technical, intellectual, and philosophical imperatives of their own, and that these dictates and constraints are probably what matters most to the specialized producers of culture. Nonetheless, in architecture, the complexity, the great cost, and the immediate political implications of large buildings pose particular problems to the investigation of cultural change from a production perspective. This is what I will discuss in these pages.

My recounting has two overlapping parts: one reflexive, the other self-critical. I will try, first, to tell as candidly as possible what I wanted to do in my writing on architectural postmodernism, and how I figured I would go about doing it. Reflexivity is at the same time ingenuous (what use can it be to explain "the production perspective" if one does not explain the real tricks and difficulties of doing it?); and it is disingenuous, for narrating research as a *process* underscores its limits and constraints, implicitly beginning to justify the work. Therefore, I will try in the end to be more direct in responding to criticism. Above all, I will try to be more self-critical, and to distinguish what I did not do because I did not choose to, from what I was not able to do.

I was interested in the uniqueness of the architectural profession even before I started to consider the professional phenomenon in the United States and England. My work proposed a different way of reading the story of professionalization in the Anglo-American world from what sociology had advanced. I emphasized the active project of the professional reformers, and how their pursuit of status, autonomy, and social esteem in the world of work depended on the achievement of a solid, protected foothold in the burgeoning markets of specialized professional services of the nineteenth and early twentieth centuries. In my analysis, profession appeared as an emergent structure that linked the sphere of formal education to protected markets of labor and services, and the success of professionalization was contingent on many factors, including the favor of the state and the conquest of affluent clienteles (Larson, 1977).

The project on professions was going to culminate into a study of employed architects, but my research on architecture happened only later and from a different perspective (Larson, 1983a, b). Slowly, over the years, I saw more architecture, talked with more architects, and read more about them and their work. Those were the years in which spokesmen for the profession were becoming celebrities, and making a lot of noise about the "postmodern turn" or, more broadly, the revision of the modern. Others did too: philosophers like Habermas and Jean-François Lyotard took the shift in architectural mood and form as indicative of a much larger cultural shift, as also did the geographer David Harvey, in a better reasoned and empirically grounded argument (Habermas, 1985; Harvey, 1989; Lyotard, 1986). The critic Fredric Jameson also wrote about architectural ideology, and devoted several pages to the analysis of John Portman's Bonaventura Hotel in Los Angeles in his famous article "Postmodernism, The Cultural Logic of Late Capitalism" (Jameson, 1987). The ubiquitous fame of this article prompted me to look at architecture from a "production perspective."

It was striking, indeed, to see Jameson take the Bonaventura as a foremost emblem of alienation, the very symbol of powerlessness and seduction in late capitalist America, without ever mentioning the conditions in which the hotel was designed and produced. John Portman, in fact, was one of the first, and probably the most successful, architects to emancipate himself from the client by becoming his own developer and client. If the Bonaventura signified all that Jameson thought it did, the architect would have been here more directly responsible than elsewhere for what his building could be made to mean. I thought it was important to know what the self-proclaimed *producers* of architecture – the designers – were doing and thinking during the postmodern shift. Since we held them responsible for one of the most significant postmodern manifestations, it seemed logical to find out what postmodernism meant to them.

I thought, moreover, that understanding how the shift had come about in a specific field, describing with exactitude the dynamics of one movement, could clarify the question of what similar or dissimilar processes were covered by the postmodern label in fields other than architecture. I admit that my intention was much more reductive than I would now have liked it to be. Looking at the conditions of production of a cultural shift, I hoped to illuminate underlying commonalities with other fields. In any case, reductive and "marxisant" as it is to look for postmodernism in changing conditions of production, I figured that I knew how to do it. I mistrust the explanations that "read" in a building, as in any other text, vague and undemonstrable correlations between formal traits, or subjective responses of the interpreter, and the vaster processes that are presumably transforming the *Zeitgeist*. Mine was not a fully conscious theoretical choice, but a preference, reaching out naturally, as it were, for basic tools of our trade in the sociology of work, the sociology of organizations and the sociology of knowledge. Perhaps theory emerges from the problems we find in trying to ply our trade.

My first problem was that even though I knew full well that the "creators of form" are but a very small minority in a still small profession, and that the latter is more concerned with selling a service than making art, I still could not avoid going along with what we may call the "art historians' story": the inordinate importance that the designer elite acquires (and gives itself) in the official and unofficial discourse of the profession. Not only the history books, but the architecture journals (and often, in the 1970s and 1980s, the mass media) are full of famous *men* or, more exactly, of men whose claim to fame is based on conceiving buildings mostly for other men (singly or in committees). The architectural elite is anointed by critics, historians, and certainly not the least by other architects. Their standing is thus established by relatively autonomous players in a discursive field within which the statements – words *and* stone – of the famous architects have the authority to *constitute* architecture: they make it, by declaring not only what good architecture is but also who are the producers worth considering. The revision of the modern had *protagonists*. In 1987, when I started my research (for which eternal thanks are due to the National Science Foundation's Visiting Professorship for Women Scientists, a most generous and intelligent program), the movement already had a scholarly history and the main protagonists had been named (Klotz, 1984 and 1988). Obviously, the "art historians' story" is only partial, mystified, though not entirely mythical; but I could not avoid dealing with the actors, still productive and very much alive, whom it identified.

When I started writing my book, I had not read Pierre Bourdieu's extension to "cultural fields" of his earlier path-breaking analysis of the logic of the scientific field (Bourdieu, 1976, 1993). Thus, I adapted on my own the logic of symbolic capital to the field of architecture. As every sociologist knows by now, Bourdieu argues that cultural fields, which characteristically "reverse the economic world," allocate recognition or *symbolic capital* to agents who occupy the positions of producers in that field. The principles and mechanisms of recognition are specific to each field, based on changing criteria of worth. Positions, recognition, and the standards of good work are the stakes of the competitive struggle among producers. It follows that cultural agents who start from "strong" or strategically favorable positions have more chances than others to accumulate symbolic capital, except that heretics who come almost literally from "left field" can succeed in splitting the field up, and even, ultimately, in taking it over. Cultural fields, endowed with their own logic and asserting a particular form of "economic reversal," are nevertheless *subordinate* to larger fields of domination. In classic sociological tradition these are the field of power, and the even more encompassing field of class relations which, in Bourdieu's perspective, is ultimately based on the distribution of economic resources. Taking from Weber's sociology of religion, Bourdieu explains that the more "the literary and artistic field" gains autonomy,

the more it tends to suspend or reverse the dominant principle of hierarchization; but also that whatever its degree of independence, it continues to be affected by the laws of the field which encompasses it, those of economic and political profit. The more autonomous the field becomes, the more favorable the symbolic power balance is to the most autonomous producers, and the more clear-cut is the division between the field of restricted production, in which the producers produce for other producers, and the field of large-scale production, which is *symbolically* excluded and discredited . . . Because it is a good measure of the degree of autonomy, and therefore of presumed adherence to the disinterested values which constitute the specific law of the field, the degree of success is no doubt the main differentiating factor. But lack of success is not in itself a sign and guarantee of election.   (Bourdieu, 1993: 39)

Famous architects are in a dominant position within a field configured by the changing outcome of competitive struggles for symbolic capital. Uncontestably, they have prestige and influence across the whole field. Power, however, is another matter. Architecture is never, and cannot be, an autonomous field, for buildings cannot be mere drawings. For architecture to be, in Le Corbusier's words, "the masterly, correct and magnificent play of masses brought together in light," buildings must be *realized* (Le Corbusier, 1960: 31). In most cases, architects must design *for someone*; moreover, modern building depends not on executants only, but on masters of complex techniques. Elite architects may have as much trouble finding clients as anyone else, and sometimes more, because they are expensive, and reputed to let budgets run out of control. This means that they are as dependent as anyone else upon the "client class," and the latter is dominant in the larger field of class relations within which architecture as expert service is subsumed.

Because this is a profession with expert authority and institutionalized avenues of recognition, architects control the discourse of architecture. The elite has the power to anoint a lesser architect, co-opting him (or even her, in this extremely male profession) to its ranks.[2] But elite architects do not in themselves have the power to consecrate officially the next generation of proficient architects; schools and licensing boards do that. The power of the architectural elite is power over the discourse of architecture, the capacity both to exercise and distribute cultural authority. Power in this cultural field does not mean autonomy, however, for the canon defined by architects, critics, and historians is a collection of *realized exemplars*, which depend for their very existence on the antecedent trust, judgment, and economic capital of a client. Furthermore, even the power over a more autonomous discourse must be *constituted* by those over whom it is exercised: to be subjects of the elite's power, other architects must care about symbolic capital; they must care in one way or another about participating in the discourse of architecture, about playing in the field where struggle determines the standards of architectural beauty and worth. This is a very small part of a small professional field, in which the large majority of architects and firms deliver service and utility to their clients. Treating architecture *as a field* was a theoretical decision that needed justification, and I may have provided it too lightly, as in passing.

Yet, in other research, I had gathered suggestive evidence that architecture is a field. I was investigating for NSF and the Research Corporation of the American Institute of Architects what architectural offices with very large billings (quite unrelated to their symbolic capital in the field) call "design research." In a series of East Coast interviews, I found that the closer an office was to the field of "architecture-as-art" – roughly measured by type of commission, geographic location, elite training of the principal and of the staff – the more likely the principal was to express resentment of the "profession's darlings." Second, *all* the designers traveled, if they could, to look at finished buildings or, at least, searched the professional journals for plans and inspiring type-forms (Larson, 1978). The practical "big volume" architects may have resented their artistic *confrères* but could not ignore them, and the acknowledgement went deeper than the formal inspiration they received.

The "artists," I argued, may appropriate (or even usurp, as was intimated) the *telos* of architecture, the aesthetic component which makes it an art, superior to *technē*, the know-how of construction. Engineers captured *technē* for themselves a long time ago, and good craftsmen mastered it in traditional building. *Telos* is architectural form, and form can be beautiful. The functions and the aesthetics of architecture express a culture, and the designers' interpretation of a canon and a code of beauty. It is possible that elite architects do not master *technē*, the panoply of instruments and their applications, as well as others do; it is possible that they do not know "how to build a building that works"; but the public recognizes them as the masters of architectural aesthetics, as the creators of forms that transcend their function. That recognition means that there still *is* a *telos*, something that ordinary builders cannot provide, and which therefore makes *all* architects necessary. The practical architects were complaining in 1978 that the windows kept falling off I. M. Pei's Prudential skyscraper in Boston; yet I. M. Pei and his design awards were still important for a profession always threatened by a sense of its own superfluity.

The field is held together by discourse. The deference that schools, professional societies, foundations, institutes, editorial boards, specialized publishers, museums, art galleries, critics, and cognoscenti bestow upon the architectural elite attests to the existence of a tenuous but shared frame of reference. In this cultural field, it was not difficult to locate the significant players, since architectural histories, architecture encyclopedias, professional journals, professional awards, and expert authorities have as their task the identification, and the classification, of notable architects.

Finding a way to contact the significant players seemed to be the difficulty. I composed a representative list and submitted it repeatedly to experts. I was able to interview over thirty American architects in seven cities, only three of whom were women. Fifteen, including two women, were profiled in the international encyclopedia *Contemporary Architects* (Morgan, 1987), a sort of sophisticated "Who's who" of the elite of world architects, but nineteen had played a significant role in the revision of the modern. Three men had been important in the development of modernist architecture in America: Gordon Bunshaft, who was retired when I interviewed him but had been the architect of Lever House in New York and partner at SOM-New York; Bruce Graham, the designer of the Sears tower in Chicago and partner at SOM-Chicago; and, last but not least, Philip Johnson, who created with Henry Russell Hitchcock the term "International Style," the founder of the architectural design section of the Museum of Modern Art, the associate of Mies van der Rohe in the design of New York's Seagram Building, who had become in the 1970s and 1980s a provider of eclectic skyscrapers, including the AT&T, featured in 1979 on the first page of the *New York Times* and the cover of *Time* magazine.

I had defined 1966 and 1985 as the inner and outer boundaries of the period under study: 1966 because it is the date in which American postmodernism acquired its manifesto with the publication of Robert Venturi's *Complexity and Contradiction in Architecture* (Venturi, 1966), which I believe represents a sign of maturity in a shift that begins in discourse; 1985 as a more arbitrary limit, chosen because historicist postmodernism "peaks" in 1980, and enters the thoroughly "modernist" world of corporate firms (SOM-Chicago, in fact) some years later. I had thought at first that I would try to interview the architects who had received repeat awards from their peers in the period whose boundaries I had determined. There was many more of them than of recognized protagonists, they were not all famous or important, and I could therefore risk many rejections without exhausting the pool of respondents. However, after my first meeting with Philip Johnson I changed my mind. Renowned for his erudition, his wit, and his political mistakes, Johnson embodied then fifty-five years of American architecture. He was gracious and generous beyond anything I could have expected. My project interested him, although he did not quite believe I would *really* write a book;[3] he encouraged me to use his name with everyone I wished to see, and his name, attesting to the smallness of social networks, opened almost every door (White, 1993: 2–4). I could interview the protagonists themselves. Although I also spoke to some ten rising (or once rising) architects, the in-depth interviews with the protagonists provided the clearest insight and the richest material for three crucial chapters. They discuss the architects' typical careers, and the "indigenous" concepts they use to describe the structural constraints that weigh on their work (Larson, 1993: ch. 4); different ways architects have of understanding the *telos* of architecture in their pursuit of transcendence (Larson, 1993: ch. 5); and some of the architects' own accounts of the design process, which I then connect with architecture's discourse, and its transition from modernism to postmodernism.

The interviews were long, ranging from one to two hours. I went into them with some themes that I wanted to touch – beginnings, career narrative, design philosophy and possible changes, narrative of the recent past and the present of architecture. Apart from that, since I knew the respondent, having read everything I could find by or about him or her, I let the interview unfold in a fluid form, like a conversation, in which I also asked specific questions about *that* architect and his or her work. By the end of 1988, I had my own set of primary sources to add to the mountain of primary and secondary sources that I had read. My texts were almost too rich. I was on a tight schedule, and I could not afford to invest the time in the consultation of qualitative analysis textbooks.

After a year of teaching, I was looking in September of 1990 to a semester of freedom in Sweden.[4] In my hands I had a book outline, a book contract, a good draft of the introduction and the background chapters, as well as a sketch of some of the chapters to be based on an exhaustive analysis of the *Progressive Architecture* awards. The book was taking the form of an analytical social history of the postmodern shift in American architecture, although it did not have a unified narrative; I saw it rather as a series of probes, and loosely coupled at that. The first, and perhaps the most difficult to write because of the amount of studying it required, was my own synthesis of "*what happened in architecture.*" There I even dared to present ideas about architecture, space, and materials in modernism and postmodernism, combining them in a way that made sense to me, although the ideas were borrowed from architects and historians (Larson, 1993: ch. 2). The second probe delved into the political economy of the urban environment; drawing on urban sociology, American political science, and the analysis of real estate dynamics, it placed architecture decisively *in cities.* This, I believe, is a partisan position that I did not justify enough in the book: it is in cities, I believe, that architecture is the most ineluctably public, visible, and therefore political. Western architecture begins as an urban art, and the aesthetic nothingness of suburbs confirms, by opposition, the intimate tie of a civilization with its architecture.

I had analyzed the *Progressive Architecture* awards from 1965 to 1985. The great variety of buildings chosen, and especially, the excerpts of juries' comments and debates, made them a trove. I could see already that they would give me the year-by-year materials I needed for a micro-history of the shift, seen from inside the profession by individuals constituted as gatekeepers, and therefore given, at least for a while, the "anointing" function that the elites have, but I had not done anything yet with the interviews, except read them over and over again.

In Sweden, I cross-coded them: for each interview, I first listed all the important topics (those I had raised myself and those that had just come up) and their exact location; then, for each topic, I listed the speaker who brought it up and the places where this happened. The latter was heuristically more important, for I could see clearly on paper that all the interviewees (even those who were retired, like Bunshaft or Joe Esherick) talked at great length and with vivid emphasis about the *business of architecture* or, more broadly, about what it takes for an architect and his firm to keep doing architecture. There was no time at all to worry about the *Zeitgeist* in the "rollercoaster" of architecture – hard work, from which not even the elite designers were exempt, and harder still when there was no work. The architects' narratives were similarly patterned by what I call "vernacular concepts," indigenous terms that recur in the architects' discourse. Terms like "roller-coaster," "breakthrough," "track record" appeared in practically all the narratives, giving them similar profiles and similar thresholds; but the resolution of those problems had led the architects in different directions, and the speakers imbued them with different meaning. Different types of careers, and different approaches to architecture as something *more* than a business and a job were beginning to emerge.

The architects' account of the change in the nature of the clients – from an individual to a collective (a committee), from a corporation or an institution building for itself, to a developer building for sheer profit – looked, with some disquiet, to both "the inside" and "the outside." Toward the inside, the account of how clients had changed translated, for instance, into an old and important concern of the profession: what was the potential for a "repeat" versus a "one shot" commission? Toward the outside, the account echoed the transformations in the political economy of cities that I had described: a lot more work, perhaps, for many more architects; but a lot less control over the product. I would have drawn, if I had been able, a much tighter parallel between the transformations of the political economy and those of the architects' official discourse than is suggested by the verb "echoed," but I am not entirely sure today of what this would have involved. I could have listed for each architect I interviewed the buildings for which his or her firm had been responsible, and then matched their date and location with the type of building permits recorded by the Construction Census for that place (or with the county's construction records). But, even if I had been able to do that by myself with the time and money I had available, that still would not have told me exactly who the client was, so I let the protagonists speak about their experiences and their anxieties, satisfied that their accounts reversed the angle of vision from which I had looked at building in American cities. From the changing structure of demand to the individual experience of designing in a changing context, from a pretendedly neutral "author's" voice to the personal, engaged voice of the producer, from a bird's eye view to a view that looks up from the trenches, the architects had *lived* those structural changes. That, after all, is what culture, making sense of social life, is about.

I think that the chapters based on the interviews with the "protagonists" are strong examples of the "production of culture" perspective. Indeed, as I analyzed my interviews, I did not think of the speakers as history-book protagonists any more, but as struggling producers of architecture, not only trying to make something good, and to make it "by Wednesday," but also to make it beautiful, often *despite* the client.[5] By the end of my work on "lived structures" I could describe with exactitude two types of elite career: the individualistic type associated with entrepreneurial "idea firms," and the corporate type, bringing design excellence to excellent "strong service" firms. I could also see, as the architects talked about the predominance of individual stars (themselves, in many cases!) and manufactured charisma, that they were haunted by something – image – over which they had no control, and which went farther and deeper than the making of celebrities.[6]

The tension between image and substance, look and building, being hired to create an appearance and control over working drawings, loomed larger and larger over the course of *Progressive Architecture* awards debates I analyzed, but the interviews had already alerted me to it, for another stream in my speakers' narratives concerned the *telos* of their work. I saw in their words and in their work three main ways of seeking transcendence, sometimes compatible, though often in tension among themselves: through signification, through an artifact's perfection, and through the enhancement of the users' lives.

The interviews with protagonists confirmed, once again, what had been my contention since my first incursions into the sociology of architecture: because these producers of art offer at the same time shelter and service, their position in the social division of labor pertains to construction, a crucial sector of the political economy. The ancient claim that architecture is an art "owned" by the architect as its essential producer can neither augment nor insure his role in construction. Today, even visual artists, traditionally weaker than architects, can dispute the architects' control, if the client so disposes. About the collaboration between art and architecture, the artist Robert Irwin remarks:

Every single architect said he wanted to be seen as an artist. But if architects are artists, by the same reasoning, are artists architects? Even if I built my own house, that does not make me an architect. There's something more complex and profound involved, having to do with ethics, expertise, and intention. But the architects dismissed this kind of thinking out of hand. My point was, if you're already an artist, what is it that I bring to the table? What do you need me for?   (in Schwartzman, 1997: 57)

Yet Richard Meier bitterly complains that in the design of the Getty Center's central garden, the same Robert Irwin, "was being treated as an artist while I was being relegated to the secondary status of architect. His creative work was regarded as sacrosanct and subject to only token cost control, while my contribution was fair game for everyone" (in Davis, 1997: 36). Thus, ultimately, any change in the discourse of architecture, any substantial transformation in the reigning conception of what architecture is and does *as an art*, implicitly addresses the architect's fragile hold upon the economy of construction. Behind the façade of the aesthetics and the theory lies the "real world" of a struggling occupation, and they live in the same world.

In our century, modernism in Northern Europe (and only very partially in the United States) dreamt of a new aesthetic for a *social* architecture, interested in creating a "radiant city" for all its dwellers, as well as work for all its architects. Acclimatized in the United States, German modernism provided from here the imperious look of the postwar reconstruction of the world under American hegemony. The glass tower symbolized not a new role for the architect, who had always been the servant of power, but his successful subordination to new corporate masters. The architect dressed up economic efficiency (maximum rental space per square foot of land) in the shining semiotic semblance of technical efficiency. In the 1950s and 1960s, the architects' ambition was physically embedded in the large scale and modern look of the truly International Style projects. The new corporate architecture rebuilt war-torn Europe, gave to the Third World the westernized face that fit its subordination, and ripped North American cities up and apart.

The heroes of the times were the architectural firms (mostly American) that could handle the mammoth projects. The small entrepreneurial firms which did not count as "players" were, on the other hand, immune to the economic downturns that hit in the early seventies. The postmodern revision came mostly from them, architects whose academic positions in elite universities distinguished them from the mass and may have given them a voice of small range, but who, Robert Gutman writes, "had not yet become sufficiently recognized to compete for jobs of any consequence beyond a house addition or an occasional small vacation house." Gutman offers this remark in his acute review of my book, but perhaps misses the point I make, that therein lay the postmodernists' strength: they were, indeed, "too far removed from opportunities for big jobs to be affected by shifts in building production" (Gutman, 1996: 587).

Despite the large scale destruction/reconstruction upon which the late version of the International Style presided, the circumstances of modern architectural practice seldom allow architects to "build cities."[7] Even the largest projects are single, and sometimes isolated, ventures, and the attack on the individual house with which the distinguished historian and critic Vincent Scully opened the *Progressive Architecture*'s jury debates in 1966 was thereby unfair.[8] But there was something about the small house in those years that simply did not measure up to what the juries expected of a "real" and "distinguished" (or "really distinguished") architect. I noted early in my research that *Complexity and Contradiction in Architecture*, Robert Venturi's "gentle manifesto" of 1966, is addressed to architects who, like himself, cannot yet aspire to more than small projects or well-publicized entries in interesting competitions (Larson, 1993: 53–59; 1994). The award juries' debates document how colleagues who were *not*, at the beginning of the period, of a "postmodern" persuasion came to accept the new ideas, no matter how small or trivial the projects seemed that embodied them.

I had problems dealing with the projects that the juries chose, and which they discussed in excerpts that the journal's editorial staff selected, no doubt, among the most quotable quotes of the jury's hard workdays. I could see, as anyone could, that the new names appeared among the winners, and that the license they had given to architects uneasy with modernist obeisance was penetrating the awards. But in order to detect the main phases of the story I was trying to tell, I needed to follow *one* strand, and not a dozen. This was the analytical significance of my concentration on the individual house, in a section I called "The private house as barometer of change." Robert Gutman misses the tactical reasons for this methodological choice: yes, the individual house was always important in launching the career of world-famous architects, and not only in the United States, paradise of the private individual dwelling unit (Gutman rightly cites Rietveld, Mies, Le Corbusier beside Frank Lloyd Wright). But it is significant that the private house was downplayed in the 1950s and reestablished from the late 1960s on, when aesthetic experimentation was emphasized above scale and type of projects, and a new kind of architect seized the protagonist role. If I may be allowed to quote myself at some length, the focus on the house told me the outline of a story, which I was then able to flesh out in the full context of the juries' debates from 1966 to 1985:

By keeping the building type constant, my focus on the single-family house allows a clearer view of the contending positions in a self-transforming professional discourse. The juries start with a technocratic notion of social responsibility, expressed in a modernist bias toward large-scale work. While they do not critique urban renewal projects directly (in part because exemplars seldom reach PA's contest), their critique appears indirectly in the revaluation of the private house. It proceeds from two main sources: One is the priority accorded to design over program, thus overriding the service aspects and the social function of architecture; the other is a concern with preservation, opposed by definition to the wholesale demolition of the existing stock of buildings.

(Larson, 1993: 194)

Whatever its privileged source, architectural discourse tends in either case to mistake the success of buildings – on all counts, the aesthetic, the functional, the economic – for "success" (that is harmony, serenity, utopian dis-alienation or whatever positive measure) in the social relations those buildings were to shelter and serve.

Focusing *only* on the house, I could detect the penetration of revisionism, the assertion of formalism ("architectural supremacism" as Richard Pommer called the current most clearly represented in those juries by Peter Eisenman in

1975), and the accommodation to unsolvable eclecticism after then. The procedure is reductionist but so is systematic analysis. I may have missed the "true
story" of postmodern revisionism in American architecture, but I believe I read
correctly the story that those juries' gate-keeping was telling in those years. It
is the story of a cultural shift that begins with stirrings, earlier and more varied
than I could have detected from outside the field, by architects discontent with
what the modernist dogma had to offer.[9] The dogma is frayed when "young
Turks," who came from other sectors of the profession than the elites, consolidate the revisionist message and make serious forays into the domain of
discourse. What prompts them forward is a crisis of both the corporate modernist aesthetic and the model corporate role of the architect. Postmodernism in
American architecture partakes of the general sense of challenge, political and
ideological, carried forth by "the heirs-apparent," the generation of students or
alumni of elite architectural schools which had, in fact, displaced and replaced
the reigning schools of old (Princeton and Yale above Harvard and MIT by way
of California).[10]

The different brands of architectural aesthetics proposed by the postmodern
revisionists meet with different degrees of success but they are all, to some
extent, coopted as their proponents' careers develop – with unusual rapidity,
thanks to the building boom of the 1980s. Yet revisionism does not end. I used
the label "postmodern" for the whole revisionist challenge (architects reserve
it for the historicist variety whose heyday was in the 1970s) because it was a
challenge against the aesthetic project of architectural modernism, and because
the latter, varied as it was in its manifestations (except perhaps the last one, the
corporate architecture that postwar America visited upon the world), projected
a unified and totalizing ambition in its rhetoric. If meta-narratives are dead, then
postmodernism is, in one sense, still alive.

Did I write the book I intended to write? Yes, in large part: to be quite can-
did, I hoped to write an empirical study related to a subject – the revision of
modernism – which, in my humble opinion, had been made intellectually
unbearable by the abstract verbiage poured upon it.[11] I confess to having had
the much less humble hope of showing that *in sociology* good theory comes out
of good research and seldom, if ever, develops from ungrounded ruminations
(mostly pseudo-philosophical). I believe that I have dealt with the intellectual
and aesthetic issues of postmodernism as a sociologist of culture should have
done, from a production perspective: moving behind the façade, as I announced
in the title I would do.[12]

Yet I am guilty of wearing my sociological theory too lightly, perhaps, to
admit justification. I believe that theory enables us to *see*, and subsequently

analyze and interpret, social facts that would not have been selected or set up as "facts" if it were not for antecedent theory, but I did not set out to apply or test any theory, not even my own (about the reasons for the weak market control obtained in the profession of architecture, for instance). I would have hated to read and to write a book that purported to apply "Prof. X's or Prof. Y's theory of cultural change to the case of architecture." I have always turned away, out of laziness, from that kind of exercise, beloved of good graduate students. Yet I recognize that network theory is eminently applicable to the architectural elite, and that I could have mapped the relative centrality of each node and each network against the awards and commissions that individuals and networks received. I believe this would have made my work more sophisticated from a structural point of view, and that it might even have contributed to network theory in the sense suggested by Emirbayer and Goodwin (1994). But I did not know enough network theory, and not enough about the architects' networks to do it without a great investment of time. In fact, network theory would have strengthened my theoretical position: as Bourdieu pointed out, actors define and explain themselves in a cultural field by taking positions in it, and the dynamics of the field impress themselves differentially upon their actions and productions (Bourdieu, 1993). Indeed, for cultural producers, class origins explain very little. But the schools people attended, and the different patterns of accumulation of symbolic capital these schools permitted, including, first and foremost, access to privileged networks, explain very much. My narrative would have been much stronger if I had followed this analytical path, but it would not have been what I thought it would be: a readable social history, whose levels of analysis took shape rapidly in my mind almost as concentric circles of overdetermination.

Neither did I provide, as one critic would have wanted me to, the means to generalize from architecture to a theory of professions (Stevens, 1994: 1696). It is possible that many stronger professions than architecture, including medicine and the law, may be confronting now in their still protected markets what I called the characteristic *heteronomy* of architecture (as the opposite of the professional drive for *autonomy*). Yet this would not be heteronomy of quite the same kind, pervading the very canon of the profession, but one derived from the parallel effect of subordination (as physicians in HMOs) and standardization (through the codification of medical procedures that is presupposed by the HMOs or third parties' review). This is an important idea, and I am glad the critic mentioned it; in fact, I tried to develop some of its implications myself in a paper entitled "Reflections on Precarious Orders."[13] At most, I thought that an accessory outcome of the research would be that of providing an original case study for the theory of professions. My goal was to build a bridge between the sociology of professions and the sociology of culture, and not to remain imprisoned by a theoretical perspective I had spent a decade in revising.

The situation of architecture seemed to me strongly reminiscent of that of artists in the culture industries. As I wrote in conclusion, architects propose alternative designs to clients, and clients select a restricted sample for building. The search for saleable new "images" and new "scenes" in the built environment, prompted by the economy of cities and by fiscal factors, has pushed the architect's task closer to the rapidly exhausted trends of fashion and the culture industries (Larson, 1993: 249–250). Howard Becker, struck by the parallel between the situation in architecture and the relationship between movie producer and composer studied by Robert Faulkner (Faulkner, 1983), suggested that I develop the comparison, but I did not have the stamina to take his advice by the time I received it.

In fact, it was Becker's work in *Art Worlds* that I had taken more than any other as a guide (Becker, 1982). It was of extreme importance to me that Becker, who was one of the readers for the press as I was told later, should have thought in his first review that I had succeeded in "connecting specific social situations of work to ideas"; he said, moreover, that this "is almost never done in studies of the arts and related disciplines." I had tried to reconstitute the art world of architecture as he teaches us to do, and that had been, indeed, my intention and my theoretical ambition. If I succeeded to any extent, it is because I was as attentive to the architects' objective professional situation as subordinate practitioners, as I was sensitive to their efforts and their cultural ambitions. I listened with extreme care, over and over again, to their voices, and they, not I, made the connection. Becker's criticisms, which I tried very hard to meet, were as important as his praise; thanks to him, I made the effort to be more forthrightly sociological, especially in concluding with a critique of what is presented as theory of postmodernism, and a statement for placing theory on solid empirical ground.

I am keenly aware of another shortcoming: this study of architecture talks very little about buildings. If I try to remember where, now, without going back to the book, I would say that I talk about architectural form in my own voice when I discuss the creation of modernism as an architecture, and as an ideology of architecture (Larson, 1993: ch. 2); when I describe Peter Eisenman's Wexner Center for the Arts at Ohio State University (Larson, 1993: ch. 8); and, in the last page of the book, when I say what I like about Swedish planned suburbs, and my emotion in front of Maya Lin's Vietnam Veterans' Memorial in Washington, DC. Why should I have talked about buildings, plans, and drawings? First of all, because I had made in the introduction an incomplete theoretical statement about the *discourse* of architecture, in which I defined its sociological base but not its boundaries or contents. I wrote:

[D]iscourse includes all that a particular category of agents say (or write) in a specific capacity and in a definable thematic area . . . The discourse of architecture is constructed autonomously, by experts who are accountable only to other experts. However, in order to continue "formulating fresh propositions" [the words and the idea belong to Michel Foucault], disciplines need to show how their rules become embodied in a canon, and the canon of architecture consists of beautiful or innovative *built exemplars*. These buildings are not and cannot be exemplars of the architect's autonomous application of knowledge and talent alone.   (1993: 5)

The implication here is that buildings are part of the discourse. The implication is greatly reinforced by my discussion of the *Progressive Architecture* awards as "architecture on paper," an autonomous process in which drawings and plans are submitted to a jury of one's peers. So, I must now make amends for both vagueness and incompetence: yes, I do believe that the discourse of architecture *includes* the architects' products. These artifacts are, moreover, that for which architects ultimately reserve their passion, and they are what *we, the public*, call architecture; they are what we love or hate or ignore, in this art that can be not the decoration but the setting of life.

Robert Gutman, who knows how to write competently and sensitively about form, points out that "the book relies so much on words in the ordinary sense: on statements architects make about their work and careers in interviews, in what they and others write and say about their work, and their comments during deliberations at awards juries. So maybe the author does believe that only what architects say and write can be the material for sociological analysis. This would represent a considerable diminution of the scope of the sociology of art" (Gutman, 1996: 589). I could not agree more with Gutman that this is one of the great limitations of my study. In any sociology of art, the discourse of the producers includes the language of form, but I did not feel that it was accessible, in this case, to me. I am not a sociologist of art, and I ignored the artifacts to which architects devote their lives. *Mea culpa*.

I wonder – not as an exculpation but as a question – if any writing can reproduce the experience of architecture. It involves us (perhaps "in a state of distraction" as Walter Benjamin said) by sight and movement into a building, in which our steps can take the form of a procession (in Philip Johnson's words), in which our eyes gather a palpable knowledge of textures and our feet a tactile impression of the ground, while we glory inadvertently in forms hollow or full, which invent volume, reinvent space, discover for us the light. If not even photography can portray it, can that experience be *said*? Since buildings are three-dimensional and unmovable, I believe we should try to convey the experience of architecture.[14] I am convinced that architects, when they talk candidly about the artifacts they love, and some critics with the gift of limpid and lucid prose, can describe that experience as I could not do, as even picture books cannot do. Later, I did try to respond to criticism (and self-criticism!) and I did pay attention to the architectural object; but I still borrowed their words to describe architecture more than I relied on my own (Larson, 1997).

Finally, does this shift away from the aesthetic dogma of modernism have any profound consequences? In itself, I do not believe it has. If neo-classical decoration and historicist allusions were the "feel good" emblems of the age of Reagan, as some architects and critics have suggested, then the wheel has turned. Since the beginning of the postmodern shift, the modernist aesthetic was allowed to play its part as just another source of aesthetic inspiration. For a while, in the brief reign of "deconstructivist" aesthetics, the "design supremacists" oriented themselves toward abstract pictorial forms drawn from Russian art in the 1920s (Wigley, 1988). Their clash of diagonal lines and surprising angles may have cleansed architectural vocabulary of pediments, columns, curved walls, and applied decoration, but it is not likely that the deconstructivists' dislocated forms will age much better than the historicist affectations. After all, it may well be, as Herbert Muschamp keenly suggests, that both currents made their most profound impression on architecture schools through the power of beautiful and new drawings (the historicists through Michael Graves', the deconstructivists through Zaha Hadid's). In any case, the revisionist shift has neither changed the role of the architect in construction, nor arrested the profession's conversion from an actor in production to an actor in marketing strategies; all our economy and all our culture have swerved in that direction. The "discursive wars" that I connected to architectural practices mattered very little beyond the circle of architects and cognoscenti. If, however, the clients (as I argued) welcomed any turn in architecture that facilitated the marketing of real estate, a larger public may have found a back entrance (though I doubt it) into making its preferences felt.

Unlike other disciplines and other arts engaged in the discursive battles of the various *post-s*, architecture matters for much larger numbers of people than does painting, say, or philosophy, or even dance or poetry. But it matters as building, *as type form*, not as form. I wrote, and I stand firmly by it: "When architects and critics scoff at traditional postmodernism as an architecture 'for the age of Reagan,' they refer mainly to *style* . . . Yet the architectural sign of the period was less a style than the overabundance of office and retail space, luxury hotels, rich men's homes, and cultural institutions for the elite" (Larson, 1993: 243–244). Type refers to program, and program refers to clients. Many contemporary architects claim the sociological legacy of the modernist movement which, in its heroic phase, sought to make the whole society its client. We should be grateful to those who believe that striving for beauty, that mysterious and elusive thing, is the most intelligent way of serving that whole client. I wanted my book to respect the complexity of what they do, as a way of saying thanks. Durable artifacts charged with symbolic power are objects of art; the objects created by architecture serve us, while trying to give form to our civilization. That always seems to me more important than sociological analysis.

Notes

I would particularly like to thank Harvey Molotch and José Gámez for their acute discussion of my book (Larson, 1993) at The Cultural Turn Conference (February 1997), and all the participants in the session, notably Roger Friedland, and Paul Hirsch.

1. The Getty Center in Los Angeles, designed by Richard Meier and built at the cost of one billion dollars, encountered relentless opposition from the affluent residents of Brentwood, the neighborhood now crowned by the massive beige and white pile of the Getty. The urban critic Mike Davis, reviewing Richard Meier's account for *The Nation* (Davis, 1997), writes that in 1987, before starting construction, Meier and the clients had "to surrender to 107 points of revision in an extraordinary agreement devised by the homeowners' lawyers." These included: a drastic reduction of height, which "entailed enormous excavations to contain the rest of the museum's bulk"; a shuffling around of mountains of dirt because the neighbors objected to a convoy of dump trucks; a ban on Meier's favorite glossy white surfaces for the exterior; and accommodation to the neighbors' obsession "that the center would be used as an observation platform for voyeurs." Nor was that Meier's only ordeal, for in all but cost he had to submit to the chairman of the Getty Trust and the museum director (Davis, 1997: 34–35). The story is different, but no less political, with the other museum marvel of the 1990s, the Bilbao Guggenheim Museum, designed by Frank Gehry of Los Angeles in the Basque country of Spain. The Bilbao Guggenheim is expected to invigorate the deindustrialized city, and push it toward a radiant cosmopolitan future of services and culture. In a highly charged political context, the museum will cost each of the inhabitants of Bilbao $700 a piece; it will require a minimum annual subsidy equivalent to half the budget of the public Basque University, with 3,500 professors and 60,000 students; and the deal was concluded in a secret agreement between the Guggenheim and the Basque authorities. Before opening, the museum had already become a target for the terrorists of ETA (Zulaika, 1997: 61–62).

2. In fact, when we hear complaints about one of these famous architects' abuse of power, it is because he has favorites, or because he has blacklisted someone whose work he dislikes, most often in an architectural competition, or in academic hiring (Larson, 1994).

3. He told me after seeing the finished book that he had thought it would be like his friend Eisenman's never finished "Terragni book."

4. This is as good a place as any to express once again my gratitude to SCASSS, the Swedish Collegium for Advanced Study in the Social Sciences, not only for being SCASSS (as close to a scholar's paradise as I had known) but for being in Uppsala, one of the prettiest towns in the world, and in Sweden, where everything I ever thought was possible in the making of humane urban environments is often achieved.

5. I remember hearing George Kassabaum, of the large Saint Louis firm HOK (Helmut Obata Kassabaum), saying at a conference that there are two types of client, "those who want it good, and those who want it Wednesday." I would believe after this research that good clients want both things. Whether they allow for beauty is another story.

6. For a full treatment of the important topic of celebrity, see Gamson (1994).

7. The partial, and always cited exceptions are Brasilia, first and above all (on which see Holston, 1989), Chandigarh, and Dhaka.

8. Scully said: "There are only four cases where an individual house is not embarrassing [note the qualifier!]: (1) if it is a specially useful prototype of a mass urbanistic development; (2) if it does something really important on a street or a square, to teach us something about urban design; (3) if it represents a breakthrough in plastic imagination, even if it might not be justifiable in terms of a house; or (4) if it is ironic, and thus expresses the human condition" Scully (1966: 162).

9. See the important book by Alexander Tzonis, Liane Lefaivre, and Richard Diamond, which appeared after mine was written (Tzonis et al., 1995).

10. On this subject, see the acute essays in Huyssen (1986).

11. I was struck, at the time, by an example which is among the most lucid. In the conclusion to his essay for the Deconstructivist Architecture exhibit, Mark Wigley writes: "The nightmare of deconstructivist architecture inhabits the unconscious of pure form rather than the unconscious of the architect . . . Each architect releases different inhibitions in order to subvert form in radically different ways. Each makes thematic a different dilemma of pure form. In so doing, they produce a devious architecture, a slippery architecture that slides uncontrollably from the familiar into the unfamiliar toward an uncanny realization of its own alien nature" (Wigley, 1988: 20).

12. Max Steuer says that I do not do what the title announces (Steuer, 1995). Britain has shown enough abstract concern with "the aesthetics and intellectual issues of postmodernism" to nourish the whole English-speaking world.

13. The paper was presented in 1995 at the meetings of the American Sociological Association in Washington, and appears in Larson 2002.

14. The critic Herbert Muschamp, who always writes with uncommon elegance, comments: "I am uncomfortable writing about buildings I have not seen first-hand; but I am writing for an audience that most likely will not get to visit these buildings; and it is not necessary to do so in order to furnish our minds. Architecture is perhaps the most public of the arts, and yet I think that much of its public life is about the mental furnishing made possible by images" (Muschamp, 1990: 106).

References

Becker, Howard. 1982. *Art Worlds*. Berkeley, CA: University of California Press.

Bourdieu, Pierre. 1976. "Le champ scientifique." *Actes de la Recherche en Sciences Sociales* 2–3:88–104.

1993. *The Field of Cultural Production*. New York: Columbia University Press.

Davis, Mike. 1997. "Serene and Sterile." *The Nation* 15:34–36.

Emirbayer, Mustapha, and Jeff Goodwin. 1994. "Network Analysis, Culture, and the Problem of Agency." *American Journal of Sociology* 99/6:1411–1454.

Gamson, Joshua. 1994. *Claims to Fame: Celebrity in Contemporary America*. Berkeley, CA: University of California Press.

Ginzburg, Carlo. 1989. *Clues, Myth, and the Historical Method*. Baltimore, MD: Johns Hopkins University Press.

Gutman, Robert. 1996. Review of M. S. Larson, *Behind the Postmodern Façade*. *Theory and Society* 25:583–589.

Habermas, Jurgen. 1985. "Modern and Postmodern Architecture," in John Forrester, ed. *Critical Theory and Public Life*. Cambridge, MA: MIT Press.

Harvey, David. 1989. *The Condition of Postmodernity*. Oxford: Basil Blackwell.

Holston, James. 1989. *The Modernist City: An Anthropological Critique of Brasilia*. Chicago, IL: University of Chicago Press.

Huyssen, Andreas. 1986. *After the Great Divide*. Bloomington, IN: University of Indiana Press.

Jameson, Fredric. 1987. "Postmodernism, the Cultural Logic of Late Capitalism." *New Left Review* 146:53–92.

Klotz, Heinrich. 1987. *The History of Postmodern Architecture*, trans. Radka Donnell. Cambridge, MA: MIT Press.

Larson, Magali Sarfatti. 1977. *The Rise of Professionalism: A Sociological Analysis*. Berkeley, CA: University of California Press.

1978. *Social Structure and Research Priorities in the Architectural Field*. Report to the American Institute of Architects Research Corporation and NSF.

1983a. "Emblem and Exception: the Historical Definition of the Architect's Professional Role," in Judith Blau, Mark La Gory, and John Pipkin, eds. *Professionals and Urban Form*. Albany, NY: State University of New York Press.

1983b. "The Professional Supply of Design: A Descriptive Study of Architectural Firms" (with George Leon and Jay Bolick), in Judith Blau, Mark La Gory, and John Pipkin, eds. *Professional and Urban Form*. Albany, NY: State University of New York Press.

1993. *Behind the Postmodern Façade: Architectural Change in Late Twentieth Century America*. Berkeley, CA: University of California Press.

1994. "Architectural Competitions as Discursive Events." *Theory and Society* 23/4.

1997. "Reading Architecture in the Holocaust Memorial Museum: a Method and Empirical Illustration," in Elizabeth Long, ed. *Cultural Studies and Sociology*. Oxford: Basil Blackwell.

2002. "Professions' Nomic Functions and the End of Modernity." *European Yearbook in the Sociology of Law*.

Morgan, Ann, ed. 1987. *Contemporary Architects*. Chicago, IL: St. James's Press.

Muschamp, Herbert. 1990. "Proliferations," in K. Michael Hays and Carol Burns, eds. *Thinking the Present: Contemporary American Architecture*. New York: Princeton Architectural Press.

Peterson, Richard. 1994. "Culture Studies through the Production Perspective," in Diana Crane, ed. *The Sociology of Culture*. Oxford: Basil Blackwell.

Schwartzman, Allan. 1997. "Art vs. Architecture." *Architecture* 86:56–59.

Scruton, Roger. 1979. *The Aesthetics of Architecture*. Princeton, NJ: Princeton University Press.

Steuer, Max. 1995. *Journal of Sociology* 46:1.

Stevens, Mitchell. 1994. Review of *Behind the Postmodern Façade. American Journal of Sociology* 99/6:1695–1697.

Tzonis, Alexander, Liane Lefaivre, and Richard Diamond. 1995. *Architecture in North America since 1960*. Boston, MA: Little, Brown and Co.

Venturi, Robert. 1966. *Complexities and Contradictions in Architecture*. New York: Museum of Modern Art.

White, Harrison. 1993. *Careers and Creativity: Social Forces in the Arts*. Boulder, CO: Westview.

Wigley, Marc. 1988. "Deconstructivist Architecture," in Philip Johnson and Mark Wigley, eds. *Deconstructivist Architecture*. New York: Museum of Modern Art.

Zevi, Bruno. 1961. *Storia dell'Architettura Moderna*. Torino: Einaudi.

Zulaika, Joseba. 1997. "The Seduction of Bilbao." *Architecture* 86:61–62.

13

How art works: form and function
in the stuff of life

Harvey Molotch

Design professionals continuously discuss the relative significance of "form" versus "function" in making a good product or a worthy career. Practitioners argue whether it is "art" or "engineering" that matters most or should matter most. Hardly a parochial professional issue or even one restricted to the nature of commercial commodities, the debate involves profound matters of general life priorities – making sense of what to value and why. While worthy of interest in itself, I am also using the field of product design to examine the nature of these larger tensions between the "soft" of life – art, aesthetics, symbolism, whimsy – on the one hand, versus the "hard" – technology, mechanics, economy, and rationality, on the other.

After several years of fieldwork among designers, including interviews with many dozens of them, I have found extremists on both sides. I heard a prominent and commercially successful ceramics designer proclaim to an audience of her peers they had deserted the ideals of enhancing life by creating goods without soul; they should "bring back the beauty and glory of the tabernacle" into the products they create. But I have also heard more engineering-oriented designers ridicule the "beret types" who create "phantom products" – things that nobody will buy because nobody can use them. The most common view is more pragmatic and moderate: something succeeds because it is more functional as well as aesthetically appropriate and achieving this dual goal is one's chief responsibility. Designers observe a correlation between artifacts they judge as having good form and stuff with good functionality – and also of people who they think do both well. Within the profession's sometimes "uneasy mix" of aesthetics and technique – similar to that found in architecture (Brain, 1997: 247) – product designers think "it's both," they say. With this last pronouncement, I agree, but probably for different reasons or at least additional reasons than those usually put forward. This chapter aims for concepts and evidence that can better specify just how "it's both," not just in designers' work but in the more general way that art and the economy are mutually embedded.

Most arguments, even some varieties of "it's both," presume at least a conceptual opposition between the two domains, implying the need either to take sides or figure out a reconciliation. This stance has been at least as common outside the world of product design as in. For art connoisseurs, practical considerations may be necessary to sustain artists, but they are otherwise a threat to aesthetic expression. Indeed, noticing instances of art serving business is enough to rule it out as art altogether. As Max Eastman said of artists who have "gone over" to commerce, the use of their work in advertisements is "an obituary notice of these men as artists" (quoted in Bogart, 1995: 54). Commercial art is an oxymoron, because economic goods, with few exceptions, are – as in the words of eminent critic, Nikolaus Pevsner – hopelessly "shoddy and hideous" (Pevsner, 1960: 46). The resulting schlock degrades sensibilities, encouraging the kind of moral failings that come when commercial kitsch replaces truth and beauty. Under these conditions, art has to be an autonomous antidote to the commercial, not corrupted in its service.

From the left, art's value comes from its potential to *oppose* the economy, at least the economy under capitalism. However ironic, given elite championing of their careers, many prominent artists worked, in their art and politics, against the status quo. Within the Marxian frame, art is supposed to build socialism or at least expose social evils under capitalism. When not obviously doing just this, some kind of hegemonic trick may be afloat. Aesthetics may be dangerous because it deflects workers' attention from the conditions of their exploitation. David Harvey says that "in periods of confusion and uncertainty, the turn to aesthetics (of whatever form) becomes more pronounced" (Harvey, 1989: 328). As another kind of mischief of domination, elites use high art to demean the lower classes; "custodians of culture" (Silverman, 1986) make their artistic "island of the sacred" inaccessible to those from lower strata (Bourdieu, 1990: 134). Such cultural capital not only enhances elite prestige but also sustains financial fortunes across generations (capital goes to capital across spheres and over time) – still another unhappy art–economy mixture.

The most popular stance is that art may be OK, even a good thing, but is ephemeral to the production process – the froth (or maybe even glory) that comes when the business is done. Rather than a first cause of economic innovation, some schools of anthropology (but not all) hold that art happens only when material surplus frees up time and consciousness for the non-essentials. "Men eat before they reason" – and that means well before they decorate, something even further down the Marxian schedule. In one late nineteenth-century view, decoration was even an imitation of practical goods; decorative motifs like the geometric zigzag were thought to have been drawn or carved by "early people" mimicking the fiber courses and cross-hatching they saw in the weaving of their utilitarian (and plain) baskets and clothing.[1] In this version of materialist thought, not only is there no role for art in the creation of industry, it is the industry that inspires the art. In his book on the history of artifacts as well as more contemporary modes of invention, scholar–engineer Henry Petroski argues that the evolution of products comes from their "usefulness," by which he means utility quite apart from any "aesthetic considerations." Such issues of aesthetics, he says:

> may certainly influence, in some cases even dominate, the process whereby a designed object comes finally to look the way it does, but they are seldom the first causes of shape and form, with jewelry and objets d'art being notable exceptions. Utilitarian objects can be streamlined and in other ways made more pleasing to the eye, but such changes are more often than not cosmetic to a mature or aging artifact.

"Design games," he says with seeming pride, "are of little concern to this book" (Petroski, 1992: 32).

In the division of labor, and this is still another symptom of art's marginality, the making and appreciating of art goes to those who take up the unessential tasks, women and effete or neurotic men. Women are relegated to decoration and craft, the arty men more noted for their offbeat genius (as when they cut off an ear). "Ornamentation and emotion," as Dennis Altman observes, are regions "that western and particularly Anglo-Saxon society has defined as feminine preoccupations" (Altman, 1982: 154); see also Wilson (1993). This makes the art teacher, seldom a "real" man, the last hired and first fired. The business-minded give credit to the muscular virtues of competitive drive, including the exploitation of natural resources and others' labor. They keep their effete in the closet.

So what is Art?

Against this background, I need to make the case for art so as to get it out of the production doghouse. I need to get it "up there" with economics so that I can show just how form and function interconnect and indeed constitute one another in making up goods. And to make that possible, I have to say what, at least for my purposes, I think art is. Despite so many noble versions, from Keats to Kant, I need my own not-so-noble variant to help the conceptual job of relating art to economies, forms to functions.

For me, whether or not something is a "work of art" does not lie simply in the thing itself, a painting or dance or melody that in some objective sense transcends. I am with Baudelaire in trying "to establish a rational and his-torical theory of beauty, in contrast to the academic theory of an unique and absolute beauty" (Baudelaire, 1970: 3). Any work (or act) of art must possess, to follow Baudelaire, a "double composition"(Baudelaire 1970: 2). Something wonderful is indeed in the work itself, but whatever that wonderful might be needs its appropriate social and cultural context to be meaningful – "the age, its fashions, its morals, its emotions." Without this second element, which Baudelaire describes as "the amusing, enticing, appetizing icing on the divine cake," the first elements would be beyond "our powers of digestion or appreciation" (Baudelaire, 1970: 3). Rather than ignoring trends of the moment, Baudelaire says, the truly great artist extracts from it "whatever element it may contain of *poetry within history*" (Baudelaire, 1970: 12; my emphasis). I recognize Baudelaire's "divine" in the strong, forceful, and mysterious reactions one has to art, responses that seem to transcend mundane sentiment; but objects do this, in my view, through their capacity to draw upon social–psychological associations that are so richly compressed they come to be experienced as transcendental. In other words, the magic of art is in the way complex social and psychological stimuli are made to conjoin, a kind of *lash-up*² of sensualities.

At a moment, compressed in time and space, come large and small dramas of life juxtaposed in spectacularly particular ways as objects' connotations come into consciousness: stormy nights, sexual thrill, a flowerpot, eating rice crispies, coming home from school, World War II, and all other art one has ever seen before. The list of potential elements is bounded only by lived and imagined experience; each person's response to the object is thus to some degree unique, but, since culture and biographies also have shared elements, each person's response is also, to some degree, a common one. The appeal of an art piece hinges on just who is touched by its assembled meanings.

So complicated, indeed, is the melding in each piece or performance, and this is an essential aspect, that the mechanism of the accomplishment is discursively lost. Art happens when observers feel they cannot know how their response came to be; it is mysterious. This mystery refracts back upon the senses, in an ongoing, instant-by-instant reflexive loop, intensifying the experience of wonder. Whether it is a religious idol whose decoration and form invoke higher beings, a "magnificent" painting hallowed in western cannon, an awesome rendition of "Melancholy Baby" sung to piano, or a good magic trick, art represents uncanny accomplishment. One cannot easily think, "oh, I could do that" by this or that procedure. Beyond proficient craftsmanship, there is, as Alfred Gell put it, "the spectator's inability mentally to rehearse" how to make it happen – a "blockage" in cognition that creates "fascination" or "captivation" (Gell, 1998: 71).

Building on Gell's formulation, we can see art as a sociology of amazement; art involves encapsulating social forces in a form that yields a knowing ignorance. It follows, again with Baudelaire, that what is or is not art depends on the rise and fall of human experience and appreciations of all sorts. The fashion system and the art system are thus inextricably combined. As "the idea of beauty which man creates for himself imprints itself on his whole attire, crumples or stiffens his dress, rounds off or squares his gesture, and in the long run even ends by subtly penetrating the very features of his face" (Baudelaire, 1970). Mounted on top of all the human sensing, and this is underplayed in Baudelaire, are institutional mechanisms to support, celebrate, undermine, and denigrate – all part of the "art worlds," as Becker analyzes it (Becker, 1982). There are also various plots, nefarious and otherwise, as different social classes and cultural groups advocate their versions, sometimes to the disadvantage of others – as Bourdieu so patiently explains (Bourdieu, 1984).

With all this in mind, it becomes easier to see how ordinary goods operate as art. Since every object, and each aspect of every object, is rich with meaning, the right combination – even in goods not considered artistic – carries affect. Sometimes, and in ways inexplicable to those who produce or experience it, the "charge" can be especially strong because of the diverse social–psychological elements bound up with it. A great looking car or dress can tweak the observers' consciousness by embodying feelings that reach beyond more routine acts of taking things in. It is more or less thrilling depending on circumstance: a teenager's first car carries more magic than a professor's final Volvo; a gown for the ball means something different than work pants; a bikini for Club Med has a distinct frisson compared to a hospital smock. This is all true right down to the details in each such object, and, even in mundane things, the rich sensuality is there, including angst or shame when having to make do with things too shoddy, too unoriginal, too conservative or otherwise "not right." At whatever market level, the producer's hoped-for magic involves avoiding such dissatisfactions by hitting a "sweet spot" of linkages across remembrances and anticipations, social projects and duties. Compressing just the right sensual cues into a product is an application of art. From the standpoint of consumers, this makes shopping – accepting this, avoiding that – a kind of art appreciation. Even if the result is nefarious in terms of human and natural destruction – *indeed precisely because it so often is* – we need to see just how the power of art works to do it. I offer evidence of its significance and suggest different ways it happens across a range of products and modes of activity.

Representation

In a way so obvious it is usually invisible, art has to represent what stuff can be before it exists. Modern production presumes effective representations in the form of drawings or models (or computer-based images). Representations do not just show what will be present, but how it will work – perhaps with arrows designating which direction levers go, wheels turn, or hands crank and what moves what – to use an old-fashioned mechanical example. The patent office needs all this and more. In mass production, specificity becomes especially important because extensive investment has to be made up front before a single item comes into being. The breakthrough of the assembly line required accurate renderings, in this case of the tooling apparatuses, the production flow, as well as of the parts used and products to result. For clients, backers, or sometimes retailers, buying-in involves coming to "see" it all before hand – how it will work, feel, or sound. Sometimes the envisioned item is put before venture capitalists. If they do not see in it what the designers want them to see ("get it," as people now say), there will not be money to make it happen. If the product is to go before focus groups, the model, sketch, or prototype must be clear or the research will be invalid.

The development of a textile industry in the early USA was thwarted by a lack of personnel who could understand how machinery, smuggled successfully out of Britain and into the new country after 1783, could be made to work. After four years of effort – the story is told about one incident – machinery parts were shipped back to England unused, and it was another generation before migrant artisans as well as appropriate drawings finally arrived (Basalla, 1988: 83; Jeremy, 1973). A lack of drawing skill in the USA held back the country's industrial development at least until the late nineteenth century (Korzenik, 1985). This led to a movement of remedial drawing classes for workers in the USA, as well as the advent of drawing classes in elementary schools (Korzenik, 1985).

The precise mode of representation, the skills at hand, and the conventions in use, affect the product outcome (see Laffitte, 1995). Concomitant with other aspects of industrial growth, sophistication grew in use of multiple perspectives, shadings, and the other artistic tricks that can communicate proportionality and physical and kinetic relations. The manner of doing this is open to whatever artistic and cultural trends are going on; technical drawing underwent "the same sequence of styles in the fifteenth through nineteenth centuries as the other graphic arts" (Szostak, 1999, paraphrasing Klingender, 1947). It was not until well into the twentieth century that cross-sectional or "cut-away" drawing came about, the first examples being Max Miller's aircraft drawings for plane manufacturing in the UK in the inter-war years (Museum, 1999). Art movements like Dada encouraged greater freedom in representing objects, allowing technical drawings to present images that would never exist in the final product.

Consistent with the general role of art but here in a very direct way, drawings and models integrate across time because they provide a way for different actors to come into the process at different moments. Drawings also integrate across space as they travel from one location to another within a factory, from one factory to another, or across regions. Even as computer graphics substitute for hand drawings, there must be a way for each operative to "check the plans." Many lay people have had a chance to see the process when watching workers combine in constructing or remodeling a house.

Art as pioneer

Beyond drawings and models, another way that art comes first is by providing a "first version" that only later has its practical, economic pay-off. Things now seen as functional developed out of things not evidently functional at all, indeed precisely because – in some cases – they appeared "merely" arty or playful. No one has argued the point more boldly than the eminent MIT metallurgist Cyril Stanley Smith who turned from what today we call materials science to larger analytic frameworks as his career matured. Cultivating and transplanting flowers, says Smith, preceded crop agriculture, while "playing with pets probably gave the knowledge that was needed for purposeful animal husbandry" (Smith, 1981: 329). He speculates that "pleasurable interactive communal activities like singing and dancing" gave birth to language itself. This leads him to the idea that "aesthetic curiosity has been central to both genetic and cultural evolution"(Smith, 1981: 329).

In terms of technological advance, Smith further argues for the primacy of "play domains." Those who first molded baked clay, *circa* 20,000 BC, were making aesthetically pleasing fertility figures (Smith, 1981: 194) – not utilitarian objects. The technology then became the basis for pots, cups, and vessels. Smith describes a host of metallurgical discoveries in which the aesthetic presaged the mechanical (Smith, 1981: 210). Humans used copper metallurgy to make ornaments prior to creating knives and weapons (Smith, 1981: 328). Blast lamps to make decorative beads led to the modern welding torch, forming the basis for modern steel production. Coating base metals by means of electrolytic currents began with depositing gold, silver, or copper to produce jewelry and decorative medals. The copper-coated "bronzes" at the Paris Opera house are examples (Smith, 1981: 215, 230). Objects with such high per-unit costs and difficult technologies get made either because they fulfill the whim of a rich patron or because they are treasured objects of some larger group willing to pay more for something extraordinary. Early electrolytic plating kept a practice around that could explode in importance with the development of better energy sources than the early primitive batteries. Then it became possible to plate mundane objects like tableware and cutlery. The electrical generator and, eventually, the whole electric-power industry thus owe much of their origin to decoration (Smith, 1981: 215, 230). Almost all copper and aluminum came to be produced through electrolytic reduction. Further along, the same process led to inexpensive production of conductors and integrated electronic microcircuits, including those used in computers and microwave equipment (Smith,

1973: 43). While it may take some leaps of faith to accept some of Smith's assertions about prehistory, the evidence from within the industrial era is quite clear-cut – which also makes his Stone Age cases more plausible. It is simply not the case that, as Petroski puts it, "tools are generally acknowledged to be the first artifacts of civilization" (Petroski, 1992: 114). The bias in our thinking is evident in the way we put the burden of proof on the idea that the art could have come first.

Here are some other cases of art preceding the advance of more mundane goods:

> Decorative fountains, particularly those at Versailles, provided the R & D for the means to drain mines and make other advances in hydraulic and nautical engineering.
>
> The desire to replicate Asian glazes, superior in hardness, color, and clarity, led to European advances not just in bone china, but to basic chemical discoveries and geological finds. High-temperature glazing experiments at the British Wedgwood china factory stimulated development of the pyrometer which allowed temperature measurement in environments beyond the capacity of ordinary thermometers – a tool used in other technologies, including by Faraday in his experiments.
>
> Finding ways to alter the taste, appearance, smell, and texture of food made the kitchen, in effect, the "first laboratory" (Goody, 1982: 101) and determined the available equipment for the alchemists (Forbes, 1954, as cited in Goody, 1982) and then early pharmacists and perfumers.
>
> Fun fireworks and their skyward spectacle were the inspiration and technical precursor for all manner of chemical experimentation, as well as modern explosives and missiles (Smith, 1981: 202).
>
> Glass beading was around for centuries prior to the need of scientific equipment, as used in biology and chemistry, to take on complex tubing configurations and transparency. In the world of plastics, the first successful applications of a commercial artificial polymer were for making decorative medallions. Alexander Parkes made "Parkesine" in the early 1860s for this purpose and then others went on to billiard balls and piano keys as the start of the plastics industry (Kaufman, 1963, as cited in Smith 1973: 21).

When something comes along ahead of its time, its art helps keep it around until other elements arrive to make it useful. Materials and techniques that have spiritual, playful, or aesthetic value help hold a place, providing the space for improvements to develop, for the consequentiality to take hold, and maybe for what is later regarded as the efficient solution to come into being. For success to occur, a given element has to be kept in play until the other pieces arrive. Then, when the complementary elements do come together, they can lock-in or lash-up, and a new inertia sets in; they become "interactively stabilized" (Pickering, 1995:17).

Building markets

Markets depend on people wanting things and art, in one form or another, massively involved guides wants toward one thing or the other. Whether seen as involving illegitimate seduction or simply the way the world always works, markets cannot be understood as existing without their sensual dimension. In the pleasure of driving a car, feeling the texture of a door knob, hearing the sound of a computer click, or taking in the look of a dental drill, the sensual makes stuff worth having and in that sense adds to goods' functionality. Again, we have an illustrative list and I invite the consumer/reader to skip about to the goods of most appeal given personal niche and amount of time to read this chapter.

Clothing

A taste for printed textiles created demand for hand-blocked designs on cotton from India (calico) and massive imports into Britain, but political conflict in India caused a supply shortage starting in the mid-eighteenth century. The "rage for calico" could not be satisfied, threatening sectors of the British textile industry that depended upon shipments of the fabric. In response, Chandra Mukerji argues (Mukerji, 1983; see also L. C. A Knowles as cited in Mukerji, 1983: 221), Hargreaves invented the spinning jenny and Arkwright (then a wig maker), the waterframe almost simultaneously in the 1760s. The result made possible an inexpensive British-made cotton fabric with a texture smooth and strong enough to take printing. This was followed by the invention of the Bell engraved cylinder system that machine-rolled designs on to the fabric. British consumers could have their florals and Britain maintain its industrial hegemony – another case of art in the lead.

   A strong British desire for color, in clothing and other goods in the early nineteenth century, generated the search for natural dyes that led to the first systematic botanical investigations. These were precursors to scientific classification and a stimulant to hybridization for agricultural as well as ornamental purposes. Within a few decades of the first British advances, German experimenters created the synthetic-dye industry that was to "revolutionize the relationship between science and technology by employing research scientists to advance industrial goals" (Basalla, 1988). This propelled German firms into chemical leadership. By the new century, the same avenue of research led to German primacy in synthetic fertilizer production as well as other commodities (Chapman, 1991), forming companies like Bosch and BASF.

Clothing makers today see their sales rise and fall depending upon how well they can satisfy ongoing and ever-changing sensibilities. Sometimes, the very fact of clothing is a fashion "extra." Even in colder zones, clothing is not necessarily forced by the need to survive. Indigenous peoples in cold climates of Australia and Tierra del Fuego kept warm through diet and appropriate exercise.[3] At least to a degree, clothing is an alternative means of protection, one that decreases the body's ability to protect itself and, especially in the absence of regular laundering facilities, incubates disease. Rudofsky points out that ankle support was thought to be a health necessity at the turn of the century, thus creating high-top shoes for women, whose ankles, in fact, became weak. Maybe arch supports and shoe padding are also mistakes. Shoes do little for most people, even purportedly comfortable ones. After aesthetic preferences create dependence, aesthetics further take over in shaping the solutions.

The sartorial rules of colonials in the tropics ("mad dogs and Englishmen") are only one outlandish example of people dressing without regard to functional need. Under the taste tyranny they then imposed, native peoples had to wear clothing appropriate to European climates and sensibilities. Of course, such garments were "adjusted" for the lower standing of the indigenous peoples, while also taking in local tastes. The muu-muus of Hawaiian women, now something of an "indigenous" tradition, reflect missionaries' need to cover up a lot of flesh of people who had little money, but in a land of color. This has now blended into a garment of island pleasure, part of summer wardrobes across the US.

However misguided and based in unjust dominance, the colonials were doing what they "thought best," given their moment and space of life. Making others, as with oneself, into "proper" people is a never-ending mission of manipulating appearances to display gender, status, community, activity, season, and time of day. In all these regards, there is no time out. Getting even minor matters wrong marks a betrayal of "sartorial conscience," and may imply severe effrontery (Bell, 1947; as quoted in Entwistle and Wilson, 1998). A man walking around outside in his briefs undercuts a whole life of competent living. People have nightmares about going to work without clothes, maybe just without socks, or simply mismatched ones. The desires for the right thing at the right time can be intense. As the US cross-dresser Rue Paul has said, we are each born naked and all the rest is drag. Working the drag, an art in itself, becomes a matter of social and even physical necessity.

Spice and gold

People's desire for spice and glitter stimulated the great treks and voyages over the earth, forever changing all that came after. Starting at least as far back as Roman trade in the time of Alexander, sponsors were looking to enhance pleasure in the food they ate rather than increasing yields or adding caloric value. Marco Polo found the southern Sung capital dense with restaurants and inns serving a wide range of exotic ingredients to populations hierarchically organized by taste preference and wealth, signaling the importance of food aesthetics and a spice trade already in operation (Goody, 1982). First coming to Europe from India and then from the eastern Mediterranean via the Crusades, mass taste for sugar led to slave plantations of the New World, among other social and economic consequences (Mintz, 1979). Taste for coffee and tea brought analogous transformations in domestic production systems and population displacements, including the transformation of Latin American peoples into virtual coffee slaves (Pendergrast, 1999). These crops lack nutritional value or industrial application. Gold, of course, is also an aesthetic product. Perhaps because of their very sensual nature, spice and gold tend to be forgotten as transforming the world; "progress" is instead recorded as milestones in navigational technology rather than as evolutions in decor and gastronomy.

Baked goods

In the US, people's desire for white bread over dark altered not only the rural plains but also the future of the urban Midwest. As Cronon explains: "Because people had long associated white flour with diets of the wealthy, it had a higher status than other flours did" (Cronon, 1991: 376). In trying to meet this desire, the Minnesota and Dakota areas suffered an agricultural disadvantage because their wheat had a hard kernel (the bran) "which tended to clog and burn in ordinary millstones." This so-called "winter wheat" could not be milled to produce the preferred whiter flour – a type produced in the milder climates to the south in Kansas, Illinois, and Indiana; but the northern producers responded by adapting machines from Eastern Europe that separated the heavy bran and wheat germ from the rest of the grain, resulting in the "new process" flour with a whiteness even "purer" than that produced from competing places. Minneapolis (and then geographically similar Battle Creek, Michigan – home of Kellogg's) became the largest centers for flour processing, breakfast cereals, and baked goods in the world, with Pillsbury and General Mills the huge milling and baking corporations. Intersecting with the technological changes it helped create, the new process altered the kind of farming that would be done on the land, the firms that prospered, as well as certain aspects of human physiology and ailments associated with a low-fiber diet.

Restaurants

Some of the appeal of eating out comes from utility, like inns for traders, but much came about just to enhance life's diversions. The Frenchman Jean-Anthelme Brillat-Savarin may have exaggerated only slightly when he said in 1825, referring to taxes paid on spices and innkeeper fees, that "gourmands are the chief mainstay of every nation's wealth" (Brillat-Savarin, 1970: 134). What we think of today as restaurants (as opposed to roadside inns) had their European beginnings as places where the emerging commercial elites could experience sumptuous surroundings that only the aristocracies could command. Especially in the grand hotels that often housed the best restaurants in the latter part of the nineteenth century, new types of foods and styles of eating were opened to larger audiences (Finkelstein, 1989).

Today, restaurants are among the largest economic sectors (US sales are above $150 billion annually),[4] Operators concern themselves with details of the sociability being served up – the age and cultural niche of the clientele, the type of events taking place – dating, family dinners, celebrations (see Zukin, 1995). Even at the level of fast-food operations, "ambiance," "presentation," and choreography matter; professionals help determine the kind of music, if any, as well as type and level of ambient "noise" that should be heard. The food itself is in a fashion system, judged better or worse by reckoning of culinary commentators and gossip among the clientele.

Furniture

The bed is anthropologically odd: "where it exists, its readily traced ancestor is the throne," says Brendan Gill (1989: 42). Chairs are also unusual among world peoples over history most of whom squat, sit flat on the ground, use hammocks, or recline on platform-type structures. Islamic peoples traditionally did without furniture almost completely, creating both home and public life on elaborate rugs. From the archaeological evidence, chairs existed as early as the Neolithic Age, but as an expression of authority rather than for relief from standing (Cranz, 1999: 32). Pervasive among the Greek and Roman citizens, slaves did not use them nor did those who were conquered in the colonies. The Last Supper is fraudulent in its depiction of the diners as sitting. Jesus and his group were too lowly to be using chairs; they would be reclining on that night just as they would on other nights. The chair disappeared even in the West during the medieval period for purposes other than to signal status, as in ecclesiastical settings. When

European chairs spread to Africa, first by the Portuguese, they were again taken up as signifiers of prestige and power.[5] It is a misunderstanding to think of today's furniture reproductions of "period" pieces as simulating prior ways of life without realizing they were used by only a small segment of the population at the time – and for different purposes than they are now put.

That children hate to sit, Cranz points out, is a developmental cue to the superfluousness of chairs (Cranz, 1999). Mao had it right, quoting a Han poet, that: "When one travels in a sedan chair, the body begins to decay" (quoted in Gell, 1998: 149). The chair's danger to posture, bone development, and healthy defecation is evidence that something other than inherent functionality lies behind it. Having lost the technique and muscle power to squat, Europeans and North Americans now are so dependent upon them that they must resort to sitting on dirty steps – something that can strike chair-free peoples as disgusting. For so many, the chair, like the bed, clothes, and shoes, has become a necessary prosthetic device. The aesthetic has invaded (and snatched) their bodies.

Through the items they buy and how they place them, people make their homes into arenas of precision consumption and cultural production "rather than a site of anxious coccooning" (Williams, 1982: 9). As with a museum curator who must contend with competing demands and an amalgam of goals, people acquire and insert their choices into an evolving context with a connoisseur's eye. They also put up with and participate in a discourse of critique, with some of their productions more or less successful and some individuals and groups more or less talented. Neighborhood consumption gossip contains judgments, schools of thought, and realms of contestation – including summary praise and condemnations of particular ethnicities, races, social classes, and genders.

Goods tend to imply one another, on grounds of both taste and sentiment (things have "style" compatibility), but also because of physical mutuality. With the coming of chairs came the commode as well as the manufacture of tables of an appropriate height. Higher seating altered the location and nature of decoration and detailing, placement of windows, and design of other architectural elements. All this, once in place, comes back to reinforce the chair as an appropriate element of the interior tableau. As Cranz points out from woeful personal experience, the naturalization of the chair becomes evident to those who might otherwise ease their back pain by lying on the floor to conduct business.

Automobiles

Of all the realms of productive seduction, automobiles are perhaps the most noticed. Roland Barthes recorded the "intense amorous studiousness" with which attendees at a 1950s Paris exhibition admired a new model Citroen car: "the bodywork, the lines of union are touched, the upholstery palpated, the seats tried, the doors caressed, the cushions fondled" (Barthes, 1993: 90). Barthes continued:

I think that cars today are almost exactly the equivalent of the great Gothic cathedrals: I mean the supreme creation of an era, conceived with passion by unknown artists, and consumed in image if not in usage by a whole population which appropriates in them a wholly magical object.

(Barthes, 1993: 88)

The history of car production displays what goes wrong when makers think the car is a practical device for transit rather than permeated by artistic projects. Understanding the car as magical object was not in Henry Ford's repertoire. Amply celebrated for his innovations in parts standardization, the assembly line, and the $5-a-day wage, Ford's artistic obtuseness almost cost him the company. His great success with the Model T – at one point, half the world's cars were Model Ts – caused him to think in terms of a standard product as the permanent basis of the industry. Even as he recounts these events, the prominent industrial historian David Hounshell seems to echo Ford's mistaken view that, whereas furniture involves "a deeply personal statement of a consumer's taste and personality," cars do not (Hounshell, 1984). But I figure consumers accepted the Model T because for most, the alternative was a horse, a wagon, a trolley, or their feet – not another kind of car. Any car that actually ran went faster than just about anything else on earth; it was a kick and a social marker. When they could buy a car that even more closely allowed them to express their "taste and personality," they went for it.

Adhering to the transportation theory of cars, Ford's production equipment gave no consideration to the design changes that would become a regular mark of the car business. Hence "the boxy body of the Model T . . . was maintained long after the technology was available for a more streamlined design because the metal stamping machines that were installed in the Ford plants could not create curved panels."[6] Ford's production tools could do only one thing, albeit one thing well; half of them had to be scrapped when he finally did make the move toward "styling." Because his machines were also placed so close together on the shop floor, altering or removing one piece of machinery meant dislodging others. Perhaps most problematic, the company had only a weak organizational capacity for planning new models and figuring out how to change sourcing, marketing, or handle the dealer network in connection with conversions. As a result, Ford had to resort to long and massive layoffs during the first model changeovers in the latter 1920s. To retool for its first style-oriented car, the Model A, Ford lost $18 million, providing "the most expensive art lesson in history" (Meikle, 1990: 52). Henry Ford's philosophy of "any color you want as long as it's black," lowered his company's market share from 55 per cent in the early 1920s to less than 15 per cent in 1927 (Hounshell, 1984: 276). In terms of corporate health, this was entirely dysfunctional.

General Motors was the chief beneficiary. Its cars outsold Ford's, and at higher prices. The business and social science experts usually attribute GM's success to the supposed organizational brilliance of the multi-divisional form – GM as a series of competing car divisions under the same corporate roof (Chandler, 1977). Whatever validity that view may have, the aesthetic was a distinct – and unsung – GM edge. At about the same time in the late 1920s that the multi-division form was up and running, GM got into style in a big way. The company brought in Harley Earl who had earlier fame customizing cars for movie stars in Los Angeles. Beginning with his inaugural project, the 1927 La Salle car, and leading to the world's first automobile styling department set up under his direction, GM enjoyed its first solid run of profitability. Earl would become a GM vice-president, and his "taste for 'Hollywood' styling" – as General Motors president, Alfred P. Sloan, Jr., approvingly called it – took love of cars and the amount people will pay for them to higher levels. This role of design has fallen between the cracks because industry critics take seduction for granted and have little interest in its competitive advantage, while business experts, preoccupied with rational efficiencies, have some trouble acknowledging seduction even when it hits them over the head.

After first innovating with color, including two-tone styling and coordination of interior and exteriors, Earl moved GM into deeper changes in body shapes and engineering details. To get a more rakish line, Earl smoothed steel over a built-in luggage compartment (today's "trunk" or "boot") to replace what had begun as, in fact, a bolted-on trunk (Bayley, 1983: 116). This also became the place to put the spare tire that could then come off the car's exterior. To mold steel into the shapes he needed, engineers created dye casts to follow the desired forms, including the GM hardtop arrangement. GM developed a special steel simultaneously "flexible enough and strong enough to endure the tremendous strain" of the molding processes (Pound, 1934: 293–294). The streamline look, with a rolled steel body, enhanced the car's aerodynamic efficiency, decreased the number of its parts, lowered labor costs, increased security against theft, and quieted the ride. Analogous taste and engineering changes were moving through other product realms. Raymond Loewy designed the first streamlined locomotives for Pennsylvania Railroad, eliminating rivets he thought made the train look "unfinished and clumsy" (quoted in Petroski, 1992: 168) and in so doing saved millions in fabricating costs.

Although the technologies did not go backward, some aspects of car fashion did. While the spare tire stayed inside the car, later nostalgic turns in taste favored at least its simulation on the rear exteriors of some luxury models, like the Lincoln Continental, Cadillac Biarritz, and Buick Riviera. Thus a tire on the exterior, which was considered neither functional nor attractive (which is why Earl removed it), came back as a signal of luxury, only to disappear again from view. As I write, the exterior spare has returned again, this time on sports utility vehicles (not a simulation this time). Perhaps they help SUV drivers tell the world they are beyond conventional suburbanism, capable of rough country searches for lost arks or endangered species. Even here, as with prior stylistic modifications, the practical inventions caused by prior taste change continued "underneath." At no point was there reversion to prior modes of fabrication or technology.

Eventually all of the big US car companies were to get the styling message, with Ford becoming as enthusiastic as any other maker. By the 1950s, GM and Ford moved into what art historian Edson Armi calls "more irregularly sculpted cars (that) have more in common with the automatism of postwar expressionist painters and their biomorphic fantasies" (Armi, 1990: 53) with, in the case of the flagship 1957 Cadillac, "Duchamp, Gropius and Marinetti all commingled in the tail fin" (Varnedoe and Gopnik, 1991: 407). These were giddy days of exuberance and profit, but, as happens, things changed (again). While not the only issue involved, design weakness led the Big Three to lose out to foreign producers who eschewed their chrome bucket reruns. Designers often disagree on aesthetic issues, but in neither print nor conversation, in the US or another part of the world, have I seen designer praise for US autos of the late 1970s and 1980s. *Fortune* magazine, in a 1988 review of "five products U.S. Companies Design Badly," listed cars, making an exception for the then new Ford Taurus (Dumaine, 1988: 130).[7] Cars from Germany, Italy, and most triumphantly Japan have been more highly regarded for their styling as well as fuel efficiency and – with the Italian exception – reliability. The combination of failings in the US product cost hundreds of thousands of manufacturing jobs, devastated Midwest economies, and eroded billions in corporate worth. All this because, at least in part, US makers were unable to find the right art when they needed it.

The Japanese and German designers faced no form–function trade-off in making such successful models, and it is just as clear that US cars were not made ugly so as to be more functional; for decades, *Consumer's Guide* (as well as numbers of class action law suits) documented US failures across the board, including lack of safety. It may be that aesthetics do not dictate car reliability or a quieter ride, but a larger aesthetic sensibility may make more likely the imaginings of forms that allow for such advances to occur. Aesthetic speculation, carried out with focused enthusiasm, may offer frameworks for technologies that otherwise would not exist. Loving a look stimulates dissatisfaction, experimentation, and reconfiguration thereby increasing technical skills and capacities; design dissatisfaction does not just come, as Petroski argues (1992: 32), because a product works less well.

Visions

Getting to a new thing, even if only involving small and incremental steps, requires leaps toward something that does not yet exist. Art helps leaps. Necessity is *not*, Smith emphasizes, the mother of invention:

a man desperately in search of a weapon or food is in no mood for discovery; he can only exploit what is already known to exist. Discovery requires aesthetically motivated curiosity, not logic, for new things can acquire validity only by interaction in an environment that has yet to be.   (Smith, 1981: 325)

Children, Baudelaire explains, are always "drunk" with inspiration, always "in a state of newness," and ready to take on the world unburdened by practicalities or conventions. This is the element that even in adulthood makes the creative difference; "genius," says Baudelaire, "is nothing more nor less than childhood recovered at will" (Baudelaire, 1970: 8).

For those working toward design solutions, visual representations "hit," sometimes in a flash, and stimulate more precise resolutions. Such "pre-analytic visions" (Schumpeter, quoted in Daly, 1996: 6) offer a glimpse of how something could work, the form it might take, and, for the creator, the thrill that goads even tedious efforts to work out the details. The desired outcome becomes "a standard for discovery" (Rothstein, 1999) – a kind of template that causes one solution to replace another, a basis for judging alternatives. "There is no doubt," Terry Smith reflects, "that nonscientific, even nonverbal, thought plays a crucial role in all invention, including that of engineers" (Smith, 1993). A vast amount of testimony from various discoverers lines up in support. Physicist P. A. M. Dirac (1963; quoted in Arnheim, 1994: 35) wrote "it is more important to have beauty in one's equations than to have them fit experiment." Statistician C. Radhakrisna Rao says: "No discovery of great importance has ever been made by logical deduction. A necessary condition for creativity is to let the mind wander unfettered by the rigidities of accepted knowledge" (1994). Andrew Strominger, the contemporary pioneer of string theory in physics, is guided by "a sense of aesthetics, of what would be the most satisfying possible answer to the problem." Then he works backward toward a solution. "Another physicist would say: If A and B, then C. And he's out to prove it. I would say: Gosh, Wouldn't C be nice? And then try to prove it" (Cole, 1997). Similar testimonies have come from the likes of Benoit Mandelbrot, Richard Feynman, Leo Szilard, Jonas Salk, and Einstein himself (Damasio, 1994).[8]

Physical objects, whether viewed in the mind or seen with the eyes, provide stability for otherwise abstract and difficult notions. Experiments show it is harder to learn logical propositions when expressed formally ("If a, then b") compared to expressions that incorporate "real" objects ("If Socrates is a man . . . then Socrates is mortal") (D'Andrede, 1989). Similarly, it is easier to solve analytic problems based on assumptions of speed, time, and distance by attaching a scenario of trains leaving stations than trying to hold it all as mathematical symbols. By utilizing known cultural objects, including spatial and geographic phenomena, people can more easily manipulate dynamic scenarios: "In order to remember a long sequence of ideas, one associates the ideas, in order, with a set of landmarks in the physical environment" (Hutchins, 1999: 9). The desktop metaphor in Macintosh and Windows computing mobilizes this advantage. These objects and landmarks that so serve thought do their job because of the compressed cultural meanings, including emotional and aesthetic valences, attached to them. The common stereotype is wrong that art and utility reside as separate realms lodged in different parts of the brain, left vs. right. More advanced cognitive science poses a different imagery. For people to proceed in any kind of problem solving, "feeling" must be present. At a very basic level of brain functioning, art and utility not only operate in conjunction, but also presuppose one another. People who have had accidents that leave lesions in their ventromedial frontal segment of the brain show severe loss of affect along with diminished capacity to reason their way through ordinary life problems. Writing of experimental results on such individuals, Damasio (1994: 54) remarks that "the powers of reason and the experience of emotions decline together," even when other skills such as memory for facts and language remain strong. Feelings, based on emotional sensations, act as "somatic markers" (Damasio, 1994) that help establish priorities of what to think about and in what order. They are:

> boosters to maintain and optimize working memory and attention concerned with scenarios of the future. In short, you cannot formulate and use adequate "theories" for your mind and for the mind of others if something like the somatic marker fails you.
>
> (Damasio, 1994: 219)

Since a great enemy of the ability to display rational competence is the multitude of possible courses of action at every life juncture, the discriminating force of emotion becomes an indispensable resource. I speculate that every cognized object or element of an object carries some sort of feeling; these serve to better hold them in memory and hence make them available for complex combinations over time. We think through objects, but objects are helpful because of the sentiments with which they come.

This makes it quite obvious that whether as designer or consumer, people do not cognize form and function as separate elements to be weighed as more or less valuable compared to one another. They come as a single gestalt or "blend" (Fauconnier and Turner, 1998, passim), rather than as separable "additives." This explains why people often have trouble explaining just why they like something and why designers often have trouble explaining where they gain their ideas. Cognizing a chair may take in the fact of a certain durability; it also might take in rest for a weary body. Such perceptions contain the practical as well as the sensual: the durability may bring a feeling of having acted soundly in acquiring (or designing) such a chair; anticipating a resting place invokes past rests, necking, or just a well-deserved "taking a load off." When apprehending an object, aesthetics and practicality combine as the very nature of the thing.

There is one way that the aesthetic must be the more basic and that is in motivating people to do all this combining. Smith sums it up: "Paradoxically man's capacity for aesthetic enjoyment may have been his most practical characteristic for it is at the root of his discovery of the world about him, and it makes him want to live" (Smith, 1971, as cited in Postrel, 1998: 134). Life is a job, including the moment to moment cognitive work involved in doing all this unceasing blending. A search for thrills and ecstasies is more than an accessory of a high material standard of living; the poor seek and experience them too. People do even dangerous things, regardless of their impracticality, maybe even because of it. In Klein's strong statement, "cigarettes are sublime" (Klein, 1993). Pleasure comes not just through biologic addiction, but through social and symbolic appeal; cigarettes – given time and place – can signal status, gender, sophistication, maturity, daring, and sexiness.[9] "To be on the wire is life; the rest is waiting," the acrobat Karl Wallenda explained in returning to the high wire after his troupe's fatal Detroit accident (Goffman, 1967). The high drama of high wires aside, products are not merely a matter of function or thrill, but both in a single case and across all the stuff that comes our way.

Fine art

Among the objects that act as landmarks for thinking, especially for certain kinds of people, are works of fine art. For product designers, the art world is a kind of vision R & D center. The avant-garde, Crowe says, "searches out areas of social practice not yet completely available to efficient manipulation and makes them discrete and visible" (Crowe, 1983: 25). The painting and sculpture collections of the Museum of Modern Art have been called "an immense quarry from which designers of every sort could draw inspiration for one or another of their practical ends" (Danto, 1992: 152). It is evidence, flattering in my view, that the museum lives outside its walls not only in the material it takes in but also in what it gives off. One upshot is that what goes on in the art world influences, through the designers, what stuff can be.

More directly and self-consciously than in other realms, designers of textiles and clothing go directly to the fine arts for possibilities. Such designers often have backgrounds in art and this gives them access to the whole panoply of period dress displayed in the history of art – something which they can then draw upon in influencing a next set of styles (Hollander, 1988). Recognized avant-garde artists, like Sonia Delaunay and Natalia Goncharova, ended up in Parisian couture in the 1920s. There were numbers of others who played roles in design and production: Leger, Dufy, Oskar Schlemmer, and other artists associated with movements like the Wiener Werkstatte, Bauhaus, futurism, and constructivism. Because clothing is a product people have in multiples and change often, each moment in art history can register.

Elsa Schiaparelli, the woman who dominated Paris fashion in the 1920s, surrounded herself with the famous Surrealists, in some cases commissioning them to come up with design ideas for her collections. At the extreme, Dali designed a woman's hat in the form of an inverted high-heeled shoe and a man's dinner jacket with external bra and hanging cocktail glasses. Wild concoctions use impractical materials, like cellophane, steel mail, or ephemeral thistledown. Unwearable and outrageous, they are tamed and made commercial, sometimes by the same designers who did the originals. The Italian futurist, Thayhat, working with couturier Madeleine Vionnet used the bias cut to create dresses with a close fit and the fluid kinetic look idealized by futurism. Chanel acted as a vehicle for modernism, celebrated by Hollander for "the working beauty of the garment in wear" (quoted in Wollen, 1998: 13). In the mid 1960s Yves Saint Laurent turned Mondrian directly into a cocktail dress.

The theatre is another halfway point for goods from art (Clark, 1998). The "visual excesses" of the Ballets Russes scandalized Paris in 1909 and set off a rage for the "mode orient" in women's clothing, including ankle-tight hobble skirts, short minaret-shaped tunics, and wide belts. These styles traveled into other theatre productions and the movies through Paul Poiret, "king of Paris fashion," and designer of US-made pictures. Among his contributions was the invention, in 1912, of the brassiere. Besides their work as set designers, modern artists created stage curtains and character costumes – again, people like Matisse, Leger, Chagall, Picasso, Miro, Depero, and – in the present day – David Hockney. Isadora Duncan's neo-Greek costumes helped launch the Hellenistic dress styles that we associate with the post-World War I years (Wollen, 1998), as with the Fortuny "classic." This style later became the "flapper look" as it drifted further from the Greek prototype. In the current moment, the deconstruction movement in architecture, criticism, the theatre, and other creative realms finds a parallel in the emerging arena of "contradictory clothes" (Wollen, 1998: 16) – the uses of bulges and hangings that distort the presentation of the human body.

At the pole opposite that of frivolous clothes, new visions in art can translate into new visions for war. Besides innovations in painting, literature, song,

Figure 13.1   Tub study, inspired by Matisse. © Studio Levien.

poems, and theatricals to encourage fighting and sacrifice, World War I also marked the coming of a different mode of battledress and choreography. Overhead bombing, new at the time (from long-range artillery and then planes) turned visibility from an advantage into a liability. Intimidation through displays of fierce regalia or redcoat power dressing was over. It was a time for camouflage, which came to the French Army via cubism. The developer of the technique, Guirand de Scevola, was explicit:

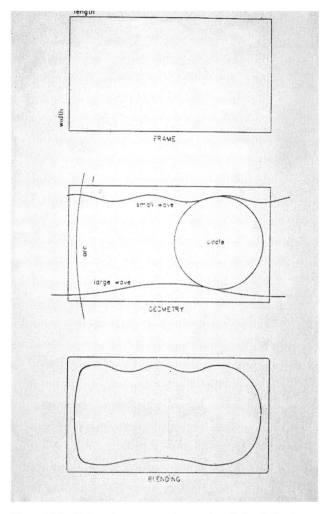

Figure 13.2   Tub study – ergonomic exercise. © Studio Levien.

In order to totally deform objects, I employed the means Cubists used to represent them – later this permitted me, without giving reasons, to hire in my (army) section some painters, who, because of their very special vision, had an aptitude for denaturing any kind of form whatsoever.   (Kern, 1983: 155)

By the end of the war, 3000 artists were at work as camoufleurs.

The Maginot Line was another artistic vision. The war engineers adapted bent-steel molds that avant-garde architects had used to form concrete into fanciful shapes; some of the miseries of the defenders took place within these types of battlements. The technologies of concrete forming, beginning in nineteenth-century France, were pushed forward by abstract sculpture as well as interrelated engineering discoveries (Gabetti and Marconi, 1968 as cited in Guillen, 1997: 705). The twin technologies, camouflage and Maginot Line, probably prolonged the war to end all wars by enhancing defense; otherwise artillery, air bombing, and tanks would have wiped out bright armies less secure than those surrounded by molded concrete. The preanalytic visions of the artists of new ways to paint and sculpt became shelf items for the art-savvy warmakers.

Art helps war along in other ways too. The *International Herald Tribune* art critic pronounced an exhibit of Italian armor "one of the most beautiful shows ever at the Met" (Melikian, 1998: 9), referring both to the quality of the installation as well as its content. According to the Smith and Wesson handgun product manager Herb Belin, "A firearm is no different from any other product . . . Its design is based on engineering and aesthetic needs." Bullish on business, he explained in 1996, "there is a whole new uninitiated consumer group and they are very influenced by aesthetic presentation" (Owen, 1996: 57). Perhaps it is easier to shoot a handsomely designed US, M16, or German G3 rifle than a clumsy Soviet-styled submachine gun Kalashnikov AK47.[10] War goods derive from art, but then – as in the case, say, of Italian futurists spellbound by bombs and bomber planes used in World War I, come back into art forms, which then go up again into missiles and other armaments.

Sometimes, it seems, art can itself become the war. Just as people can use goods in more or less bad ways to show off, they can use art in more or less bad ways to dominate one another. According to Gell: "the Maori found themselves unable to compete with one another (or Europeans) via the traditional warlike means. Their competitive spirit focused more and more on the construction of large, elaborately carved and painted meeting houses, each Maori community trying, so far as lay within its power, to outdo its neighbors and rivals in this respect" (Gell, 1992: 251). Building palaces, creating vast art collections and erecting elaborate tombs may be still other ways that art operates as aggression, but minus the blood.

In routine peace times, some design activists consciously advocate particular art movements as appropriate for goods' inspiration. In the famous late nineteenth-century British version of the "Arts and Crafts" school, William Morris and his associates created a complete home inventory of products – furniture, wallpaper, dishware, fabrics, and bedding – modeled after paintings and crafts of the day. Adherents mimicked romantic paintings, like the idyllic nature scenes of Gwynn-Jones and Lord Leighton, as well as the popular renditions of natural forms like flowers, leaves, and acorns. There were other variants across Europe and North America of explicit match-ups between art currents and merchandise – De Stijl in the Netherlands, Mackintosh in Scotland, Secessionism in Vienna, Art Nouveau in France. The creators at Bauhaus, more than any others, explicitly and consequentially advocated linkage of art and merchandise. Funded by the German government, and active between the world wars until closed down by the Nazis, the Bauhaus studios housed painters, sculptors, architects, and the type of people later to be called industrial designers. Many of the most successful commercial designs, measured by retail sales, foreign exports, and value of the imitations, owe their success to the resident artists like Kandinsky, Albers, and Klee. Entire institutions and vast public facilities (corporate headquarters, airports, and dormitories) continue to be outfitted with these products. Although the classics have been sales successes, the still greater economic consequence has come from the many imitations of them and in the way their stylistic elements influence other wares. The appliance designs inspired by those that Hans Gugelot and Dieter Rams did for Braun, a company that emerged as Germany's post-war successor to the Bauhaus at The Ulm Institute, continue to make money for the firm, just as they shaped the whole world of home appliances (and much else), first from German makers (Krupps, besides Braun), and then virtually all producers.

Fine art works its preanalytic vision from afar as well as through direct contact. The design authority Penny Sparke says Russian sculptor Alexander Archipenko inspired a table thermos by the American industrial designer, Henry Dreyfuss (Sparke et al., 1986: 103). Operating more or less independently in the US, Henry Bertoia, himself a life-long artist, attributed his classic steel rod or "diamond" chairs to Marcel Duchamp. "I wanted my chair to rotate, change with movement, like the body in Duchamp's 'Nude Descending the Staircase,'" Bertoia said.[11] This chair has been vastly imitated, with the wire back making its way into kitchen dinette sets, folding card-table sets, and a vast run of garden furniture. In the late 1990s, the New York designer Ayse Birsel, of Olive Design, created her "Miro pole" – a narrow column with protuberances for lights, power outlets, sound speakers. Chairs by Charles and Rae Eames invoke organic forms of Arp and his predecessors. Italian Ettore Scotsass, a famous designer for Olivetti and other companies, says pop art influenced his products (Centre, 1992, wall copy).

I came across a contemporary design office's careful documentation, in a 37-page booklet, of the way fine art helped solve a bathtub problem for American Standard. As the designer, Robin Levien, explained to me, the tub was becoming "the center of the bathroom" but it was the competing Jacuzzi Corporation that was making it happen. American Standard had sold much of its product line as ensemble: tub, sinks, toilet, en suite. So a loss of tub share threatened the

Figure 13.3   "Wave" bathtub as marketed. © Studio Levien.

rest of the line, especially if a firm like Jacuzzi were to buy up a sink/toilet maker that would then give them a complete range. For their design to be bold enough to assert their client's high-design presence, the designer needed distinction. He took Thomas Jefferson's serpentine walls at the University of Virginia, along with forms borrowed from Matisse and Kandinsky to create the "single geometric alphabet" of circular arc, large wave, small wave, and straight line that went into the tub's "playful balance" (see Fig. 13.3). They called it the "Wave" series, produced in a variety of models.

The influence path is seldom so neat or straight – and probably often not known even to the creators. Besides the fact that mundane products have influenced the fine arts and even some of the so-called "tribal art" that they also admire, the designers no doubt often can "see" the great art in their products only after the fact. They come to be reminded of Picasso as they look upon what is in front of them, which does not mean that images of Picasso were not also part of the imagination, just that it is an open issue of just how.

The semiotic handle

The seductive nature of objects is not a simple "yes–no" issue, but a matter of the specific ways aesthetic qualities facilitate or inhibit acquisition and use.

To be functional an object must convey the right kind of feeling to make the transaction occur. In this sense, decoration is not only something short of a "crime," as some of the modernists claimed, but a mechanism for function to be realized. The polka dots on a child's bedding or a favorite Disney motif are more likely to secure a comfortable night's sleep (for both child and parent) than putatively more "functional" hospital whites (Gell, 1998). When decoration is a "technology of enchantment" (Gell, 1992), it is as efficacious as any other form of technology. This kind of utility is why Gell, a social anthropologist, can find that "most non-modernist, non-puritan civilizations value decorativeness and allot it a specific role in the mediation of social life, the creation of attachment between persons and things" (Gell, 1998: 83).

From contemporary experience, we know the enchantment details have to be just right, not just to make a product appealing in general but to make it usable *in situ*. Users can be attracted to an object, but "wrongly" attracted. Form may induce a pull on the wrong lever, or in the wrong order, or for an inappropriate application. A can opener works best when its look, feel, and even sound imply the shape and material content of cans it can deal with (not beer cans, for example), as well as the physical strength needed to work it, and the general conditions of its use – how to stand, where to look, when to stop. The feelings an object arouses guide the hand (or foot, or head, or back – just as it does the smile or frown) in a certain direction, with a particular force, in a specific sequence. Every material object thus works through its *semiotic handle* that makes it attractive in the first place and specifically useful in practice.

The look, feel, and sounds of even industrial equipment influence its effectiveness and market success. In a hospital, the wrong appearance can dissuade a clinically appropriate approach, by patient or health professional. Making controls and levers more inviting and intuitive can decrease accidents. Contrast for example the device for open-heart surgery before and after it was redesigned by Heimstra Design (see Figs. 13.4, 13.5, and 13.6). The mechanistic version (the "before design") might have been intuitively approachable in the late nineteenth century when gears and screw-turns were of the moment, but not for contemporary people. In contrast, the redesign would have been mysterious in an earlier era, perhaps even frightening. Getting it right must take into account the specifics of time, place, and niche.

The aesthetics of so prosaic an object as the forklift trucks that move goods around in warehouses, industrial yards, and factories do matter. Crown Fork Lift Trucks broke the industry mold by hiring a design consultant for its product in the early 1960s. The first "designed" fork-lift won the year's major award from the Industrial Designers Society of America (an IDSA "gold," shared with the Ford Mustang) and launched the company toward market dominance (with

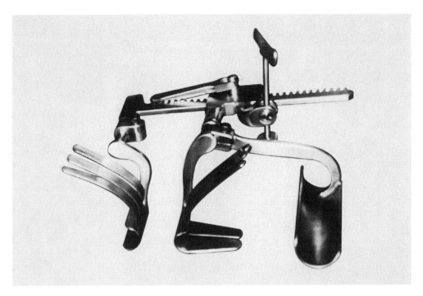

Figure 13.4   Heart surgery appliance (before design). Minimally Invasive Coronary Bypass Device. Photograph © Hiemstra Product Development, LLC.

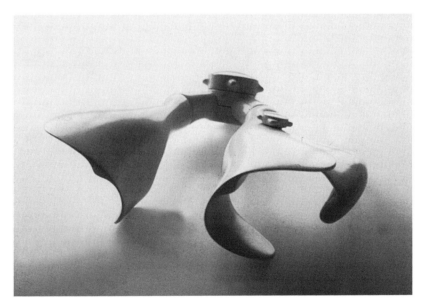

Figure 13.5   Heart surgery appliance (after design). Minimally Invasive Coronory Bypass Device. Photograph © Hiemstra Product Development, LLC.

Figure 13.6   Simulated application. Minimally Invasive Coronary Bypass
Device. Photograph © Hiemstra Product Development, LLC.

annual sales well above half a billion dollars). The founder and CEO, Thomas
Bidwell, says that although he is "from an industry that bends heavy metal . . .
we used design to build our company . . . design was our edge." He recalls that
people said his customers "are the tough guys who chew cigars." But "I never
did buy that . . . This guy buys suits. He doesn't turn his senses off when he
goes to work."[12] Hence capital goods are not immune from the interpenetration
of art and artifact.

   Designers provide other examples of heavy industry depending on the aesthetic. Factory workers, they say, may gain a sense they are making a quality

product if their equipment looks, feels, and performs like it is itself quality. A designer told me sales of his $30,000 ocular lathe, used by opticians to grind lenses, needs to look like the company that made it "will be around in five years" to maintain it. Good design may be seen as better for worker safety (designers certainly think it is); a Mexican designer reports that one of the reasons the oil monopoly Pemex hired his firm to work on control system on off-shore oil platforms was to lower its insurance costs at Lloyds (Alvarez, 1998).

In contrast to my view is that put forth by Donald Norman in his influential book, *The Design of Everyday Things* (1988). Norman evaluated various products in terms of how their design made them more or less useful. A positive example for him are the faucet handles on some airplane washbasins; indentations that cradle the finger invite downward pressure without the need for signs that say "push." A need for writing represents a failure of the physical object to communicate for itself (VCRs are notorious tragedies). Physical cues should provide the guide as to which buttons to push, or pull, or slide, and in what order. These all seem worthwhile points, but I think there is a subtext in Norman's work that "aesthetics" get in the way of the practical solutions he supports. I think Norman is making a polemic *for a particular version* of how aesthetics should be mobilized to enhance functionality. Creating the right semiotic handle for an object is an aesthetic accomplishment – including in the goods he praises. It is all about "come-ons." But the right semiotics will be of one form for an airplane sink, another for a skateboard, and still different again for a chair certain people will find worth sitting in. Decoration, as evident from my prior examples, makes goods acceptable and accessible. In whatever way it is managed, it "is intrinsically functional, or else its presence would be inexplicable," as Gell succinctly put it (Gell, 1998: 74).

The practicality of art

A reason high quality in form and function may inhere in the same goods and by the same designers is that just as doing science or engineering involves an aesthetic dimension, being "arty" means having to deal with the practical. Artists are not so effete as they are made out to be, or even as they sometimes present themselves. Every artist must face the mundane. There are material matters of pigments, solvents, durability, weights, scale, and interrelations among parts (Becker, 1982). There are organizational issues having to do with agents, dealers, galleries, preparators, critics, and patrons without which the work could not successfully exist. Speaking of his experience in theater, Beck remarks that the collective nature of virtually all aesthetic work means that "somebody's artistic freedom is somebody else's tyranny, the abridgment of somebody else's creative space" (Beck, 1988: 45). The artistic output at the end stands as an encapsulation of the practical vicissitudes through which it has come to exist – as well, of course, as the "magic" the artist brings to bear in making the combination happen. If the art is a solution, it cannot occur without the problems it has come to solve and those problems are, in considerable degree, practical ones. In the words of the novelist Richard Stern, "one's signature" becomes what one makes of such limits (Atlas, 1999: 43).

This again shows a way creative accomplishments involve solving for form and function simultaneously. Da Vinci did top-grade weapons as well as frescoes and the same talents that made his works recognizably excellent by art connoisseurs plausibly helped make his products more effective in war. His notebooks make clear the Renaissance Man never stopped, including in his assiduous efforts pitching his projects – some art, some science, some in combination – to patrons. Given the history of goods and the findings of cognitive science, this makes some sense as a model for how many operate post-Renaissance: it misleads to think of people, groups, or brain parts as hyper-specialized to one kind of talent as opposed to the other. What might be going on instead, in Zen terms, is "mindfulness" – the propensity to focus and, in effect, let all parts of the individual brain as well as group intelligence work through toward effective innovation.

Making love

In da Vinci's day as now, productive projects require coordination among diverse actors; there must be a way to "get it together" – to enlist enthusiasm as well as create a common understanding as to what that enthusiasm should serve. Art coordinates diverse individuals and groups, across both time and space, by tacitly providing shared understanding of "what this is all about," both in general and in specific terms. We know the details involved in even a single life project are always too numerous to state explicitly, that no list of rules can incorporate all that needs to be known (Garfinkel, 1967). Some alternative mechanism is required to seduce diverse agencies and actors into a coherent effort and to give them "the feel," as we sometimes say, for the kind of outcome that is supposed to result. It is "art" – sometimes a painting (like a Matisse bather), a metaphor (like "the tabernacle"), or an ambitious narrative ("we will go to the moon") that radiates visions that span across actors and industrial segments. Mutual "enrollments," as Bruno Latour says (Latour, 1987: 108), have to take place.

Nobody, not even Edison, could have "invented" electric lighting; it was a genuine problem for the necessary elements to fall into place, the diverse enrollments to occur. Art helped not only by creating early applications and "holding" them for still wider utilization, but also by providing the excitement and vision to keep the love alive (Bazerman, 1999; Hughes, 1989). Swan had developed a paper filament bulb in his laboratory as early as 1848. Edison overtook him not just in coming upon a superior technique of fabrication, but in his capacities to organize other aspects of the industry into being – investors, power sources, and government cooperation to stage street-lighting exhibitions. Edison had to convince others to put the pieces in place – no doubt part of the "perspiration" he said was the important ingredient of his success. As reported in first-hand accounts, seeing streets lit by electricity filled hearts with rapture, helping overcome not only organizational impediments but also fears of so inexplicable and potentially dangerous a technology. Colored glass, soon evolving into Tiffany lampshades would add further glory in the dark. As enrollments gather steam, I imagine, a bandwagon builds as people find it easier to love something others also love. A crowd of affections becomes a virtuous mob, as aesthetic contagion spreads through co-appreciations, akin to the special pleasure of participating in an enthusiastic ovation (see Atkinson, 1984). In good part because of Edison's organizational and theatrical skills, he rather than Swan made sure electricity got going.

Taking up the case of a *failed* big project, Latour examined why, after expensive and ambitious investments, its French sponsors gave up on an automated railway project called "Aramis." Many setbacks occurred, some overcome, but, in the end, the project could no longer hold together because not enough of the stakeholders – politicians, bureaucrats, financiers, technologists, media, and public groups – sufficiently "loved" it. There could not be the persistence needed to roll the great boulder up the hill. It is a boulder, not so much because of sheer size but because of the many pieces that need to be kept together more or less at once and over an extended period. The simultaneity of complimentary visions came to erode. In his invoking of "love," Latour embraces the word used by Smith in explaining why toys as well as art projects have so well served technological advance:

All big things grow from little things, but new little things will be destroyed by their environment unless they are cherished for reasons more like love than purpose.

(Smith, 1981: 331)

Chickens and eggs

I have now provided my versions of why "it's both." Aesthetics have power equal to that of functionality. It can be seen in historic ordering, in the way art holds technologies in place, how it indispensably builds markets for particular products and whole classes of commodities. It supplies the visions that make technical solutions possible and provides the coordinating affections through which diverse actors remain on board. It is part of the very process of cognizing objects and their use. Humans accomplish all tasks, whether noticed as artistic or economic, or not noticed at all, by drawing on the entire panoply of human emotional and sensate capacities. We are, with form and function, with art and economy, at home not just with chicken and egg, but chicken in egg and egg in chicken. There are no *independent* variables in this analytic hen house.

People cling to the assumption that conventional rationality guides effective human activity, something reinforced not only by academic fields like formal logic and economics, but by most everyone's retrospective accounts of their behavior. Whether in science articles, history books, or even therapy sessions, folks "clean-up" their mess to provide an orderly story. In part this is because it is nearly impossible to capture in discourse the complex textures that make up human agency and in part because we are supposed to have performed in a way sufficiently "rational" to make a tidy accounting possible. We are constrained to mesh our accounts "with the juridical, ethical or grammatical legalism to which the observer is inclined by his own situation" (Bourdieu [1990: 91]; see also Garfinkel [1967]). Indeed, to try and make conscious the artful mechanisms through which practice occurs undermines the very capacity to succeed at that practice – like trying to ride a bike by thinking through how it can happen.

Nobody has a good theory of novelty, says Basalla, because such a theory "would have to encompass the irrationality of the playful and fantastic, the rationality of the scientific, the materialism of the economic, and the diversity of the social and cultural" (Basalla, 1988: 134). Without the advantage of theorists like Latour and Becker or evidence from cognitive science, Basalla is exactly right, which is why I have had to invoke so many different ideas and threads of scholarship to make sense of the form–function process. Still short of grand theory, I can at least assert that products have no essential form or essential function, separate from specific time and circumstance. It is the *mode of form–function combination* that makes something more or less worthy and to whom. Having just the right mix at just the right moment puts something out and sustains it, determining as well – for good or for ill – whether it lasts on markets and in living rooms for decades or only an instant. Because any creating and consuming "does both," any industry is both a "culture industry" and one that serves practical ends. Parallel to the way the expressive and practical cohere in the human mind and all social life, all art does work and all markets are art markets.

Notes

For detailed critiques of prior drafts and ongoing discussions, I am indebted to Howard Becker, Deirdre Boden, Mitchell Duneier, Daniel Miller, and Glenn Wharton.

1. Much of Alois Riegl's life work was directed against views like this, so dominant among his intellectual contemporaries; Riegl (1992).
2. Law (1984). Bruno Latour attributes this phrase to John Law who evidently used it in an early draft of a paper that was later published without it. See Law (1986).
3. Rubinstein (1995) cites Newburgh (1968) and Bazett (1968).
4. Statistical Abstract, 1990. Washington, DC: United States Department of Commerce. P. 769.
5. Sieber (1980), as cited in Cranz (1998); see also Rybczynski (1986).
6. Schwartz and Romo (forthcoming), who cite Ford (1926: 186–188) and others.
7. The other badly designed product types cited were small appliances, home furniture, stoves, and air conditioners. The products cited as "America's best designs" were Deere & Co. lawnmowers, a TV educational toy from Texas Instruments, the Macintosh computer, Ray-Ban sunglasses, and a set of Corning cookware.
8. For still other testimonials, see: Ball (1998); Barrow (1995); Coen (1999); Greene (1999); and Rothstein (1996). From the more mundane realm of economics, Szostak (1999) gives countless examples of the zeal for elegant models trumping a search for accurate description.
9. Failure to acknowledge such pleasures hinders efforts to solve problems like delinquency, family "irresponsibility," drug use, and crime. People live for pleasure, in some sense, no matter what excuse they give for living. That is why it may be better to go for the thrill of a street deal, a hit on a pipe, or some other ecstatic move; Katz (1988).
10. Thanks to Tom Armbruster for this comparison.
11. Source: Interactive computer program at London Design Museum, accessed April 4, 1993.
12. Comments by Thomas Bidwell, "Natural Resources," Annual Conference, Industrial Designers Society of America. Santa Fe, NM, September 16, 1995.

References

Altman, D. 1982. *The Homosexualization of America*. New York: St. Martin's Press.
Alvarez, M. 1998. "Remarks." San Diego, CA, Paper presented at Annual Meeting, Industrial Designers Society of America.
Armi, E. 1990. *The Art of American Car Design*. University Park, PA: Pennsylvania State University.
Arnheim, Rudolf. 1994. *Art and Visual Perception: A Psychology of the Creative Eye*. Berkeley: University of California Press.
Atkinson, J. M. 1984. *Our Masters' Voices: the Language and Body Language of Politics*. New York: Methuen.

Ball, P. 1998. *The Self-Made Tapestry*. Oxford: Oxford University Press.

Barthes, R. 1993 [1957]. *Mythologies*. London: Vintage.

Basalla, G. 1988. *The Evolution of Technology*. Cambridge: Cambridge University Press.

Baudelaire, C. 1970. *The Painter of Modern Life*. London: Phaidon.

Bayley, S. 1983. *Harley Earl and the Dream Machine*. New York: Knopf.

Bazett, H. C. 1968. "The Regulation of Body Temperature," in L. H. Newburgh, ed. *The Physiology of Heat Regulation and the Science of Clothing*. New York: Stretchet Haffner. Pp. 109–117.

Beck, B. 1988. *Reflections on Art and Inactivity*. Evanston, IL: CIRA. Seminar Series Monograph, Culture and the Arts Workgroup. Center for Interdisciplinary Research in the Arts. Northwestern University. 1: 43–66.

Becker, H. 1982. *Art Worlds*. Berkeley, CA: University of California Press.

Bell, Q. 1947. *On Human Finery*. London: Hogarth Press.

Bourdieu, P. 1984. *Distinction: A Social Critique of the Judgement of Taste*. Cambridge, MA: Harvard University Press.

1990. *The Logic of Practice*. Cambridge: Polity Press.

Brain, D. 1997. *From Public Housing to Private Communities. Public and Private in Thought and Practice: Perspectives on a Grand Dichotomy*, ed. J. Weintraub and K. Kumar. Chicago, IL: University of Chicago Press.

Brillat-Savarin, J. A. 1970 [1825]. *The Physiology of Taste: Meditations on Transcendental Gastronomy*. New York: Liveright.

Centre, G. P. 1992. *Manifeste*. Paris: Centre Pompidou.

Chandler, A. 1977. *The Visible Hand: The Managerial Revolution in American Business*. Cambridge, MA: Harvard University Press.

Chapman, K. 1991. *The International Petrochemical Industry*. Cambridge, MA: Blackwell.

Clark, J. 1998. *Kinetic Beauty: the Theatre of the 1920s. Addressing the Century: 100 Years of Art and Fashion*, P. Wollen. London: Hayward Gallery. Pp. 79–87.

Coen, E. 1999. *The Art of Genes*. Oxford: Oxford University Press.

Cole, K. C. 1997. "A Career Boldly Tied by String." *Los Angeles Times* February 4: 1.

Cranz, G. 1998. *The Chair: Rethinking Culture, Body and Design*. New York: Norton.

Cronon, W. 1991. *Nature's Metropolis: Chicago and the Great West*. New York: W. W. Norton.

D'Andrade, R. 1989. *Culturally Based Reasoning. Cognition in Social Worlds*, ed. A. Gellatly, D. Rogers, and J. Sloboda. New York: McGraw-Hill.

Daly, Herman 1996. *Beyond Growth: The Economics of Sustainable Development*. Boston, MA: Beacon Press.

Damasio, A. 1994. *Descartes' Error: Emotion, Reason, and the Human Brain*. New York: Plenum.

Danto, Arthur. 1992. *Beyond the Brillo Book*. New York: Farrar, Straus & Giroux.

Dumaine, B. 1988. "Five Products U.S. Companies Design Badly." *Fortune*: 130.

Fauconnier, G. and M. Turner. 1998. "Conceptual Integration Networks." *Cognitive Science* 22/2:133–187.

Finkelstein, J. 1989. *Dining Out*. New York: New York University Press.

Forbes, R. J. 1954. "Chemical, Culinary and Cosmetic Arts," in C. Singer et al., eds. *A History of Technology, vol. 1: From Early Times to Fall of Ancient Empires*. Oxford.

Garfinkel, H. 1967. *Studies in Ethnomethodology*. Englewood Cliffs, NJ: Prentice-Hall.

Gell, A. 1992. "The Technology of Enchantment and the Enchantment of Technology," in J. Coote and A. Shelton, eds. *Anthropology, Art, and Aesthetics*. Oxford: Clarendon Press. Pp. 40–67.

  1998. *Art and Agency*. Oxford: Clarendon.

Gill, B. 1989. "California: Hats, Beds, and Houses." *Architectural Digest*, 36–44.

Goffman, E. 1967. *Interaction Ritual: Essays in Face-to-Face Behavior*. Chicago, IL: Aldine.

Goody, J. 1982. *Cooking, Cuisine and Class*. Cambridge: Cambridge University Press.

Greene, B. 1999. *The Elegant Universe*. New York: Norton.

Guillen, R. 1997. "The Air-Force, Missiles, and the Rise of the Los Angeles Aerospace Technopole." *Journal of the West* 36/3:60–66.

Hollander, A. 1988. *Seeing Through Clothes*. New York: Penguin.

Hounshell, D. 1984. *From the American System to Mass Production 1800–1932*. Baltimore, MD: Johns Hopkins University Press.

Hughes, T. 1989. *American Genesis: A Century of Invention and Technological Enthusiasm, 1870–1970*. New York: Viking.

Hutchins, E. 1999. "Mental Models as an Instrument for Bounded Rationality." San Diego, CA, Distributed Cognition and HCI Laboratory, Department of Cognitive Science, UCSD. Dalem Workshop on Bounded Rationality: The Adaptive Toolbox.

Katz, J. 1988. *Seductions of Crime: Moral and Sensual Attractions in Doing Evil*. New York: Basic Books.

Kern, S. 1983. *The Culture of Time and Space, 1880–1918*. Cambridge, MA: Harvard University Press.

Klein, R. 1993. *Cigarettes are Sublime*. Durham, NC: Duke University Press.

Klingender, F. 1947. *Art and the Industrial Revolution*. Frogmore: Paladin.

Korzenik, D. 1985. *Drawn to Art: a Nineteenth-Century American Dream*. Hanover, NH: University Press of New England.

Laffitte, B. 1995. *Drawing as a Natural Resource in Design*. Natural Resources, Santa Fe, NM. Industrial Designers Society of America. Pp. 41–45.

Law, J. 1984. "On Ships and Spices: Technology, Power and the Portuguese Route to India." Paris, France: Centre de Sociologie de l'Innovation, Ecole des Mines de Paris.

  1986. "On the Methods of Long-Distance Control: Vessels, Navigation, and the Portuguese Route to India," in J. Law, ed. *Power, Action, and Belief: a New Sociology of Knowledge?*, London; Boston: Routledge and Kegan Paul. Pp. 234–263.

Meikle, J. 1990. "From Celebrity to Anonymity: The Professionalization of American Industrial Design," in A. Schönberger, ed. *Raymond Loewy: Pioneer of American Industrial Design*. Berlin: Prestel. Pp. 51–62.

Melikian, S. 1998. "Designs in Shining Armor." *International Herald Tribune*. Paris. P. 9.

Mintz, S. 1979. "Time, Sugar and Sweetness." *Marxist Perspectives* 2:56–73.

Mukerji, C. 1983. *From Graven Images: Patterns of Modern Materialism*. New York: Columbia University Press.

Museum, N. 1999. *Beneath the Skin: Technical Artists*. London: National Museum of Science and Industry.

Newburgh, L. H., ed. 1968. *The Physiology of Heat Regulation and the Science of Clothing*. New York: Stretchet Haffner.

Norman, D. 1988. *The Design of Everyday Things*. New York: Doubleday.

Owen, W. 1996. "Design for Killing: The Aesthetic of Menace Sells Guns to the Masses." *I.D. Magazine*, September/October: 54–61.

Pendergrast, M. 1999. *Uncommon Grounds: the History of Coffee and how it Transformed our World*. New York: Basic Books.

Petroski, H. 1992. *The Evolution of Useful Things*. New York: Random House.

Pickering, A. 1995. *The Mangle of Practice: Time, Agency and Science*. Chicago, IL: University of Chicago Press.

Postrel, V. 1998. *The Future and its Enemies: the Growing Conflict over Creativity, Enterprise, and Progress*. New York: Free Press.

Rao, C. R. (Calyampudi Radhakrishna). 1994. *Selected Papers of C. R. Rao*, ed. S. Das Gupta et al. New York: Wiley.

Riegl, A. [1893] 1992. *Problems of Style: Foundations for a History of Ornament*. Princeton, NJ: Princeton University Press.

Rothstein, E. 1996. *Emblems of Mind*. New York: Avon.

1999. "Recurring Patterns, The Sinews of Nature." *New York Times*. New York: A15, 17.

Rubinstein, R. 1995. *Dress Codes*. Boulder, CO: Westview.

Rybczynski, W. 1986. *Home: A Short History of an Idea*. New York: Penguin.

Schwartz, M. and F. Romo (forthcoming). *The Rise and Fall of Detroit*. Berkeley, CA: University of California Press.

Smith, C. S. 1971. "Art, Technology, and Science: Notes on Their Historical Interaction," in D. H. D. Roller, ed. *Perspectives in the History of Science and Technology*. Norman, Oklahoma: University of Oklahoma Press. Pp. 166–194.

1981. *A Search for Structure: Selected Essays on Science, Art, and History*. Cambridge, MA: MIT Press.

Smith, T. 1993. *Making the Modern: Industry, Art, and Design in America*. Chicago, IL: University of Chicago Press.

Sparke, P., F. Hodges, E. D. Coad, and A. Stone 1986. *Design Source Book*. Secaucus, NJ: Chartwell Books.

Szostak, R. 1999. *Econ-Art*. London: Pluto Press.

Varnedoe, K. and A. Gopnik 1991. *High & Low*. New York: The Museum of Modern Art.

Williams, Rosalind H. 1982. *Dream Worlds: Mass Consumption in Late Nineteenth-Century France*. Berkeley: University of California Press.

Wilson, E. 1993. "Fashion and the Postmodern Body," in J. Ash and E. Wilson, eds. *Chic Thrills: A Fashion Reader*. Berkeley, CA: University of California Press. Pp. 3–16.

Wollen, P., ed. 1998. *Addressing the Century*. London: Hayward Gallery.

Zukin, S. 1995. *The Cultures of Cities*. Cambridge, MA: Blackwell.

14

Ethnosympathy: reflections on an American dilemma

Jon D. Cruz

When first asked to submit a chapter for this volume, a number of thematic options came to mind, but the one I settled upon grew out of the first Cultural Turn conference at Santa Barbara at which I presented some of the main ideas in a book that was in progress and which has now since been published as *Culture on the Margins: The Black Spiritual and the Rise of American Cultural Interpretation.*[1] Since then, I have had some time to think about the work I undertook in writing the book, and of the issues that began to emerge only toward its completion. In a way, writing about a completed book is supposed to feel like a celebration, after all, the best public moments of intellectual life and the pursuit of knowledge include the pleasure of sharing the fruit of one's work with others. This moment marks something of the sunny side of intellectual work with conferences, forums, and publishing. Yet, less emphasis seems to be paid to the nagging problems that never quite go away – of reaching certain horizons where the pleasure of discovery is eclipsed by even larger issues that beg attention, and with the sobering feeling that some hard-won accomplishments can bring a new sense of actually feeling dumber. Perhaps this problem is neglected because it registers always as a part of that realm of private doubt better kept from public acclaim. We are at our public best when we convey ourselves to be good confidence men and women, better to parade the finished work, hide the ragged beginnings, avoid the boulders unturned, and strut one's "findings," all in the good form of presentation of professional self.

But intellectual work is often, I suspect, less ordered and surefooted, and is more likely comprised of staggering lurches and precarious and doubtful acts of balance. Such was the case for me in writing the book. In this study I tried to show how the black spiritual was central to the first modern "cultural turn" in the second half of the nineteenth century. I went into this project much like a critical abolitionist from the North during the Civil War – to hear music and to cast my hand at cultural interpretation. I ran, instead, into the roar of ideological clashes and social movements and the din generated by the interplay of race, culture, and modernity, and I stumbled upon a fragile sensibility in the making – what I call "ethnosympathy" (my working definition of which will unfold in this chapter). In the process of completing the book, I have come to see ethnosympathy as one of the core victories to come out of that much-maligned event called modernity; but this is to put the cart before the horse. Let me start elsewhere.

I began research on the book with an acceptable inheritance – the received schemas and classifications of cultural goods that have been bequeathed by a century and a half of cultural analysis and interpretation (or reified categories stamped by the conditions of their sociohistorical emerge, as Georg Lukács would say). I was also primarily interested in the relationship between cultural expressions and modern technology. I was concerned particularly with how market, corporate, and institutional forces managed to annex significant aspects of the cultural sphere. I was going to examine black music as a font of cultural meanings, and then I was going to track how this important body of expressivity was annexed by the processes of modern commodification. A number of thematics would come into play: cultural voicing as public spheres; technological innovations that overtake publics and resell meaning back to publics; the evolution of modern corporate and media culture industries; how capitalism adeptly exploits popular vernaculars but also archives such vernaculars through cultural production; and, of course, the ongoing struggles over the control of cultural goods. These interconnected issues remain important in their own right, but this was not the kind of book I ended up writing.

Given where I started, I had no idea that in the thick of study I would be working my way through the tortuous logic of Cotton Mather's attempt to justify Christian teaching with slavery. I certainly did not plan to look at the way in which the Great Awakenings of the early nineteenth century produced a critical elevation of emotional outpouring, which served as both the preferred language of the soul, and a refutation of the staid formalism of establishment theology. Nor did I think I would have to look at how this massive sphere of emotionality would legitimate the emotive pain of slaves as they reworked the religious franchise to their expressive advantage. I did not plan to look at the way in which the Protestant religious franchise was given to slaves and how this franchise would greatly expand the cultural terrain enabling slaves to use the dominant ideology to interrogate the dominant ideology. I did not anticipate from the outset that I would have to confront the larger problem of the rise of modern selfhood and subjectivity which would go beyond its earlier religious roots to posit and then explore the newly conceptualized cultural interior of modern subjects. Nor did I anticipate that I would have to make some sense of the antimodernist impulses that were engendered by the coming of market society and early industrialization, impulses that would rupture an older Protestant consensus and spawn renegade ministers and social movements that, in turn, would create cultural opportunities for women, workers, and slaves to emerge as subjects to be redeemed – in themselves and for themselves, and as useful to other moral, ethical, and political entrepreneurs – against the backdrop of a social order that had lost its moral mandate. I was oblivious at the outset to the role that American transcendentalism would play as it cut a deal between a spiritualized notion of natural history and the crisis-driven theophilosophical search for truths in nature, a search that would predispose a very small but highly influential cadre of cultural hunters and gatherers to seek their redemption in the newly discovered black culture on the margins. I had not planned to take a look at that fateful marriage between romanticism and humanitarian reformism, a marriage that would produce as offspring a congenitally ambivalent science of folklore that would vacillate between a desire to expose its hard-won insights into the machinations of social power and the use of such insight to support and justify the dominant forms of social order. Into this nexus I staggered. All of these points – these lines of cultural force – situated the discovery and ensuing edification of the black spiritual in the period surrounding the Civil War. These points intersected black music and shaped its initial modern discovery. Black music, particularly the *spiritual*, appeared at the very heart of the formation of modern cultural interpretation.

I went in to interpret; I ended up struggling to interpret the interpreters, and attempting to explain how the discovery of black music, especially the edification of religious singing, was central to modern American cultural interpretation. And I had to confront how such an important evolution of interpretive benevolence could embrace an acceptable kind of modern subject appreciated for certain strains of cultural performativity, and yet remain relatively disengaged from the more elaborate political voices, writings, and struggles of black Americans and other peoples to address their fate within American society. In the process, I was forced to come to terms with the formation of the interpretive paradigms that had informed my initial inquiry. I ended up with an account of an interpretive formation and writing a study of the sociology of knowledge applied to a fateful chapter of American cultural modernity.

Ethnosympathy was not a notion or idea that I had planned to investigate at the outset; and, once it became clearer to me that this was a central issue, I was not able to expand my views upon it as far as I would have liked. What I came upon has continued to feel like the nagging of messy and unfinished business. I do want to nudge the concept along a bit more here. To do so, I will summarize some of the ground covered in the book, but also note how some thoughts provoked by W. E. B. Du Bois proved useful in recasting the ties between the nineteenth century and our new century's tensions that surround the fate as well as promise of modern critical ethnosympathy.

Early on in writing *Culture on the Margins* it became evident that any kind of sociology of music is bound to become a venture upon very difficult terrain. The difficulties multiply when one leaves the neat confines of ready-made genres (which are too often simply inherited and adopted from industry and market logics), and begins to grapple with music as a point of entry into a much larger cultural formation. To speak of formations is fundamentally a historical problem, and, when one tries to bring something like a "cultural formation"[2] into visibility, one is quickly confronted with something rather fantastic – how cultural phenomena actually sprawl across history and society, and spill over and beyond the neatness that is so often presumed to come with adopting a "disciplined" approach to study. I wanted to begin to unpack some of this sprawl, this cultural complex, within a sociological enterprise (feeling all the while both abandoned by sociology and needing also to abandon sociology, or at least the reified paradigmatic forms that seem to get so much attention among the definers of the sociology of culture), in order to do sociology.

Clearly, I knew I was after some process rather than some product. What was I actually looking at? I thought that I was going to center on the meaning of black music, for, in most of my conversations with others about my research, such expectation was always presumed. After all, we do have something of a canon at our disposal, a full century of writings that tell us what this or that music is, where it comes from, what it says, what it does for its practitioners, and the forms that it has taken over time. In my view, such work represents a hard-won victory of restoring the presence of social actors to the study of cultural forms. Why not just get on board? It was not fear and trembling, but ragged beginnings and doubt that made me hesitant to add to the canon. Did I have anything to add to the already eloquent assessments by W. E. B. Du Bois, Carter Woodson, Langston Hughes, Zora Neale Hurston, John Lovell, Lawrence Levine, Sterling Stuckey, Eugene Genovese, Eileen Southern, Albert Raboteau, and, more recently, Angela Davis, George Lipsitz, Tricia Rose? The answer was no. I could make good on effort, but I knew from the onset that I would at best produce a grace note to an already wonderful array of compositions.

My plans really began to shift when I reread (many times) some passages from Du Bois' 1903 classic, *The Souls of Black Folk*, and tried at the same time to get at what Raymond Williams called the "structure of feeling" that informed Du Bois' words as a historically situated critical reflection. There was another problem that began to trouble me – a sense of lament and loss flagged by Du Bois. I felt I had to get my head around this sensibility. Du Bois wrote:

The nineteenth was the first century of human sympathy, – the age when half wonderingly we began to descry in others that transfigured spark of divinity which we call Myself; when clodhoppers and peasants, and tramps and thieves, and millionaires and – sometimes – Negroes, became throbbing souls whose warm pulsing life touched us so nearly that we half gasped with surprise, crying, "Thou too! Hast Thou seen sorrow and the dull waters of Hopelessness? Hast Thou known Life?" And then all helplessly we peered into those Other-worlds, and wailed, "O World of Worlds, how shall man make you one?[3]

We can look forward from Du Bois into our century, and appreciate how central he is to what we today would call "ethnic studies" and critical race relations analysis. We can also see that what Du Bois was charting was not just a voyage into the *Souls of Black Folk*, but a voyage into the rather unexplored regions of America history, society, culture, and modernity.

But there was a nagging tension between looking forward and looking back historically. We could look forward from Du Bois and talk about the modern canon of sympathetic cultural interpretation. In doing so, we would have to come to terms with why the historical scholarship that is touched by the challenge presented by Du Bois, contains an anguish, an urgency, and certainly a struggle over the very intellectual modalities that inform so many acts of cultural interpretation. Cutting through so much of the sympathetic writings of the twentieth century is the sense that something fragile needs to be retrieved, salvaged, restored, and protected. Invariably, the writings speak to the connection between the expressions of people and the need to comprehend the human fingerprints upon social fate. So much of the good critical and interpretive scholarship continues the valuable work of retrieving obscured voices and aiding the unfinished business of reinscribing into history the subjects ignored by official history. We could look forward from Du Bois – or we could look backward with Du Bois. I was puzzled by why Du Bois was looking backward. What was it that had been there, but was there no longer?

Consider the look back. This "first century of human sympathy" was certainly a cultural watershed. It was fed by the powerful currents of eighteenth- and early nineteenth-century romanticism, which mark crucial responses to modernity. In the lament over the disappearance of environments, lives, and livelihoods, romantic criticism spurred, in turn, the humanitarian reformist impulses of the nineteenth century; and it was on the heels of the cultural and political work of romanticism and reformism that classical social theory was able to secure the idea that society itself was an object that could be brought into critical discernment. Social science made it possible to shift the notion of individual, collective, and human fate from teleological to social explanations (which is not to say that social theory abandoned teleology). By and large, fate was not inevitable; it had human fingerprints; it could be challenged. A socially and historically informed sympathy could right the human errors that were responsible for the irrational dimension of human suffering.

What Du Bois seemed to harbor was a desire to bring into visibility something deeply dialogical and dialectical – dialogical in that he signified the reflexive entwinement of self, collective identity, history, and social structure; dialectical in that he attempted to articulate a fragile social vision, a *conscious desire* as well as a *desired consciousness* that would enable an understanding of social fate and an attempt to struggle with that fate in relationship to our being able to comprehending things that are socially systemic. To put the issue this way involves some conceptual double-duty. On the one hand, there is the distinct inwardly *subjective* turn, the attempt to bring the meanings of group lives into view. On the other hand, there is a *social* turn, an attempt to examine groups as social sites that help highlight even larger horizons of social life. Such double-duty entails linking the problem of meaning with social and historical forces and structures. It is an act of "understanding" (in the Weberian sense of *verstehen*), which involves deciphering the problem of meaning by amplifying the relationship between collectivities and the more difficult problem of envisioning social life.[4] The twofold task thus entails a conscious desire as well as a desired consciousness which, entwined, reaches toward a comprehension of meaning and structure, subjects and history, group fate and societal envelopment. Bridging these two frameworks is the task of critical ethnosympathy.

Yet, when Du Bois wrote this passage, the kind of sympathy he had in mind had fallen into massive disrepair. The early years of the twentieth century showed nothing of the more than tolerant multicultural celebration that Walt Whitman had envisioned. What triumphed instead was a Social Darwinism that conceptualized modernity and progress by distancing itself from, or seeking to subordinate, the myriad of lesser groups and peoples whose presumed absence of fit from within the centers of modernity made them all the more likely to be seen as fit to be absent. Sympathy – not as sentiment but as substantive democratic inclusion – appeared to be in fast retreat. Nowhere was this more deeply registered than upon the black American heirs of an aborted Reconstruction and Native Americans sequestered within reservations, and with excluding implications that kept the women's struggle for the franchise at bay.

There was another set of passages in Du Bois' early book, in which he looks back. In the last chapter, "Of the Sorrow Songs," Du Bois writes of black song-making. Though he does not mention former slave Frederick Douglass, the very title of this chapter echoes words written by Douglass. After all it was Douglass who in 1845 penned the first extensive discussion by a former slave on the music of slaves – which he called "the Songs of Sorrow." Similar to other slave narratives, Douglass' narrative was a book of revelation, and an invitation for sympathetic abolitionists to join him in something of a protoethnographic voyage into the cultural logic and inner lives of slaves. In Douglass' words, the "songs of sorrow" – he did not call them spirituals – "told a tale of woe which was then altogether beyond my feeble comprehension; they were tones loud, long, and deep, they breathed the prayer and complaint of souls boiling over with the bitterest anguish. Every tone was testimony against slavery, and a prayer to God for deliverance from chains," and hearing them always filled him with "ineffable sadness." The songs were gateways that led to seeing the social: "If any one wishes to be impressed with the soul-killing effects of slavery, let him go to Colonel Lloyd's plantation on allowance-day, place himself in the deep pine woods, and there let him, in silence analyze the sounds that shall pass through the chambers of his soul, – and if he is not thus impressed it will only be because 'there is no flesh in his obdurate heart.'"[5]

What Douglass and other black authors of the narratives did was to open a window upon black phenomenology, to provide, in social science parlance, "thick descriptions" of overdetermined "habituses" and "dispositions," and to illuminate the crossing of historical forces and collective biography. They also anchored a broader white audience, already informed by the much larger structure of feeling that drew critically from romanticism and reformism, to the plight of blacks, free or enslaved. What impressed me was the fact that the writing on slavery by an ex-slave treated music in a modern framework that appears to have launched a *sociology of music*. After Douglass, black music in the United States emerged as a cultural practice worthy of social analysis.

What did this new knowledge signify? Where did this new ethos of pathos, this new ethnosympathy, come from? Douglass launched a paradigm shift of tremendous importance. I had to consider Douglass' contribution in contrast to other modes of hearing. To do so meant backing up historically to ask what kind of hearing greeted black song making prior to Douglass' protoethnographic revelations.

From this point on, I began to let go of the received categories of the sorrow songs and spirituals as distinctive genres (though it is quite important to consider them as such) and began to rethink them as a new cultural site coming into view, and as a new cultural arena taking form. I needed to rethink them from the vantage point of how this music became the *cultural object* of new practices of hearing; that is, as an increasingly legitimate and hence discoverable cultural entity. In this discovery, the turn toward the inner life and meanings of groups and the establishment of particular modalities of cultural interpretation were intertwined. To get at shifts in hearing, I posed the question: how did the music making of slaves come to be heard as more than alien "noise?" The noise of black soundings was certainly the earliest interpretive framework that slavers, owners, overseers, and most other observers employed in their extremely limited reception of black expressivity. But, more importantly, I asked how slave "noise" was transformed into "meaningful sound." In unpacking these questions, I covered the following ground. I showed how crucial the Abolitionist movement was in developing the view of slave music making as a new indicator of black subjectivity. Of course, from the owners' perspective, slaves were not subjects, but objects representing property. The new hearing, however, developed in tandem with slaves being attributed with subjectivity, and with slaves also cultivating their own sense of subjectivity.

What first stood out to me among the emerging and shifting schemas of appropriating black music were three distinct modalities that characterized the different kinds of hearing: *incidental*, *instrumental*, and *pathos-oriented* orientations toward black vocalizations. Prior to the 1830s, the music making of slaves was considered mainly as alien "noise." Yet, by the time of the Civil War, abolitionists were busy elevating black religious song making as a newly found cultural good. More important, they selected among black cultural goods and found what they thought was the ultimate "good" of black culture – the spirituals. How do we get from "bad noise" to "good culture?" To answer this question, we must note some key features of available and changing schemas of hearing. Briefly, incidental listening is the earliest and oldest schema. In incidental listening, slave music is not sought out as if it were a thing to apprehend; rather, it is heard inadvertently, accidentally. By and large, slave traders, owners, overseers, and a variety of accidental tourists simply happened upon black music, which to them was entirely novel. They tended to perceive it primarily as "noise" – unintelligible, unfathomable, devoid of meaning. Black soundings were intriguing, but early listeners tended to hear everything negatively – as aberrant, grotesque, unpleasant, and undesirable.

However, there was a dimension of emotional recognition, though feeble, that entered into this early schema for hearing. We detect a bit of an ear for what I call "emotional noise." Early observations of black music tend to evoke two interpretive poles. On the one hand, observers readily admit an inability, even failure, to understand slave music, often on account of language barriers. On the other, they display an emergent comprehension of inner meanings that were attributed to the feelings of the black individuals or groups in whose singing they hear fairly well defined emotions, and offer interpretations of what these emotions might mean. Slave singing was interpreted as "doleful," "mournful," "melancholy," "monotonous," and "sad," but, of the two sets of attributes, it is *noise* that overrides the nascent perception of meaning within emotional noise.

With *instrumental* or *utilitarian hearing*, owners and overseers approach music in a more calculated sense. Intentionality replaces the accidental. Music is used in ways that coincide with the progressive institutionalization of slavery. Examples include the demand that slaves sing and dance as a way of exercising them during transit, to ready their presentation for the auction block, to help set the pace and regulation of the labor process, to monitor their soundings, and to procure entertainment. Slave music is also discursively treated (that is, carefully talked about) for reasons related to surveillance, repression, and even the attempted eradication of slave culture. Like incidental hearing, instrumental hearing registers the gamut of impressions – from awe to revulsion – but, unlike incidental hearing, instrumental hearing is tied to strategies of intentional listening and is bound up with goal-oriented managerialism.

However, the third kind, *pathos-oriented hearing*, interests me because it breaks older sound barriers. It definitely emerges with the growing efficacy of antislavery sentiments, and provides a direct link to the larger developments of romantic and reformist currents within the larger cultural watershed that produced ethnosympathy. Rather than hearing music as aberrant sound, as ancillary to labor exploitation, racial domination, pecuniary gain, or with an overt concern for domestic maintenance, *pathos-oriented hearing marks the origins of hearing black music as a new and valuable moral, intellectual, political, and cultural "discovery."* What was being discovered in the abolitionist conjuncture was the inner world of slaves as subjects, as makers of meaning, as possessors of authenticity, and as producers of cultural goods. These goods served as windows into the cultural realm of slaves. Motivated by antislavery sentiment and a sense of social crisis, pathos-oriented hearing not only helped form and launch a distinctive cultural turn (in this case toward crisis-ridden subjects on the margins); it also enabled critics to pivot upon this cultural turn by linking cultural interpretation to a grammar that was critical as well of social forces, institutions, and structures. In essence, this critical pathos performed the double-duty of ethnosympathy – of connecting inner and outer, history and biography, subject and structure. Like some modern interpreters of our century, the most critical abolitionists were working with a *conscious desire* as well as a *desired consciousness* that enables an understanding of social fate and an attempt to struggle with that fate in relationship to comprehending things that are socially systemic.

What makes ethnosympathy and the early cultural turn so intertwined is the way in which two cultural currents – proselytization and the psychic and cultural opportunity structure made available to slaves – impact one another. As possessors of souls, slaves could expand their new subjectivity. Black Christianity in general, and the religiously inflected slave narratives in particular, signify, in part, these important developments. Many of the slave narratives worked this tenuous ground, as they mined the core ideology of Christianity in ways that challenged the religious justifications for slavery and racial domination.

As public literature, the slave narratives were, arguably, well fitted to the literary tastes of many inquisitive (if not liberal) white Americans in the North. As literature, the narratives penned by former slaves shared similarities with travel narratives, which were a very popular genre in the nineteenth century. In their main form, travel narratives entail visits to strange and distant places; they provide reportage of a voyage to places hitherto not experienced; they map new experience; they bring the reader to the foreign, the distant, the exotic; their authority resides in the narrator, the central and trustworthy source of rendering true statements in keeping with authentic experience.

One might think of an eighteenth- or nineteenth-century travel narrative and a slave narrative as worlds apart, but consider how the slave narratives are frequently about inner, psychic movement, of coming into a realization about the lines of force that have moved (and moved through) one's life; they are recollections of being shackled, with nowhere to go except psychically inward (as autobiography) and morally outward (as social crisis literature). Their inner travel covers moral and emotional geography rather than physical geography. In this inner geography the recently acquired soul (an internalized attribution that coincided with institutional initiatives) merges with the expressive authenticity of the newly acquired status of being redeemable in the form of the modern political subject. The ports, terrain, and horizons that are toured for the reader are both alien, distant, and foreign as well as psychically and morally repugnant. Yet the psychic, moral, and emotional geographies are inescapably *familiar*, *domestic*, and *homely*. They are *American*, and, for the very sympathetic reader, much too close for comfort – for the hitherto presumed domain of *subculture* had been undeniably transmogrified into a vision of *dominant culture*. But what I wish to highlight is that fact that the slave narratives opened up – indeed demanded – a dialogue on the deepest and widely embraced (hegemonic) notions of religious consciousness, politics, struggles over reform, and social and racial justice.

In the North, schisms within unitarianism, which also produced the important transcendentalist movement, made it possible for ex-ministers and kindred moral and political entrepreneurs to "discover" and exonerate the new black subjectivity. Nowhere is this better forged than in the rise of black and white radical abolitionists. These two currents – religious transformation of subjectivities and the social and political movements affiliated with abolitionism – were grounded in the Garrisonian wing of the antislavery movement in which Frederick Douglass was an early and key participant.

The shift that begins to produce a fragile ethnosympathy was thus rooted first in the Protestant religious crisis in which slaveholders were obligated to proselytize slaves and to minister to their souls. This, I argued, led inadvertently to attributing black objects with an identity of being human subjects. Second, this emergent and ambivalent development took on greater velocity as the abolitionist movement gained ground to become the most critical social movement in the nineteenth century.

When the Civil War erupted, the spiritual quickly became a major symbol for a very small group of radical abolitionists. Those who were first attracted to the spirituals and who tried to capture them through observation and transcription were largely Unitarians with strong transcendentalist leanings. In the process, their forays into black music launched what I argue were some of the earliest protoethnographically modern approaches on American soil. What was being discovered in the abolitionist conjuncture was the inner world of slaves – as subjects, as makers of meaning, as possessors of authenticity, as producers of cultural goods. These goods helped establish an early American cultural semiotics, with the spirituals serving as windows into the cultural realm of slaves. Such windows into the cultural margins are also forms of cultural projection. From a sociology of knowledge point of view, the new, pathos-oriented attention to slave expressions provided a window into the disenchanted among the northern cultural bourgeoisie. Pathos-oriented hearing helped abolitionists launch a distinctive cultural turn (in this case toward crisis-ridden subjects on the margins); but it also enabled critics to proceed in multiple directions. Radical abolitionists could rail against the industrial machines that the new captains of the economy were bringing into the hitherto tranquil gardens that supposedly belonged to the self-acclaimed "natural aristocracy" of an idealized Jeffersonian gentlemen yeomanry. In ways similar to the young Marx's neo-Rousseauian quest for an innocent *species being*, they could pursue the transcendentalist-inspired quest for "Nature" and poetry by stripping away the veneer and artifice of convention.

Protoethnographic sensibilities arguably can be found much earlier in many travel narratives, but what marks the interest in the spirituals, apart from travel narratives in general, is how this interest is also joined by a desire to fathom the inner worlds and the hermeneutical dimensions of blacks as meaning-making subjects. These investigations took hold after the Civil War, and were continued by the new black schools and colleges that were organized soon after slavery was dismantled. Institutions like Fisk, Hampton, and Tuskegee kept alive the cultural retrieval work for quite some time until professional folklorists annexed it. I want to summarize this swathe of developments.

Pathos-oriented writings on black music had already appeared in a number of publications, including Garrison's political organ, *The Liberator*, and highbrow journals like the *Atlantic Monthly* and *John Dwight's Journal of Music*. But two key books – Thomas Higginson's *Army Life in a Black Regiment* (1870) and William Allen [et al.]'s *Slave Songs of the United States* (1867) – represent the most elaborate and modern treatments. Taken together, these two works embody an important division of labor. Higginson's book taps an older romanticism. He likens his discovery of black music to Sir Walter Scott's earlier discovery of Scottish borderland ballads. But black soldiers are, with an

American twist, music making "natural Transcendentalists." Higginson provides a remarkable example of what today we would call "field work." He lived with his subjects, his troops. He observed, noted, probed, gathered, and transcribed songs with the kind of lived proximity to his work and to his subjects that would become important to the modern professional ethnographer and anthropologist. He carried out what, today, some call the methodology of "participant observation." Higginson relays how he obtained black songs – how he observed from both distance and intimacy, how he approached his subjects as unobtrusively as possible while maximizing his closeness to them, how he indulged in small talk to get big answers and insights, or asked straight out how they actually made new songs. He queried singers for their own meanings and interpretations, and juxtaposed black song making to a wider variety of comparative examples.

Allen, on the other hand, was much more concerned with facticity than nostalgia, with categorization and typology than with ruminations upon the inner life. *Slave Songs of the United States* was the first major compilation of songs that included not just lyrics, but also professionally transcribed notation. Containing one hundred and thirty six songs, it was the most extensive collection to date of black songs ever assembled.

Yet, both books register the loss of ethnosympathy that Douglass had tried to champion. Both reflect the shift in reframing black culture and expressivity in ways that weakened its ties to the larger social criticisms that had been championed by the slave narratives and their critical reception. The reframing involves the narrowing embrace of restricted musical performativity. This is the high point of discovery, and in its inauguration of other protofolkloristic and protoethnographic interests it contains an irony: the spiritual begins to get loved to social death. By social death, I do not mean that black religious song making died. What I mean to say is that a particular kind of interpretation flourished and became rationalized as a new interpretive impulse that had the deadening effect of splitting off song making from its originating engagement with a much larger arena of meaning (reification).

Filtered through a lens that refracted idealized religious performativity, the interest in black music making began to circle around the newly legitimated discovery of *black cultural goods*. The result was a cultural and interpretive enclosure around black culture and expressivity that limited discovery to a preference for the spiritual as *good black culture*. Moreover, this preference began to cut the ties between black expressions and the critical–dialogical and socially interrogating dimensions of an emergent black intelligentsia. The new interpretive developments embraced a *politics of redemption* that simultaneously abrogated a *politics of vision*. Put another way, a *culturalism* that was academically sanctioned emerged with an intellectual disposition that was professional and thus adequate in and for itself. It could dispense with the larger moral and political tensions that had surrounded the early cultural turn. The preferred reading – of the good culture of performative subjects – facilitated the cultural and interpretive enclosure, and also cut the ties that black expression had to the critical–dialogical dimensions of the slave narratives. The spiritual as acceptable performance was beckoned and received with open arms, but the existing political grammars that probed the problem of post-bellum social fate were turned away, not to surface in any substantial way until the irruption of the Civil Rights movement in the 1960s.

Nonetheless, this appreciation of the spirituals was full of pathos; it manifested at the time the most sympathetic and progressive embrace of black expressivity. But it was a culturalism that was shaped in the context of the new racial chasm that emerged in the rubble of Reconstruction. On one side of the chasm were the emancipated but now economically and politically stranded African Americans (joined in a rather inchoate racial formation with Native Americans sequestered on reservations, Mexicans politically annexed and disenfranchised as landholders, and Asian immigrants barred from US citizenship). On the other side were the new consortium of Social Darwinist populism, the formation of new ethnic hierarchies, the saber-rattling new imperialism of the Spanish–American War, and the emergent power of the military–industrial state. Rounding out the new marriage of power and knowledge was the institutionalization of professional social science in general with its most focused treatment of the racial formation carried out by the various ethnoscientific branches within the major disciplines. The problem of fate in general, and the critical dialogue that the narratives tried to champion in particular, withered precisely as a truncated appreciation for culture anchored in the preference for religious performativity flourished.

The fledgling black schools and colleges inherited these retrievalist strategies, but over time they, too, gave the quest to the new professional folklorists. In 1874, Hampton Institute's director of music, Thomas P. Fenner, was concerned with the retention of slave songs for posterity's sake. He also noted how difficult it was to grasp the full meaning of songs when they were pulled out of their collective, socially embedded practices. Songs, argued Fenner, ought be recognized as activities and practices. Dislodging songs from their context and repositioning them through musical transcription invariably resulted in the loss of meaning.[6] Fenner had voiced his concerns with regard to retrieving black song making fourteen years before the American Folklore Society emerged as a professional body. When the American Folklore Society did emerge in 1888, it emphasized in the opening pages of its official publication, *The Journal of American Folklore*, its mission to preserve and collect disappearing English ballads, and the songs of former slaves and Native Americans. The black schools attempted to keep alive the work of cultural retrieval and collection, but they were soon outperformed, outpaced, and out-professionalized by the academic-based social scientists. In 1897, Hampton Institute sent Alice Bacon to attend the America Folklore Society's annual meeting. Representing Hampton's own Folklore Society, Bacon reiterated the problems that arose when the testimonies of black music were overtaken by pressures that lead to reification and carica-turization. Each song, she stated, "has its place and its history, and the work of our Society must be to find the place and the history of each song." What was to be avoided was what was becoming an all too common practice – of finding a "beautiful new plantation song," having it transcribed by the music teacher, and then drilling the student choir to learn it. The results, Bacon insisted, were twofold. Ripped from context, the song "becomes a totally different thing"; and the process undermined what she believed was the authenticity of the spiritual.[7] Bacon's criticism could have just as well been applied to the contemporary surge of interest that the new professional folklorists were bringing to black expres-sions. As an enterprise birthed by science, the capture of artifacts was leading to the death of meaning, but, to remain in the graces of the new profession-als, Bacon concluded her presentation by acknowledging the need for more and better science. Hampton's problem, she admitted, was that there was not a single scientific folklorist in its membership. One need only read the early and numerous articles on black music in the *Journal of American Folklore* to see how fully the new scientized culturalism had gutted the potential of criti-cal ethnosympathy. In the sophisticated but nullifying prose, little was left of what was once a desired consciousness and a conscious desire to link cultural practices to statements of social fate.

By the end of the century, the academy had come into prominence. Its modern impulses prompted and deepened the schism between a humanistic soppiness that championed the residues of an older romantic and sentimental sensibil-ity, and an emergent scientism that reduced the problem of fate and culture to an empirical enterprise crowned by the language and method of taxonomy. Douglass had insisted that songs expressed collective life and refracted the crisis of a social structure governed by despised institutions (the social sys-tem of slavery). Now they were reduced to relics that represented the last rites of a dying culture. Slavery had been eradicated, but the problem of the fate of black Americans and other *racialized* groups was left unresolved as it became more complex and subordinated to the larger struggles of forging an appeasement among a northern industrial bourgeoisie, a southern agrarian power structure, and a new increasingly complex but tenuously integrated *ethnic* formation.

This juncture governs the cultural eclipse that Du Bois inherits. Du Bois tried to open up the dialogic and the dialectic, to rekindle the urgency of bringing together what had been wrenched apart. In one of his most important essays he wrote of the awareness of being "an outcast and a stranger." But, if Du Bois is an outcast and stranger, he conveys a knowledge that demonstrates an intellectual intimacy similar to the interpretive and analytical depth that many of the slave narratives possessed. He framed "knowing" as "double-consciousness," of having a "second sight," in his case the result of being a black person in an "American world, – a world which yields him no true consciousness, but only lets him see himself through the revelation of the other world." Double-consciousness was a way of "always looking at one's self through the eyes of others, of measuring one's soul by the tape of a world that looks on in amused contempt and pity."[8] This pained reflexivity accompanied the attempt to confront the fact that a fragile yet important sympathy had been overtaken by a new numbness and indifference, if not also by a brazen animosity toward black Americans and other marginalized groups. Du Bois attempted to assess the psychic and cultural damage done to people – in his case, African Americans – sidelined by the forces of history. His significance lies, in part, with his attempt to retrieve a waning sensibility through the lens of a critically ethnosympathetic appraisal of the knotted relationship between subculture and dominant culture.

Both Douglass and Du Bois spoke of things cultural, but not in terms of isolating marginalized lives, and not in ways that reduced *verstehen* to wholly self-contained, encapsulated *identities* devoid of sociohistorical engagement. Rather, their use of the cultural was fully ethnosympathetic, and was aimed at understanding social structure and ideologies through cultural forms and situated vocabularies. To borrow from Antonio Gramsci, their cultural turn was designed to link vernacular and dominant culture to the "ensemble of social relations" that form the historical bloc, moment, or whole way of life. They pointed from black lives to American society. What had to be confronted and resisted was the much more dominant tendencies with the larger culture's social and institutionally constructed classificatory schemas that were designed to serve normative and managerial impulses rather than critical social vision. The largest task facing the emergent ethnosympathy was the confrontation with its cultural opposite – the antipathy of an intractable modern racism. At stake in this early cultural turn was the fledgling ethnosympathy that deployed social subjects in ways that tried to bring the larger social system into visibility.

How is it that testimonies of and from the lives of people can become artifacts severed from the living? How is it that the vibrancy of a slave narrative, serialized in an abolitionist paper in the 1840s, can culminate in an article within the new professional social scientific journals of the late nineteenth century, where discussion between cultural expressivity and struggles over social fate evapo-rates? How can a writer in 1919 speak with such passionate engagement of the transcendental beauty of black songs, comment on "the Emersonian oversoul: is it to be found in Negro music?" when that very year, the lynching of blacks had reached such an atrocious level to warrant James Weldon Johnson calling it the "Red Summer"?

Histories have ways of hanging around, thus there are always lessons to be pulled from this that speak not just to the nineteenth century, but to the twentieth and beyond. How is it that in the mid-1950s the US government could sponsor tours of black jazz musicians whose mission during the Cold War was to aid anticommunism and court the hearts and minds of the non-aligned, and yet at home, remain largely indifferent to the struggles of black citizens attempt-ing to vote? How do we make sense of the ease with which our society can elevate black athletes as superheroes – who possess a discipline that delivers them as politically consumable embodiments of Republican virtue, as promot-ers of corporate goods, and whose pictures deserve to be on children's cereal boxes – and yet remain deaf to what many are now calling the deeply racialized "prison-industrial complex?"

I now want to expand upon some of the implications of critical ethnosym-pathy. Ethnosympathy is certainly a peculiar term. At first glance, it would appear to be the concatenated outcome of two quite familiar words – "ethno" and "sympathy." While its etiology is old, "ethno" as the scientized signifier of "man" has a rather important modern meaning. It is central to the rise of the human sciences in the nineteenth century. Today, however, we know this term particularly as the root component in a number of important knowledge orienta-tions: "ethnology," "ethnography," "ethnomethodology," and "ethnic studies." It is important to note that, within the historical issues I have already raised, an early American "ethnic studies" actually appears to have flowered during the high point of abolitionism. This perspective confronts a current view that considers ethnic studies a modern aberration, or, from the vantage point of an amnesia aided by a convenient cynicism, as a runaway shop inimical to the traditional intellectual labor practices of modern social science and humani-ties disciplines. It would appear, however, that something like ethnic studies was on the scene *before* the advent of modern, institutionally based, social sci-ence. In this regard, the current view of ethnic studies as something like an unwanted child or an impoverished relative, one who will never quite mature, or who will remain something of a chronic poacher, is not merely obscuran-tist and ahistorical; it fails to recognize that ethnosympathy helped parent the modern social scientific enterprise. This dimension of cultural repression and disavowal embedded in the late modern knowledge enterprise has only begun to be examined.

The second component, *sympathy*, connotes a sensibility, a sensitivity associated with feelings of compassion and commiseration. These aspects of sympathy are old as well, and span rather unwieldy historical domains that have been diffused and rationalized along numerous cultural fronts – religious, modern reformist, social scientific, normative–managerial, and critical. They reach back to earlier religious notions of compassion, as the dutiful expression of those who occupy status locations marked by rights but also obligations to exercise beneficence. Sympathy is central to the Romantic movement of the eighteenth and nineteenth centuries where it becomes codified in modern form with Rousseau, Herder, Chateaubriand, the Romantic poets, and the early novelists, all of whom, when taken together, register the early modern sense of loss or disappearance of an earlier, sometimes idealized, but fragile world. As modern virtue, sympathy appears in Scottish moralism, where it is a key construct in the philosophy of David Hume, and in Adam Smith's *Theory of Moral Sentiments* (but evacuated by Smith in *The Wealth of Nations*, an indication of how the earlier critical phenomenology is nipped in the bud and trumped by ascendant egoistic utilitarianism). As a sensibility, sympathy represents an attempt to adjudicate the rupturing of social life by modernity and industrialization; it serves as a modern virtue comprised of critical and reflexive apprehension, nostalgia, and lament. And it is deeply endemic to, or we might say it even permeates, though unevenly, much of nineteenth- and twentieth-century humanitarian reformism's two major and deeply contradictory fronts – the *critical* penchant, on the one hand, to indict society and to criticize it for what it does to individuals and groups; and the *normative* drive, on the other, to construct categories of the social into modes of knowledge conducive to institutionalized modes of modern managerialism. Put another way, these fronts appear as ongoing critical disenchantment or utopianist striving, or as an embracing of order, if not discipline and punishment.

Ethnosympathy, however, is much more than a merger of non-reflexive pity and a consideration for a particular people. It connotes a quite complicated *cultural complex of modernity*, with a history that is fused with the coming into being of *society* as a social object and as a backdrop against which discrete, specific, collective groups are positioned. Indeed, as a crucial modern construct, ethnosympathy brings society into focus to examine the stakes behind the social fact that some groups wield tremendous social power and some groups register society's most horrible effects of that power. As a cultural complex, the contours of ethnosympathy are already present with the rise of the social or human sciences in the late nineteenth century. Indeed, with its nascent understanding of the connections between social order, social change, and social crisis, ethnosympathy *presupposes* them.

All of this makes ethnosympathy a contentious and conflicted sensibility. It coincides with – because it is historically entwined with – the modern notion of *subculture*. Ethnosympathy entails, after all, an interest in the way knowledge of group life brings the social much more crucially into focus, but ethnosympathy and subculture study are not simply interchangeable. The important distinction, as noted earlier, is between normative and critical applications behind the terms. Both Douglass and Du Bois take the critical cultural turn and pry open the American dilemma by probing the critical dimension of ethnosympathy. Yet they refuse the normative limits that are often implied as well as applied in the notion of *sub*culture. As I have argued, both sought the crucial move – the critical recuperation of a conscious desire as well as a desired consciousness to achieve a synthetic but yet tentative understanding of subjective fate in relationship to comprehending what is socially systemic.

Douglass may have helped sow the seeds of what has since flourished in American subcultural analysis. But what becomes immediately important is that the term "subculture," when resituated along the historical lines I have presented, becomes something of a misnomer, for, if the slave narratives signify anything, it is the rather knotty problem of a subcultural problem that actually spills over, under, and beyond the containing walls implied in the very term "subculture." In this case, the so-called "sub" was actually fully societal, not marginal but central, and undeniably national (consider, for example, the fact that up to the present the narratives, if acknowledged, remain categorically marginalized – for example as "ethnic literature" or "minority discourse") in spite of their formation within, and their profound interrogation of, the core crises that culminated in something as massively national as the crisis-ridden social structure of antebellum society and the ensuing civil war. This spilling over from *sub to core* belies the *sub as core* as it involves an important kind of dislocating and relocating of black cultural practices as well as white cultural practices (the practices of hearing and of interpretive appropriation) in relationship to a politics of social vision – which was precisely what Douglass' narrative (and, later, Du Bois' essays) tried to kindle and articulate.

This brings me to some final comments on the relationship between ethnosympathy and the notion of "subculture." Though the modern use of the term "subculture" derives from the Chicago School, its practical usage was prefigured in the second half of the nineteenth century when the critical expressions of slaves (along with those of Native Americans, and with implications for women, wage laborers, and others groups) were being progressively translated into a disconnected culturalism that culminated in the normative managerialism of professional ethnology. It received major reinvigoration in the wake of the Civil Rights movement during the context of the 1960s – the refusal of the

Southern states to permit blacks to exercise their constitutional rights to the franchise, the campaigns of state-sanctioned violence, the political killings of American youth who tried to bring national attention to an American apartheid, the bombing of black churches, the snarling dogs, the blood-spattered batons, and armed military formations deployed to prevent the collective presentation of racialized publics – calling into visibility the social diseases that flourished in the shadows of the cornucopia of American democratic capitalism. Again, there was, if it might be put this way, a presumably subcultural problem that spilled over, under, and beyond the containing walls implied in the very term "subculture" as in what was supposedly *subordinate, subservient, subaltern, subnormal,* and *subversive*; and which was to be *subverted* and *subjugated* under the watchful eye of *supervision*. What links the Civil Rights movement to the older racialized American case of the fate of the spirituals is the way culture and crisis converge practically, and in how they mark new, then disappearing, then reemergent intellectual reflections based upon a desire and a capacity to see something of the larger society *from* the vantage point of distinct groups and collective subjects – as when a subculture actually operates as a lens that brings into focus, and enables a broader range of people to grasp, something much larger, more systemic, transinstitutional, and deeply historical.

Ethnosympathy has a peculiar elasticity – to say the least. It can foster an expansive and acute vision of the social; but, as a historical tendency, it is more likely to shrivel to the narrow toleration of ethnicity as selective cultural performance. The challenge, however, is to grasp ethnosympathy as a capacity to conceptualize society's deepest dilemmas which fundamentally involve relationships among groups and collective life. The critical emergence of groups and the intellectual reflections that involve them have everything to do with the opportunities to broaden our ethnosympathetic social vision, and, in this regard, collective groups and subcultures matter. But the history of how they matter is complicated and contentious. Two tendencies, one indisputably dominant, the other fragile and marginal, loom in this history of how they have mattered. On the one hand, groups come to matter from a dominant–normative perspective because they represent affronts to established social, political, moral, and institutional comfort; they invoke antagonisms to social order, violations of rule and custom. The cultural work of how they come to matter is how they are *othered* through surveillance, intervention, and discipline. Such cultural work is essentially the normative business of social regulation and management. On the other hand, collective groups can come to matter quite differently, not so much as when they are the objects of discipline, but rather when they engender the kind of cultural work – in movement and in intellectual reach – that can bring society into view in new and critical ways. Collective subjects are invariably situated between these two modalities, and are crucial insofar as their emergence and their being used socially become enmeshed in strategies of maintenance as well as in disruptive vision. The tension between these tendencies constitutes the American dilemma of ethnosympathy. While the study of culture straddles the divide, it is disruptive vision that poses the most important challenges to a social studies that wishes for something more than to be party to the deeper managerial and dominant–institutional impulses of the knowledge enterprise.

One implication of the historical connections I have sketched here is that the contemporary debates around the study of culture, and for that matter, the "cultural turn" (understood too narrowly as a set of theoreticist trajectories launched by the "linguistic turn"[9]), may actually present a history that starts too late; that is, it is not historical enough. As Hayden White has recently pointed out (again), the attention to history is not in itself a critical advance as long as history is induced by a social science that sees its role modeled after the natural sciences, and where preoccupations with methods and objectivism are subordinated to illusions of "disinterest." In the case of the much earlier cultural turn in the second half of the nineteenth century, the result, as I argue in *Culture on the Margins*, was precisely the very bifurcation between a rational science of objects and an irrational politics of subjects. White is right to raise skepticism toward the call to problematic history. The problem, as I have sketched here, is not simply to look back to find a starting point uncontaminated by ideology. Rather, it is the problem of how, when, and why history is invoked, studied, and incorporated in relationship to the larger challenge of critical vision; it is how history is placed in the retrieval of dialogic and dialectic sensibility. In the case presented here, the problem concerns the extent to which historicism includes the problem of ethnosympathy.[10] Contemporary attempts that account for the turn to the study of culture can overlook the *formation* in which modes of study (theories, paradigms, new intellectual orientations, etc.) are inextricably linked to the crises in which group life emerges as part of social and historical development. In leaving this aspect of group emergence and knowledge development aside, they perpetuate a blind spot with regard to how cultural study is shaped in part by the conditions under which groups actually emerge and perhaps become eclipsed. This was the fate at the end of the last century that produced an academic capturing of black culture severed from the engagement of everyday politics. It is a history that American society has not been able fully to confront, save in fits and starts. It is a history that continues to haunt the present as that nagging numbness that lurks beneath the canonical confidence of rationalist celebration in the pursuit of the finishing touches of this or that explanatory model. It is a history full of "unfinished business."

Notes

I wish to thank my colleagues Roger Friedland and John Mohr for the invitation and opportunity to write reflexively.
1. Cruz (1999).
2. Raymond Williams' discussion of the concept of formation remains the provocative read. Cf. Williams (1997: 115–120; 1982: 57–86).
3. Du Bois (1969: 235–236).
4. On the one hand, understanding (*verstehen*) involves the attempt to comprehend "the *subjective* meaning, the meaning intended by the actor himself as an ultimate, concrete, empirically graspable reality, not some thought structure that is speculatively superimposed upon reality." See Weber (1988), p. 677. Cf. also Gerth and Mills (1946), p. 55. Taken together, the problem of meaning as lived, and the epistemological capacity to draw the latter toward envisioning the social, moves us beyond the built-in limitations of treating meaning as the problem of an inner culture reducible to psychological habitus and disposition. *Verstehen* pivots on meaning, but simultaneously reaches outward toward a *reflexive reexamination* of what the observations of collective life actually produce – the prospect of critical social vision. Du Bois' double-duty enterprise was consistent with Weber's notion of *verstehen*. Such insights, however, seemed to have lost their urgency in American sociology through the first half of the twentieth century (replaced by neutralized notions of "systems"), until C. Wright Mills reinvested them in his famous couplet of "history/biography." Cf. Mills (1959).
5. Douglass (1982: 57–58).
6. See Fenner (1973: iii–iv).
7. See Bacon (1897: 17–21).
8. Du Bois (1969: 45).
9. See the introduction in Bonnell and Hunt (1999).
10. Cf. White, "Afterword" in Bonnell and Hunt (1999: 315–324).

References

Bacon, Alice Mabel. 1897. "Work and Methods of the Hampton Folk-Lore Society." *Journal of American Folk-Lore* 11/40:17–21.

Bonnell, Victoria E. and Lynn Hunt, eds. 1999. *Beyond the Cultural Turn: New Directions in the Study of Society and Culture*. Berkeley, CA: University of California Press.

Cruz, Jon. 1999. *Culture on the Margins: The Black Spiritual and the Rise of American Cultural Interpretation*. Princeton, NJ: Princeton University Press.

Douglass, Frederick. [1845] 1982. *Narrative of the Life of Frederick Douglass, an American Slave, Written by Himself*. New York: Penguin Books.

Du Bois, W. E. B. 1969 [1903]. *The Souls of Black Folk*. New York: NAL Penguin.

Fenner, Thomas P. [1874] 1973. *Religious Folk Songs of the Negro*. New York: AMS Press.

Gerth, Hans and C. Wright Mills. 1946. *From Max Weber: Essays in Sociology*. New York: Oxford University Press.

Mills, C. Wright. 1959. *The Sociological Imagination*. London: Oxford University Press.

Weber, Marianne. 1988. *Max Weber: A Biography*, trans. Harry Zohn. New Brunswick, NJ: Transaction Books.

White, Hayden. 1999. "Afterword," in Bonnell and Hunt, eds. *Beyond the Cultural Turn*. Berkeley, CA: University of California Press. Pp. 315–324.

Williams, Raymond. 1977. *Marxism and Literature*. Oxford: Oxford University Press.

1982. *The Sociology of Culture*. New York: Schocken Books.

Index

MICHAEL MULKAY, *The Embryo Research Debate*
0 521 57180 4 hardback 0 521 57683 0 paperback
LYNN RAPAPORT, *Jews in Germany after the Holocaust*
0 521 58219 9 hardback 0 521 58809 X paperback
CHANDRA MUKERJI, *Territorial Ambitions and
the Gardens of Versailles*
0 521 49675 6 hardback 0 521 59959 8 paperback
LEON H. MAYHEW, *The New Public*
0 521 48146 5 hardback 0 521 48493 6 paperback
VERA L. ZOLBERG AND JONI M. CHERBO
(eds.), *Outsider Art*
0 521 58111 7 hardback 0 521 58921 5 paperback
SCOTT BRAVMANN, *Queer Fictions of the Past*
0 521 59101 5 hardback 0 521 59907 5 paperback
STEVEN SEIDMAN, *Difference Troubles*
0 521 59043 4 hardback 0 521 59970 9 paperback
RON EYERMAN AND ANDREW JAMISON,
Music and Social Movements
0 521 62045 7 hardback 0 521 62966 7 paperback
MEYDA YEGENOGLU, *Colonial Fantasies*
0 521 48233 X hardback 0 521 62658 7 paperback
LAURA DESFOR EDLES, *Symbol and Ritual in the New Spain*
0 521 62140 2 hardback 0 521 62885 7 paperback
NINA ELIASOPH, *Avoiding Politics*
0 521 58293 8 hardback 0 521 58759 X paperback
BERNHARD GIESEN, *Intellectuals and the German Nation*
0 521 62161 5 hardback 0 521 63996 4 paperback
PHILIP SMITH (ed.), *The New American Cultural Sociology*
0 521 58415 9 hardback 0 521 58634 8 paperback
S. N. EISENSTADT, *Fundamentalism, Sectarianism and Revolution*
0 521 64184 5 hardback 0 521 64586 7 paperback
MARIAM FRASER, *Identity without Selfhood*
0 521 62357 X hardback 0 521 62579 3 paperback
LUC BOLTANSKI, *Distant Suffering*
0 521 57389 0 hardback 0 521 65953 1 paperback
PYOTR SZTOMPKA, *Trust*
0 521 59144 9 hardback 0 521 59850 8 paperback
SIMON J. CHARLESWORTH, *A Phenomenology
of Working-Class Culture*
0 521 65066 6 hardback 0 521 65915 9 paperback

ROBIN WAGNER-PACIFICI, *Theorizing the Standoff*
0 521 65244 8 hardback 0 521 65479 3 paperback
RONALD R. JACOBS, *Race, Media and the Crisis of Civil Society*
0 521 62360 X hardback 0 521 62578 5 paperback
ALI MIRSEPASSI, *Intellectual Discourse and
the Politics of Modernization*
0 521 65000 3 hardback 0 521 65997 3 paperback
RON LEMBO, *Thinking Through Television*
0 521 58465 5 hardback 0 521 58577 5 paperback
MICHÈLE LAMONT AND LAURENT THÉVENOT
(eds.), *Rethinking Comparative Cultural Sociology*
0 521 78263 5 hardback 0 521 78794 7 paperback
STEPHEN M. ENGEL, *The Unfinished Revolution:
Social Movement Theory and the Gay and Lesbian Movement*
0 521 80287 3 hardback 0 521 00377 6 paperback
RON EYERMAN, *Cultural Trauma: Slavery and
the Formation of African American Identity*
0 521 80828 6 hardback 0 521 00437 3 paperback
KRISHAN KUMAR, *The Making of English National Identity*
0 521 77188 9 hardback 0 521 77736 4 paperback